3D Imaging, Analysis and Applications

Nick Pears · Yonghuai Liu · Peter Bunting
Editors

3D Imaging, Analysis and Applications

 Springer

Editors
Nick Pears
Department of Computer Science
University of York
York, UK

Peter Bunting
Institute of Geography and Earth Sciences
Aberystwyth University
Aberystwyth, UK

Yonghuai Liu
Institute of Geography and Earth Sciences
Aberystwyth University
Aberystwyth, UK

ISBN 978-1-4471-6024-3   ISBN 978-1-4471-4063-4 (eBook)
DOI 10.1007/978-1-4471-4063-4
Springer London Heidelberg New York Dordrecht

© Springer-Verlag London 2012
Softcover reprint of the hardcover 1st edition 2012
Chapter 3—Active 3D Imaging Systems, pp. 95–138 © Her Majesty the Queen in Right of Canada 2012
Chapter 10—High-Resolution Three-Dimensional Remote Sensing for Forest Measurement, pp. 417–443
© Springer-Verlag London (outside the USA) 2012

This work is subject to copyright. All rights are reserved by the Publisher, whether the whole or part of the material is concerned, specifically the rights of translation, reprinting, reuse of illustrations, recitation, broadcasting, reproduction on microfilms or in any other physical way, and transmission or information storage and retrieval, electronic adaptation, computer software, or by similar or dissimilar methodology now known or hereafter developed. Exempted from this legal reservation are brief excerpts in connection with reviews or scholarly analysis or material supplied specifically for the purpose of being entered and executed on a computer system, for exclusive use by the purchaser of the work. Duplication of this publication or parts thereof is permitted only under the provisions of the Copyright Law of the Publisher's location, in its current version, and permission for use must always be obtained from Springer. Permissions for use may be obtained through RightsLink at the Copyright Clearance Center. Violations are liable to prosecution under the respective Copyright Law.
The use of general descriptive names, registered names, trademarks, service marks, etc. in this publication does not imply, even in the absence of a specific statement, that such names are exempt from the relevant protective laws and regulations and therefore free for general use.
While the advice and information in this book are believed to be true and accurate at the date of publication, neither the authors nor the editors nor the publisher can accept any legal responsibility for any errors or omissions that may be made. The publisher makes no warranty, express or implied, with respect to the material contained herein.

Printed on acid-free paper

Springer is part of Springer Science+Business Media (www.springer.com)

Dr. Philip Batchehor (1967–2011)

Mathematicians are born, not made
Jules Henri Poincaré

This book is dedicated to the memory of Dr. Philip Batchelor, who tragically died in a climbing accident while close to completing work on Chapter 11. Born in Cornwall in England but brought up in Vouvry in Switzerland he was always proud of both sides to his heritage. A truly gifted mathematician, he devoted his talents to medical imaging, where he made many valuable contributions. He discovered a matrix formalization of motion in MRI, which inspired the field of non-rigid MRI motion correction. In diffusion imaging, he provided a mathematical framework for the treatment of tensors, leading to the geodesic anisotropy measure. More recently, he and co-workers made significant progress in tackling the hugely difficult task of diffusion tensor imaging of the beating heart. A popular senior lecturer in Imaging Sciences at King's College London, he was highly valued for his teaching as well as his research. He always had time for students, colleagues and anyone who sought his advice. His insight into problems in three dimensions and higher benefited many who were lucky enough to work with him. He would have been delighted to pass on some of his knowledge in this book. Beyond his scientific abilities, it is his warmth, generosity of spirit and consistent smile that will be remembered with affection by colleagues, friends and family alike.

Preface

This book is primarily a graduate text on 3D imaging, shape analysis and associated applications. In addition to serving masters-level and doctoral-level research students, much of the text is accessible enough to be useful to final-year undergraduate project students. Also, we hope that it will serve wider audiences; for example, as a reference text for professional academics, people working in commercial research and development labs and industrial practitioners.

We believe that this text is unique in the literature on 3D imaging in several respects: (1) it provides a wide coverage of topics in 3D imaging; (2) it pays special attention to the clear presentation of well-established core techniques; (3) it covers a wide range of the most promising recent techniques that are considered to be state-of-the-art; (4) it is the first time that so many world-leading academics have come together on this range of 3D imaging topics.

Firstly, we ask: why is 3D imaging so interesting to study, research and develop? Why is it so important to our society, economy and culture? In due course, we will answer these questions but, to provide a wide context, we need consider the development of biological vision systems, the development of visual representations and the role of digital images in today's information society. This leads us to the field of computer vision and ultimately to the subject of this book: 3D imaging.

Biological Vision Systems

It is worth reflecting on the obvious fact that the importance of images, in their very general sense (paintings, digital photographs, etc.), is rooted in our ability to see. The ability to sense light dates back to at least the Cambrian period, over half a billion years ago, as evidenced by fossils of trilobites' compound eyes in the Burgess shale. For many animals, including humans, the eye-brain vision system constitutes an indispensable, highly information rich mode of sensory perception. The evolution of this system has been driven by aspects of our particular optical world: with the Sun we have a natural source of light; air is transparent, which allows our environment to be illuminated; the wavelength of light is small enough to be scattered by most surfaces, which means that we can gather light reflected off them from many different viewpoints, and it is possible to form an image with a relatively simple structure such as a convex lens. It is easy to appreciate the utility and advantages of visual perception, which provides a means to sense the environment in a comprehensive, non-contact way. Indeed, evolutionary biologists have proposed that the development of vision intensified predation and sparked an evolutionary arms race between predators and prey. Thus biological vision systems exist as a result of evolutionary survival and have been present on Earth for a very long time.

Today, there is comprehensive research literature in visual psychophysics, the study of eyesight. Visual illusions suggest that, for some 3D cues, humans use a lot of assumptions about their environment, when inferring 3D shape. The study of how depth perception depends on several visual and oculomotor cues has influenced the development of modern techniques in 3D imaging. Ideas have also flowed in the opposite direction: results from computer vision indicate what information can be extracted from raw visual data, thereby inspiring theories of human visual perception.

Visual Representations from Paintings to Photographs

A drawing, painting or photograph can be viewed as a form of visual expression and communication. Drawing and painting has a very long history and several discoveries of very old cave paintings have been made, for example, those in the Chauvet cave (France) are more than 32,000 years old. Throughout the history of mankind, the use of paintings, drawings and automatically captured images has been culturally important in many different ways. In terms of the subject matter of this book, the advent of photography in the early 19th century was an important milestone, enabling light reflected from an object or scene to be recorded and retained in a durable way. Photographs have many advantages, such as an accurate, objective visual representation of the scene and a high level of autonomy in image capture. Once photography was born, it was soon realized that measurements of the imaged scene could be made; for example, a map could be built from photographs taken from a balloon. Thus the field of photogrammetry was born, which focuses on extracting accurate measurements from images (this is now often included under the banner of *remote sensing*). The work done in this field, from the mid-19th to the mid-20th century, is an essential historical precursor to the material presented in this book.

The Role of Digital Images in Today's Information Society

Today we live in an *information society*, which is characterized by the economic and cultural importance of information in its many forms. The creation, distribution, analysis and intelligent use of digital information now has a wide range of impacts on everyone in the developed world, throughout all stages of their lives. This can be anything from the way in which we do our jobs, to the way our health is managed by our doctors; to how our safety is secured on public transport, during air travel and in public spaces; to how our financial systems work; to how we manage our shopping and leisure time. Of course, many of these impacts have been brought about by the advances in computing and communications technology over the past few decades, with the most obvious examples being the Internet, the world wide web and, more recently, mobile access to these resources over wide-bandwidth, wireless technologies.

The information that we use is often described as being *multi-media*, in the sense that it includes text, audio, graphical figures, images, video and interactive content. Of these different forms, images have always played a hugely important role for obvious reasons: they can convey a huge amount of information in a compact form, they clarify concepts and ideas that are difficult to describe in words, they draw in their audience by making documents more visually appealing and they relate directly to our primary non-contact mechanism for sensing our environment (we humans live and interact in a visual world). For these reasons, images will always be important, but recent advances in both hardware and software technologies are likely to amplify this. For example, digital cameras are now embedded in many devices such as smartphones and the relatively recent explosion in social networking allows groups of people to share images.

Computer Vision

The information society brings with it such a large number of images that we can not hope to analyze them all manually-consider for example the number of images from the security surveillance of a large city over a 24 hour period. The goal of computer vision is to automate the analysis of images through the use of computers and the material presented in this book fits that high level aim. Since there are a large number of ways in which we use images, there is a correspondingly large number of applications of computer vision. In general, automation can improve image analysis performance (people get bored), it increases coverage, it reduces operating costs and, in some applications, it leads to improved safety (e.g. robots working in hazardous environments). The last four decades has seen the rapid evolution of imaging technology and computing power, which has fed the growth of the field of computer vision and the related fields of image analysis and pattern recognition.

The Limitations of Standard 2D Images

Most of the images in our information society are standard 2D color-texture images (i.e. the kind of images that we capture from our mobile phones and digital cameras), or they are effectively sequences of such images that constitute videos. Although this is sufficient for many of the uses that we have described, particularly if the images/video are for direct viewing by a human (e.g. for entertainment or social network use), single, standard 2D images have a number of difficulties when being analyzed by computers. Many of these difficulties stem from the fact that the 3D world is projected down onto a 2D image, thus losing depth information and creating ambiguity. For example, in a 2D image: how do we segment foreground objects from the background? How can we recognize the same object from different viewpoints? How do we deal with ambiguity between object size and distance from the camera? To compound these problems, there is also the issue of how to deal with varying illumination, which can make the same object appear quite different when imaged.

3D Imaging, Analysis and Applications

To address the problems of standard 2D images, described above, 3D imaging techniques have been developed within the field of computer vision that *automatically* reconstruct the 3D shape of the imaged objects and scene. This is referred to as a 3D scan or 3D image and it often comes with a registered color-texture image that can be pasted over the captured shape and rendered from many viewpoints (if desired) on a computer display.

The techniques developed include both active systems, where some form of illumination is projected onto the scene and passive systems, where the natural illumination of the scene is used. Perhaps the most intensively researched area of 3D shape acquisition has been focused on stereo vision systems, which, like the human visual system, uses a pair of views (images) in order to compute 3D structure. Here, researchers have met challenging problems such as the establishment of correspondences between overlapping images for the dense reconstruction of the imaged scene. Many applications require further processing and data analysis, once 3D shape data has been acquired. For example, identification of salient points within the 3D data, registration of multiple partial 3D data scans, computation of 3D symmetry planes and matching of whole 3D objects.

It is one of today's challenges to design a technology that can cover the whole pipeline of 3D shape capture, processing and visualization. The different steps of this pipeline have raised important topics in the research community for decades, owing to the numerous theoretical and technical problems that they induce. Capturing the 3D shape, instead of just a 2D projection as a standard camera does, makes an extremely wide array of new kinds of application possible. For instance, 3D and free-viewpoint TV, virtual and augmented reality, natural user interaction based on monitoring gestures, 3D object recognition and 3D recognition for biometry, 3D medical imaging, 3D remote sensing, industrial inspection, robot navigation, to name just a few. These applications, of course, involve much more technological advances than just 3D shape capture: storage, analysis, transmission and visualization of the 3D shape are also part of the whole pipeline.

3D imaging and analysis is closely associated with computer vision, but it also intersects with a number of other fields, for example: image processing, pattern recognition, computer graphics, computational geometry and physics. It involves building sensors, modeling them and then processing the output images. In particular, 3D image analysis bridges the gap between low-level and high-level vision in order to deduce high-level (semantic) information from basic 3D data.

Book Objective and Content

The objective of this book is to bring together a set of core topics in 3D imaging, analysis and applications, both in terms of well-established fundamental techniques and the most promising recent techniques. Indeed, we see that many similar techniques are being used in a variety of subject areas and applications and we feel that we can unify a range of related ideas, providing clarity to both academic and industrial practitioners, who are acquiring and processing 3D datasets. To ensure the quality of the book, all contributors have attained a world-class standing by publishing in the top conferences and journals in this area. Thus, the material presented in this book is informative and authoritative and represents mainstream work and opinions within the community.

After an introductory chapter, the book covers 3D image capture methods, particularly those that use two cameras, as in passive stereo vision, or a camera and light projector, as in active stereo vision. It also covers how 3D data is represented, stored and visualized. Later parts of the book cover the analysis and processing of 3D images, firstly in a general sense, which includes feature extraction, shape registration and shape matching, and then with a view to a range of applications including 3D object recognition, 3D object retrieval (shape search), 3D face recognition, 3D mapping and 3D medical imaging.

The idea to produce a new book on 3D imaging was originated by Yonghuai Liu, while Nick Pears was responsible for coordinating the authoring.

Acknowledgements

We would like to express our sincere gratitude to all chapter authors for their contributions, their discussions and their support during the book preparation. It has been our honor to work with so many truly world leading academics and, without them, the production of this book would have not been possible.

We would also like to thank all of the chapter reviewers for their insightful comments, which have enabled us to produce a high quality book. In particular we thank Jean-Yves Guillemaut, Wolfgang Sepp, Fabio Remondino, Zhanyi Hu, Ralph Martin, Yucel Yemez, Paul Rosin, Akihiro Sugimoto, M. Fatih Demirci, George Passalis, Bill Buckles, Xiaoye Liu, Jenny Lovell, Sorin Popescu, Isabelle Bloch and Gianni

Frisardi. Special thanks to Adrien Bartoli and Umberto Castellani for contributing ideas to the preface of this book.

We are grateful for the support of our publisher, Springer; in particular, we would like to thank Helen Desmond, Ben Bishop, Beverley Ford and Catherine Moore from Springer UK, who worked with us in a friendly and effective way throughout all stages of the book production process.

Yonghuai Liu and Nick Pears
with Pete Bunting

Contents

1 **Introduction** 1
  Reinhard Koch, Nick Pears, and Yonghuai Liu

Part I 3D Imaging and Shape Representation

2 **Passive 3D Imaging** 35
  Stephen Se and Nick Pears

3 **Active 3D Imaging Systems** 95
  Marc-Antoine Drouin and Jean-Angelo Beraldin

4 **Representing, Storing and Visualizing 3D Data** 139
  William A.P. Smith

Part II 3D Shape Analysis and Processing

5 **Feature-Based Methods in 3D Shape Analysis** 185
  Alexander M. Bronstein, Michael M. Bronstein, and Maks Ovsjanikov

6 **3D Shape Registration** 221
  Umberto Castellani and Adrien Bartoli

7 **3D Shape Matching for Retrieval and Recognition** 265
  Benjamin Bustos and Ivan Sipiran

Part III 3D Imaging Applications

8 **3D Face Recognition** 311
  Ajmal Mian and Nick Pears

9 **3D Digital Elevation Model Generation** 367
  Hong Wei and Marc Bartels

10 **High-Resolution Three-Dimensional Remote Sensing for Forest Measurement** 417
   Hans-Erik Andersen

11 **3D Medical Imaging** 445
   Philip G. Batchelor, P.J. "Eddie" Edwards, and Andrew P. King

Index 497

Contributors

Hans-Erik Andersen United States Department of Agriculture Forest Service, Pacific Northwest Research Station, Seattle, WA, USA

Marc Bartels Computational Vision Group, School of Systems Engineering, University of Reading, Reading, UK

Adrien Bartoli Université d'Auvergne, Clermont-Ferrand, France

Philip G. Batchelor King's College, London, UK

Jean-Angelo Beraldin National Research Council of Canada, Ottawa, Ontario, Canada

Alexander M. Bronstein Department of Computer Science, Technion—Israel Institute of Technology, Haifa, Israel

Michael M. Bronstein Department of Computer Science, Technion—Israel Institute of Technology, Haifa, Israel

Benjamin Bustos Department of Computer Science, University of Chile, Santiago, Chile

Umberto Castellani University of Verona, Verona, Italy

Marc-Antoine Drouin National Research Council of Canada, Ottawa, Ontario, Canada

Andrew P. King King's College, London, UK

Reinhard Koch Institute of Computer Science, Christian-Albrechts-University of Kiel, Kiel, Germany

Yonghuai Liu Department of Computer Science, Aberystwyth University, Aberystwyth, Ceredigion, UK

Ajmal Mian School of Computer Science and Software Engineering, University of Western Australia, Crawley, WA, Australia

Maks Ovsjanikov Department of Computer Science, Stanford University, Stanford, CA, USA

Nick Pears Department of Computer Science, University of York, York, UK

Stephen Se MDA Systems Ltd., Richmond, BC, Canada

Ivan Sipiran Department of Computer Science, University of Chile, Santiago, Chile

William A.P. Smith Department of Computer Science, University of York, York, UK

Hong Wei Computational Vision Group, School of Systems Engineering, University of Reading, Reading, UK

P.J. "Eddie" Edwards Imperial College, London, UK

Chapter 1
Introduction

Reinhard Koch, Nick Pears, and Yonghuai Liu

Abstract *3D Imaging, Analysis and Applications* is a comprehensive textbook on 3D shape capture, 3D shape processing and how such capture and processing can be used. Eleven chapters cover a broad range of concepts, algorithms and applications and they are split into three parts, as follows: Part I, *3D Imaging and Shape Representation*, presents techniques for capture, representation and visualization of 3D data; Part II, *3D Shape Analysis and Processing* presents feature-based methods of analysis, registration and shape matching and, finally, Part III, *3D Imaging Applications* presents application areas in 3D face recognition, remote sensing and medical imaging. This introduction provides the reader with historical and background information, such as that relating to the development of computer vision; in particular, the development of automated 3D imaging. It briefly discusses general depth estimation principles for 3D imaging, details a selection of seminal papers, sketches applications of 3D imaging and concludes with an outline of the book's remaining chapters.

1.1 Introduction

Three-dimensional (3D) imaging seeks to capture the 3D structure of scenes and objects within our environment. The computed set of data points in 3D space is often accompanied by color-texture information in the form of a registered 2D image, typically obtained from standard digital image capture. Such 3D data, with or

---

R. Koch (✉)
Institute of Computer Science, Christian-Albrechts-University of Kiel, Kiel, Germany
e-mail: rk@informatik.uni-kiel.de

N. Pears
Department of Computer Science, University of York, Deramore Lane, York YO10 5GH, UK
e-mail: nick.pears@york.ac.uk

Y. Liu
Department of Computer Science, Aberystwyth University, Aberystwyth, Ceredigion SY23 3DB, UK
e-mail: yyl@aber.ac.uk

without accompanying color/texture, is referred to by various names, such as a *3D model*,[1] a *3D scan*[2] or a *3D image*.[3]

The output of a 3D imaging process can be analyzed and processed to extract information that supports a wide range of applications, such as object recognition, shape search on the web, face recognition for security and surveillance, robot navigation, mapping of the Earth's surface, forests or urban regions, and clinical procedures in medicine.

Chapter Outline Firstly, in Sect. 1.2, we present a historical perspective on 3D imaging. Since this subject is most widely studied in the context of the modern field of *computer vision*, Sect. 1.3 briefly outlines the development of computer vision and recommends a number of general texts in this area. In Sect. 1.4, we outline acquisition techniques for 3D imaging. This is followed by a set of twelve relatively modern (post 1970) research papers that we think are significant milestones in 3D imaging and shape analysis and, finally, in Sect. 1.6, we outline some applications of 3D imaging. This chapter concludes by giving a 'road map' for the remaining chapters in this book.

1.2 A Historical Perspective on 3D Imaging

To understand the roots of 3D imaging, we first need to consider the history of the more general concepts of image formation and image capture. After this, the remainder of this section discusses binocular depth perception and stereoscopic displays.

1.2.1 Image Formation and Image Capture

Since ancient times, humans have tried to capture their surrounding 3D environment and important aspects of social life on wall paintings. Early drawings, mostly animal paintings, are thought to date back 32,000 years, such as the early works in the Chauvet Cave, France. Drawings in the famous Lascaux Caves near Montinac, France are also very old and date back to around 17,000 years [12]. These drawings were not correct in terms of perspective, but did capture the essence of the objects in an artistic way.

A rigorous mathematical treatment of vision was postulated by Euclid[4] in his book *Optics* [10]. Thus, already early on in history, some aspects of perspectivity

---

[1]Typically, this term is used when the 3D data is acquired from multiple viewpoint 2D images.

[2]Typically, this term is used when a scanner acquired the 3D data, such as a laser stripe scanner.

[3]Typically, this term is used when the data is ordered in a regular grid, such as the 2D array of depth values in a range image, or a 3D array of data in volumetric medical imaging.

[4]Euclid of Alexandria, Greek mathematician, also referred to as the *Father of Geometry*, lived in Alexandria during the reign of Ptolemy I (323–283 BC).

were known. Another very influential mathematical text was the *Kitab al-Manazir* (Book of Optics) by Alhazen[5] [47].

In parallel with the mathematical concepts of vision and optics, physical optics developed by the use of lenses and mirrors, forming the basis of modern optical instruments. Very early lenses were found as polished crystals, like the famous *Nimrud lens* that was discovered by Austen Henry Layard.[6] The lens quality is far from perfect but allows light focusing at a focal point distance of 110 mm. Lenses were used as *burning lenses* to focus sunlight and as magnification lenses. Early written record of such use is found with Seneca the Younger[7] who noted:

> Letters, however small and indistinct, are seen enlarged and more clearly through a globe or glass filled with water [33].

Thus, he describes the effect of a spherical convex lens. Early on, the use of such magnification for observing distant objects was recognized and optical instruments were devised, such as corrective lenses for bad eye-sight in the 13th to 15th century CE and the telescope at the beginning of the 17th century. It is unclear who invented the telescope, as several lens makers observed the magnification effects independently. The German born Dutch lens maker Hans Lippershey (1570–1619) from Middelburg, province Zealand, is often credited as inventor of the telescope, since he applied for a patent, which was denied. Other lens makers like his fellow Middelburg lens maker Zacharias Janssen also claiming the invention [28]. Combined with the camera obscura, optically a pinhole camera, they form the basic concept of modern cameras. The *camera obscura*, Latin for *dark room*, has been used for a long time to capture images of scenes. Light reflected from a scene enters a dark room through a very small hole and is projected as an image onto the back wall of the room. Already Alhazen had experimented with a camera obscura and it was used as a drawing aid by artists and as a visual attraction later on. The name *camera* is derived from the camera obscura. The pinhole camera generates an inverse image of the scene with a scale factor $f = i/o$, where i is the image distance between pinhole and image and o is the object distance between object and pinhole. However, the opening aperture of the pinhole itself has to be very small to avoid blurring. A light-collecting and focusing lens is then used to enlarge the opening aperture and brighter, yet still sharp images can be obtained for thin convex lenses.[8] Such lenses follow the Gaussian thin lens equation: $1/f = 1/i + 1/o$, where f is the focal length of the lens. The drawback, as with all modern cameras, is the limited depth of field, in which the image of the scene is in focus.

---

[5] Alhazen (Ibn al-Haytham), born 965 CE in Basra, Iraq, died in 1040. Introduced the concept of *physical optics* and experimented with lenses, mirrors, camera obscura, refraction and reflection.

[6] Sir Austen Henry Layard (1817–1894), British archaeologist, found a polished rock crystal during the excavation of ancient Nimrud, Iraq. The lens has a diameter of 38 mm, presumed creation date 750–710 BC and now on display at the British Museum, London.

[7] Lucius Annaeus Seneca, around 4 BC–65 CE, was a Roman philosopher, statesman, dramatist, tutor and adviser of Nero.

[8] Small and thin bi-convex lenses look like lentils, hence the name *lens*, which is Latin for *lentil*.

Until the mid-19th century, the only way to capture an image was to manually paint it onto canvas or other suitable background. With the advent of photography,[9] images of the real world could be taken and stored for future use. This invention was soon expanded from monochromatic to color images, from monoscopic to stereoscopic[10] and from still images to film sequences. In our digital age, electronic sensor devices have taken the role of chemical film and a variety of electronic display technologies have taken over the role of painted pictures.

It is interesting to note, though, that some of the most recent developments in digital photography and image displays have their inspiration in technologies developed over 100 years ago. In 1908, Gabriel Lippmann[11] developed the concept of *integral photography*, a camera composed of very many tiny lenses side by side, in front of a photographic film [34]. These lenses collect view-dependent light rays from all directions onto the film, effectively capturing a three-dimensional field of light rays, the *light field* [1]. The newly established research field of *computational photography* has taken on his ideas and is actively developing novel multilens-camera systems for capturing 3D scenes, enhancing the depth of field, or computing novel image transfer functions. In addition, the reverse process of projecting an integral image into space has led to the development of lenticular sheet 3D printing and to auto-stereoscopic (glasses-free) multiview displays that let the observer see the captured 3D scene with full depth parallax without wearing special purpose spectacles. These 3D projection techniques have spawned a huge interest in the display community, both for high-quality auto-stereoscopic displays with full 3D parallax as used in advertisement (3D signage) and for novel 3D-TV display systems that might eventually conquer the 3D-TV home market. This is discussed further in Sect. 1.2.3.

1.2.2 Binocular Perception of Depth

It is important to note that many visual cues give the perception of depth, some of which are monocular cues (occlusion, shading, texture gradients) and some of which are binocular cues (retinal disparity, parallax, eye convergence). Of course, humans, and most predator animals, are equipped with a very sophisticated binocular vision system and it is the binocular cues that provide us with accurate short range depth

---

[9]Nicéphore Niépce, 1765–1833, is credited as one of the inventors of photography by solar light etching (Heliograph) in 1826. He later worked with Louis-Jacques-Mandé Daguerre, 1787–1851, who acquired a patent for his Daguerreotype, the first practical photography process based on silver iodide, in 1839. In parallel, William Henry Fox Talbot, 1800–1877, developed the calotype process, which uses paper coated with silver iodide. The calotype produced a negative image from which a positive could be printed using silver chloride coated paper [19].

[10]The Greek word *stereos* for solid is used to indicate a spatial 3D extension of vision, hence stereoscopic stands for a 3D form of visual information.

[11]Gabriel Lippmann, 1845–1921, French scientist, received the 1908 Nobel price in Physics for his method to reproduce color pictures by interferometry.

1 Introduction

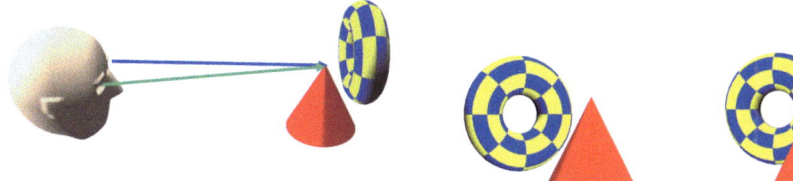

Fig. 1.1 *Left*: Human binocular perception of 3D scene. *Right*: the perceived images of the left and right eye, showing how the depth-dependent disparity results in a parallax shift between foreground and background objects. *Both* observed images are fused into a 3D sensation by the human eye-brain visual system

perception. Clearly it is advantageous for us to have good depth perception to a distance at least as large as the length of our arms. The principles of binocular vision were already recognized in 1838 by Sir Charles Wheatstone,[12] who described the process of binocular perception:

> ...the mind perceives an object of three dimensions by means of the two dissimilar pictures projected by it on the two retinae... [54]

The important observation was that the binocular perception of two correctly displaced 2D-images of a scene is equivalent to the perception of the 3D scene itself.

Figure 1.1 illustrates human binocular perception of a 3D scene, comprised of a cone in front of a torus. At the right of this figure are the images perceived by the left and the right eye. If we take a scene point, for example the tip of the cone, this projects to different positions on the left and right retina. The difference between these two positions (retinal correspondences) is known as *disparity* and the disparity associated with nearby surface points (on the cone) is larger than the disparity associated with more distant points (on the torus). As a result of this difference between foreground and background disparity the position (or alignment) of the foreground relative to the background changes as we shift the viewpoint from the left eye to the right eye. This effect is known as parallax.[13]

Imagine now that the 3D scene of the cone in front of the torus is observed by a binocular camera with two lenses that are separated horizontally by the inter-eye distance of a human observer. If these images are presented to the left and right eyes of the human observer later on, she or he cannot distinguish the observed real scene from the binocular images of the scene. The images are fused inside the binocular perception of the human observer to form the 3D impression. This observation led

---

[12] Sir Charles Wheatstone, 1802–1875, English physicist and inventor.

[13] The terms disparity and parallax are sometimes used interchangeably in the literature and this misuse of terminology is a source of confusion. One way to think about parallax is that it is induced by the difference in disparity between foreground and background objects over a pair of views displaced by a translation. The end result is that the foreground is in alignment with different parts of the background. Disparity of foreground objects and parallax then only become equivalent when the distance of background objects can be treated as infinity (e.g. distant stars), in this case the background objects are stationary in the image.

to the invention of the stereoscope by Sir David Brewster[14] [9], where two displaced images could convey 3D information to the human observer.

1.2.3 Stereoscopic Displays

Since Brewster's stereoscope, a wealth of technical devices for presenting stereoscopic images to the human observer have been designed. Virtually all of modern stereoscopic display technologies are based on the same principle, namely that of presenting two different views to the two eyes on a single display. To do this, techniques have been employed that:

- separate views by color-coding (the anaglyph technique with red-green glasses or spectral comb filters),
- use polarization properties of light (circularly or linearly polarized eye glasses),
- perform time-coding with left-right time-interleaving and actively synchronized shutter glasses, or
- exploit lens systems to project the different images directly into the eyes of the observer.

While the first three techniques all use separating glasses to be worn by the user, the latter lens projection systems allow glasses-free, auto-stereoscopic perception, even for more than two different views. Figure 1.2 sketches the stereoscopic perception with either two-view stereoscopic or glasses-free auto-stereoscopic multiview displays. In the binocular display, polarization serves to decouple left and right eye information. The auto-stereoscopic display exploits optical lenticular sheet lenses or light barrier systems to selectively project the displaced images into different angular sections in front of the display. If the observer moves in front of the display, each eye receives a differently displaced image, resulting in a look-around capability.

Binocular stereoscopic movies and selected stereoscopic television programs have now entered the market quite successfully. These display techniques are commonly given the branding *3D*, but actually they do not contain or need true 3D information. In a stereo movie recording, two displaced movie cameras are synchronously used to capture left and right eye views and stereoscopic digital movie projectors utilize polarization filters to separate both views. The spectator needs to wear a similar set of polarized glasses for binocular perception. The perceived depth impression is fixed by the inter-camera eye distance of the recording stereo camera and can only be adjusted during recording. This is a drawback of binocular stereo camera recordings because it is difficult to scale depth perception later on. Hence, different recordings must be undertaken for large screen movie theaters and for home TV settings. Even more severe is the stereoscopic image capture for auto-stereoscopic displays. In this case, not two but many slightly displaced views need

---

[14] Sir David Brewster, 1781–1868, Scottish physicist and inventor.

1 Introduction

Fig. 1.2 *Left*: Stereoscopic displays use glasses-based polarization light separators to produce the two images required for stereoscopic reception. *Right*: Lens-based auto-stereoscopic displays project multiple, slightly displaced images by use of lenses or parallax barrier systems, allowing glasses-free stereoscopic reception. Such systems allow for slight head motion

to be recorded simultaneously. Typical displays require 8 to 28 simultaneous views and it is not feasible to record all views directly, because the amount of data would grow enormously. Also, the design of such multi-ocular cameras is difficult and expensive. Instead, a true 3D movie format is needed that allows us to synthesize the required views from a generic 3D image format. Currently, 3D data formats like Multi-View Depth (MVD) or Layered Depth Video (LDV) are under discussion [3]. MVD and LDV record both depth and color from few camera positions that capture the desired angular sections in front of the display. The many views needed to drive the display are then rendered by depth-compensated interpolation from the recorded data. Thus, a true 3D format will greatly facilitate data capture for future 3D-TV systems.

There is another obstacle to binocular perception that was not discussed in early binocular display systems. The observed disparity is produced on the image plane and both eyes of the human observer are accommodating their focus on the display plane. However, the binocular depth cue causes the eyes to physically converge towards the virtual 3D position of the object, which may be before or behind the display plane. Both, eye accommodation and eye convergence angle, are strong depth cues to our visual system and depth is inferred from both. In the real world, both cues coincide since the eyes focus and converge towards the same real object position. On a binocular display, the eyes always accommodate towards the display, while the convergence angle varies with depth. This conflict causes visual discomfort and is a major source of headaches when watching strong depth effects, especially in front of the screen. Stereographers nowadays take great care to balance these effects during recording. The only remedy to this disturbing effect is to build volumetric displays where the image is truly formed in 3D space rather than on the 2D display. In this case, the convergence and accommodation cues coincide and yield stress-free stereoscopic viewing. There is an active research community underway developing volumetric or holographic displays, that rely either on spatial pattern interference, on volume-sweeping surfaces, or on 3D lightfields. Blundell and Schwarz give a good classification of volumetric displays and sketch current trends [7]. All these 3D displays need some kind of 3D scene representation and binocular imaging is not sufficient. Hence, these displays also are in need of true 3D data formats.

1.3 The Development of Computer Vision

Although the content of this book derives from a number of research fields, the field of computer vision is the most relevant large-scale research area. It is a diverse field that integrates ideas and methods from a variety of pre-existing and co-existing areas, such as: image processing, statistics, pattern recognition, geometry, photogrammetry, optimization, scientific computing, computer graphics and many others. In the 1960s–1980s, Artificial Intelligence was the driving field that tried to exploit computers for understanding the world that, in various ways, corresponded to how humans understand it. This included the interpretation of 3D scenes from images and videos.

The process of scene understanding was thought of as a hierarchy of vision levels, similar to visual perception, with three main levels [38], as follows:

Low-level vision: early 2D vision processes, such as filtering and extraction of local image structures.
Mid-level vision: processes such as segmentation, generation of 2.5D depth, optical flow computation and extraction of regional structures.
High-level vision: semantic interpretation of segments, object recognition and global 3D scene reasoning.

This general approach is still valid, but it was not successful at the first attempt, because researchers underestimated the difficulties of the first two steps and tried to directly handle high-level vision reasoning. In his recent textbook *Computer Vision: Algorithms and Applications* [49], Rick Szeliski reports an assignment of Marvin Minsky, MIT, to a group of students to develop a computer vision program that could reason about image content:

> According to one well-known story, in 1966, Marvin Minsky at MIT asked his undergraduate student Gerald Jay Sussman to "spend the summer linking a camera to a computer and getting the computer to describe what it saw".[15]

Soon, it became clear that Minsky underestimated this challenge. However, the attempts to resolve the various problems of the three levels proved fruitful to the field of computer vision and very many approaches to solve partial problems on all levels have appeared. Although some vision researchers follow the path of cognitive vision that is inspired by the working of the human brain, most techniques today are driven by engineering demands to extract relevant information from the images.

Computer vision developed roughly along the above-mentioned three levels of vision. Research in low-level vision has deepened the understanding of local image structures. Digital images can be described without regard of scanning resolution by the image scale space [55] and image pyramids [50]. Image content can be described in the image domain or equivalently in the frequency (Fourier) domain, leading to a theory of filter design to improve the image quality and to reduce noise. Local

---

[15]Szeliski, Computer Vision: Algorithms and Applications, p. 10 [49].

structures are defined by their intrinsic dimension[16] [4], which leads to interest operators [20] and to feature descriptors [6].

Regional relations between local features in an image or between images are powerful descriptions for mid-level vision processes, such as segmentation, depth estimation and optical flow estimation. Marr [38] coined the term *2.5D model*, meaning that information about scene depth for a certain region in an image exists, but only viewed from a single view point. Such is the case for range estimation techniques, which includes stereo, active triangulation or time-of-flight depth measurement devices, where not a full 3D description is measured but a range image $d(u, v)$ with one distance value per image pixel. This range value, along with some intrinsic parameters of the range sensing device, allows us to invert the image projection and to reconstruct scene surfaces. Full 3D depth can be reconstructed from multiview range images if suitably fused from different viewpoints.

The special branch of computer vision that deals with viewing a scene from two or more viewpoints and extracting a 3D representation of the geometry of the imaged scene is termed *geometric computer vision*. Here, the camera can be thought of as a measurement device. Geometric computer vision developed rapidly in the 1990s and 2000s and was influenced strongly by geodesy and photogrammetry. In fact, those disciplines are converging. Many of the techniques well known in photogrammetry have found their way into computer vision algorithms. Most notably is the method of bundle adjustment for optimally and simultaneously estimating camera parameters and 3D point estimates from uncertain image features [51].

Combining the geometric properties of scene objects with image based reflectance measurements allows us to model the visual-geometric appearance of scenes. There is now a strong relationship between computer vision and computer graphics that developed during the last decade. While computer graphics displays computer-defined objects with given surface properties by projecting them into a synthetic camera, vision estimates the surface properties of real objects as seen by a real camera. Hence, vision can be viewed as the inverse problem of graphics. One of the key challenges in computer vision is that, due to the projection of the objects into the camera, the range information is lost and needs to be recovered. This makes the inverse problem of recovering depth from images especially hard and often ill-posed. Today, both disciplines are still converging, for example in the area of image-based rendering in computer graphics and by exploiting the computing capabilities of Graphics Processing Units for computer vision tasks.

High-level vision attempts to interpret the observed scene and to assign semantic meaning to scene regions. Much progress has been made recently in this field, starting with simple object detection to object recognition, ranging from individual objects to object categories. Machine learning is vital for these approaches to work reliably and has been exploited extensively in computer vision over the last decade [43]. The availability of huge amounts of labeled training data from databases and the Web, and advances in high-dimensional learning techniques, are keys to the success

---

[16]Intrinsic Image Dimension (IID) describes the local change in the image. Constant image: 0D, linear structures: 1D, point structures: 2D.

of machine learning techniques. Successful applications range from face detection, face recognition and biometrics, to visual image retrieval and scene object categorization, to human action and event analysis. The merging of machine learning with computer vision algorithms is a very promising ongoing development and will continue to solve vision problems in the future, converging towards the ultimate goal of visual scene understanding. From a practical point of view, this will broaden the range of applications from highly controlled scenes, which is often the necessary context for the required performance in terms of accuracy and reliability, to natural, uncontrolled, real-world scenes with all of their inherent variability.

1.3.1 Further Reading in Computer Vision

Computer vision has matured over the last 50 years into a very broad and diverse field and this book does not attempt to cover that field comprehensively. However, there are some very good textbooks available that span both individual areas as well as the complete range of computer vision. An early book on this topic is the above-mentioned text by David Marr: *Vision. A Computational Investigation into the Human Representation and Processing of Visual Information* [38]; this is one of the forerunners of computer vision concepts and could be used as a historical reference. A recent and very comprehensive text book is the work by Rick Szeliski: *Computer Vision: Algorithms and Applications* [49]. This work is exceptional as it covers not only the broad field of computer vision in detail, but also gives a wealth of algorithms, mathematical methods, practical examples, an extensive bibliography and references to many vision benchmarks and datasets. The introduction gives an in-depth overview of the field and of recent trends.[17] If the reader is interested in a detailed analysis of geometric computer vision and projective multi-view geometry, we refer to the standard book *Multiple View Geometry in Computer Vision* by Richard Hartley and Andrew Zisserman[21]. Here, most of the relevant geometrical algorithms as well as the necessary mathematical foundations are discussed in detail. Other textbooks that cover the computer vision theme at large are *Computer Vision: a modern approach* [16], *Introductory Techniques for 3-D Computer Vision* [52], or *An Invitation to 3D Vision: From Images to Models* [36].

1.4 Acquisition Techniques for 3D Imaging

The challenge of 3D imaging is to recover the distance information that is lost during projection into a camera, with the highest possible accuracy and reliability, for every pixel of the image. We define a *range image* as an image where each pixel stores the distance between the imaging sensor (for example a 3D range camera)

---

[17] A pdf version is also available for personal use on the website http://szeliski.org/Book/.

and the observed surface point. Here we can differentiate between passive and active methods for range imaging, which will be discussed in detail in Chap. 2 and Chap. 3 respectively.

1.4.1 Passive 3D Imaging

Passive 3D imaging relies on images of the ambient-lit scene alone, without the help of further information, such as projection of light patterns onto the scene. Hence, all information must be taken from standard 2D images. More generally, a set of techniques called *Shape from X* exists, where X represents some visual cue. These include:

- Shape from focus, which varies the camera focus and estimates depth pointwise from image sharpness [39].
- Shape from shading, which uses the shades in a grayscale image to infer the shape of the surfaces, based on the reflectance map. This map links image intensity with surface orientation [24]. There is a related technique, called *photogrammetric stereo*, that uses several images, each with a different illumination direction.
- Shape from texture, which assumes the object is covered by a regular surface pattern. Surface normal and distance are then estimated from the perspective effects in the images.
- Shape from stereo disparity, where the same scene is imaged from two distinct (displaced) viewpoints and the difference (disparity) between pixel positions (one from each image) corresponding to the same scene point is exploited.

The most prominent, and the most detailed in this book, is the last mentioned of these. Here, depth is estimated by the geometric principle of triangulation, when the same scene point can be observed in two or more images. Figure 1.3 illustrates this principle in detail. Here, a rectilinear stereo rig is shown where the two cameras are side by side with the principal axes of their lenses parallel to each other. Note that the origin (or center) of each camera is the optical center of its lens and the *baseline* is defined as the distance between these two camera centers. Although the real image sensor is behind the lens, it is common practice to envisage and use a conceptual image position in front of the lens so that the image is the same orientation as the scene (i.e. not inverted top to bottom and left to right) and this position is shown in Fig. 1.3. The term *triangulation* comes from the fact that the scene point, $\mathbf{X}$, can be reconstructed from the triangle[18] formed by the baseline and the two coplanar vector directions defined by the left camera center to image point $\mathbf{x}$ and the right camera center to image point $\mathbf{x}'$. In fact, the depth of the scene is related to the disparity between left and right image correspondences. For closer objects, the disparity is greater, as illustrated by the blue lines in Fig. 1.3. It is clear from this figure that the

---

[18] This triangle defines an *epipolar plane*, which is discussed in Chap. 2.

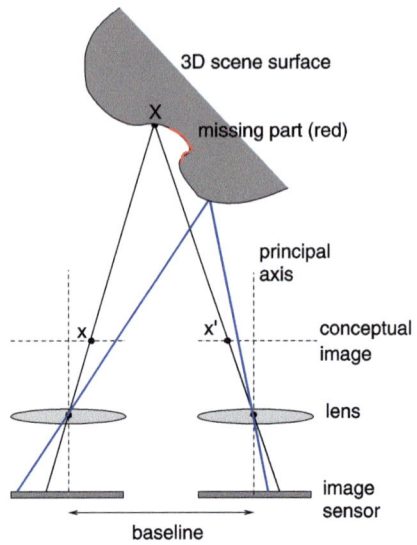

Fig. 1.3 A rectilinear stereo rig. Note the increased image disparity for the near scene point (*blue*) compared to the far scene point (*black*). The scene area marked in *red* can not be imaged by the right camera and is a 'missing part' in the reconstructed scene

scene surface colored red can not be observed by the right camera, in which case no 3D shape measurement can be made. This scene portion is sometimes referred to as a *missing part* and is the result of self-occlusion or occlusion by a different foreground object. Image correspondences are found by evaluating image similarities through image feature matching, either locally or globally over the entire image. Problems might occur if the image content does not hold sufficient information for unique correspondences, for example in smooth, textureless regions. Hence, a dense range estimation cannot be guaranteed and, particularly in man-made indoor scenarios, the resulting range images are often sparse. Algorithms, test scenarios and benchmarks for such systems may be found in the Middlebury database [42] and Chap. 2 in this book will discuss these approaches in detail. Note that many stereo rigs turn the cameras towards each other so that they are *verged*, which increases the overlap between the fields of view of the camera and increases the scene volume over which 3D reconstructions can be made. Such a system is shown in Fig. 1.4.

1.4.2 Active 3D Imaging

Active 3D imaging avoids some of the difficulties of passive techniques by introducing controlled additional information, usually controlled lighting or other electromagnetic radiation, such as infrared. Active stereo systems, for example, have the same underlying triangulation geometry as the above-mentioned passive stereo systems, but they exchange one camera by a projector, which projects a spot or a stripe, or a patterned area that does not repeat itself within some local neighborhood. This latter type of non-scanned system is called a *structured light* projection. Advances in optoelectronics for the generation of structured light patterns and other

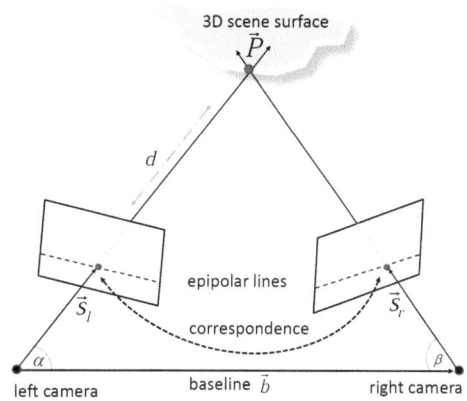

Fig. 1.4 A verged stereo system. Note that this diagram uses a simplified diagrammatic structure seen in much of the literature where only camera centers and conceptual image planes are shown. The intersection of the epipolar plane with the (image) planes defines a pair of epipolar lines. This is discussed in detail in Chap. 2. Figure reprinted from [29] with permission

illumination, accurate mechanical laser scanning control, and high resolution, high sensitivity image sensors have all had their impact on advancing the performance of active 3D imaging.

Note that, in structured light systems, all of the image feature shift that occurs due to depth variations, which causes a change in disparity, appears in the sensor's one camera, because the projected image pattern is fixed. (Contrast this with a passive binocular stereo system, where the disparity change, in general, is manifested as feature movement across two images.) The projection of a pattern means that smooth, textureless areas of the scene are no longer problematic, allowing dense, uniform reconstructions and the correspondence problem is reduced to finding the known projected pattern. (In the case of a projected spot, the correspondence problem is removed altogether.) In general, the computational burden for generating active range triangulations is relatively light, the resulting range images are mostly dense and reliable, and they can be acquired quickly.

An example of such systems are coded light projectors that use either a time-series of codes or color codes [8]. A recent example of a successful projection system is the Kinect-camera[19] that projects an infrared dot pattern and is able to recover dense range images up to several meters distance at 30 frames per second (fps). One problem with all triangulation-based systems, passive and active, is that depth accuracy depends on the triangulation angle, which means that a large baseline is desirable. On the other hand, with a large baseline, the 'missing parts' problem described above is exacerbated, yielding unseen, occluded regions at object boundaries. This is unfortunate, since precise object boundary estimation is important for geometric reconstruction.

An alternative class of active range sensors that mitigates the occlusion problem are coaxial sensors, which exploit the time-of-flight principle. Here, light is emitted from a light source that is positioned in line with the optical axis of the receiving sensor (for example a camera or photo-diode) and is reflected from the object sur-

---

[19] *Kinect* is a trademark of Microsoft.

Fig. 1.5 Active coaxial time-of-flight range estimation by phase shift correlation. Figure reprinted from [29] with permission

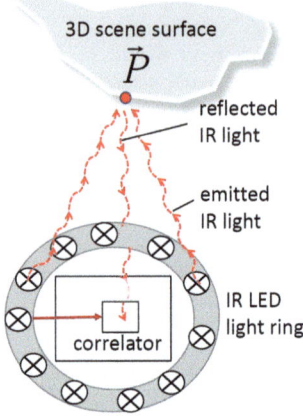

face back into the sensor. Figure 1.5 gives a schematic view of an active coaxial range sensor.[20] The traveling time delay between outgoing and reflected wave is then measured by phase correlation or direct run-time shuttering, as a direct measure of object distance. Classical examples of such devices are laser-based systems, such as the *LIght Detection And Ranging* (LIDAR) scanner for long-distance depth estimation. The environment is scanned by deflecting a laser with a rotating mirror and distances are measured pointwise, delivering 3D point clouds. Recently, camera-based receivers are utilized that avoid the need for coherent laser light but use inexpensive LED light sources instead. (Such light sources are also easier to make eye-safe.) Again, the time shift of the reflected light is measured, either by gating very short light pulses directly, or by phase correlation of the time shift between the emitted and reflected light of a modulated continuous LED light source. Such range cameras [44] are depth estimation devices that, in principle, may deliver dense and accurate depth maps in real-time and can be used for depth estimation of dynamic time-varying scenes [31, 32]. Active sensing devices will be discussed in more detail in Chap. 3 and in Chap. 9 in the context of remote sensing.

1.4.3 Passive Stereo Versus Active Stereo Imaging

What are the relative merits of passive and active stereo imaging systems? In summary, since the computational burden of passive correspondences is alleviated, it is generally easier to build active systems that can generate dense range images at high frames rates (e.g. 30 fps for the Kinect). Lack of surface features or sufficiently

---

[20]Figures are a preprint from the forthcoming Encyclopedia of Computer Vision [29].

large-scale texture on the scene object can result in passive stereo giving low density 3D reconstructions, at least in the local regions where the surface texture or features (e.g. corners) are missing. This has a number of effects. Firstly, it makes it difficult to comprehensively determine the size and shape of the imaged object. Secondly, it is difficult to get good shape visualizations, when the imaged object is rendered from many different viewpoints. In contrast, as long as the surface is not too dark (low reflectivity) or specular, and does not have too many deep concavities ('missing parts'), active stereo systems allow comprehensive shape measurements and give good renderings for multi-viewpoint visualizations. Thus, when the density of features is low, or the resolution of image sensing is low compared to the scale of the imaged texture, an active stereo system is the preferred solution. However, the need to scan a laser spot or stripe or to project a structured light pattern brings with it extra complexity and expense, and potential eye-safety issues. The use of spot or stripe scanning also brings with it additional reliability issues associated with moving parts.

There is another side to this discussion, which takes into account the availability of increasingly high resolution CCD/CMOS image sensors. For passive stereo systems, these now allow previously smooth surfaces to appear textured, at the higher resolution scale. A good example is the human face where the random pattern of facial pores can be extracted and hence used to solve the correspondence problem in a passive system. Of course, higher resolution sensors bring with them higher data rates and hence a higher computational burden. Thus, to achieve reasonable real-time performance, improved resolution is developing in tandem with faster processing architectures, such as GPUs, which are starting to have a big impact on dense, real-time passive stereo [56].

1.5 Twelve Milestones in 3D Imaging and Shape Analysis

In the development towards the current state-of-the-art in 3D imaging and analysis systems, we now outline a small selection of scientific and technological milestones. As we have pointed out, there are many historical precursors to this modern subject area, from the ancient Greeks referring to the optical projection of images (Aristotle, circa 350 BC) to Albrecht Duerer's first mechanical perspective drawing (1525 CE) to Hauck's establishment of the relationship between projective geometry and photogrammetry (1883 CE). Here, however, we will present a very small selection of relatively modern milestones[21] from circa 1970 that are generally thought to fall within the fields of computer vision or computer graphics.

---

[21] Twelve milestones is a small number, with the selection somewhat subjective and open to debate. We are merely attempting to give a glimpse of the subject's development and diversity, not a definitive and comprehensive history.

Fig. 1.6 Extracted stripe deformation when scanning a polyhedral object. Figure reprinted from [45] with permission

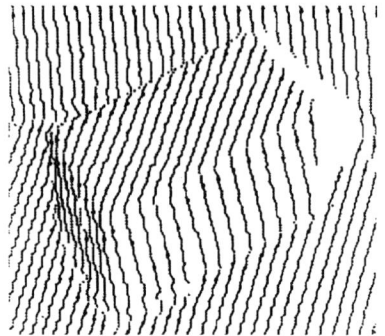

1.5.1 Active 3D Imaging: An Early Optical Triangulation System

The development of active rangefinders based on optical triangulation appears regularly in the literature from the early 1970s. In 1972, Shirai [45] presented a system that used a stripe projection system and a TV camera to recognize polyhedral objects. The stripe projector is rotated in steps so that a vertical plane of light passes over a polyhedral object of interest. A TV camera captures and stores the deformation of the projected stripe at a set of projection angles, as shown in Fig. 1.6. A set of processing steps enabled shapes to be recognized based on the interrelation of their scene planes. The assumption of polyhedral scene objects reduced the complexity of their processing, which suited the limitations of the available computational power at that time.

1.5.2 Passive 3D Imaging: An Early Stereo System

One of the first computer-based passive stereo systems employed in a clearly defined application was that of Gennery who, in 1977, presented a stereo vision system for an autonomous vehicle [18]. In this work, interest points are extracted and area-based correlation is used to find correspondences across the stereo image pair. The relative pose of the two cameras is computed from these matches, camera distortion is corrected and, finally, 3D points are triangulated from the correspondences. The extracted point cloud is then used in the autonomous vehicle application to distinguish between the ground and objects above the ground surface.

1.5.3 Passive 3D Imaging: The Essential Matrix

When 8 or more image correspondences are given for a stereo pair, captured by cameras with known intrinsic parameters, it is possible to linearly estimate the relative position and orientation (pose) of the two viewpoints from which the two projective images were captured. Once these relative viewpoints are known, then the 3D structural information of the scene can be easily recovered from the image correspondences. The origin of this approach, where the relative viewpoint pose is captured in a 3×3 *Essential Matrix*, is due to Longuet-Higgins in his 1981 *Nature* paper entitled: *A computer algorithm for reconstructing a scene from two projections* [35]. It was previously known that relative camera viewpoints could be determined iteratively with just 5 correspondences, but the extra correspondences allowed Longuet-Higgins to present a much more direct linear solution. Note that, only the direction of the displacement between the two viewpoints can be recovered, which means that the absolute scale of the 3D scene reconstruction is unknown. (Put simply, shape but not size is recovered, but the correct scale can be determined with a known dimension in the scene.)

1.5.4 Model Fitting: The RANSAC Approach to Feature Correspondence Analysis

Matching corresponding features between images or surfaces is essential for both 3D shape reconstruction methods and 3D shape matching techniques. Selecting, for example, a set of 8 correct correspondences is vital to the estimation of the Essential Matrix. Unfortunately, this is a very difficult problem and often mismatches occur. Hence, robust selection of feature correspondences is of utmost importance. The 1981 seminal paper by M.A. Fishler and R.C. Bolles: *Random Sample Consensus: A Paradigm for Model Fitting with Applications to Image Analysis and Automated Cartography* [37] opened the way to handle correspondence errors with a large percentage of outliers. From the available set of n candidate correspondences, which are matched on the basis of local properties, random subsets of $p = 8$ correspondences are drawn and a candidate Essential Matrix is computed for each. The other $n - p$ candidate correspondences are then tested against the random set solutions and the solution with the largest 'consensus' (i.e. the most support in terms of the number of inliers) is selected as the best solution. Although computationally expensive, it yields excellent results. From the 1990s, many variants of this basic algorithm, with improved performance, have been employed in computer vision and 3D shape analysis.

1.5.5 Active 3D Imaging: Advances in Scanning Geometries

The practical development of 3D laser range sensors closely follows the availability of new electronic components and electro-optical technologies. A novel active triangulation method was proposed by Rioux in 1984 [40]. To obtain a large field of view using small triangulation angles, without sacrificing precision, the concept of synchronized scanners was proposed. Such a system has the advantage that the number of 'missing parts' (i.e. the 'shadow effect') can be reduced. These occur where parts of the scene are not simultaneously accessible to both the laser and the image sensor. Using a special scanning mirror arrangement, both the emitted laser beam and receiver optics are rotated simultaneously, in a synchronized fashion, so that the laser spot in the sensor plane can be maintained closer to the image center, while the projected beam remains inherently in focus over a large depth of field and high resolution can be maintained despite a short physical baseline.

1.5.6 3D Registration: Rigid Transformation Estimation from 3D Correspondences

Given a set of surface correspondences between two 3D data sets of the same or similar objects in different poses, how do we compute the 6 degree of freedom rigid transformation between them? If we have this rotation and translation information, we can bring the two scans into alignment; a process called *registration*. In the second half of the 1980s, several researchers presented solutions to this problem; for example, both Faugeras and Hebert [15] and Horn [25] derived formulations where the rigid body rotation is represented using quaternions. In Horn's work, an optimal unit quaternion (4-vector) is estimated as the eigenvector corresponding to the maximum eigenvalue of a matrix. Once the rotation has been estimated, it is trivial to compute the estimated translation using this rotation and the centroids of the two point clouds.

The singular value decomposition (SVD) approach of Arun et al. [2] is also very widely used. Here, a 3×3 cross-covariance matrix H is formed using the correspondences and an SVD of this matrix, $H = USV^T$, yields the estimated rotation matrix as $\hat{R} = UV^T$.

Rigid body transformation estimation forms the core of rigid 3D registration algorithms, such as Iterative Closest Points, which is described next.

1.5.7 3D Registration: Iterative Closest Points

As long as three or more correspondences in a general position (non-collinear) are given between two overlapping 3D point clouds, then the resulting rigid body transformation can be estimated, using one of several methods, as previously mentioned. In 1992, Besl and McKay proposed the seminal iterative closest point (ICP) algorithm [5]. Algorithms based on the ICP algorithm are currently the *de facto* standard for rigid 3D shape registration tasks. The basis of the algorithm is that it iterates two steps until convergence: tentative correspondences establishment via 'closest points' across the two shapes, and rigid transformation parameters update. As long as the initial rotational and translational displacement between a pair of 3D shapes is sufficiently small, then convergence to a global minimum is always possible and

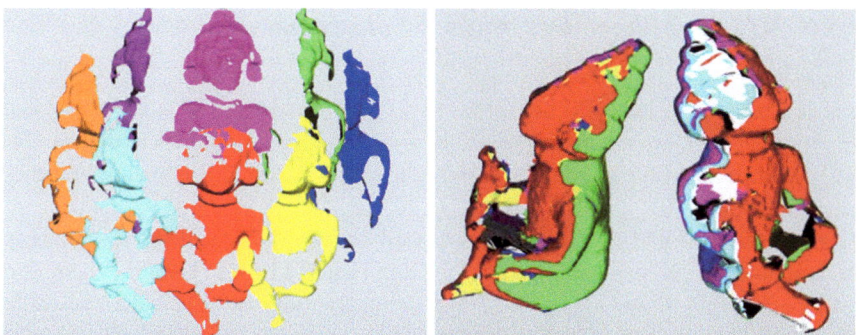

Fig. 1.7 Example of model reconstruction. Partial 3D views of the object of interest are acquired (*left*). After registration all the 3D views are transformed to the common reference system and merged (*right*). Figure generated by Alessandro Negrente, reproduced from [17]

high quality correspondences can be established. Over the last two decades, many variants of ICP have been proposed to improve the speed and accuracy of the registration process. An example of the registration required for model construction from partial 3D views is given in Fig. 1.7.

1.5.8 Passive 3D Imaging: The Fundamental Matrix and Camera Self-calibration

In 1992 Luong, Faugeras, and Maybank extended the Essential Matrix to uncalibrated cameras through the Fundamental Matrix. While for the Essential Matrix estimation, the camera intrinsic parameters had to be known in advance, now arbitrary cameras could be used and calibrated from the image data alone. The papers by Faugeras:*What can be seen in three dimensions with an uncalibrated stereo rig?* [13] and by Faugeras, Luong and Maybank: *Camera self-calibration: Theory and experiments* [14] started a new research area within computer vision that today allows us to reconstruct large 3D environments from arbitrary image collections; for example, those taken by tourists and uploaded to the web. There are even web services available that enable us to simply upload our pictures of a scene and obtain 3D representations from them.

The basic algorithm for estimating the Fundamental Matrix from 8 correspondences was rather sensitive to correspondence errors and researchers were sceptical about its usability in noisy imaging conditions. This problem was tackled in 1995 by Richard Hartley in his famous work entitled *In Defense of the 8-Point Algorithm* [22] [23]. Hartley showed that image normalization is vital for practical Fundamental Matrix estimation.

1.5.9 3D Local Shape Descriptors: Spin Images

The ICP algorithm fails if it converges to a local minimum that is not the global minimum of the least-squares registration error. A common approach to prevent this is to determine a sparse set of three or more strong local descriptor (feature) matches across the pair of 3D shapes, which allows coarse 3D registration to within the convergence basin of ICP. Probably the most well-known 3D local shape descriptor is the spin image [26], presented by Johnson and Hebert in 1997. Here the local normal of a 3D point is used to encode neighbouring points by measuring their height in the direction of the normal and their radius in the tangential plane described by the normal. Thus a spin image encodes the relative positions of neighboring points in a cylindrical-polar coordinate system. The neighbor's angles in the tangential plane are discarded in order to give pose-invariance to the descriptor and the heights and radius values of the neighbors are built into a two-dimensional histogram, which forms the spin image descriptor. A large number of experiments in the literature have shown that the spin images are powerful for several tasks that include the registration of overlapping shapes, 3D object recognition and 3D shape retrieval (shape search).

Figure 1.8 shows some examples of spin images computed on 3D captures of human faces [11]. In this case, the spin images are taken over a limited local range, as the 3D face surfaces are partial scans taken from a single viewpoint (there is no scanned surface for the back of the head). In the figure, the spin images for a given landmark appear quite similar across two different faces. For complete 3D scans, it is possible for spin images to encode the full extent of the object.

1.5.10 Passive 3D Imaging: Flexible Camera Calibration

Camera calibration is the process whereby *intrinsic* camera parameters are established, such as the focal length of the lens and the size and aspect ratio of the image sensor pixels. The position and orientation of the camera relative to the scene is also established and the parameters describing this are referred to as *extrinsic* parameters. Many current approaches to camera calibration are based on the easy-to-use, yet accurate approach presented by Zhang in 2000,[22] where calibration can be achieved from n-views of a calibration grid of known grid dimensions [57]. This calibration grid is a planar 'chessboard' pattern of alternate black and white squares which can be freely moved as the calibration images are captured, the motion between the captures is not required, hence the system is easy

---

[22]Zhang's seminal work is pre-dated by a large body of pioneering work on calibration, such as D.C. Brown's work in the context of photogrammetry, which dates back to the 1950s and many other works in computer vision, such as the seminal two-stage method of Tsai [53].

1 Introduction

Fig. 1.8 Example spin images computed for 14 landmarks on two different faces from the FRGC dataset. Here a bin size of 5 mm is used. The size of the spin image is 18×9 pixels. The *middle top part* of the spin image is the 3D surface point whose local shape we are encoding; the *left part* of the spin image corresponds to points above this 3D point in the direction of the normal; the *right part* corresponds to points below, using this same direction. The vertical direction in the spin image corresponds to the radius in the tangential plane. Figure adapted from [11], courtesy of Clement Creusot

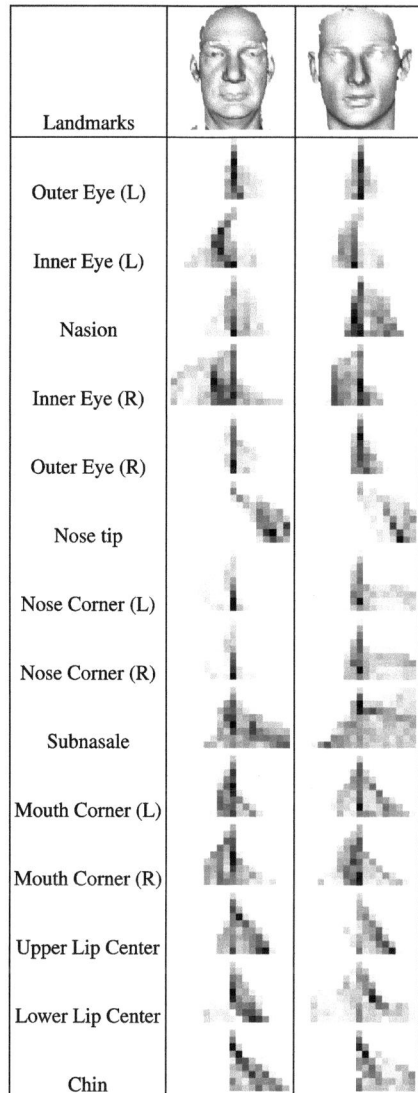

to use. Although the minimum number of images captured is 2, around 20 are commonly used for improved accuracy. The estimation is in two-stages: firstly, a closed-form linear solution for the camera's parameters is used, followed by a non-linear refinement based on the maximum-likelihood criterion. In the first stage, lens distortion is assumed to be zero, whereas the second stage provides a mechanism for radial distortion parameters to be estimated, if required. Figure 1.9 illustrates a typical set of calibration plane positions to calibrate a camera and a standard corner detector is used to find each junction of four squares on each chess-

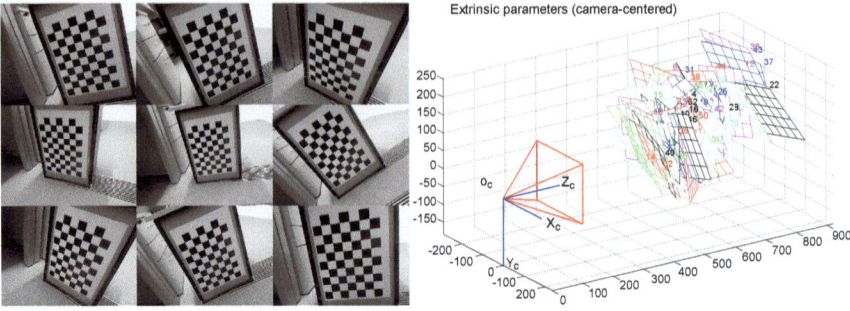

Fig. 1.9 *Left*: calibration targets used in a camera calibration process, images courtesy of Hao Sun. *Right*: after calibration, it is possible to determine the positions of the calibration planes using the estimated extrinsic parameters. Figure generated by the *Camera Calibration Toolbox for Matlab*, webpage at http://www.vision.caltech.edu/bouguetj/calib_doc/, accessed 22nd Dec 2011. Page maintained by Jean-Yves Bouguet

board image. The same corner position input data can be used to calibrate a stereo rig, whereby two sets of intrinsic parameters are established and the extrinsic parameters define the 6 degree-of-freedom rigid pose of one camera relative to another.

1.5.11 3D Shape Matching: Heat Kernel Signatures

One problem with spin images and other local shape descriptors is that they are encoded in Euclidean space and are only valid for rigid local shapes. Understanding shapes in terms of their geodesic distances[23] can yield more generic approaches that are not degraded by the bending of the shape (i.e. they are isometric invariant). In 2009, Sun et al. [48] presented a multi-scale shape signature that is isometric invariant. It is based on the properties of the heat diffusion process over a meshed surface and belongs to a class of methods known as diffusion geometry approaches. The concise signature is obtained by restricting the heat kernel to the temporal domain. This technique and other approaches involving diffusion geometry enable high performance 3D shape matching under isometric deformation and are thus finding their way into 3D object recognition and 3D shape retrieval (search) applications. Figure 1.10 shows heat kernel signatures extracted on two instances of an isometrically deformed shape.

---

[23] A geodesic distance between two points on a surface is the minimal across-surface distance.

1 Introduction

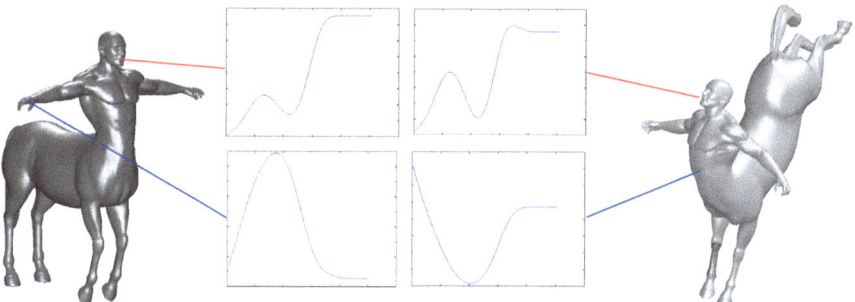

Fig. 1.10 Heat kernel signatures calculated on two isometric shapes. The *top row* shows that signatures at corresponding points look very similar. The *bottom row* shows that signatures at different points on the mesh differ. Figure reproduced from Chap. 7, courtesy of Benjamin Bustos

1.5.12 A Seminal Application: Real-Time Human Pose Recognition

In 2011, Shotton et al. [46] presented a system that was able to segment the whole body into a set of parts based on a single range image (i.e. no temporal information is used) and thereby determine, in real-time, the position of human body joints. This process is illustrated in Fig. 1.11. A design aim was high frame rates and they achieved 200 frames per second on consumer hardware. The system can run comfortably using an inexpensive 3D camera and the algorithm forms a core component

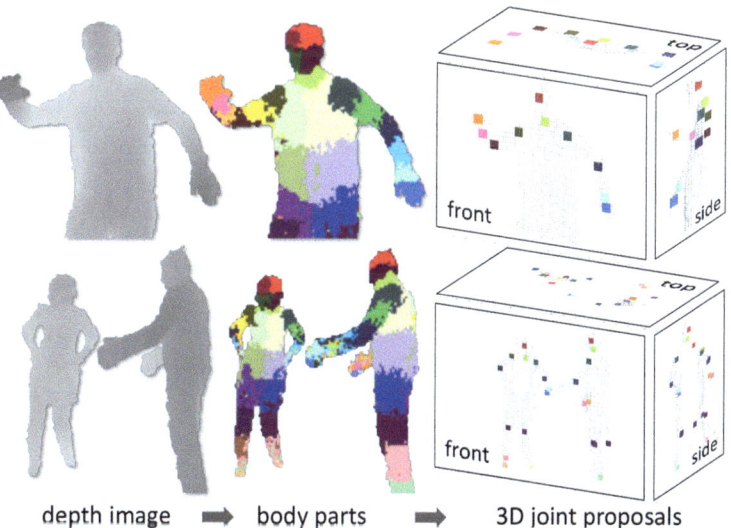

Fig. 1.11 From a single depth image, range pixels can be labeled as belonging to certain body parts, which are colored differently in the figure. From this labeling, 3D joint positions can be inferred. Figure courtesy of [46]

of the Kinect-XBox gaming platform. To achieve high frame rates, extremely simple and computationally cheap 3D features were employed based on depth comparisons and randomized decision forest classifiers were trained and implemented to run on a GPU. The training data uses 100,000 captured poses, each of which generates a synthetic set of 15 base meshes, spanning a range of different body sizes, shapes, viewpoints, clothing and hairstyle. This system is an archetypal modern, successful 3D recognition system that shows what can be achieved when machine learning techniques, a large corpus of training data and fast computational architectures are brought together.

1.6 Applications of 3D Imaging

Probably the most mature techniques in range sensing are 3D scanner applications in geodetic, architectural and industrial surveys. Airborne LIDAR systems are being used routinely now to survey building structures in cities leading to the generation of digital elevation maps (DEMs). High-precision DEMs of rural regions and forest areas are also produced for various purposes. Multiple reflection response LIDAR systems record and evaluate multiple reflections in forest areas that arise from height differences between the solid forest floor and the foliage. These systems are combined with photogrammetric DEM estimation and semantic segmentation from aerial imagery to automate map generation (e.g. for navigation) and topographic map creation. Figure 1.12 depicts an example of a 3D DEM, mapped with texture from a satellite image. Chapters 9 and 10 will explicitly deal with these applications.

Ground-based 3D scanner stations are used to reconstruct 3D structures, such as buildings (indoor and outdoor) for the purpose of documentation and mensuration. One application area is preservation and electronic documentation of cultural heritage, such as scanning of 3D models from famous buildings, old castles, churches and archaeological artifacts. The conversion of these data into 3D models and their

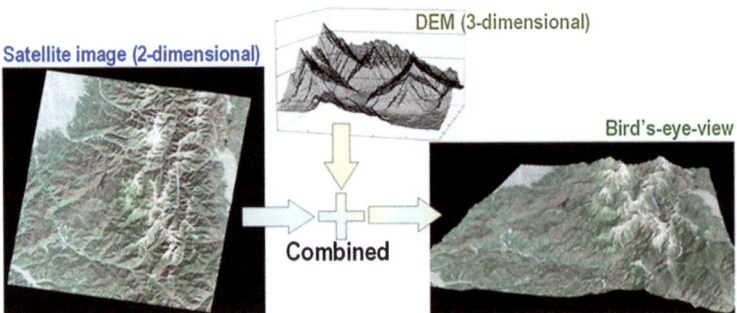

Fig. 1.12 Bird's eye view of a mountainous area from a 3D DEM mapped with texture from a satellite image. Copyright METI/NASA, reprinted with permission from ERSDAC (Earth Remote Sensing Data Analysis Center), http://www.ersdac.or.jp/GDEM/E/2.html

1 Introduction

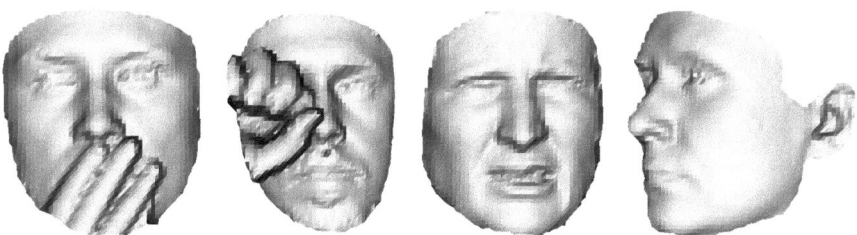

Fig. 1.13 Example 3D scans from the Bosphorus dataset with occlusions, expression variations and pose variations [41]. Figure adapted from [11]

presentation by electronic means will help to preserve cultural diversity and will enable online access to such sites. Another application area is the precise 3D documentation of industrial sites and fabrication plants for as-built control and quality control. It is very important to document the changes in building structures and industrial plants, since this will greatly facilitate planning and integration of new structures. A challenge for reconstructing complete sites from range imaging devices is the need to fuse all surface data into a consistent 3D representation and to extract functional objects from the 3D points. This involves the registration of partial surfaces into complete models, as was illustrated in Fig. 1.7.

The handling of dynamic and time-varying 3D shapes is another emerging field which heavily relies on 3D imaging techniques. With the advent of range video cameras that capture depth at video frame rates, like the ToF 3D range cameras or the Kinect sensor, it becomes possible to observe deforming shapes over time and to model these deformations accordingly [27]. Of particular interest is the tracking and modeling of human motion, expression and behavior. Much work investigated traditional dynamic shape techniques, such as active motion capture systems using markers, or markerless multiview shape from silhouette for human motion capture and much has already been achieved regarding motion and behavior modeling. Novel and improved range imaging technology is now facilitating and significantly influencing motion and behavior modeling. As already discussed, a recent example is the very successful combination of the Kinect sensor with the XBox human motion capture system[24] for interactive games. Prior approaches that utilized 2D images only are significantly inferior to the detailed tracking of body and limbs that is becoming available with range data.

In addition to human pose and gesture tracking, the analysis of human faces and face recognition systems are gaining importance. In particular, face recognition can be improved significantly if 3D face models and 3D face data are available. Systems based on 3D face shape are much more robust when dealing with changing illumination and pose, and facial views can be normalized for better recognition. Figure 1.13 shows a set of rendered face scans from the Bosphorus dataset [41]. Current research aims to provide 3D face recognition under occlusion, facial ex-

---

[24]Kinect and XBox are trademarks of Microsoft Corporation.

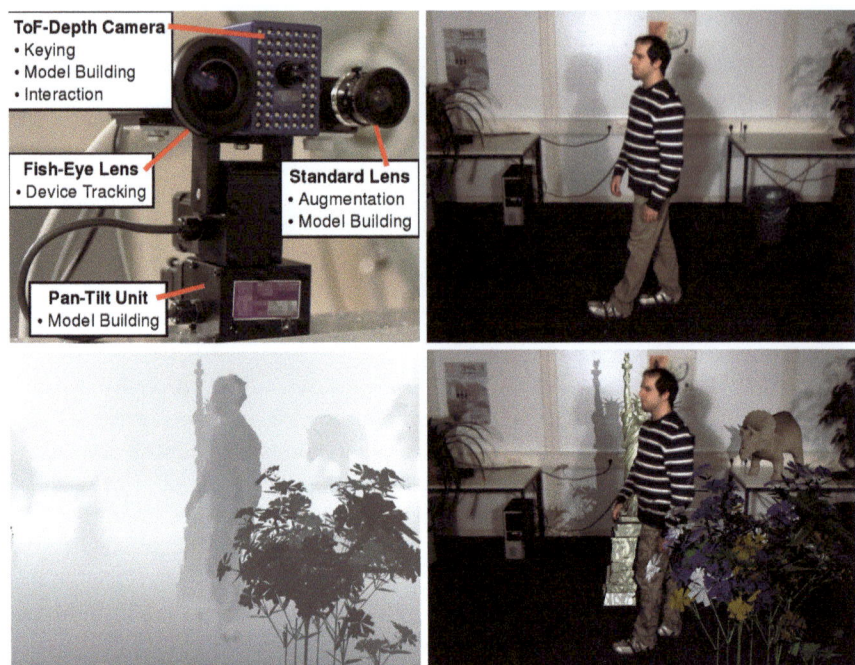

Fig. 1.14 Depth-based 3D virtual studio application. *Top left*: Hybrid range-color camera system. *Top right*: one original color view of the scene. *Bottom left*: range image with mixed real and virtual content. *Bottom right*: automatic composition of real and virtual content, including mutual occlusion, color and shadow mixing. Images reprinted from [30] with permission

pression variations and pose variations. Chapter 8 discusses this research area in detail.

The exploitation of range data will open new opportunities to automate data processing and to address new application areas. One such area is digital post processing of film and video. The insertion of virtual content into a movie is an important part of film production and a substantial cost factor as well. Traditionally, 2D color keying is used to separate objects from the background, or to insert virtual content into a 3D scene and dynamic objects are even segmented out manually in the post production process. If range data is available, then the concept of *depth keying* can be applied, where a person is separated from its background by distance evaluation. This is much more robust than traditional 2D image-based color keying or motion segmentation approaches in unconstrained environments. As an example, Fig. 1.14 gives an overview of such a hybrid system that directly exploits a dynamic 3D range camera based on the time-of-flight principle, in addition to a set of color cameras for visualization [30]. This technique may be used in 3D virtual studios that mix virtual and real content for TV and film production. The system reconstructs a 3D environment model, together with depth and color of moving persons. Since all data contains both depth and color, it is easy to separate dynamically moving objects from the static environment and even to insert additional virtual content for video post production. Figure 1.14 shows the camera system, one of the original views, the depth and color views from the enhanced scene, including real and virtual content. Without range data, such scene composition is a tedious manual task, as used in traditional video post processing today. With the use of depth information, there is a wealth of opportunities to facilitate and to automate data processing.

Although many different techniques have been proposed for a wide variety of 3D imaging applications, many of them work well only in constrained scenarios and over a subset of the available datasets. Many techniques still fail on challenging data and techniques with more robustness and better overall performance still need to be developed. Deeper insights into various 3D imaging, analysis and application problems are required for the development of such novel techniques.

1.7 Book Outline

We conclude this chapter with a roadmap of the remaining chapters of this book. Although there is a natural order to the chapters, they are relatively self-contained, so that they can also be read as standalone chapters. The book is split into three parts: Part I is comprised of Chaps. 2–4 and it presents the fundamental techniques for the capture, representation and visualization of 3D data; Part II is comprised of Chaps. 5–7 and is concerned with 3D shape analysis, registration and matching; finally, Part III is comprised of Chaps. 8–11 and discusses various application areas in 3D face recognition, remote sensing and medical imaging.

1.7.1 Part I: 3D Imaging and Shape Representation

Chapter 2 describes passive 3D imaging, which recovers 3D information from camera systems that do not project light or other electromagnetic radiation onto the imaged scene. An overview of the common techniques used to recover 3D information from camera images is presented first. The chapter then focuses on 3D recovery from multiple views, which can be obtained using two or more cameras at the same time (stereo), or a single moving camera at different times (structure from motion). The aim is to give a comprehensive presentation that covers camera modeling, camera calibration, image rectification, correspondence search and the triangulation to compute 3D scene structure. Several 3D passive imaging systems and their real-world applications are highlighted later in this chapter.

In Chap. 3, active 3D imaging is discussed. These systems do project light, infrared or other electromagnetic radiation (EMR) onto the scene and they can be based on different measurement principles that include time-of-flight, triangulation and interferometry. While time-of-flight and interferometry systems are briefly discussed, an in-depth description of triangulation-based systems is provided, which have the same underlying geometry as the passive stereo systems presented in Chap. 2. The characterization of such triangulation-based systems is discussed using both an error propagation framework and experimental protocols.

Chapter 4 focuses on 3D data representation, storage and visualization. It begins by providing a taxonomy of 3D data representations and then presents more detail on a selection of the most important 3D data representations and their processing, such as triangular meshes and subdivision surfaces. This chapter also discusses the local differential properties of surfaces, mesh simplification and compression.

1.7.2 Part II: 3D Shape Analysis and Processing

Chapter 5 presents feature-based methods in 3D shape analysis, including both classical and the most recent approaches to interest point (keypoint) detection and local surface description. The main emphasis is on heat-kernel based detection and description algorithms, a relatively recent set of methods based on a common mathematical model and falling under the umbrella of diffusion geometry.

Chapter 6 details 3D shape registration, which is the process of bringing together two or more 3D shapes, either of the same object or of two different but similar objects. This chapter first introduces the classical Iterative Closest Point (ICP) algorithm [5], which represents the gold standard registration method. Current limitations of ICP are addressed and the most popular variants of ICP are described to improve the basic implementation in several ways. Challenging registration scenarios are analyzed and a taxonomy of promising alternative registration techniques is introduced. Three case studies are described with an increasing level of difficulty, culminating with an algorithm capable of dealing with deformable objects.

Chapter 7 presents 3D shape matching with a view to applications in shape retrieval (e.g. web search) and object recognition. In order to present the subject, four approaches are described in detail with good balance among maturity and novelty, namely the depth buffer descriptor, spin images, salient spectral geometric features and heat kernel signatures.

1.7.3 Part III: 3D Imaging Applications

Chapter 8 gives an overview of 3D face recognition and discusses both well-established and more recent state-of-the-art 3D face recognition techniques in terms of their implementation and expected performance on benchmark datasets. In contrast to 2D face recognition methods that have difficulties when handling changes in illumination and pose, 3D face recognition algorithms have been more successful in dealing with these challenges. 3D face shape data is used as an independent cue for face recognition and has also been combined with texture to facilitate multimodal face recognition.

The next two chapters discuss related topics in remote sensing and segmentation. Chapter 9 presents techniques used for generation of 3D Digital Elevation Models (DEMs) from remotely sensed data. Three methods, and their accuracy evaluation, are presented in the discussion: stereoscopic imagery, Interferometric Synthetic Aperture Radar (InSAR) and LIght Detection and Ranging (LIDAR).

Chapter 10 discusses 3D remote sensing for forest measurement and applies 3D DEM data to 3D forest and biomass analysis. Several techniques are described that can be used to detect and measure individual tree crowns using high-resolution remote sensing data, including aerial photogrammetry and airborne laser scanning (LIDAR). In addition, the chapter presents approaches that can be used to infer aggregate biomass levels within areas of forest (plots and grid cells), using LIDAR information on the 3D forest structure.

Finally, Chap. 11 describes imaging methods that aim to reconstruct the inside of the human body in 3D. This is in contrast to optical methods that try to reconstruct the surface of viewed objects, though there are similarities in some of the geometries and techniques used. The first section gives an overview of the physics of data acquisition, where images come from and why they look the way they do. The next section illustrates how this raw data is processed into surface and volume data for viewing and analysis. This is followed by a description of how to put images in a common coordinate frame, and a more specific case study illustrating higher dimensional data manipulation. Finally some clinical applications are described to show how these methods can be used to affect the treatment of patients.

References

1. Adelson, E.H., Bergen, J.R.: The plenoptic function and the elements of early vision. In: Landy, M., Movshon, J.A. (eds.) Computational Models of Visual Processing (1991)
2. Arun, K.S., Huang, T.S., Blostein, S.D.: Least-squares fitting of two 3d point sets. IEEE Trans. Pattern Anal. Mach. Intell. **9**(5), 698–700 (1987)
3. Bartczak, B., Vandewalle, P., Grau, O., Briand, G., Fournier, J., Kerbiriou, P., Murdoch, M., Mller, M., Goris, R., Koch, R., van der Vleuten, R.: Display-independent 3d-TV production and delivery using the layered depth video format. IEEE Trans. Broadcast. **57**(2), 477–490 (2011)
4. Bennet, R.: Representation and Analysis of Signals. Part xxi: The Intrinsic Dimensionality of Signal Collections, Rep. 163. The Johns Hopkins University, Baltimore (1965)
5. Besl, P., McKay, N.D.: A method for registration of 3D shapes. IEEE Trans. Pattern Anal. Mach. Intell. **14**(2), 239–256 (1992)
6. Bigun, J., Granlund, G.: Optimal orientation detection of linear symmetry. In: First International Conference on Computer Vision, pp. 433–438. IEEE Computer Society, New York (1987)
7. Blundell, B., Schwarz, A.: The classification of volumetric display systems: characteristics and predictability of the image space. IEEE Trans. Vis. Comput. Graph. **8**, 66–75 (2002)
8. Boyer, K., Kak, A.: Color-encoded structured light for rapid active ranging. IEEE Trans. Pattern Anal. Mach. Intell. **9**(1) (1987)
9. Brewster, S.D.: The Stereoscope: Its History, Theory, and Construction with Applications to the fine and useful Arts and to Education. John Murray, Albemarle Street, London (1856)
10. Brownson, C.D.: Euclid's optics and its compatibility with linear perspective. Arch. Hist. Exact Sci. **24**, 165–194 (1981). doi:10.1007/BF00357417

11. Creusot, C.: Automatic landmarking for non-cooperative 3d face recognition. Ph.D. thesis, Department of Computer Science, University of York, UK (2011)
12. Curtis, G.: The Cave Painters. Knopf, New York (2006)
13. Faugeras, O.: What can be seen in three dimensions with an uncalibrated stereorig? In: Sandini, G. (ed.) Computer Vision: ECCV'92. Lecture Notes in Computer Science, vol. 588, pp. 563–578. Springer, Berlin (1992)
14. Faugeras, O., Luong, Q., Maybank, S.: Camera self-calibration: theory and experiments. In: Sandini, G. (ed.) Computer Vision: ECCV'92. Lecture Notes in Computer Science, vol. 588, pp. 321–334. Springer, Berlin (1992)
15. Faugeras, O.D., Hebert, M.: The representation, recognition and locating of 3-d objects. Int. J. Robot. Res. **5**(3), 27–52 (1986)
16. Forsyth, D., Ponce, J.: Computer Vision: A Modern Approach. Prentice Hall, Upper Saddle River (2003)
17. Fusiello, A.: Visione computazionale. Appunti delle lezioni. Pubblicato a cura dell'autore (2008)
18. Gennery, D.B.: A stereo vision system for an autonomous vehicle. In: Proc. 5th Int. Joint Conf. Artificial Intell (IJCAI), pp. 576–582 (1977)
19. Gernsheim, H., Gernsheim, A.: The History of Photography. Mc Graw-Hill, New York (1969)
20. Harris, C., Stephens, M.J.: A combined corner and edge detector. In: Alvey Vision Conference (1988)
21. Hartley, R., Zisserman, A.: Multiple View Geometry in Computer Vision. Cambridge University, Cambridge (2003). ISBN 0-521-54051-8
22. Hartley, R.I.: In defence of the 8-point algorithm. In: Proceedings of the Fifth International Conference on Computer Vision, ICCV'95, p. 1064. IEEE Computer Society, Washington (1995)
23. Hartley, R.I.: In defence of the 8-point algorithm. IEEE Trans. Pattern Anal. Mach. Intell. **19**(6), 580–593 (1997)
24. Horn, B.K.P.: Shape from shading: a method for obtaining the shape of a smooth opaque object from one view. Ph.D. thesis, MIT, Cambridge, MA, USA (1970)
25. Horn, B.K.P.: Closed-form solution of absolute orientation using unit quaternions. J. Opt. Soc. Am. A **4**(4), 629–642 (1987)
26. Johnson, A.E., Hebert, M.: Using spin images for efficient object recognition in cluttered 3d scenes. IEEE Trans. Pattern Anal. Mach. Intell. **21**(5), 433–449 (1997)
27. Jordt, A., Koch, R.: Fast tracking of deformable objects in depth and colour video. In: Proceedings of the British Machine Vision Conference (BMVC) (2011)
28. King, H.: The History of Telescope. Griffin, London (1955)
29. Koch, R.: Depth estimation. In: Ikeuchi, K. (ed.) Encyclopedia of Computer Vision. Springer, New York (2013)
30. Koch, R., Schiller, I., Bartczak, B., Kellner, F., Koeser, K.: Mixin3d: 3d mixed reality with ToF-camera. In: Dynamic 3D Imaging DAGM 2009 Workshop, Dyn3D, Jena, Germany. Lecture Notes in Computer Science, vol. 5742, pp. 126–141 (2009)
31. Kolb, A., Barth, E., Koch, R., Larsen, R.: Time-of-flight cameras in computer graphics. Comput. Graph. Forum **29**(1), 141–159 (2010)
32. Kolb, A., Koch, R.: Dynamic 3D Imaging. Lecture Notes in Computer Science, vol. 5742. Springer, Berlin (2009)
33. Kriss, T.C., Kriss, V.M.: History of the operating microscope: from magnifying glass to microneurosurgery. Neurosurgery **42**(4), 899–907 (1998)
34. Lippmann, G.: La photographie integrale (English translation Fredo Durant, MIT-csail). In: Academy Francaise: Photography-Reversible Prints. Integral Photographs (1908)
35. Longuet-Higgins, H.C.: A computer algorithm for re-constructing a scene from two projections. Nature **293**, 133–135 (1981)
36. Ma, Y., Soatto, S., Kosecka, J., Sastry, S.: An Invitation to 3D Vision: From Images to Geometric Models. Springer, Berlin (2003)

37. Fischler, M.A., Bolles, R.C.: Random sample consensus: a paradigm for model fitting with applications to image analysis and automated cartography. Commun. ACM **24**, 381–395 (1981)
38. Marr, D.: Vision. A Computational Investigation Into the Human Representation and Processing of Visual Information. Freeman, New York (1982)
39. Nayar, S.K., Watanabe, M., Noguchi, M.: Real-time focus range sensor. IEEE Trans. Pattern Anal. Mach. Intell. **18**(12), 1186–1198 (1996)
40. Rioux, M.: Laser range finder based on synchronized scanners. Appl. Opt. **23**(21), 3837–3844 (1984)
41. Savran, A., Alyuz, N., Dibeklioglu, H., Celiktutan, O., Gokberk, B., Sankur, B., Akarun, L.: Bosphorus database for 3d face analysis. In: Biometrics and Identity Management. Lecture Notes in Computer Science, vol. 5372, pp. 47–56 (2008)
42. Scharstein, D., Szeliski, R.: A taxonomy and evaluation of dense two-frame stereo correspondence algorithms. Int. J. Comput. Vis. **47**, 7–42 (2002)
43. Schölkopf, B., Smola, A.: Learning with Kernels: Support Vector Machines, Regularization, Optimization and Beyond. MIT Press, Cambridge (2002)
44. Schwarte, R., Xu, Z., Heinol, H.G., Olk, J., Klein, R., Buxbaum, B., Fischer, H., Schulte, J.: New electro-optical mixing and correlating sensor: facilities and applications of the photonic mixer device (PMD). In: Proc. SPIE, vol. 3100 (1997)
45. Shirai, Y.: Recognition of polyhedrons with a range finder. Pattern Recognit. **4**, 243–250 (1972)
46. Shotton, J., Fitzgibbon, A., Cook, M., Sharp, T., Finocchio, M., Moore, R., Kipman, A., Blake, A.: Real-time human pose recognition in parts from single depth images. In: CVPR (2011)
47. Smith, A.M.: Alhacen's theory of visual perception: a critical edition, with English translation and commentary, of the first three books of Alhacen's de aspectibus, the medieval Latin version of Ibn al-Haytham's Kitab al-Manazir. Trans. Am. Philos. Soc. **91** (2001)
48. Sun, J., Ovsjanikov, M., Guibas, L.: A concise and provably informative multi-scale signature based on heat diffusion. Comput. Graph. Forum **28**(5), 1383–1392 (2009)
49. Szeliski, R.: Computer Vision, Algorithms and Applications. Springer, Berlin (2010)
50. Tanimoto, S., Pavlidis, T.: A hierarchal data structure for picture processing. Comput. Graph. Image Process. **4**, 104–113 (1975)
51. Triggs, B., McLauchlan, P.F., Hartley, R.I., Fitzgibbon, A.W.: Bundle adjustment—a modern synthesis. In: Proceedings of the International Workshop on Vision Algorithms: Theory and Practice, ICCV'99, pp. 298–372. Springer, London (2000). http://portal.acm.org/citation.cfm?id=646271.685629
52. Trucco, E., Verri, A.: Introductory Techniques for 3-D Computer Vision. Prentice Hall, New York (1998)
53. Tsai, R.Y.: A versatile camera calibration technique for high accuracy 3d machine vision metrology using off-the-shelf TV cameras and lenses. IEEE J. Robot. Autom. **3**(4), 323–344 (1987)
54. Wheatstone, C.: Contributions to the physiology of vision. Part the first. On some remarkable, and hitherto unobserved, phenomena of binocular vision. In: Philosophical Transactions of the Royal Society of London, pp. 371–394 (1838)
55. Witkin, A.P.: Scale-space filtering. In: Proceedings of the Eighth International Joint Conference on Artificial Intelligence, vol. 2, pp. 1019–1022. Morgan Kaufmann, San Francisco (1983). http://portal.acm.org/citation.cfm?id=1623516.1623607
56. Yang, R., Pollefeys, M.: A versatile stereo implementation on commodity graphics hardware. Real-Time Imaging **11**, 7–18 (2005)
57. Zhang, Z.: A flexible new technique for camera calibration. IEEE Trans. Pattern Anal. Mach. Intell. **22**(11), 1330–1334 (2000)

Part I
3D Imaging and Shape Representation

In this part, we discuss 3D imaging using both passive techniques (Chap. 2) and active techniques (Chap. 3). The former uses ambient illumination (i.e. sunlight or standard room lighting), whilst the latter projects its own illumination (usually visible or infra-red) onto the scene. Both chapters place an emphasis on techniques that employ the geometry of range triangulation, which requires cameras and/or projector stationed at two (or more) viewpoints. Chapter 4 discusses how to represent the captured data, both for efficient algorithmic 3D data processing and efficient data storage. This provides a bridge to the following part of the book, which deals with 3D shape analysis and processing.

Chapter 2
Passive 3D Imaging

Stephen Se and Nick Pears

Abstract We describe passive, multiple-view 3D imaging systems that recover 3D information from scenes that are illuminated only with ambient lighting. Much of the material is concerned with using the geometry of stereo 3D imaging to formulate estimation problems. Firstly, we present an overview of the common techniques used to recover 3D information from camera images. Secondly, we discuss camera modeling and camera calibration as an essential introduction to the geometry of the imaging process and the estimation of geometric parameters. Thirdly, we focus on 3D recovery from multiple views, which can be obtained using multiple cameras at the same time (stereo), or a single moving camera at different times (structure from motion). Epipolar geometry and finding image correspondences associated with the same 3D scene point are two key aspects for such systems, since epipolar geometry establishes the relationship between two camera views, while depth information can be inferred from the correspondences. The details of both stereo and structure from motion, the two essential forms of multiple-view 3D reconstruction technique, are presented. Towards the end of the chapter, we present several real-world applications.

2.1 Introduction

Passive 3D imaging has been studied extensively for several decades and it is a core topic in many of the major computer vision conferences and journals. Essentially, a *passive* 3D imaging system, also known as a passive 3D vision system, is one in which we can recover 3D scene information, without that system having to project its own source of light or other source of electromagnetic radiation

---

S. Se (✉)
MDA Systems Ltd., 13800 Commerce Parkway, Richmond, BC V6V 2J3, Canada
e-mail: sse@mdacorporation.com

N. Pears
Department of Computer Science, University of York, Deramore Lane, York YO10 5GH, UK
e-mail: nick.pears@york.ac.uk

(EMR) onto that scene. By contrast, an *active* 3D imaging system has an EMR projection subsystem, which is commonly in the infra-red or visible wavelength region.

Several passive 3D information sources (cues) relate closely to human vision and other animal vision. For example, in stereo vision, fusing the images recorded by our two eyes and exploiting the difference between them gives us a sense of depth. The aim of this chapter is to present the fundamental principles of passive 3D imaging systems so that readers can understand their strengths and limitations, as well as how to implement a subset of such systems, namely those that exploit multiple views of the scene.

Passive, multiple-view 3D imaging originates from the mature field of photogrammetry and, more recently, from the younger field of computer vision. In contrast to photogrammetry, computer vision applications rely on fast, automatic techniques, sometimes at the expense of precision. Our focus is from the computer vision perspective.

A recurring theme of this chapter is that we consider some aspect of the geometry of 3D imaging and formulate a linear least squares estimation problem to estimate the associated geometric parameters. These estimates can then optionally be improved, depending on the speed and accuracy requirements of the application, using the linear estimate as an initialization for a non-linear least squares refinement. In contrast to the linear stage, this non-linear stage usually optimizes a cost function that has a well-defined geometric meaning.

Chapter Outline We will start with an overview of various techniques for passive 3D imaging systems, including single-view and multiple-view approaches. However, the main body of this chapter is focused on 3D recovery from multiple views, which can be obtained using multiple cameras simultaneously (stereo) or a single moving camera (structure from motion). A good starting point to understand this subject matter is knowledge of the image formation process in a single camera and how to capture this process in a camera model. This modeling is presented in Sect. 2.3 and the following section describes camera calibration: the estimation of the parameters in the developed camera model. In order to understand how to search efficiently for left-right feature pairs that correspond to the same scene point in a stereo image pair (the *correspondence* problem), a good understanding of two-view geometry is required, which establishes the relationship between two camera views. Hence Sect. 2.5 details this geometry, known as *epipolar geometry*, and shows how it can be captured and used in linear (vector-matrix) form. Following this, we can begin to consider the correspondence problem and the first step is to simplify the search to be across the same horizontal scanlines in each image, by warping the stereo image pair in a process known as *rectification*. This is described in Sect. 2.6. The following section then focuses on the correspondence search itself and then Sect. 2.8 details the process of generating a 3D point cloud from a set of image correspondences.

With increasing computer processing power and decreasing camera prices, many real-world applications of passive 3D imaging systems have been emerging in recent years. Thus, later in the chapter (Sect. 2.9), some recent applications involving such systems are presented. Several commercially available stereo vision systems will first be presented. We then describe 3D modeling systems that generate photo-realistic 3D models from image sequences, which have a wide range of applications. Later in this section, passive 3D imaging systems for mobile robot pose estimation and obstacle detection are described. Finally, multiple-view passive 3D imaging systems are compared to their counterpart within active 3D imaging systems. This acts as a bridge to Chap. 3, where such systems will be discussed in detail.

2.2 An Overview of Passive 3D Imaging Systems

Most cameras today use either a *Charge Coupled Device* (CCD) image sensor or a *Complementary Metal Oxide Semiconductor* (CMOS) sensor, both of which capture light and convert it into electrical signals. Typically, CCD sensors provide higher quality, lower noise images whereas CMOS sensors are less expensive, more compact and consume less power. However, these stereotypes are becoming less pronounced. The cameras employing such image sensors can be hand-held or mounted on different platforms such as *Unmanned Ground Vehicles* (UGVs), *Unmanned Aerial Vehicles* (UAVs) and optical satellites.

Passive 3D vision techniques can be categorized as follows: (i) Multiple view approaches, (ii) Single view approaches. We outline each of these in the following two subsections.

2.2.1 Multiple View Approaches

In multiple view approaches, the scene is observed from two or more viewpoints, by either multiple cameras at the same time (stereo) or a single moving camera at different times (structure from motion). From the gathered images, the system is to infer information on the 3D structure of the scene.

Stereo refers to multiple images taken simultaneously using two or more cameras, which are collectively called a stereo camera. For example, binocular stereo uses two viewpoints, trinocular stereo uses three viewpoints, or alternatively there may be many cameras distributed around the viewing sphere of an object. *Stereo* derives from the Greek word *stereos* meaning *solid*, thus implying a 3D form of visual information. In this chapter, we will use the term *stereo vision* to imply a binocular stereo system. At the top of Fig. 2.1, we show an outline of such a system.

If we can determine that imaged points in the left and right cameras correspond to the same scene point, then we can determine two directions (3D rays) along which the 3D point must lie. (The camera parameters required to convert the 2D image positions to 3D rays come from a camera calibration procedure.) Then, we can intersect the 3D rays to determine the 3D position of the scene point, in a process

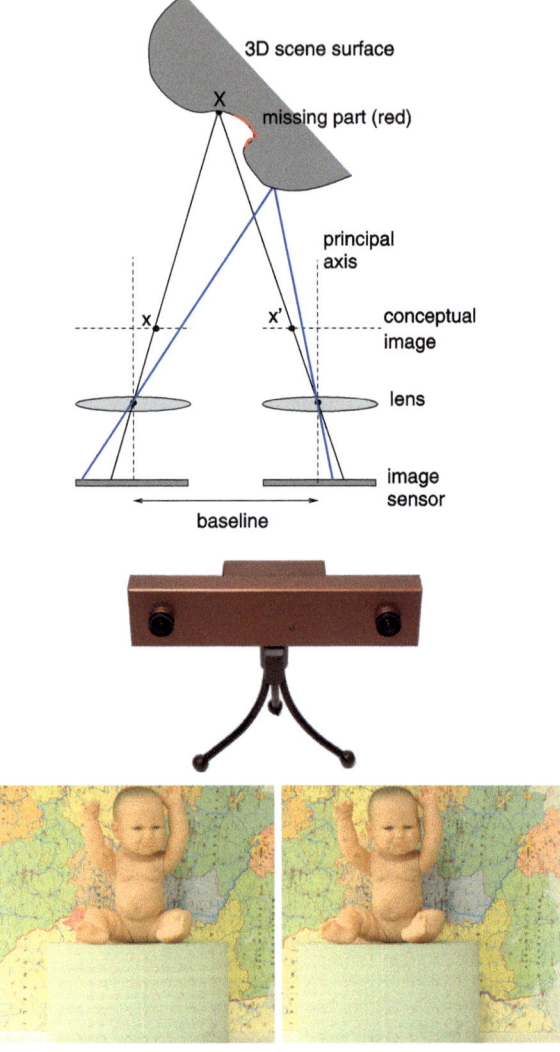

Fig. 2.1 *Top*: Plan view of the operation of a simple stereo rig. Here the optical axes of the two cameras are parallel to form a rectilinear rig. However, often the cameras are rotated towards each other (verged) to increase the overlap in their fields of view. *Center*: A commercial stereo camera, supplied by Videre Design (figure courtesy of [59]), containing SRI's Small Vision System [26]. *Bottom*: *Left* and *right* views of a stereo pair (images courtesy of [34])

known as *triangulation*. A scene point, **X**, is shown in Fig. 2.1 as the intersection of two rays (colored black) and a nearer point is shown by the intersection of two different rays (colored blue). Note that the difference between left and right image positions, the *disparity*, is greater for the nearer scene point. Note also that the scene surface colored red cannot be observed by the right camera, in which case no 3D shape measurement can be made. This scene portion is sometimes referred to as a *missing part* and is the result of self-occlusion. A final point to note is that, although the real image sensor is behind the lens, it is common practice to envisage and use a conceptual image position in front of the lens so that the image is the same orientation as the scene (i.e. not inverted top to bottom and left to right) and this position is shown in the figure.

Despite the apparent simplicity of Fig. 2.1(top), a large part of this chapter is required to present the various aspects of stereo 3D imaging in detail, such as calibration, determining left-to-right image correspondences and dense 3D shape reconstruction. A typical commercial stereo camera, supplied by Videre Design,[1] is shown in the center of Fig. 2.1, although many computer vision researchers build their own stereo rigs, using off-the-shelf digital cameras and a slotted steel bar mounted on a tripod. Finally, at the bottom of Fig. 2.1, we show the left and right views of a typical stereo pair taken from the Middlebury webpage [34].

In contrast to stereo vision, *structure from motion* (SfM) refers to a single moving camera scenario, where image sequences are captured over a period of time. While stereo refers to fixed relative viewpoints with synchronized image capture, SfM refers to variable viewpoints with sequential image capture. For image sequences captured at a high frame rate, optical flow can be computed, which estimates the motion field from the image sequences, based on the spatial and temporal variations of the image brightness. Using the local brightness constancy alone, the problem is under-constrained as the number of variables is twice the number of measurements. Therefore, it is augmented with additional global smoothness constraints, so that the motion field can be estimated by minimizing an energy function [23, 29]. 3D motion of the camera and the scene structure can then be recovered from the motion field.

2.2.2 Single View Approaches

In contrast to these two multiple-view approaches, 3D shape can be inferred from a single viewpoint using information sources (cues) such as shading, texture and focus. Not surprisingly, these techniques are called *shape from shading*, *shape from texture* and *shape from focus* respectively.

Shading on a surface can provide information about local surface orientations and overall surface shape, as illustrated in Fig. 2.2, where the technique in [24] has been used. Shape from shading [22] uses the shades in a grayscale image to infer the shape of the surfaces, based on the reflectance map which links image intensity with surface orientation. After the surface normals have been recovered at each pixel, they can be integrated into a depth map using regularized surface fitting. The computations involved are considerably more complicated than for multiple-view approaches. Moreover, various assumptions, such as uniform albedo, reflectance and known light source directions, need to be made and there are open issues with convergence to a solution. The survey in [65] reviews various techniques and provides some comparative results. The approach can be enhanced when lights shining from different directions can be turned on and off separately. This technique is

---

[1] http://www.videredesign.com.

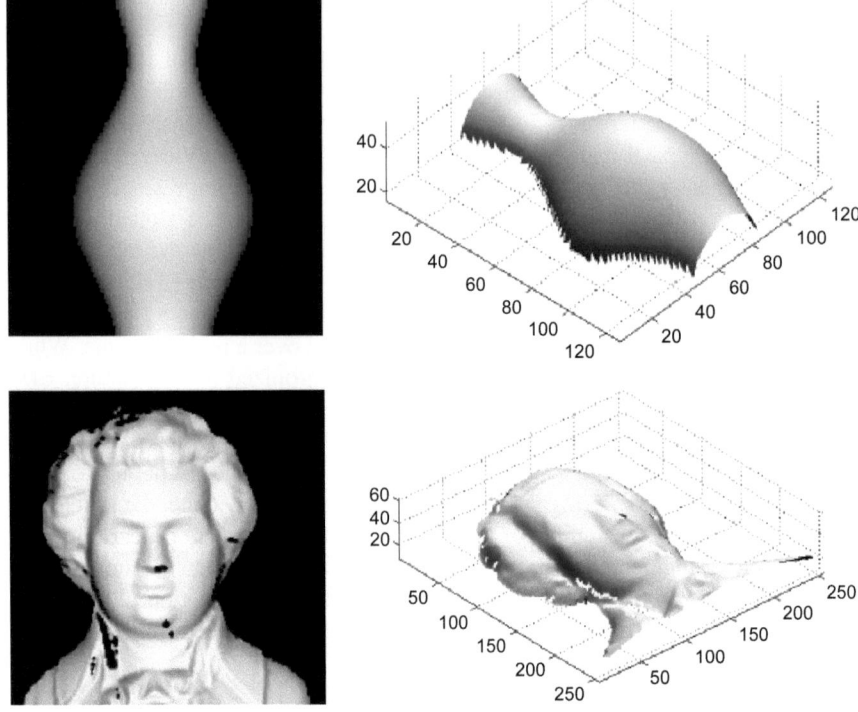

Fig. 2.2 Examples of synthetic shape from shading images (*left column*) and corresponding shape from shading reconstruction (*right column*)

known as *photometric stereo* [61] and it takes two or more images of the scene from the same viewpoint but under different illuminations in order to estimate the surface normals.

The foreshortening of regular patterns depends on how the surface slants away from the camera viewing direction and provides another cue on the local surface orientation. Shape from texture [17] estimates the shape of the observed surface from the distortion of the texture created by the imaging process, as illustrated in Fig. 2.3. Therefore, this approach works only for images with texture surfaces and assumes the presence of a regular pattern. Shape from shading is combined with shape from texture in [60] where the two techniques can complement each other. While the texture components provide information in textured region, shading helps in the uniform region to provide detailed information on the surface shape.

Shape from focus [37, 41] estimates depth using two input images captured from the same viewpoint but at different camera depths of field. The degree of blur is a strong cue for object depth as it increases as the object moves away from the camera's focusing distance. The relative depth of the scene can be constructed from

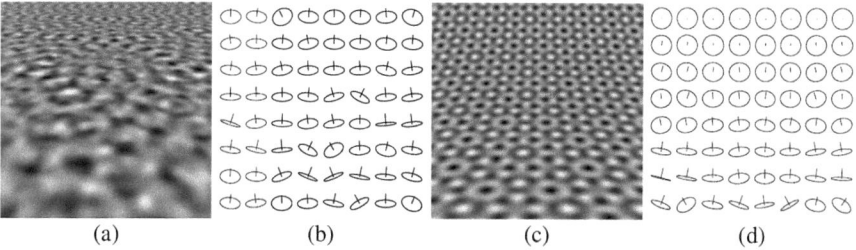

Fig. 2.3 Examples of synthetic shape from texture images (**a**, **c**) and corresponding surface normal estimates (**b**, **d**). Figure courtesy of [17]

the image blur where the amount of defocus can be estimated by averaging the squared gradient in a region.

Single view metrology [13] allows shape recovery from a single perspective view of a scene given some geometric information determined from the image. By exploiting scene constraints such as orthogonality and parallelism, a vanishing line and a vanishing point in a single image can be determined. Relative measurements of shape can then be computed, which can be upgraded to absolute metric measurements if the dimensions of a reference object in the scene are known.

While 3D recovery from a single view is possible, such methods are often not practical in terms of either robustness or speed or both. Therefore, the most commonly used approaches are based on multiple views, which is the focus of this chapter. The first step to understanding such approaches is to understand how to model the image formation process in the cameras of a stereo rig. Then we need to know how to estimate the parameters of this model. Thus camera modeling and camera calibration are discussed in the following two main sections.

2.3 Camera Modeling

A camera is a device in which the 3D scene is projected down onto a 2D image. The most commonly used projection in computer vision is 3D perspective projection. Figure 2.4 illustrates perspective projection based on the pinhole camera model, where **C** is the position of the pinhole, termed the camera center or the *center of projection*. Recall that, although the real image plane is behind the camera center, it is common practice to employ a virtual image plane in front of the camera, so that the image is conveniently at the same orientation as the scene.

Clearly, from this figure, the path of imaged light is modeled by a ray that passes from a 3D world point **X** through the camera center. The intersection of this ray with the image plane defines where the image, $\mathbf{x}_c$, of the 3D scene point, **X**, lies. We can reverse this process and say that, for some point on the image plane, its corresponding scene point must lie somewhere along the ray connecting the center of projection, **C**, and that imaged point, $\mathbf{x}_c$. We refer to this as *back-projecting* an image point to an infinite ray that extends out into the scene. Since we do not know

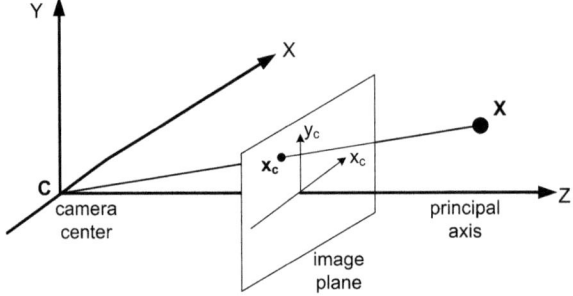

Fig. 2.4 Projection based on a pinhole camera model where a 3D object is projected onto the image plane. Note that, although the real image plane is behind the camera center, it is common practice to employ a virtual image plane in front of the camera, so that the image is conveniently at the same orientation as the scene

how far along the ray the 3D scene point lies, explicit depth information is lost in the imaging process. This is the main source of geometric ambiguity in a single image and is the reason why we refer to the recovery of the depth information from stereo and other cues as *3D reconstruction*.

Before we embark on our development of a mathematical camera model, we need to digress briefly and introduce the concept of homogeneous coordinates (also called projective coordinates), which is the natural coordinate system of analytic projective geometry and hence has wide utility in geometric computer vision.

2.3.1 Homogeneous Coordinates

We are all familiar with expressing the position of some point in a plane using a pair of coordinates as $[x, y]^T$. In general for such systems, n coordinates are used to describe points in an n-dimensional space, $\mathbb{R}^n$. In analytic projective geometry, which deals with algebraic theories of points and lines, such points and lines are typically described by *homogeneous coordinates*, where $n + 1$ coordinates are used to describe points in an n-dimensional space. For example, a general point in a plane is described as $\mathbf{x} = [x_1, x_2, x_3]^T$, and the general equation of a line is given by $\mathbf{l}^T \mathbf{x} = 0$ where $\mathbf{l} = [l_1, l_2, l_3]^T$ are the homogeneous coordinates of the line.[2] Since the right hand side of this equation for a line is zero, it is an homogeneous equation, and any non-zero multiple of the point $\lambda[x_1, x_2, x_3]^T$ is the same point, similarly any non-zero multiple of the line's coordinates is the same line. The symmetry in this

---

[2]You may wish to compare $\mathbf{l}^T \mathbf{x} = 0$ to two well-known parameterizations of a line in the (x, y) plane, namely: $ax + by + c = 0$ and $y = mx + c$ and, in each case, write down homogeneous coordinates for the point $\mathbf{x}$ and the line $\mathbf{l}$.

equation is indicative of the fact that points and lines can be exchanged in many theories of projective geometry; such theories are termed *dual* theories. For example, the cross product of two lines, expressed in homogeneous coordinates, yields their intersecting point, and the cross-product of a pair of points gives the line between them.

Note that we can easily convert from homogeneous to inhomogeneous coordinates, simply by dividing through by the third element, thus $[x_1, x_2, x_3]^T$ maps to $[\frac{x_1}{x_3}, \frac{x_2}{x_3}]^T$. A key point about homogeneous coordinates is that they allow the relevant transformations in the imaging process to be represented as linear mappings, which of course are expressed as matrix-vector equations. However, although the mapping between homogeneous world coordinates of a point and homogeneous image coordinates is linear, the mapping from homogeneous to inhomogeneous coordinates is non-linear, due to the required division.

The use of homogeneous coordinates fits well with the relationship between image points and their associated back-projected rays into the scene space. Imagine a mathematical (virtual) image plane at a distance of one metric unit in front of the center of projection, as shown in Fig. 2.4. With the camera center, **C**, the homogeneous coordinates $[x, y, 1]^T$ define a 3D scene ray as $[\lambda x, \lambda y, \lambda]^T$, where λ is the unknown distance ($\lambda > 0$) along the ray. Thus there is an intuitive link between the depth ambiguity associated with the 3D scene point and the equivalence of homogeneous coordinates up to an arbitrary non-zero scale factor.

Extending the idea of thinking of homogeneous image points as 3D rays, consider the cross product of two homogeneous points. This gives a direction that is the normal of the plane that contains the two rays. The line between the two image points is the intersection of this plane with the image plane. The dual of this is that the cross product of two lines in the image plane gives the intersection of their associated planes. This is a direction orthogonal to the normals of both of these planes and is the direction of the ray that defines the point of intersection of the two lines in the image plane. Note that any point with its third homogeneous element zero defines a ray parallel to the image plane and hence meets it at infinity. Such a point is termed a *point at infinity* and there is an infinite set of these points $[x_1, x_2, 0]^T$ that lie on the *line at infinity* $[0, 0, 1]^T$; Finally, note that the 3-tuple $[0, 0, 0]^T$ has no meaning and is undefined. For further reading on homogeneous coordinates and projective geometry, please see [21] and [12].

2.3.2 Perspective Projection Camera Model

We now return to the perspective projection (central projection) camera model and we note that it maps 3D world points in standard metric units into the pixel coordinates of an image sensor. It is convenient to think of this mapping as a cascade of three successive stages:

1. A 6 degree-of-freedom (DOF) rigid transformation consisting of a rotation, R (3 DOF), and translation, **t** (3 DOF), that maps points expressed in world coordinates to the same points expressed in camera centered coordinates.

2. A perspective projection from the 3D world to the 2D image plane.
3. A mapping from metric image coordinates to pixel coordinates.

We now discuss each of these projective mappings in turn.

2.3.2.1 Camera Modeling: The Coordinate Transformation

As shown in Fig. 2.4, the camera frame has its (X, Y) plane parallel to the image plane and Z is in the direction of the principal axis of the lens and encodes depth from the camera. Suppose that the camera center has *inhomogeneous* position $\tilde{\mathbf{C}}$ in the world frame[3] and the rotation of the camera frame is R_c relative to the world frame orientation. This means that we can express any *inhomogeneous* camera frame points as:

$$\tilde{\mathbf{X}}_c = \mathsf{R}_c^T (\tilde{\mathbf{X}} - \tilde{\mathbf{C}}) = \mathsf{R}\tilde{\mathbf{X}} + \mathbf{t}. \qquad (2.1)$$

Here $\mathsf{R} = \mathsf{R}_c^T$ represents the rigid rotation and $\mathbf{t} = -\mathsf{R}_c^T \tilde{\mathbf{C}}$ represents the rigid translation that maps a scene point expressed in the world coordinate frame into a camera-centered coordinate frame. Equation (2.1) can be expressed as a projective mapping, namely one that is linear in homogeneous coordinates, to give:

$$\begin{bmatrix} X_c \\ Y_c \\ Z_c \\ 1 \end{bmatrix} = \begin{bmatrix} \mathsf{R} & \mathbf{t} \\ \mathbf{0}^T & 1 \end{bmatrix} \begin{bmatrix} X \\ Y \\ Z \\ 1 \end{bmatrix}.$$

We denote P_r as the 4×4 homogeneous matrix representing the rigid coordinate transformation in the above equation.

2.3.2.2 Camera Modeling: Perspective Projection

Observing the similar triangles in the geometry of perspective imaging, we have

$$\frac{x_c}{f} = \frac{X_c}{Z_c}, \quad \frac{y_c}{f} = \frac{Y_c}{Z_c}, \qquad (2.2)$$

where (x_c, y_c) is the position (metric units) of a point in the camera's image plane and f is the distance (metric units) of the image plane to the camera center. (This is usually set to the focal length of the camera lens.) The two equations above can be written in linear form as:

$$Z_c \begin{bmatrix} x_c \\ y_c \\ 1 \end{bmatrix} = \begin{bmatrix} f & 0 & 0 & 0 \\ 0 & f & 0 & 0 \\ 0 & 0 & 1 & 0 \end{bmatrix} \begin{bmatrix} X_c \\ Y_c \\ Z_c \\ 1 \end{bmatrix}.$$

---

[3] We use a tilde to differentiate n-tuple inhomogeneous coordinates from $(n+1)$-tuple homogeneous coordinates.

We denote $\mathbf{P}_p$ as the 3×4 perspective projection matrix, defined by the value of f, in the above equation. If we consider an abstract image plane at $f = 1$, then points on this plane are termed *normalized image coordinates*[4] and from Eq. (2.2), these are given by

$$x_n = \frac{X_c}{Z_c}, \quad y_n = \frac{Y_c}{Z_c}.$$

2.3.2.3 Camera Modeling: Image Sampling

Typically, the image on the image plane is sampled by an image sensor, such as a CCD or CMOS device, at the locations defined by an array of pixels. The final part of camera modeling defines how that array is positioned on the $[x_c, y_c]^T$ image plane, so that pixel coordinates can be generated. In general, pixels in an image sensor are not square and the number of pixels per unit distance varies between the x_c and y_c directions; we will call these scalings m_x and m_y. Note that pixel positions have their origin at the corner of the sensor and so the position of the principal point (where the principal axis intersects the image plane) is modeled with pixel coordinates $[x_0, y_0]^T$. Finally, many camera models also cater for any skew,[5] s, so that the mapping into pixels is given by:

$$\begin{bmatrix} x \\ y \\ 1 \end{bmatrix} = \begin{bmatrix} m_x & s & x_0 \\ 0 & m_y & y_0 \\ 0 & 0 & 1 \end{bmatrix} \begin{bmatrix} x_c \\ y_c \\ 1 \end{bmatrix}.$$

We denote $\mathbf{P}_c$ as the 3×3 projective matrix defined by the five parameters m_x, m_y, s, x_0 and y_0 in the above equation.

2.3.2.4 Camera Modeling: Concatenating the Projective Mappings

We can concatenate the three stages described in the three previous subsections to give

$$\lambda \mathbf{x} = \mathbf{P}_c \mathbf{P}_p \mathbf{P}_r \mathbf{X}$$

or simply

$$\lambda \mathbf{x} = \mathbf{P} \mathbf{X}, \tag{2.3}$$

where λ is non-zero and positive. We note the following points concerning the above equation

---

[4] We need to use a variety of image coordinate normalizations in this chapter. For simplicity, we will use the same subscript n, but it will be clear about how the normalization is achieved.

[5] Skew models a lack of orthogonality between the two image sensor sampling directions. For most imaging situations it is zero.

1. For any homogeneous image point scaled to $\lambda[x, y, 1]^T$, the scale λ is equal to the imaged point's depth in the camera centered frame ($\lambda = Z_c$).
2. Any non-zero scaling of the projection matrix $\lambda_P \mathsf{P}$ performs the same projection since, in Eq. (2.3), any non-zero scaling of homogeneous image coordinates is equivalent.
3. A camera with projection matrix P, or some non-zero scalar multiple of that, is informally referred to as *camera P* in the computer vision literature and, because of point 2 above, it is referred to as being defined *up to scale*.

The matrix P is a 3×4 projective camera matrix with the following structure:

$$\mathsf{P} = \mathsf{K}[\mathsf{R}|\mathbf{t}]. \tag{2.4}$$

The parameters within K are the camera's *intrinsic parameters*. These parameters are those combined from Sects. 2.3.2.2 and 2.3.2.3 above, so that:

$$\mathsf{K} = \begin{bmatrix} \alpha_x & s & x_0 \\ 0 & \alpha_y & y_0 \\ 0 & 0 & 1 \end{bmatrix},$$

where $\alpha_x = fm_x$ and $\alpha_y = fm_y$ represent the focal length in pixels in the x and y directions respectively. Together, the rotation and translation in Eq. (2.4) are termed the camera's *extrinsic parameters*. Since there are 5 DOF from intrinsic parameters and 6 DOF from extrinsic parameters, a camera projection matrix has only 11 DOF, not the full 12 of a general 3×4 matrix. This is also evident from the fact that we are dealing with homogeneous coordinates and so the overall scale of P does not matter.

By expanding Eq. (2.3), we have:

$$\lambda \underbrace{\begin{bmatrix} x \\ y \\ 1 \end{bmatrix}}_{\substack{homogeneous \\ image \\ coordinates}} = \underbrace{\begin{bmatrix} \alpha_x & s & x_0 \\ 0 & \alpha_y & y_0 \\ 0 & 0 & 1 \end{bmatrix}}_{\substack{intrinsic \\ camera \\ parameters}} \underbrace{\begin{bmatrix} r_{11} & r_{12} & r_{13} & t_x \\ r_{21} & r_{22} & r_{23} & t_y \\ r_{31} & r_{32} & r_{33} & t_z \end{bmatrix}}_{\substack{extrinsic \\ camera \\ parameters}} \underbrace{\begin{bmatrix} X \\ Y \\ Z \\ 1 \end{bmatrix}}_{\substack{homogeneous \\ world \\ coordinates}}, \tag{2.5}$$

which indicates that both the intrinsic and extrinsic camera parameters are necessary to fully define a ray (metrically, not just in pixel units) in 3D space and hence make absolute measurements in multiple-view 3D reconstruction. Finally, we note that any non-zero scaling of scene homogeneous coordinates $[X, Y, Z, 1]^T$ in Eq. (2.5) gives the same image coordinates[6] which, for a single image, can be interpreted as ambiguity between the scene scale and the translation vector **t**.

---

[6]The same homogeneous image coordinates *up to scale* or the same inhomogeneous image coordinates.

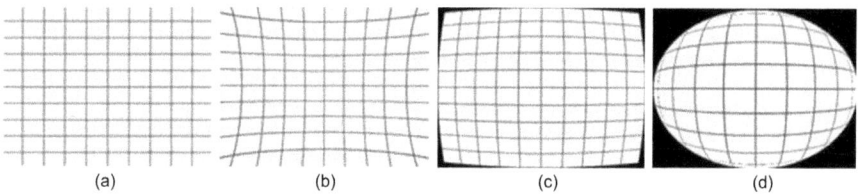

Fig. 2.5 Examples of radial distortion effects in lenses: (**a**) No distortion (**b**) Pincushion distortion (**c**) Barrel distortion (**d**) Fisheye distortion

2.3.3 Radial Distortion

Typical cameras have a lens distortion, which disrupts the assumed linear projective model. Thus a camera may not be accurately represented by the pinhole camera model that we have described, particularly if a low-cost lens or a wide field-of-view (short focal length) lens such as a fisheye lens is employed. Some examples of lens distortion effects are shown in Fig. 2.5. Note that the effect is non-linear and, if significant, it must be corrected so that the camera can again be modeled as a linear device. The estimation of the required distortion parameters to do this is often encompassed within a camera calibration procedure, which is described in Sect. 2.4. With reference to our previous three-stage development of a projective camera in Sect. 2.3.2, lens distortion occurs at the second stage, which is the 3D to 2D projection, and this distortion is sampled by the image sensor.

Detailed distortion models contain a large number of parameters that model both radial and tangential distortion [7]. However, radial distortion is the dominant factor and usually it is considered sufficiently accurate to model this distortion only, using a low-order polynomial such as:

$$\begin{bmatrix} x_{nd} \\ y_{nd} \end{bmatrix} = \begin{bmatrix} x_n \\ y_n \end{bmatrix} + \begin{bmatrix} x_n \\ y_n \end{bmatrix} (k_1 r^2 + k_2 r^4),$$

where $[x_n, y_n]^T$ is the undistorted image position (i.e. that obeys our linear projection model) in normalized coordinates, $[x_{nd}, y_{nd}]^T$ is the distorted image position in normalized coordinates, k_1 and k_2 are the unknown radial distortion parameters, and $r = \sqrt{x_n^2 + y_n^2}$. Assuming zero skew, we also have

$$\begin{bmatrix} x_d \\ y_d \end{bmatrix} = \begin{bmatrix} x \\ y \end{bmatrix} + \begin{bmatrix} (x - x_0) \\ (y - y_0) \end{bmatrix} (k_1 r^2 + k_2 r^4), \tag{2.6}$$

where the distorted position $[x_d, y_d]^T$ is now expressed in pixel coordinates and $[x, y]^T$ are the usual pixel coordinates predicted by the linear pinhole model. Note that r is still defined in normalized image coordinates and so a non-unity aspect ratio ($m_x \neq m_y$) in the image sensor does not invalidate this equation. Also note that both Eq. (2.6) and Fig. 2.5 indicate that distortion increases away from the center of the image. In the barrel distortion, shown in Fig. 2.5(c), distortion correction requires that image points are moved slightly towards the center of the image, more so if they are near the edges of the image. Correction could be applied to the whole image, as in dense stereo, or just a set of relevant features, such as extracted corner points. Clearly, the latter process is computationally cheaper.

Now that we have discussed the modeling of a camera's image formation process in detail, we now need to understand how to estimate the parameters within this model. This is the focus of the next section, which details camera calibration.

2.4 Camera Calibration

Camera calibration [8] is the process of finding the parameters of the camera that produced a given image of a scene. This includes both extrinsic parameters R, t and intrinsic parameters, comprising those within the matrix K and radial distortion parameters, k_1, k_2. Once the intrinsic and extrinsic camera parameters are known, we know the camera projection matrix P and, taking into account of any radial distortion present, we can back-project any image pixel to a 3D ray in space. Clearly, as the intrinsic camera calibration parameters are tied to the focal length, changing the zoom on the lens would make the calibration invalid. It is also worth noting that calibration is not always required. For example, we may be more interested in approximate shape, where we need to know what objects in a scene are co-planar, rather than their absolute 3D position measurements. However, for stereo systems at least, camera calibration is commonplace.

Generally, it is not possible for an end-user to get the required calibration information to the required accuracy from camera manufacturer's specifications and external measurement of the position of cameras in some frame. Hence some sort of camera calibration procedure is required, of which there are several different categories. The longest established of these is *photogrammetric calibration*, where calibration is performed using a scene object of precisely known physical dimensions. Typically, several images of a special 3D target, such as three orthogonal planes with calibration grids (chessboard patterns of black and white squares), are captured and precise known translations may be used [58]. Although this gives accurate calibration results, it lacks flexibility due to the need for precise scene knowledge.

At the other end of the spectrum is *self-calibration* (auto-calibration) [21, 35], where no calibration target is used. The correspondences across three images of the same rigid scene provide enough constraints to recover a set of camera parameters which allow 3D reconstruction up to a similarity transform. Although this approach is flexible, there are many parameters to estimate and reliable calibrations cannot always be obtained.

Between these two extremes are 'desktop' camera calibration approaches that use images of planar calibration grids, captured at several unknown positions and orientations (i.e. a single planar chessboard pattern is manually held at several random poses and calibration images are captured and stored). This gives a good compromise between the accuracy of photogrammetric calibration and the ease of use of self-calibration. A seminal example is given by Zhang [64].

Although there are a number of publicly available camera calibration packages on the web, such as the Caltech camera calibration toolbox for MATLAB [9] and in the OpenCV computer vision library [40], a detailed study of at least one approach is essential to understand calibration in detail. We will use Zhang's work [64] as a seminal example and this approach consists of two main parts:

(1) A *basic* calibration that is based on linear least squares and hence has a closed-form solution. In the formulation of the linear problem, a set of 9 parameters needs to be estimated. These are rather complicated combinations of the camera's intrinsic parameters and the algebraic least squares minimization to determine them has no obvious geometric meaning. Once intrinsic parameters have been extracted from these estimated parameters, extrinsic parameters can be determined using the projective mapping (homography) associated with each calibration grid image.

(2) A *refined* calibration that is based on non-linear least squares and hence has an iterative solution. Here it is possible to formulate a least squares error between the observed (inhomogeneous) image positions of the calibration grid corners and the positions predicted by the current estimate of intrinsic and extrinsic camera parameters. This has a clear geometric interpretation, but the sum of squares function that we wish to minimize is non-linear in terms of the camera parameters. A standard approach to solving this kind of problem is the *Levenberg-Marquardt* (LM) algorithm, which employs gradient descent when it is far from a minimum and Gauss-Newton minimization when it gets close to a minimum. Since the LM algorithm is a very general procedure, it is straightforward to employ more complex camera models, such as those that include parameters for the radial distortion associated with the camera lens.

The iterative optimization in (2) above needs to be within the basin of convergence of the global minimum and so the linear method in (1) is used to determine an initial estimation of camera parameters. The raw data used as inputs to the process consists of the image corner positions, as detected by an automatic corner detector [18, 52], of all corners in all calibration images and the corresponding 2D world positions, $[X, Y]^T$, of the corners on the calibration grid. Typically, correspondences are established by manually clicking one or more detected image corners, and making a quick visual check that the imaged corners are matched correctly using overlaying graphics or text. A typical set of targets is shown in Fig. 2.6.

In the following four subsections we outline the theory and practice of camera calibration. The first subsection details the estimation of the planar projective mapping between a scene plane (calibration grid) and its image. The next two subsections closely follow Zhang [64] and detail the basic calibration and then the refined calibration, as outlined above. These subsections refer to the case of a single camera and so a final fourth subsection is used to describe the additional issues associated with the calibration of a stereo rig.

2.4.1 Estimation of a Scene-to-Image Planar Homography

A homography is a projective transformation (*projectivity*) that maps points to points and lines to lines. It is a highly useful imaging model when we view planar scenes,

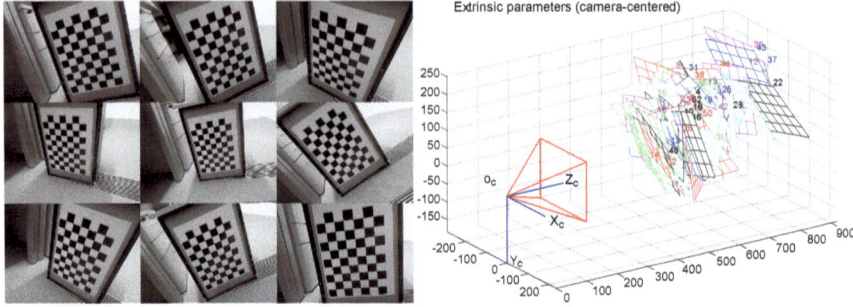

Fig. 2.6 *Left*: calibration targets used in a camera calibration process, image courtesy of Hao Sun. *Right*: after calibration, it is possible to determine the positions of the calibration planes using the estimated extrinsic parameters (Figure generated by the *Camera Calibration Toolbox for Matlab*, webpage maintained at Caltech by Jean-Yves Bouguet [9])

which is common in many computer vision processes, including the process of camera calibration.

Suppose that we view a planar scene, then we can define the (X, Y) axes of the world coordinate system to be within the plane of the scene and hence $Z = 0$ everywhere. Equation (2.5) indicates that, as far as a planar scene is concerned, the imaging process can be reduced to:

$$\lambda \mathbf{x} = \mathsf{K}[\mathbf{r}_1 \quad \mathbf{r}_2 \quad \mathbf{t}][X, Y, 1]^T,$$

where $\mathbf{r}_1$ and $\mathbf{r}_2$ are the first and second columns of the rotation matrix R, hence:

$$\lambda \mathbf{x} = \mathsf{H}[X, Y, 1]^T, \qquad \mathsf{H} = \mathsf{K}[\mathbf{r}_1 \quad \mathbf{r}_2 \quad \mathbf{t}]. \tag{2.7}$$

The 3×3 matrix H is termed a planar homography, which is defined up to a scale factor,[7] and hence has eight degrees of freedom instead of nine.

By expanding the above equation, we have:

$$\lambda \begin{bmatrix} x \\ y \\ 1 \end{bmatrix} = \begin{bmatrix} h_{11} & h_{12} & h_{13} \\ h_{21} & h_{22} & h_{23} \\ h_{31} & h_{32} & h_{33} \end{bmatrix} \begin{bmatrix} X \\ Y \\ 1 \end{bmatrix}. \tag{2.8}$$

If we map homogeneous coordinates to inhomogeneous coordinates, by dividing through by λ, this gives:

$$x = \frac{h_{11}X + h_{12}Y + h_{13}}{h_{31}X + h_{32}Y + h_{33}} \tag{2.9}$$

$$y = \frac{h_{21}X + h_{22}Y + h_{23}}{h_{31}X + h_{32}Y + h_{33}}. \tag{2.10}$$

---

[7]Due to the scale equivalence of homogeneous coordinates.

From a set of four correspondences in a general position,[8] we can formulate a set of eight linear equations in the eight unknowns of a homography matrix. This is because each correspondence provides a pair of constraints of the form given in Eqs. (2.9) and (2.10).

Rearranging terms in four pairs of those equations allows us to formulate the homography estimation problem in the form:

$$\mathbf{Ah} = \mathbf{0}, \qquad (2.11)$$

where A is an 8×9 data matrix derived from image and world coordinates of corresponding points and $\mathbf{h}$ is the 9-vector containing the elements of the homography matrix. Since A has rank 8, it has a 1-dimensional null space, which provides a non-trivial (non-zero vector) solution for Eq. (2.11). This can be determined from a Singular Value Decomposition (SVD) of the data matrix, which generates three matrices (U, D, V) such that $\mathsf{A} = \mathsf{UDV}^T$. Here, D is a diagonal matrix of singular values and U, V are orthonormal matrices. Typically, SVD algorithms order the singular values in descending order down the diagonal of D and so the required solution, corresponding to a singular value of zero, is extracted as the last column of V. Due to the homogeneous form of Eq. (2.11), the solution is determined up to a non-zero scale factor, which is acceptable because H is only defined up to scale. Often a unit scale is chosen (i.e. $\|\mathbf{h}\| = 1$) and this scaling is returned automatically in the columns of V.

In general, a larger number of correspondences than the minimum will not exactly satisfy the same homography because of image noise. In this case, a least squares solution to $\mathbf{h}$ can be determined in an over-determined system of linear equations. We follow the same procedure as above but this time the data matrix is of size $2n \times 9$ where $n > 4$ is the number of correspondences. When we apply SVD, we still select the last column of V corresponding to the smallest singular value in D. (Note that, in this case, the smallest singular value will be non-zero.)

Data normalization prior to the application of SVD is *essential* to give stable estimates [21]. The basic idea is to translate and scale both image and world coordinates to avoid orders of magnitude difference between the columns of the data matrix. Image points are translated so that their centroid is at the origin and scaled to give a root-mean-squared (RMS) distance of $\sqrt{2}$ from that origin, so that the 'average' image point has coordinates of unity magnitude. Scene points should be normalized in a similar way except that they should be scaled to give an RMS distance of $\sqrt{3}$.

When using homogeneous coordinates, the normalizations can be applied using matrix operators N_i, N_s, such that new *normalized* coordinates are given as:

$$\mathbf{x}_n = \mathsf{N}_i \mathbf{x}, \qquad \mathbf{X}_n = \mathsf{N}_s \mathbf{X}$$

for the image points and scene points respectively. Suppose that the homography computed from normalized coordinates is $\tilde{\mathsf{H}}$, then the homography relating the original coordinates of the correspondences is given as

$$\mathsf{H} = \mathsf{N}_i^{-1} \tilde{\mathsf{H}} \mathsf{N}_s.$$

---

[8] No three points collinear.

2.4.2 Basic Calibration

From the known planar scene target and the resulting image, a scene-to-image planar homography can be estimated as described in the previous subsection. Suppose that we describe such a homography as a set of 3×1 column vectors, i.e. $H = [\mathbf{h}_1\ \mathbf{h}_2\ \mathbf{h}_3]$, then comparing this to Eq. (2.7) we have:

$$\lambda_H \mathbf{h}_1 = K\mathbf{r}_1, \qquad \lambda_H \mathbf{h}_2 = K\mathbf{r}_2, \qquad (2.12)$$

where λ_H is a scale factor, accounting for the particular scale of an estimated homography. Noting that the columns of the rotation matrix, $\mathbf{r}_1, \mathbf{r}_2$ are orthonormal:

$$\mathbf{r}_1^T \mathbf{r}_2 = \mathbf{h}_1^T K^{-T} K^{-1} \mathbf{h}_2 = 0, \qquad (2.13)$$

$$\mathbf{r}_1^T \mathbf{r}_1 = \mathbf{r}_2^T \mathbf{r}_2 \Rightarrow \mathbf{h}_1^T K^{-T} K^{-1} \mathbf{h}_1 = \mathbf{h}_2^T K^{-T} K^{-1} \mathbf{h}_2. \qquad (2.14)$$

These equations provide one constraint each on the intrinsic parameters.

We construct a symmetric matrix B such that

$$B = K^{-T} K^{-1} = \begin{bmatrix} B_{11} & B_{12} & B_{13} \\ B_{12} & B_{22} & B_{23} \\ B_{13} & B_{23} & B_{33} \end{bmatrix}.$$

Let the ith column vector of H be $\mathbf{h}_i = [h_{1i}, h_{2i}, h_{3i}]^T$, we have:

$$\mathbf{h}_i^T B \mathbf{h}_j = \mathbf{v}_{ij}^T \mathbf{b},$$

where

$$\mathbf{v}_{ij} = [h_{1i}h_{1j}, h_{1i}h_{2j} + h_{2i}h_{1j}, h_{2i}h_{2j}, h_{3i}h_{1j} + h_{1i}h_{3j}, h_{3i}h_{2j} + h_{2i}h_{3j}, h_{3i}h_{3j}]^T$$

and $\mathbf{b}$ is the vector containing six independent entries of the symmetric matrix B:

$$\mathbf{b} = [B_{11}, B_{12}, B_{22}, B_{13}, B_{23}, B_{33}]^T.$$

Therefore, the two constraints in Eqs. (2.13) and (2.14) can be rewritten as:

$$\begin{bmatrix} \mathbf{v}_{12}^T \\ (\mathbf{v}_{11} - \mathbf{v}_{22})^T \end{bmatrix} \mathbf{b} = \mathbf{0}.$$

If n images of the planar calibration grid are observed, n sets of these equations can be stacked into a matrix-vector equation as:

$$V\mathbf{b} = \mathbf{0},$$

where V is a $2n \times 6$ matrix. Although a minimum of three planar views allows us to solve for $\mathbf{b}$, it is recommended to take more and form a least squares solution. In this case, the solution for $\mathbf{b}$ is the eigenvector of $V^T V$ associated with the smallest eigenvalue. Once $\mathbf{b}$ is estimated, we know the matrix B up to some unknown scale factor, λ_B, and all of the intrinsic camera parameters can be computed by expanding the right hand side of $B = \lambda_B K^{-T} K^{-1}$ in terms of its individual elements. Although this is somewhat laborious, it is straightforward algebra of simultaneous equations, where five intrinsic camera parameters plus one unknown scale factor can be derived from the six parameters of the symmetric matrix B. Zhang [64] presents the solution:

$$y_0 = \frac{(B_{12}B_{13} - B_{11}B_{23})}{(B_{11}B_{22} - B_{12}^2)}$$

$$\lambda_B = B_{33} - \frac{[B_{13}^2 + y_0(B_{12}B_{13} - B_{11}B_{23})]}{B_{11}}$$

$$\alpha_x = \sqrt{\frac{\lambda_B}{B_{11}}}$$

$$\alpha_y = \sqrt{\frac{\lambda_B B_{11}}{(B_{11}B_{22} - B_{12}^2)}}$$

$$s = \frac{-B_{12}\alpha_x^2 \alpha_y}{\lambda_B}$$

$$x_0 = \frac{s y_0}{\alpha_y} - \frac{B_{13}\alpha_x^2}{\lambda_B}.$$

Once K is known, the extrinsic camera parameters for each image can be computed using Eq. (2.12):

$$\mathbf{r}_1 = \lambda_H \mathsf{K}^{-1} \mathbf{h}_1$$
$$\mathbf{r}_2 = \lambda_H \mathsf{K}^{-1} \mathbf{h}_2$$
$$\mathbf{r}_3 = \mathbf{r}_1 \times \mathbf{r}_2$$
$$\mathbf{t} = \lambda_H \mathsf{K}^{-1} \mathbf{h}_3,$$

where

$$\lambda_H = \frac{1}{\|\mathsf{K}^{-1}\mathbf{h}_1\|} = \frac{1}{\|\mathsf{K}^{-1}\mathbf{h}_2\|}.$$

The vectors $\mathbf{r}_1$, $\mathbf{r}_2$ will not be exactly orthogonal and so the estimated rotation matrix does not exactly represent a rotation. Zhang [64] suggests performing SVD on the estimated rotation matrix so that $\mathsf{USV}^T = \mathsf{R}$. Then the closest pure rotation matrix in terms of Frobenius norm to that estimated is given as $\mathsf{R}' = \mathsf{UV}^T$.

2.4.3 Refined Calibration

After computation of the linear solution described above, it can be iteratively refined via a non-linear least squares minimization using the *Levenberg-Marquardt* (LM) algorithm. As previously mentioned, the camera parameters can be extended at this stage to include an estimation for the lens distortion parameters, to give us the following minimization:

$$\hat{\mathbf{p}} = \min_{\mathbf{p}} \left\{ \sum_{i=1}^{n} \sum_{j=1}^{m} \|\mathbf{x}_{i,j} - \hat{\mathbf{x}}_{i,j}(\mathsf{K}, k_1, k_2, \mathsf{R}_i, \mathbf{t}_i, \mathbf{X}_j)\|^2 \right\},$$

where $\mathbf{x}_{i,j}$ is the image of world point $\mathbf{X}_j$ in image i and $\hat{\mathbf{x}}_{i,j}$ is the predicted projection of the same world point according to Eq. (2.7) (using estimated intrinsic and extrinsic camera parameters) followed by radial distortion according to Eq. (2.6).

The vector $\mathbf{p}$ contains all of the free parameters within the planar projection (homography) function plus two radial distortion parameters k_1 and k_2 as described in Sect. 2.3.3. Initial estimates of these radial distortion parameters can be set to zero. LM iteratively updates all parameters according to the equation:

$$\mathbf{p}_{k+1} = \mathbf{p}_k + \delta \mathbf{p}_k$$
$$\delta \mathbf{p}_k = -\left(\mathsf{J}^T \mathsf{J} + \lambda_J \operatorname{diag}\left(\mathsf{J}^T \mathsf{J}\right)\right)^{-1} \mathsf{J}^T \mathbf{e},$$

where J is the Jacobian matrix containing the first derivatives of the residual $\mathbf{e}$ with respect to each of the camera parameters.

Thus computation of the Jacobian is central to LM minimization. This can be done either numerically or with a custom routine, if analytical expressions for the Jacobian entries are known. In the numerical approach, each parameter is incremented and the function to be minimized (the least squares error function in this case) is computed and divided by the increment, which should be the maximum of 10^{-6} and $10^{-4} \times |p_i|$, where p_i is some current parameter value [21]. In the case of providing a custom Jacobian function, the expressions are long and complicated in the case of camera calibration, and so the use of a symbolic mathematics package can help reduce human error in constructing the partial differentials.

Note that there are LM implementations available on many platforms, for example in MATLAB's optimization toolbox, or the C/C++ `levmar` package. A detailed discussion of iterative estimation methods including LM is given in Appendix 6 of Hartley and Zisserman's book [21].

2.4.4 Calibration of a Stereo Rig

It is common practice to choose the optical center of one camera to be the origin of a stereo camera's 3D coordinate system. (The midpoint of the stereo baseline, which connects the two optical centers is also occasionally used.) Then, the relative rigid location of cameras, [R, t], within this frame, along with both sets of intrinsic parameters, is required to generate a pair of projection matrices and hence a pair of 3D rays from corresponding image points that intersect at their common scene point.

The previous two subsections show how we can calculate the intrinsic parameters for any single camera. If we have a stereo pair, which is our primary interest, then we would compute a pair of intrinsic parameter matrices, one for the left camera and one for the right. In most cases, the two cameras are the same model and hence we would expect the two intrinsic parameter matrices to be very similar.

Also, we note that, for each chessboard position, two sets of extrinsic parameters, [R, t], are generated, one for the left camera's position relative to the calibration plane and one for the right. Clearly, each left-right pair of extrinsic parameters should have approximately[9] the same relationship, which is due to the fixed rigid rotation and translation of one camera relative to another in the stereo rig.

Once two sets of intrinsic parameters and *one* set of extrinsic parameters encoding the *relative* rigid pose of one camera relative to another has been computed, the results are often refined in a global stereo optimization procedure, again using the Levenberg-Marquardt approach. To reduce n sets of relative extrinsic parameters to one set, we could choose the set associated with the closest calibration plane or compute some form of robust average.

All parameter estimates, both intrinsic and extrinsic, can be improved if the LM optimization is now performed over a minimal set of parameters, since the extrinsic parameters are reduced from 12 (two rotations and two translations) to 6 (one rotation and one translation) per calibration grid location. This approach ensures global rigidity of the stereo rig going from left to right camera. An implementation of global stereo optimization to refine stereo camera parameters is given in the Caltech camera calibration toolbox for MATLAB [9].

2.5 Two-View Geometry

3D reconstruction from an image pair must solve two problems: the correspondence problem and the reconstruction problem.

- *Correspondence problem.* For a point $\mathbf{x}$ in the left image, which is the corresponding point $\mathbf{x}'$ in the right image, where $\mathbf{x}$ and $\mathbf{x}'$ are images of the same physical scene point $\mathbf{X}$?
- *Reconstruction problem.* Given two corresponding points $\mathbf{x}$ and $\mathbf{x}'$, how do we compute the 3D coordinates of scene point $\mathbf{X}$?

Of these problems the correspondence problem is significantly more difficult as it is a search problem whereas, for a stereo camera of known calibration, reconstruction to recover the 3D measurements is a simple geometric mechanism. Since we have sets of three unique points, $(\mathbf{x}, \mathbf{x}', \mathbf{X})$, this mechanism is called triangulation (not to be confused with surface mesh triangulation, described in Chap. 4).

This section is designed to give the reader a good general grounding in two-view geometry and estimation of the key two-view geometric relations that can be useful even when extrinsic or intrinsic camera calibration information is not available.[10] As long as the concept of epipolar geometry is well understood, the remaining main sections of this chapter can be followed easily.

---

[9] 'Approximately', because of noise in the imaged corner positions supplied to the calibration process.

[10] Extrinsic parameters are always not known in a structure from motion problem, they are part of what we are trying to solve for. Intrinsic parameters may or may not be known, depending on the application.

2.5.1 Epipolar Geometry

Epipolar geometry establishes the relationship between two camera views. When we have calibrated cameras and we are dealing with metric image coordinates, it is dependent only on the relative pose between the cameras. When we have uncalibrated cameras and we are dealing with pixel-based image coordinates, it is additionally dependent on the cameras' intrinsic parameters, however, it is independent of the scene.

Once the epipolar geometry is known, for any image point in one image, we know that its corresponding point (its match) in the other image, must lie on a line, which is known as the *epipolar line* associated with the original point. This epipolar constraint greatly reduces the correspondence problem from a 2D search over the whole image to a 1D search along the epipolar line only, and hence reduces computational cost and ambiguities.

The discussion here is limited to two-view geometry only. A similar constraint called the *trifocal tensor* is applicable for three views, but is outside the scope of this chapter. For further information on the trifocal tensor and n-view geometries, please refer to [21].

As shown in Fig. 2.7(a), the image points **x** and **x**′, world point **X** and the camera centers are co-planar and this plane is called the epipolar plane, which is shaded in the figure. If we only know **x**, how is the corresponding point **x**′ constrained? The line **l**′ is the intersection of the epipolar plane with the second image plane. **l**′ is called the epipolar line, which is the image in the second view of the ray back-projected from **x**. As the point **x**′ lies on **l**′, the correspondences search does not need to cover the entire image but can be restricted only to the line **l**′. In fact, if any point on epipolar line **l** has a corresponding point in the second image, it must lie on epipolar line **l**′ and vice-versa. Thus **l** and **l**′ are called *conjugate* epipolar lines.

The epipole is the point of intersection of the line joining the camera centers with the image plane. The epipole **e** is the projection of the second camera center on the first image, while the epipole **e**′ is the projection of the first camera center on the second image.

In essence, two-view epipolar geometry describes the intersection of the image planes with the pencil of planes having the baseline as the pencil axis, as illustrated in Fig. 2.7(b). Note that the baseline is the line joining the two camera centers.[11] All epipolar lines intersect at the epipole of the respective image to give a pencil of epipolar lines in each image. Note that the epipoles are not necessarily within the boundaries of the image. A special case is when the cameras are oriented in the same direction and they are separated by a translation parallel to both image planes. In this case, the epipoles are at infinity and the epipolar lines are parallel. Furthermore, if the translation is in the X direction only and the cameras have the same intrinsic parameters, the conjugate epipolar lines lie on the same image rows. This is an ideal set up when we search for correspondences between the two images. However, we

---

[11] The length of the baseline is the magnitude of the extrinsic translation vector, **t**.

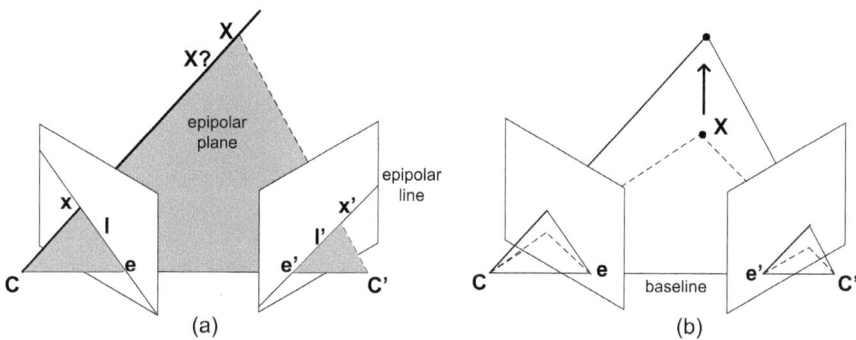

Fig. 2.7 (a) The epipolar geometry establishes the relationship between the two camera views. (b) The epipolar planes rotate around the baseline and all epipolar lines intersect at the epipole

may prefer some camera vergence to improve the field-of-view overlap between the two cameras and, in this case, the images need to be warped so that the epipolar lines become horizontal again. This *rectification* process is discussed later in the chapter.

The epipolar constraint can be represented algebraically by a 3×3 matrix called the *fundamental matrix* (F), when we are dealing with raw pixel coordinates, and by the *essential matrix* (E) when the intrinsic parameters of the cameras are known and we are dealing with metrically expressed coordinates (e.g. millimeters) in the image plane.

2.5.2 Essential and Fundamental Matrices

Both the essential and fundamental matrices derive from a simple co-planarity constraint. For simplicity it is best to look at the epipolar relation using the essential matrix first and then adapt it using the camera intrinsic parameters to obtain a relation for pixel-based image coordinates, which involves the fundamental matrix.

Referring to Fig. 2.8, we have a world point $\mathbf{X}$ that projects to points $\mathbf{x}_c$ and $\mathbf{x}'_c$ in the image planes. These image plane points are expressed as 3-vectors, so that they are effectively the 3D positions of the imaged points expressed metrically in their own camera frame, hence the subscript c. (Note also that they can be regarded as normalized homogeneous image coordinates, with the scale set to the focal length, f, although any non-zero scale would suffice.) We know that the three vectors $\mathbf{Cx}_c$, $\mathbf{C}'\mathbf{x}'_c$ and $\mathbf{t}$ are co-planar, so we can choose one of the two camera frames to express this co-planarity, using the scalar triple product. If we choose the right frame (primed), then we must rotate vector $\mathbf{Cx}_c$ using rotation matrix R, to give:

$$\mathbf{x}'^T_c (\mathbf{t} \times \mathsf{R}\mathbf{x}_c) = 0.$$

Expressing the cross product with $\mathbf{t}$ by the multiplication with the skew-symmetric matrix $[\mathbf{t}]_x$, we have:

$$\mathbf{x}'_c [\mathbf{t}]_x \mathsf{R}\mathbf{x}_c = 0,$$

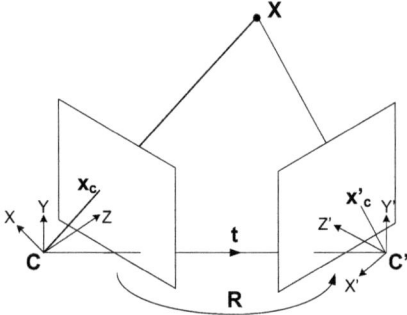

Fig. 2.8 The essential matrix $E = [t]_x R$ encodes the epipolar geometry. It is used to relate the correspondences x_c and x'_c between two images, when these image locations are expressed in metric units. If pixel-based coordinates are used (for example, if intrinsic camera parameters are unknown) epipolar geometry is encoded by the fundamental matrix F

where

$$[t]_x = \begin{bmatrix} 0 & -t_z & t_y \\ t_z & 0 & -t_x \\ -t_y & t_x & 0 \end{bmatrix}$$

and thus we have:

$$E = [t]_x R \tag{2.15}$$

and

$$x_c'^T E x_c = 0. \tag{2.16}$$

Thus the essential matrix encapsulates only extrinsic parameters, namely, the rotation and translation associated with the *relative* pose of the two cameras. The implication of this is that, in applications where R and t have not been computed in a calibration procedure, they may be recoverable from an estimate of E, which will be discussed further in Sect. 2.8.2 in the context of structure from motion.

In many practical situations, we also need to deal with uncalibrated cameras where the intrinsic parameters are unknown (i.e. the mapping between metric image coordinates and raw pixel values is unknown). The shifting and scaling operations required for this conversion can be encapsulated in matrices K and K′, as follows:

$$x = K x_c, \quad x' = K' x'_c,$$

where K and K′ are the 3×3 matrices containing the intrinsic camera parameters for the two cameras. Inserting these relations into Eq. (2.16) gives:

$$x'^T K'^{-T} E K^{-1} x = 0$$
$$x'^T F x = 0$$

thus

$$F = K'^{-T} E K^{-1} = K'^{-T} [t]_x R K^{-1}$$

and we can see that the fundamental matrix encapsulates both intrinsic and extrinsic parameters. The interpretation of the epipolar constraint given by the fundamental matrix, is that, if points $\mathbf{x}$ and $\mathbf{x}'$ correspond, then $\mathbf{x}'$ must lie on the epipolar line given by $\mathbf{l}' = \mathsf{F}\mathbf{x}$ and therefore the dot product between $\mathbf{x}'$ and $\mathsf{F}\mathbf{x}$ is zero.

Some key properties of the fundamental matrix are summarized below:

- If F is the fundamental matrix between camera P and camera P', then F^T is the fundamental matrix between camera P' and camera P.
- F is a projective mapping taking a point to a line. If $\mathbf{l}$ and $\mathbf{l}'$ are corresponding (i.e. conjugate) epipolar lines, then any point $\mathbf{x}$ on $\mathbf{l}$ maps to the same line $\mathbf{l}'$. Hence, there is no inverse mapping (zero determinant, rank 2).
- F has seven degrees of freedom. While a 3×3 homogeneous matrix has eight independent ratios, there is also an additional constraint that the determinant of F is zero (F is rank 2), which further removes one degree of freedom.
- For any point $\mathbf{x}$ in the first image, the corresponding epipolar line in the second image is $\mathbf{l}' = \mathsf{F}\mathbf{x}$. Similarly, $\mathbf{l} = \mathsf{F}^T \mathbf{x}'$ represents the epipolar line in the first image corresponding to $\mathbf{x}'$ in the second image.
- The epipoles are determined as the left and right nullspaces of the fundamental matrix. This is evident, since each epipole is on every epipolar line in their respective image. This is written as $\mathbf{e}'^T \mathbf{l}' = \mathbf{e}'^T \mathsf{F}\mathbf{x} = 0 \; \forall \mathbf{x}$, hence $\mathbf{e}'^T \mathsf{F} = 0$. Similarly $\mathbf{l}^T \mathbf{e} = \mathbf{x}'^T \mathsf{F} \mathbf{e} = 0 \; \forall \mathbf{x}'$, hence $\mathsf{F}\mathbf{e} = 0$.
- The SVD (*Singular Value Decomposition*) of F is given as $\mathsf{F} = \mathsf{U} \, \mathrm{diag}(\sigma_1, \sigma_2, 0) \, \mathsf{V}^T$ where $\mathsf{U} = [\mathbf{u}_1, \mathbf{u}_2, \mathbf{e}']$, $\mathsf{V} = [\mathbf{v}_1, \mathbf{v}_2, \mathbf{e}]$. Thus finding the column in V that corresponds to the zero singular value gives a simple method of computation of the epipoles from the fundamental matrix.
- For cameras with some vergence (epipoles not at infinity) to give camera projection matrices: $\mathsf{P} = \mathsf{K}[\mathsf{I}|0]$ and $\mathsf{P}' = \mathsf{K}'[\mathsf{R}|\mathbf{t}]$, then we have: $\mathsf{F} = \mathsf{K}'^{-T}[\mathbf{t}]_\times \mathsf{R}\mathsf{K}^{-1} = [\mathsf{K}'\mathbf{t}]_\times \mathsf{K}'\mathsf{R}\mathsf{K}^{-1} = \mathsf{K}'^{-T}\mathsf{R}\mathsf{K}^T [\mathsf{K}\mathsf{R}^T \mathbf{t}]_\times$ [21].

2.5.3 The Fundamental Matrix for Pure Translation

If the two identical cameras ($\mathsf{K} = \mathsf{K}'$) are separated by a pure translation ($\mathsf{R} = \mathsf{I}$), the fundamental matrix has a simple form, which can be shown to be [21]:

$$\mathsf{F} = [\mathsf{K}\mathbf{t}]_\times = [\mathbf{e}']_\times = \begin{bmatrix} 0 & -e'_z & e'_y \\ e'_z & 0 & -e'_x \\ -e'_y & e'_x & 0 \end{bmatrix}.$$

In this case, the epipoles are at the same location in both images. If the translation is parallel to the image plane, the epipoles are at infinity with $e_z = e'_z = 0$ and the epipolar lines are parallel in both images. When discussing rectilinear stereo rigs and rectification later, we will be particularly interested in the case when the translation is parallel to the camera's x-axis, in which case the epipolar lines are parallel and horizontal and thus correspond to image scan (raster) lines. In this case $\mathbf{e}' = [1, 0, 0]^T$ and the fundamental matrix is:

$$\mathsf{F} = \begin{bmatrix} 0 & 0 & 0 \\ 0 & 0 & -1 \\ 0 & 1 & 0 \end{bmatrix}$$

and hence the relationship between corresponding points $\mathbf{x}$ and $\mathbf{x}'$ is given by $\mathbf{x}'^T \mathsf{F} \mathbf{x} = 0$ which reduces to $y = y'$.

2.5.4 Computation of the Fundamental Matrix

As the fundamental matrix is expressed in terms of corresponding image points, F can be computed from image correspondences alone. No camera calibration information is needed and pixel coordinates are used directly. Note that there are degenerate cases in the estimation of F. These occur in two common and well-known instances: (i) when the relative pose between the two views can be described by a pure rotation and (ii) when the scene is planar. For now we consider scenarios where such degeneracies do not occur and we return to them later.

By expanding $\mathbf{x}'^T \mathsf{F} \mathbf{x} = 0$ where $\mathbf{x} = [x, y, 1]^T$ and $\mathbf{x}' = [x', y', 1]^T$ and

$$\mathsf{F} = \begin{bmatrix} f_{11} & f_{12} & f_{13} \\ f_{21} & f_{22} & f_{23} \\ f_{31} & f_{32} & f_{33} \end{bmatrix}$$

we obtain:

$$x'x f_{11} + x'y f_{12} + x' f_{13} + y'x f_{21} + y'y f_{22} + y' f_{23} + x f_{31} + y f_{32} + f_{33} = 0.$$

As each feature correspondence provides one equation, for n correspondences, we get the following set of linear equations:

$$\begin{bmatrix} x'_1 x_1 & x'_1 y_1 & x'_1 & y'_1 x_1 & y'_1 y_1 & y'_1 & x_1 & y_1 & 1 \\ \vdots & \vdots & \vdots & \vdots & \vdots & \vdots & \vdots & \vdots & \vdots \\ x'_n x_n & x'_n y_n & x'_n & y'_n x_n & y'_n y_n & y'_n & x_n & y_n & 1 \end{bmatrix} \begin{bmatrix} f_{11} \\ f_{12} \\ f_{13} \\ f_{21} \\ f_{22} \\ f_{23} \\ f_{31} \\ f_{32} \\ f_{33} \end{bmatrix} = \mathbf{0} \quad (2.17)$$

or more compactly,

$$\mathsf{A}\mathbf{f} = \mathbf{0},$$

where A is termed the data matrix and $\mathbf{f}$ is the vector of unknown elements of F.

The eight-point algorithm[12] [27] can be used as a very simple method to solve for F linearly using eight correspondences. As this is a homogeneous set of equations, **f** can only be determined up to a scale factor. With eight correspondences, Eq. (2.17) can be solved by linear methods, where the solution is the nullspace of A. (This can be found from the column in V that corresponds to the *zero* singular value in D in the singular value decomposition $A = UDV^T$.) However, a solution with a minimal set of correspondences is often inaccurate, particularly if the correspondences are not well spread over the images, or they may not provide enough strong constraints if some of them are near-collinear or co-planar. It is preferable to use more than eight correspondences, then the least squares solution for **f** is given by the singular vector corresponding to the *smallest* singular value of A.

Note that this approach is similar to that for determining the homography matrix, discussed earlier in Sect. 2.4.1. As with that approach, it is essential to normalize the pixel coordinates of each image before applying SVD [19, 21], using a mean-centering translation and a scaling so that the RMS distance of the points to the origin is $\sqrt{2}$. When using homogeneous coordinates, this normalization can be applied using matrix operators N, N′, such that new *normalized* image coordinates are given as $\mathbf{x}_n = N\mathbf{x}$, $\mathbf{x}'_n = N'\mathbf{x}'$.

In general the solution for F_n (the subscript n now denotes that we have based the estimate on normalized image coordinates) will not have zero determinant (its rank will be 3 and not 2), which means that the epipolar lines will not intersect at a single point. In order to enforce this, we can apply SVD a second time, this time to the initially estimated fundamental matrix so that $F_n = UDV^T$. We then set the smallest singular value (in the third row and third column of D) to zero to produce matrix D′ and update the estimate of the fundamental matrix as $F_n = UD'V^T$.

Of course, the estimate of F_n maps points to epipolar lines in the normalized image space. If we wish to search for correspondences within the original image space, we need to de-normalize the fundamental matrix estimate as $F = N'^T F_n N$.

Typically, there are many correspondences between a pair of images, including mostly inliers but also some outliers. This is inevitable, since matching is a local search and ambiguous matches exist, which will be discussed further in Sect. 2.7. Various robust methods for estimating the fundamental matrix, which address the highly corrupting effect of outliers, are compared in [55]. In order to compute F from these correspondences automatically, a common method is to use a robust statistics technique called Random Sample Consensus (RANSAC) [16], which we now outline:

1. Extract features in both images, for example, from a corner detector [18].
2. Perform feature matching between images (usually over a local area neighborhood) to obtain a set of potential matches or *putative correspondences*.
3. Repeat the following steps N times:

---

[12]There are several other approaches, such as the seven-point algorithm.

Table 2.1 Number of samples required to get at least one good sample with 99 % probability for various sample size s and outlier fraction ε

Sample size s	$\varepsilon = 10\%$	$\varepsilon = 20\%$	$\varepsilon = 30\%$	$\varepsilon = 40\%$	$\varepsilon = 50\%$
4	5	9	17	34	72
5	6	12	26	57	146
6	7	16	37	97	293
7	8	20	54	163	588
8	9	26	78	272	1177

- Select eight putative correspondences randomly.
- Compute F using these eight points, as described above.
- Find the number of inliers[13] that support F.

4. Find the F with the highest number of inliers (largest support) among the N trials.
5. Use this F to look for additional matches outside the search range used for the original set of putative correspondences.
6. Re-compute a least squares estimate of F using all inliers.

Note that re-computing F in the final step may change the set of inliers, as the epipolar lines are adjusted. Thus, a possible refinement is to iterate computation of a linear least squares estimate of F and its inliers, until a stable set of inliers is achieved or some maximum number of iterations is reached. The refinement achieved is often considered to be not worth the additional computational expense if processing time is considered important or if the estimate of F is to be used as the starting point for more advanced iterative non-linear refinement techniques, described later.

In the RANSAC approach, N is the number of trials (putative F computations) needed to get at least one good sample with a high probability (e.g. 99 %). How large should N be? The probability p of getting a good sample is given by:

$$p = 1 - \left(1 - (1-\varepsilon)^s\right)^N,$$

where ε is the fraction of outliers (incorrect feature correspondences) and s is the number of correspondences selected for each trial. The above equation can be re-arranged as:

$$N = \frac{\log(1-p)}{\log(1-(1-\varepsilon)^s)}. \tag{2.18}$$

The number of samples required for various sample size and outlier fraction based on Eq. (2.18) are shown in Table 2.1. It can be seen that the number of samples gets higher as the outlier fraction increases.

By repeatedly selecting a group of correspondences, the inlier support would be high for a correct hypothesis in which all the correspondences within the sample

---

[13] An inlier is a putative correspondence that lies within some threshold of its expected position predicted by F. In other words image points must lie within a threshold from their epipolar lines generated by F.

size, s, are correct. This allows the robust removal of outliers and the computation of F using inliers only. As the fraction of outliers may not be known in advance, an adaptive RANSAC method can be used where the number of outliers at each iteration is used to re-compute the total number of iterations required.

As the fundamental matrix has only seven degrees of freedom, a minimum of seven correspondences are required to compute F. When there are only seven correspondences, $\det(\mathsf{F}) = 0$ constraint also needs to be imposed, resulting in a cubic equation to solve and hence may produce up to three solutions and all three must be tested for support. The advantage of using seven correspondences is that fewer trials are required to achieve the same probability of getting a good sample, as illustrated in Table 2.1.

Fundamental matrix refinement techniques are often based on the Levenberg-Marquardt algorithm, such that some non-linear cost function is minimized. For example a geometric cost function can be formulated as the sum of the squared distances between image points and the epipolar lines generated from their associated corresponding points and the estimate of F. This is averaged over both points in a correspondence and over all corresponding points (i.e. all those that agree with the estimate of F). The minimization can be expressed as:

$$\mathsf{F} = \min_{\mathsf{F}} \left(\frac{1}{N} \sum_{i=1}^{N} \left(d(\mathbf{x}'_i, \mathsf{F}\mathbf{x}_i)^2 + d(\mathbf{x}_i, \mathsf{F}^T \mathbf{x}'_i)^2 \right) \right),$$

where $d(\mathbf{x}, \mathbf{l})$ is the distance of a point $\mathbf{x}$ to a line $\mathbf{l}$, expressed in pixels. For more details of this and other non-linear refinement schemes, the reader is referred to [21].

2.5.5 Two Views Separated by a Pure Rotation

If two views are separated by a pure rotation around the camera center, the baseline is zero, the epipolar plane is not defined and a useful fundamental matrix cannot be computed. In this case, the back-projected rays from each camera cannot form a triangulation to compute depth. This lack of depth information is intuitive because, under rotation, all points in the same direction move across the image in the same way, regardless of their depth. Furthermore, if the translation magnitude is small, the epipolar geometry is close to this degeneracy and computation of the fundamental matrix will be highly unstable.

In order to model the geometry of correspondences between two rotated views, a *homography*, described by a 3×3 matrix H, should be estimated instead. As described earlier, a homography is a projective transformation (*projectivity*) that maps points to points and lines to lines. For two identical cameras ($\mathsf{K} = \mathsf{K}'$), the scene-to-image projections are:

$$\mathbf{x} = \mathsf{K}[\mathsf{I}|\mathbf{0}]\mathbf{X}, \qquad \mathbf{x}' = \mathsf{K}[\mathsf{R}|\mathbf{0}]\mathbf{X}$$

hence

$$\mathbf{x}' = \mathsf{K}\mathsf{R}\mathsf{K}^{-1}\mathbf{x} = \mathsf{H}\mathbf{x}. \tag{2.19}$$

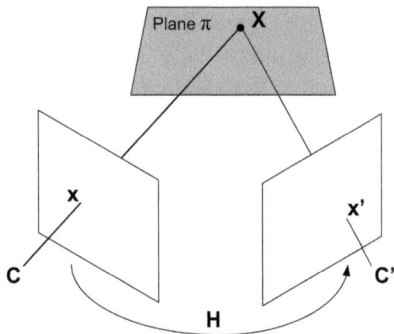

Fig. 2.9 The homography induced by a plane π, where a point **x** in the first image can be transferred to the point **x**′ in the second image

We can think of this homography as a mapping of image coordinates onto normalized coordinates (centered on the principal point at a unit metric distance from the camera). These points are rotated and then multiplying by K generates the image coordinates on the focal plane of the second, rotated camera.

2.5.6 Two Views of a Planar Scene

A homography should also be estimated for planar scenes where correspondences cannot uniquely define the epipolar geometry and hence the fundamental matrix. Similar to Eq. (2.7), the *2D-to-2D* projection of the world plane π in Fig. 2.9 to the left and right images are given by:

$$\lambda_x \mathbf{x} = \mathsf{H}_x \mathbf{X}, \qquad \lambda_{x'} \mathbf{x}' = \mathsf{H}_{x'} \mathbf{X},$$

where $\mathsf{H}_x, \mathsf{H}_{x'}$ are 3×3 homography matrices (homographies) and $\mathbf{x}, \mathbf{x}'$ are homogeneous image coordinates. The planar homographies form a group and hence we can form a composite homography as $\mathsf{H} = \mathsf{H}_{x'} \mathsf{H}_x^{-1}$ and it is straightforward to show that:

$$\lambda \mathbf{x}' = \mathsf{H}\mathbf{x}.$$

Figure 2.9 illustrates this mapping from **x** to **x**′ and we say that a homography is induced by the plane π. Homography estimation follows the same approach as was described in Sect. 2.4.1 for a scene-to-image planar homography (replacing **X** with **x** and **x** with **x**′ in Eqs. (2.8) to (2.10)).

Note that a minimum of four correspondences (no three points collinear in either image) are required because, for the homography, each correspondence generates a pair of constraints. Larger numbers of correspondences allow a least squares solution to an over-determined system of linear equations. Again suitable normalizations are required before SVD is applied to determine the homography.

A RANSAC-based technique can also be used to handle outliers, similar to the fundamental matrix estimation method described in Sect. 2.5.4. By repeatedly selecting the minimal set of four correspondences randomly to compute H and counting the number of inliers, the H with the largest number of inliers can be chosen.

Additional matches that are not in the original set of putative correspondences can be obtained using the best H. Then, H can be re-computed using all supporting matches in a linear least squares minimization using SVD.

Finally we note that, as in the case of the fundamental matrix, a non-linear optimization can be applied to refine the homography solution, if required by the application. The interested reader is referred to [21] for the details of the geometric cost function to be minimized.

2.6 Rectification

Typically, in a stereo rig, the cameras are horizontally displaced and rotated towards each other by an equal amount (verged), in order to overlap their fields of view. In this case, epipolar lines lie at a variety of angles across the two images, complicating the search for correspondences. In contrast, if these cameras had their principal axes parallel to each other (no vergence) and the two cameras had identical intrinsic parameters, conjugate (corresponding) epipolar lines would lie along the same horizontal scanline in each image, as observed in Sect. 2.5.3. This configuration is known as a standard rectilinear stereo rig. Clearly it is desirable to retain the improved stereo viewing volume associated with verged cameras and yet have the simplicity of correspondence search associated with a rectilinear rig.

To achieve this we can warp or *rectify* the raw images associated with the verged system such that corresponding epipolar lines become collinear and lie on the same scanline. A second advantage is that the equations for 3D reconstruction are very simply related to image disparity after image rectification, since they correspond to those of a simple rectilinear stereo rig. This triangulation computation is described later in the chapter.

Rectification can be achieved either with camera calibration information, for example in a typical stereo application, or without calibration information, for example in a typical structure from motion application. We discuss the calibrated case in the following subsection and give a brief mention of uncalibrated approaches in Sect. 2.6.2.

2.6.1 Rectification with Calibration Information

Here we assume a calibrated stereo rig, where we know both the intrinsic and the extrinsic parameters. Knowing this calibration information gives a simple rectification approach, where we find an image mapping that generates, from the original images, a pair of images that would have been obtained from a rectilinear rig. Of course, the field of view of each image is still bound by the real original cameras, and so the rectified images tend to be a different shape than the originals (e.g. slightly trapezoidal in a verged stereo rig).

Depending on the lenses used and the required accuracy of the application, it may be considered necessary to correct for radial distortion, using estimated parameters k_1 and k_2 from the calibration. To do the correction, we employ Eq. (2.6) in order to compute the unknown, undistorted pixel coordinates, $[x, y]^T$, from the known distorted coordinates, $[x_d, y_d]^T$. Of course, an iterative solution is required for this non-linear equation and the undistorted pixel coordinates can be initialized to the distorted coordinates at the start of this process.

Assuming some vergence, we wish to map the image points onto a pair of (virtual) image planes that are parallel to the baseline and in the same plane. Thus we can use the homography structure in Eq. (2.19) that warps images between a pair of rotated views. Given that we already know the intrinsic camera parameters, we need to determine the rotation matrices associated with the rectification of the left and right views. We will assume that the origin of the stereo system is at the optical center of the left camera and calibration information gives [R, t] to define the rigid position of the right camera relative to this. To get the rotation matrix that we need to apply to image points of the left camera, we define the rectifying rotation matrix as:

$$R_{rect} = \begin{bmatrix} \mathbf{r}_1^T \\ \mathbf{r}_2^T \\ \mathbf{r}_3^T \end{bmatrix},$$

where $\mathbf{r}_i$, $i = 1\ldots 3$ are a set of mutually orthogonal unit vectors. The first of these is in the direction of the epipole or, equivalently, the direction of the translation to the right camera, $\mathbf{t}$. (This ensures that epipolar lines will be horizontal in the rectified image.) Hence the unit vector that we require is:

$$\mathbf{r}_1 = \frac{\mathbf{t}}{\|\mathbf{t}\|}.$$

The second vector $\mathbf{r}_2$ is orthogonal to the first and obtained as the cross product of $\mathbf{t}$ and the original left optical axis $[0, 0, 1]^T$ followed by a normalization to unit length to give:

$$\mathbf{r}_2 = \frac{1}{\sqrt{t_x^2 + t_y^2}} [-t_y, t_x, 0]^T.$$

The third vector is mutually orthogonal to the first two and so is computed using the cross product as $\mathbf{r}_3 = \mathbf{r}_1 \times \mathbf{r}_2$.

Given that the real right camera is rotated relative to the real left camera, we need to apply a rotation RR_{rect} to the image points of the right camera. Hence, applying homographies to left and right image points, using the form of Eq. (2.19), we have:

$$\mathbf{x}_{rect} = KR_{rect}K^{-1}\mathbf{x}$$
$$\mathbf{x}'_{rect} = K'RR_{rect}K'^{-1}\mathbf{x}',$$

where K and K' are the 3 × 3 matrices containing the intrinsic camera parameters for the left and right cameras respectively. Note that, even with the same make and

Fig. 2.10 An image pair before rectification (**a**) and after rectification (**b**). The overlay shows that the corresponding *left* and *right* features lie on the same image row after rectification. Figure courtesy of [43]

model of camera, we may find that the focal lengths associated with K and K′ are slightly different. Thus we need to scale one rectified image by the ratio of focal lengths in order to place them on the same focal plane.

As the rectified coordinates are, in general, not integer, *resampling* using some form of interpolation is required. The rectification is often implemented in reverse, so that the pixel values in the new image plane can be computed as a bilinear interpolation of the four closest pixels values in the old image plane. Rectified images give a very simple triangulation reconstruction procedure, which is described later in Sect. 2.8.1.2.

2.6.2 Rectification Without Calibration Information

When calibration information is not available, rectification can be achieved using an estimate of the fundamental matrix, which is computed from correspondences within the raw image data. A common approach is to compute a pair of rectifying homographies for the left and right images [20, 33] so that the fundamental matrix associated with the rectified images is the same form as that for a standard rectilinear rig and the 'new cameras' have the same intrinsic camera parameters. Since such rectifying homographies map the epipoles to infinity ($[1, 0, 0]^T$), this approach fails when the epipole lies within the image. This situation is common in structure from motion problems, when the camera translates in the direction of its Z-axis. Several authors have tackled this problem by directly resampling the original images along their epipolar lines, which are specified by an estimated fundamental matrix. For example, the image is reparameterized using polar coordinates around the epipoles to reduce the search ambiguity to half epipolar lines [42, 43]. Figure 2.10 shows an example of an image pair before and after rectification for this scheme, where the corresponding left and right features lie on the same image row afterwards. Specialized rectifications exist, for example [10] which allows image matching over large forward translations of the camera although, in this scheme, rotations are not catered for.

2.7 Finding Correspondences

Finding correspondences is an essential step for 3D reconstruction from multiple views. The correspondence problem can be viewed as a search problem, which asks, given a pixel in the left image, which is the corresponding pixel in the right image? Of course there is something of a circular dependency here. We need to find correspondences to determine the epipolar geometry, yet we need the epipolar geometry to find (denser) correspondences in an efficient manner. The RANSAC sampling approach described earlier, showed us how to break into this loop. Once we have the epipolar geometry constraint, the search space is reduced from a 2D search to the epipolar line only.

The following assumptions underpin most methods for finding correspondences in image pairs. These assumptions hold when the distance of the world point from the cameras is much larger than the baseline.

- Most scene points are visible from both viewpoints.
- Corresponding image regions are similar.

Two questions are involved: what is a suitable image element to match and what is a good similarity measure to adopt? There are two main classes of correspondence algorithms: correlation-based and feature-based methods. Correlation-based methods recover dense correspondences where the element to match is an image window centered on some pixel and the similarity measure is the correlation between the windows. Feature-based methods typically establish sparse correspondences where the element to match is an image feature and the similarity measure is the distance between descriptors of the image features.

2.7.1 Correlation-Based Methods

If the element to match is only a single image pixel, ambiguous matches exist. Therefore, windows are used for matching in correlation-based methods and the similarity criterion is a measure of the correlation between the two windows. A larger window gives larger image context which can reduce the probability of ambiguities, but this has its own problems which will be discussed in Sect. 2.8.1.1. The selected correspondence is given by the window that maximizes a similarity criterion or minimizes a dissimilarity criterion within a search range. Once a match is found, the offset between the two windows can be computed, which is called the *disparity* from which the depth can be recovered. Some commonly used criteria for correlation-based methods are described next.

Based on the rectified images in Fig. 2.11, we define the window function, where m, an odd integer, is the image window size so that:

$$W_m(x, y) = \left\{ (u, v) \Big| x - \frac{(m-1)}{2} \leq u \leq x + \frac{(m-1)}{2}, \right.$$
$$\left. y - \frac{(m-1)}{2} \leq v \leq y + \frac{(m-1)}{2} \right\}. \tag{2.20}$$

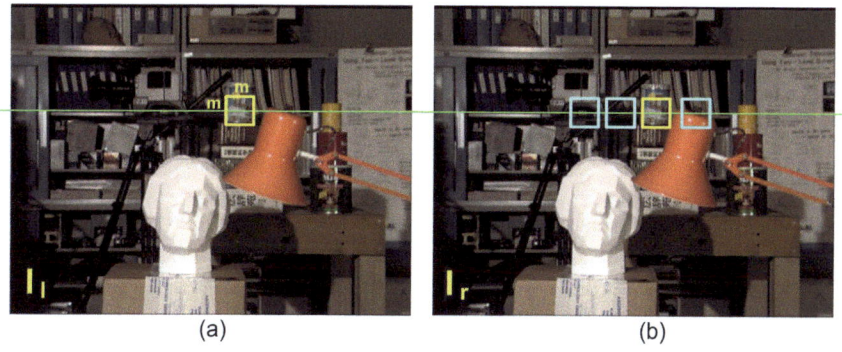

Fig. 2.11 Correlation-based methods look for the matching image window between the *left* and *right* rectified images. An *m* by *m* window centering at the pixel is used for correlation (Raw image pair courtesy of the Middlebury Stereo Vision Page [34], originally sourced from Tsukuba University)

The dissimilarity can be measured by the *Sum of Squared Differences* (SSD) cost for instance, which is the intensity difference as a function of disparity d:

$$SSD(x, y, d) = \sum_{(u,v) \in W_m(x,y)} \left[I_l(u, v) - I_r(u - d, v) \right]^2,$$

where I_l and I_r refer to the intensities of the left and right images respectively.

If two image windows correspond to the same world object, the pixel values of the windows should be similar and hence the SSD value would be relatively small. As shown in Fig. 2.11, for each pixel in the left image, correlation-based methods would compare the SSD measure for pixels within a search range along the corresponding epipolar line in the right image. The disparity value that gives the lowest SSD value indicates the best match.

A slight variation of SSD is the *Sum of Absolute Differences* (SAD) where the absolute values of the differences are added instead of the squared values:

$$SAD(x, y, d) = \sum_{(u,v) \in W_m(x,y)} \left| I_l(u, v) - I_r(u - d, v) \right|.$$

This cost measure is less computationally expensive as it avoids the multiplication operation required for SSD. On the other hand, the SSD cost function penalizes the large intensity difference more due to the squaring operation.

The intensities between the two image windows may vary due to illumination changes and non-Lambertian reflection. Even if the two images are captured at the same time by two cameras with identical models, non-Lambertian reflection and differences in the gain and sensitivity can cause variation in the intensity. In these cases, SSD or SAD may not give a low value even for the correct matches. For these reasons, it is a good idea to normalize the pixels in each window. A first level of normalization would be to ensure that the intensities in each window are zero-mean. A second level of normalization would be to scale the zero-mean intensities so that they either have the same range or, preferably, unit variance. This can be achieved by dividing each pixel intensity by the standard deviation of window pixel intensities, after the zero mean operation, i.e. normalized pixel intensities are given as:

$$I_n = \frac{I - \bar{I}}{\sigma_I},$$

where $\bar{I}$ is the mean intensity and σ_I is the standard deviation of window intensities. While SSD measures the dissimilarity and hence the smaller the better, *Normalized Cross-Correlation* (NCC) measures the similarity and hence, the larger the better. Again, the pixel values in the image window are normalized first by subtracting the average intensity of the window so that only the relative variation would be correlated. The NCC measure is computed as follows:

$$NCC(x, y, d) = \frac{\sum_{(u,v) \in W_m(x,y)} (I_l(u, v) - \bar{I}_l)(I_r(u - d, v) - \bar{I}_r)}{\sqrt{\sum_{(u,v) \in W_m(x,y)} (I_l(u, v) - \bar{I}_l)^2 (I_r(u - d, v) - \bar{I}_r)^2}},$$

where

$$\bar{I}_l = \frac{1}{m^2} \sum_{(u,v) \in W_m(x,y)} I_l(u, v), \qquad \bar{I}_r = \frac{1}{m^2} \sum_{(u,v) \in W_m(x,y)} I_r(u, v).$$

2.7.2 Feature-Based Methods

Rather than matching each pixel, feature-based methods only search for correspondences to a sparse set of features, such as those located by a repeatable, well-localized interest point detector (e.g. a corner detector). Apart from locating the features, feature extraction algorithms also compute some sort of feature descriptors for their representation, which can be used for the similarity criterion. The correct correspondence is given by the most similar feature pair, the one with the minimum distance between the feature descriptors.

Stable features are preferred in feature-based methods to facilitate matching between images. Typical examples of image features are edge points, lines and corners. For example, a feature descriptor for a line could contain the length, the orientation, coordinates of the midpoint or the average contrast along the edge line. A problem with linear features is that the matching can be poorly localized along the length of a line particularly if a linear feature is fragmented (imagine a smaller fragment from the left image sliding along a larger fragment from the right image). This is known as the aperture problem, referring to the fact that a *local* match 'looks through' a small aperture.

As a consequence, point-based features that are well-localized in two mutually orthogonal directions, have been preferred by researchers and practitioners in the field of computer vision. For example, the Harris corner detector [18] extracts points

Fig. 2.12 Wide baseline matching between two images with SIFT. The size and orientation of the squares correspond to the scale and orientation of the matching SIFT features

that differ as much as possible from neighboring points. This is achieved by looking for high curvatures in two mutually orthogonal directions, as the gradient is ill-defined in the neighborhood of corners. The corner strength or the grayscale values in a window region around each corner could be used as the descriptor. Another corner detector SUSAN [52] detects features based on the size, centroid and second moments of the local areas. As it does not compute image derivatives, it is robust to noise and does not require image smoothing.

Wide baseline matching refers to the situation where the two camera views differ considerably. Here, matching has to operate successfully over more difficult conditions, since there are larger geometric and photometric variations between the images.

In recent years, many interest point detection algorithms have been proposed that are scale invariant and viewpoint invariant to a certain extent which facilitates wide baseline matching. An interest point refers to an image feature that is stable under local and global perturbation and the local image structure is rich in terms of local image contents. These features are often described by a distinctive feature descriptor which is used as the similarity criterion. They can be used even when epipolar geometry is not yet known, as such distinctive descriptors allow correspondences to be searched over the whole image relatively efficiently.

For example, the *Scale Invariant Feature Transform* (SIFT) [28] and the *Speeded-Up Robust Feature* (SURF) [2] are two popular features which were developed for image feature generation in object recognition applications. The SIFT feature is described by a local image vector with 128 elements, which is invariant to image translation, scaling, rotation and partially invariant to illumination changes and affine or 3D projections.

Figure 2.12 shows an example of matching SIFT features across large baseline and viewpoint variation. It can be seen that most matches are correct, thanks to the invariance and discriminative nature of SIFT features.

Table 2.2 Different types of 3D reconstruction

A priori knowledge	3D reconstruction
Intrinsic and extrinsic parameters	Absolute 3D reconstruction
Intrinsic parameters only	Metric 3D reconstruction (up to a scale factor)
No information	Projective 3D reconstruction

2.8 3D Reconstruction

Different types of 3D reconstruction can be obtained based on the amount of *a priori* knowledge available, as illustrated in Table 2.2. The simplest method to recover 3D information is stereo where the intrinsic and extrinsic parameters are known and the *absolute metric* 3D reconstruction can be obtained. This means we can determine the actual dimensions of structures, such as: *height of door* $= 1.93$ m.

For structure from motion, if no such prior information is available, only a projective 3D reconstruction can be obtained. This means that 3D structure is known only up to an arbitrary projective transformation so we know, for example, how many planar faces the object has and what point features are collinear, but we do not know anything about the scene dimensions and angular measurements within the scene. If intrinsic parameters are available, the projective 3D reconstruction can be upgraded to a metric reconstruction, where the 3D reconstruction is known up to a scale factor (i.e. a scaled version of the original scene). There is more detail to this hierarchy of reconstruction than we can present here (for example *affine* 3D reconstruction lies between the metric and projective reconstructions) and we refer the interested reader to [21].

2.8.1 Stereo

Stereo vision refers to the ability to infer information on the 3D structure and distance of a scene from two or more images taken from different viewpoints. The disparities of all the image points form the *disparity map*, which can be displayed as an image. If the stereo system is calibrated, the disparity map can be converted to a 3D point cloud representing the scene.

The discussion here focuses on binocular stereo for two image views only. Please refer to [51] for a survey of multiple-view stereo methods that reconstruct a complete 3D model instead of just a single disparity map, which generates *range image* information only. In such a 3D imaging scenario, there is at most one depth per image plane point, rear facing surfaces and other self-occlusions are not imaged and the data is sometimes referred to as 2.5D.

2 Passive 3D Imaging

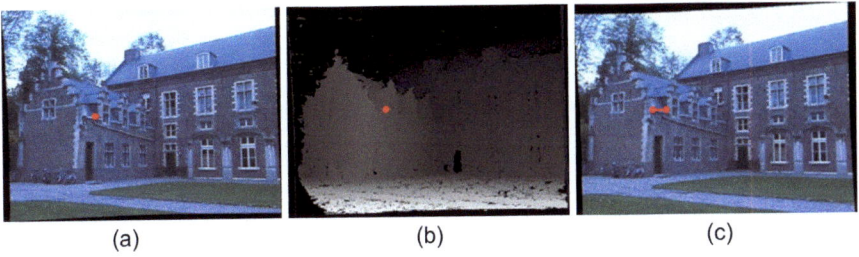

(a) (b) (c)

Fig. 2.13 A sample disparity map (**b**) obtained from the left image (**a**) and the right image (**c**). The disparity value for the pixel highlighted in *red* in the disparity map corresponds to the length of the line linking the matching features in the right image. Figure courtesy of [43]

2.8.1.1 Dense Stereo Matching

The aim of dense stereo matching is to compute disparity values for all the image points from which a dense 3D point cloud can be obtained. Correlation-based methods provide dense correspondences while feature-based methods only provide sparse correspondences. Dense stereo matching is more challenging than sparse correspondences as textureless regions do not provide information to distinguish the correct matches from the incorrect ones. The quality of correlation-based matching results depends highly on the amount of texture available in the images and the illumination conditions.

Figure 2.13 shows a sample disparity map after dense stereo matching. The disparity map is shown in the middle with disparity values encoded in grayscale level. The brighter pixels refer to larger disparities which mean the object is closer. For example, the ground pixels are brighter than the building pixels. An example of correspondences is highlighted in red in the figure. The pixel itself and the matching pixel are marked and linked on the right image. The length of the line corresponds to the disparity value highlighted in the disparity map.

Comparing image windows between two images could be ambiguous. Various matching constraints can be applied to help reduce the ambiguity, such as:

- Epipolar constraint
- Ordering constraint
- Uniqueness constraint
- Disparity range constraint

The epipolar constraint reduces the search from 2D to the epipolar line only, as has been described in Sect. 2.5. The ordering constraint means that if pixel b is to the right of a in the left image, then the correct correspondences a' and b' must also follow the same order (i.e. b' is to the right of a' in the right image). This constraint fails if there is occlusion.

The uniqueness constraint means that each pixel has at most one corresponding pixel. In general, there is a one-to-one correspondence for each pixel, but there is none in the case of occlusion or noisy pixels.

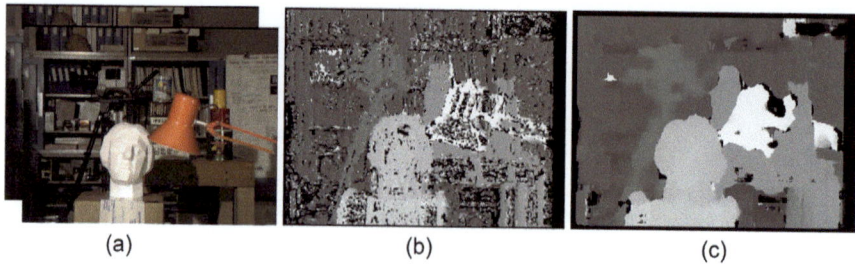

Fig. 2.14 The effect of window size on correlation-based methods: (**a**) input images (**b**) disparity map for a small correlation window (**c**) disparity map for a large correlation window (Raw image pair courtesy of the Middlebury Stereo Vision Page [34], originally sourced from Tsukuba University)

The disparity range constraint limits the disparity search range according to the prior information of the expected scene. Maximum disparity sets how close the object can be while the minimum disparity sets how far the object can be. Zero disparity refers to objects at infinity.

One important parameter for these correlation-based methods is the window size m in Eq. (2.20). While using a larger window size provides more intensity variation and hence more context for matching, this may cause problems around the occlusion area and at object boundaries, particularly for wide baseline matching.

Figure 2.14 shows the effect of window size on the resulting disparity map. The disparity map in the middle is for a window size of 3×3. It can be seen that, while it captures details well, it is very noisy, as the smaller window provides less information for matching. The disparity map on the right is for a window size of 15×15. It can be seen that while it looks very clean, the boundaries are not well-defined. Moreover, the use of a larger window size also increases the processing time as more pixels need to be correlated. The best window size is a trade-off between these two effects and is dependent on the level of fine detail in the scene.

For local methods, disparity computation at a given point depends on the intensity value within a local window only. The best matching window is indicated by the lowest dissimilarity measure or the highest similarity measure which uses information in the local region only. As pixels in an image are correlated (they may belong to the same object for instance), global methods could improve the stereo matching quality by making use of information outside the local window region.

Global methods perform optimization across the image and are often formulated as an energy minimization problem. Dynamic programming approaches [3, 5, 11] compute the minimum-cost path through the matrix of all pair-wise matching costs between two corresponding scanlines so that the best set of matches that satisfy the ordering constraint can be obtained. Dynamic programming utilizes information along each scanline independently, therefore, it may generate results that are not consistent across scanlines.

Graph cuts [6, 25] is one of the current state-of-the-art optimization techniques. These approaches make use of information across the whole image and produce high quality disparity maps. There is a trade-off between stereo matching quality and the processing time. Global methods such as graph cuts, max flow [45], and belief propagation [53, 54] produce better disparity maps than local methods but they are very computationally intensive.

Apart from the algorithm itself, the processing time also depends on the image resolution, the window size and the disparity search range. The higher the image resolution, the more pixels need to be processed to produce the disparity map. The similarity measure needs to correlate more pixels for a larger window size. The disparity search range affects how many such measures need to be computed in order to find the correct match.

Hierarchical stereo matching methods have been proposed by down-sampling the original image into a pyramid [4, 44]. Dense stereo matching is first performed on the lowest resolution image and disparity ranges can be propagated back to the finer resolution image afterwards. This coarse-to-fine hierarchical approach allows fast computation to deal with a large disparity range, as a narrower disparity range can be used for the original image. Moreover, the more precise disparity search range helps to obtain better matches in the low texture areas.

The Middlebury webpage [34] provides standard datasets with ground truth information for researchers to benchmark their algorithms so that the performance of various algorithms can be evaluated and compared. A wide spectrum of dense stereo matching algorithms have been benchmarked, as illustrated in Fig. 2.15 [46]. Researchers can submit results of new algorithms which are ranked based on various metrics, such as RMS error between computed disparity map and ground truth map, percentage of bad matching pixels and so on. It can be observed from Fig. 2.15 that it is very difficult to understand algorithmic performance by qualitative inspection of disparity maps and the quantitative measures presented in [46] are required.

2.8.1.2 Triangulation

When the corresponding left and right image points are known, two rays from the camera centers through the left and right image points can be back-projected. The two rays and the stereo baseline lie on a plane (the epipolar plane) and form a triangle, hence the reconstruction is termed 'triangulation'. Here we describe triangulation for a rectilinear arrangement of two views or, equivalently, two rectified views.

After image rectification, the stereo geometry becomes quite simple as shown in Fig. 2.16, which shows the top-down view of a stereo system composed of two pinhole cameras. The necessary parameters, such as baseline and focal length, are obtained from the original stereo calibration. The following two equations can be obtained based on the geometry:

$$x'_c = f \frac{X}{Z}$$
$$x_c = f \frac{X+B}{Z},$$

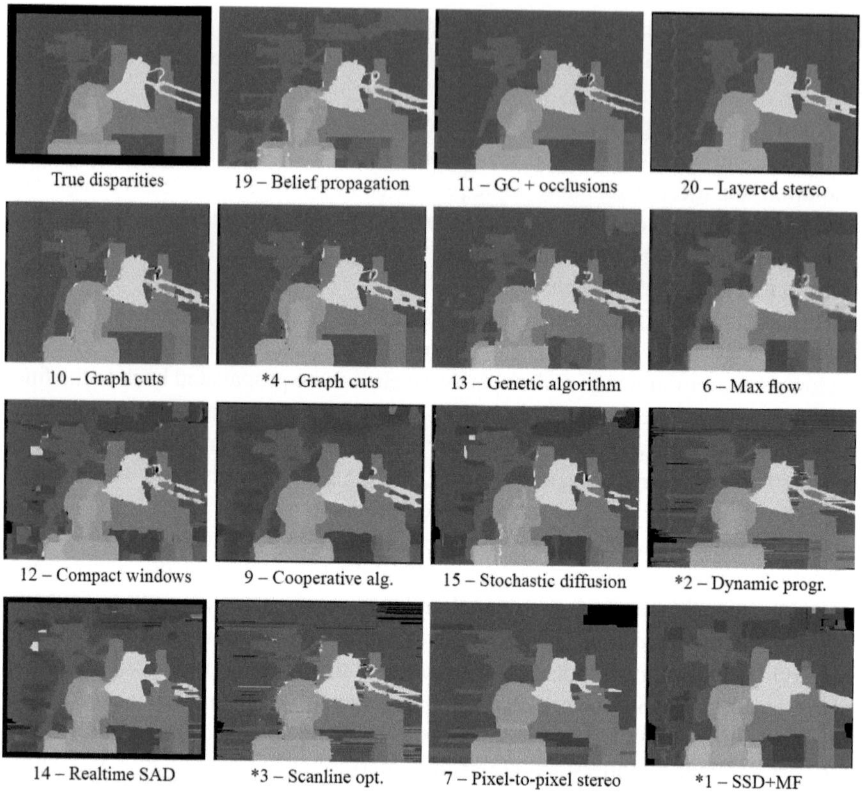

Fig. 2.15 Comparative disparity maps for the top fifteen dense stereo matching algorithms in [46] in decreasing order of performance. The *top left* disparity map is the ground truth. Performance here is measured as the percentage of bad matching pixels in regions where there are no occlusions. This varies from 1.15 % in algorithm 19 to 5.23 % in algorithm 1. Algorithms marked with a ∗ were implemented by the authors of [46], who present a wider range of algorithms in their publication. Figure courtesy of [46]

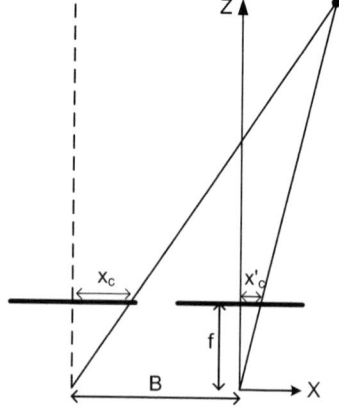

Fig. 2.16 The stereo geometry becomes quite simple after image rectification. The world coordinate frame is arbitrarily centered on the right camera. B is the stereo baseline and f is the focal length. Disparity is given by $d = x_c - x'_c$

where x'_c and x_c are the corresponding horizontal image coordinates (in metric units) in the right and left images respectively, f is the focal length and B is the baseline distance.

Disparity d is defined as the difference in horizontal image coordinates between the corresponding left and right image points, given by:

$$d = x_c - x'_c = \frac{fB}{Z}.$$

Therefore,

$$Z = \frac{fB}{d},$$
$$X = \frac{Zx'_c}{f}, \quad Y = \frac{Zy'_c}{f},$$
(2.21)

where y'_c is the vertical image coordinates in the right image.

This shows that the 3D world point can be computed once disparity is available: $(x'_c, y'_c, d) \mapsto (X, Y, Z)$. Disparity maps can be converted into depth maps using these equations to generate a 3D point cloud. It can be seen that triangulation is straightforward compared to the earlier stages of computing the two-view relations and finding correspondences.

Stereo matches are found by seeking the minimum of some cost functions across the disparity search range. This computes a set of disparity estimates in some discretized space, typically integer disparities, which may not be accurate enough for 3D recovery. 3D reconstruction using such quantized disparity maps leads to many thin layers of the scene. Interpolation can be applied to obtain sub-pixel disparity accuracy, such as fitting a curve to the SSD values for the neighboring pixels to find the peak of the curve, which provides more accurate 3D world coordinates.

By taking the derivatives of Eq. (2.21), the standard deviation of depth is given by:

$$\Delta Z = \frac{Z^2}{Bf} \Delta d,$$

where Δd is the standard deviation of the disparity. This equation shows that the depth uncertainty increases quadratically with depth. Therefore, stereo systems typically are operated within a limited range. If the object is far away, the depth estimation becomes more uncertain. The depth error can be reduced by increasing the baseline, focal length or image resolution. However, each of these has detrimental effects. For example, increasing the baseline makes matching harder and causes viewed objects to self-occlude, increasing the focal length reduces the depth of field, and increasing image resolution increases processing time and data bandwidth requirements. Thus, we can see that design of stereo cameras typically involves a range of performance trade-offs, where trade-offs are selected according to the application requirements.

Figure 2.17 compares the depth uncertainty for three stereo configuration assuming a disparity standard deviation of 0.1 pixel. A stereo camera with higher

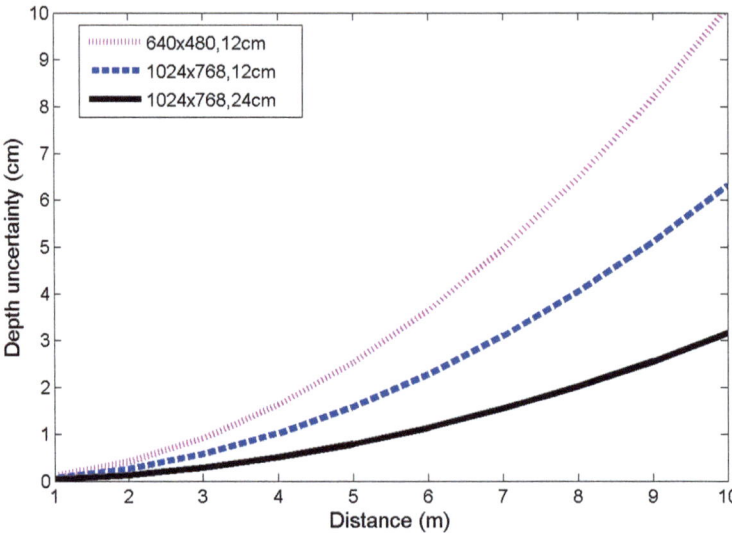

Fig. 2.17 A plot illustrating the stereo uncertainty with regard to image resolution and baseline distance. A larger baseline and higher resolution provide better accuracy, but each of these has other costs

resolution (dashed line) provides better accuracy than the one with lower resolution (dotted line). A stereo camera with a wider baseline (solid line) provides better accuracy than the one with a shorter baseline (dashed line).

A quick and simple method to evaluate the accuracy of 3D reconstruction, is to place a highly textured planar target at various depths from the sensor, fit a least squares plane to the measurements and measure the residual RMS error. In many cases, this gives us a good measure of depth repeatability, unless there are significant systematic errors, for example from inaccurate calibration of stereo camera parameters. In this case, more sophisticated processes and ground truth measurement equipment are required. Capturing images of a target of known size and shape at various depths, such as a textured cube, can indicate how reconstruction performs when measuring in all three spatial dimensions.

2.8.2 Structure from Motion

Structure from motion (SfM) is the simultaneous recovery of 3D structure and camera relative pose (position and orientation) from image correspondences and it refers to the situation where images are captured by a moving camera. There are three sub-problems in structure from motion.

- Correspondence: which elements of an image frame correspond to which elements of the next frame.

- Ego-motion and reconstruction: determination of camera motion (sometimes called ego-motion) and structure of the observed world.
- Segmentation: extraction of regions corresponding to one or more moving objects.

The third sub-problem is a relatively recent problem in structure from motion, where some objects in the scene may have moved between frames. For dynamic scenes, features belonging to moving objects could be identified and removed as outliers. Alternatively one could consider an environment to contain an unknown number (n) of independently moving objects and a static environment as $n + 1$ SfM sub-problems, each having their own F matrix. However, for the following discussion, we assume that the scene is static, without any moving objects.

By matching features between frames, we obtain at least eight correspondences from which the fundamental matrix can be recovered as described in Sect. 2.5.4. Without camera calibration parameters, only the projective reconstruction can be obtained where orthogonal lines in the world may not be reconstructed as orthogonal. While this may be useful by itself, most practical applications require at least metric reconstruction where the reconstructed 3D model is a scaled version of the real scene.

Metric reconstruction requires camera intrinsic parameters which can be estimated from the images themselves using self-calibration (auto-calibration) techniques [21, 35] developed in recent years. Such methods exploit some prior information of the scene itself such as parallel lines, vanishing points and so on. For better accuracy and more robustness, the camera intrinsic parameters can be obtained with a calibration procedure using a known calibration grid, as discussed in Sect. 2.4.

Once the camera intrinsic parameters are known, the essential matrix E can be computed from the fundamental matrix. According to Eq. (2.15), the motion can be recovered from E, where **t** is determined up to a scale factor only (since we can multiply Eq. (2.16) by an arbitrary non-zero scale factor). The physical insight into this is that the same image disparity between a pair of views can occur for a point close to the camera positions and a point n-times the distance away with n-times the translation. Effectively we have scaled similar triangles in the triangulation-based reconstruction process.

SVD can be applied to extract **t** and R from E as follows [21]. Application of SVD gives the factorization $E = UDV^T$. By defining:

$$W = \begin{bmatrix} 0 & -1 & 0 \\ 1 & 0 & 0 \\ 0 & 0 & 1 \end{bmatrix}, \quad Z = \begin{bmatrix} 0 & 1 & 0 \\ -1 & 0 & 0 \\ 0 & 0 & 0 \end{bmatrix},$$

the solution is given by:

$$R = UWV^T \quad \text{or} \quad UW^TV^T$$

$$\mathbf{t} = \pm\mathbf{u}_3,$$

where $\mathbf{u}_3$ is the third column of matrix U. With two possible choices of R and **t**, there are four possible solutions. Testing with a single point to determine if it is in front of both cameras is sufficient to decide among the four different solutions. For further details, please refer to [21].

Once **t** (up to scale) and R have been extracted from E, the sparse scene structure can be recovered by computing the intersection between the back-projected rays. In general, due to measurement noise, these will not intersect in 3D space. The simplest solution is to compute the mid-point of the shortest perpendicular line between the two rays. However, a refined solution is to choose a reconstructed scene point **X**, such that it minimizes the sum of square errors between the actual image positions and their positions predicted by their respective camera projection matrices. The scene structure is only determined up to a scale factor but in some applications this could be constrained, for example, if some measurement is known in the scene, or the translation can be estimated from the wheel odometry of a mobile robot. In summary, this method first estimates the intrinsic camera parameters (or uses an existing calibration) after which the extrinsic camera parameters are recovered. Both the intrinsic and extrinsic camera parameters are then used to compute the scene structure.

Alternatively, *bundle adjustment*[14] offers a more accurate method that simultaneously optimizes the 3D structure and the 6-DOF camera pose (extrinsic camera parameters) for each view in an image sequence [57]. Sometimes the intrinsic camera parameters are also refined in the procedure. This is a batch process that iteratively refines the camera parameters and the 3D structure in order to minimize the sum of the reprojection errors. (A reprojection error is the Euclidean distance between an image feature and its reprojection into the image plane after computing the 3D world coordinate and the camera pose associated with that image point.) Since a specific reprojection error is only dependent on its own scene point and own viewpoint, the structure of the equations is sparse. Thus, even though bundle adjustment is thought to be fairly computationally expensive, exploitation of sparse linear algebra algorithms can significantly mitigate this. Such procedures are referred to as *sparse bundle adjustment*.

Using consecutive video frames gives poor 3D accuracy due to the very short baseline. An image pair formed by a larger time increment would provide better 3D information. However, if the time increment is too large, the camera could have moved significantly and it would be harder to establish correct correspondences. One possible solution to this is to track features over several short baseline frames using a small, local area-based search, before computing 3D from a pair of frames tracked over a significantly longer baseline.

2.9 Passive Multiple-View 3D Imaging Systems

Examples of passive multiple-view 3D imaging systems and their applications will now be presented, including stereo cameras, 3D modeling and mobile robot naviga-

---

[14]Bundle adjustment methods appeared several decades ago in the photogrammetry literature and are now used widely in the computer vision community.

tion. 3D modeling systems generate photo-realistic 3D models from sequences of images and have a wide range of applications. For mobile robot applications, passive multiple-view 3D imaging systems are used for localization, building maps and obstacle avoidance.

2.9.1 Stereo Cameras

Stereo cameras can be custom-built by mounting two individual cameras on a rigid platform separated by a fixed baseline. However, it is important that, for non-static scenes or for mobile platforms, the two cameras are synchronized so that they capture images at the same time. In order to obtain absolute 3D information, as discussed earlier in Table 2.2, the stereo camera needs to be calibrated to recover the intrinsic and extrinsic parameters. It is also critical that the relative camera pose does not change over time, otherwise, re-calibration would be required.

Commercial off-the-shelf (COTS) stereo vision systems have been emerging in recent years. These cameras often have a fixed baseline and are pre-calibrated by the vendor. Typically, they are nicely packaged and convenient to use and an example was given earlier in Fig. 2.1. The Point Grey Research Bumblebee camera[15] is another example, which comes pre-calibrated and an application programming interface (API) is provided to configure the camera and grab images, as well as rectify the images and perform dense stereo matching.

It is desirable to obtain disparity maps in real-time in many applications, for example obstacle detection for mobile robots. Hardware-accelerated correlation-based stereo systems are now commercially available, which can offer a high update rate required for mobile robot navigation, as well as to free up the processor for other tasks.

The Tyzx DeepSea G2 stereo vision system[16] provides real-time embedded 3D vision processing without the use of separate computer. The custom image processing chip (an *Application-Specific Integrated Circuit* or ASIC), a *Field Programmable Gate Array* (FPGA) and an embedded PowerPC are all enclosed in the self-contained camera package. Different baselines and lens options are available. Real-time 3D depth data can be obtained via an Ethernet connection. Figure 2.18 shows that the Tyzx system is used on a rugged military *Unmanned Ground Vehicle* (UGV) for obstacle detection [62].

Videre Design [59] offers fixed baseline and variable baseline stereo cameras, as well as a stereo camera with onboard processing. Their *stereo on a chip* (STOC) camera performs stereo processing onboard the camera and these are available with different fixed baselines. The fixed baseline cameras are pre-calibrated at the factory while the variable baseline cameras can be field-calibrated, offering flexibility for different range requirements.

---

[15] http://www.ptgrey.com/products/stereo.asp.
[16] http://www.tyzx.com/products/DeepSeaG2.html.

Fig. 2.18 A military UGV (Unmanned Ground Vehicle) equipped with the Tyzx DeepSea G2 stereo vision system [62]. Image courtesy of iRobot Corporation

Dense stereo matching can be highly parallelized, therefore such algorithms are highly suitable to run on graphics processing units (GPUs) to free up the CPU for other tasks. GPUs have a parallel throughput architecture that supports executing many concurrent threads, providing immense speed-up for highly parallelized algorithms. A dense stereo matching algorithm has been implemented on a commodity graphics card [63] to perform several hundred millions of disparity evaluations per second. This corresponds to 20 Hz for 512×512 image resolution with 32 disparity search range, therefore real-time performance can be achieved without the use of specialized hardware.

2.9.2 3D Modeling

The creation of photo-realistic 3D models of observed scenes has been an active research topic for many years. Such 3D models are very useful for both visualization and measurements in various applications such as planetary rovers, defense, mining, forensics, archeology and virtual reality.

Pollefeys et al. [43] and Nister [38] presented systems which create surface models from a sequence of images taken with a hand-held video camera. The camera motion is recovered by matching corner features in the image sequence. Dense stereo matching is carried out between the frames. The input images are used as surface texture to produce photo-realistic 3D models. These monocular approaches only output a scaled version of the original scene, but can be scaled with some prior information. Moreover, it requires a long processing time.

The objective of the DARPA Urbanscape project [36] is to develop a real-time data collection and processing system for the automatic geo-registered 3D reconstruction of urban scenes from video data. Multiple video streams as well as *Global Positioning System* (GPS) and *Inertial Navigation System* (INS) measurements are collected to reconstruct photo-realistic 3D models and place them in geo-registered coordinates. An example of a large-scale 3D reconstruction is shown in Fig. 2.19.

Fig. 2.19 An example of 3D modeling of urban scene from the Urbanscape project. Figure courtesy of [36]

Fig. 2.20 The user points the stereo camera freely at the scene of interest (*left*) and the photo-realistic 3D model of the scene is generated (*right*). Figure adapted from [47]

A stereo-camera based 3D vision system is capable of quickly generating calibrated photo-realistic 3D models of unknown environments. *Instant Scene Modeler* (iSM) can process stereo image sequences captured by an unconstrained handheld stereo camera [47]. Dense stereo matching is performed to obtain 3D point clouds from each stereo pair. 3D point clouds from each stereo pair are merged together to obtain a color 3D point cloud. Furthermore, a surface triangular mesh is generated from the point cloud. This is followed by texture mapping, which involves mapping image textures to the mesh triangles. As adjacent triangles in the mesh may use different texture images, seamlines may appear unless texture blending is performed. The resulting photo-realistic 3D models can be visualized from different views and absolute measurements can be performed on the models. Figure 2.20 shows the user pointing the hand-held COTS stereo camera to freely scan the scene and the resulting photo-realistic 3D model, which is a textured triangular mesh.

For autonomous vehicles and planetary rovers, the creation of 3D terrain models of the environment is useful for visualization and path planning [1]. Moreover, the 3D modeling process achieves significant data compression, allowing the transfer of data as compact surface models instead of raw images. This is beneficial for plane-

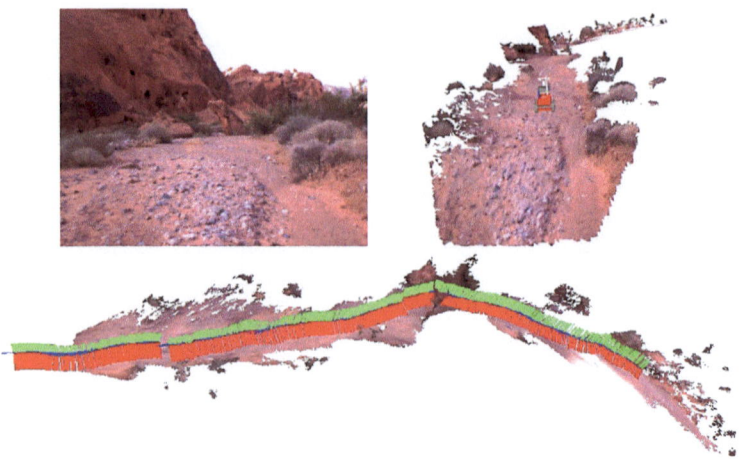

Fig. 2.21 First image of a sequence captured by an autonomous rover in a desert in Nevada (*left*). Terrain model generated with virtual rover model inserted (*right*). Resulting terrain model and rover trajectory (*bottom*). Figure courtesy of [1]

Fig. 2.22 Mars Exploration Rover stereo image processing (*left*) and the reconstructed color 3D point cloud (*right*), with a virtual rover model inserted. Figure courtesy of [31]

tary rover exploration due to the limited bandwidth available. Figure 2.21 shows a photo-realistic 3D model created from a moving autonomous vehicle that traveled over 40 m in a desert in Nevada.

One of the key technologies required for planetary rover navigation is the ability to sense the nearby 3D terrain. Stereo cameras are suitable for planetary exploration thanks to their low power and low mass requirements and the lack of moving parts. The NASA *Mars Exploration Rovers* (MERs), named *Opportunity* and *Spirit*, both use passive stereo image processing to measure geometric information about the environment [31]. This is done by matching and triangulating pixels from a pair of rectified stereo images to generate a 3D point cloud. Figure 2.22 shows an example of the stereo images captured and the color 3D point cloud generated which represents the imaged terrain.

Fig. 2.23 3D model of a mock crime scene obtained with a hand-held stereo camera. Figure courtesy of [48]

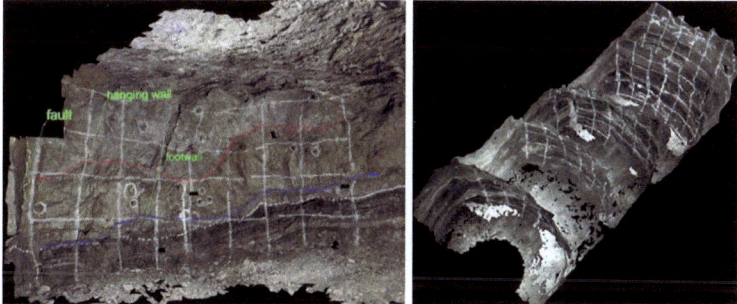

Fig. 2.24 Underground mine 3D model (*left*) and consecutive 3D models as the mine advances (*right*). The *red* and *blue* lines on the *left* are geological features annotated by geologists to help with the ore body modeling. Figure courtesy of [48]

Documenting crime scenes is a tedious process that requires the investigators to record vast amounts of data by using video, still cameras and measuring devices, and by taking samples and recording observations. With passive 3D imaging systems, 3D models of the crime scene can be created quickly without much disturbance to the crime scene. The police can also perform additional measurements using the 3D model after the crime scene is released. The 3D model can potentially be shown in court so that the judge and the jury can understand the crime scene better. Figure 2.23 shows a 3D reconstruction of a mock crime scene generated from a hand-held stereo sequence within minutes after acquisition [48].

Photo-realistic 3D models are useful for survey and geology in underground mining. The mine map can be updated after each daily drill/blast/ore removal cycle to minimize any deviation from the plan. In addition, the 3D models can also allow the mining companies to monitor how much ore is taken at each blast. Figure 2.24 shows a photo-realistic 3D model of an underground mine face annotated with ge-

Fig. 2.25 3D reconstruction of a building on the ground using video (*left*) and using infra-red video (*right*) captured by an UAV (Unmanned Aerial Vehicle). Figure courtesy of [50]

ological features and consecutive 3D models of a mine tunnel created as the mine advances [48].

Airborne surveillance and reconnaissance are essential for successful military missions. *Unmanned Aerial Vehicles* (UAVs) are becoming the platform of choice for such surveillance operations and video cameras are among the most common sensors onboard UAVs. Photo-realistic 3D models can be generated from UAV video data to provide situational awareness as it is easier to understand the scene by visualizing it in 3D. The 3D model can be viewed from different perspectives and allow distance measurements and line-of-sight analysis. Figure 2.25 shows a 3D reconstruction of a building on the ground using video and infra-red video captured by an UAV [50]. The photo-realistic 3D models are geo-referenced and can be visualized in 3D *Geographical Information System* (GIS) viewers such as Google Earth.

2.9.3 Mobile Robot Localization and Mapping

Mobile robot localization and mapping is the process of simultaneously tracking the position of a mobile robot relative to its environment and building a map of the environment. Accurate localization is a prerequisite for building a good map and having an accurate map is essential for good localization. Therefore, *Simultaneous Localization and Mapping* (SLAM) is a critical underlying capability for successful mobile robot applications. To achieve a SLAM capability, high resolution passive vision systems can capture images in milliseconds, hence they are suitable for moving platforms such as mobile robots.

Stereo vision systems are commonly used on mobile robots, as they can measure the full six degrees of freedom (DOF) of the change in robot pose. This is known as visual odometry. By matching visual landmarks between frames to recover the robot motion, visual odometry is not affected by wheel slip and hence is more accurate than the wheel-based odometry. For outdoor robots with GPS receivers, visual odometry can also augment the GPS to provide better accuracy, and it is also valuable in environments where GPS signals are not available.

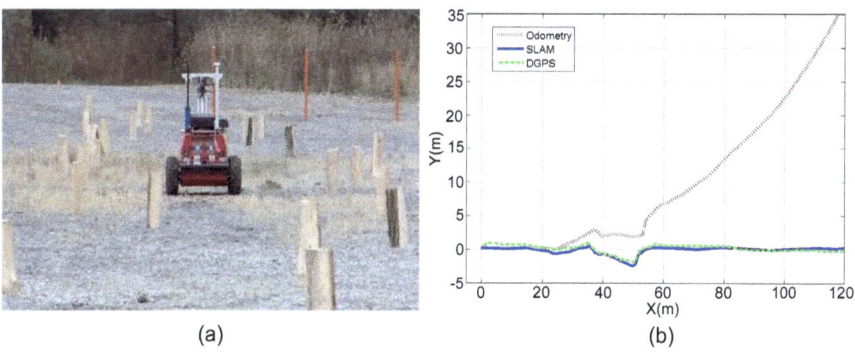

Fig. 2.26 (a) Autonomous rover on a gravel test site with obstacles (b) Comparison of the estimated path by SLAM, wheel odometry and DGPS (Differential GPS). Figure courtesy of [1]

Unlike in 3D modeling where correlation-based dense stereo matching is typically performed, feature-based matching is sufficient for visual odometry and SLAM; indeed, it is preferable for real-time robotics applications, as it is computationally less expensive. Such features are used for localization and a feature map is built at the same time.

The MERs *Opportunity* and *Spirit* are equipped with visual odometry capability [32]. An update to the rover's pose is computed by tracking the motion of autonomously-selected terrain features between two pairs of stereo images. It has demonstrated good performance and successfully detected slip ratios as high as 125 % even while driving on slopes as high as 31 degrees.

As SIFT features [28] are invariant to image translation, scaling, rotation, and fairly robust to illumination changes and affine or even mild projective deformation, they are suitable landmarks for robust SLAM. When the mobile robot moves around in an environment, landmarks are observed over time but from different angles, distances or under different illumination. SIFT features are extracted and matched between the stereo images to obtain 3D SIFT landmarks which are used for indoor SLAM [49] and for outdoor SLAM [1]. Figure 2.26 shows a field trial of an autonomous vehicle at a gravel test site with obstacles and a comparison of rover localization results. It can be seen that the vision-based SLAM trajectory is much better than the wheel odometry and matches well with the *Differential GPS* (DGPS).

Monocular visual SLAM applications have been emerging in recent years and these only require a single camera. The results are up to a scale factor, but can be scaled with some prior information. MonoSLAM [14] is a real-time algorithm which can recover the 3D trajectory of a monocular camera, moving rapidly through a previously unknown scene. The SLAM methodology is applied to the vision domain of a single camera, thereby achieving real-time and drift-free performance not offered by other structure from motion approaches.

Apart from localization, passive 3D imaging systems can also be used for obstacle/hazard detection in mobile robotics. Stereo cameras are often used as they can recover the 3D information without moving the robot. Figure 2.27 shows the stereo

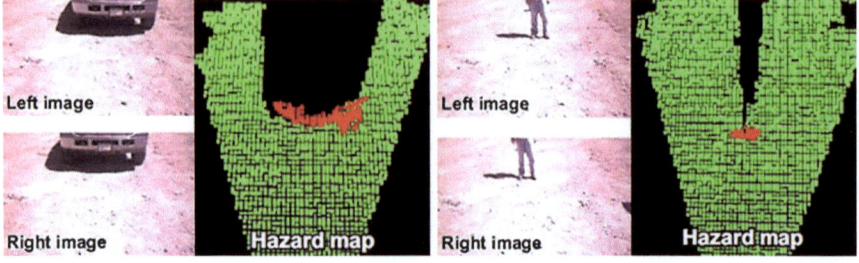

Fig. 2.27 Examples of hazard detection using stereo images: a truck (*left*) and a person (*right*)

images and the hazard maps for a truck and a person respectively. Correlation-based matching is performed to generate a dense 3D point cloud. Clusters of point cloud that are above the ground plane are considered as hazards.

2.10 Passive Versus Active 3D Imaging Systems

Before concluding, we briefly compare passive multiple-view 3D imaging systems and their active imaging counterpart, as a bridge between this and the following chapter. Passive systems do not emit any illumination and only perceive the ambient light reflected from the scene. Typically this is reflected sunlight when outdoors, or the light reflected from standard room lighting when indoors. On the other hand, active systems include their own source of illumination, which has two main benefits:

- 3D structure can be determined in smooth, textureless regions. For passive stereo, it would be difficult to extract features and correspondences in such circumstances.
- The correspondence problem either disappears, for example a single spot of light may be projected at any one time, or is greatly simplified by controlling the structure of the projected light.

The geometric principle of determining depth from a light (or other EMR) projector (e.g. laser) and a camera is identical to the passive binocular stereo situation. The physical difference is that, instead of using triangulation applied to a pair of back-projected rays, we apply triangulation to the axis of the projected light and a single back-projected ray.

Compared with active approaches, passive systems are more computationally intensive as the 3D data is computed from processing the images and matching image features. Moreover, the depth data could be noisier as it relies on the natural texture in the scene and ambient lighting condition. Unlike active scanning systems such as laser scanners, cameras could capture complete images in milliseconds, hence they can be used as mobile sensors or operate in dynamic environments. The cost, size, mass and power requirements of cameras are generally lower than those of active sensors.

2.11 Concluding Remarks

One of the key challenges for 3D vision researchers is to develop algorithms to recover accurate 3D information robustly under a wide range of illumination conditions which can be done by humans so effortlessly. While 3D passive vision algorithms have been maturing over the years, this is still an active topic in the research community and at major computer vision conferences. Many algorithms perform reasonably well with test data but there are still challenges to handle scenes with uncontrolled illumination. Other open issues include efficient global dense stereo matching, multi-image matching and fully automated accurate 3D reconstruction from images.

Passive 3D imaging systems are becoming more prevalent as cameras are getting cheaper and computers are fast enough to handle the intensive processing requirements. Thanks to hardware acceleration and GPUs, real-time applications are more common, leading to a growing number of real-world applications.

After working through this chapter, you should be able to:

- Explain the fundamental concepts and challenges of passive 3D imaging systems.
- Explain the principles of epipolar geometry.
- Solve the correspondence problem by correlation-based and feature-based techniques (using off-the-shelf feature extractors).
- Estimate the fundamental matrix from correspondences.
- Perform dense stereo matching and compute a 3D point cloud.
- Explain the principles of structure from motion.
- Provide example applications of passive 3D imaging systems.

2.12 Further Reading

Two-view geometry is studied extensively in [21], which also covers the equivalent of epipolar geometry for three or more images. The eight-point algorithm was proposed in [19] to compute the fundamental matrix, while the five-point algorithm was proposed in [39] for calibrated cameras. Reference [57] provides a good tutorial and survey on bundle adjustment, which is also covered in textbooks [15, 21] and a recent survey article [35].

Surveys such as [46] serve as a guide to the extensive literature on stereo imaging. Structure from motion is extensively covered in review articles such as [35]. A step-by-step guide to 3D modeling from images is described in detail in [30]. Non-rigid structure from motion for dynamic scenes is discussed in [56].

Multiple-view 3D vision continues to be a highly active research topic and some of the major computer vision conferences include: the International Conference on Computer Vision (ICCV), IEEE Conference on Computer Vision and Pattern Recognition (CVPR) and the European Conference on Computer Vision (ECCV). Some of the relevant major journals include: International Journal of Computer

Vision (IJCV), IEEE Transactions on Pattern Analysis and Machine Intelligence (PAMI) and Image and Vision Computing (IVC).

The International Society for Photogrammetry and Remote Sensing (ISPRS) proceedings and archives provide extensive literature on photogrammetry and related topics.

The following web sites provide comprehensive on-line resources for computer vision including 3D passive vision topics and are being updated regularly.

- CVonline (http://homepages.inf.ed.ac.uk/rbf/CVonline/) provides an on-line compendium of computer vision.
- VisionBib.Com (http://www.visionbib.com) contains annotated bibliography on a wide range of computer vision topics, as well as references to available datasets.
- Computer Vision online (http://www.computervisiononline.com) is a portal with links to software, hardware and datasets.
- OpenCV (http://opencv.willowgarage.com) is an open-source computer vision library.

2.13 Questions

1. What are the differences between passive and active 3D vision systems?
2. Name two approaches to recover 3D from single images and two approaches to recover 3D from multiple images.
3. What is the epipolar constraint and how can you use it to speed up the search for correspondences?
4. What are the differences between essential and fundamental matrices?
5. What is the purpose of rectification?
6. What are the differences between correlation-based and feature-based methods for finding correspondences?
7. What are the differences between local and global methods for dense stereo matching?
8. What are the differences between stereo and structure from motion?
9. What are the factors that affect the accuracy of stereo vision systems?

2.14 Exercises

Experimenting with stereo imaging requires that you have two images of a scene from slightly different viewpoints, with a good overlap between the views, and a significant number of well distributed corner features that can be matched. You will also need a corner detector. There are many stereo image pairs and corner detector implementations available on the web [40]. Of course, you can collect your own images either with a pre-packaged stereo camera or with a pair of standard digital cameras. The following programming exercises should be implemented in a language of your choice.

1. *Fundamental matrix with manual correspondences.* Run a corner detector on the image pair. Use a point-and-click GUI to manually label around 20 well distributed correspondences. Compute the fundamental matrix and plot the conjugate pair of epipolar lines on the images for each correspondence. Experiment with different numbers and combinations of correspondences, using a minimum of eight in the eight-point algorithm. Observe and comment on the sensitivity of the epipolar lines with respect to the set of correspondences chosen.
2. *Fundamental matrix estimation with outlier removal.* Add 4 incorrect corner correspondences to your list of 20 correct ones. Observe the effect on the computed fundamental matrix and the associated (corrupted) epipolar lines. Augment your implementation of fundamental matrix estimation with the RANSAC algorithm. Use a graphical overlay on your images to show that RANSAC has correctly identified the outliers, and verify that the fundamental matrix and its associated epipolar lines can now be computed without the corrupting effect of the outliers.
3. *Automatic feature correspondences.* Implement a function to *automatically* match corners between two images according to the *Sum of Squared Differences* (SSD) measure. Also, implement a function for the *Normalized Cross-Correlation* (NCC) measure. Compare the matching results with test images of similar brightness and also of different brightness.
4. *Fundamental matrix from automatic correspondences.* Use your fundamental matrix computation (with RANSAC) with the automatic feature correspondences. Determine the positions of the epipoles and, again, plot the epipolar lines.

The following additional exercises require the use of a stereo rig, which could be a pre-packaged stereo pair or a home-made rig with a pair of standard digital cameras. The cameras should have a small amount of vergence to overlap their fields of view.

5. *Calibration.* Create your own calibration target by printing off a chessboard pattern and pasting it to a flat piece of wood. Use a point-and-click GUI to semi-automate the corner correspondences between the calibration target and a set of captured calibration images. Implement a camera calibration procedure for a stereo pair to determine the intrinsic and extrinsic parameters of the stereo rig. If you have less time available you may choose to use some of the calibration libraries available on the web [9, 40].
6. *Rectification.* Compute an image warping (homography) to apply to each image in the stereo image pair, such that conjugate epipolar lines are horizontal (parallel to the x-axis) and have the same y-coordinate. Plot a set of epipolar lines to check that this rectification is correct.
7. *Dense stereo matching.* Implement a function to perform local dense stereo matching between left and right rectified images, using NCC as the similarity measure, and hence generate a disparity map for the stereo pair. Capture stereo images for a selection of scenes with varying amounts of texture within them and at varying distances from the cameras, and compare their disparity maps.
8. *3D reconstruction.* Implement a function to perform a 3D reconstruction from your disparity maps and camera calibration information. Use a graphics tool to visualize the reconstructions. Comment on the performance of the reconstructions for different scenes and for different distances from the stereo rig.

References

1. Barfoot, T., Se, S., Jasiobedzki, P.: Vision-based localization and terrain modelling for planetary rovers. In: Howard, A., Tunstel, E. (eds.) Intelligence for Space Robotics, pp. 71–92. TSI Press, Albuquerque (2006)
2. Bay, H., Ess, A., Tuytelaars, T., Van Gool, L.: SURF: speeded up robust features. Comput. Vis. Image Underst. **110**(3), 346–359 (2008)
3. Belhumeur, P.N.: A Bayesian approach to binocular stereopsis. Int. J. Comput. Vis. **19**(3), 237–260 (1996)
4. Bergen, J.R., Anandan, P., Hanna, K.J., Hinogorani, R.: Hierarchical model-based motion estimation. In: European Conference on Computer Vision (ECCV), Italy, pp. 237–252 (1992)
5. Birchfield, S., Tomasi, C.: Depth discontinuities by pixel-to-pixel stereo. Int. J. Comput. Vis. **35**(3), 269–293 (1999)
6. Boykov, Y., Veksler, O., Zabih, R.: Fast approximate energy minimization via graph cuts. IEEE Trans. Pattern Anal. Mach. Intell. **23**(11), 1222–1239 (2001)
7. Brown, D.C.: Decentering distortion of lenses. Photogramm. Eng. **32**(3), 444–462 (1966)
8. Brown, D.C.: Close-range camera calibration. Photogramm. Eng. **37**(8), 855–866 (1971)
9. Camera Calibration Toolbox for MATLAB: http://www.vision.caltech.edu/bouguetj/calib_doc/. Accessed 20th October 2011
10. Chen, Z., Pears, N.E., Liang, B.: Monocular obstacle detection using Reciprocal-Polar rectification. Image Vis. Comput. **24**(12), 1301–1312 (2006)
11. Cox, I.J., Hingorani, S.L., Rao, S.B., Maggs, B.M.: A maximum likelihood stereo algorithm. Comput. Vis. Image Underst. **63**(3), 542–567 (1996)
12. Coxeter, H.S.M.: Projective Geometry, 2nd edn. Springer, Berlin (2003)
13. Criminisi, A., Reid, I., Zisserman, A.: Single view metrology. Int. J. Comput. Vis. **40**(2), 123–148 (2000)
14. Davison, A., Reid, I., Molton, N., Stasse, O.: MonoSLAM: real-time single camera SLAM. IEEE Trans. Pattern Anal. Mach. Intell. **29**(6), 1052–1067 (2007)
15. Faugeras, O., Luong, Q.T.: The Geometry of Multiple Images. MIT Press, Cambridge (2001)
16. Fischler, M.A., Bolles, R.C.: Random sample consensus: a paradigm for model fitting with applications to image analysis and automated cartography. Commun. ACM **24**(6), 381–395 (1981)
17. Garding, J.: Shape from texture for smooth curved surfaces in perspective projection. J. Math. Imaging Vis. **2**, 329–352 (1992)
18. Harris, C., Stephens, M.J.: A combined corner and edge detector. In: Alvey Vision Conference, pp. 147–152 (1988)
19. Harley, R.I.: In defense of the 8-point algorithm. IEEE Trans. Pattern Anal. Mach. Intell. **19**(6), 580–593 (1997)
20. Hartley, R.I.: Theory and practice of projective rectification. Int. J. Comput. Vis. **35**(2), 115–127 (1999)
21. Hartley, R.I., Zisserman, A.: Multiple View Geometry in Computer Vision, 2nd edn. Cambridge University Press, Cambridge (2004)
22. Horn, B.K.P., Brooks, M.J. (eds.): Shape from Shading. MIT Press, Cambridge (1989)
23. Horn, B.K.P., Schunck, B.G.: Determining optical flow. Artif. Intell. **17**, 185–203 (1981)
24. Huang, R., P, S.W.A.: A shape-from-shading framework for satisfying data-closeness and structure-preserving smoothness constraints. In: Proceedings of the British Machine Vision Conference (2009)
25. Kolmogorov, V., Zabih, R.: Computing visual correspondence with occlusions using graph cuts. In: International Conference on Computer Vision (ICCV), Vancouver, pp. 508–515 (2001)
26. Konolige, K.: Small vision system: hardware and implementation. In: Proc. Int. Symp. on Robotics Research, Hayama, Japan, pp. 111–116 (1997)
27. Longuet-Higgins, H.C.: A computer algorithm for re-constructing a scene from two projections. Nature **293**, 133–135 (1981)

28. Lowe, D.G.: Distinctive image features from scale-invariant keypoints. Int. J. Comput. Vis. **60**(2), 91–110 (2004)
29. Lucas, B.D., Kanade, T.: An interactive image registration technique with an application in stereo vision. In: International Joint Conference on Artificial Intelligence (IJCAI), Vancouver, pp. 674–679 (1981)
30. Ma, Y., Soatto, S., Kosecka, J., Sastry, S.S.: An Invitation to 3-D Vision. Springer, New York (2003)
31. Maimone, M., Biesiadecki, J., Tunstel, E., Cheng, Y., Leger, C.: Surface navigation and mobility intelligence on the Mars Exploration Rovers. In: Howard, A., Tunstel, E. (eds.) Intelligence for Space Robotics, pp. 45–69. TSI Press, Albuquerque (2006)
32. Maimone, M., Cheng, Y., Matthies, L.: Two years of visual odometry on the mars exploration rovers. J. Field Robot. **24**(3), 169–186 (2007)
33. Mallon, J., Whelan, P.F.: Projective rectification from the fundamental matrix. In: Image and Vision Computing, pp. 643–650 (2005)
34. The Middlebury stereo vision page: http://vision.middlebury.edu/stereo/. Accessed 16th November 2011
35. Moons, T., Van Gool, L., Vergauwen, M.: 3D reconstruction from multiple images. Found. Trends Comput. Graph. Vis. **4**(4), 287–404 (2010)
36. Mordohai, P., et al.: Real-time video-based reconstruction of urban environments. In: International Workshop on 3D Virtual Reconstruction and Visualization of Complex Architectures (3D-ARCH), Zurich, Switzerland (2007)
37. Nayar, S.K., Nakagawa, Y.: Shape from focus. IEEE Trans. Pattern Anal. Mach. Intell. **16**(8), 824–831 (1994)
38. Nister, D.: Automatic passive recovery of 3D from images and video. In: International Symposium on 3D Data Processing, Visualization and Transmission (3DPVT), Thessaloniki, Greece, pp. 438–445 (2004)
39. Nister, D.: An efficient solution to the five-point relative pose problem. IEEE Trans. Pattern Anal. Mach. Intell. **26**(6), 756–770 (2004)
40. Open source computer vision library: http://opencv.willowgarage.com/wiki/. Accessed 20th October 2011
41. Pentland, A.P.: A new sense for depth of field. IEEE Trans. Pattern Anal. Mach. Intell. **9**(4), 523–531 (1987)
42. Pollefeys, M., Koch, R., Van Gool, L.: A simple and efficient rectification method for general motion. In: International Conference on Compute Vision (ICCV), Kerkyra, Greece, pp. 496–501 (1999)
43. Pollefeys, M., Van Gool, L., Vergauwen, M., Verbiest, F., Cornelis, K., Tops, J., Koch, R.: Visual modeling with a hand-held camera. Int. J. Comput. Vis. **59**(3), 207–232 (2004)
44. Quam, L.H.: Hierarchical warp stereo. In: Image Understanding Workshop, New Orleans, pp. 149–155 (1984)
45. Roy, S., Cox, I.J.: A maximum-flow formulation of the N-camera stereo correspondence problem. In: International Conference on Computer Vision (ICCV), Bombay, pp. 492–499 (1998)
46. Scharstein, D., Szeliski, R.: A taxonomy and evaluation of dense two-frame stereo correspondence algorithms. Int. J. Comput. Vis. **47**(1/2/3), 7–42 (2002)
47. Se, S., Jasiobedzki, P.: Photo-realistic 3D model reconstruction. In: IEEE International Conference on Robotics and Automation, Orlando, Florida, pp. 3076–3082 (2006)
48. Se, S., Jasiobedzki, P.: Stereo-vision based 3D modeling and localization for unmanned vehicles. Int. J. Intell. Control Syst. **13**(1), 47–58 (2008)
49. Se, S., Lowe, D., Little, J.: Mobile robot localization and mapping with uncertainty using scale-invariant visual landmarks. Int. J. Robot. Res. **21**(8), 735–758 (2002)
50. Se, S., Firoozfam, P., Goldstein, N., Dutkiewicz, M., Pace, P.: Automated UAV-based video exploitation for mapping and surveillance. In: International Society for Photogrammetry and Remote Sensing (ISPRS) Commission I Symposium, Calgary (2010)
51. Seitz, S., Curless, B., Diebel, J., Scharstein, D., Szeliski, R.: A comparison and evaluation of multi-view stereo reconstruction algorithms. In: IEEE Conference on Computer Vision and Pattern Recognition (CVPR), New York, pp. 519–526 (2006)

52. Smith, S.M., Brady, J.M.: SUSAN—a new approach to low level image processing. Int. J. Comput. Vis. **23**(1), 45–78 (1997)
53. Sun, J., Zheng, N., Shum, H.: Stereo matching using belief propagation. IEEE Trans. Pattern Anal. Mach. Intell. **25**(7), 787–800 (2003)
54. Tappen, M.F., Freeman, W.T.: Comparison of graph cuts with belief propagation for stereo, using identical MRF parameters. In: International Conference on Computer Vision (ICCV), Nice, France, pp. 900–907 (2003)
55. Torr, P.H.S., Murray, D.: The development and comparison of robust methods for estimating the fundamental matrix. Int. J. Comput. Vis. **24**(3), 271–300 (1997)
56. Torresani, L., Hertzmann, A., Bregler, C.: Non-rigid structure-from-motion: estimating shape and motion with hierarchical priors. IEEE Trans. Pattern Anal. Mach. Intell. **30**(5), 878–892 (2008)
57. Triggs, B., McLauchlan, P.F., Hartley, R.I., Fitzigibbon, A.W.: Bundle adjustment—a modern synthesis. In: International Workshop on Vision Algorithms, Kerkyra, Greece, pp. 298–372 (1999)
58. Tsai, R.Y.: A versatile camera calibration technique for high-accuracy 3D machine vision metrology using off-the-shelf TV cameras and lenses. IEEE J. Robot. Autom. **3**(4), 323–344 (1987)
59. Videre Design: http://www.videredesign.com/. Accessed 16th November 2011
60. White, R., Forsyth, D.A.: Combining cues: shape from shading and texture. In: IEEE Conference on Computer Vision and Pattern Recognition (CVPR), New York, pp. 1809–1816 (2006)
61. Woodham, R.J.: Analysing images of curved surfaces. Artif. Intell. **17**, 117–140 (1981)
62. Yamauchi, B.: Autonomous urban reconnaissance using man-portable UGVs. In: Unmanned Systems Technology. Orlando, Florida, SPIE, vol. 6230 (2006)
63. Yang, R., Pollefeys, M.: A versatile stereo implementation on commodity graphics hardware. Real-Time Imaging **11**(1), 7–18 (2005)
64. Zhang, Z.: A flexible new technique for camera calibration. IEEE Trans. Pattern Anal. Mach. Intell. **22**(11), 1330–1334 (2000)
65. Zhang, R., Tsai, P.S., Cryer, J.E., Shah, M.: Shaping from shading: a survey. IEEE Trans. Pattern Anal. Mach. Intell. **21**(8), 690–706 (1999)

Chapter 3
Active 3D Imaging Systems

Marc-Antoine Drouin and Jean-Angelo Beraldin

Abstract Active 3D imaging systems use artificial illumination in order to capture and record digital representations of objects. The use of artificial illumination allows the acquisition of dense and accurate range images of textureless objects that are difficult to acquire using passive vision systems. An active 3D imaging system can be based on different measurement principles that include time-of-flight, triangulation and interferometry. While time-of-flight and interferometry systems are briefly discussed, an in-depth description of triangulation-based systems is provided. The characterization of triangulation-based systems is discussed using both an error propagation framework and experimental protocols.

3.1 Introduction

Three-dimensional (3D) imaging systems (also known as 3D vision systems) capture and record a digital representation of the geometry and appearance (e.g. color-texture) information of visible 3D surfaces of people, animals, plants, objects and sites. This digital surrogate of the physical world is then processed in order to extract useful information from the raw data and finally, communicate the results. *Active* 3D imaging systems use an artificial illumination, usually either a spatially coherent light source (e.g. laser) or an incoherent one (e.g. halogen lamp), to acquire dense range maps with a minimum of ambiguity. The term is also used for systems that project non-visible electromagnetic radiation, such as near infra-red onto the scene. The use of an artificial light source makes it possible for active 3D imaging systems to generate a model of a surface geometry even when the surface appears featureless to the naked eye or to a photographic/video camera and, hence, require minimal operator assistance. Furthermore, the 3D information can be made relatively insensitive to ambient illumination and surface color. They are, by their

---

M.-A. Drouin (✉) · J.-A. Beraldin
National Research Council of Canada, Ottawa, Ontario, Canada
e-mail: Marc-Antoine.Drouin@nrc-cnrc.gc.ca

J.-A. Beraldin
e-mail: Jean-Angelo.Beraldin@nrc-cnrc.gc.ca

nature, non-contact measurement instruments and produce a quantifiable 3D digital representation (e.g. point cloud or range image) of a surface in a specified finite volume of interest and with a particular measurement uncertainty.

3.1.1 Historical Context

The desire to capture and record shape using optical instruments can be traced back to the invention of rudimentary surveying instruments and the camera obscura [60]. The invention of photography, in which images are recorded on semi-permanent recording media, is certainly the catalyst of modern methods. In the 1860s, François Willème invented a process known as photo-sculpture that used many cameras [49, 65]. Profiles of the subject to be reproduced were taken on photographic plates, projected onto a screen, and transferred to a piece of clay using a pantograph. The process supplied many profiles, which were used to rough down the piece of clay, leaving a large amount of manual work. Commercial applications developed rapidly and studios stayed in operation from 1863 to 1867, when it was realized that the photo-sculpture process was not more economical than the traditional sculpture technique. A professional sculptor was needed and the photo-sculpture process required a significant investment in cameras, projection and reproduction systems, and skilled labour to operate them.

It is only with the advances made during the last 50 years in the field of solid-state electronics, photonics, computer vision and computer graphics that the process of capturing and recording detailed shapes by optical means regained substantial interest. Indeed, obvious changes have been instrumental in the growth of active 3D imaging systems technology i.e. the availability of affordable and fast digital computers and reliable light sources (lasers, halogen lamps, LED). It is now possible to build reliable, accurate, high-resolution 3D active vision systems that can capture large amounts of 3D data. In addition, the ability to process these dense point clouds in an efficient and cost-effective way has opened up a myriad of applications in areas as diverse as military, medical, entertainment, industrial and commercial activities.

3.1.2 Basic Measurement Principles

Active three-dimensional (3D) imaging systems can be based on different measurement principles. The three most used principles in commercially available systems are time-of-flight, interferometry and triangulation. Seitz describes time-of-flight as based on an accurate clock, interferometry as one that uses accurate wavelengths and triangulation as a method based on geometry[59]. Figure 3.1 summarizes the typical accuracy of each type of active 3D imaging system technology found on the market as a function of the operating distance. It can be observed from that figure that each optical technique covers a particular range of operation. Many in-depth classifications of optical distance measurement principles have been published in important references in the field of 3D vision, e.g. [14, 16, 43, 50].

3 Active 3D Imaging Systems

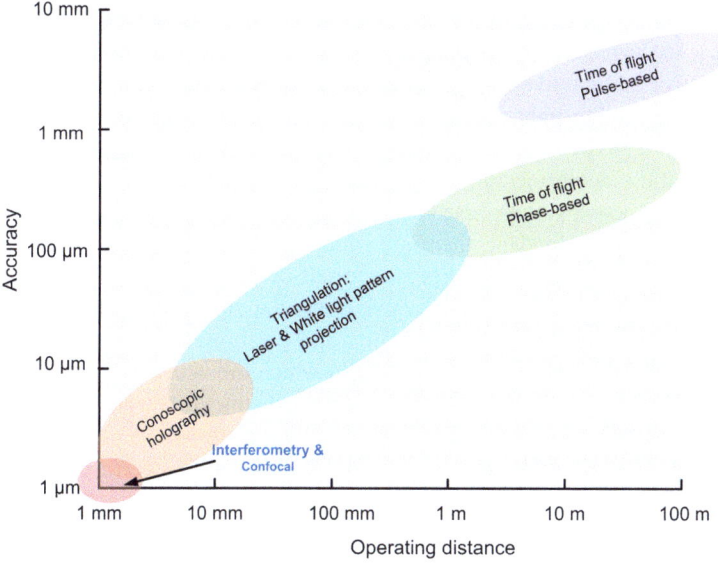

Fig. 3.1 Diagram showing typical accuracy at different operating distances of the most common active 3D imaging technologies for surface digitization. Figure courtesy of [56]

The fundamental work on time-of-flight systems can be traced back to the era of RADAR, which is based on radio waves. With the advent of lasers in the late 1950s, it became possible to image a surface with angular and range resolutions much higher than possible with radio waves. Different strategies have been devised to exploit this basic measurement principle of time-of-flight [7, 10, 43]. Figure 3.1 shows two of them.

Interferometry is based on the superposition of two beams of light [43]. Typically, a laser beam is split into two paths. One path is of known length, while the other is of unknown length. The difference in path lengths creates a phase difference between the light beams. The two beams are then combined together before reaching a photo-detector. The interference pattern seen by the detector resulting from the superposition of those two light beams depends on the path difference (a distance). Note that commercially available systems based on other principles such as conoscopic holography are available for small operating distances (see Fig. 3.1).

The remainder of this chapter will focus on triangulation-based methods which use the same principle as the passive triangulation systems presented in the previous chapter. The reader can find more information on interferometry-based methods in [43] and time-of-flight methods are described in [7, 10, 14, 43].

3.1.3 Active Triangulation-Based Methods

In the previous chapter, passive triangulation systems were presented, namely standard stereo configurations and structure-from-motion. In this chapter, we assume that the reader is familiar with camera calibration and the epipolar geometry of two camera views, as presented in Chap. 2.

Both active and passive triangulation systems are based on the same geometric principle: intersecting light rays in 3D space. Typically, an active system replaces one camera of a passive stereo system by a projection device. This projection device can be a digital video projector, an analogue slide projector or a laser. (Note, however, that many active systems use two cameras with a projection device. Although this is at first sight redundant, there are sound reasons behind this design choice, such as a reduction in 'missing parts' due to self-occlusion.)

There are many ways to classify active triangulation sensors, according to their opto-mechanical components, construction and performance. One of the key dimensions within this taxonomy is the way in which the active 3D imaging system illuminates the scene. Here we will consider three distinct categories: spot scanners, stripe scanners and systems that use structured light patterns.

The simplest of these is the spot scanner (also known as a point-based scanner) where, typically, a collimated or focused laser beam illuminates a very small circular or elliptical part of the scene for each image capture. One advantage of this approach is that the spatial correspondence problem is non-existent, because the illumination of the object's surface is spread temporally (i.e. in the time dimension). Moreover, a spot scanner allows us to control the spatial sampling on the scene surfaces. The laser power can also be controlled on a per 3D sample basis. However, this is at the expense of additional opto-mechanical complexity because the spot must be scanned either by mounting the sensor on a 2D translation stage, or by orienting the laser around two axes of rotation using two galvanometer-mounted mirrors.

Typically, in the second type of scanner, a collimated laser beam is passed through a cylindrical lens in order to generate a 'sheet of light' which illuminates the scene with a thin stripe. Other implementations are possible, for example the cylindrical lens could be replaced by a diffractive optical element (DOE) or a diffraction grating. This stripe now only needs to be scanned in one direction relative to the scene in order to assemble a range image and, again, this may be done by translation of the sensor (or, alternatively, the object) or the rotation of a single mirror. These 3D imaging devices are called stripe scanners or profile scanners. Note that although the complexity of scanning has reduced from two-dimensional to one-dimensional, some ambiguity in the direction of illumination is introduced, which needs to be resolved using the epipolar constraint.

The final type of scanner that we discuss is the type that projects a structured light pattern onto the scene [43]. These 3D imaging devices are also known as area scanners [2]. Typically these systems do not scan the projected light over the scene object at all, since the object is usually completely illuminated by the pattern, although the term 'scanner' is often still applied in an informal sense. These systems provide the advantage of the shortest capture times, thus minimizing distortion due to motion in dynamic scenes. The correspondence problem, however, is more challenging (although not as difficult as for passive stereo) and the projected light is structured either spatially, temporally, or both in order to determine which part of the projected pattern corresponds to which part of the imaged pattern.

When working with coherent light sources (lasers) eye-safety is of paramount importance and one should never operate laser-based 3D imaging sensors without appropriate eye-safety training. Many 3D imaging systems use a laser in the visible spectrum where fractions of a milliwatt are sufficient to cause eye damage, since the laser light density entering the pupil is magnified, at the retina, through the lens. For an operator using any laser, an important safety parameter is the maximum permissible exposure (MPE) which is defined as the level of laser radiation to which a person may be exposed without hazardous effect or adverse biological changes in the eye or skin [4]. The MPE varies with wavelength and operating conditions of a system. We do not have space to discuss eye safety extensively here and refer the reader to the *American National Standard for Safe use of Lasers* [4]. Note that high power low coherence (and non-coherent) light sources can also pose eye safety issues.

3.1.4 Chapter Outline

Firstly, we will present spot scanners and this will be followed by stripe scanners. Those types of scanners are used to introduce the concepts needed for the presentation of structured light systems in Sect. 3.4. In the following section, we discuss the calibration of active 3D imaging systems. Then, the measurement uncertainty associated with triangulation systems is presented. This section is optional advanced material and may be omitted on the first reading. The experimental characterization of active 3D imaging systems is then presented. In Sect. 3.8, further advanced topics are included and this section also may be omitted on the first reading. Towards the end of the chapter, we present the main challenges for future research, concluding remarks and suggestions for further reading. Finally a set of questions and exercises are presented for the reader to develop and consolidate their understanding of active 3D imaging systems.

3.2 Spot Scanners

Usually, spot scanners use a laser. We limit the discussion to this type of technology and in order to study the basic principle of triangulation, we assume an infinitely thin laser beam diameter and constrain the problem to the plane (X, Z), i.e. $Y = 0$. The basic geometrical principle of optical triangulation for a spot scanner is shown in Fig. 3.2 and is identical to the one of passive stereo discussed in Chap. 2.

In Fig. 3.2, a laser source projects a beam of light on a surface of interest. The light scattered by that surface is collected from a vantage point spatially distinct from the projected light beam. This light is focused (imaged) onto a linear spot

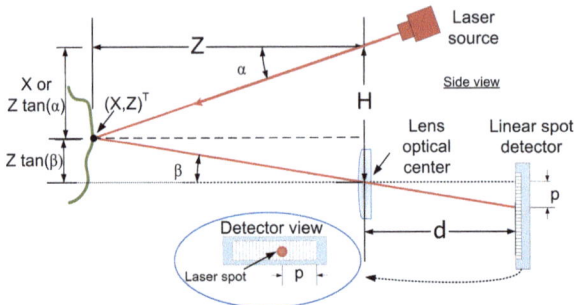

Fig. 3.2 Schematic diagram of a single point optical triangulation sensor based on a laser beam and a linear spot detector. The baseline is H and d is the distance between the lens and the linear spot detector. The projection angle is α. The collection angle is β and it is computed using the distance d and the position p on the linear spot detector. The point $[X, Z]^T$ is determined by the baseline H, the projection angle α and the collection angle β. Figure courtesy of [11]

detector.[1] The knowledge of both projection and collection angles (α and β) relative to a baseline (H) determines the $[X, Z]^T$ coordinate of a point on a surface. Note that it is assumed that the only light that traverses the lens goes through the optical center, which is the well-known *pinhole* model of the imaging process. Furthermore, we refer to *projection* of the laser light onto the scene and we can think of the imaged spot position on the detector and the lens optical center as a *back-projected* ray, traveling in the opposite direction to the light, back into the scene. This intersects with the projected laser ray to determine the 3D scene point.

The linear spot detector acts as an angle sensor and provides signals that are interpreted as a position p. Explicitly, given the value of p, the value of β in radians is computed as

$$\beta = \arctan\left(\frac{p}{d}\right) \qquad (3.1)$$

where d is the distance between the laser spot detector and the collection lens. (Typically this distance will be slightly larger than the focal length of the lens, such that the imaged spot is well focused at the depth at which most parts of the object surface are imaged. The relevant thin lens equation is discussed in Sect. 3.8.1.)

The position of p on the linear spot detector is computed using a peak detector which will be described later. Using simple trigonometry, one can verify that

$$Z = \frac{H}{\tan\alpha + \tan\beta} \qquad (3.2)$$

and

$$X = Z\tan\alpha. \qquad (3.3)$$

---

[1] A linear spot detector can be conceptually viewed as a conventional camera that has a singe row of pixels. Many linear spot detectors have been proposed in the past for 3D imaging [11].

Substituting Eq. (3.1) into Eq. (3.2) gives

$$Z = \frac{Hd}{p + d \tan \alpha}. \tag{3.4}$$

In order to acquire a complete profile without using a translation stage, the laser beam can be scanned around some $[X, Z]^T$ coordinate using a mirror mounted on a mechanical scanner (typically a galvonometer drive). In this case, the angle α is varied according to a predefined field of view. For practical reasons, the total scanned angle for a configuration like the one in Fig. 3.2 is about 30 degrees. Larger angles may be scanned by more sophisticated optical arrangements called synchronized scanners, where the field of view of the camera is scanned using the same mirror that scans the laser. Sometimes the reverse side of a double sided mirror is used [21, 54].

3.2.1 Spot Position Detection

It is crucial to obtain the position of the laser spot on the linear spot detector to sub-pixel accuracy. In order to accomplish this, the image of the laser spot must be a few pixels wide on the detector which is easy to achieve in a real system. Many peak detectors have been proposed to compute the position of the laser spot and two studies compare different peak detectors [34, 48]. We examine two peak detectors [18, 34, 48]. The first one localizes the 'center of mass' of the imaged spot intensity. In this method, the pixel i_M with the maximum intensity is found in the 1D image which is denoted I. Then a window of size $2N+1$ centered on i_M is used to compute the centroid position. Explicitly, the peak position p is defined as

$$p = i_M + \frac{\sum_{i=-N}^{N} I(i_M + i) i}{\sum_{i=-N}^{N} I(i_M + i)}. \tag{3.5}$$

The second peak detector uses convolution with a derivative filter, followed by a linear interpolation. Explicitly, for each pixel, i, let

$$g(i) = \sum_{j=-N}^{N} I(i - j) F(j + N) \tag{3.6}$$

where $F = [1, 1, 1, 1, 0, -1, -1, -1, -1]$ and $N = 4$. Finally, the linear interpolation process is implemented as

$$p = i_0 + \frac{g(i_0)}{g(i_0) - g(i_0 + 1)} \tag{3.7}$$

where i_0 is a pixel such that $g(i_0) \geq 0$ and $g(i_0 + 1) < 0$. Moreover, F has the property of filtering out some of the frequency content of the image [18]. This makes it possible to filter out the ambient illumination and some of the noise and interference introduced by the linear detector electronics. Note that other filters could be used. It has been shown that the second peak detector outperforms the first in an actual implementation of laser triangulation [18].

3.3 Stripe Scanners

As shown previously, spot scanners intersect a detection direction (a line in a plane, which is a back-projected ray) with a projection direction (another line in the same plane) to compute a point in a 2D scene space. Stripe scanners and structured light systems intersect a back-projected 3D ray, generated from a pixel in a conventional camera, and a projected 3D plane of light, in order to compute a point in the 3D scene. Clearly, the scanner baseline should not be contained within the projected plane, otherwise we would not be able to detect the deformation of the stripe. (In this case, the imaged stripe lies along an epipolar line in the scanner camera.)

A stripe scanner is composed of a camera and a laser 'sheet-of-light' or plane, which is rotated or translated in order to scan the scene. (Of course, the object may be rotated on a turntable instead, or translated, and this is a common set up for industrial 3D scanning of objects on conveyer belts.) Figure 3.3 illustrates three types of stripe scanners. Note that other configurations exist, but are not described here [16]. In the remainder of this chapter, we will discuss systems in which only the plane of projected light is rotated and an image is acquired for each laser plane orientation. The camera pixels that view the intersection of the laser plane with the scene can be transformed into observation directions (see Fig. 3.3). Depending on the roll orientation of the camera with respect to the laser plane, the observation directions in the camera are obtained by applying a peak detector on each row or column of the camera image. We assume a configuration where a measurement is performed on each row of the camera image using a peak detector.

Next, the pinhole camera model presented in the previous chapter is revisited. Then, a laser-plane-projector model is presented. Finally, triangulation for a stripe scanner is described.

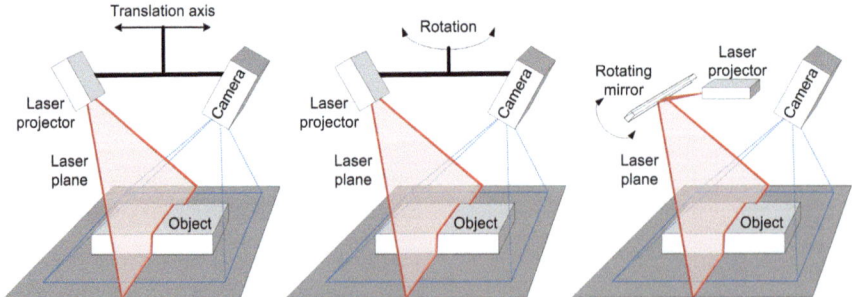

Fig. 3.3 (*Left*) A stripe scanner where the scanner head is translated. (*Middle*) A stripe scanner where the scanner head is rotated. (*Right*) A stripe scanner where a mirror rotates the laser beam. Figure courtesy of the National Research Council (NRC), Canada

3 Active 3D Imaging Systems

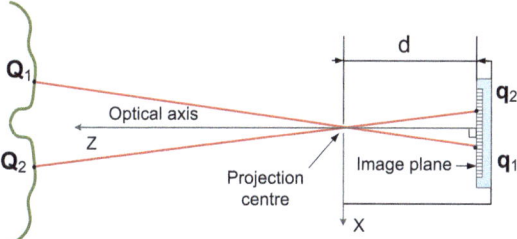

Fig. 3.4 Cross-section of a pinhole camera. The 3D points $\mathbf{Q}_1$ and $\mathbf{Q}_2$ are projected into the image plane as points $\mathbf{q}_1$ and $\mathbf{q}_2$ respectively. Finally, d is the distance between the image plane and the projection center. Figure courtesy of NRC Canada

3.3.1 Camera Model

The simplest mathematical model that can be used to represent a camera is the pinhole model. A pinhole camera can be assembled using a box in which a small hole (i.e. the aperture) is made on one side and a sheet of photosensitive paper is placed on the opposite side. Figure 3.4 is an illustration of a pinhole camera. The pinhole camera has a very small aperture so it requires long integration times; thus, machine vision applications use cameras with lenses which collect more light and hence require shorter integration times. Nevertheless, for many applications, the pinhole model is a valid approximation of a camera. In this mathematical model, the aperture and the photo-sensitive surface of the pinhole are represented respectively by the center of projection and the image plane. The center of projection is the origin of the camera coordinate system and the optical axis coincides with the Z-axis of the camera. Moreover, the optical axis is perpendicular to the image plane and the intersection of the optical axis and the image plane is the principal point (image center). Note that when approximating a camera with the pinhole model, the geometric distortions of the image introduced by the optical components of an actual camera are not taken into account. Geometric distortions will be discussed in Sect. 3.5. Other limitations of this model are described in Sect. 3.8.

A 3D point $[X_c, Y_c, Z_c]^T$ in the camera reference frame can be transformed into pixel coordinates $[x, y]^T$ by first projecting $[X_c, Y_c, Z_c]^T$ onto the normalized camera frame using $[x', y']^T = [X_c/Z_c, Y_c/Z_c]^T$. This normalized frame corresponds to the 3D point being projected onto a conceptual imaging plane at a distance of one unit from the camera center. The pixel coordinates can be obtained from the normalized coordinates as

$$\begin{bmatrix} x \\ y \end{bmatrix} = d \begin{bmatrix} \frac{x'}{s_x} \\ \frac{y'}{s_y} \end{bmatrix} + \begin{bmatrix} o_x \\ o_y \end{bmatrix} \qquad (3.8)$$

where s_x and s_y are the dimensions of the sensor in millimeters divided by the number of pixels along the X and Y-axis respectively. Moreover, d is the distance in millimeters between the aperture and the sensor chip and $[o_x, o_y]^T$ is the position in pixels of the principal point (image center) in the image. The parameters s_x, s_y, d, o_x and o_y are the intrinsic parameters of the camera. Note that the camera model used in this chapter is similar to the one used in the previous chapter, with one minor difference: fm_x and fm_y are replaced by d/s_x and d/s_y respectively. This change is partly notational ($m_x = \frac{1}{s_x}, m_y = \frac{1}{s_y}$) and partly to do with where the image is in focus relative to the camera center (in general, d and f are not equal, with d often being slightly larger). This will be discussed further in Sect. 3.8. Note that intrinsic camera parameters can be determined using the method described in Chap. 2.

The extrinsic parameters of the camera must be defined in order to locate the position and orientation of the camera in the world coordinate system. This requires three parameters for the rotation and three parameters for the translation. (Note that in many design situations, we can define the world coordinate system such that it coincides with the camera coordinate system. However, we still would need to estimate the pose of the light projection system, which can be viewed as an *inverse camera*, within this frame. Also, many active 3D imaging systems use multiple cameras, which can reduce the area of the 'missing parts' caused by self occlusion.)

The rotation is represented using a 3 × 3 rotation matrix

$$R_c = \begin{bmatrix} 1 & 0 & 0 \\ 0 & \cos\theta_x & -\sin\theta_x \\ 0 & \sin\theta_x & \cos\theta_x \end{bmatrix} \begin{bmatrix} \cos\theta_y & 0 & \sin\theta_y \\ 0 & 1 & 0 \\ -\sin\theta_y & 0 & \cos\theta_y \end{bmatrix} \begin{bmatrix} \cos\theta_z & -\sin\theta_z & 0 \\ \sin\theta_z & \cos\theta_z & 0 \\ 0 & 0 & 1 \end{bmatrix}$$
(3.9)

where θ_x, θ_y and θ_z are the rotation angles around the X, Y, and Z axis and translation is represented by a vector $\mathbf{T}_c = [T_x, T_y, T_z]^T$. Note that the rotation matrix R_c is orthogonal (i.e. $R_c^T = R_c^{-1}$) and $\det(R) = 1$.

A 3D point $\mathbf{Q}_w = [X_w, Y_w, Z_w]^T$ in the world reference frame can be transformed into a point $\mathbf{Q}_c = [X_c, Y_c, Z_c]^T$ of the camera reference frame by using

$$\mathbf{Q}_c = R_c \mathbf{Q}_w + \mathbf{T}_c.$$
(3.10)

Then, the point $\mathbf{Q}_c$ is projected onto the normalized camera frame $[x', y']^T = [X_c/Z_c, Y_c/Z_c]^T$. Finally, the point in the normalized camera frame $[x', y']^T$ can be transformed into the pixel coordinate $[x, y]^T$ using Eq. (3.8). Explicitly, the transformation from $\mathbf{Q}_w$ to pixel $[x, y]^T$ is

$$\begin{bmatrix} x \\ y \end{bmatrix} = \begin{bmatrix} \frac{d}{s_x} \frac{(r_{11},r_{12},r_{13})\mathbf{Q}_w + T_x}{(r_{31},r_{32},r_{33})\mathbf{Q}_w + T_z} \\ \frac{d}{s_y} \frac{(r_{21},r_{22},r_{23})\mathbf{Q}_w + T_y}{(r_{31},r_{32},r_{33})\mathbf{Q}_w + T_z} \end{bmatrix} + \begin{bmatrix} o_x \\ o_y \end{bmatrix}$$
(3.11)

where the r_{ij} are the elements of matrix R_c. Note that a pixel $[x, y]^T$ can be transformed into the normalized camera frame using

$$\begin{bmatrix} x' \\ y' \end{bmatrix} = \frac{1}{d} \begin{bmatrix} s_x(x - o_x) \\ s_y(y - o_y) \end{bmatrix}.$$
(3.12)

Moreover, one may verify using Eq. (3.10) that a point in the camera reference frame can be transformed to a point in the world reference frame by using

$$\mathbf{Q}_w = \mathsf{R}_c^T [\mathbf{Q}_c - \mathbf{T}_c]. \qquad (3.13)$$

3.3.2 Sheet-of-Light Projector Model

In the projective-geometry framework of the pinhole camera, a digital projector can be viewed as an inverse camera and both share the same parameterization. Similarly, a sheet-of-light projection system can be geometrically modeled as a pinhole camera with a single infinitely thin column of pixels. Although this parameterization is a major simplification of the physical system, it allows the presentation of the basic concepts of a sheet-of-light scanner using the same two-view geometry that was presented in Chap. 2. This column of pixels can be back-projected as a plane in 3D and the projection center of this simplified model acts as the laser source (see Sect. 3.8.5).

In order to acquire a complete range image, the laser source is rotated around a rotation axis by an angle α. The rotation center is located at $\mathbf{T}_\alpha$ and R_α is the corresponding rotation matrix.[2] For a given α, a point $\mathbf{Q}_\alpha$ in the laser coordinate frame can be transformed into a point $\mathbf{Q}_w$ in the world coordinate frame using

$$\mathbf{Q}_w = \mathbf{T}_\alpha + \mathsf{R}_\alpha [\mathbf{Q}_\alpha - \mathbf{T}_\alpha]. \qquad (3.14)$$

In a practical implementation, a cylindrical lens can be used to generate a laser plane and optical components such as a mirror are used to change the laser-plane orientation.

3.3.3 Triangulation for Stripe Scanners

Triangulation for stripe scanners essentially involves intersecting the back-projected ray associated with a camera pixel with the sheet of light, projected at some angle α. Consider a stripe scanner, where projector coordinates are subscripted with 1 and camera coordinates are subscripted with 2. Suppose that an unknown 3D scene point, $\mathbf{Q}_w$, is illuminated by the laser for a given value of α and this point is imaged in the scanner camera at *known* pixel coordinates $[x_2, y_2]^T$. The normalized camera point $[x_2', y_2']^T$ can be computed from $[x_2, y_2]^T$ and the intrinsic camera parameters

---

[2]The rotation matrix representing a rotation of θ around an axis $[a, b, c]^T$ of unit magnitude is

$$\mathsf{R}_\theta = \begin{bmatrix} a^2(1-\cos\theta)+\cos\theta & ab(1-\cos\theta)-c\sin\theta & ac(1-\cos\theta)+b\sin\theta \\ ab(1-\cos\theta)+c\sin\theta & b^2(1-\cos\theta)+\cos\theta & bc(1-\cos\theta)-a\sin\theta \\ ac(1-\cos\theta)-b\sin\theta & bc(1-\cos\theta)+a\sin\theta & c^2(1-\cos\theta)+\cos\theta \end{bmatrix}.$$

(known from a camera calibration) using Eq. (3.12). Considering the sheet-of-light projector model, described above, the 3D scene point $\mathbf{Q}_w$ is back-projected to an *unknown* normalized coordinate $[0, y'_1]^T$ for the given value of α.

Clearly there are three unknowns here, which includes the depth associated with the back-projected camera ray to the 3D scene point, and a pair of parameters that describe the planar position in the projected sheet-of-light of the 3D scene point. If we can form an independent equation for each of the coordinates X_w, Y_w, Z_w of $\mathbf{Q}_w$, then we can solve for that point's unknown 3D scene position.

By rearranging Eq. (3.13) and Eq. (3.14), one may obtain

$$\mathbf{Q}_w = \mathsf{R}_\alpha \left[0, \lambda_1 y'_1, \lambda_1\right]^T + \mathbf{T}_\alpha - \mathsf{R}_\alpha \mathbf{T}_\alpha = \mathsf{R}_c^T \left[\left[\lambda_2 x'_2, \lambda_2 y'_2, \lambda_2\right]^T - \mathbf{T}_c\right] \quad (3.15)$$

where λ_1 and λ_2 are the range (i.e. the distance along the Z-axis) between the 3D point $\mathbf{Q}_w$ and the laser source and the camera respectively. Moreover, R_α and $\mathbf{T}_\alpha$ are the parameters related to the laser plane orientation and position and R_c and $\mathbf{T}_c$ are the extrinsic parameters of the camera. (Note that these can be simplified to the 3 × 3 identity matrix and the zero 3-vector, if the world coordinate system is chosen to coincide with the camera coordinate system.) When R_α and $\mathbf{T}_\alpha$ are known, the vector equality on the right of Eq. (3.15) is a system of three equations with three unknowns λ_1, λ_2 and y'_1. These can easily be determined and then the values substituted in the vector equality on the left of Eq. (3.15) to solve for the unknown $\mathbf{Q}_w$.

For a given α, a 3D point can be computed for each row of the camera. Thus, in Eq. (3.15) the known y_2 and α and the measured value of x_2 which is obtained using a peak detector can be used to compute a 3D point. A range image is obtained by taking an image of the scene for each value of α. In the next section, we examine scanners that project structured light patterns over an area of the scene.

3.4 Area-Based Structured Light Systems

The stripe scanner presented earlier requires the head of the scanner to be rotated or translated in order to produce a range image (see Fig. 3.3). Other methods project many planes of light simultaneously and use a coding strategy to recover which camera pixel views the light from a given plane. There are many coding strategies that can be used to establish the correspondence [57] and it is this coding that gives the name *structured* light. The two main categories of coding are spatial coding and temporal coding, although the two can be mixed [29]. In temporal coding, patterns are projected one after the other and an image is captured for each pattern. Matching to a particular projected stripe is done based only on the time sequence of imaged intensity at a particular location in the scanner's camera. In contrast, spatial coding techniques project just a single pattern, and the greyscale or color pattern within a local neighborhood is used to perform the necessary correspondence matching. Clearly this has a shorter capture time and is generally better suited to dynamic scene capture. (One example could be the sequence of 3D face shapes that constitute changes in facial expression.) However, due to self occlusion, the required local area around a pixel is not always imaged, which can pose more difficulty when the object surface is complex, for example with many surface concavities. Moreover, systems based on spatial coding usually produce a sparse set of correspondences, while systems based on temporal coding produce a dense set of correspondences.

Usually, structured light systems use a non-coherent projector source (e.g. video projector) [9, 64]. We limit the discussion to this type of technology and we assume a digital projection system. Moreover, the projector images are assumed to contain vertical lines referred to as *fringes*.[3] Thus the imaged fringes cut across the camera's epipolar lines, as required. With L intensity levels and F different projection fringes to distinguish, $N = \lceil \log_L F \rceil$ patterns are needed to remove the ambiguity. When these patterns are projected temporally, this strategy is known as a *time-multiplexing codification* [57]. Codes that use two (binary) intensity levels are very popular because the processing of the captured images is relatively simple. The *Gray code* is probably the best known time-multiplexing code. These codes are based on intensity measurements. Another coding strategy is based on phase measurement and both approaches are described in the remainder of this section. For spatial neighborhood methods, the reader is referred to [57].

3.4.1 Gray Code Methods

Gray codes were first used for telecommunication applications. Frank Gray from Bell Labs patented a telecommunication method that used this code [39]. A structured light system that used Gray codes was presented in 1984 by Inokuchi et al. [41]. A Gray code is an ordering of 2^N binary numbers in which only one bit changes between two consecutive elements of the ordering. For $N > 3$ the ordering is not unique. Table 3.1 contains two ordering for $N = 4$ that obey the definition of a Gray code. The table also contains the natural binary code. Figure 3.5 contains the pseudo-code used to generate the first ordering of Table 3.1.

Let us assume that the number of columns of the projector is 2^N, then each column can be assigned to an N bit binary number in a Gray code sequence of 2^N elements. This is done by transforming the index of the projector column into an element (i.e. N-bit binary number) of a Gray code ordering, using the pseudocode of Fig. 3.5. The projection of darker fringes is associated with the binary value of 0 and the projection of lighter fringes is associated with the binary value of 1. The projector needs to project N images, indexed $i = 1 \ldots N$, where each fringe (dark/light) in the ith image is determined by the binary value of the ith bit (0/1) within that column's N-bit Gray code element. This allows us to establish the correspondence

---

[3]Fringe projection systems are a subset of structured light systems, but we use the two terms somewhat interchangeably in this chapter.

Table 3.1 Two different orderings with $N = 4$ that respect the definition of a Gray Code. Also, the natural binary code is also represented. Table courtesy of [32]

Ordering 1	Binary	0000	0001	0011	0010	0110	0111	0101	0100	1100	1101	1111	1110	1010	1011	1001	1000
	Decimal	0	1	3	2	6	7	5	4	12	13	15	14	10	11	9	8
Ordering 2	Binary	0110	0100	0101	0111	0011	0010	0000	0001	1001	1000	1010	1011	1111	1101	1100	1110
	Decimal	6	4	5	7	3	2	0	1	9	8	10	11	15	13	12	14
Natural binary	Binary	0000	0001	0010	0011	0100	0101	0110	0111	1000	1001	1010	1011	1100	1101	1110	1111
	Decimal	0	1	2	3	4	5	6	7	8	9	10	11	12	13	14	15

CONVERSION FROM GRAY TO BINARY($gray[0 \ldots n]$)
$bin[0] = gray[0]$
for $i = 1$ **to** n **do**
　$bin[i] = bin[i-1]$　**xor**　$gray[i]$
end for
return bin

CONVERSION FROM BINARY TO GRAY($bin[0 \ldots n]$)
$gray[0] = bin[0]$
for $i = 1$ **to** n **do**
　$gray[i] = bin[i-1]$　**xor**　$bin[i]$
end for
return gray

Fig. 3.5 Pseudocode allowing the conversion of a natural binary code into a Gray code and vice versa. Figure courtesy of [32]

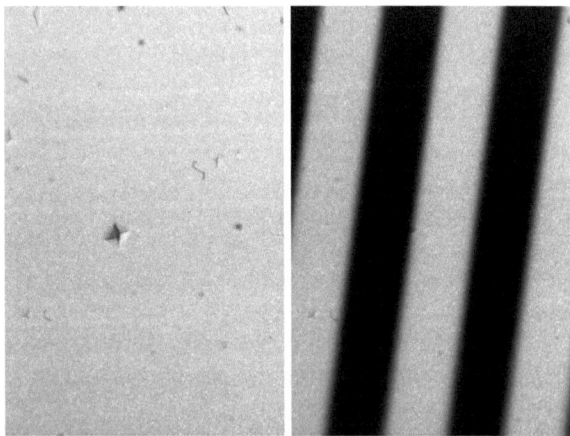

Fig. 3.6 (*Left*) an image of the object with surface defects. (*Right*) An image of the object when a Gray code pattern is projected. Figure courtesy of NRC Canada

between the projector fringes and the camera pixels. Figure 3.6 contains an example of a Gray code pattern. Usually, the image in the camera of the narrowest projector fringe is many camera pixels wide and all of these pixels have the same code. It is possible to compute either the centers of the fringes or the edges between adjacent fringes in order to define the projector plane with which triangulation is performed. Generally edge based schemes give better performance [57].

3.4.1.1 Decoding of Binary Fringe-Based Codes

Two algorithms for transforming the camera images into correspondences between projector fringes and camera pixels are presented. In the first algorithm, the camera pixels are at known positions and the projector fringe for those positions are measured. In the second algorithm, the fringe indices are known in the projector and for each row of the camera the fringe transitions are measured.

The first algorithm uses a simple thresholding approach where a threshold is computed individually for each pixel of the camera [57]. The threshold values are computed using the images of the projection of a white and a black frame. For every camera pixel, the mean value of the white and black frames is used as the threshold value. This method does not allow a sub-pixel localization of the boundary between fringes, which is important in order to increase the precision of the system (see Sect. 3.6). This method simply classifies the camera pixel as being lit by which projector pixel and supports other coding strategies such as phase measurement methods covered in Sect. 3.4.2.

The second algorithm provides a robust way for achieving sub-pixel accuracy [63]. The method requires the projection of both a Gray code and the associated reverse Gray code (white fringes are replaced by black ones and vice versa). Figure 3.7 illustrates the process of computing the position of a stripe's transition into the camera image. An intensity profile is constructed using linear interpolation for both the images of a Gray code and those of the associated reverse Gray code (left side and middle of Fig. 3.7). The intersection of both profiles is the sub-pixel location of the fringe transition (right side of Fig. 3.7).

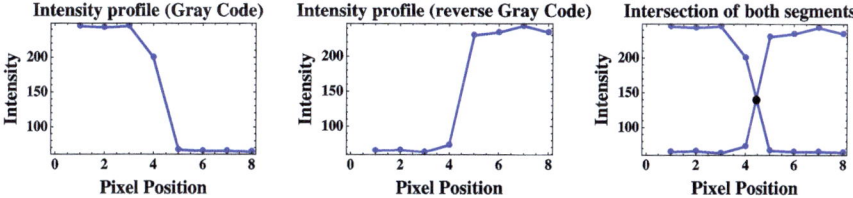

Fig. 3.7 (*Left*) Intensity profile of a white-to-black transition in the image of a Gray code. The values between pixels are obtained using linear interpolation. The transition is located between the 4th and 5th pixel. (*Middle*) The same intensity profile for the associated reverse Gray code. (*Right*) The two previous graphs are superimposed and the intersection is marked with a *dot*. The transition is localized at pixel 4.45. Figure courtesy of NRC Canada

3.4.1.2 Advantage of the Gray Code

The Gray code offers a significant advantage over the natural binary code when using the previously described thresholding algorithm with noisy images. The reason for this is that more decoding errors occur on fringe transitions, namely pixels where the pattern changes from dark to light or light to dark. For the Gray code, there are significantly fewer fringe transitions over the N patterns when compared to the natural binary code. In fact the natural binary code has the highest possible frequency of transitions in the Nth projected pattern, which corresponds to the least significant bit of the code.

Let us assume that the probability of getting an error when thresholding a camera image at a pixel located at a fringe transition is p, and that the probability of getting an error when no transition occurs is q, the probability of getting an error using a Gray code is $p \times q^{N-1}$ for all camera pixels located at a transition independent of the transition location. In this case, the Gray code results in a uniform distribution of error at the transition which is not the case with the natural binary code. The natural binary code has a probability of getting an error at a transition that ranges from p^N to $p \times q^{N-1}$. As an example, the probability of getting an error at the transition between 7 and 8 and between 0 and 1 in the natural binary code shown in Table 3.1 are p^4 (all bits change) and $p \times q^3$ respectively (only one bit changes). As we have already mentioned, in a fringe projection system, it is expected that p is larger than q. Thus, the mean error rate at fringe transitions when using a Gray code is expected to be smaller than the one obtained using a natural binary code.

The narrowest fringes of a Gray code may be difficult to decode and are error-prone when the images are out-of-focus (see Sect. 3.8). For this reason, a Gray code is often used to establish a coarse correspondence using the widest patterns and another code based on *phase measurement* replaces the narrowest patterns. Phase measurement methods (also known as phase shift) outperform Gray code methods when the patterns are out-of-focus. Phase shift methods are presented next.

3.4.2 Phase Shift Methods

While a Gray code is binary in nature (through a suitable thresholding of intensity images), phase shift approaches use patterns containing periodic and smooth variations in greyscale level. The phase shift patterns contain vertical fringes and each projector column, x_2, is associated with a phase value $\phi(x_2)$ using

$$\phi(x_2) = \frac{2\pi}{\omega} \mod (x_2, \omega) \qquad (3.16)$$

where ω is the spatial period of the pattern and mod is the modulo operator.

The intensity profile for each row is defined by $I(x_2) = A + B\cos(\phi(x_2) - \theta)$ where A and B are constants and θ is a phase offset. Many patterns with different

Fig. 3.8 (*Left*) the camera image of a phase shift pattern. (*Right*) the recovered phase for each camera pixel coded in greyscale level. The image is of the surface defect shown in Fig. 3.6(*Left*). Figure courtesy of NRC Canada

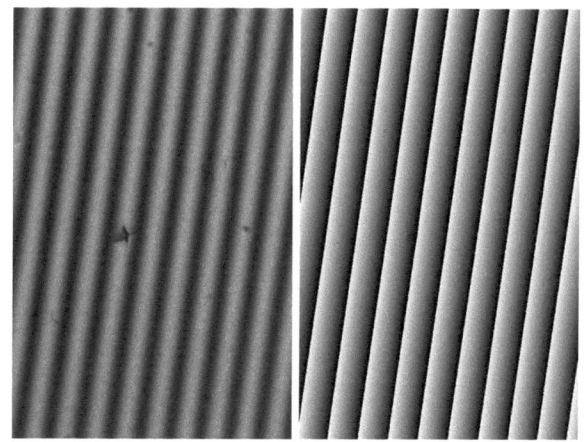

phase offset, θ, are required to establish the correspondence between the phase measured at a camera pixel and the phase associated with a projector fringe. Note that, because the modulo operator is used, this mapping is not unique and an extra unwrapping step is necessary to establish an unambiguous correspondence. Figure 3.8 shows a phase shift pattern and the recovered phase.

The intensity of each pixel of the camera viewing the projected phase shift patterns can be modeled using the following system of equations:

$$
\begin{aligned}
I_0(x_1, y_1) &= A(x_1, y_1) + B(x_1, y_1)\cos\bigl(\phi(x_1, y_1) - \theta_0\bigr) \\
I_1(x_1, y_1) &= A(x_1, y_1) + B(x_1, y_1)\cos\bigl(\phi(x_1, y_1) - \theta_1\bigr) \\
&\ldots \\
I_{N-1}(x_1, y_1) &= A(x_1, y_1) + B(x_1, y_1)\cos\bigl(\phi(x_1, y_1) - \theta_{N-1}\bigr)
\end{aligned}
\tag{3.17}
$$

where $A(x_1, y_1)$, $B(x_1, y_1)$ and $\phi(x_1, y_1)$ are unknowns and θ_i are the known phase offsets in the projector. The number of patterns is N. $I_i(x_1, y_1)$ is the measured image intensity for camera pixel $[x_1, y_1]^T$ when the pattern with the phase offset θ_i is projected. Using the trigonometric identity $\cos(\alpha - \beta) = \cos\alpha\cos\beta + \sin\alpha\sin\beta$, the previous system of equations is equivalent to

$$
\begin{aligned}
I_0(x_1, y_1) &= A(x_1, y_1) + B_1(x_1, y_1)\cos(\theta_0) + B_2(x_1, y_1)\sin(\theta_0) \\
I_1(x_1, y_1) &= A(x_1, y_1) + B_1(x_1, y_1)\cos(\theta_1) + B_2(x_1, y_1)\sin(\theta_1) \\
&\ldots \\
I_N(x_1, y_1) &= A(x_1, y_1) + B_1(x_1, y_1)\cos(\theta_{N-1}) + B_2(x_1, y_1)\sin(\theta_{N-1})
\end{aligned}
\tag{3.18}
$$

where

$$
B_1(x_1, y_1) = B(x_1, y_1)\cos\bigl(\phi(x_1, y_1)\bigr)
\tag{3.19}
$$

and
$$B_2(x_1, y_1) = B(x_1, y_1)\sin(\phi(x_1, y_1)). \qquad (3.20)$$

Since the θ_i are known, $\cos\theta_i$ and $\sin\theta_i$ are scalar coefficients. The following more compact matrix notation can be used

$$\mathbf{MX}(x_1, y_1) = \mathbf{I}(x_1, y_1) \qquad (3.21)$$

where $\mathbf{I}(x_1, y_1) = [I_0(x_1, y_1), I_1(x_1, y_1), \ldots, I_{N-1}(x_1, y_1)]^T$,

$$\mathbf{M} = \begin{bmatrix} 1 & \cos(\theta_0) & \sin(\theta_0) \\ 1 & \cos(\theta_1) & \sin(\theta_1) \\ \vdots & \vdots & \vdots \\ 1 & \cos(\theta_{N-1}) & \sin(\theta_{N-1}) \end{bmatrix} \qquad (3.22)$$

and $\mathbf{X}(x_1, y_1) = [A(x_1, y_1), B_1(x_1, y_1), B_2(x_1, y_1)]^T$. In the presence of noise and when using more than three patterns, the system of equations may have no solution. In this case, the vector $\mathbf{X}(x_1, y_1)$ is obtained using the pseudoinverse and explicitly,

$$\mathbf{X}(x_1, y_1) = (\mathbf{M}^T\mathbf{M})^{-1}\mathbf{M}^T\mathbf{I}(x_1, y_1). \qquad (3.23)$$

Note that $\mathbf{M}^T\mathbf{M}$ is invertible when $\mathbf{M}$ has rank 3. Alternative presentations can be found in [31, 51]. Once $\mathbf{X}(x_1, y_1)$ is computed,

$$B(x_1, y_1) = \sqrt{B_1(x_1, y_1)^2 + B_2(x_1, y_1)^2} \qquad (3.24)$$

and
$$\phi(x_1, y_1) = \arctan(B_2(x_1, y_1), B_1(x_1, y_1)) \qquad (3.25)$$

where $\arctan(n, d)$ represents the usual $\arctan(n/d)$ where the sign of n and d are used to determinate the quadrant.

We provide the details for the case $\theta_i = \frac{2\pi i}{N}$ for which

$$\mathbf{M}^T\mathbf{M} = \begin{bmatrix} N & 0 & 0 \\ 0 & \frac{N}{2} & 0 \\ 0 & 0 & \frac{N}{2} \end{bmatrix} \quad \text{and} \quad \mathbf{M}^T\mathbf{I}(x_1, y_1) = \begin{bmatrix} \sum_{i=0}^{N-1} I_i(x_1, y_1) \\ \sum_{i=0}^{N-1} I_i(x_1, y_1)\cos(\frac{2i\pi}{N}) \\ \sum_{i=0}^{N-1} I_i(x_1, y_1)\sin(\frac{2i\pi}{N}) \end{bmatrix}.$$

Explicitly, $A(x_1, y_1)$, $B_1(x_1, y_1)$ and $B_2(x_1, y_1)$ are computed using

$$A(x_1, y_1) = \frac{1}{N}\sum_{i=0}^{N-1} I_i(x_1, y_1) \qquad (3.26)$$

$$B_1(x_1, y_1) = \frac{2}{N}\sum_{i=0}^{N-1} I_i(x_1, y_1)\cos\left(\frac{2i\pi}{N}\right) \qquad (3.27)$$

$$B_2(x_1, y_1) = \frac{2}{N} \sum_{i=0}^{N-1} I_i(x_1, y_1) \sin\left(\frac{2i\pi}{N}\right) \quad (3.28)$$

and $\phi(x_1, y_1)$ and $B(x_1, y_1)$ are computed using Eq. (3.25) and Eq. (3.24) respectively.

3.4.2.1 Removing the Phase Ambiguity

Once the phases have been computed, projector position x_2 corresponding to the camera pixel $[x_1, y_1]^T$ is given as

$$x_2 = \frac{\omega}{2\pi} \phi(x_1, y_1) + k(x_1, y_1) \quad (3.29)$$

where $k(x_1, y_1)$ is an unknown integer that represents the phase ambiguity. The value of $k(x_1, y_1)$ must be recovered in order to compute the location of the 3D points. We will briefly describe two different approaches that allow the removal of this phase ambiguity.

Fiducial markers can be embedded into the phase shift patterns. Those markers can simply be a white or black point. When there is only one marker, the 3D position of the surface on which the fiducial maker is projected can be computed by triangulation. This allows one to know the k values for the camera pixels around a fiducial marker. It is then possible to propagate this information to neighboring pixels using a phase unwrapping algorithm. Phase unwrapping is frequently encountered in other fields such as synthetic aperture radar and interferometry. This is a complex subject and an entire book is devoted to it [37]. For these reasons, phase unwrapping will not be discussed further. When the projection patterns contain many fiducial markers, the epipolar constraint and the ordering constraint which are described in the previous chapter can be used to establish unambiguous matches between fiducial markers. Note that a similar fiducial approach is implemented in [42].

The second approach combines phase shift and Gray codes [58]. Binary codes, such as the Gray code, are often used to establish a coarse correspondence between projector and camera pixels using the thresholding algorithm presented previously. The patterns with the smallest stripes are not projected and are replaced by phase shift patterns whose spatial periods are selected to match the smallest stripes projected. Combining binary and phase shift code is a solution used in many experimental [57] and commercial scanners.

3.4.3 Triangulation for a Structured Light System

In the projective-geometry framework of the pinhole camera, a digital projector can be viewed as an inverse camera and both share the same parametrization. Each implementation of an analogue slide projector can have its own parametrization.

Nevertheless, they remain similar to a pinhole camera. Two commercial implementations are presented in [42] and [22]. Again, we consider an area-based scanner composed of a digital projector and a digital camera where phase shift patterns are used. It is assumed that the projected fringes are vertical.

Suppose that the world coordinate system of the camera coincides with the world coordinate system and the extrinsic parameters of the projector are R_p and T_p. A point in the camera is at a known position $[x_1, y_1]^T$ and one coordinate in the projector (i.e. x_2) is measured using phase shift. Again, x_1', y_1' and x_2' can be computed from x_1, y_1 and x_2 using Eq. (3.12). Moreover, the x_1', y_1' and x_2' provide the three following constraints on the 3D point $[X_w, Y_w, Z_w]^T$:

$$\begin{bmatrix} x_1' \\ y_1' \\ x_2' \end{bmatrix} = \begin{bmatrix} \frac{X_w}{Z_w} \\ \frac{Y_w}{Z_w} \\ \frac{(r_{11}, r_{12}, r_{13})[X_w, Y_w, Z_w]^T + T_x}{(r_{31}, r_{32}, r_{33})[X_w, Y_w, Z_w]^T + T_z} \end{bmatrix} \quad (3.30)$$

where the r_{ij} are the elements of matrix R_p and $[T_x, T_y, T_z]^T = T_p$. Assuming that, x_1' and y_1' define a known position in the camera, that x_2' is measured in the projector and that the three previous equations are linearly independent, we denote the 3D point $[X_w, Y_w, Z_w]^T$ corresponding to $[x_1', y_1']^T$ as $\mathbf{Q}_{(x_1', y_1')}(x_2')$. Explicitly, using Eq. (3.30) we obtain

$$\mathbf{Q}_{(x_1', y_1')}(x_2') = \frac{(T_x - x_2' T_z)}{-x_1' r_{11} - y_1' r_{12} - r_{13} + x_2' x_1' r_{31} + x_2' y_1' r_{32} + x_2' r_{33}} \begin{bmatrix} x_1' \\ y_1' \\ 1 \end{bmatrix}. \quad (3.31)$$

3.5 System Calibration

There are three types of method that can be used to calibrate a triangulation-based scanner. Some methods are purely parametric, others are non-parametric, and, finally, some methods combine parametric and non-parametric elements. Non-parametric methods are well adapted to small reconstruction volumes and to the modeling of local distortions that can include mirror surface defects, or other non-linearities that may be difficult to identify or model. Parametric methods make it possible to modify some parameters of the system without requiring a full recalibration. For example, the baseline of the system could be changed. The recalibration procedure would only need to recompute the pose between the camera and projection system; clearly, the intrinsic parameters would remain the same. This is not possible with non-parametric methods. While different cameras may use the same parametric model, an area-based digital projection system has a parameterization that is significantly different from a sheet-of-light laser projection system. We present a hybrid parametric and non-parametric method that could be adapted for the calibration of a large class of stripe and area-based triangulation scanners. Here, we will assume a fringe-projection scanner that uses phase shift. The calibration of other scanners will be discussed briefly at the end of this section.

A parametric model is used to represent the camera while the projection system is viewed as a black box and a look-up table is built in order to calibrate the system. This method requires a calibration bench consisting of an auxiliary camera and a planar surface mounted on a translation stage. Firstly, the scanner camera and the auxiliary camera, which together form a passive stereo rig, are calibrated using the methods described in Chap. 2. Given a pixel from the scanner camera and using the epipolar geometry presented in the previous chapter, it is possible to identify the corresponding epipolar line in the auxiliary camera. Moreover, the scanner-camera pixel and the corresponding point on this line must be lit by the same point of the projection system. The projection system is used to remove the ambiguity in the matching between the two cameras and the 3D points can be easily and accurately computed using this setup [29]. This two-camera-and-one-projector system is another type of triangulation scanner and products based on this principle are commercially available. Here, we use this two-camera setup only during the calibration stage. The planar surface is moved to different positions in the reconstruction volume. At each position i, a range image is produced using the method described above and the coordinate system of the scanner camera is used as the world coordinate system. Each 3D point is associated with a scanner camera pixel $[x_1, y_1]^T$ and a measured position x_2 in the projection system. Two tables of the form $t_i(x_1, y_1) = x_2$ and $t'_i(x_1, y_1) = Z$ can be filled for each plane position i. Once the tables are filled, the auxiliary camera is no longer needed and the scanner can be used to acquire range images of unknown objects. For a given pixel $[x_1, y_1]^T$ in the camera and a measured position x_2 in the projector, one can find the entries $t_j(x_1, y_1)$ and $t_{j+1}(x_1, y_1)$ such that $t_j(x_1, y_1) < x_2 \leq t_{j+1}(x_1, y_1)$. Once those entries are found, the value of Z can be interpolated using $t'_j(x_1, y_1)$ and $t'_{j+1}(x_1, y_1)$ and the values of X and Y can be computed using Eq. (3.30). Note that the computation of the pixel coordinates $[x, y]^T$ from the normalized coordinates $[x', y']^T$ of Eq. (3.8) does not take into account the lens distortion. The following transformation takes into account lens distortion

$$\begin{bmatrix} x \\ y \end{bmatrix} = \begin{bmatrix} \frac{d}{s_x} & 0 \\ 0 & \frac{d}{s_y} \end{bmatrix} \left[k' \begin{bmatrix} x' \\ y' \end{bmatrix} + \begin{bmatrix} 2k_3 x' y' + k_4(r^2 + 2x'^2) \\ k_3(r^2 + 2y'^2) + 2k_4 x' y' \end{bmatrix} \right] + \begin{bmatrix} o_x \\ o_y \end{bmatrix} \quad (3.32)$$

where $r^2 = x'^2_2 + y'^2_2$, $k' = 1 + k_1 r^2 + k_2 r^4 + k_5 r^6$ and the k_i are the radial and tangential distortion coefficients. This model is known as the Brown-Conrady model [23] and is widely used. Camera calibration packages often use similar distortion models. The computation of pixel coordinates from normalized coordinates is straightforward. However, the reverse computation, which is what we need, requires the use of iterative algorithms such as Levenberg Marquardt and can be time consuming. At calibration time, another table can be computed. This table, given a camera pixel $[x_1, y_1]^T$, provides the distortion-free normalized coordinates $[x'_1, y'_1]^T$ that are used to compute X and Y using Eq. (3.31).

A sheet-of-light system such as the one illustrated at Fig. 3.3(right) can be calibrated similarly by replacing the tables $t_i(x_1, y_1) = x_2$ and $t'_i(x_1, y_1) = Z$ by $t_i(\alpha, y_2) = x_2$ and $t'_i(\alpha, y_2) = Z$ where α is the angle controlling the orientation of the laser plane, y_2 is a row of the camera and x_2 is the measured laser peak position for the camera row y_2. Systems that use a Gray code with sub-pixel localization of the fringe transitions could be calibrated similarly. Note that tables t_i and t'_i can be large and the values inside those tables may vary smoothly. It is, therefore, possible to fit a *non-uniform rational B-spline* (NURBS) surface or polynomial surface over those tables in order to reduce the memory requirement. Moreover, different steps are described in [25] that make it possible to reduce the sensitivity to noise of a non-parametric calibration procedure.

3.6 Measurement Uncertainty

In this section, we examine the uncertainty associated with 3D points measured by an active triangulation scanner. This section contains advanced material and may be omitted on first reading. Some errors are systematic in nature while others are random. Systematic errors may be implementation dependent and an experimental protocol is proposed to detect them in Sect. 3.7. In the remainder of this section, random errors are discussed. This study is performed for area-based scanners that use phase shift. An experimental approach for modeling random errors for the Gray code method will be presented in Sect. 3.7. Moreover, because the description requires advanced knowledge of the image formation process, the discussion of random errors for laser-based scanners is postponed until Sect. 3.8.

In the remainder of this section, we examine how the noise in the images of the camera influences the position of 3D points. First, the error propagation from image intensity to pixel coordinate is presented for the phase shift approach described in Sect. 3.4.2. Then, this error on the pixel coordinate is propagated through the intrinsic and extrinsic parameters. Finally, the error-propagation chain is used as a design tool.

3.6.1 Uncertainty Related to the Phase Shift Algorithm

In order to perform the error propagation from the noisy images to the phase value associated with a pixel $[x_1, y_1]^T$, we only consider the $B_1(x_1, y_1)$ and $B_2(x_1, y_1)$ elements of vector $\mathbf{X}(x_1, y_1)$ in Eq. (3.23). Thus, Eq. (3.23) becomes

$$[B_1(x_1, y_1), B_2(x_1, y_1)]^T = \mathbf{M}' \mathbf{I}(x_1, y_1) \tag{3.33}$$

where $\mathbf{M}'$ is the last two rows of the matrix $(\mathbf{M}^T \mathbf{M})^{-1} \mathbf{M}^T$ used in Eq. (3.23). First, assuming that the noise is spatially independent, the joint probability density function $p(B_1(x_1, y_1), B_2(x_1, y_1))$ must be computed. Finally, the probability density function for the phase error $p(\Delta\phi)$ is obtained by changing the coordinate system from Cartesian to polar coordinates and integrating over the magnitude. Assuming that the noise contaminating the intensity measurement in the images is a zero-mean Gaussian noise, $p(B_1(x_1, y_1), B_2(x_1, y_1))$ is a zero-mean multivariate Gaussian distribution [27, 28]. Using Eq. (3.33), the covariance matrix Σ_B associated with this distribution can be computed as

$$\Sigma_B = \mathsf{M}'\Sigma_I\mathsf{M}'^T \qquad (3.34)$$

where Σ_I is the covariance matrix of the zero-mean Gaussian noise contaminating the intensity measured in the camera images [27, 28].

We give the details for the case $\theta_i = 2\pi i/N$ when the noise on each intensity measurement is independent with a zero mean and variance σ^2. One may verify that

$$\Sigma_B = \sigma^2 \begin{bmatrix} 2/N & 0 \\ 0 & 2/N \end{bmatrix}. \qquad (3.35)$$

This is the special case of the work presented in [53] (see also [52]).

Henceforth, the following notation will be used: quantities obtained from measurement will use a hat symbol to differentiate them from the unknown real quantities. As an example $B(x_1, y_1)$ is the real unknown value while $\hat{B}(x_1, y_1)$ is the value computed from the noisy images. The probability density function is

$$p\big(\hat{B}_1(x_1, y_1), \hat{B}_2(x_1, y_1)\big) = \frac{N}{4\pi\sigma^2} e^{-\gamma(x_1, y_1)} \qquad (3.36)$$

where

$$\gamma(x_1, y_1) = \frac{N((B_1(x_1, y_1) - \hat{B}_1(x_1, y_1))^2 + (B_2(x_1, y_1) - \hat{B}_2(x_1, y_1))^2)}{4\sigma^2}. \qquad (3.37)$$

Now changing to a polar coordinate system using $\hat{B}_1 = r\cos(\phi + \Delta\phi)$ and $\hat{B}_2 = r\sin(\phi + \Delta\phi)$ and $B_1 = B\cos\phi$ and $B_2 = B\sin\phi$ and integrating over r in the domain $[0, \infty]$ we obtain the probability density function

$$p(\Delta\phi) = \frac{e^{-\frac{B^2N}{4\sigma^2}}\left(2\sigma + e^{\frac{B^2N\cos^2\Delta\phi}{4\sigma^2}} B\sqrt{N\pi}\cos\Delta\phi(1 + \mathrm{erf}(\frac{B\sqrt{N}\cos\Delta\phi}{2\sigma}))\right)}{4\pi\sigma} \qquad (3.38)$$

which is independent of ϕ and where

$$\mathrm{erf}(z) = \frac{2}{\sqrt{\pi}} \int_0^z e^{-t^2}\, dt. \qquad (3.39)$$

When σ is small and B is large, $p(\Delta\phi)$ can be approximated by the probability density function of a zero-mean Gaussian distribution of variance $\frac{2\sigma^2}{B^2N}$ (see [53] for details). Assuming that the spatial period of the pattern is ω, the positional error on x_2 is a zero-mean Gaussian noise with variance

$$\sigma_{x_2}^2 = \frac{\omega^2 \sigma^2}{2\pi^2 B^2 N}. \tag{3.40}$$

The uncertainty interval can be reduced by reducing either the spatial period of the pattern, or the variance σ^2, or by increasing either the number of patterns used or the intensity ratio (i.e. B) of the projection system. Note that even if B is unknown, it can be estimated by projecting a white and a black image; however, this is only valid when the projector and camera are in focus (see Sect. 3.8).

3.6.2 Uncertainty Related to Intrinsic Parameters

When performing triangulation using Eq. (3.31), the pixel coordinates of the camera are known and noise is only present on the measured pixel coordinates of the projector. Thus, the intrinsic parameters of the camera do not directly influence the uncertainty on the position of the 3D point. The error propagation from the pixel coordinates to the normalized view coordinates for the projector can easily be computed. The transformation in Eq. (3.12) is linear and the variance associated with x_2' is

$$\sigma_{x_2'}^2 = \frac{\sigma_{x_2}^2 s_{x_2}^2}{d^2} \tag{3.41}$$

where s_{x_2} and d are intrinsic parameters of the projector and $\sigma_{x_2}^2$ is computed using Eq. (3.40). According to Eq. (3.41), as the distance d increases, or s_{x_2} is reduced, the variance will be reduced. However, in a real system, the resolution may not be limited by the pixel size but by the optical resolution (see Sect. 3.8). and increasing d may be the only effective way of reducing the uncertainty. As will be explained in

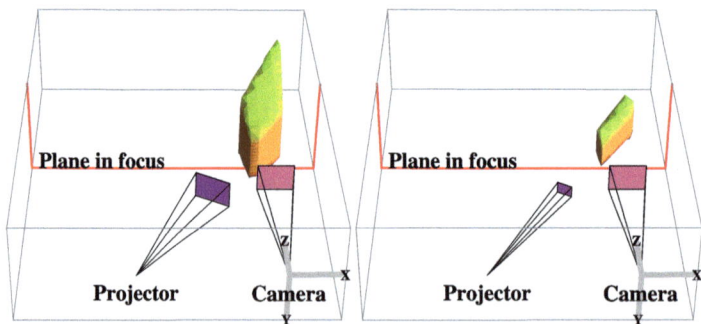

Fig. 3.9 The reconstruction volume of two systems where only the focal length of the projector is different (50 mm *at left* and 100 mm *at right*). The red lines define the plane in focus in the camera. Figure courtesy of NRC Canada

Sect. 3.8, when d is increased while keeping the standoff distance constant the focal length must be increased; otherwise, the image will be blurred. Note that when d is increased the field of view is also reduced. The intersection of the field of view of the camera and projector defines the reconstruction volume of a system. Figure 3.9 illustrates the reconstruction volume of two systems that differ only by the focal length of the projector (i.e. the value of d also varies). Thus, there is a trade off between the size of the reconstruction volume and the magnitude of the uncertainty.

3.6.3 Uncertainty Related to Extrinsic Parameters

Because the transformation of Eq. (3.31) from a normalized image coordinates to 3D points is non-linear, we introduce a first-order approximation using Taylor's expansion. The solution close to $\hat{x}'_2$ can be approximated by

$$\mathbf{Q}_{(x'_1, y'_1)}(\hat{x}'_2 + \Delta x'_2) \approx \mathbf{Q}_{(x'_1, y'_1)}(\hat{x}'_2) + \frac{d}{d\hat{x}'_2} \mathbf{Q}_{(x'_1, y'_1)}(\hat{x}'_2) \Delta x'_2 \qquad (3.42)$$

where

$$\frac{d}{d\hat{x}'_2} \mathbf{Q}_{(x'_1, y'_1)}(\hat{x}'_2)$$

$$= \frac{(-r_{33}T_x + r_{13}T_z - r_{31}T_x x'_1 + r_{11}T_z x'_1 - r_{32}T_x y'_1 + r_{12}T_z y'_1)}{(r_{13} + r_{11}x'_1 - r_{33}\hat{x}'_2 - r_{31}x'_1\hat{x}'_2 + r_{12}y'_1 - r_{32}\hat{x}'_2 y'_1)^2} \begin{bmatrix} x'_1 \\ y'_1 \\ 1 \end{bmatrix}. \qquad (3.43)$$

Since a first order approximation is used, the covariance matrix associated to a 3D point can be computed similarly as Σ_B in Eq. (3.35) [27, 28]. Explicitly, the covariance matrix associated with a 3D point is

$$\Sigma = \begin{bmatrix} x'^2_1 & x'_1 y'_1 & x'_1 \\ x'_1 y'_1 & y'^2_1 & y'_1 \\ x'_1 & y'_1 & 1 \end{bmatrix}$$

$$\times \frac{(-r_{33}T_x + r_{13}T_z - r_{31}T_x x'_1 + r_{11}T_z x'_1 - r_{32}T_x y'_1 + r_{12}T_z y'_1)^2}{(r_{13} + r_{11}x'_1 - r_{33}\hat{x}'_2 - r_{31}x'_1\hat{x}'_2 + r_{12}y'_1 - r_{32}\hat{x}'_2 y'_1)^4} \sigma^2_{x'_2} \qquad (3.44)$$

where $\sigma^2_{x'_2}$ is computed using Eq. (3.40) and Eq. (3.41).

The covariance matrix can be used to compute a confidence region which is the multi-variable equivalent to the confidence interval.[4] The uncertainty over the range

---

[4] A confidence interval is an interval within which we are $(1 - \alpha)100\ \%$ confident that a point measured under the presence of Gaussian noise (of known mean and variance) will be within this interval (we use $\alpha = 0.05$).

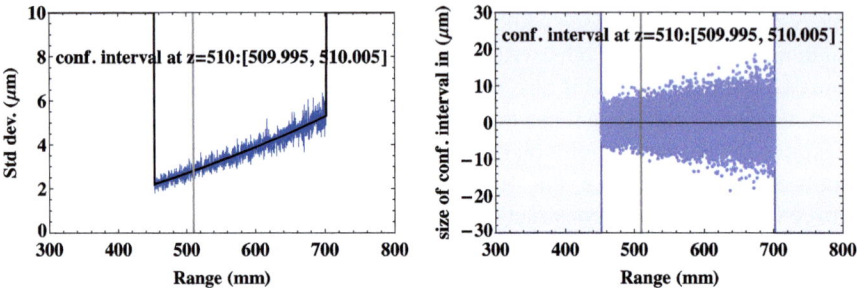

Fig. 3.10 (*Left*) The standard deviation obtained from the first-order approximation and the Monte-Carlo simulation points respectively display in *black* and *blue*. (*Right*) Confidence interval size computed for many range values using a first-order approximation. The Monte-Carlo simulation points are displayed at the top of the confidence interval. The reconstruction volume covers a range from 450 to 700 mm and is shown in Fig. 3.9(*Left*). The confidence interval for $Z = 510$ mm is given. Figure courtesy of NRC Canada

(i.e. Z-axis) is an important design characteristic. Figure 3.10(Left) illustrates the confidence interval for different range values for the geometric configuration at the left of Fig. 3.9. As the range increases, the size of the confidence interval also increases. This is a characteristic of triangulation systems and this explains why triangulation systems are often used for short range measurements [10]. Note that the results presented in Fig. 3.10 ignore many things such as the effect of optical components (see Sect. 3.8).

The usable measurement volume is the portion of the reconstruction volume for which the error on the position of a 3D point is expected to be smaller than a maximum permissible error. The depth of field of a scanner is the size of the interval of Z values inside this usable measurement volume. Note that because of optical limitations, such as blurring effects, the usable measurement volume can be significantly smaller than the reconstruction volume (see Sect. 3.8).

Since a first-order approximation is used when computing the uncertainty with Eq. (3.44), it is important to validate the results using Monte-Carlo simulations. Figure 3.10(Right) shows the results of one such simulation. The simulation process consisted of the following steps:

- 50000 values of x'_2 were generated using a uniform distribution.
- Zero-mean Gaussian noise was added to each point.
- The points were triangulated using Eq. (3.31) at $[x'_1, y'_1]^T = [0, 0]^T$.
- The variance of the range values obtained previously was compared with the one computed using the first-order approximation.

3.6.4 Uncertainty as a Design Tool

For design purposes, it is useful to fix the position of a 3D point and examine how the uncertainty varies when modifying the parameters of the system. In order to do so, it

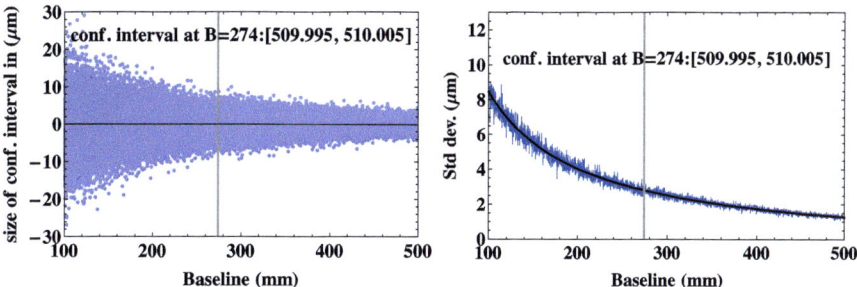

Fig. 3.11 (*Left*) The size of the confidence interval when varying both the vergence (i.e. the angle around the Y axis) and the baseline for the geometric configuration shown in Fig. 3.9(*Left*). (*Right*) The standard deviation for this geometric configuration. The confidence interval for a baseline value of 274 mm is given. This is the baseline value used by the geometric configuration shown in Fig. 3.9(*Left*). Figure courtesy of NRC Canada

is possible to modify Eq. (3.44) such that x_2' is replaced by Z_w. As the distance between the views is increased, the size of the uncertainty interval for the range value is reduced. Moreover, configurations with vergence produce lower uncertainty than those without, due to the preferable large angle that a back-projected ray intersects a projected plane of light. Note that the baseline and the vergence angle are usually varied together to minimize the variation of the shape and the position of the reconstruction volume. Figure 3.11 illustrates the impact of varying these extrinsic parameters of the system on the confidence interval for a fixed 3D point. As the distance between the views is increased, the amount of occlusion that occurs is also increased. An occlusion occurs when a 3D point is visible in one view but not in the other one. This can occur when a 3D point is outside the reconstruction volume of a scanner or when one part of the surface occludes another. Thus, there is a trade off between the size of the confidence interval and the amount of occlusion that may occur.

3.7 Experimental Characterization of 3D Imaging Systems

Manufacturers of 3D scanners and end-users are interested in verifying that their scanner performs within predetermined specifications. In this section, we will show scans of known objects that can be used to characterize a scanner. Objects composed of simple surfaces such as a plane or a sphere can be manufactured with great accuracy. These objects can then be scanned by the 3D imaging system and the measurements taken can be compared with nominal values. Alternatively, a *coordinate measuring machine* (CMM) can be used to characterize the manufactured object. This object can then be scanned by the 3D imaging system and the measurements taken can be compared with those obtained by the CMM. As a rule of thumb, the measurements acquired by the reference instrument need to be a minimum of four

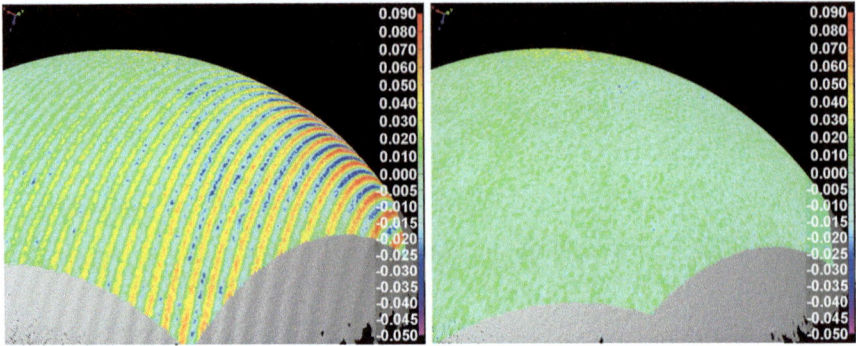

Fig. 3.12 An object scanned twice under the same conditions. A sphere was fitted to each set of 3D points. The residual error in millimeters is shown using a *color coding*. The artifacts visible in the left image are suspected to be the result of a human error. Figure courtesy of NRC Canada

times and preferably an order of magnitude more accurate than the measurements acquired by the 3D scanner.

We propose to examine four types of test for characterizing 3D imaging systems. Note that, the range images generated by a 3D imaging system are composed of 3D points usually arranged in a grid format. The first type of test looks at the error between 3D points that are contained in a small area of this grid. This type of test is not affected by miscalibration and makes it possible to perform a low level characterization of a scanner. The second type of test looks at the error introduced when examining the interactions between many small areas of the grid. This type of test makes it possible to perform a system level characterization and is significantly affected by miscalibration. The third family of test evaluates the impact of object surface properties on the recovered geometry. The last family of test is based on an industrial application and evaluates the fitness of a scanner to perform a given task.

In this section, we present the scans of objects obtained using different short-range technologies. Most of the scanners used are triangulation-based and there is currently a plethora of triangulation-based scanners available on the market. Different scanners that use the same technology may have been designed for applications with different requirements; thus, a scanner that uses a given implementation may not be representative of all the scanners that use that technology. Establishing a fair comparison between systems is a challenging task that falls outside of the scope of this chapter. The results shown in this section are provided for illustration purposes.

The human operator can represent a significant source of error in the measurement chain. The user may select a 3D imaging system whose operating range or operating conditions (i.e. direct sunlight, vibration, etc.) are inadequate for a given task. Alternatively, a user can misuse a system that is well-adapted to a given task. Usually, this is a result of lack of experience, training and understanding of the performance limitations of the instrument. As an example, in Fig. 3.12, a sphere was scanned twice by the same fringe projection system under the same environmental conditions. The scan shown on the left of the figure contains significant artifacts, while the other does not. One plausible explanation for those artifacts is that the selected projector intensity used while imaging the phase-shift patterns induces saturation for some camera pixels. Another plausible explanation is that the scanned object was inside the reconstruction volume of the scanner, but outside the usable measurement volume. Moreover, user fatigue and visual acuity for spotting details to be measured also influence the measurement chain.

3.7.1 Low-Level Characterization

Figure 3.13 shows multiple scans of a planar surface at different positions in the reconstruction volume. This type of experiment is part of a standard that addresses the characterization of the flatness measurement error of optical measurement devices [2]. When the area used to fit a plane is small with respect to the reconstruction volume, miscalibration has a very limited impact. A point-based laser triangulation scanner was used to illustrate this type of experiment. As expected from the results of the previous section, the Root Mean Square Error (RMSE) for each plane fit increases as the distance from the scanner increases (see Fig. 3.10). The RMSE values are 6.0, 7.0 and 7.5 µm. However, it is not the error value which is important but the distribution of the error which can be seen in Fig. 3.13 using a color coding. This type of experiments makes it possible to identify systematic errors that are independent of the calibration. Because of this, lens, geometric configuration and other components of the system can be changed and the system can be retested quickly. Usually, the error analysis is performed using the raw output of the scanner and not the 3D points. This makes it possible to decorrelate the different error sources and thereby simplify the identification of the error sources. As an example, for a phase-shift triangulation system, the fitting of a primitive is not performed using the $[X_w, Y_w, Z_w]^T$ points obtained from the point triangulation procedure described in Sect. 3.4.3, but using the $[x_1, y_1, x_2]^T$ directly. Moreover, in order to take into account the distortion of the lens, the rotation of the mirrors and other non-linear distortions, the raw data from the scanner is fitted to a NURBS surface rather than a plane.

We now examine an experimental protocol for measuring the error of the sub-pixel fringe localization of a Gray code fringe projection system [53]. It is assumed that no error in the decoding of Gray code occurs and the only error is in the sub-pixel localization of the fringe frontiers. Under projective geometry, the image in the camera of a projector fringe that is projected on a planar surface should remain a line. In a noise-free environment, and assuming that the line in the projector image is vertical with respect to the camera, each row y_1 of the camera should provide an equation of the form $[x_1, y_1, 1][1, a, b]^T = 0$ where x_1 is the measured frontier and a and b are the unknown parameters defining the line. Because our camera contains more than two rows and the images are noisy, it is possible to use linear regression to estimate a and b. Once the parameters a, b of the line have been estimated, it is possible to compute the variance of the error on x_1. Since the optical components introduce distortion, a projected line may no longer be a line in the camera and polynomials can be fitted rather than straight lines.

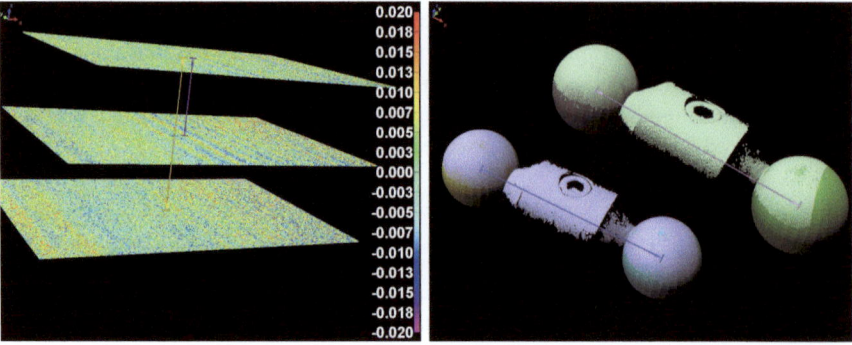

Fig. 3.13 (*Left*) A point-based laser scanner was used to scan the same plane at 3 different positions. The residual error in millimeters is shown using a *color coding*. (*Right*) A profile-based laser scanner was used to perform a center-to-center distance measurement between the centers of two spheres. The experiment was repeated at two different positions. Figure courtesy of NRC Canada

3.7.2 System-Level Characterization

While fitting a model on a small patch of 3D points is not significantly affected by miscalibration, angle measurements are very sensitive to miscalibration. Figure 3.14 contains a 3D model of a known object produced by a fringe projection system. The nominal values of the angles between the top surface and each side are known and the difference between the values measured by fringe projection system is less than 0.03 degree. Those values were obtained by first fitting planes to the 3D points produced by the scanner and then the angles were computed. All operations were performed using the Polyworks ImInspect® software from InnovMetric.[5] This experiment should be repeated using different positions and orientations of the test object. The RMSE of the plane at the right on Fig. 3.14(Top) is 10 μm.

Sphere-to-sphere measurement is part of a standard that addresses the characterization of optical measurement devices [2]. Two spheres are mounted on a bar with a known center-to-center distance. This artifact is known as a *ball bar*. This ball bar is placed at different predetermined positions in the reconstruction volume and the errors of center-to-center distance are used to characterize the scanner. Two scans of this object at two different positions are shown in Fig. 3.13. Again, this type of measurement is very sensitive to miscalibration.

3.7.3 Characterization of Errors Caused by Surface Properties

It is important to note that surface properties can significantly influence the performance of a scanner. As an example, Fig. 3.15 contains an image of a USAF resolution chart which is used to assess the lateral resolution of conventional cameras. We

---

[5] www.innovmetric.com.

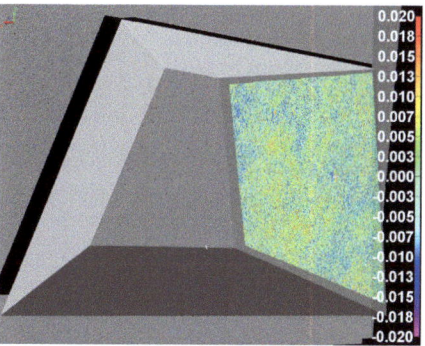

Fig. 3.14 An object scanned by a fringe projection system. The nominal values of the angles between the top surface and each side are respectively 10, 20, 30 and 40 degrees. The residual error in millimeters is shown using a color coding. Figure courtesy of NRC Canada

use the chart to evaluate the impact of sharp intensity variations on the performance of scanners. Texture changes create artifacts in the surface geometry. Moreover, the light may penetrate into the surface of an object before bouncing back to the scanner and this may influence the recovered geometry [10]. Furthermore, the object surface micro-structure combined with the light source spectral distribution can greatly influence the performance of a system. As an example, an optical flat surface was scanned with the same fringe projection system using two different light sources. The first one is a tungsten-halogen source with a large wavelength range, while the second one is a red led with a narrow wavelength range. The experimentation was conducted in complete darkness and the light source intensities were adjusted such that the intensity ratios in the camera were similar for both sources. The RMSE values obtained using the two sources are 21 and 32 μm respectively (see Sect. 3.8.4).

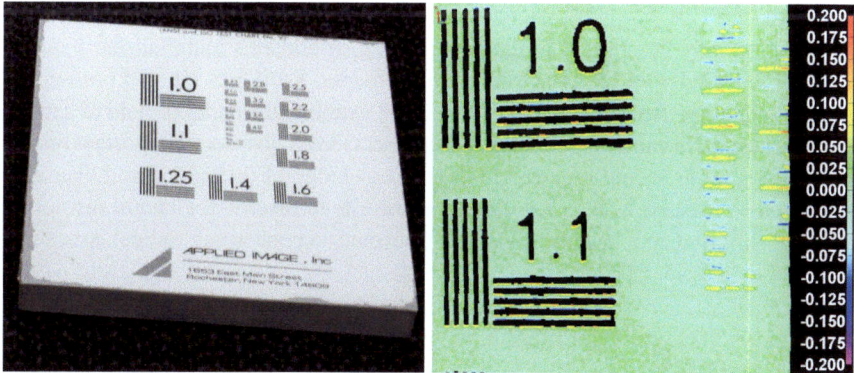

Fig. 3.15 Intensity artifacts produced by a fringe projection system. Note that in some areas (i.e. the *dark regions*) the magnitude of the sinusoidal pattern was so small that the scanner did not produce any 3D points. Again, the residual error in millimeters is shown using a *color coding*. Figure courtesy of NRC Canada

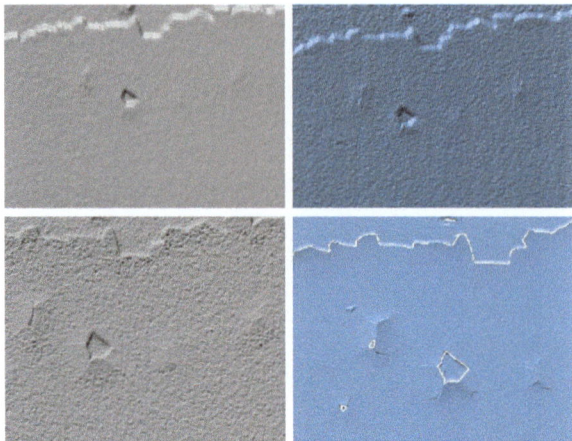

Fig. 3.16 The same surface containing defects scanned by four different scanners. (*Top left*) Point-based laser triangulation system. (*Top right*) Profile-based laser triangulation system. (*Bottom left*) Fringe projection system. (*Bottom Right*) Scanner based on conoscopic holography. Figure courtesy of [33]

3.7.4 Application-Based Characterization

We illustrate the principle behind this family of tests using a surface defect detection application. The objective of this application is to localize defects that create a variation on the surface of a product. In this type of application, the calibration of the system is not very important; however, the capability of the system to image small structural details is very important. In this test, an object which is known to contain defects is scanned and it is possible to verify the presence of those defects in the 3D data. Figure 3.16 illustrates surface defects as detected by four different systems.

3.8 Selected Advanced Topics

This section may be omitted at the first reading. It contains material that requires in-depth knowledge of the image formation process. Section 3.8.1 will present the thin lens equation. Section 3.8.2 and Sect. 3.8.3 examine the depth of field of a triangulation based 3D camera. Section 3.8.4 and Sect. 3.8.5 give some important results whose derivations would required in-depth knowledge of diffraction and Gaussian beam optics. Finally, Sect. 3.8.6 uses those results to discuss the lateral resolution of phase shift and spot scanners. Further information concerning optical issues can be found in [15, 43, 61].

3.8.1 Thin Lens Equation

Optical systems are complex and difficult to model. A very useful approximation is the thin lens equation which provides a first order approximation of a lens with

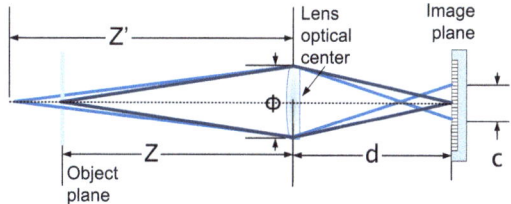

Fig. 3.17 The image of the point at distance Z from the optical center is in focus on the image plane, while the point at distance Z' from the optical center is imaged as a circle of diameter c on the image plane. The lens aperture is Φ and the distance between the image plane and the optical center is d. Figure courtesy of NRC Canada

negligible thickness. Given the distance Z between an object and the optical center of the lens and the focal length f of this lens, one may compute, using the thin lens equation the distance between the optical center and the image plane needed in order to obtain a sharp image of the object. Since optical engineering falls outside the scope of this chapter, we provide the thin lens equation without derivation (see for details [61]). The thin lens equation is

$$\frac{1}{Z} + \frac{1}{d} = \frac{1}{f} \qquad (3.45)$$

where f is the lens focal length, Z is the distance between the optical center and the object plane and d is the distance between the optical center and the image plane (i.e. the CCD or CMOS sensor).

Since $d \approx f$ when the distance between the camera and the object is sufficiently large, Chap. 2 and other textbooks use f (for focal length) rather than using d in their camera models (see Sect. 3.3.1).

Usually, 3D imaging systems are used for applications that require the scan of non-planar objects. Thus, Eq. (3.45) is not fulfilled for all the points on the surface of the object. As will be explained next, this induces out-of-focus blurring in some parts of the image.

3.8.2 Depth of Field

The point located at Z' in Fig. 3.17, will be imaged as a circle of diameter c on the image plane. This circle is named a *circle of confusion*. Using simple trigonometry and the thin lens equation, the diameter of this circle can be computed as

$$c = \Phi \frac{|Z' - Z|}{Z'} \frac{f}{Z - f} \qquad (3.46)$$

where Φ is the size of the lens aperture. The proof is left as an exercise to the reader. Given a maximum diameter c_{max} for the circle of confusion and assuming

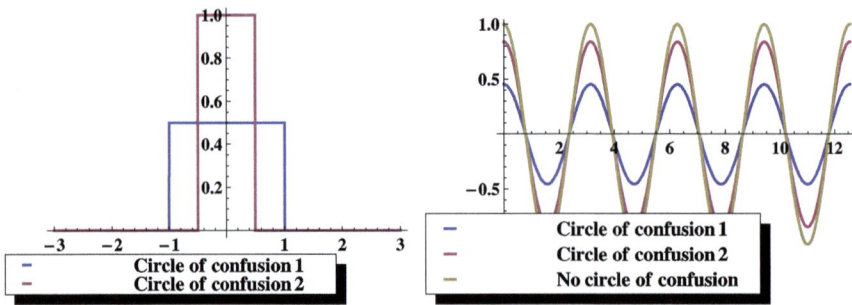

Fig. 3.18 (*Left*) The circle of confusion acts as a box filter. The diameter of the first circle of confusion is two units, while the diameter of the second one is one unit. (*Right*) Effect of blurring induced by the circles of confusion (shown left) on the magnitude of a sinusoidal pattern having a period of three units. Figure courtesy of NRC Canada

that $Z' > Z > f$, the depth of field can be computed, using Eq. (3.46), as

$$D_f = 2(Z' - Z) \qquad (3.47)$$

where

$$Z' = \frac{\Phi f Z}{\Phi f + (f - Z)c_{max}}. \qquad (3.48)$$

Thus, a large lens diameter will induce a small focusing range, even though more light is captured by the imaging system.

Figure 3.18 illustrates the impact of blurring on the magnitude of sinusoidal patterns used by a phase shift scanner. As the ratio between the circle-of-confusion diameter and spatial period of the pattern increases, the magnitude of the signal is reduced. In Eq. (3.40), it can be seen that reducing the spatial period reduces the uncertainty. However, once the optical components of the system are taken into account, one can see that reducing the spatial period, may also reduce the magnitude of the sinusoidal pattern, possibly increasing the uncertainty rather than reducing it. Furthermore, because the blurring depends on the distance of a 3D point, the magnitude of the sinusoidal pattern also depends on the distance. Thus, one should expect that the curve of standard deviation shown at Fig. 3.10, should look more like a U shape when taking into account the optically-induced blurring. It is, therefore, important to factor in the optically induced blurring and other optical related degradations when designing a system because those define the usable measurement volume, which is generally smaller than the reconstruction volume. Note than even when a system is perfectly in-focus, diffraction and aberrations induce a degradation of the image which is similar to out-of-focus blurring [61].

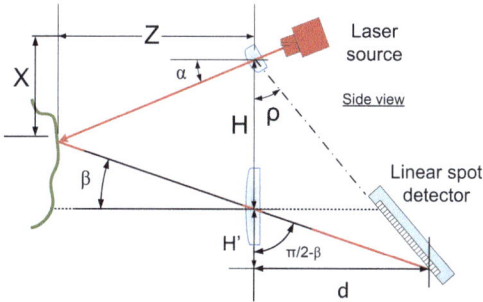

Fig. 3.19 Scheimpflug geometry for a point-based triangulation sensor. The baseline is H. The projection and collection angles are α and β respectively. The angle between the photo-detector and the collecting lens is ρ. Finally, d and H' are respectively the distance along the Z-axis and X-axis between the lens optical center and the position of the laser spot on the detector. Figure courtesy of NRC Canada

3.8.3 Scheimpflug Condition

As explained previously, a large lens diameter will induce a small focusing range. This affects all triangulation-based 3D cameras and many of them use the *Scheimpflug condition* in order to mitigate the impact of this reduced focusing range [16]. In order to simplify the discussion, the Scheimpflug condition will be presented for a point-based scanner. Nevertheless, it could be used with profile-based and area-based scanners. Figure 3.19 shows an optical geometry based on the Scheimpflug condition for the point-based scanner presented in Sect. 3.2. Note that the optical axis is no longer perpendicular to the photo-detector. The angle between the photo-detector and the collecting lens is set to ρ and, as will be shown, this ensures that for a given illumination direction (i.e. angle α) all the points along the laser beam path will be in-focus on the position detector. Using simple trigonometry, one can verify that

$$\tan \rho = \frac{d}{H + H'} \qquad (3.49)$$

and

$$H' = \frac{d}{\tan(\pi/2 - \beta)}. \qquad (3.50)$$

where H' is a line segment in Fig. 3.19. We obtain

$$d = \frac{H \tan \rho}{1 - \tan \beta \tan \rho} \qquad (3.51)$$

by substituting Eq. (3.50) in Eq. (3.49). Finally, substituting Eq. (3.51) and Eq. (3.2) in Eq. (3.45), we obtain

$$\cot \rho = \frac{H - f \tan \alpha}{f}. \qquad (3.52)$$

Thus, for a given α, the angle ρ can be computed such that any point along the laser beam path is in-focus on the position detector. This condition allows one to design a system with a large aperture to increase light collection power. As will be explained next, for a laser-based scanner, this allows the reduction of noise without affecting the focusing range.

3.8.4 Speckle and Uncertainty

In Sect. 3.6.1, the error propagation from image intensity to pixel coordinate was examined for area-based scanners that use phase shift and an expression for the variance $\sigma_{x_2}^2$ was provided. As shown, the variance $\sigma_{x_2}^2$ can then be used to compute the uncertainty on the 3D points computed by a triangulation scanner. Here, we give the result of a similar analysis performed for point-based systems that use a laser.

For laser-based system, the value of $\sigma_{x_2}^2$ depends on the type of laser spot detector used (e.g. CMOS, CCD, lateral-effect photodiode, split diodes), the laser peak detector algorithm, the signal-to-noise ratio (SNR) and the imaged laser spot shape [11]. The laser spot shape is influenced by lens aberrations, vignetting, surface artifacts, etc. In the case of discrete response laser spot sensors, assuming both a high SNR and a centroid-based method for peak detection, the dominant error source will be speckle.

Speckle is the result of the interference of many light waves having the same wavelength but having different phases. Different waves emitted by the projection system are reflected on the object at slightly different positions and thus reach the detector with slightly different phases. The light waves are added together at the detector which measures an intensity that varies. The speckle depends on the surface micro-structure or roughness (of the order of the source wavelength) of the object which is scanned. Note that, speckle noise is more a multiplicative noise source than an additive source. Explicitly, the variance $\sigma_{x_2}^2$ can be approximated as

$$\sigma_{x_2}^2 \approx \frac{\lambda^2 d^2}{2\pi \Phi^2} \tag{3.53}$$

where Φ is the lens aperture diameter, λ is the laser wavelength and d is the distance between the laser spot detector and the collection lens [16]. The effects of speckle on the peak detection have also been studied by [8, 30, 45]. Note that when substituting Eq. (3.53) back into Eq. (3.41), one can verify that the presence of speckle noise caused by a laser does not depend on d. When λ is reduced or when Φ is increased, the uncertainty is reduced. While a large lens diameter reduces the uncertainty, it also limits the focusing range when a Scheimpflug condition is not used.

Note that speckle can be an important error source even for a fringe projection system that uses a low-coherence light source with a relatively long coherence length. The coherence length is proportional to the square of the nominal wavelength of the source and inversely proportional to the wavelength range [45].

3 Active 3D Imaging Systems

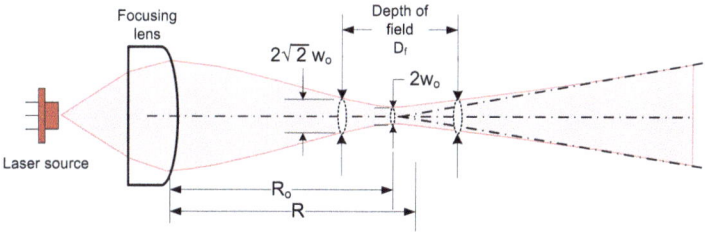

Fig. 3.20 The focus of an actual laser beam is governed by diffraction. We show the case of a focused laser beam with a Gaussian shape transversal profile. The minimum beam diameter is $2w_0$ and R_0 is the distance from the lens to the point at which the beam diameter is minimal. A maximum beam diameter of $2\sqrt{2}w_0$ is used to compute the depth of field, D_f, of the laser. Figure courtesy of NRC Canada

3.8.5 Laser Depth of Field

Until now, the laser beam and collected ray were assumed to be infinitely thin. Though convenient to explain the basic principles, this is an over-simplification. Taking into account the properties of Gaussian beams associated with lasers is fundamental to understanding the limitations of some 3D laser-based vision systems [17, 20, 55]. As a result of diffraction, even in the best laser emitting conditions, a laser beam does not maintain focus with distance (see Fig. 3.20). Note that in many close-range 3D laser scanners, a focused laser beam is the preferred operating mode. This is a complex topic whose details fall outside the scope of this chapter. Nevertheless, because it is fundamental to understanding the resolution limitations of some 3D imaging systems, we give two important results concerning Gaussian beam propagation. Using the Gaussian beam propagation formula, the beam radius measured orthogonally to the beam axis, denoted by $w(R)$ at the e^{-2} irradiance contour in the direction of propagation R is

$$w(R) = w_0 \sqrt{1 + \left(\frac{\lambda(R-R_0)}{\pi w_0^2}\right)^2} \qquad (3.54)$$

where the distance R_0 is the distance from the lens to the point at which the beam radius is minimal. The minimum radius is denoted by w_0 and λ is the wavelength of the laser source. More details information concerning Eq. (3.54) can be found in [15, 43, 61]. In accordance with the Rayleigh criterion, the depth of field D_f for a focused Gaussian beam is $R_{max} - R_{min}$ where $w(R_{max}) = w(R_{min}) = \sqrt{2}w_0$ and $R_{min} < R_{max}$ and explicitly,

$$D_f = \frac{2\pi w_0^2}{\lambda}. \qquad (3.55)$$

For a point-based scanner, the depth of field D_f, the distance R_0 and the angular interval for the scanning angle α can be used to compute the usable measurement

Table 3.2 Approximate depth of field as a function of a few beam radii. The laser wavelength is 0.633 μm. Table courtesy of NRC Canada

Beam radius (w_0)	Approximate depth of field (D_f)
10 μm	1 mm
100 μm	100 mm
1 mm	10 m

volume of the scanner. Moreover, the usable measurement volume of a sheet-of-light scanner could be computed similarly.

3.8.6 Lateral Resolution

Intuitively, the lateral resolution is the capability of a scanner to discriminate two adjacent structures on the surface of a sample. A formal definition can be found in [3]. For some applications such as the one presented in Sect. 3.7.4, it is critical to use a 3D scanner with sufficient lateral resolution. The lateral resolution is limited by two factors which are the structural and the spatial resolution [3].

For a phase-shift system, when working out-of-focus, the lateral resolution of a system is not limited by the camera resolution (spatial resolution), but by the optical resolution (structural resolution) of the camera lens. Thus, to increase the lateral resolution, one may have to reduce the depth of field of the scanner or the lens aperture size. When a digital projector is used, artifacts induced by inter-pixel gaps and discretization may limit the lateral resolution of the system. Note that it is possible to alleviate those artifacts by using the hybrid hardware-software solution presented in [33].

For a laser spot scanner, the knowledge of the beam radius on the scene allows one to determine the structural component of the lateral resolution of the system. The spatial resolution is the smallest possible variation of the scan angle α. Increasing the angular resolution of α can improve the lateral resolution as long as the spatial resolution does not exceed the structural one. Thus, reducing the beam radius may be the only way to increase the lateral resolution. When the beam radius is reduced, the depth of field is also reduced unless an auto-focusing method is used while measuring. Thus, there is a trade off between lateral resolution and the depth of field. Table 3.2 gives some numerical examples of beam radii.

3.9 Research Challenges

In Sect. 3.6 we presented the error propagation from the image formation to the 3D points for some area scanners. To the best of our knowledge, no commercial scanner associates to each 3D point a covariance matrix that can be used for performing a first-order error propagation. An important research issue is the understanding and modeling of error propagation from the calibration step to the visualization step of the modeling pipeline. This is challenging because the modeling pipeline can contain a significant amount of geometric processing such as the fusion of multiple scans, the transformation of point clouds into meshes, the decimation of triangles, and the fitting of geometric primitives.

As the individual components of 3D imaging systems continue to improve, it is expected that the spatial resolution of 3D imaging systems will increase up to the limits imposed by physics. As an example, in recent years the resolution of cameras has significantly increased. This had a significant impact on the performance of fringe projection systems; however, there are physical limitations that make further improvement of a 3D scanner impossible. As an example, a laser point scanner can be designed to reduce the effect of speckle, but speckle cannot be removed as it is a physical limit of any system that uses coherent light. Another example of physical limitations is the diffraction introduced by the finite size of a lens aperture. Thus, one of the main challenges in the development of 3D imaging systems is to combine the improvements in commercially available components with innovative new designs and algorithms in order to bring the performance of the system as close as possible to the physical limits. Another interesting area of research is the design of systems for niche applications which are required to work in harsh environments or that must scan very challenging objects, such as translucent objects, objects with grooves or other surface concavities, and underwater objects.

3.10 Concluding Remarks

Many of the traditional measurement instruments like theodolites and CMMs are being replaced by non-contact optical scanners based on triangulation, time-of-flight, or interferometry technology. This sudden change in process design and quality assurance practices needs to be addressed by research organizations and companies. When the goal of a business is to make a quality product for a profit, then metrology will have a direct impact on that business. The quality of measurements planned in the design stage, applied during manufacturing and performed during inspection directly affect the quality of a product. Poor measurements (those without an accuracy statement) may even lead to creating waste with scrapped products. Conversely, precise measurements (those with an accuracy statement) lead to superior products. The dimensional deviations between as-designed, as-built and as-measured devices can only be understood and controlled if traceable measurements can be made in compliance with clear standards. While 3D imaging systems are more widely available, standards, best practices and comparative data are limited. In the near future, we expect to see more comparative data in scientific publications and industrial standards aimed at active 3D imaging systems.

3.11 Further Reading

One of the earliest papers on triangulation-based spot scanning for the capture and recording of 3D data was published by Forsen in 1968 [36]. Kanade presents a collection of chapters from different authors that describe a number of close-range active 3D imaging systems [44]. Many survey papers that review range sensors have been published [7, 16]. The geometric description of the point and profile based system presented a simple scanner. Mirrors can be used to fold the baseline such that the baseline of a system is larger than the physical scanner and where the mirrors dynamically modify the field of view of the camera such that the sensor only sees a small area around the laser spot [54]. The calibration of point-based triangulation scanner is discussed in [12, 13, 25].

An article published by Salvi et al. [57] presents an in-depth classification of different types of structured light patterns. Davis et al. [29] present a unifying framework within which one can categorize 3D triangulation sensors, for example on the basis of their coding within the spatial and temporal domains. Moreover, an analysis of the uncertainty of a white light fringe projection based on Gray codes is presented in [63]. Many analyses of the impact of random noise on phase shift methods have been conducted [31, 40, 53, 62].

The two authoritative texts on the matter of uncertainty and vocabulary related to metrology are the *Guide to the Expression of Uncertainty in Measurement* (GUM) and the *International Vocabulary of Metrology* (VIM) [1, 5]. The document designated E 2544 from the American Society for Testing and Materials (ASTM) provides the definition and description of terms for 3D imaging systems [6]. Moreover, the VDI 2634 is a document from a standardization body that addresses the characterization of optical distance sensors [2]. Error propagation in the context of multiple-view geometry is discussed in [28]. The characterization of active 3D imaging systems is discussed in [19, 24, 26, 27, 35, 38, 45–47].

3.12 Questions

1. Name and explain three categories of triangulation scanner, based on different methods of scene illumination.
2. In recent years, the resolution of cameras has significantly increased. What are the impacts of this on each type of triangulation scanner?
3. What are the impacts on the 3D data of varying the baseline of a laser stripe scanner without recalibrating the system?
4. What are the impacts on the 3D data of varying the distance, d (the distance between the camera center and image plane) of a laser stripe scanner without recalibrating the system?
5. What are the values of R_p, T_p, x'_1, y'_1 and x'_2 for which the three constraints in Eq. (3.30) are not linearly independent?
6. What are the elements that can limit the lateral resolution of a stripe scanner? Classify those elements as belonging to the spatial or structural resolution.

3.13 Exercises

1. Using a programming environment of your choice, develop a 2D simulator of a phase shift fringe projection scanner that can reproduce the intensity artifact shown in Fig. 3.15. Assume that optical-induced blurring is only present in the camera images and that the camera has an infinite spatial resolution. Repeat the experiment for a fringe projection system that uses a Gray code.
2. Modify the previously developed prototype in order to apply it to a stripe scanner. Plot a graph that shows the variation of error due to the width of the stripe.
3. For a stripe-based scanner, an occlusion occurs when the linear detector does not see the laser spot. However, since the spot size is not infinitesimal, there are intermediate situations where only a fraction of the spot is seen by the detector. Using a prototyping environment, develop a model to evaluate the impact of this on the recovered geometry.
4. Perform the error propagation computation for a stripe scanner that includes uncertainty on the angles α.
5. Using Fig. 3.17, trigonometry and the thin lens equation, give the derivation of Eq. (3.46).
6. Modify the camera model presented in Sect. 3.3.1 to incorporate a Scheimpflug condition.

References

1. ISO Guide 98-3: Uncertainty of Measurement Part 3: Guide to the Expression of Uncertainty in Measurement (gum 1995) (1995)
2. VDI 2634: Part 2: Optical 3-d Measuring Systems Optical System Based on Area Scanning (2002)
3. VDI 2617: Part 6.2: Accuracy of Coordinate Measuring Machines Characteristics and Their Testing Guideline for the Application of DIN EN ISO 10360 to Coordinate Measuring Machines with Optical Distance Sensors. Beuth Verlag GmbH (2005)
4. ANSI z136: Part 1–6: American National Standard for Safe Use of Lasers (2007)
5. CGM 200:2008: International Vocabulary of Metrology Basic and General Concepts and Associated Terms (VIM) (2008)
6. ASTM e2544-10: Standard Terminology for Three-Dimensional (3d) Imaging Systems (2010)
7. Amann, M.C., Bosch, T., Lescure, M., Myllylä, R., Rioux, M.: Laser ranging: a critical review of usual techniques for distance measurement. Opt. Eng. **40**(1), 10–19 (2001)
8. Baribeau, R., Rioux, M.: Influence of speckle on laser range finders. Appl. Opt. **30**(20), 2873–2878 (1991)
9. Benoit, P., Mathieu, E., Hormire, J., Thomas, A.: Characterization and control of three-dimensional objects using fringe projection techniques. Nouv. Rev. Opt. **6**(2), 67–86 (1975)
10. Beraldin, J.A., Blais, F., Lohr, U.: Laser scanning technology. In: Vosselman, G., Mass, H.-G. (eds.) Airborne and Terrestrial Laser Scanning. Whittles Publishers, Dunbeath (2010)
11. Beraldin, J.A., Blais, F., Rioux, M., Domey, J., Gonzo, L., Nisi, F.D., Comper, F., Stoppa, D., Gottardi, M., Simoni, A.: Optimized position sensors for flying-spot active triangulation systems. In: Proc. Int. Conf. 3D Digital Imaging and Modeling, pp. 29–36 (2003)

12. Beraldin, J.A., El-Hakim, S.F., Cournoyer, L.: Practical range camera calibration. In: Videometrics. SPIE Proceedings, vol. II, pp. 21–31 (1993)
13. Beraldin, J.A., Rioux, M., Blais, F., Godin, G., Baribeau, R.: Model-Based Calibration of a Range Camera (1992)
14. Besl, P.J.: Active, optical range imaging sensors. Mach. Vis. Appl. **1**(2), 127–152 (1988)
15. Blahut, R.E.: Theory of Remote Image Formation. Cambridge University Press, Cambridge (2004)
16. Blais, F.: Review of 20 years of range sensor development. J. Electron. Imaging **13**(1), 231–243 (2004)
17. Blais, F., Beraldin, J.A.: Recent developments in 3d multi-modal laser imaging applied to cultural heritage. Mach. Vis. Appl. **17**(3), 395–409 (2006)
18. Blais, F., Rioux, M.: Real-time numerical peak detector. Signal Process. **11**(2), 145–155 (1986)
19. Boehler, W., Marbs, A.: Investigating scanner accuracy. Tech. rep, German University FH, Mainz (2003)
20. Born, M., Wolf, E.: Principles of Optics: Electromagnetic Theory of Propagation, Interference and Diffraction of Light, 7th edn. Cambridge University Press, Cambridge (1999)
21. Bosch, T., Lescure, M. (eds.): Selected Papers on Laser Distance Measurements, vol. 115. SPIE Milestone Series (1995). B.J. Thompson (General editor)
22. Breuckmann: GmbH: Projector for an arrangement for three-dimensional optical measurement of object. United State Patent Office 7532332 (2009)
23. Brown, D.: Decentering distortion of lenses. Photom. Eng. **32**(3), 444–462 (1966)
24. Brownhill, A., Brade, R., Robson, S.: Performance study of non-contact surface measurement technology for use in an experimental fusion device. In: 21st Annual IS&T/SPIE Symposium on Electronic Imaging (2009)
25. Bumbaca, F., Blais, F.: Real-time correction of three-dimensional non-linearities for a laser range finder. Opt. Eng. (1986)
26. Carrier, B., Mackinnon, D., Cournoyer, L., Beraldin, J.A.: Proposed NRC portable target case for short-range triangulation-based 3-d imaging systems characterization. In: 23st Annual IS&T/SPIE Symposium on Electronic Imaging (2011)
27. Cox, M.G., Siebert, B.R.L.: The use of a Monte Carlo method for evaluating uncertainty and expanded uncertainty. Metrologia **43**(4), S178 (2006)
28. Criminisi, A.: Accurate Visual Metrology from Single and Multiple Uncalibrated Images. Springer, New York (2001)
29. Davis, J., Nehab, D., Ramamoorthi, R., Rusinkiewicz, S.: Spacetime stereo: A unifying framework for depth from triangulation. IEEE Trans. Pattern Anal. Mach. Intell. **27**(2), 296–302 (2005)
30. Dorsch, R.G., Häusler, G., Herrmann, J.M.: Laser triangulation: fundamental uncertainty in distance measurement. Appl. Opt. **33**(7), 1306–1314 (1994)
31. Dorsch, R.G., Häusler, G., Herrmann, J.M.: Fourier-transform method of phase-shift determination. Appl. Opt. **40**(17), 2886–2894 (2001)
32. Drouin, M.A.: Mise en correspondance active et passive pour la vision par ordinateur multivue. Université de Montréal (2007)
33. Drouin, M.A., Blais, F.: Method and System for Alleviating the Discretization and Inter-Pixel Gaps Effect of a Digital Fringe Projection System (2011). United State Patent Office 13/108,378 (Application)
34. Fisher, R.B., Naidu, D.K.: A comparison of algorithms for subpixel peak detection. In: Image Technology, Advances in Image Processing, Multimedia and Machine Vision, pp. 385–404. Springer, Berlin (1996)
35. Forbes, A.B., Hughes, B., Sun, W.: Comparison of measurements in co-ordinate metrology. Measurement **42**(10), 1473–1477 (2009)

36. Forsen, G.: Processing visual data with an automaton eye. In: Pictorial Pattern Recognition, pp. 471–502 (1968)
37. Ghiglia, D.C., Pritt, M.D.: Two-Dimensional Phase Unwrapping Theory, Algorithms ans Software. Wiley, New York (1998)
38. Goesele, M., Fuchs, C., Seidel, H.P.: Accuracy of 3d range scanners by measurement of the slanted edge modulation transfer function. In: International Conference on 3D Digital Imaging and Modeling, vol. 37 (2003)
39. Gray, F.: Pulse code communication. United State Patent Office 2632058 (1953)
40. Hibino, K.: Susceptibility of systematic error-compensating algorithms to random noise in phase-shifting interferometry. Appl. Opt. **36**(10), 2084–2093 (1997)
41. Inokuchi, S., Sato, K., Matsuda, F.: Range imaging system for 3-D object recognition. In: Proc. Int. Conf. Pattern Recognition, pp. 806–808 (1984)
42. Inspect, Inc.: Optional 3d digitizer, system and method for digitizing an object. United State Patent Office 6493095 (2002)
43. Jahne, B., Haussecker, H.W., Geissler, P.: Handbook of Computer Vision and Applications. 1. Sensors and Imaging. Academic Press, San Diego (1999)
44. Kanade, T. (ed.): Three-Dimensional Machine Vision. Kluwer Academic, Norwell (1987)
45. Leach, R. (ed.): Optical Measurement of Surface Topography. Springer, Berlin (2011)
46. Luhmann, T., Bethmann, F., Herd, B., Ohm, J.: Comparison and verification of optical 3-d surface measurement systems. In: The International Archives of the Photogrammetry, Remote Sensing and Spatial Information Sciences, vol. XXXVII, Part B5, Beijing (2008)
47. MacKinnon, D., Aitken, V., Blais, F.: Review of measurement quality metrics for range imaging. J. Electron. Imaging **17** (2008)
48. Naidu, K., Fisher, R.B.: A comparative analysis of algorithms for determining the peak position of a stripe to sub-pixel accuracy. In: Proc. British Machine Vision Conf. (1991)
49. Newhall, B.: Photosculture. Image: Journal of Photography and Motion Pictures of the George Eastman House **7**(5), 100–105 (1958)
50. Nitzan, D.: Three-dimensional vision structure for robot applications. IEEE Trans. Pattern Anal. Mach. Intell. **10**(3), 291–309 (1988)
51. Ohyama, N., Kinoshita, S., Cornejo-Rodriguez, A., Tsujiuchi, J.: Accuracy of phase determination with unequal reference phase shift. J. Opt. Soc. Am. A **12**(9), 1997–2008 (1995)
52. Rathjen, C.: Optical Shop Testing. Wiley, New York (1978). Edited by Malacara
53. Rathjen, C.: Statistical properties of phase-shift algorithms. J. Opt. Soc. Am. A **12**(9), 1997–2008 (1995)
54. Rioux, M.: Laser range finder based on synchronized scanners. Appl. Opt. **23**(21), 3837–3855 (1984)
55. Rioux, M., Taylor, D., Duggan, M.: Design of a large depth of view three-dimensional camera for robot vision. Opt. Eng. **26**(12), 1245–1250 (1987)
56. Robson, S., Beraldin, A., Brownhill, A., MacDonald, L.: Artefacts for optical surface measurement. In: Society of Photo-Optical Instrumentation & Electronics & Society for Imaging Science and Technology, in Videometrics, Range Imaging, and Applications XI (2011)
57. Salvi, J., Pages, J., Batlle, J.: Pattern codification strategies in structured light systems. Pattern Recognit. **37**(4), 827–849 (2004)
58. Sansoni, G., Patrioli, A.: Noncontact 3d sensing of free-form complex surfaces. In: Proc. SPIE, vol. 4309 (2001)
59. Seitz, P.: Photon-noise limited distance resolution of optical metrology methods. In: Optical Measurement Systems for Industrial Inspection V. Proceedings of SPIE, vol. 6616 (2007)
60. Singer, C.J., Williams, T.I., Raper, R.: A History of Technology. Clarendon Press, Oxford (1954)
61. Smith, W.J.: Modern Optical Engineering, 3rd edn. McGraw-Hill, New York (2000)
62. Surrel, Y.: Additive noise effect in digital phase detection. Appl. Opt. **36**(1), 271–276 (1994)

63. Trobina, M.: Error model of a coded-light range sensor. Tech. Rep. BIWI-TR-164, ETH-Zentrum (1995)
64. Will, P.M., Pennington, K.S.: Grid coding: a novel technique for image processing. Proc. IEEE **60**(6), 669–680 (1972)
65. Willéme, F.: Photo-sculpture. United State Patent Office 43822 (1864)

Chapter 4
Representing, Storing and Visualizing 3D Data

William A.P. Smith

Abstract In this chapter, we review methods for storing, modeling and visualizing 3D data. We focus in particular on representations for raw 3D data, surface-based and solid-based models. We describe and compare the various data structures available for representing triangular meshes and formats for mesh storage. We also provide details on three different subdivision schemes and explain how differential surface properties can be computed from different surface representations. In the context of data compression, we describe in detail the Quadric Error Metric algorithm for mesh simplification. Finally, we suggest areas for future work in this area and provide some concluding remarks.

4.1 Introduction

There is a wide range of 3D acquisition technologies and applications for 3D data. Perhaps not surprisingly, there are an equally wide number of systems for 3D data representation, compression, storage, search, manipulation and visualization. 3D data representations serve as an intermediary between the data acquisition and the application, with constraints imposed from both sides.

In many cases, the method of acquisition dictates a specific native representation format. For example, classical stereo vision recovers disparity and hence depth values at each pixel and so usually is represented as a range image. On the other hand, the target application also imposes constraints on the method of representation. For example, certain operations are more efficient when a particular 3D representation is used. For this reason, it may be necessary to convert between representations, perhaps involving some level of approximation.

Examples of common 3D datasets range from the very small (molecules, microscopic tissue structures, 3D microstructures in materials science), to the human scale (3D human heart, 3D face, 3D body scans) to the large (3D modeling of buildings and landscapes) and beyond (3D modeling of astrophysical data). It is the scale, res-

---

W.A.P. Smith (✉)
Department of Computer Science, University of York, York, YO10 5GH, UK
e-mail: william.smith@york.ac.uk

olution and compression of this data that determines the volume of data stored. In turn, the challenges for storing, manipulating and visualizing this data grow as the volume increases.

Chapter Outline In this chapter, we provide an overview of how 3D data can be stored, modeled and visualized. We begin by providing a taxonomy of 3D data representations. We then present, in more detail, a selection of the most important 3D data representations. Firstly, we focus on triangular meshes, describing the data structures available for efficiently processing such data. We take, as an example, the halfedge data structure and provide some implementation details. Secondly, we describe schemes for subdivision surfaces. Having considered methods for representing 3D data, we then discuss how local differential surface properties can be computed for the most common representation. Next, we describe how 3D data can be compressed and simplified before finally discussing visualization of 3D data, providing examples of the sorts of visualizations that are available using commonly-used tools.

4.2 Representation of 3D Data

The representation of 3D data is the foundation of a number of important applications, such as computer-aided geometric design, visualization and graphics. In this section, we summarize various 3D representations which we classify as: raw data (i.e. delivered by a 3D sensing device), surfaces (i.e. 2D manifolds embedded in 3D space) and solids (i.e. 3D objects with volume).

4.2.1 Raw Data

The raw output of a 3D sensor can take a number of forms, such as points, a depth map and polygons. Often, data represented in these raw forms requires further processing prior to analysis. Moreover, these representations may permit non-manifold or noisy surfaces to be represented which may hinder subsequent analysis.

4.2.1.1 Point Cloud

In its simplest form, 3D data exists as a set of unstructured 3-dimensional coordinates called a *point cloud*, $\mathbb{P}$, where $\mathbb{P} = \{\mathbf{v}_1, \ldots, \mathbf{v}_n\}$ and $\mathbf{v}_i \in \mathbb{R}^3$. Typically, a point cloud of n points is stored as an $n \times 3$ array of floating point numbers or a linked list of n vertex records. Point clouds arise most commonly in vision as the output of multiview stereo [22] or related techniques such as SLAM (simultaneous localization and mapping) [63]. They also arise from laser range scanning devices, where the 3D positions of vertices lying along the intersection between a laser stripe and the surface are computed. Vertices may be augmented by additional information such as texture or, in the case of *oriented points*, a surface normal [28]. A visualization of a point cloud is shown in Fig. 4.21(a). In order to further process point cloud data, it is often necessary to fit a smooth surface to data in a manner which is robust to noise in the point positions. However, the direct rendering of vertex data (known as point-based rendering) has developed as a sub-field within graphics that offers certain advantages over traditional polygon-based rendering [57].

4.2.1.2 Structured Point Cloud

A more constrained representation may be used when point cloud vertices adhere to an underlying structure, namely a grid with arbitrary sampling. In this case, vertices are stored in an ordered $m \times n \times 3$ array and, for each point $i = 1..m$, $j = 1..n$, there is a corresponding 3D vertex $[x(i, j)\ y(i, j)\ z(i, j)]^T \in \mathbb{R}^3$. Moreover, the ordering of the points is such that adjacent vertices share adjacent indices. There is an implicit mesh connectivity between neighboring points and non-boundary points are always degree 6. Conversion to a triangular mesh is straightforward, by constructing an edge between all pairs of adjacent vertices. Often, there is an additional binary 2D array of size $m \times n$ which indicates the presence or absence of 3D data (for example, parts of the surface being imaged may have poor reflectance). Instead of binary value, a scalar "confidence" value can be stored providing an indication of measurement uncertainty at each point. Finally, a grayscale or color-texture image of the same dimensions may also be associated with the 3D data. In this case, the format provides an implicit correspondence between 2D pixels and 3D vertices, assuming that the 3D camera captures and stores such information. An example of a commonly used structured point cloud dataset is the 3D face data in the *Face Recognition Grand Challenge* version 2 data release [52].

4.2.1.3 Depth Maps and Range Images

A special case of structured point cloud arises when the sampling of points in the $x - y$ plane is viewer-centered. Although often used interchangeably, we define a *range image* as a structured point cloud which arises from a perspective projection and a *depth map* as an orthogonal projection and regular sampling of 3D vertices over a 2D image plane. Both representations have the advantage that they can be represented by a 2D function $z(x, y)$. Hence, these representations require less storage than those which allow variable spacing of points in the (x, y) plane and can effectively be stored (and compressed) as an image. In the case of a depth map, the only additional information required to reconstruct 3D vertex position is the fixed spacings, Δ_x and Δ_y. In the case of a range image, parameters related to the camera projection (e.g. focal length and center of projection) must also be stored. Depth maps and range images can be visualized as grayscale images, whereby image intensity represents the distance to the surface (see Fig. 4.21(d)). Alternatively, they can be converted into a triangular mesh and rendered. Since the vertices are evenly distributed over the image plane, a regular triangulation can be used. Range images are the natural representation for binocular stereo [58] where, for each pixel, a disparity value is calculated that is related to depth. In addition, range images are often computed as an intermediate representation as part of the rendering pipeline. Here they are used for z-buffering and to efficiently simulate many visual effects such as depth of field and atmospheric attenuation.

4.2.1.4 Needle map

Photometric shape reconstruction methods often recover an intermediate representation comprising per-pixel estimates of the orientation of the underlying surface $z(x, y)$. In graphics this is known as a *bump map*. This is either in the form of surface gradients, i.e. $p(x, y) = \partial_x z(x, y)$ and $q(x, y) = \partial_y z(x, y)$, or surface normals, i.e. $\mathbf{n}(x, y) = [p(x, y) \; q(x, y) \; -1]^T$. A needle map can be rendered by using a reflectance function to locally shade each pixel. Alternatively, a depth map can be estimated from surface normals via a process known as *surface integration* (see [55] for a recently reported approach). This is a difficult problem when the surface normal estimates are noisy or subject to bias. When augmented with depth estimates, potentially at a lower resolution, the two sources of information can be combined to make a robust estimate of the surface using an efficient algorithm due to Nehab et al. [45]. This approach is particularly suitable where the depth map is subject to high frequency noise (e.g. from errors in stereo correspondence) and the surface normals subject to low frequency bias (e.g. when using photometric stereo with inaccurate light source directions).

4.2.1.5 Polygon Soup

A polygon soup*Polygon soup* is, in some senses, analogous to point cloud data, but comprises polygons rather than vertices. More precisely, it is a set of unstructured polygons [44], each of which connect vertices together but which are not themselves connected in a coherent structure such as a mesh. Such models may arise in an interactive modeling system where a user creates and places polygons into a scene without specifying how the polygons connect to each other. This sort of data may contain errors such as: inconsistently oriented polygons; intersecting, overlapping or missing polygons; cracks (shared edges not represented as such); or T-junctions. This causes problems for many applications including rendering, collision detection, finite element analysis and solid modeling operations. To create a closed surface, a surface fitting algorithm must be applied to the unstructured polygons. For example, Shen et al. [60] show how to fit an implicit surface to polygon soup data.

4.2.2 Surface Representations

The vast majority of geometric algorithms in computer vision and graphics operate on representations of 3D data based on surfaces. Of these representations, by far the most common is the triangular mesh. For this reason, we focus in more detail on this representation in Sect. 4.3. For many applications in *Computer Aided Design* (CAD), it is necessary to be able to guarantee a certain class of surface smoothness. For example, this may relate to aerodynamic or aesthetic requirements. Smoothness can be categorized according to *differentiability class*. A surface belongs to class $\mathbb{C}^0$ if it is continuous (i.e. the surface or function value changes smoothly). The class $\mathbb{C}^1$ consists of all surfaces which are differentiable and whose derivative is continuous (i.e. the surface normal changes smoothly), while $\mathbb{C}^2$ surfaces have continuous second derivatives (i.e. the surface curvature changes smoothly). A representation which can provide such guarantees, as well as providing a convenient interface for interactive editing is subdivision surfaces. We focus in more detail on this representation in Sect. 4.4. Here, we give a brief overview of alternative surface representations and provide a comparison of the desirable features exhibited by each representation.

4.2.2.1 Triangular Mesh

The most common surface representation comprises 3D vertices, connected together to form triangular faces, which in turn represent or approximate a 2D manifold embedded in 3D space. A number of categorizations are possible here. An important distinction is whether the mesh is closed (i.e. the surface completely encloses a volume) or open (i.e. the mesh contains "boundary" edges that are used by only one triangle). Meshes can represent surfaces with different genera. The *genus* of a surface is an integer representing the maximum number of cuttings along non-intersecting closed simple curves without rendering the resultant manifold disconnected. For example, a sphere has genus zero, while a torus has genus 1. An important property of a triangle is that it has a single surface normal. When a mesh is used to approximate a curved surface, the differential properties of the surface, such as normals and curvature, can only be approximately computed from the mesh faces. Mesh storage and representation is discussed in more detail in Sect. 4.3.

Often, mesh vertices are augmented with *texture coordinates*, also known as UV coordinates [23]. These are most often 2D coordinates which describe a mapping from the surface to a 2D planar parameterization. 1D, 3D (volumetric) and 4D (volumetric plus time) texture coordinates are also occasionally used. Texture coordinates range over the unit square, $(u, v) \in [0, 1] \times [0, 1]$. RGB intensity (known as texture maps), surface normals (known as bump maps) or 3D displacements (known as displacement maps) are stored as images which are indexed by the texture coordinates. When rendering a polygonal mesh, texture within the interior of polygons can be looked up by interpolating the texture coordinates of the vertices of the polygon. Transforming an arbitrary mesh to a 2D parameterization with minimal distortion is a difficult problem [59].

4.2.2.2 Quadrilateral Mesh

The polygons in a mesh need not be triangular. Meshes may contain polygons of arbitrary shape and number of vertices, though non-planar polygons will require additional processing for rendering (e.g. to interpolate surface normal direction over the polygon). One commonly used polygon mesh is based on quadrilateral polygons (sometimes known as a *quadmesh*). Quadmeshes can be easily converted to a triangular mesh by diagonally subdividing each quadrilateral. Quadrilateral meshes are preferred to triangular meshes in a number of circumstances. One example is when Finite Element Analysis is used to simulate surface deformation such as in automobile crash simulation or sheet-metal forming. In these cases, the solution accuracy is improved by using a quadmesh.

4.2.2.3 Subdivision Surfaces

Subdivision surfaces are used to represent a smooth surface using a low resolution base mesh and a subdivision rule (or *refinement scheme*). When applied recursively, the subdivided surface tends towards the smooth surface. The *limit* subdivision surface is the surface produced when the refinement scheme is iteratively applied infinitely many times. The limit surface can be computed directly for most subdivision surfaces, without the need to evaluate the iterative refinement. This allows a subdivision surface to be rendered without explicitly subdividing the original base mesh. We describe a number of subdivision schemes in Sect. 4.4.

4.2.2.4 Morphable Model

A space efficient representation, which can be used to approximate members of a class of surfaces (such as human faces [6] or automobiles [36]), is the *morphable model*. This is a compact statistical representation learnt from training samples. A mesh of N vertices may be written as a long vector: $\mathbf{s} = [x_1 \ y_1 \ z_1 \ \ldots \ x_N \ y_N \ z_N]^T$. From a sample of such meshes that are in dense correspondence (i.e. the ith vertex in each mesh corresponds to a point with the same meaning, such as the tip of the nose), a mean vector, $\bar{\mathbf{s}}$, and a set of orthonormal basis vectors, $\mathbf{e}_1, \ldots, \mathbf{e}_k \in \mathbb{R}^{3N}$, are derived using Principal Components Analysis (PCA). These vectors correspond to the most common modes of variation within the training data and they are sorted by the variance captured by each mode, $\sigma_1 > \cdots > \sigma_k$. Hence, only the most important modes need be retained to explain a large proportion of the variance in the training data, i.e. $k \ll N$. Any member of the class of objects can be approximated as a linear combination of the mean vector and the principal modes of variation:

$$\mathbf{s} = \mathsf{P}\mathbf{b} + \bar{\mathbf{s}}, \qquad (4.1)$$

where $\mathsf{P} = [\mathbf{e}_1| \ldots |\mathbf{e}_k] \in \mathbb{R}^{3N \times k}$ is the matrix formed by stacking the basis vectors and $\mathbf{b} \in \mathbb{R}^k$ is a vector of weights associated with each mode. The advantage of such

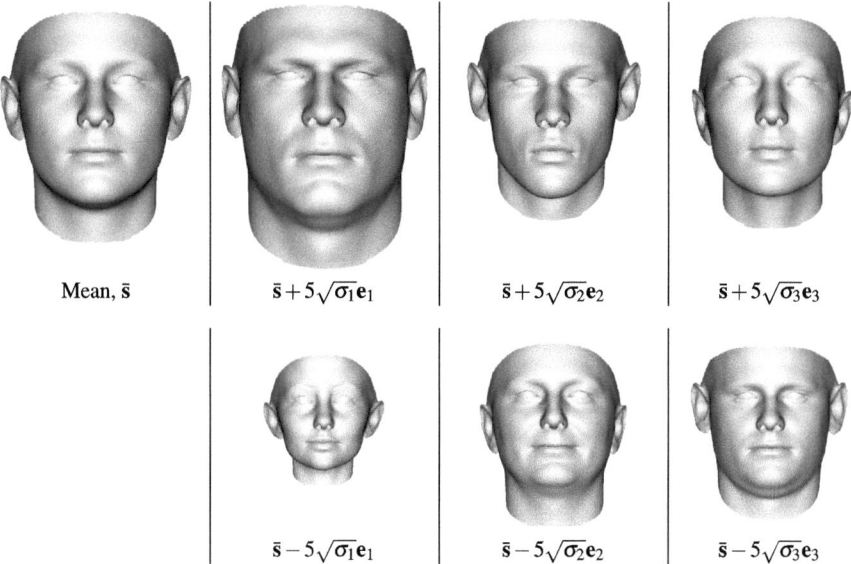

Fig. 4.1 A 3D morphable model of human faces [48]. The *top left panel* shows the mean face surface. The remainder show the mean face deformed by ±5 standard deviations along the first three principal modes of variation

a representation is that the high dimensional mesh can be approximated by the low dimensional parameter vector. Moreover, the parameter space is useful for recognition and classification and the modes themselves often correspond to meaningful global descriptors. For example, in Fig. 4.1, we show a morphable model of human faces. The first mode appears to capture the difference between adult and child faces. A morphable model is limited to representing objects from within the same class as the training data. The ability of the model to generalize to unseen samples is characterized by the *generalization error*, which is a function of the diversity of the training samples. There is also an implicit assumption that the original high dimensional data approximates a Gaussian distribution (hyperelliposoid), which can be accurately approximated by a small number of axes.

4.2.2.5 Implicit Surface

An implicit surface [8] (also known as a *level set* or an *isosurface*) is the set of all points $[x\ y\ z]^T$ which satisfy the function $f(x, y, z) = 0$. Typically, function values greater than zero indicate points that are outside the object, while negative values indicate points that are inside. For example, the surface of a sphere of radius r can be represented by the set of points satisfying $x^2 + y^2 + z^2 - r^2 = 0$. The surface normal to an implicit surface can be obtained simply by taking partial derivatives:

$$\mathbf{n}(x, y, z) = \begin{bmatrix} \partial_x f(x, y, z) & \partial_y f(x, y, z) & \partial_z f(x, y, z) \end{bmatrix}^T. \tag{4.2}$$

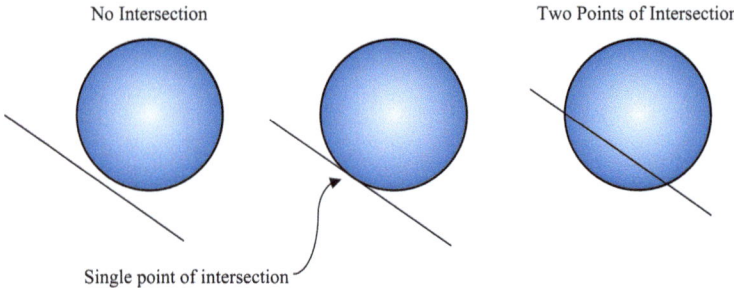

Fig. 4.2 The three possible cases for a line-sphere intersection

Inside/outside tests can also be performed efficiently by simply evaluating the sign of the surface function at a given point. One of the most attractive properties of the implicit surface representation is that intersections can be computed analytically. By substituting a parametric ray equation into the implicit surface function and solving for the parameter, all intersections can be found exactly. For example, consider the ray described by:

$$\begin{bmatrix} x \\ y \\ z \end{bmatrix} = \begin{bmatrix} x_0 \\ y_0 \\ z_0 \end{bmatrix} + t \begin{bmatrix} a \\ b \\ c \end{bmatrix}. \tag{4.3}$$

Substituting into the parametric surface for the sphere, radius r, given above yields:

$$t = \frac{-(ax_0 + by_0 + cz_0) \pm \sqrt{(ax_0 + by_0 + cz_0)^2 - (a^2 + b^2 + c^2)(x_0^2 + y_0^2 + z_0^2 - r^2)}}{(a^2 + b^2 + c^2)}. \tag{4.4}$$

There are three possible cases for this intersection (see Fig. 4.2). Two real roots means that the ray intersects the sphere in two places. One real root means the ray touches the sphere tangentially. No real roots means the ray misses the surface. Higher order surfaces involve the solution of higher order intersection equations, which may not be possible analytically.

In general, obtaining a function which exactly describes a general surface is difficult. However, for applications involving visualization of physical effects such as fluid dynamics (where functional descriptions of the dynamics are readily available) an implicit surface is a natural representation. There are a number of commonly used ways to define an implicit surface. The example above is algebraic. The most common such form is a quadric which can be used to describe regular shapes such as spheres, ellipsoids and tori.

An alternative is to derive an algebraic representation from an intermediate representation [9], which is specified by a designer or fitted to data. The most common approach is to define a control structure from primitives such as points, line segments and planar patches. A field function is defined and its value at some point is determined by the distance, r, from that point to a control structure. For example: $f(r) = \frac{1}{r^2}$. The value of this function is known as the *field strength*. The total field strength is the sum of the field strengths due to each control structure. Distances to line segments and planes is usually taken as the distance to the closest point on the structure. A single point yields a sphere whose radius is determined by the chosen contour value. Where there are more than one control point, the fields interact and the resulting isosurface bulges between points. Approaches along these lines are known variously as *metaballs*, *blobbies* and *soft objects*. Rendering isosurfaces for display is not straightforward. The most common approach is to convert to a polygonal model [7]. Alternatives include raytracing the surface [21], which involves computing ray-surface intersections, as described above, or using point sampling and point-based rendering. An implicit surface representation that is commonly used for the interpolation of 'missing parts' of surfaces is the *Radial Basis Function* [11].

4.2.2.6 Parametric Surface

A parametric surface [14] is one which is defined by parametric equations with two parameters, as follows:

$$x = f_x(u, v),$$
$$y = f_y(u, v),$$
$$z = f_z(u, v).$$

For example, the radius r sphere example given above can be described in terms of spherical coordinate parameters:

$$x = r \sin\theta \cos\alpha,$$
$$y = r \sin\theta \sin\alpha,$$
$$z = r \cos\theta.$$

A surface in such a form is easy to evaluate and, if the parametric equations are differentiable, it is straightforward to calculate differential properties of the surface. The problem is that it is very difficult to describe anything other than fairly simple shapes using an algebraic parametric description. For this reason, complex shapes are composed from piecewise parametric surfaces. These parametric patches are blended together to obtain the overall surface and each patch is defined in terms of a set of control points over the unit square. To evaluate a parametric patch at a point, the tensor product of parametric curves defined by the control points is computed. This is achieved by combining control points with polynomial blending functions. Most commonly, these are bicubic:

$$f(u, v) = \mathbf{U}\mathbf{M}\mathbf{P}\mathbf{M}^T\mathbf{V}^T \tag{4.5}$$

Fig. 4.3 A Bézier surface patch. Control points are shown in *red*, the control grid in *blue* and the interpolated surface in *black*

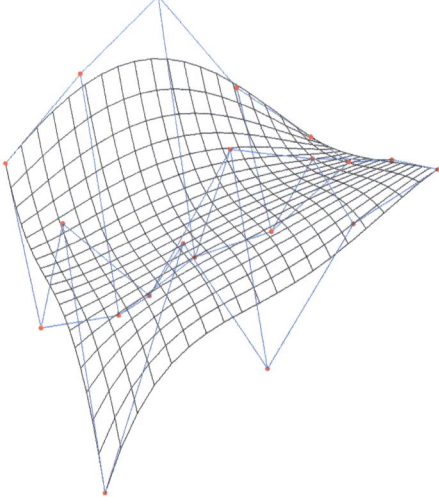

where $\mathbf{U} = [u^3\ u^2\ u\ 1]$ and $\mathbf{V} = [v^3\ v^2\ v\ 1]$ and

$$\mathbf{P} = \begin{bmatrix} P_{1,1} & P_{1,2} & P_{1,3} & P_{1,4} \\ P_{2,1} & P_{2,2} & P_{2,3} & P_{2,4} \\ P_{3,1} & P_{3,2} & P_{3,3} & P_{3,4} \\ P_{4,1} & P_{4,2} & P_{4,3} & P_{4,4} \end{bmatrix}, \tag{4.6}$$

are the function values of the control points (for a bicubic patch, these are specified by a 4 × 4 grid sampling). The matrix **M** describes a blending function for a parametric cubic curve. Two common examples include B-spline:

$$\mathbf{M}_{\text{B-Spline}} = \begin{bmatrix} \frac{-1}{6} & \frac{1}{2} & \frac{-1}{2} & \frac{1}{6} \\ \frac{1}{2} & -1 & \frac{1}{2} & 0 \\ \frac{-1}{2} & 0 & \frac{1}{2} & 0 \\ \frac{1}{6} & \frac{2}{3} & \frac{1}{6} & 0 \end{bmatrix}, \tag{4.7}$$

and Bézier:

$$\mathbf{M}_{\text{Bezier}} = \begin{bmatrix} -1 & 3 & -3 & 1 \\ 3 & -6 & 3 & 0 \\ -3 & 3 & 0 & 0 \\ 1 & 0 & 0 & 0 \end{bmatrix}. \tag{4.8}$$

Bézier patches have some useful properties. The patch will lie completely within the convex hull of its control points and the Bézier surface will pass through the control points at the corner of the patch. It does not generally pass through the other control points. They are visually intuitive and popular in interactive editing applications for this reason. An example of a Bézier patch is shown in Fig. 4.3. To achieve $\mathbb{C}^0$ continuity between adjacent patches, the boundary control points (and

Fig. 4.4 An example NURBS surface patch

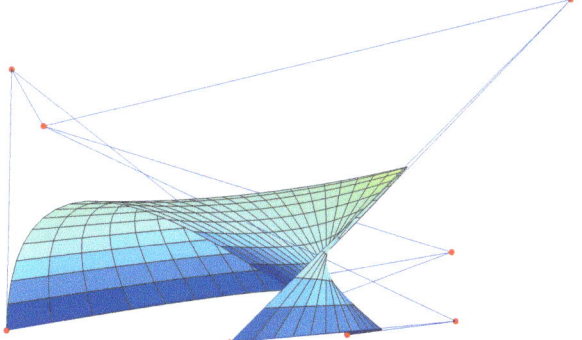

hence boundary curve) must be aligned. $\mathbb{C}^1$ continuity is achieved by aligning the boundary curve and derivatives. This requires that four sets of three control points must be collinear.

An extremely useful generalization of B-splines and Bézier surfaces are *Non-uniform Rational B-Splines* (NURBS) [53, 56]. An example of a NURBS surface patch is given in Fig. 4.4. The distribution of control points in a NURBS surface may be non-uniform. They are invariant to affine and perspective transformations, which means that such transformations can be applied to the control points to obtain the same surface as applying the transformation to the surface computed from the original control points. A NURBS surface is defined by its *order*, a weighted set of *control points* and a *knot vector*. A point on a NURBS surface is given by a weighted sum of a number of control points (usually only a small subset) determined by a polynomial blending function. The parameter space is divided up into intervals and a control point only influences certain intervals. This results in the desirable property of *local support*, which means one part of the surface can be adjusted without influencing others. The knot vector is a sequence of parameter values, which determine how and where a control point affects the NURBS surface. The order of a NURBS surface determines the number of nearby control points, which influence a point on the surface. The NURBS surface is a unifying representation that offers a single mathematical form for both standard analytical shapes (e.g. conics) and free-form surfaces.

4.2.2.7 Comparison of Surface Representations

The best choice of surface representation is application dependent. Table 4.1 summarizes some of the broad strengths and weaknesses of the surface representations discussed above. Generally speaking, polygonal meshes are the most widely used representation and the standard rendering pipeline, such as OpenGL, is optimized for their use. Subdivision surfaces are popular in animation and interactive editing applications. Parametric surfaces are widely used in CAD, as are implicit surfaces, which also find use in mathematical or scientific applications.

Table 4.1 Comparison of surface representations

	Polygonal mesh	Subdivision surface	Morphable model	Implicit surface	Parametric surface
Accuracy	✗	✓	✗	✓	✓
Space efficiency	✗	✓	✓	✓	✓
Display efficiency	✓	✓	✓	✗	✓
InterSect. efficiency	✗	✗	✗	✓	✗
Intuitive specification	✗	✗	✓	✗	✓
Ease of editing	✗	✓	✓	✗	✗
Arbitrary topology	✓	✓	✗	✗	✗
Guaranteed continuity	✗	✓	✗	✓	✓

4.2.3 Solid-Based Representations

Solid-based representations are used where either the method of acquisition is volumetric in nature or where the application dictates a requirement for solid-based computations and manipulations. For example, consider the simple problem of computing the volume of a 3D object. If the object was stored, for example, as a closed surface represented using a mesh, there is no simple way in which this can be calculated. Using some of the solid-based representations described in this section, this is trivial. Common areas of application for solid-based representations include:

1. **Medical Imaging** [62]. Imaging modalities such as MRI and CT are volumetric in nature. Analyzing and visualizing such data necessitates volumetric representations. This is discussed further in Chap. 11.
2. **Engineering**. Components must be designed not only so that they fit together, but also so that their structural properties, determined by their 3D shape, meet specifications.
3. **Scientific visualization** [46]. Volumetric data arises in fields ranging from oceanography to particle physics. In order for humans to interact with and draw inferences from such data, it must be possible to visualize it in a meaningful way.
4. **Finite-element analysis** [79]. A numerical technique for finding approximate solution of partial differential equations and integrals.
5. **Stereolithography** [2]. A process in which an ultraviolet laser is used to trace out cross-sections through a 3D object, building up layers of resin until a complete object has been fabricated. Commonly known as "3D printing".
6. **Interference fit** [35]. Designing object shapes so that two parts can be held together by friction alone.

Solids can either be represented volumetrically or by the surface which encloses them. In this section, we summarize the most common solid-based representations.

4.2.3.1 Voxels

Voxels are the 3D analog of pixels (the name is a contraction of "volumetric pixel"). They are sometimes also referred to as a spatial occupancy enumeration. Each voxel corresponds to a small cubic volume within space. At each voxel, a boolean is stored which indicates the presence or absence of the volume at that point. Alternatively, it may be more appropriate to store a scalar which represents, for example, density at that point in the volume. The precision of the representation is determined by the size of the voxel. A voxel representation is very efficient for making volumetric calculations such as clearance checking. Data storage requirements are high, since the number of voxels grows cubically with the resolution along each dimension. Voxels are the natural representation for volumetric imaging modalities. This is where the sensing device measures surface properties at discrete spatial locations over a 3D volume. Common examples include Magnetic Resonance Imaging (MRI) and Computed Tomography (CT). In vision, volumetric representations are also appropriate for methods such as space carving [33], where image cues are used to determine whether a voxel lies within the volume of an object.

There are two common ways to visualize voxel data: direct volume rendering or conversion to polygonal surface for traditional mesh rendering. In direct volume rendering, voxels are projected to a 2D viewplane and drawn from back to front using an appropriate color and opacity for every voxel. Such visualizations allow multiple layered surfaces to be visualized simultaneously (often exploited in medical imaging where skin, soft tissue and bone can all be visualized in the same image). Conversion to a polygonal mesh requires extraction of an isosurface of equal surface value throughout the volume. The most commonly used approach for this purpose is the *marching cubes* algorithm of Lorensen and Cline [40]. The algorithm proceeds by examining cubes formed by 8 neighboring voxels. Each of the 8 scalar values is treated as a bit in an 8-bit integer. If a scalar value is higher than the iso-value (i.e. inside the surface) it is set to one, otherwise it is set to zero. Hence, there are $2^8 = 256$ possible configurations. The 8-bit integer is used to access a lookup table which stores a polygon associated with each voxel configuration. The individual polygons are then fused to form a surface.

A space efficient representation for voxel data is the *octree*. This uses adaptive resolution depending on the complexity of the surface throughout the volume. The key idea is that voxels which are fully occupied or fully empty are not subdivided,

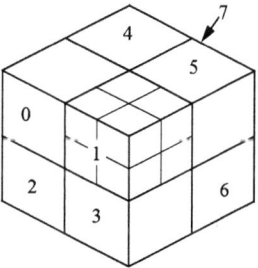

Fig. 4.5 The 8 voxels produced by an octree voxel subdivision

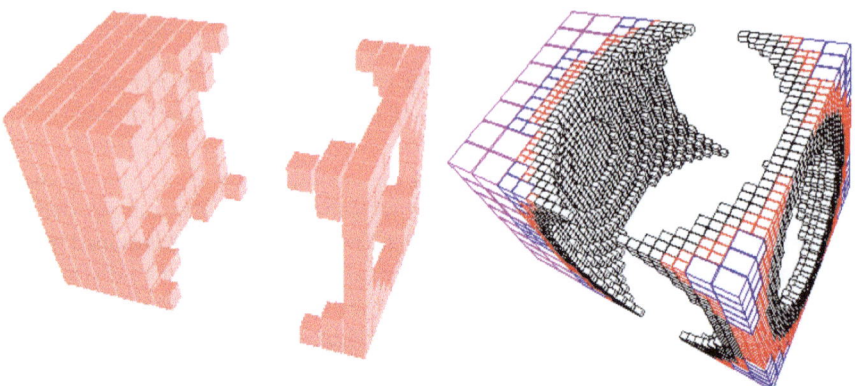

Fig. 4.6 A volume represented using equally sized voxels (*left*) and the octree adaptive representation (*right*). Figure courtesy of lecture notes in computer graphics, Department of Computer Science, University of York

while partially occupied voxels are. This continues until either all voxels are occupied or empty, or the smallest allowable voxel size is reached. Subdividing a voxel into smaller cubes results in 8 smaller voxels (see Fig. 4.5). This representation can be stored in a tree structure in which nodes have 8 children. Leaves are fully occupied or empty voxels and the root represents the complete volume in which the object lies. The finest resolution is determined by the depth of the tree. The example shown in Fig. 4.6 demonstrates how, in regions of high curvature, subdivision can continue to obtain an arbitrarily high accuracy approximation to the underlying smooth volume. A 2-dimensional analog of the octree representation in which pixels are recursively subdivided into four smaller pixels can be stored in a quadtree.

4.2.3.2 *K*-d Trees

K-dimensional trees, or *K*-d trees for short, generalize the notion of space partitioning to arbitrary, axis-aligned planes. Whereas the octree uses a regular subdivision of space, a *K*-d tree is a data structure whose interior nodes represent a partition of space along a plane which is orthogonal to one of the axes. A *K*-d tree is stored in a binary tree where interior nodes represent a partition over an axis-aligned plane and leaf nodes represent a volume in space. As well as a volumetric representation for shape, *K*-d trees are widely used for organizing points to speed up multidimensional search [3], such as nearest-neighbor searches.

For example, Fig. 4.7 shows a *K*-d tree constructed over a 3-dimensional volume (initially comprising the white boxed region). The first subdivision is shown by the red plane. Each of the two subdivided regions are then split by the green planes and finally the blue planes yield 8 leaf volumes. The canonical method of construction cycles through the axes of the space, subdividing along each in turn, before returning to the first again. So, in the example in Fig. 4.7, the next partitions would be parallel to the red plane. The position of the partitioning is chosen by the median point

Fig. 4.7 A 3D example of a K-d tree. Figure courtesy of [76]

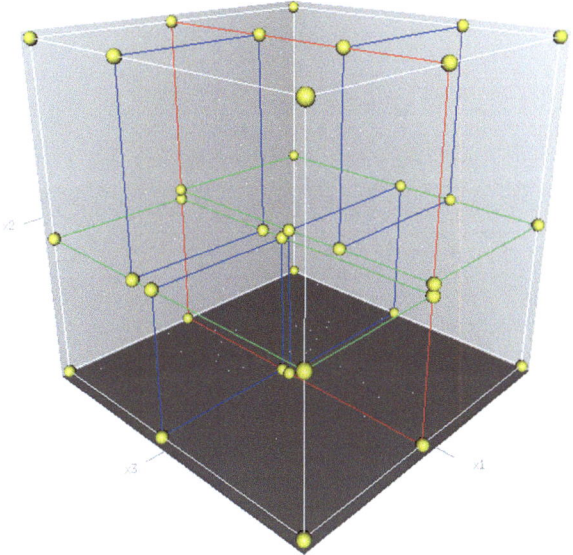

within the volume along the axis of partitioning. This strategy leads to balanced trees in which each leaf node is at the same depth.

K-d trees provide a way of reducing the complexity of nearest neighbor searches or distance-based segmentation. For example, in the problem of range searching the aim is to find all vertices which lie within a certain Euclidean distance of a target vertex (i.e. within a sphere centered on the target vertex with a radius given by the distance threshold). This is an important problem for computing local features and properties on surfaces. The brute force approach requires computation of the distance between the target vertex and all others. With a K-d tree, the volume in which the vertex lies can be found and only the distance to points within that volume need be considered. The overhead of constructing the tree becomes worthwhile when many such operations need to be performed. Note that for general range searching over a surface, the use of a distance threshold will fail for complex, highly curved surfaces (where Euclidean and geodesic distances vary greatly). In this case, it is necessary to consider vertex connectivity to ensure only connected regions of the surface are returned. This is discussed further in the next section.

4.2.3.3 Binary Space Partitioning

Binary Space Partitioning (BSP) further generalizes the notion of space partitioning to arbitrary subdivisions. Unlike the K-d tree, the cutting planes can be any orientation, thus a K-d tree is an axis-aligned BSP tree. A volume (or in 2D, an area) is represented by a series of binary tests determining which side of a plane (or in 2D, a line) a point lies on. This representation leads to a binary tree structure with the leaf nodes indicating whether a point lies inside or outside the volume

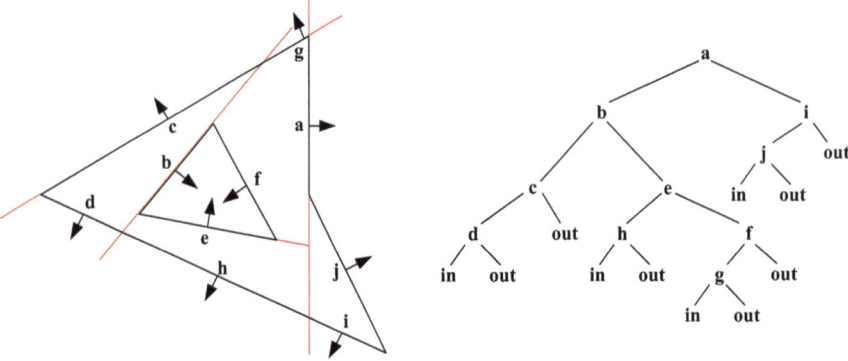

Fig. 4.8 A 2D example of a Binary Space Partitioning tree

and branching at nodes representing the outcome of the binary test. This is a simple and elegant representation on which boolean operations and point classifications are easy to compute, though it potentially results in a high memory overhead. The representation was first proposed by Fuchs et al. [16] and is a popular representation in graphics, where calculation of visible triangles from arbitrary viewpoints is required.

In Fig. 4.8, we provide an example of a BSP tree. In this case, the tree operates in 2D and hence the binary tests determine which side of each line a point lies and the resulting object is a 2D area.

4.2.3.4 Constructive Solid Geometry

Constructive Solid Geometry (CSG) [34] is a representation for solid objects based on compositions of simple primitive solids. They are combined using boolean set operations. The primitives and operations can be stored efficiently in a binary tree in which the leaves contain primitives, nodes contain operators and the represented object lies at the root. Figure 4.9 shows an example of a complex solid constructed from a small number of primitives and operations. The CSG representation is intuitive and relates well to CAD interfaces. However, representing arbitrary solids in this way can prove inefficient. In the context of 3D imaging, CSG can be useful for applications with "humans in the loop". For example, in content-based retrieval, a human must be able to construct a coarse 3D model with which to search. Another example is fitting a part-based model to 3D data (such as body parts to human motion data). In this case, the parts can be constructed by a human using CSG. Finally, for indexing 3D data, a very low-dimensional description of an object can be obtained by fitting a CSG model to the 3D data and determining similarity by comparing CSG trees.

4.2.3.5 Boundary Representations

Boundary representations (known as *B-reps*) [65] describe solids by defining the boundary between solid and non-solid. They are widely used in Computer Aided

4 Representing, Storing and Visualizing 3D Data

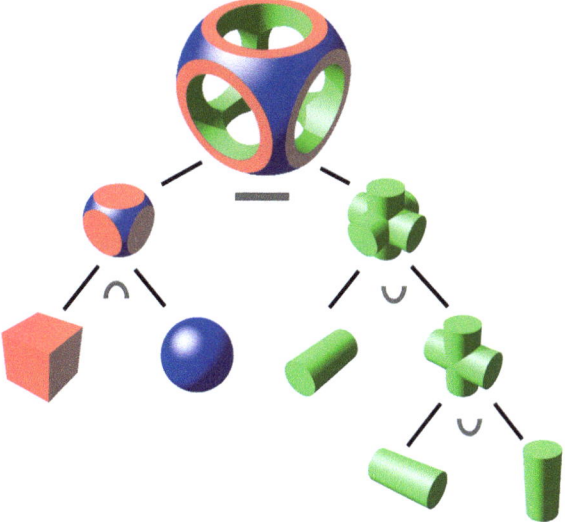

Fig. 4.9 An example of a CSG object represented by a binary tree of operations and primitives. Figure courtesy of [75]

Design. B-reps are composed of two parts. The first is the *topology*. This describes how the surface elements are connected and is specified in terms of faces, edges and vertices. See Fig. 4.10 for an example. The second part is the *geometry*, which specifies the shape of a face, edge or vertex in terms of surfaces, curves and points. A face is associated with a bounded portion of a surface and an edge with a bounded piece of a curve. The topology of a B-rep is stored in a data structure, most commonly the *winged-edge* which stores a face, edge and vertex table. Each edge stores pointers to its two vertices, the two faces adjacent to the edge and the four edges adjacent to both the edge and the adjacent faces. Each vertex and face stores a pointer to one of its adjacent edges. Adjacency relationship can therefore be computed in constant time. Compared to CSG representations, B-reps are more flexible and have a richer operation set.

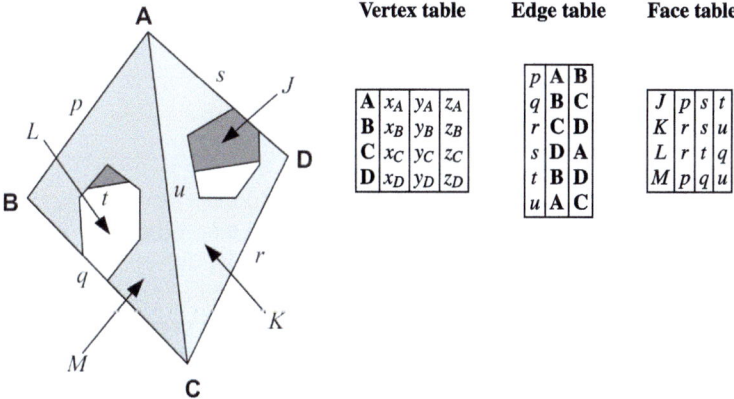

Fig. 4.10 An example of the topology of a solid described by a B-rep

4.2.4 Summary of Solid-Based Representations

The method of acquisition of 3D data determines in which of the raw representations the data is delivered. Although some operations are possible on such data (for example, point-based rendering of point clouds), most applications necessitate conversion to a higher level representation. This may require a degree of approximation, for example, integrating a depth map from surface normal data.

The choice between surface-based and solid-based representations is dictated by the nature of the data and the intended application. On the other hand, certain representations are amenable to creation and editing by hand, for example by an animator or CAD designer. The requirements here may include ease and intuition of editing operations and guarantees about the nature of the resulting surface, such as smoothness. Other factors which may influence the choice of representation include storage and processing efficiency, representational power (e.g. some representations can only describe surfaces which are manifold or continuous) and the efficiency with which the representation can be rendered for visualization.

4.3 Polygon Meshes

Polygonal meshes are of such importance and are used so ubiquitously throughout computer graphics and computer vision that we provide a more in depth discussion of the file formats and data structures available for their storage and representation. We focus particularly on triangular meshes, though the representations extend naturally to quad or arbitrary polygon meshes.

Formally, a triangular mesh of N vertices is defined as a pair: $\mathcal{M}^N = (\mathbb{K}^N, \mathbf{S})$. The topology, or connectivity, of the mesh is given by the *simplicial complex* $\mathbb{K}^N$, which is a set whose elements can be vertices $\{i\}$, edges $\{i, j\}$ or triangles $\{i, j, k\}$, with the indices $i, j, k \in [1 \ldots N]$. The actual shape of the mesh is given by the vector $\mathbf{S} \in \mathbb{R}^{3N}$, where the ith vertex is given by $\mathbf{v}_i = [S_{3i-2} \ S_{3i-1} \ S_{3i}]^T$. There is some redundancy in this representation (for example, edges can be inferred from triangles) and so not all representations store all of this information.

4.3.1 Mesh Storage

There are a wide range of open and proprietary file formats for the storage of mesh data. These can be categorized into binary and ASCII text formats. The former are more space efficient while the latter are human readable and editable. In general, these file formats all comprise a list of 3D vertices followed by a list of polygons which index into the vertex list. The files may also store vertex or face attributes such as surface normals and texture coordinates.

The most commonly used text-based formats are OBJ (originally developed by Wavefront Technologies) and VRML (Virtual Reality Modeling Language), which was designed particularly with the World Wide Web in mind. The most popular binary format is 3DS which has grown to become a *de facto* industry standard for transferring models between 3D programs. As well as 3D data, this format can also include scene properties such as lighting. Finally, the PLY format (developed at the Stanford Graphics Lab) supports both ASCII and binary storage.

As the most frequently used format for model archiving, we briefly describe the OBJ format. This is composed of up to four parts, two of which are required. The following snippet provides an example OBJ file:

```
# Vertex (x,y,z) coordinates
v 0.123 0.456 0.789
v ...
...

# Texture coordinates (u,v) coordinates
vt 0.500 0.600
vt ...
...

# Normals in (nx,ny,nz) form
vn 0.707 0.000 0.707
vn ...
...

# Face Definitions
f 1 2 3
f 3/1 4/2 5/3
f 6/4/1 3/5/3 7/6/5
f ...
...
```

Comments can appear anywhere within the file and are indicated by the line beginning with a hash symbol. The file must begin with a list of 3D vertex positions. Each is entered on a separate line, starting with "v". Then there are two optional parts: 2D texture coordinates (line begins with "vt") and 3D vertex normals (line begins with "vn"). Texture coordinates are 2D coordinates in the range [0, 1], which index into a texture map (which is typically square). Texture coordinates are scaled by the dimensions of the texture map and color values interpolated from the pixels surrounding the scaled texture coordinate position. The vertex, texture coordinate and surface normal lists should be of the same length. Texture coordinates and normals are assigned to the vertex in the corresponding position in the vertex list. The final required part comprises face definitions. Each face definition can take four possible forms, as follows:

Vertex. A valid vertex index starts from 1 and indexes into the previously defined vertex list. Faces may have more than three vertices.

```
f v1 v2 v3 v4 ...
```

Vertex/texture-coordinate. A vertex index may be followed by a texture coordinate index, separated by a slash.

```
f v1/vt1 v2/vt2 v3/vt3 ...
```

Vertex/texture-coordinate/normal. A vertex index may be followed by both a texture coordinate and surface normal index, each separated by a slash.

```
f v1/vt1/vn1 v2/vt2/vn2 v3/vt3/vn3 ...
```

Vertex/normal. A vertex index may be followed by only a surface normal index, separated by a double slash.

```
f v1//vn1 v2//vn2 v3//vn3 ...
```

An OBJ file may be augmented by a companion MTL (Material Template Library) file, which describes surface shading and material properties for the purposes of rendering.

4.3.2 Mesh Data Structures

To apply any processing to a mesh, such as rendering, manipulation or editing, we must be able to retrieve elements of the mesh and discover adjacency relationships. The most common such queries include: finding the faces/edges which are incident on a given vertex, finding the faces which border an edge, finding the edges which border a face, and finding the faces which are adjacent to a face. Mesh data structures can be classified according to how efficiently these queries can be answered. This is often traded off against storage overhead and representational power.

There are a large number of data structures available for the purpose of representing meshes. Some of the most common are summarized below.

Face list. A list of faces, each of which stores vertex positions. There is no redundancy in this representation, but connectivity between faces with shared vertices is not stored. Adjacency queries or transformations are inefficient and awkward.

Vertex-face list. A commonly used representation which is space efficient. It comprises a list of shared vertices and a list of faces, each of which stores pointers into the shared vertex list for each of its vertices. Since this is the representation used in most 3D file formats, such as OBJ, it is straightforward to load archival data into this structure.

Vertex-vertex list. A list of vertices, each containing a list to the vertices to which it is adjacent. Face and edge information is implicit and hence rendering is inefficient since it is necessary to traverse the structure to build lists of polygons. They are, however, extremely simple and are efficient when modeling complex changes in geometry [61].

Edge list. An edge list can be built from a vertex/face list in $O(M)$ time for a mesh of M faces. An edge list is useful for a number of geometric computer graphics algorithms such as computing stencil shadows.

Table 4.2 Space and time complexity of mesh data structures for a mesh of M faces and N vertices

	Vertex-face list	Vertex-vertex list	Winged-edge	Halfedge
No. pointers to store a cube	24	24	192	144
All vertices of a face	$O(1)$	$O(1)$	$O(1)$	$O(1)$
All vertices adjacent to a vertex	$O(M)$	$O(1)$	$O(1)$	$O(1)$
Both faces adjacent to an edge	$O(M)$	$O(N)$	$O(1)$	$O(1)$

Winged-edge. The best known boundary representation (B-rep). Each edge stores pointers to the two vertices at their ends, the two faces bordering them, and pointers to four of the edges connected to the end points. This structure allows edge-vertex and edge-face queries to be answered in constant time, though other adjacency queries can require more processing.

Halfedge. Also known as the FE-structure [78] or as a doubly-connected edge list (DCEL) [4], although note that the originally proposed DCEL [43] described a different data structure. The halfedge is a B-rep structure which makes explicit the notion that an edge is shared by two faces by splitting an edge into two entities. It is restricted to representing manifold surfaces. Further implementation details are given below.

Adjacency matrix. A symmetric matrix of size $N \times N$, which contains 1 if there is an edge between the corresponding vertices. Highly space inefficient for meshes but allows some operations to be performed by applying linear algebra to the adjacency matrix. This forms the basis of algebraic graph theory [5].

We provide a summary of the time and space complexity of a representative sample of mesh data structures in Table 4.2. Note that different structures that support operations with the same asymptotic complexity, may not be equally efficient in practice. For example, finding all vertices of a face using a winged-edge structure requires traversal from the face list to the edge list to the vertex list, whereas the vertex-face list structure can traverse directly from faces to vertices. Also note that, where we specify constant time, we refer to constant time per piece of information. So, for example, using a halfedge all of the edges incident on a vertex can be computed in a time which is linear in the number of edges incident on the vertex.

The halfedge structure allows all adjacency queries to be computed in constant time, while requiring only a modest overhead in storage requirements. For this reason, it is a good choice as a general purpose data structure for mesh processing. We describe the halfedge data structure in more detail in the following sections.

4.3.2.1 Halfedge Structure

The halfedge data structure comprises vertices, faces and "halfedges". Each edge in the mesh is represented by two halfedges. Conceptually, a halfedge is obtained by dividing an edge down its length. Figure 4.11 shows a small section of a mesh represented using the halfedge structure. Halfedges store pointers to the following:

Fig. 4.11 Halfedge structure

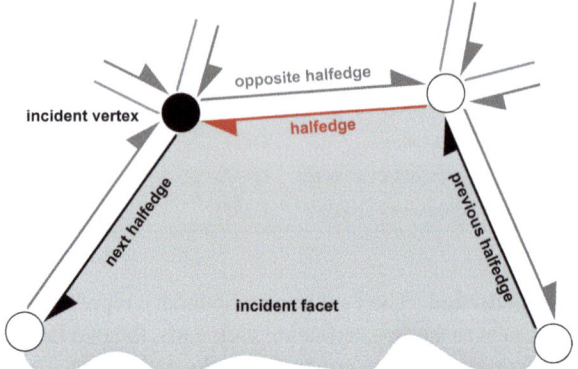

1. The next halfedge in the facet (and so they form a circularly linked list around the face).
2. Its companion "opposite" halfedge.
3. The vertex at the end of the halfedge.
4. The face that the halfedge borders.

Note that halfedges can be linked in clockwise or counterclockwise direction about a face, but this must be consistent over the mesh.

Concretely, in the C programming language, a minimal halfedge structure would be implemented as follows:

```c
struct halfedge
{
    halfedge* next;
    halfedge* opposite;
    vertex* incidentvertex;
    face* incidentfacet;
};
```

In the halfedge data structure, a vertex stores 3D position (as well as any other per-vertex information) and a pointer to one of the halfedges that uses the vertex as a starting point:

```c
struct vertex
{
    float x;
    float y;
    float z;
    // Additional per-vertex data here
    halfedge* outgoingedge;
}
```

4 Representing, Storing and Visualizing 3D Data 161

Finally, a facet stores any per-facet information (for example, face normals) and a pointer to one of the halfedges bordering the face:

```
struct face
{
    // Additional per-facet data here
    halfedge* borderedge;
}
```

With the halfedge structure to hand, traversals are achieved by simply following the appropriate pointers. In the simplest case, the vertices adjacent to an edge can be found as follows:

```
vertex* vert1 = edge->incidentvertex;
vertex* vert2 = edge->opposite->incidentvertex;
```

A similar approach can be applied for adjacent faces. Traversing the perimeter of a face is simply a case of following a circularly linked list:

```
halfedge* edge = face->borderedge;
do {
    // Process edge
    edge = edge->next;
} while (edge != face->borderedge)
```

Another useful operation is iterating over all the edges adjacent to a vertex (this is important for range searching and also for vertex deletion resulting from an edge collapse, where pointers to this vertex must be changed to point to the vertex at the other end of the deleted edge). This is implemented as follows:

```
halfedge* edge = vert->outgoingedge;
do {
    // Process edge
    edge = edge->opposite->next;
} while (edge != vert->outgoingedge)
```

Many other traversal operations can be implemented in a similar manner. In the context of range searching, edge lengths need to be considered (i.e. the Euclidean distance between adjacent vertices). Dijkstra's shortest path algorithm can be applied in this context for range searching using approximate geodesic distances or for exact geodesic distances the Fast Marching Method can be used [30]. Exercise 7 asks you to implement Dijkstra's shortest path algorithm on a halfedge structure.

4.4 Subdivision Surfaces

Subdivision surfaces are based on an iterative refinement of a base mesh according to a refinement scheme. Each iteration of the subdivision results in a mesh which is smoother than the previous. Refinement schemes are divided into two classes: *approximating* and *interpolating*. Interpolating schemes retain the positions of the original base mesh as part of the subdivided surfaces. In contrast, approximating schemes are free to adjust the positions of these vertices. Approximating schemes generally lead to smoother surfaces but allow less precise control for designers who wish to specify the exact position of control vertices.

Subdivision surfaces exhibit a number of desirable features. The base mesh provides an easily editable representation. Often a coarse base mesh is built by combining basic shapes to obtain a desired topology. Alternatively, an object may be scanned or created using NURBS surfaces. A designer may adjust vertex positions at any level of subdivision, using a visualization of the limit surface to guide vertex placement. This allows gross or fine-scale refinements to be made to the surface, which are then reflected at lower levels of subdivision. Another important feature, for both aesthetic and engineering reasons, is the guarantees that subdivision surfaces can provide about surface continuity. Finally, they can be efficiently displayed, even allowing interactive editing.

In the context of 3D imaging, subdivision surfaces provide an ideal representation for storing and interacting with 3D data, due to their space efficiency and ease of editing. However, a prerequisite step is to fit a subdivision surface to 3D data. This is a difficult problem on which much research has focussed. Popular approaches include that of Litke et al. [38], which is based on quasi-interpolation and that of Takeuchi et al. [67], which uses surface simplification to construct a control mesh. Subdivision surfaces can also be used to upsample low resolution sensed data by using measured vertices as control points and a subdivision scheme to interpolate a smooth surface.

One of the key developments in subdivision surfaces was to show that the limit surface could be efficiently evaluated directly without having to apply the iterative subdivision process. Stam [64] showed that a subdivision surface and all its derivatives can be evaluated in terms of a set of eigenbasis functions, which depend only on the subdivision scheme.

We describe the two most popular approximating schemes due to Doo and Sabin [13] and Catmull and Clark [12], which can operate on quadrilateral meshes. We also describe the approximating scheme proposed by Loop [39], which operates on triangular meshes. Popular interpolating schemes include butterfly scheme, refined by Zorin et al. [80], and the method of Kobbelt [31].

4.4.1 Doo-Sabin Scheme

Commencing with a mesh of N vertices, $\mathcal{M}^N = (\mathbb{K}^N, \mathbf{S})$, an iteration of the Doo-Sabin subdivision scheme proceeds as follows:

4 Representing, Storing and Visualizing 3D Data

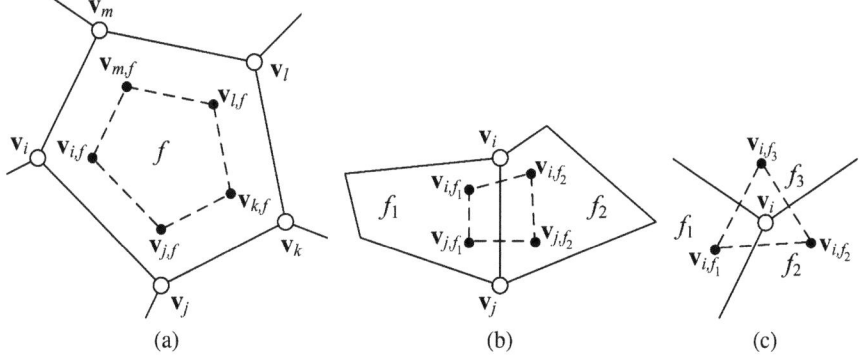

Fig. 4.12 Creation of (**a**) F-face, (**b**) E-face and (**c**) V-face in the Doo-Sabin subdivision scheme

1. Every vertex v_i, where $\{i\} \in \mathbb{K}^N$, yields a new vertex, $v_{i,f}$, for every face $f = \{i, j, k, \ldots\} \in \mathbb{K}^N$ that has v_i as a vertex. This is known as the *image of* v_i *in* f.
2. The position of $v_{i,f}$ can be computed using a number of different rules. A simple scheme sets $v_{i,f}$ to the midpoint of the centroid of f and the vertex position v_i, i.e.

$$v_{i,f} = \frac{c_f + v_i}{2}, \qquad (4.9)$$

where

$$c_f = \frac{1}{\|f\|} \sum_{j \in f} v_j. \qquad (4.10)$$

3. Image vertices are connected to form three kinds of new face, the first of which is an F-face. An F-face is a smaller version of an original face, $f = \{i, j, k, \ldots\} \in \mathbb{K}^N$, formed by connecting the image vertices of the vertices of f, i.e. $v_{i,f}, v_{j,f}, v_{k,f}, \ldots$. If f is an n-sided face then so is the resulting F-face. This process is shown in Fig. 4.12(a).
4. The second type of new face is an E-face. For every edge $\{i, j\} \in \mathbb{K}^N$ shared by two vertices f_1 and f_2, a new rectangular face is formed from the four image vertices created from the endpoints of the edge, i.e. v_{i,f_1}, v_{i,f_2}, v_{j,f_1} and v_{j,f_2}. This process is shown in Fig. 4.12(b).
5. The final type of new face is a V-face. For every vertex $\{i\} \in \mathbb{K}^N$, a new face is created by connecting the image vertices of v_i in all faces to which v_i is adjacent. If v_i has degree n then the new V-face is n-sided. This process is shown in Fig. 4.12(c).

To summarize, the subdivided mesh will comprise a quadrilateral for each edge in the original mesh, an n-sided polygon for each n-sided polygon in the original mesh and an n-sided polygon for each degree-n vertex in the original mesh. An example of applying the Doo-Sabin scheme to a quadrilateral mesh is shown in Fig. 4.13. After one round of subdivision, all vertices have degree four. Hence subsequent divisions

Fig. 4.13 Two iterations of the Doo-Sabin subdivision scheme applied to a T-shaped quadrilateral base mesh. Extraordinary points are shown in *blue* (reprinted public domain figure)

will create quadrilateral V-faces. Non-quadrilateral faces after one subdivision become *extraordinary points* in the limit surface. The limit surface is C^1 continuous, except at extraordinary points.

4.4.2 Catmull-Clark Scheme

Commencing with a mesh of N vertices, $\mathcal{M}^N = (\mathbb{K}^N, \mathbf{S})$, an iteration of the Catmull-Clark subdivision scheme proceeds as follows:

1. For each face $f = \{i, j, \dots\} \in \mathbb{K}^N$, add a new vertex to the mesh (known as a *face point*) with a position given by the centroid of the vertices of the face:

$$\mathbf{v}_f = \frac{1}{\|f\|} \sum_{i \in f} \mathbf{v}_i. \tag{4.11}$$

2. For each edge $e = \{i, j\} \in \mathbb{K}^N$ with adjacent faces f_1 and f_2, add a new vertex to the mesh (known as an *edge point*) with a position given by the average of the edge end points and adjacent face points:

$$\mathbf{v}_e = \frac{1}{4}(\mathbf{v}_i + \mathbf{v}_j + \mathbf{v}_{f_1} + \mathbf{v}_{f_2}). \tag{4.12}$$

The original edge is replaced by two new edges connected to the edge point.
3. Add edges from every edge point $\mathbf{v}_e$ to their adjacent face points, $\mathbf{v}_{f_1}$ and $\mathbf{v}_{f_2}$.
4. For each original point $\mathbf{v}_i$, where $\{i\} \in \mathbb{K}^N$, compute a new position:

$$\mathbf{v}_i^{\text{new}} = \frac{\hat{\mathbf{v}}_f + 2\hat{\mathbf{v}}_e + (F - 3)\mathbf{v}_i}{F}, \tag{4.13}$$

where $\hat{\mathbf{v}}_f$ is the average of the F face points adjacent to the original point and $\hat{\mathbf{v}}_e$ is the average of the edge points adjacent to the original point.

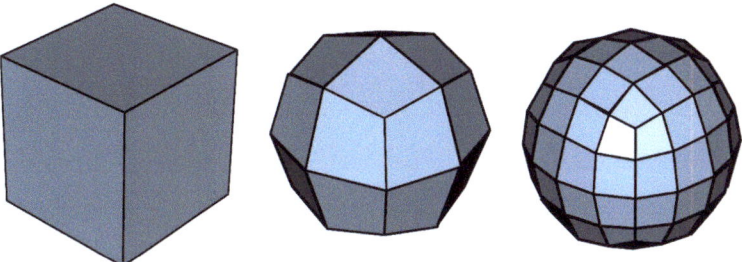

Fig. 4.14 Two iterations of the Catmull-Clark subdivision scheme applied to a cube base mesh. Figure adapted from [74]

The subdivided mesh is composed of quadrilaterals (see Fig. 4.14). In general these will not be planar surfaces. The number of vertices with a degree other than four remains constant over iterations of the subdivision process. These are known as *extraordinary points*. The limit surface can be shown to be $\mathbb{C}^2$ continuous everywhere except at extraordinary vertices, where it is $\mathbb{C}^1$ continuous.

4.4.3 Loop Scheme

Unlike the previous two subdivision schemes, Loop's method operates only on triangular meshes. Commencing with a triangular mesh of N vertices, $\mathcal{M}^N = (\mathbb{K}^N, \mathbf{S})$, an iteration of Loop's scheme proceeds as follows:

1. For every edge $e = \{i, j\} \in \mathbb{K}^N$ a new vertex $\mathbf{v}_e$ is created as a linear combination of the four vertices comprising the two faces, $f_1 = \{i, j, k_1\}$ and $f_2 = \{i, j, k_2\}$, which are adjacent to the edge as shown in Fig. 4.15(a). They are combined using the following weights:

$$\mathbf{v}_e = \frac{1}{8}\mathbf{v}_{k_1} + \frac{1}{8}\mathbf{v}_{k_2} + \frac{3}{8}\mathbf{v}_i + \frac{3}{8}\mathbf{v}_j. \quad (4.14)$$

2. The position of each original point is adjusted according to its existing position and those of its adjacent vertices, as shown in Fig. 4.15(b). For each original point $\mathbf{v}_i$, where $\{i\} \in \mathbb{K}^N$, the new position is given by:

$$\mathbf{v}_i^{\text{new}} = \alpha \left(\sum_{j \in \text{Adj}(i)} \mathbf{v}_j \right) + (1 - d_i \alpha) \mathbf{v}_i, \quad (4.15)$$

where $\text{Adj}(i) = \{j | \{i, j\} \in \mathbb{K}^N\}$ is the set of vertices adjacent to $\mathbf{v}_i$. The constant α is determined by the degree $d_i = \|\text{Adj}(i)\|$ and there are many variations

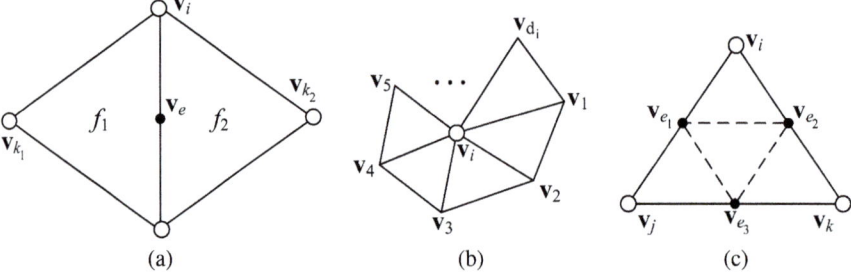

Fig. 4.15 Loop subdivision scheme: (**a**) creation of an edge vertex; (**b**) calculating new position for original points; (**c**) triangulation of new edge points

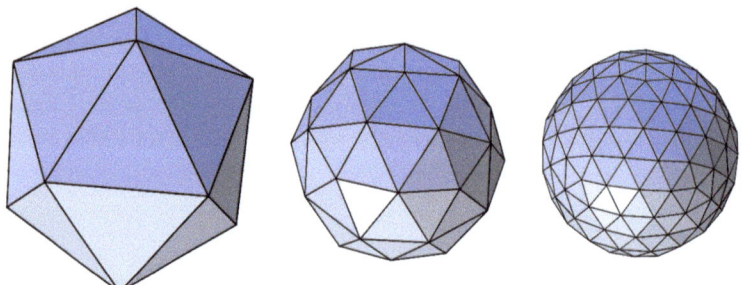

Fig. 4.16 Two iterations of the Loop subdivision scheme applied to an icosahedron base mesh. Figure adapted from [77]

available. The simplest choice is:

$$\alpha = \begin{cases} \frac{3}{16} & \text{if } d_i = 3, \\ \frac{1}{d_i}[\frac{5}{8} - (\frac{3}{8} + \frac{1}{4}\cos\frac{2\pi}{d_i})^2] & \text{if } d_i > 3. \end{cases} \quad (4.16)$$

3. The subdivided surface is given by connecting the new edge vertices and the updated original vertices as shown in Fig. 4.15(c).

After one subdivision, all vertices have degree six except those which were in the original mesh and had a degree other than six. These are the extraordinary vertices. The limit surface is C^2 continuous except at the extraordinary vertices. Figure 4.16 shows loop subdivision applied to an icosahedron base mesh.

4.5 Local Differential Properties

Many useful 3D data processing operations require the computation of local differential properties of a surface. These range from the construction of local features such as spin images [26] to the computation of geodesic paths over a manifold [30].

However, most surface representations are discrete and contain only an approximate sampling of the underlying surface. The nature of the representation determines the manner in which these properties are computed.

First order properties of the surface (normal vector and tangent plane) are most commonly used for shading (since surface reflectance is a function of orientation). Interpolation shading uses interpolated surface normals to allow a polygonal approximation of a smooth surface to appear smooth when rendered (see Fig. 4.21(g)). Second order properties (principal curvatures and directions) are often used for local characterization of the surface topology, for example the shape index [32]. Occasionally, even third order properties (directional derivatives of the principal curvatures) can be useful.

For surfaces described in functional form (such as implicit surfaces), differential properties can be computed analytically using differential calculus. On the other hand, discrete representations require the assumption that the underlying surface is smooth and differential properties can only be approximated. Such operators should converge asymptotically to the true result as the sampling density increases.

4.5.1 Surface Normals

For uniformly sampled representations such as voxels and depth maps, differential properties can easily be approximated using finite differences which consider adjacent pixels or voxels, corresponding to the local neighborhood about a point. For example, in the simplest case, the surface gradients in the x and y-directions of a surface represented as a discrete depth map, $z(x, y)$, can be approximated using single forward differences:

$$\partial_x z(x, y) \approx \frac{z(x + 1, y) - z(x, y)}{\delta_x}, \quad \partial_y z(x, y) \approx \frac{z(x, y + 1) - z(x, y)}{\delta_y}, \quad (4.17)$$

where δ_x and δ_y are the spacings on the pixel array. The surface normal vector is then given by:

$$\mathbf{n}(x, y) = \frac{[\partial_x z(x, y) \partial_y z(x, y) 1]^T}{\|[\partial_x z(x, y) \partial_y z(x, y) 1]^T\|}. \quad (4.18)$$

Note that computing gradients using only forward differences results in high sensitivity to noise. For this reason, a window about each pixel can be used in conjunction with an appropriate filter to provide a more stable estimate of the gradients [45].

In the case of an arbitrary triangular mesh, such a simple approach is not possible. If the surface is truly piecewise planar, then it is enough to associate a *face normal* with each triangular facet. For a face composed of vertices $\mathbf{v}_1$, $\mathbf{v}_2$ and $\mathbf{v}_3$, the face normal is given by:

$$\mathbf{n}_f = \frac{(\mathbf{v}_1 - \mathbf{v}_2) \times (\mathbf{v}_1 - \mathbf{v}_3)}{\|(\mathbf{v}_1 - \mathbf{v}_2) \times (\mathbf{v}_1 - \mathbf{v}_3)\|}. \quad (4.19)$$

Fig. 4.17 Computation of vertex normal by averaging adjacent face normals

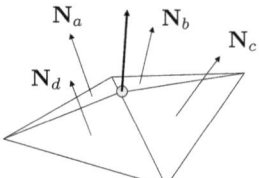

For the normal to be directed to the outside of the object, the vertices must be ordered in an anticlockwise sense when viewed from the outside.

More commonly, the underlying surface is assumed smooth and the surface normal is approximated at each vertex. There are a number of alternative approaches to computing vertex normals [25], which are based on weighted averages of the adjacent facet normals (see Fig. 4.17).

Consider a vertex whose incident edges in anticlockwise order are given by the sequence $\langle \mathbf{e}_1, \ldots, \mathbf{e}_n \rangle$. The first edge is repeated at the end of the sequence so $\mathbf{e}_1 = \mathbf{e}_n$. The most well known method which is very efficient to compute uses triangle areas as weights. The area weighted normal to a facet defined by edges $\mathbf{e}_i$ and $\mathbf{e}_{i+1}$ is given simply by $\mathbf{e}_i \times \mathbf{e}_{i+1}$. Hence, the area weighted vertex normal is:

$$\mathbf{n}_v^{\text{Area}} = \sum_{i=1}^{n-1} \mathbf{e}_i \times \mathbf{e}_{i+1}. \tag{4.20}$$

Note that this result requires normalization back to unit length. The efficiency of this approach lies in the fact that the cross product computation factors in the area weight at no extra computational cost. In particular, no trigonometric calculations are required. The downside to this approach is that a triangle with large area but small angle between the edges incident on the vertex contributes disproportionately to the result. This can lead to highly inaccurate normals under certain circumstances and the result depends heavily on the mesh triangulation (see [41] for an example).

An alternative, originally proposed by Thürmer and Wüthrich [70] uses the angle between pairs of edges incident on a vertex as the weight:

$$\mathbf{n}_v^{\text{Angle}} = \sum_{i=1}^{n-1} \arccos\left(\frac{\mathbf{e}_i \cdot \mathbf{e}_{i+1}}{\|\mathbf{e}_i\| \|\mathbf{e}_{i+1}\|} \right) \frac{\mathbf{e}_i \times \mathbf{e}_{i+1}}{\|\mathbf{e}_i \times \mathbf{e}_{i+1}\|}. \tag{4.21}$$

Again, the result requires normalization. This approach is relatively simple and accurate but requires trigonometric calculations so is unsuitable for applications involving real-time computation of vertex normals (for example interactive rendering of a deforming surface).

A method proposed by Max [41] offers a compromise. It does not require trigonometric calculations, but is more stable in the special cases where area weighting performs badly. The weight is comprised of the sine of the angle between edge vectors and the edge length reciprocal:

$$\mathbf{n}_v^{Max} = \sum_{i=1}^{n-1} \frac{\sin\alpha_i}{\|\mathbf{e}_i\|\|\mathbf{e}_{i+1}\|} \frac{\mathbf{e}_i \times \mathbf{e}_{i+1}}{\|\mathbf{e}_i \times \mathbf{e}_{i+1}\|}, \quad (4.22)$$

where

$$\sin\alpha_i = \frac{\|\mathbf{e}_i \times \mathbf{e}_{i+1}\|}{\|\mathbf{e}_i\|\|\mathbf{e}_{i+1}\|}. \quad (4.23)$$

Which simplifies to:

$$\mathbf{n}_v^{Max} = \sum_{i=1}^{n-1} \frac{\mathbf{e}_i \times \mathbf{e}_{i+1}}{\|\mathbf{e}_i\|^2\|\mathbf{e}_{i+1}\|^2}. \quad (4.24)$$

Again, the result requires normalization. The derivation follows from an assumption of a locally spherical surface. For meshes representing surfaces which are exactly locally spherical, the result is exact.

4.5.2 Differential Coordinates and the Mesh Laplacian

When a surface is represented using a mesh, a transformation can be made to differential coordinates (δ-coordinates), which provides an alternate route to the computation of differential surface properties as well as a useful representation for other operations (including mesh compression). This is most easily accomplished when the mesh is stored in an adjacency matrix. A vertex $\mathbf{v}_i$, $\{i\} \in \mathbb{K}^N$ which is a member of the mesh $\mathcal{M}^N = (\mathbb{K}^N, \mathbf{S})$ may be represented in terms of δ-coordinates. This representation describes the difference between the absolute position of the vertex and the center of mass of its adjacent vertices:

$$\delta_i = \begin{bmatrix} \delta_i^x & \delta_i^y & \delta_i^z \end{bmatrix}^T = \mathbf{v}_i - \frac{1}{\|\mathrm{Adj}(i)\|} \sum_{j \in \mathrm{Adj}(i)} \mathbf{v}_j. \quad (4.25)$$

$d_i = \|\mathrm{Adj}(i)\|$ is the degree of the vertex i. This transformation can be represented in matrix form. Given the mesh adjacency matrix $\mathbf{A}$, where

$$A_{ij} = \begin{cases} 1 & \text{if } \{i, j\} \in \mathbb{K}^N \\ 0 & \text{otherwise,} \end{cases} \quad (4.26)$$

and the diagonal degree matrix, $\mathbf{D}$, where $D_{ii} = d_i$, the *graph Laplacian matrix* (sometimes called the *topological Laplacian*) is defined by $\mathbf{L} = \mathbf{D} - \mathbf{A}$, i.e.

$$L_{ij} = \begin{cases} d_i & \text{if } i = j \\ -1 & \text{if } \{i, j\} \in \mathbb{K}^N \\ 0 & \text{otherwise.} \end{cases} \quad (4.27)$$

Fig. 4.18 The angles used in the cotangent weights scheme for surface normal computation

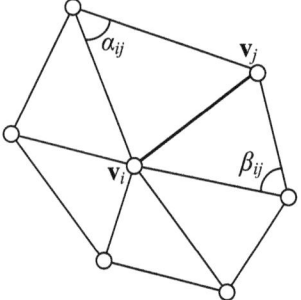

The Laplacian relates absolute and differential coordinates as follows: If the long vector $\mathbf{x} \in \mathbb{R}^N$ contains the x coordinates of the vertices then $\mathsf{L}\mathbf{x} = \mathsf{D}\delta^x$, where $\delta^x \in \mathbb{R}^N$ is a long vector of the x components of the differential coordinates of the vertices. Similarly for the y and z coordinates. Note that spectral analysis of the Laplacian can be used to perform signal processing operations on an irregularly triangulated mesh [68].

From differential geometry it is known that an infinitesimal curvilinear integral about a point on a smooth surface is related to the mean curvature $H(\mathbf{v}_i)$ at $\mathbf{v}_i$ and the surface normal $\mathbf{n}_i$:

$$\lim_{|\gamma| \to 0} \frac{1}{|\gamma|} \int_{\mathbf{v} \in \gamma} (\mathbf{v}_i - \mathbf{v}) dl(\mathbf{v}) = -H(\mathbf{v}_i)\mathbf{n}_i, \qquad (4.28)$$

where γ is a closed simple surface curve $l(\mathbf{v})$ around $\mathbf{v}_i$. By rewriting the differential coordinate vector, it can be seen that a discrete approximation to this integral can be made:

$$\frac{1}{\|\mathrm{Adj}(i)\|} \sum_{j \in \mathrm{Adj}(i)} (\mathbf{v}_i - \mathbf{v}_j) \approx -H(\mathbf{v}_i)\mathbf{n}_i. \qquad (4.29)$$

Hence, the direction of the differential coordinate vector approximates the surface normal and the magnitude is proportional to the mean curvature [68]. This provides an alternative means to surface normal calculation for a mesh which is motivated by differential geometry. A final alternative proposed by Meyer et al. [42] is based on *cotangent weights*:

$$\delta_i^{\mathrm{cot}} = \frac{1}{|\Omega_i|} \sum_{j \in \mathrm{Adj}(i)} \frac{1}{2}(\cot \alpha_{ij} + \cot \beta_{ij})(\mathbf{v}_i - \mathbf{v}_j), \qquad (4.30)$$

where $|\Omega_i|$ is the size of the Voronoi cell of i and α_{ij} and β_{ij} denote the two angles opposite the edge $\{i, j\}$ (see Fig. 4.18).

4.6 Compression and Levels of Detail

Broadly speaking, the storage requirements for 3D data can be reduced in two ways: storing a 3D representation in less space (compression) or deriving a lower resolution representation that approximates the original data. We have already seen some representations that lead to space efficient storage of 3D data. For example, subdivision surfaces require only the storage of a low resolution base mesh and subdivision rule, while the octree representation uses adaptive resolution depending on the complexity of the volume. Compression of 3D data in general [1, 49] is a more challenging problem than is solved by the relatively mature technologies available for compression of audio, image and video data. Techniques for 3D data compression can be categorized into three classes of approach:

Mesh-based methods. These methods involve traversal of a polygonal mesh and encoding of the mesh structure in a manner that can be compressed. An example of such an approach is *topological surgery* [69]. This method proceeds by quantizing vertex positions within the desired accuracy. A vertex spanning tree is then used to predict the position of each vertex from 2, 3 or 4 of its ancestors in the tree. Finally, the correction vectors required to recover the original positions are entropy encoded. Another popular approach is based on a spectral analysis of the mesh Laplacian [27]. An eigendecomposition of the Laplacian matrix (see Sect. 4.5.2) yields an orthonormal set of basis vectors onto which the geometry signals (vectors of x, y and z components) can be projected. By discarding high frequency components of the decomposition (i.e. those eigenvectors with small eigenvalues), the mesh can be compressed such that only high frequency detail is lost.

Progressive and hierarchical methods. We have already seen subdivision surfaces that fall into this category. Another important approach is the *compressed progressive mesh* [24]. In the original progressive mesh, a mesh is encoded as a form of reverse simplification. The opposite of an edge collapse operation is a vertex split, in which a vertex is divided into two and additional edges and faces are added to the mesh. A progressive mesh represents a high resolution mesh as a series of vertex split operations starting from a base mesh. Although this allows progressive transmission of increasingly detailed mesh data, there is a storage overhead, which means space requirements increase. Pajarola and Rossignac [47] showed how this representation can be compressed.

Imaged-based methods. A 3D surface may be represented in image space. This can either be native to the representation (in the case of a range image or bump map) or via a process known as surface parameterization or surface flattening [59]. Once represented as an image, any existing image compression algorithm may be applied to the data. However, it is important to note that the objectives of lossy image compression may not yield correspondingly high quality results in the surface domain since the redundancies in the two data sources may not be the same. One example of an image-based approach is *geometry images* [20]. Geometry is captured as a 2D array of quantized points. To transform a mesh to this representation, an arbitrary mesh is cut along a network of edge paths and the resulting single chart is parameterized onto a square. Face connectivity is implicit in the representation and bump maps or texture can be stored in the same parameterization. Compressing the resulting data using an image wavelet-encoder allows dramatic reductions in storage requirements without severely affecting the resulting geometry.

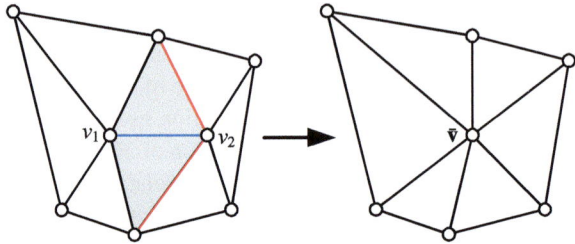

Fig. 4.19 An edge collapse operation

As suggested above, an alternative to using compression to store a high resolution mesh in less space is to derive a lower resolution mesh which approximates the original. This is known as mesh simplification and is described in the following section.

4.6.1 Mesh Simplification

Mesh simplification or *mesh decimation* is the process of iteratively removing vertices, edges and faces from a mesh to reduce its complexity and storage requirements. As well as reducing storage requirements by removing redundant structures, simplified meshes can also be processed or rendered more efficiently. Most mesh simplification algorithms proceed using iterative edge collapse.

4.6.1.1 Edge Collapse

A pair contraction $(\mathbf{v}_1, \mathbf{v}_2) \to \bar{\mathbf{v}}$, transforms a pair of vertices $\mathbf{v}_1$ and $\mathbf{v}_2$ to a new position $\bar{\mathbf{v}}$, connects all their incident edges to $\mathbf{v}_1$ and deletes the vertex $\mathbf{v}_2$. Any edges or faces which became degenerate after the contraction are removed. An example is shown in Fig. 4.19.

Starting with the original high resolution mesh $\mathcal{M}^N = (\mathbb{K}^N, \mathbf{S})$, a sequence of pair contractions is applied until the simplification goals are satisfied (for example, the target number of vertices is reached). Each contraction corresponds to a local incremental modification of the complex $\mathbb{K}^N$ and shape vectors $\mathbf{S}$. The algorithm generates a sequence of meshes $\mathcal{M}^N, \mathcal{M}^{N-1}, \mathcal{M}^{N-2}, \ldots$ with decreasing resolution.

In general, only *edge* pairs are considered valid for contraction, i.e. where $\{i, j\} \in \mathbb{K}^N$. When an edge is contracted: $(\mathbf{v}_i, \mathbf{v}_j) \to \bar{\mathbf{v}}_{ij}$, the simplicial complex, $\mathbb{K}^N$, describing the mesh topology is modified. Degenerate faces (those that no longer have 3 distinct vertices) and duplicate edges are removed as well as the collapsed edge and redundant vertex j:

$$\mathbb{K}^{N-1} = \mathbb{K}^N \setminus \{\{j\}, \{i, j\}, \{j, k\}, \{i, j, k\} : \{i, j, k\} \in \mathbb{K}^N\}. \tag{4.31}$$

The shape vector of each individual mesh is also modified as the result of an edge collapse. The vertex $\mathbf{v}_j$ is deleted and $\mathbf{v}_i$ is moved to $\bar{\mathbf{v}}_{ij}$.

4.6.1.2 Quadric Error Metric

Edge collapse algorithms operate by selecting the next edge for collapse as the one whose deletion will result in the least increase in error. The choice of error measure determines the nature of the simplification. For example, it may seek to preserve volume or surface orientation. The most successful and widely used error measure is based on the *Quadric Error Metric* (QEM), as proposed by Garland and Heckbert [18] in their QSlim algorithm.

Each vertex is a solution of a set of triangles (planes), which meet at that vertex. Hence we can define the error of the vertex with respect to this set as the sum of squared distances to each triangle. Given a triangular plane $\mathbf{p}$ defined by the equation $ax + by + cz + d = 0$, where $\mathbf{n} = [a, b, c]$ is the plane normal and d is a scalar constant. A fundamental quadric is defined as

$$Q = \left(\mathbf{n}\mathbf{n}^T, d\mathbf{n}, d^2\right) = (\mathbf{A}, \mathbf{b}, c), \tag{4.32}$$

where $\mathbf{A}$ is a 3×3 matrix, $\mathbf{b}$ is a 3-vector and c is a scalar. The quadric Q assigns a value $Q(\mathbf{v})$ to every point in space $\mathbf{v}$ by the second order equation

$$Q(\mathbf{v}) = \mathbf{v}^T \mathbf{A} \mathbf{v} + 2\mathbf{b}^T \mathbf{v} + c. \tag{4.33}$$

Note that the level surface $Q(\mathbf{v}) = \varepsilon$, which is a set of all points whose error with respect to Q is ε, is a quadratic surface. Also the value of this quadratic $Q(\mathbf{v})$ is precisely the squared distance of $\mathbf{v}$ to a given plane. The addition of quadrics can be naturally defined component-wise: $Q_1(\mathbf{v}) + Q_2(\mathbf{v}) = (Q_1 + Q_2)(\mathbf{v})$ where $(Q_1 + Q_2) = (\mathbf{A}_1 + \mathbf{A}_2, \mathbf{b}_1 + \mathbf{b}_2, c_1 + c_2)$. Thus, given a set of fundamental quadrics, determined by a set of planes, the quadric error at each vertex $\mathbf{v}_i$ is completely determined by

$$E_{Q_i}(\mathbf{v}_i) = \sum_p Q_p(\mathbf{v}_i) = Q_i(\mathbf{v}_i), \tag{4.34}$$

where $Q_i = \sum_p Q_p$ is the sum of the fundamental quadrics of all the planes incident on a vertex $\mathbf{v}_i$. Using this additive rule, for an edge collapse $(\mathbf{v}_i, \mathbf{v}_j) \to \bar{\mathbf{v}}_{ij}$, we can associate a quadric Q_{i+j} which approximates the error at $\bar{\mathbf{v}}_{ij}$, where $Q_{i+j} = Q_i + Q_j$. This simple additive rule is one of the reasons for the efficiency of this approach.

When considering the contraction of an edge $(\mathbf{v}_i, \mathbf{v}_j)$, we need to determine the target position $\bar{\mathbf{v}}_{ij}$. We select the optimum position $(\bar{\mathbf{v}})$ as the one that minimizes Eq. (4.33). Since Eq. (4.33) is a quadratic, finding its minimum is a linear problem. Taking partial derivatives of Eq. (4.33)

$$\nabla Q(\bar{\mathbf{v}}) - 2\mathbf{A}\bar{\mathbf{v}} + 2\mathbf{b}. \tag{4.35}$$

Solving for $\nabla Q(\bar{\mathbf{v}}) = 0$, we find the optimum position to be

$$\bar{\mathbf{v}} = -\mathbf{A}^{-1}\mathbf{b}. \tag{4.36}$$

Finally, after removal of t vertices the next edge to be collapsed is chosen as the one with minimal quadric error:

$$\{i^*, j^*\} = \arg\min_{\{i,j\}\in \mathbb{K}^{N-t}} Q_{i+j}(\bar{\mathbf{v}}_{ij}). \tag{4.37}$$

Note that the algorithm is implemented efficiently by placing edges onto a priority queue. Priority is determined by the QEM for each edge. After each edge collapse, the QEM scores of edges sharing vertices with either end of the collapsed edge are updated (using the simple additive rule given above). Since an edge collapse is constant time complexity, the whole simplification is $O(n\log n)$, where the $\log n$ term corresponds to removing an edge from the queue. There are some additional technical considerations such as the preservation of an object boundary which are described in detail in the thesis of Garland [17].

4.6.2 QEM Simplification Summary

The QEM simplification algorithm is summarized as follows:

1. Compute quadrics for all triangles in the mesh (Eq. (4.32)).
2. Compute errors associated with all edges $\{i, j\}$: $Q_{i+j}(\bar{\mathbf{v}}_{ij})$ and place edge errors on a priority queue.
3. Delete edge with minimal error from priority queue, contract edge in mesh structure (removing redundant vertices and faces) and update QEM scores for adjacent edges.
4. If simplification goals are not met, go to step 3.

4.6.3 Surface Simplification Results

In Fig. 4.20, we show results of applying the QEM simplification algorithm to a mesh containing 172,974 vertices. The original mesh is shown on the left. The middle image shows the surface after edges have been collapsed until the number of vertices has been reduced by 80 % (to 34,595 vertices). Notice that there is almost no visual degradation of the rendering despite the large decrease in resolution. On the right, the original mesh has been simplified until the number of vertices has been reduced by 90 % (17,296 vertices remain).

4.7 Visualization

To enable humans to explore, edit and process 3D data, we require a means of visualization. The visualization of data in general is a broad and important topic

Fig. 4.20 Simplification results using the Quadric Error Metric. From *left* to *right*: original mesh (172,974 vertices), simplified by 80 % (34,595 vertices) and simplified by 90 % (17,296 vertices)

[29, 54] with applications in statistics and applications to scientific and medical datasets. Visualizing 3D data in particular has attracted considerable research attention, specifically where the aim is to create realistic renderings. This has been the target of computer graphics for many decades [51]. However, visualization in general encompasses a broader set of aims beyond only simulating the physics of real world image formation. For example, we may wish to navigate massive and complex datasets [71] where only a small fraction can be observed at any one time. Alternatively, our dataset may be volumetric and acquired in slices [37]. Such data can either be viewed as 2D images, formed by sampling over a plane that intersects the dataset, or rendered as 3D surfaces by applying surface fitting techniques to the raw data.

Many free tools exist for the visualization of data. In the domain of mesh data, these include *MeshLab* and *Graphite*, while for volumetric data include *MicroView*. In Fig. 4.21 we demonstrate some of the most common means of visualizing 3D mesh data. We begin by plotting vertices as 2D points, i.e. a point cloud. Although difficult to interpret, such visualizations can be used with raw data and give an overview of sampling density. In (b) and (c) we draw only edges, in the latter case only drawing edges which are not occluded by other faces. This gives an impression of a solid model and is easier to interpret than the raw wireframe. In (d) we show the object projected to a 2D depth map where darker indicates further away. Note that the depth data appears smooth and it is difficult to visualize small surface features when rendered in this way. In (e) we plot the vertex normals at each vertex as a blue line. Note that we use a simplified version of the surface here in order to be able to draw all of the vertex normals. In (f) we plot the principal curvature directions for the same simplified mesh as blue and red vectors. In (g) we show a smooth-shaded rendering of the original high resolution data. By varying material properties and illumination, this is the classical rendering approach used in computer graphics. In (h) we show a flat shaded rendering of the low resolution version of the mesh. In this case, triangles are shaded with a constant color which destroys the effect of a smooth surface. However, this view can be useful for inspecting the geometry of the surface without the deceptive effect of interpolation shading. Finally, in (i) we show an example of coloring the surface according to the output of a function, in

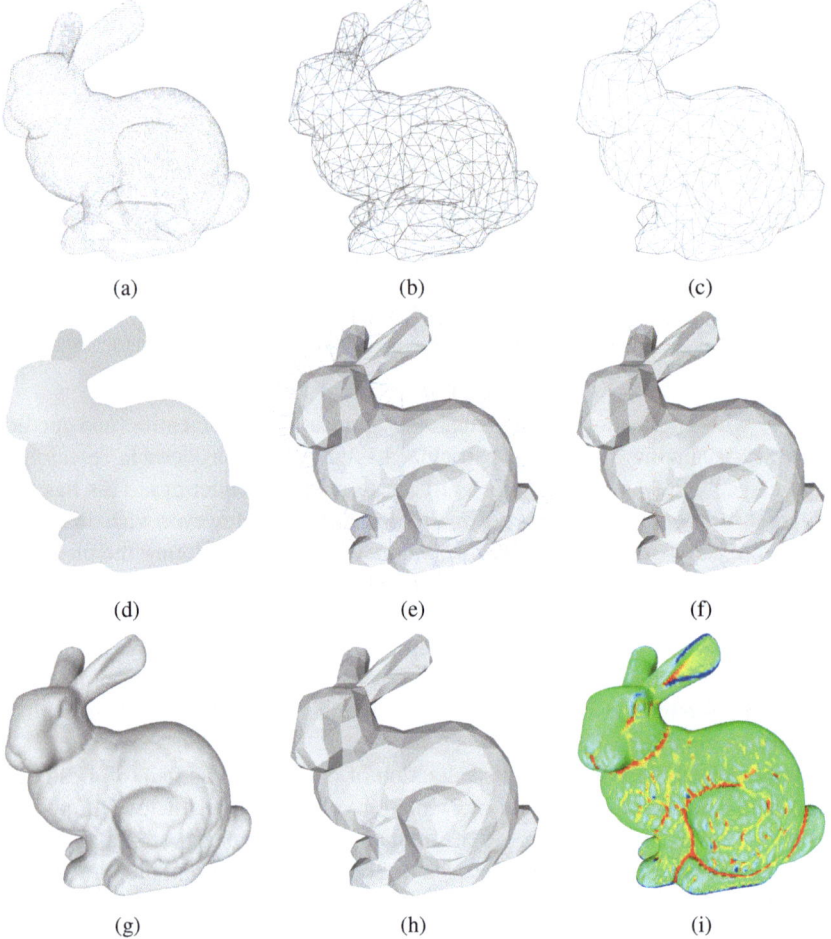

Fig. 4.21 Visualization examples for mesh data: (**a**) point cloud, (**b**) wireframe, (**c**) wireframe with hidden surfaces removed, (**d**) depth map (*darker* indicates further away), (**e**) vertex normals drawn in *blue*, (**f**) principal curvature directions drawn in *red* and *blue*, (**g**) *smooth shaded*, (**h**) *flat shaded*, (**i**) surface color heat mapped to represent function value (in this case mean curvature)

this case mean curvature. This visualization can be useful for many surface analysis tasks. Note that the extreme red and blue values follow the lines of high curvature.

4.8 Research Challenges

Although the representation, storage and visualization of 3D data has been considered for many decades, there are still some major challenges to be faced. On the one hand, the size of 3D datasets is continuing to grow as sensing technology improves (e.g. the resolution of medical imaging devices) and we begin to process large sequences of dynamic data (acquired through 4D capture) or databases of meshes. Large databases arise in applications such as 3D face recognition where fine surface detail is required to distinguish faces, yet many millions of subjects may be enrolled in the database. Not only must the database be stored efficiently but it must be possible to perform queries in real-time to be of use in real-world applications. The progressive mesh representations described above allow progressive transmission of 3D data, but this must be extended to dynamic data. Moreover, the transformation of a mesh into a progressive mesh is expensive and may not be viable for huge datasets. The growing trend to outsource storage and processing of data to "the cloud" necessitates 3D representations that can be stored, interacted with and edited in a distributed manner.

However, on the other hand, there is a growing wish to be able to access such data in a resource limited environment. For example, over bandwidth-limited network connections or on mobile devices with limited computational power. The advances in rendering technology exhibited in computer generated movie sequences will begin to find its way into consumer products such as game consoles and mobile devices. These platforms are highly resource limited in terms of both processing power and storage. Hence, the efficiency of the data structures used to store and process 3D data will be of critical importance in determining performance.

Statistical representations of 3D surfaces (such as the 3D morphable model [6]) have proven extremely useful in vision applications, where their compactness and robustness allow them to constrain vision problems in an efficient way. However, their application is limited because of *model dominance* whereby low frequency, global modes of variation dominate appearance. Extensions to such statistical representations that can capture high frequency local detail while retaining the compact storage requirements are a significant future challenge. A related challenge is how such models can be learnt from a sparse set of samples within a very high dimensional space, so that the model's generalization capabilities can be improved.

4.9 Concluding Remarks

Representations of 3D data provide the interface between acquisition or sensing of 3D data and ultimately processing the data in a way that enables the development of useful applications. Anyone involved in 3D imaging and processing must be aware of the native representations used by sensing devices and the various advantages and limitations of higher level surface and volume based representations. In many cases, data in a raw representation must be preprocessed before conversion to the desired higher level format, for example through surface fitting, smoothing or resampling. Subsequently, in choosing the most suitable representation for a particular application, it must be established what operations need to be performed on the data and what requirements exist in terms of computational and storage efficiency. Whether involved with the low level design of 3D sensors or interpreting and processing high level 3D data, understanding these issues is important. Finally, as sensors and applications continue to develop, the need for new representations and methods for compression and visualization mean this remains an active research area.

4.10 Further Reading

An introductory level text covering mathematics related to geometry processing is by Vince [72]. 3D representations in general are covered in some detail in the computer graphics textbooks of Watt [73] and Foley et al. [15]. A number of textbooks focus in more detail on specific representations. For example, meshes, geometry processing algorithms including error removal, mesh creation, smoothing, conversion and morphing are covered in detail in the textbook of Botsch et al. [10]. NURBS are described in detail in the textbook of Piegl and Tiller [53], subdivision surfaces are covered by Peters and Reif [50], implicit curves and surfaces are examined by Gomes et al. [19] and the textbook of Suetens [66] deals with volumetric representations in the context of medical imaging. A popular textbook describing techniques for visualization is by Post et al. [54].

4.11 Questions

1. Compare and contrast K-d point cloud structuring and octree structuring. When might one method be preferable over the other?
2. For each of the following methods and devices for 3D acquisition, explain what is the most suitable raw data representation. Justify your answer. You may need to research how each method operates.

   - Time-of-flight camera.
   - Multi-view stereo.
   - Shape from shading.
   - Structured light.
   - MRI scanner (consider structural, functional and diffusion tensor modalities).

3. For a 3D imaging application of your choice, list the operations that would need to be applied to the data and use this to guide selection of an appropriate 3D representation. Explain any difficulties that may arise in converting to this representation from the raw data acquired in your chosen application.
4. What considerations are relevant when selecting a data structure for 3D meshes?
5. Describe an application in which lossy compression of 3D data is acceptable and an application in which only lossless compression is acceptable.
6. Explain three situations in which 3D data needs to be visualized. Each situation should employ a different visualization of the data.

4.12 Exercises

1. Derive an algorithm for extracting a list of edges from a triangular mesh stored in a vertex-face list. The complexity should be linear in the number of triangles.
2. Using a data structure of your choice, show how to compute a vertex normal for a triangular mesh. You should choose one of the methods described in Sect. 4.5.1 to compute the normals.
3. In Sect. 4.3.2.1, code is given for traversing the edges incident on a vertex in a halfedge structure. Provide similar code for traversing the faces incident on a vertex.
4. Describe how to implement the *edge collapse* operation in a halfedge structure. The collapsed edge and one of the vertices must be removed from the structure, edges incident on the deleted vertex must be altered so that they are incident on the retained vertex and finally any degenerate faces must be removed.
5. A sphere can be represented as a subdivision surface using the following rule. The base mesh is a polyhedron, in this case use an icosahedron. The subdivision rule divides each triangle into four smaller triangles by adding vertices halfway along each edge. The new vertices are translated such that their distance from the sphere center is equal to the radius of the sphere. Derive a rule for computing the number of edges, faces and vertices in the representation as a function of the number of iterative subdivisions. Now, using a triangle mesh data structure of your choice, derive a similar rule for computing the number of pointers required to store the representation at each level of iteration.
6. Using a mesh representation of your choice, show how to evaluate the quadric error metric at a vertex.
7. A mesh can be considered as a weighted graph, where edge weights correspond to Euclidean distance between the end nodes. Describe how to implement Dijkstra's shortest path algorithm in order to achieve fast range searching over a mesh graph stored in a halfedge structure. Given a distance threshold over which to range search, what is the stopping criteria for this algorithm?

References

1. Alliez, P., Gotsman, C.: Recent advances in compression of 3d meshes. In: Dodgson, N., Floater, M., Sabin, M. (eds.) Advances in Multiresolution for Geometric Modeling, pp. 3–26. Springer, Berlin (2005)
2. Asberg, B., Blanco, G., Bose, P., Garcia-Lopez, J., Overmars, M., Toussaint, G., Wilfong, G., Zhu, B.: Feasibility of design in stereolithography. Algorithmica **19**(1–2), 61–83 (1997)
3. Bentley, J.L.: Multidimensional binary search trees used for associative searching. Commun. ACM **18**(9), 509–517 (1975)
4. de Berg, M., van Kreveld, M., Overmars, M., Schwarzkopf, O.: Computational Geometry: Algorithms and Applications. Springer, Berlin (1997)
5. Biggs, N.: Algebraic Graph Theory. Cambridge University Press, Cambridge (1993)
6. Blanz, V., Vetter, T.: A morphable model for the synthesis of 3D faces. In: Proc. SIGGRAPH, pp. 187–194 (1999)

7. Bloomenthal, J.: Polygonization of implicit surfaces. Comput. Aided Geom. Des. **5**(4), 341–355 (1988)
8. Bloomenthal, J., Bajaj, C., Blinn, J., Cani-Gascuel, M.P., Rockwood, A., Wyvill, B., Wyvill, G. (eds.): Introduction to Implicit Surfaces. Morgan Kaufmann, San Mateo (1997)
9. Bloomenthal, J., Wyvill, B.: Interactive techniques for implicit modeling. In: Proc. Symposium on Interactive 3D Computer Graphics (1990)
10. Botsch, M., Kobbelt, L., Pauly, M., Alliez, P., Levy, B.: Polygon Mesh Processing. AK Peters/CRC Press, Wellesley/Boca Raton (2011)
11. Carr, J.C., Beatson, R.K., Cherrie, J.B., Mitchell, T.J., Fright, W.R., McCallum, B.C., Evans, T.R.: Reconstruction and representation of 3d objects with radial basis functions. In: Proc. SIGGRAPH, pp. 67–76 (2001)
12. Catmull, E., Clark, J.: Recursively generated b-spline surfaces on arbitrary topological meshes. Comput. Aided Des. **10**(6), 350–355 (1978)
13. Doo, D., Sabin, M.: Behavior of recursive division surfaces near extraordinary points. Comput. Aided Des. **10**(6), 356–360 (1978)
14. Farin, G.: Curves and Surfaces for CAGD: A Practical Guide. Morgan Kaufmann, San Mateo (2002)
15. Foley, J.D., van Dam, A., Feiner, S.K., Hughes, J.F.: Computer Graphics. Addison Wesley, Reading (1995)
16. Fuchs, H., Kedem, Z.M., Naylor, B.F.: On visible surface generation by a priori tree structures. ACM Comput. Graph., 124–133 (1980)
17. Garland, M.: Quadric-based polygonal surface simplification. Ph.D. thesis, Computer Science Department, Carnegie Mellon University (1999)
18. Garland, M., Heckbert, P.S.: Surface simplification using quadric error metrics. In: Proc. SIGGRAPH, pp. 209–216 (1997)
19. Gomes, A.J.P., Voiculescu, I., Jorge, J., Wyvill, B., Galbraith, C.: Implicit Curves and Surfaces: Mathematics, Data Structures and Algorithms. Springer, Berlin (2009)
20. Gu, X., Gortler, S., Hoppe, H.: Geometry images. ACM Trans. Graph. **21**(3) (2002) (Proceedings of SIGGRAPH)
21. Hart, J.C.: Ray tracing implicit surfaces. In: SIGGRAPH Course Notes (1993)
22. Hartley, R., Zisserman, A.: Multiple View Geometry in Computer Vision. Cambridge University Press, Cambridge (2000)
23. Heckbert, P.S.: Survey of texture mapping. IEEE Comput. Graph. Appl. **6**(11), 56–67 (1986)
24. Hoppe, H.: Efficient implementation of progressive meshes. Comput. Graph. **22**(1), 27–36 (1998)
25. Jin, S., Lewis, R.R., West, D.: A comparison of algorithms for vertex normal computations. Vis. Comput. **21**(1–2), 71–82 (2005)
26. Johnson, A., Spin-images: A representation for 3-d surface matching. Ph.D. thesis, Robotics Institute, Carnegie Mellon University (1997)
27. Karni, Z., Gotsman, C.: Spectral compression of mesh geometry. In: Proc. SIGGRAPH, pp. 279–286 (2000)
28. Kazhdan, M.: Reconstruction of solid models from oriented point sets. In: Proc. Eurographics Symposium on Geometry Processing (2005)
29. Keller, P.R., Keller, M.M.: Visual Cues: Practical Data Visualization. IEEE Comput. Soc., Los Alamitos (1993)
30. Kimmel, R., Sethian, J.A.: Computing geodesic paths on manifolds. Proc. Natl. Acad. Sci. **95**(15), 8431–8435 (1998)
31. Kobbelt, L.: Interpolatory subdivision on open quadrilateral nets with arbitrary topology. Comput. Graph. Forum **15**(3), 409–420 (1996)
32. Koenderink, J.J., van Doorn, A.J.: Surface shape and curvature scales. Image Vis. Comput. **10**(8), 557–565 (1992)
33. Kutulakos, K.N., Seitz, S.M.: A theory of shape by space carving. Int. J. Comput. Vis. **38**(3), 199–218 (2000)

34. Laidlaw, D.H., Trumbore, W.B., Hughes, J.F.: Constructive solid geometry for polyhedral objects. In: Proc. SIGGRAPH, pp. 161–170 (1986)
35. Lebeck, A.O.: Principles and Design of Mechanical Face Seals. Wiley-Interscience, New York (1991)
36. Leotta, M.J., Mundy, J.L.: Predicting high resolution image edges with a generic, adaptive, 3-d vehicle model. In: Proc. CVPR, pp. 1311–1318 (2009)
37. Levoy, M.: Display of surfaces from volume data. IEEE Comput. Graph. Appl. **8**(3), 29–37 (1988)
38. Litke, N., Levin, A., Schröder, P.: Fitting subdivision surfaces. In: Proc. Conference on Visualization (2001)
39. Loop, C.: Smooth subdivision surfaces based on triangles. Master's thesis, University of Utah (1987)
40. Lorensen, W.E., Cline, H.E.: Arching cubes: a high resolution 3d surface construction algorithm. Comput. Graph. **21**(4) (1987)
41. Max, N.: Weights for computing vertex normals from facet normals. J. Graph. Tools **4**(2), 1–6 (1999)
42. Meyer, M., Desbrun, M., Schröder, P., Barr, A.H.: Discrete differential-geometry operators for triangulated 2-manifolds. Vis. Math. **3**(7), 35–57 (2002)
43. Muller, D.E., Preparata, F.P.: Finding the intersection of two convex polyhedra. Theor. Comput. Sci. **7**, 217–236 (1978)
44. Murali, T.M., Funkhouser, T.A.: Consistent solid and boundary representations from arbitrary polygonal data. In: Proc. Symposium on Interactive 3D Graphics (1997)
45. Nehab, D., Rusinkiewicz, S., Davis, J.E., Ramamoorthi, R.: Efficiently combining positions and normals for precise 3D geometry. ACM Trans. Graph. **24**(3), 536–543 (2005) (Proceedings of SIGGRAPH)
46. Nielson, G.M., Hagen, H., Müller, H.: Scientific Visualization: Overviews, Methodologies, and Techniques. IEEE Computer Society Press, New York (1997)
47. Pajarola, R., Rossignac, J.: Compressed progressive meshes. IEEE Trans. Vis. Comput. Graph. **6**(1), 79–93 (2000)
48. Paysan, P., Knothe, R., Amberg, B., Romdhani, S., Vetter, T.: A 3D face model for pose and illumination invariant face recognition. In: Proc. IEEE Intl. Conf. on Advanced Video and Signal based Surveillance (2009)
49. Peng, J., Kim, C.S., Kuo, C.C.J.: Technologies for 3d mesh compression: a survey. J. Vis. Commun. Image Represent. **16**(6), 688–733 (2005)
50. Peters, J., Reif, U.: Subdivision Surfaces. Springer, New York (2008)
51. Pharr, M., Humphreys, G.: Physically Based Rendering: From Theory to Implementation. Morgan Kaufmann, San Mateo (2010)
52. Phillips, P.J., Flynn, P.J., Scruggs, T., Bowyer, K.W., Chang, J., Hoffman, K., Marques, J., Jaesik, M., Worek, W.: Overview of the face recognition grand challenge. In: Proc. CVPR, pp. 947–954 (2005)
53. Piegl, L., Tiller, W.: The NURBS Book. Springer, Berlin (1996)
54. Post, F.H., Nielson, G.M., Bonneau, G.P. (eds.): Data Visualization: The State of the Art. Springer, Berlin (2002)
55. Reddy, D., Agrawal, A., Chellappa, R.: Enforcing integrability by error correction using ℓ_1-minimization. In: Proc. CVPR (2009)
56. Rogers, D.F.: An Introduction to NURBS with Historical Perspective. Morgan Kaufmann, San Mateo (2001)
57. Rusinkiewicz, S., Levoy, M.: Qsplat: a multiresolution point rendering system for large meshes. In: Proc. SIGGRAPH, pp. 343–352 (2000)
58. Scharstein, D., Szeliski, R.: A taxonomy and evaluation of dense two-frame stereo correspondence algorithms. Int. J. Comput. Vis. **47**(1–3), 7–42 (2002)
59. Sheffer, A., Praun, E., Rose, K.: Mesh parameterization methods and their applications. Found. Trends Comput. Graph. Vis. **2**(2), 105–171 (2006)

60. Shen, C., O'Brien, J.F., Shewchuk, J.R.: Interpolating and approximating implicit surfaces from polygon soup. In: Proc. SIGGRAPH, pp. 896–904 (2004)
61. Smith, C.: On vertex-vertex systems and their use in geometric and biological modeling. Ph.D. thesis, University of Calgary (2006)
62. Smith, N.B., Webb, A.: Introduction to Medical Imaging: Physics, Engineering and Clinical Applications. Cambridge University Press, Cambridge (2010)
63. Smith, R.C., Cheeseman, P.: On the representation and estimation of spatial uncertainty. Int. J. Robot. Res. **5**(4), 56–68 (1986)
64. Stam, J.: Exact evaluation of Catmull–Clark subdivision surfaces at arbitrary parameter values. In: Proc. SIGGRAPH, pp. 395–404 (1998)
65. Stroud, I.: Boundary Representation Modeling Techniques. Springer, Berlin (2006)
66. Suetens, P.: Fundamentals of Medical Imaging. Cambridge University Press, Cambridge (2009)
67. Takeuchi, S., Kanai, T., Suzuki, H., Shimada, K., Kimura, F.: Subdivision surface fitting with QEM-based mesh simplification and reconstruction of approximated b-spline surfaces. In: Proc. Pacific Conference on Computer Graphics and Applications, pp. 202–212 (2000)
68. Taubin, G.: A signal processing approach to fair surface design. In: Proc. SIGGRAPH, pp. 351–358 (1995)
69. Taubin, G., Rossignac, J.: Geometric compression through topological surgery. ACM Trans. Graph. **17**(2), 84–115 (1998)
70. Thürmer, G., Wüthrich, C.A.: Computing vertex normals from polygonal facets. J. Graph. Tools **3**(1), 43–46 (1998)
71. Unwin, A., Theus, M., Hofmann, H.: Graphics of Large Datasets: Visualizing a Million. Springer, Berlin (2006)
72. Vince, J.A.: Mathematics for Computer Graphics. Springer, Berlin (2010)
73. Watt, A.: 3D Computer Graphics. Addison Wesley, Reading (1999)
74. Wikipedia: http://en.wikipedia.org/wiki/Catmull-Clark_subdivision_surface. Accessed 23rd January 2012
75. Wikipedia: http://en.wikipedia.org/wiki/Constructive_solid_geometry. Accessed 23rd January 2012
76. Wikipedia: http://en.wikipedia.org/wiki/K-d_tree. Accessed 23rd January 2012
77. Wikipedia: http://en.wikipedia.org/wiki/Loop_subdivision_surface. Accessed 23rd January 2012
78. Weiler, K.: Edge-based data structures for solid modeling in a curved surface environment. IEEE Comput. Graph. Appl. **5**(1), 21–40 (1985)
79. Zienkiewicz, O.C., Taylor, R.L., Zhu, J.Z.: The Finite Element Method: Its Basis and Fundamentals. Butterworth-Heinemann, Stoneham (2005)
80. Zorin, D., Schröder, P., Sweldens, W.: Interpolating subdivision for meshes with arbitrary topology. In: Proc. SIGGRAPH, pp. 189–192 (1996)

Part II
3D Shape Analysis and Processing

In the following chapter, we discuss how we can analyze and process imaged 3D objects, by providing a sparse set of interest-points (keypoints) on the surface and then building (local) 3D shape descriptors at these points. This is essential in order to be able to find corresponding surface points on pairs of 3D scans in a reasonable computational time. Chapter 6 then discusses 3D shape registration, which is the process of bringing one 3D shape into alignment with another similar 3D shape. The discussion centers on the well-known *Iterative Closest Points* algorithm of Besl and McKay and its variants. Both chapters include advanced approaches that allow the scanned scene objects to deform. Finally, in Chap. 7, we discuss the 3D shape matching processes that allow us to build applications in both 3D shape retrieval (e.g. in shape search engines) and 3D object recognition. Although this chapter is largely application-based, we kept it within this book part (rather than the following part on applications), as it contains some basic concepts in 3D shape matching and provides a better balance of material across the three parts.

Chapter 5
Feature-Based Methods in 3D Shape Analysis

Alexander M. Bronstein, Michael M. Bronstein, and Maks Ovsjanikov

Abstract The computer vision and pattern recognition communities have recently witnessed a surge in feature-based methods for numerous applications including object recognition and image retrieval. Similar concepts and analogous approaches are penetrating the world of 3D shape analysis in a variety of areas including non-rigid shape retrieval and matching. In this chapter, we present both mature concepts and the state-of-the-art of feature-based approaches in 3D shape analysis. In particular, approaches to the detection of interest points and the generation of local shape descriptors are discussed. A wide range of methods is covered including those based on curvature, those based on difference-of-Gaussian scale space, and those that employ recent advances in heat kernel methods.

5.1 Introduction

In computer vision and pattern recognition jargon, the term *features* is often used to refer to persistent elements of a 2D image (such as corners or sharp edges), which capture most of the relevant information and allow one to perform object analysis. In the last decade, feature-based methods (such as the scale invariant feature transform (SIFT) [51] and similar algorithms [4, 55]) have become a standard and broadly-used paradigm in various applications, including retrieval and matching (e.g. for multiview geometry reconstruction), due to their relative simplicity, flexibility, and excellent performance in practice.

A similar trend is emerging in 3D shape analysis in a variety of areas including non-rigid shape retrieval and shape matching. While in some cases computer

---

A.M. Bronstein (✉) · M.M. Bronstein
Department of Computer Science, Technion—Israel Institute of Technology, Haifa 32000, Israel
e-mail: bron@cs.technion.ac.il

M.M. Bronstein
e-mail: mbron@cs.technion.ac.il

M. Ovsjanikov
Department of Computer Science, Stanford University, Stanford, CA, USA
e-mail: maks@stanford.edu

vision methods are straightforwardly applicable to 3D shapes [45, 50], in general, some fundamental differences between 2D and 3D shapes require new and different methods for shape analysis.

One of the distinguishing characteristics that make computer vision techniques that work successfully in 2D image analysis not straightforwardly applicable in 3D shape analysis is the difference in shape representations. In computer vision, it is common to work with a 2D image of a physical object, representing both its geometric and photometric properties. Such a representation simplifies the task of shape analysis by reducing it to simple image processing operations, at the cost of losing information about the object's 3D structure, which cannot be unambiguously captured in a 2D image. In computer graphics and geometry processing, it is assumed that the 3D geometry of the object is explicitly given. Depending on application, the geometric representation of the object can differ significantly. For example, in graphics it is common to work with triangular meshes or point clouds; in medical applications with volumes and implicit representations.

Furthermore, 3D shapes are usually poorer in high-frequency information (such as edges in images), and being generally non-Euclidean spaces, many concepts natural in images (edges, directions, etc.), do not straightforwardly generalize to shapes.

Most feature-based approaches can be logically divided into two main stages: location of stable, repeatable points that capture most of the relevant shape information (*feature detection*[1]) and representation of the shape properties at these points (*feature description*). Both processes depend greatly on shape representation as well as on the application at hand.

In 2D image analysis, the typical use of features is to describe an object independently of the way it is seen by a camera. Features found in images are geometric discontinuities in the captured object (edges and corners) or its photometric properties (texture). Since the difference in viewpoint can be *locally* approximated as an affine transformation, feature detectors and descriptors in images are usually made *affine invariant*.

In 3D shape analysis, features are typically based on geometry rather than appearance. The problems of shape correspondence and similarity require the features to be stable under natural transformations that an object can undergo, which may include not only changes in pose, but also non-rigid bending. If the deformation is inelastic, it is often referred to as *isometric* (distance-preserving), and feature-based methods coping with such transformations as *isometry-invariant*; if the bending also involves connectivity changes, the feature detection and description algorithms are called *topology-invariant*.

The main challenge of feature-based 3D shape analysis can be summarized as finding a set of features that can be found repeatably on shapes undergoing a wide class of transformations on the one hand and carry sufficient information to allow using these features to find correspondence and similarity (among other tasks) on the other.

---

[1] In some literature, this is also known as *interest point* detection or *keypoint detection*.

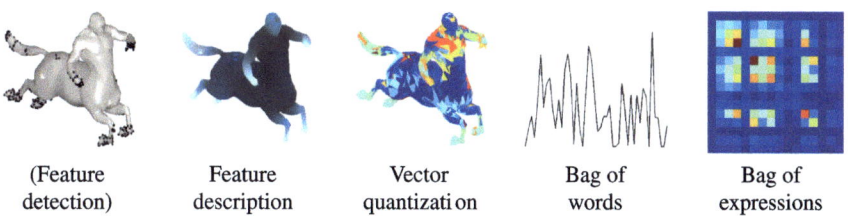

(Feature detection) — Feature description — Vector quantization — Bag of words — Bag of expressions

Fig. 5.1 Construction of bags of features for feature-based shape retrieval

5.1.1 Applications

Two archetypal problems in shape analysis addressed by feature-based methods are *shape similarity* and *correspondence*. The former underlies many pattern recognition applications, where we have to distinguish between different geometric objects (e.g. in 3D face recognition [15]). A particularly challenging setting of the shape similarity problem appears in *content-based shape retrieval*, an application driven by the availability of large public-domain databases of 3D models, such as *Google 3D Warehouse*, which have created the demand for shape search and retrieval algorithms capable of finding similar shapes in the same way a search engine responds to text queries (detailed discussion of this application appears in Chap. 7).

One of the notable advantages of feature-based approaches in shape retrieval is the possibility of representing a shape as a collection of primitive elements ("geometric words"), and using the well-developed methods from text search such as the *bag of features* (BOF) (or *bag of words*) paradigm [23, 75]. Such approaches are widely used in image retrieval and have been introduced more recently to shape analysis [19, 83]. The construction of a bag of features is usually performed in a few steps, depicted in Fig. 5.1. Firstly, the shape is represented as a collection of local feature descriptors (either dense or computed as a set of stable points following an optional stage of feature detection). Secondly, the descriptors are represented by *geometric words* from a *geometric vocabulary* using vector quantization. The geometric vocabulary is a set of representative descriptors, precomputed in advance. This way, each descriptor is replaced by the index of the closest geometric word in the vocabulary. Computing the histogram of the frequency of occurrence of geometric words gives the bag of features. Alternatively, a two-dimensional histogram of co-occurrences of pairs of geometric words (*geometric expressions*) can be used [19]. Shape similarity is computed as a distance between the corresponding bags of features. The bag of features representation is usually compact, easy to store and compare, which makes such approaches suitable for large-scale shape retrieval. Evaluation of shape retrieval performance (e.g. the robust large-scale retrieval benchmark [13] from the Shape Retrieval Contest (SHREC)) tests the robustness of retrieval algorithms on a large set of shapes with different simulated transformations, including non-rigid deformations.

Another fundamental problem in shape analysis is that of *correspondence* consisting of finding relations between similar points on two or more shapes. Finding correspondence between two shapes that would be invariant to a wide variety of transformations is usually referred to as *invariant shape correspondence*. Correspondence problems are often encountered in shape synthesis applications such as morphing. In order to morph one shape into the other, one needs to know which point on the first shape will be transformed into a point on the second shape, in other words, establishing a correspondence between the shapes. A related problem is *registration*, where the deformation bringing one shape into the other is explicitly sought for.

Feature-based methods for shape correspondence are based on first detecting features on two shapes between which correspondence is sought, and then match them by comparing the corresponding descriptors. The feature-based correspondence problem can be formulated as finding a map that maximizes the similarity between corresponding descriptors. The caveat of such an approach is that it may produce inconsistent matches, especially in shapes with repeating structure or symmetry: for example, points on the right and left sides of a human body can be swapped due to bilateral symmetry. A way to cope with this problem is to add some *global structure*, for example, pairwise geodesic or diffusion distance preservation constraint. Thus, this type of *minimum-distortion correspondence* tries to match simultaneously local structures (descriptors) and global structures (metrics), and can be found by an extension of the generalized multidimensional scaling (GMDS) algorithm [16, 82] or graph labeling [78, 84, 85]. Evaluation of correspondence finding algorithms typically simulates a one-to-one shape matching scenario, in which one of the shapes undergoes multiple modifications and transformations, and the quality of the correspondence is evaluated as the distance on the shape between the found matches and the known groundtruth correspondence. Notable benchmarks are the SHREC robust correspondence benchmark [14] and the Princeton correspondence benchmark [41].

5.1.2 Chapter Outline

In this chapter, we present an overview of feature-based methods in 3D shape analysis and their applications, classical as well as most recent approaches. The main emphasis is on heat-kernel based detection and description algorithms, a relatively recent set of methods based on a common mathematical model and falling under the umbrella of *diffusion geometry*. Detailed description, examples, figures, and problems in this chapter allows the implementation of these methods.

The next section outlines some prerequisite mathematical background, describing our notation and a number of important concepts in differential and diffusion geometry. Then the two main sections are presented: Sect. 5.3 discusses feature detectors, while Sect. 5.4 describes feature descriptors. The final sections give concluding remarks, research challenges and suggested further reading.

5.2 Mathematical Background

Throughout this chapter, an object is some subset of the ambient Euclidean space, $\Omega \subset \mathbb{R}^3$. In many cases (e.g. data acquired by a range scanner), we can access only the *boundary* $\partial \Omega$ of the object, which can be modeled as a two-dimensional smooth *manifold* or *surface*, denoted here by $\mathbb{X}$. Photometric information is given as a scalar or a vector field $\alpha : \mathbb{X} \to \mathbb{R}^d$ on the manifold and referred to as *texture*. If the surface is sampled at some discrete set of points $\{x_1, \ldots, x_N\} \subset \mathbb{X}$, then this representation is called a *point cloud*; if, in addition, connectivity information is available in the form of a simplicial complex (*triangulation*, consisting of a set of *edges* $(x_i, x_j) \in \mathbb{E}$ and *faces* $(x_i, x_j, x_k) \in \mathbb{F}$), such a representation is called a *mesh*.

In medical applications, such as tomographic data analysis, information about the internal structure of the object in addition to its boundary is often available. A common representation in such applications is a *volumetric image*, which can be represented as a 3D matrix, where each voxel (3D pixel) describes the properties of the object (e.g. its penetrability by X-ray radiation). Segmentation algorithms applied to volumetric data used in medical applications often extract boundaries of 3D objects in *implicit form*, represented as level-sets of some function $f : \mathbb{R}^3 \to \mathbb{R}$.

5.2.1 Differential Geometry

Both the two-dimensional boundary surface and the three-dimensional volume enclosed by it can be modeled as, respectively, two- and three-dimensional complete Riemannian sub-manifolds of $\mathbb{R}^3$. Every point $\mathbf{x}$ on the manifold $\mathbb{X}$ is assigned a *tangent space* $T_x\mathbb{X}$. For two dimensional surfaces, the vector $\mathbf{N}$ orthogonal to $T_x\mathbb{X}$ is called the *normal* to the surface at $\mathbf{x}$. The tangent space at each point is associated with a smooth inner product $g_x : T_x\mathbb{X} \times T_x\mathbb{X} \to \mathbb{R}$, usually referred to as the *metric tensor*. Denoting by $\mathbf{x} : \mathbb{U} \subseteq \mathbb{R}^2 \to \mathbb{R}^3$ the regular map embedding $\mathbb{X}$ into $\mathbb{R}^3$, the metric tensor can be expressed in coordinates as

$$g_{ij} = \frac{\partial \mathbf{x}^T}{\partial u_i} \frac{\partial \mathbf{x}}{\partial u_j}, \tag{5.1}$$

where u_i are the coordinates of U. The metric tensor relates infinitesimal displacements du in the parametrization domain $\mathbb{U}$ to displacement on the manifold,

$$dp^2 = g_{11}du_1^2 + 2g_{12}du_1du_2 + g_{22}du_2^2. \tag{5.2}$$

This quadratic form is usually referred to as the *first fundamental form* and it provides a way to define length structures on the manifold. Given a curve $C : [0, T] \to X$, its length can be expressed as

$$L(C) = \int_0^T g(\dot{C}(t), \dot{C}(t))_{C(t)}^{1/2} dt, \tag{5.3}$$

where $\dot{C}$ denotes the velocity vector. *Minimal geodesics* are the minimizers of $L(C)$, giving rise to the *geodesic distances*

$$d(\mathbf{x}, \mathbf{x}') = \min_{C \in \Gamma(\mathbf{x},\mathbf{x}')} L(C), \qquad (5.4)$$

where $\Gamma(\mathbf{x}, \mathbf{x}')$ is the set of all admissible paths between the points $\mathbf{x}$ and $\mathbf{x}'$ on the surface $\mathbb{X}$ (due to completeness assumption, the minimizer always exists). Structures expressible solely in terms of the metric tensor g are called *intrinsic*. For example, the geodesic can be expressed in this way. The importance of intrinsic structures stems from the fact that they are invariant under isometric transformations (bendings) of the shape. In an isometrically bent shape, the geodesic distances are preserved, which is a property that allows the design of isometrically invariant shape descriptors [31].

The metric tensor also allows the definition of differential operations on the tangent space. Given a smooth scalar field $f : \mathbb{X} \to \mathbb{R}$, its *(intrinsic) gradient* $\nabla_\mathbb{X} f$ at point $\mathbf{x}$ is defined through the relation $f(\mathbf{x} + d\mathbf{v}) = f(\mathbf{x}) + g_x(\nabla_\mathbb{X} f(\mathbf{x}), d\mathbf{v})$, where $d\mathbf{v} \in T_x^*\mathbb{X}$ is an infinitesimal tangent vector. For a given tangent vector $\mathbf{v}$, the quantity

$$D_v f = \lim_{\varepsilon \to 0} \frac{f(\mathbf{x} + \varepsilon \mathbf{v}) - f(\mathbf{x})}{\varepsilon \sqrt{g_x(\mathbf{v}, \mathbf{v})}} \qquad (5.5)$$

is called the *directional derivative* of f at point $\mathbf{x}$ in the direction $\mathbf{v}$.

5.2.2 Curvature of Two-Dimensional Surfaces

Given a curve $\gamma : [0, L] \to \mathbb{R}^3$, its first-order and second-order derivatives with respect to the parameter, $\dot{\gamma}$ and $\ddot{\gamma}$, are called the *tangent* and *curvature* vectors, respectively. The magnitude of $\ddot{\gamma}(t)$ measures the curvature of γ at a point. The curvature of a surface at a point $\mathbf{x}$ can be expressed in terms of curves passing through it confined to the surface. Every direction $\mathbf{v} \in T_x\mathbb{X}$ can be associated with a curve γ such that $\gamma(0) = \mathbf{x}$ and $\dot{\gamma}(0) = \mathbf{v}$, and, thus, with a curvature vector $\ddot{\gamma}(0)$. The projection of the curvature vector on the tangent plane is called the *geodesic curvature*, and it vanishes if and only if γ is a geodesic. The projection $\kappa_n = \mathsf{P}_N\ddot{\gamma}(0)$ of the curvature vector on the normal is called the *normal curvature*. The minimum and the maximum values of κ_n are called the *principal curvatures* $\kappa_1 \leq \kappa_2$, and the corresponding directions the *principal directions*. The average of the two principal curvatures $H = \frac{1}{2}(\kappa_1 + \kappa_2)$ is called the *mean curvature*, and their product $K = \kappa_1 \kappa_2$ is called the *Gaussian curvature*.

Surprisingly enough, though the principal curvatures are *extrinsic* quantities (i.e. quantities depending on the way the surface is embedded into the Euclidean space), the Gaussian curvature is an *intrinsic quantity*, that is, it can be fully expressed in terms of the metric of the surface. One of such definitions considers the perimeter $P(r)$ of a geodesic circle of radius r centered at a point $\mathbf{x}$ on the surface. On a Euclidean surface, $P(r) = 2\pi r$, while on curved surfaces a different quantity is measured. The defect of the perimeter is governed by the Gaussian curvature according to

$$K = \lim_{r \to 0} \frac{3(2\pi r - P(r))}{\pi r^3}. \tag{5.6}$$

5.2.3 Discrete Differential Geometry

The discretization of differential geometric quantities such as tangent and normal vectors, principal directions and curvatures, gradients, and the Laplace-Beltrami operator requires some attention, as straightforward differentiation with respect to some parametrization coordinates usually amplifies noise to unreasonable levels. In what follows, we briefly overview naïve and more robust methods for estimation of such quantities. The simplest discrete representation of a two-dimensional surface is a *point cloud* consisting of a set $\mathbb{X} = \{\mathbf{x}_1, \ldots, \mathbf{x}_n\}$ of discrete points in $\mathbb{R}^3$ taken from the underlying continuous surface. Local connectivity information can be introduced by defining an *edge set* $\mathbb{E} \subset \mathbb{X} \times \mathbb{X}$ indicating for each pair of samples $(\mathbf{x}, \mathbf{x}')$ in the cloud whether they are adjacent (i.e., $(\mathbf{x}, \mathbf{x}') \in E$) or not. This leads to an undirected graph representation. It is frequently convenient to approximate a continuous surface by a piecewise-planar one, consisting of a collection of polygonal patches glued together along their edges. A particular case of such polyhedral approximations are *triangular meshes* in which all faces are triangles built upon triples of points in the point cloud. Each triangle $\mathbf{x}_i, \mathbf{x}_j, \mathbf{x}_k$ can be associated with the normal vector

$$\mathbf{N} = \frac{(\mathbf{x}_j - \mathbf{x}_i) \times (\mathbf{x}_k - \mathbf{x}_i)}{\|(\mathbf{x}_j - \mathbf{x}_i) \times (\mathbf{x}_k - \mathbf{x}_i)\|}. \tag{5.7}$$

The normal at a vertex of the mesh can be computed by averaging the normals to the triangles sharing that vertex, possibly weighted by the triangle areas. Such a neighborhood of a vertex is usually referred to as the 1-*ring*.

In the presence of noisy samples, the support of the 1-rings can be insufficient to reliably approximate the normal vectors. As an alternative, given a vertex $\mathbf{x}$, we can consider the r-neighborhood $\mathbb{N}_r(\mathbf{x}) = \mathbb{B}_r(\mathbf{x}) \cap \mathbb{X}$ where the ball $\mathbb{B}_r(\mathbf{x})$ is with respect to the Euclidean metric. The samples in $\mathbb{N}_r(\mathbf{x})$ can be further weighted inversely proportionally to their Euclidean distances from $\mathbf{x}$. The weighted second-order moment matrix

$$\mathbf{M} = \sum_{\mathbf{y} \in \mathbb{N}_r(\mathbf{x})} \alpha(\mathbf{y})(\mathbf{y} - \mathbf{x})(\mathbf{y} - \mathbf{x})^\mathrm{T} \tag{5.8}$$

represents the orientation of the surface in the vicinity of $\mathbf{x}$. Here, $\alpha(\mathbf{y})$ are assumed to be non-negative weights summing to one. The two largest eigenvectors $\mathbf{T}_1$ and

T_2 of M span the tangent plane $T_x \mathbb{X}$, while the third, smallest, eigenvector **N** corresponds to the normal. The tradeoff between sensitivity to small geometric features and robustness to noise is controlled by the local neighborhood radius r.

In the same way that local plane fitting constitutes a robust tool for the approximation of normals and tangents, fitting of a quadratic surface allows the estimation of second-order quantities related to curvature. For that purpose, the points in $\mathbb{N}_r(\mathbf{x})$ are first transformed so that **x** coincides with the origin, the z axis coincides with the normal, and the x and y axes coincide with the tangent vectors (i.e., a point y is represented as $\mathbf{y} = \mathbf{x} + u\mathbf{T}_1 + v\mathbf{T}_2 + w\mathbf{N}$). A paraboloid

$$w(u,v) = au^2 + buv + cv^2 \tag{5.9}$$

is then fit using weighted least squares. The Gaussian and mean curvatures can now be estimated using the closed-form expressions $K = 4ac - b^2$ and $H = a + c$; the principal curvatures and directions are obtained in a similar way [9]. For a comprehensive overview of curvature discretization methods, the reader is referred to [52].

5.2.4 Diffusion Geometry

The positive semi-definite self-adjoint *Laplace-Beltrami operator* Δ_X associated with the metric tensor g is defined by the identity

$$\int f \Delta_X h\, d\mathrm{vol} = -\int g_x(\nabla_X f, \nabla_X h) d\mathrm{vol}, \tag{5.10}$$

which holds for any pair of smooth scalar fields $f, h : \mathbb{X} \to \mathbb{R}$;. Here, $d$vol denotes the differential area or volume element of the manifold, depending, respectively, whether the latter is 2D or 3D.

The Laplace-Beltrami operator can be expressed in the parametrization coordinates as

$$\Delta_X = -\frac{1}{\sqrt{\det g}} \sum_{ij} \partial_i \sqrt{\det g}\, g_{ij}^{-1} \partial_j. \tag{5.11}$$

When the metric is Euclidean ($g_{ij} = \mathbf{I}$), the operator reduces to the familiar

$$\Delta f = -\left(\frac{\partial^2 f}{\partial u_1^2} + \frac{\partial^2 f}{\partial u_2^2} \right) \tag{5.12}$$

(note that, in this chapter, we define the Laplacian with the minus sign in order to ensure its positive semi-definiteness).

The Laplace-Beltrami operator gives rise to the partial differential equation

$$\left(\frac{\partial}{\partial t} + \Delta_X \right) f(t, \mathbf{x}) = 0, \tag{5.13}$$

called the *heat equation*. The heat equation describes the propagation of heat on the surface and its solution $f(t, \mathbf{x})$ is the heat distribution at a point $\mathbf{x}$ in time t. The initial condition of the equation is some initial heat distribution $f(0, \mathbf{x})$; if $\mathbb{X}$ has a boundary, appropriate boundary conditions must be added. The solution of (5.13) corresponding to a point initial condition $f(0, \mathbf{x}) = \delta(\mathbf{x} - \mathbf{x}')$, is called the *heat kernel* and represents the amount of heat transferred from $\mathbf{x}$ to $\mathbf{x}'$ in time t due to the diffusion process. Using spectral decomposition, the heat kernel can be represented as

$$k_t(\mathbf{x}, \mathbf{x}') = \sum_{i \geq 0} e^{-\lambda_i t} \phi_i(\mathbf{x}) \phi_i(\mathbf{x}'), \tag{5.14}$$

where ϕ_i and λ_i are, respectively, the eigenfunctions and eigenvalues of the Laplace-Beltrami operator satisfying $\Delta \phi_i = \lambda_i \phi_i$ (without loss of generality, we assume λ_i to be sorted in increasing order starting with $\lambda_0 = 0$). Since the Laplace-Beltrami operator is an *intrinsic* geometric quantity (i.e. it can be expressed solely in terms of the metric of $\mathbb{X}$), its eigenfunctions and eigenvalues as well as the heat kernel are invariant under isometric transformations of the manifold.

The value of the heat kernel $k_t(\mathbf{x}, \mathbf{x}')$ can be interpreted as the transition probability density of a random walk of length t from the point $\mathbf{x}$ to the point $\mathbf{x}'$. This allows the construction of a family of intrinsic metrics known as *diffusion metrics*,

$$\begin{aligned} d_t^2(\mathbf{x}, \mathbf{x}') &= \int \left(k_t(\mathbf{x}, \cdot) - k_t(\mathbf{x}', \cdot) \right)^2 d\mathrm{vol} \\ &= \sum_{i > 0} e^{-\lambda_i t} \left(\phi_i(\mathbf{x}) - \phi_i(\mathbf{x}') \right)^2, \end{aligned} \tag{5.15}$$

which measure the "connectivity rate" of the two points by paths of length t.

The parameter t can be given the meaning of *scale*, and the family $\{d_t\}$ can be thought of as a scale-space of metrics. By integrating over all scales, a *scale-invariant* version of (5.15) is obtained,

$$\begin{aligned} d_{\mathrm{CT}}^2(\mathbf{x}, \mathbf{x}') &= 2 \int_0^\infty d_t^2(\mathbf{x}, \mathbf{x}') dt \\ &= \sum_{i > 0} \frac{1}{\lambda_i} \left(\phi_i(\mathbf{x}) - \phi_i(\mathbf{x}') \right)^2. \end{aligned} \tag{5.16}$$

This metric is referred to as the *commute-time distance* and can be interpreted as the connectivity rate by paths of any length. We will broadly call constructions related to the heat kernel, diffusion and commute time metrics as *diffusion geometry*.

5.2.5 Discrete Diffusion Geometry

The discretization of the heat kernel k_t and the associated diffusion geometry constructs is performed using formula (5.14), in which a finite number of eigenvalues

Fig. 5.2 One ring of a point $\mathbf{x}_i$, adjacent point $\mathbf{x}_j$ and the angles α_{ij} and β_{ij} used in the cotangent weight scheme to discretize the Laplace-Beltrami operator

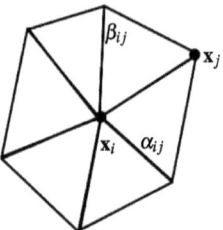

and eigenfunctions of the discrete Laplace-Beltrami operator are taken. The latter can be computed directly using the finite elements method [70], of by discretization of the Laplace operator on the mesh followed by its eigendecomposition. For a manifold discretized as a vertex set $\mathbb{V}$, a discrete Laplace-Beltrami operator is expressed in the following generic form,

$$(\Delta_X f)_i = \frac{1}{a_i} \sum_j w_{ij}(f_i - f_j), \qquad (5.17)$$

where w_{ij} are weights, a_i are normalization coefficients and the elements $f_i = f(v_i)$ of the vector $\mathbf{f}$ represent a scalar function on the manifold (e.g. the heat distribution) sampled at the vertex set.

In matrix notation, (5.17) can be written as $\Delta_X \mathbf{f} = \mathsf{A}^{-1}\mathsf{W}\mathbf{f}$, where $\mathbf{f}$ is an $N \times 1$ vector, $\mathsf{A} = \mathrm{diag}(a_i)$ and $\mathsf{W} = \mathrm{diag}(\sum_{l \neq i} w_{il}) - (w_{ij})$. The discrete eigenfunctions and eigenvalues are found by solving the *generalized eigendecomposition* [48] $\mathsf{W}\Phi = \mathsf{A}\Phi\Lambda$, where $\Lambda = \mathrm{diag}(\lambda_l)$ is a diagonal matrix of eigenvalues and $\Phi = (\phi_l(v_i))$ is the matrix of the corresponding eigenvectors.

Different choices of A and W have been studied, depending on which continuous properties of the Laplace-Beltrami operator one wishes to preserve [32, 86]. For triangular meshes, a popular choice adopted in this chapter is the *cotangent weight* scheme [57, 65], in which

$$w_{ij} = \begin{cases} (\cot \alpha_{ij} + \cot \beta_{ij})/2 & (\mathbf{v}_i, \mathbf{v}_j) \in \mathbb{E}; \\ 0 & \text{else,} \end{cases} \qquad (5.18)$$

where α_{ij} and β_{ij} are the two angles opposite to the edge between vertices $\mathbf{v}_i$ and $\mathbf{v}_j$ in the two triangles sharing the edge, and a_i are the discrete area elements (see Fig. 5.2).

In many cases, the discretized Laplacian operator is only a means for the computation of its eigenfunctions and eigenvalues used to approximate the heat kernels. The family of finite elements methods (FEM) constitutes an alternative approach, allowing direct discretization of the eigendecomposition of the Laplace-Beltrami operator. Firstly, a set of M locally-supported basis functions $\{f_i(x)\}$ spanning a sufficiently smooth subspace of L^2 functions on the manifold is selected. Linear or cubic functions are the typical choice. An eigenfunction ϕ_i of the Laplacian admits the following weak form identity

$$\langle \nabla_X \phi_i, f_j \rangle = \lambda_i \langle \phi_i, f_j \rangle \tag{5.19}$$

for every basis function f_j. Expressing ϕ_i as a linear combination $\phi_i(x) \approx u_{i1} f_1(x) + \cdots + u_{iM} f_M(x)$, we arrive at the following system of equations:

$$\sum_{j=1}^{M} u_{ji} \langle \nabla_X f_i, f_j \rangle = \sum_{j=1}^{M} u_{ji} \lambda_i \langle f_i, f_j \rangle. \tag{5.20}$$

As the function α_i are fixed, the terms $a_{ij} = \langle \nabla_X f_i, f_j \rangle$ and $b_{ij} = \langle f_i, f_j \rangle$ are pre-computed forming the generalized eigendecomposition problem $\mathsf{AU} = \Lambda \mathsf{BU}$, where A and B are the $N \times M$ matrices with the elements a_{ij} and b_{ij}, respectively, and U is the $M \times M$ matrix with the elements u_{ij}. Once U is computed, the corresponding eigenfunctions can be found using the columns of U as the coefficients of linear combinations of the basis functions.

For volumetric data, the Laplace-Beltrami operator is usually discretized on a regular Cartesian grid using finite differences.

5.3 Feature Detectors

The goal of a feature detector is to find stable points or regions on a shape. The main requirements of a feature detector are that the points that it selects are (i) *repeatable*, that is, in two instances of a shape, ideally the same set of corresponding points is detected, and (ii) *informative*, that is, descriptors built upon these points contain sufficient information to distinguish the shape from others. The outputs of a feature detector are sometimes called *interest points* or *keypoints*.

Since there is no single way to define a feature, the construction of the detector depends very much on the shape representation and the application at hand, or more specifically, the desired invariance properties.

5.3.1 A Taxonomy

In the most trivial case, no feature detection is performed and the feature descriptor is computed at all the points of the shape [19] or at some densely sampled subset thereof. The descriptor in this case is usually termed *dense*. Dense descriptors bypass the problem of repeatability, at the price of increased computational cost and potentially introducing many unimportant points that clutter the shape representation.

Many detectors assume to be given some scalar-valued or vector-valued function defined on the surface. The function can be either *photometric* information (texture) or a *geometric* quantity such as curvature. With this concept in mind, feature detection on shapes resembles very much that in images and many attempts to import methods from image processing and computer vision have been described in the literature. Several methods for feature detection have been inspired by the *difference of Gaussians* (DOG), a classical feature detection approach used in computer vision. Zaharescu et al. [87] introduce the *mesh DOG* approach by first applying Gaussian filtering to scalar functions (e.g. mean or Gauss curvature) defined on the shape. This allows representation of the function in scale space and feature points are prominent maxima of the scale space across scales. Castellani et al. [21] apply Gaussian filtering directly on the mesh geometry and create a scale space describing the displacement of the mesh points in the normal direction.

A different class of feature detection methods tries to find stable components or regions in the analyzed shape. In the computer vision and image analysis community, stable component detection is used in the maximally stable extremal regions (MSER) algorithm [55]. MSER represents intensity level sets as a component tree and attempts to find level sets with the smallest area variation across intensity; the use of area ratio as the stability criterion makes this approach affine-invariant, which is an important property in image analysis, as it approximates viewpoint transformations. Methods similar to MSER have been explored in the works on topological persistence [30]. Persistence-based clustering [22] was used by Skraba et al. [76] to perform shape segmentation. In [27, 49] MSER-like features for meshes and volumes have been studied.

Because many feature detectors operate locally on a function defined on the shape, they are usually not very sensitive to non-rigid deformations. Nevertheless, there exist several geometric quantities based on the intrinsic properties of the manifold and thus theoretically invariant to isometric deformations by construction. Feature detectors based on such quantities are called *intrinsic* and also *isometry-invariant* or *bending-invariant*. Examples of intrinsic geometric quantities are the Gaussian curvature (which has been used in several settings of [87]), and heat kernels [33, 81]. Feature detection methods based on the heat kernel define a function on the shape, measuring the amount of heat remaining at a point $\mathbf{x}$ after large time t, given a point source at $\mathbf{x}$ at time 0, and detect features as local maxima of this function.

Another type of transformation, of interest in practical applications, is changes in topology, manifested as the presence of holes, missing parts, or changes in connectivity. Feature detectors insensitive to such changes (typically, a simpler case of point-wise connectivity change) are referred to as *topology-invariant*.

Table 5.1 summarizes the properties of known feature detectors, some of which are detailed in what follows.

5.3.2 Harris 3D

An efficient feature detection method, called Harris operator, first proposed for the use in images [36] was extended to 3D shapes by Glomb [35] and Sipiran and Bustos

5 Feature-Based Methods in 3D Shape Analysis

Table 5.1 Comparison of 3D feature detectors

Descriptor	Representation	Invariance			
		Scale	Rigid	Bending	Topology
Dense	Any	Yes	Yes	Yes	Yes
Harris 3D [74]	Any	No	Yes	Approx	Approx
Mesh DOG [87]	Mesh	No	Yes	Approx[a]	Approx
Salient features [21]	Mesh	No	Yes	Approx	Approx
Heat kernel [81]	Any	No	Yes	Yes	Approx
MSER [27, 49]	Mesh, volume	Yes	Yes	Yes	Approx

[a]Unless truly intrinsic quantities are used

[74]. This method is based on measuring variability of the shape in a local neighborhood of the point, by fitting a function to the neighborhood, and identifying feature points as points where the derivatives of this function are high [12]. Unlike images, 3D data might have arbitrary topology and sampling, which complicates the computation of derivatives.

For each point **x** on the shape, a neighborhood of radius ρ (typically, a k-ring in mesh representation) is selected. The neighborhood points are brought into a canonical system of coordinates by first subtracting the centroid. Next, a plane is fitted to the translated points by applying PCA and choosing the direction corresponding to the smallest eigenvalues as the direction of the normal. The points are rotated so that the normal is aligned with the z-axis. A quadratic function of the form $f(u,v) = \mathbf{a}^\mathrm{T}(u^2, uv, v^2, u, v, 1)$ is then fitted to the set of transformed points, yielding a parametric representation of the local extrinsic surface properties. Here, u and v denote the tangent plane coordinates, and **a** stands for the quadratic patch parameters.

A 2×2 symmetric matrix

$$\mathsf{E} = \frac{1}{\sqrt{2\pi}\sigma} \int_{\mathbb{R}^2} e^{-\frac{u^2+v^2}{2\sigma^2}} \begin{bmatrix} f_u^2(u,v) & f_u(u,v)f_v(u,v) \\ f_u(u,v)f_v(u,v) & f_v^2(u,v) \end{bmatrix} du\, dv \quad (5.21)$$

is computed. The *3D Harris operator* is defined as the map assigning $\mathsf{H}(\mathbf{x}) = \det(\mathsf{E}) - 0.04\mathrm{tr}^2(\mathsf{E})$ to each point **x** on the shape. A fixed percentage of points with the highest values of $H(\mathbf{x})$ are selected as the feature points.

In [74], the neighborhood radius ρ (alternatively, the k-ring width k) and the Gaussian variance σ are performed adaptively for each point in order to make the method independent on sampling and triangulation.

5.3.3 Mesh DOG

The Mesh DOG descriptor introduced in Zaharescu et al. [87] assumes the shape in mesh representation and in addition to be given some function f defined on the mesh vertices. The function can be either photometric information (texture) or a geometric quantity such as curvature.

Given a scalar function f on the shape, its *convolution* with a radially-symmetric kernel $k(r)$ is defined as

$$(f * k)(\mathbf{x}) = \int k(d(\mathbf{x}, \mathbf{y})) f(\mathbf{y}) d\mathbf{y}, \qquad (5.22)$$

where $d(\mathbf{x}, \mathbf{y})$ is the geodesic distance between points $\mathbf{x}$ and $\mathbf{y}$. Zaharescu et al. [87] propose the following r-ring approximation:

$$(f * k)(\mathbf{x}) = \frac{\sum_{\mathbf{y} \in \mathbb{N}_r(\mathbf{x})} k(\|\mathbf{x} - \mathbf{y}\|) f(\mathbf{y})}{\sum_{\mathbf{y} \in \mathbb{N}_r(\mathbf{x})} k(\|\mathbf{x} - \mathbf{y}\|)}, \qquad (5.23)$$

which assumes a uniformly sampled mesh. Here, $\mathbb{N}_r(\mathbf{x})$ denotes the r-ring neighborhood of the point $\mathbf{x}$.

By subsequently convolving a function f with a Gaussian kernel g_σ of width σ, a scale space $f_0 = f$, $f_k = f_{k-1} * g_\sigma$ is constructed. The *difference of Gaussians* (DOG) operator at scale k is defined as $DOG_k = f_k - f_{k-1}$.

Feature points are selected as the maxima of the DOG scale space across scales, followed by non-maximum suppression, using the one ring neighborhood in the current and the adjacent scales. A fixed percentage of points with the highest values of DOG are selected. To further eliminate unstable responses, only features exhibiting *corner-like* characteristics are retained. For this purpose, the *Hessian* operator at every point $\mathbf{x}$ is computed as

$$\mathsf{H} = \begin{bmatrix} f_{uu}(\mathbf{x}) & f_{uv}(\mathbf{x}) \\ f_{uv}(\mathbf{x}) & f_{vv}(\mathbf{x}), \end{bmatrix} \qquad (5.24)$$

where f_{uu}, f_{uv} and f_{vv} are the second-order partial derivatives of f at $\mathbf{x}$. Second order derivatives are estimated w.r.t. some local system of coordinates u, v (e.g., by fixing $\mathbf{u}$ to be the direction of the gradient, $\mathbf{u} = \nabla_X f(\mathbf{x})$, and $\mathbf{v}$ perpendicular to it) by applying the directional derivative twice,

$$f_{uv}(\mathbf{x}) = \langle \nabla_X \langle \nabla_X f(\mathbf{x}), \mathbf{u} \rangle, \mathbf{v} \rangle. \qquad (5.25)$$

The condition number $\lambda_{\max}/\lambda_{\min}$ of H (typically, around 10) is independent of the selection of the local system of coordinates and is used to threshold the features.

5.3.4 Salient Features

In Mesh DOG, the scale space is built by filtering a scalar function on the mesh while keeping the mesh geometry intact. Castellani et al. [21] proposed to create a scale space by filtering the shape itself.

Let $\mathbb{X}^0 = \{\mathbf{x}_i\} \subset \mathbb{R}^3$ denote the extrinsic coordinates of points on a surface. For example, if the shape is represented as a mesh, $\mathbb{X}^0$ is the point cloud comprising the mesh vertices. One can apply a Gaussian kernel g_σ to this point cloud, obtaining a new set of points $\mathbb{X}^1 = \mathbb{X}^0 * g_\sigma$, where

$$\mathbf{x}_i^1 = \sum_j g_\sigma\big(\|\mathbf{x}_i - \mathbf{x}_j\|\big)\mathbf{x}_j. \tag{5.26}$$

Applying the kernel several times creates a scale space of "blurred" shapes $\mathbb{X}^k$. One can naturally define a vector-valued DOG scale space on the original surface by assigning a vertex $\mathbf{x}_i$ the difference of the corresponding blurred coordinates, $\mathbf{d}_i^k = \mathbf{x}_i^k - \mathbf{x}_i^{k-1}$. By projecting $\mathbf{d}_i^k$ onto the normal $\mathbf{N}(\mathbf{x}_i)$ at the point $\mathbf{x}_i$, a scalar-valued DOG scale space, referred to as the *scale map* by the authors, is created. From this stage on, an approach essentially identical to Mesh DOG is undertaken. The authors do not use filtering by Hessian operator response and propose to use a robust method inspired by [37] to detect the feature points.

5.3.5 Heat Kernel Features

Recently, there has been increased interest in the use of *diffusion geometry* for shape recognition [17, 53, 56, 62, 67, 71]. In particular, the spectral decomposition (5.14) of the heat kernel is especially attractive as there exists efficient and stable methods to discretize the Laplace-Beltrami operator and its eigendecomposition.

The diagonal of the heat kernel at different scales, $k_t(\mathbf{x}, \mathbf{x})$, referred to as the *heat kernel signature* (HKS), can be interpreted as a multi-scale notion of the Gaussian curvature. Local maxima of the HKS for a large time parameter correspond to tips of protrusions that can be used as stable features as recently proposed by Sun et al. [81] and Gebal et al. [33].

In the simplest setting, feature points are found as two-ring local maxima of $k_t(\mathbf{x}, \mathbf{x})$ at a sufficiently large scale t [81]. In a more sophisticated setting, the persistence diagram of $k_t(\mathbf{x}, \mathbf{x})$ is computed, as described in the sequel, and features with insufficiently large distance between birth and death times are filtered out [12, 26, 76].

5.3.6 Topological Features

A different variety of feature-based techniques have been inspired by topological, rather than geometrical, shape analysis [61]. The most common tool used in applying topological methods to feature-based shape analysis is the notion of *topological persistence* introduced and formalized by Edelsbrunner et al. [30]. In its most basic form, topological persistence allows the definition of a pairing between critical values of a function defined on a topological domain (such as a simplicial complex) in a canonical way. This pairing defines a persistence value associated with each critical point, which provides a principled way of distinguishing prominent local maxima and minima from noise. Thus, these techniques fit naturally into the feature-based shape analysis framework, where both feature detection and description are often obtained via analysis of critical values of some function. Several techniques have been recently proposed for finding stable feature points by applying topological persistence to different functions defined on the shape, including the Heat Kernel Signature [26, 76] and the eigenfunctions of the Laplace-Beltrami operator [69].

Let w be some non-negative scalar function defined on the surface (e.g., the heat kernel $k_t(\mathbf{x}, \mathbf{x})$ for a moderate time scale t). A *super-level set* of w is defined as $\{\mathbf{x} : w(\mathbf{x}) \geq \tau\}$. By sweeping τ from zero to infinity, either new connected components of the level sets are born, or previously existing components merge. Each connected component can be associated with a local maximum of w, when the component is first born. Merging of two components corresponding to two local maxima $\mathbf{x}_1$ and $\mathbf{x}_2$ occurs at τ such that there exists a path connecting $\mathbf{x}_1$ and $\mathbf{x}_2$ along which $f(\mathbf{x}) \geq \tau$. We say that the component corresponding to a smaller local maximum $\mathbf{x}_1 < \mathbf{x}_2$ dies at time τ, that is, is merged into the component corresponding to the larger local maximum $\mathbf{x}_2$. The *persistence diagram* represents the births and deaths of all the connected components by assigning to each component a point in $[0, \infty]^2$, with the x and y coordinates representing the birth and the death time, respectively. The persistence of a local maximum is defined as the difference between its death and birth times. Maxima that never die have infinite persistence.

An excellent application of topological persistence to shape analysis and shape matching was demonstrated by Agarwal et al. [1], who used it to define a feature detector and descriptor, by defining a function on a surface, which approximately captures the concavity and convexity at each point in a parameter-free way. For every point $\mathbf{x}$ on the surface, the authors use topological persistence to find a canonical pair $\mathbf{y}$ which shares the normal direction with $\mathbf{x}$. Then the *elevation function* at $\mathbf{x}$ is simply the difference of the height values of $\mathbf{x}$ and $\mathbf{y}$ in this normal direction. Elevation function is invariant to rigid deformations and allows the analysis of both concavities and convexities in a unified fashion. Prominent minima and maxima of the elevation function can also be used as natural stable features of a shape. Persistent maxima of the heat kernel $k_t(\mathbf{x}, \mathbf{x})$ have also been shown to constitute robust and repeatable feature points [26]. Applying methods from computational topology to feature-based shape analysis is an active and potentially fruitful area of research and we refer the interested reader to a recent book [29].

5.3.7 Maximally Stable Components

Another class of methods, introduced in [27, 49], detects stable regions of the shape as an alternative to detecting stable points. For the discussion, we will assume that the shape is represented by a graph $G = (\mathbb{X}, \mathbb{E})$ weighted by a non-negative *vertex weight* $w : \mathbb{X} \to \mathbb{R}$ or *edge weight* $d : \mathbb{E} \to \mathbb{R}$. The graph is said to be *connected* if there exists a path between every pair of vertices in it. A graph $G' = (\mathbb{X}' \subseteq \mathbb{X}, \mathbb{E}' \subseteq \mathbb{E})$ is called a *subgraph* of G and denoted by $G' \subseteq G$. A maximal connected subgraph is called a *component* of $\mathbb{X}$. Given $\mathbb{E}' \subseteq \mathbb{E}$, the graph induced by $\mathbb{E}'$ is the graph $G' = (\mathbb{X}', \mathbb{E}')$ whose vertex set is made of all vertices belonging to an edge in $\mathbb{E}'$, that is, $\mathbb{X}' = \{\mathbf{x} \in \mathbb{X} : \exists \mathbf{x}' \in \mathbb{X}, (\mathbf{x}, \mathbf{x}') \in \mathbb{E}'\}$. Given a vertex-weighted graph (G, w) with a weighting function w, the ℓ-*cross-section* of G is defined as the graph induced by $E_\ell = \{(\mathbf{x}_1, \mathbf{x}_2) \in \mathbb{E} : w(\mathbf{x}_1), w(\mathbf{x}_2) \leq \ell\}$ for some $\ell \geq 0$. In the same way, a cross-section of an edge-weighted graph (G, d) is induced by the edge subset $E_\ell = \{e \in \mathbb{E} : d(e) \leq \ell\}$. A connected component of the cross-section is called an ℓ-level set of the weighted graph. The *altitude* of a component C is defined as the minimal ℓ for which C is a component of the ℓ-cross-section of G. Altitudes establish a partial order relation on the connected components of G as any component C is contained in a component with higher altitude. The set of all such pairs $(\ell(C), C)$ therefore forms a *component tree*.

Given a sequence $\{(\ell, C_\ell)\}$ of nested components forming a branch in the component tree, the *stability* of C_ℓ is defined as

$$s(\ell) = \frac{\text{vol}(C_\ell)}{\frac{d}{d\ell}\text{vol}(C_\ell)}, \qquad (5.27)$$

where vol(C) denotes the area of the component C (or its volume in case of a three-dimensional manifold). In other words, the more the relative volume of a component changes with the change of ℓ, the less stable it is. A component C_{ℓ^*} is called *maximally stable* if the stability function has a local maximum at ℓ^*. Maximally stable components are widely known in the computer vision literature under the name of *maximally stable extremal regions* (*MSER*) [55], with $s(\ell^*)$ usually referred to as the region *score*. The construction of weighted component trees is based on the observation that the vertex set $\mathbb{V}$ can be partitioned into disjoint sets which are merged together going up in the tree. Maintaining and updating such a partition is done using the *union-find* algorithm and related data structures with $\mathcal{O}(n \log n)$ complexity [60]. Such an approach is used to implement single-link agglomerative clustering which is adopted here for the construction of the component tree.

Using vertex-weighting, any scalar function that distinguishes between vertices and captures the local geometrical properties such as mean curvature [27] can be used. For non-rigid shape analysis, diffusion-geometric weights have a clear advantage being deformation-invariant [76] and easily computed through the heat kernel. The simplest vertex weight is obtained as the diagonal of the heat kernel $w(\mathbf{x}) = k_t(\mathbf{x}, \mathbf{x})$, which, up to a monotonic transformation, can be thought of as an approximation of the Gaussian curvature at t. The choice of the parameter t defines the scale of such an approximation [81]. A scale-invariant version of this weight (the *commute-time kernel*) is obtained by integrating k_t over all time scales in the range $[0, \infty]$,

$$w(\mathbf{x}) = \sum_{i=0}^{\infty} \lambda_i^{-1} \phi_i^2(\mathbf{x}). \qquad (5.28)$$

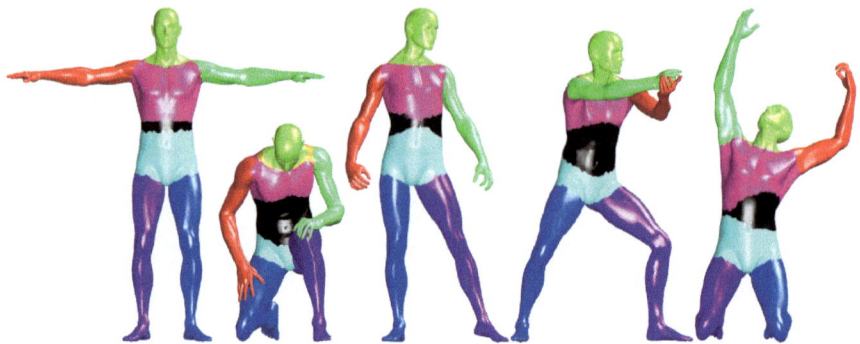

Fig. 5.3 Edge-weighted MSER. Figure reproduced from [49]

Edge weights offer more flexibility allowing the expression of dissimilarity relations between adjacent vertices. Examples of edge-weighted MSER extraction are given in Fig. 5.3. Since the heat kernel $k_t(\mathbf{x}_1, \mathbf{x}_2)$ represents the proximity or "connectivity" of two vertices $\mathbf{x}_1, \mathbf{x}_2$, any function of the form $d(\mathbf{x}_1, \mathbf{x}_2) = \eta(k^{-1}(\mathbf{x}_1, \mathbf{x}_2))$ can define an edge weight inversely proportional to the heat kernel value (here η denotes a non-negative monotonic function). Another natural way of defining edge weights is the *diffusion distance* (5.15) or its scale-invariant version, the *commute time distance* (5.16).

While the original formulation of shape MSER detectors focused on meshes, in principle there exists no limitation to extend it to other representations as well. Recently, an extension of the method to volumetric data has been proposed, with the volumetric heat kernels and diffusion distances used as the weighting functions.

5.3.8 Benchmarks

An ideal feature detector should be repeatable under the desired class of shape transformations and also detect "rich" feature points from which informative descriptors can be drawn. While the latter is largely application and data-dependent, the repeatability of the detector can be evaluated quantitatively on a set of representative shape transformations. SHREC'10 robust feature detection and description benchmark [12] evaluates the detector repeatability by running the detector on a set of reference shapes. The detected features are used as reference locations. Then, detection is performed on the same shapes undergoing simulated transformations of different types (non-rigid bending, different types of noise, holes, etc.), for which groundtruth correspondence with the reference shapes is known. Repeatability is evaluated by counting the fraction of features that are consistently detected in the proximity of the reference locations. Different varieties of the heat kernel methods achieved the best results on this benchmark.

5.4 Feature Descriptors

Given a set of feature points (or, in the case of a dense descriptor, all the points on the shape), a local descriptor is then computed. There exists a plethora of different shape descriptor algorithms, which depend very much on the representation in which the shape is given (e.g. mesh or point cloud), the kind of information available and its quality (e.g. sampling resolution), and the application in mind. A descriptor can be characterized by its (i) "informativity", i.e., the information content that can be used for shape discrimination; (ii) invariance to some class of shape transformations, such as deformations or noise, (iii) computational complexity, (iv) compactness of descriptor and complexity of comparison of two descriptors (e.g. in shape matching applications). In addition, if the descriptor is used in combination with a feature detector, its sensitivity to feature location (detector repeatability) might be important. There are many tradeoffs between these properties that can be made in feature-based shape analysis applications.

5.4.1 A Taxonomy

Descriptors can be categorized as *geometric* or *photometric* (or both, referred to as *hybrid*), depending whether they rely only on the 3D geometry of the shape, or also make use of the texture. Some photometric descriptors can be adapted to work with geometric information, where some geometric property (e.g. curvature) is used in place of the texture [87]. A wide variety of geometric quantities such as local patches [58], local moments [24] and volume [34], spherical harmonics [73], and contour and edge structures [45, 63] trying to emulate comparable features in images, can be used for geometric descriptors.

Multiscale descriptors (e.g. [20, 68, 81]) look at the shape at multiple levels of resolution, thus capturing different properties manifested at these scales. This is opposed to *single scale* or *scalar* descriptors, such as conformal factor [6].

Descriptors which are not altered by global scaling of the shape are called *scale-invariant*. Such an invariance can in some cases be achieved by shape normalization; a better approach is to build scale-invariance into the descriptor construction.

Because typically a descriptor operates locally around the feature point, feature descriptors are usually not very sensitive to non-rigid deformations of the shape. Nevertheless, there exist several geometric descriptors which are based on intrinsic properties of the manifold and thus theoretically invariant to isometric deformations by construction. Examples of intrinsic descriptors include histograms of local geodesic distances [10, 66], conformal factors [6], some settings of [87], and heat kernels [20, 81]. Such descriptors are called *intrinsic* and also *isometry-invariant* or *bending-invariant*.

Another type of transformation, of interest in practical applications, is changes in topology, manifested as the presence of holes, missing parts, or changes in connectivity. Descriptors insensitive to such changes (typically, a simpler case of point-wise connectivity change) are referred to as *topology-invariant*.

Table 5.2 Comparison of 3D feature descriptors

Descriptor	Representation	Invariance			
		Scale	Rigid	Bending	Topology
Gaussian curvature	Any	No	Yes	Yes	Approx[c]
Shape index [43]	Any	Yes	Yes	No	Approx[c]
Integral volume [34]	Volume, Mesh[a]	No	Yes	No	Approx[c]
Local histograms [66]	Any	No[b]	Yes	Yes	No[b]
HKS [81]	Any	No	Yes	Yes	Approx[c]
SIHKS [20]	Any	Yes	Yes	Yes	Approx[c]
CHKS [47]	Any+Texture	Yes	Yes	Yes	Approx[c,h]
VHKS [68]	Volume, Mesh[a]	No	Yes	Yes	Approx[c]
Spin image [39]	Any	No[i]	Yes	No[g]	Yes
Shape context [5]	Any	No	Yes	No	Yes
MeshHOG [87]	Mesh (+Texture)	Yes[d]	Yes	Approx[e]	Approx[d]
Conformal factor [6]	Mesh	No	Yes	Yes	No[f]

[a]Involving mesh rasterization

[b]Assuming geodesic distances. Different invariance properties can be achieved using diffusion or commute-time distances

[c]Point-wise connectivity changes have only a local effect and do not propagate to distant descriptors

[d]If photometric texture is used; in general, depending on the texture choice

[e]Triangulation-dependent

[f]Defined for shapes with fixed topology (e.g. watertight)

[g]Can be made approximately invariant using small support

[h]The use of photometric information can reduce the sensitivity to topological noise compared to HKS

[i]Can be made scale invariance as in [44]

Finally, some authors [34] make a distinction between *high-dimensional* (or *rich*) and *low-dimensional* descriptors. The former refers to descriptors providing a fairly detailed description of the shape properties around the point such as [5, 39], while the latter computes only a few values per point and typically are curvature-like quantities such as *shape index* [42] and *curvedness* [43]. We find this division somewhat misleading, as there is no direct relation between the descriptor "richness" and dimensionality (recent works in computer vision on descriptor hashing and dimensionality reduction [79] demonstrate that rich descriptors such as SIFT can be compactly represented in much lower dimensions without losing much information). The question whether the "richness" of a descriptor is sufficient depends in general on the application and the data.

Table 5.2 summarizes the theoretical properties of known descriptors, some of which are detailed in what follows. The invariance properties of many descriptors were evaluated quantitatively in the SHREC robust feature detection and description benchmark [12], testing the descriptor variability under simulated transformations of different types (non-rigid bending, different types of noise, holes, etc.).

We devote particular attention in this section to different varieties of the recently introduced heat kernel signatures, which we consider to be one of the most versatile descriptors currently available, possessing provable invariance properties, as well as a promising and interesting field for future research.

5.4.2 Curvature-Based Descriptors (HK and SC)

The simplest and perhaps earliest shape descriptors based on curvature (also referred to as HK descriptors) were introduced by Besl [8, 9]. The combination of the mean curvature $H = \frac{1}{2}(\kappa_1 + \kappa_2)$ and the Gaussian curvature $K = \kappa_1 \cdot \kappa_2$ allow the classification of the type of a local surface patch as saddle valley ($K, H < 0$), saddle ridge ($K < 0, H > 0$), concave or convex cylinder ($K = 0, H < 0$ and $K = 0, H > 0$, respectively), concave or convex ellipsoid ($K > 0, H < 0$ and $K > 0, H > 0$, respectively), or plane ($K = H = 0$). The values of H and K depend on the shape scale.

Koenderink and van Doorn [43] defined a different descriptor (referred to as SC) which decouples the type and strength of local shape curvature as follows: The *shape index* $S = \frac{2}{\pi} \text{atan}(\frac{\kappa_1 + \kappa_2}{\kappa_1 - \kappa_2})$ is a scale-invariant continuous gradation of concave ($-1 < S < -0.5$), hyperbolic ($-0.5 < S < 0.5$) and convex ($0.5 < S < 1$) shapes. The *curvedness* $C = \sqrt{(\kappa_1^2 + \kappa_2^2)/2}$ measures how strong the curvature of a particular local shape type is at a point. Planar shapes have indeterminate shape index and can be determined from the curvedness $C = 0$.

Both the HK and SC descriptors make use of the mean curvature, which is not intrinsic and hence not deformation invariant.

5.4.3 Spin Images

The *spin image* descriptor [2, 3, 39] represents the neighborhood of a point on a shape by fitting an oriented coordinate system at the point. The local system of cylindrical coordinates at point **x** is defined using the normal and tangent plane: the radial coordinate α defined as the perpendicular distance to the line through the surface normal $\mathbf{n}(\mathbf{x})$, and the elevation coordinate β, defined as the signed perpendicular distance to the tangent plane. The cylindrical angular coordinate is omitted because it cannot be defined robustly and unambiguously on many surface patches, such as those where the curvature is the similar in all directions.

A spin image is a histogram of points in the *support region* represented in α, β coordinates. The bins can be in linear or logarithmic scale. The support region is defined by limiting the range of the values of α and β (thus looking at points **y** within some distance from **x**) and requiring that $\cos^{-1}\langle \mathbf{n}(\mathbf{x}), \mathbf{n}(\mathbf{y}) \rangle < \varepsilon$ (limiting

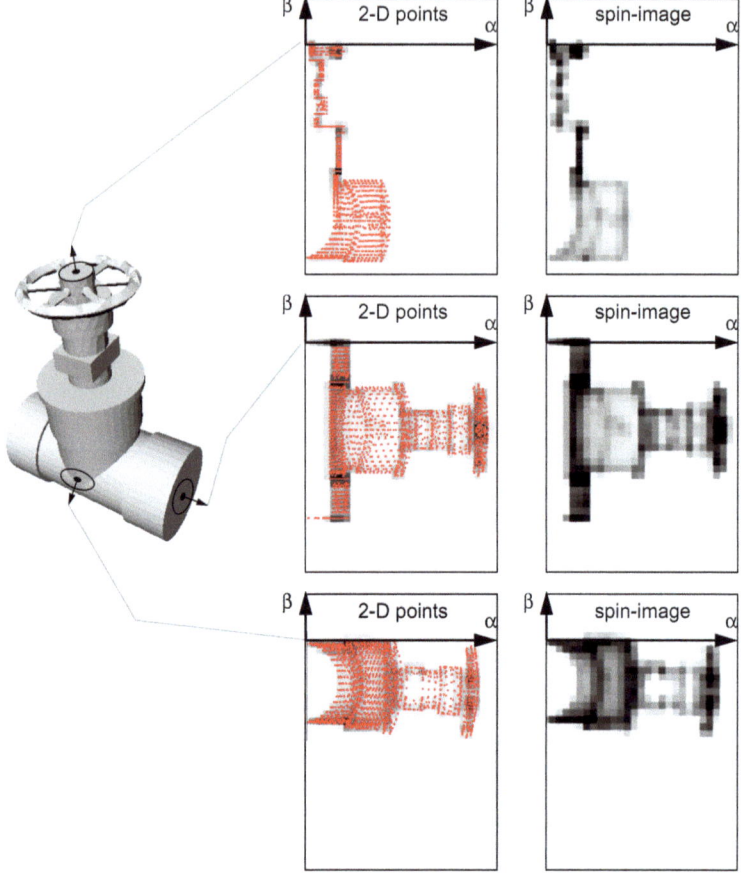

Fig. 5.4 Example of spin image descriptor computation. Figure reproduced from [38] with permission from Andrew E. Johnson

self occlusion artifacts). The histogram can be represented as a 2D image, hence the name of the descriptor (Fig. 5.4).

The spin image is applicable to any shape representation in which the point coordinates are explicitly given and normals and tangent planes can be computed (e.g., meshes or point clouds). Because of dependence on the embedding coordinates, such a descriptor is not deformation-invariant.

5.4.4 Shape Context

The concept of the *shape context* descriptor was first introduced in [5] for image analysis, though it is directly applicable to 3D shapes [46]. The shape context describes the structure of the shape as relations between a point to the rest of the points.

5 Feature-Based Methods in 3D Shape Analysis

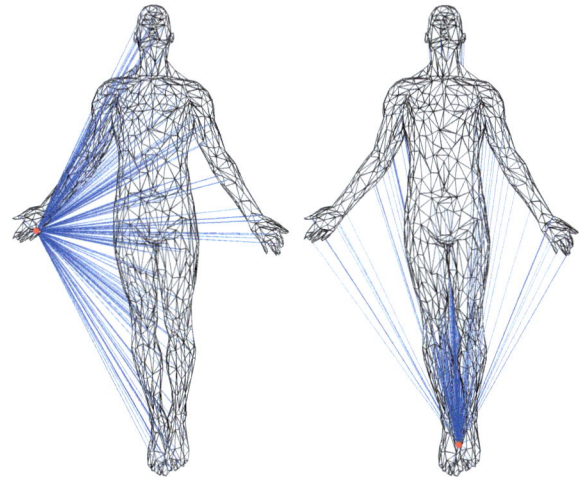

Fig. 5.5 Example of shape context computation. Shown in red is the reference point $\mathbf{x}$, and in blue the rays $\mathbf{y} - \mathbf{x}$

Given the coordinates of a point $\mathbf{x}$ on the shape, the shape context descriptor is constructed as a histogram of the direction vectors from $\mathbf{x}$ to the rest of the points, $\mathbf{y} - \mathbf{x}$. Typically, a log-polar histogram is used. The descriptor is applicable to any shape representation in which the point coordinates are explicitly given, such as mesh, point cloud, or volume. Such a descriptor is not deformation-invariant, due to its dependence on the embedding coordinates. An example of shape context computation is shown in Fig. 5.5.

5.4.5 Integral Volume Descriptor

The *integral volume* descriptor, used in [34], is an extension to 3D shapes of the concept of integral invariants introduced for image description in [54]. Given a solid object Ω with a boundary $X = \partial\Omega$, the descriptor measures volume contained in a ball of fixed radius r,

$$V_r(\mathbf{x}) = \int_{B_r(\mathbf{x}) \cap \Omega} d\mathbf{x}. \tag{5.29}$$

If $B_r(\mathbf{x}) \cap \Omega$ is simply connected, the volume descriptor can be related to the mean curvature $H(\mathbf{x})$ as $V_r(\mathbf{x}) = \frac{2\pi}{3} r^3 - \frac{\pi}{4} H r^4 + \mathcal{O}(r^5)$ [34]. Since the mean curvature is not intrinsic, the descriptor is sensitive to deformations of the shape. Varying the value of r, a multi-scale descriptor can be computed. Numerically, the descriptor is efficiently computed in a voxel representation of the shape, by means of convolution with the ball mask.

5.4.6 Mesh Histogram of Gradients (HOG)

MeshHOG [87] is a shape descriptor emulating SIFT-like image descriptors [51], referred to as *histograms of gradients* or *HOG*. The descriptor assumes the shape in mesh representation and in addition to be given some function f defined on the mesh vertices. The function can be either photometric information (texture) or a geometric quantity such as curvature. The descriptor at point $\mathbf{x}$ is computed by creating a local histogram of gradients of f in an r-ring neighborhood of $\mathbf{x}$. The gradient ∇f is defined extrinsically as a vector in $\mathbb{R}^3$ but projected onto the tangent plane at $\mathbf{x}$ which makes it intrinsic. The descriptor support is divided into four polar slices (corresponding to 16 quadrants in SIFT). For each of the slices, a histogram of 8 gradient orientations is computed. The result is a 32-dimensional descriptor vector obtained by concatenating the histogram bins.

The MeshHOG descriptor works with mesh representations and can work with photometric or geometric data or both. It is intrinsic in theory, though the specific implementation in [87] depends on triangulation.

5.4.7 Heat Kernel Signature (HKS)

The *heat kernel signature* (HKS) was proposed in [81] as an intrinsic descriptor based on the properties of heat diffusion and defined as the diagonal of the heat kernel. Given some fixed time values $t_1, \ldots, t_n$, for each point x on the shape, the HKS is an n-dimensional descriptor vector

$$p(\mathbf{x}) = \big(k_{t_1}(\mathbf{x}, \mathbf{x}), \ldots, k_{t_n}(\mathbf{x}, \mathbf{x})\big). \tag{5.30}$$

Intuitively, the diagonal values of the heat kernel indicate how much heat remains at a point after certain time (or alternatively, the probability of a random walk to remain at a point if resorting to the probabilistic interpretation of diffusion processes) and is thus related to the "stability" of a point under diffusion process.

The HKS descriptor is intrinsic and thus isometry-invariant, captures local geometric information at multiple scales, is insensitive to topological noise, and is informative (if the Laplace-Beltrami operator of a shape is non-degenerate, then any continuous map that preserves the HKS at every point must be an isometry). Since the HKS can be expressed in the Laplace-Beltrami eigenbasis as

$$k_t(\mathbf{x}, \mathbf{x}) = \sum_{i \geq 0} e^{-t\lambda_i} \phi_i^2(\mathbf{x}), \tag{5.31}$$

it is easily computed across different shape representations for which there is a way to compute the Laplace-Beltrami eigenfunctions and eigenvalues.

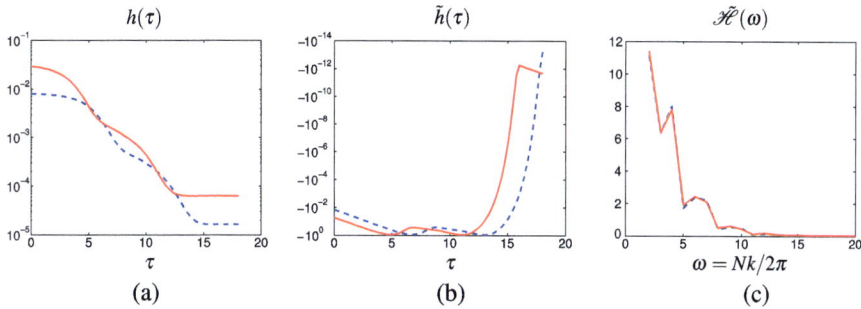

Fig. 5.6 Construction of the Scale-Invariant HKS: (**a**) we show the HKS computed at the same point, for a shape that is scaled by a factor of 11 (*blue dashed plot*); please notice the log-scale. (**b**) The signal $\tilde{h}(\tau)$, where the change in scale has been converted into a shifting in time. (**c**) The first 10 components of $|\tilde{\mathscr{H}}(\omega)|$ for the two signals; the descriptors computed at the two different scales are virtually identical

5.4.8 Scale-Invariant Heat Kernel Signature (SI-HKS)

A disadvantage of the HKS is its dependence on the global scale of the shape. If $\mathbb{X}$ is globally scaled by β, the corresponding HKS is $\beta^{-2}k_{\beta^{-2}t}(\mathbf{x}, \mathbf{x})$. In some cases, it is possible to remove this dependence by *global* normalization of the shape.

A *scale-invariant HKS* (SI-HKS) based on *local* normalization was proposed in [20]. Firstly, the heat kernel scale is sampled logarithmically with some basis α, denoted here as $k(\tau) = k_{\alpha^\tau}(x, x)$. In this scale-space, the heat kernel of the scaled shape becomes $k'(\tau) = a^{-2}k(\tau + 2\log_\alpha a)$ (Fig. 5.6a). Secondly, in order to remove the dependence on the multiplicative constant a^{-2}, the logarithm of the signal followed by a derivative w.r.t. the scale variable is taken,

$$\frac{d}{d\tau}\log k'(\tau) = \frac{d}{d\tau}\left(-2\log a + \log k(\tau + 2\log_\alpha a)\right)$$

$$= \frac{d}{d\tau}\log k(\tau + 2\log_\alpha a)$$

$$= \frac{\frac{d}{d\tau}k(\tau + 2\log_\alpha a)}{k(\tau + 2\log_\alpha a)}. \quad (5.32)$$

Denoting

$$\tilde{k}(\tau) = \frac{\frac{d}{d\tau}k(\tau)}{h(\tau)} = \frac{-\sum_{i\geq 0}\lambda_i \alpha^\tau \log \alpha e^{-\lambda_i \alpha^\tau}\phi_i^2(\mathbf{x})}{\sum_{i\geq 0}e^{-\lambda_i \alpha^\tau}\phi_i^2(\mathbf{x})}, \quad (5.33)$$

one thus has a new function $\tilde{k}$ which transforms as $\tilde{k}'(\tau) = \tilde{k}(\tau + 2\log_\alpha a)$ as a result of scaling (Fig. 5.6b). Finally, by applying the Fourier transform to $\tilde{k}$, the shift becomes a complex phase,

$$\mathscr{F}[\tilde{k}'](\omega) = \tilde{\mathscr{K}}'(\omega) = \tilde{\mathscr{K}}(\omega)e^{-j\omega 2\log_\alpha a}, \quad (5.34)$$

Fig. 5.7 *Top*: three components of the HKS (*left*) and the proposed SI-HKS (*right*), represented as *RGB color* and shown for different shape transformations (null, isometric deformation+scale, missing part, topological transformation). *Bottom*: HKS (*left*) and SI-HKS (*right*) descriptors at three points of the shape (marked with *red*, *green*, and *blue*). Dashed line shows the null shape descriptor

and taking the absolute value in the Fourier domain (Fig. 5.6c),

$$\left|\tilde{\mathcal{K}}'(\omega)\right| = \left|\tilde{\mathcal{K}}(\omega)\right|, \tag{5.35}$$

produces a scale-invariant descriptor (Fig. 5.7).

5.4.9 Color Heat Kernel Signature (CHKS)

If, in addition, *photometric* information is available, given in the form of *texture* $\alpha : X \to \mathcal{C}$ in some m-dimensional colorspace $\mathcal{C}$ (e.g. $m = 1$ in case of grayscale texture and $m = 3$ in case of color texture), it is possible to design diffusion processes that take into consideration not only geometric but also photometric information [47, 77]. For this purpose, let us assume the shape X to be a submanifold of some $(m+3)$-dimensional manifold $\mathcal{E} = \mathbb{R}^3 \times \mathcal{C}$ with the Riemannian metric tensor g, embedded by means of a diffeomorphism $\xi : X \to \xi(X) \subseteq \mathcal{E}$. A Riemannian metric on the manifold X induced by the embedding is the *pullback metric* $(\xi^*g)(r,s) = g(d\xi(r), d\xi(s))$ for $r, s \in T_x X$, where $d\xi : T_x X \to T_{\xi(x)}\mathcal{E}$ is the differential of ξ, and T denotes the tangent space. In coordinate notation, the pullback metric is expressed as $(\xi^*g)_{\mu\nu} = g_{ij}\partial_\mu\xi^i\partial_\nu\xi^j$, where the indices $i, j = 1, \ldots, m+3$ denote the embedding coordinates.

The structure of $\mathcal{E}$ is to model joint geometric and photometric information. The geometric information is expressed by the embedding coordinates $\xi_g = (\xi^1, \ldots, \xi^3)$; the photometric information is expressed by the embedding coordinates $\xi_p = (\xi^4, \ldots, \xi^{3+m}) = (\alpha^1, \ldots, \alpha^m)$. In a simple case when $\mathcal{C}$ has a Euclidean structure (for example, the Lab colorspace has a natural Euclidean metric), the pullback metric boils down to $(\xi^*g)_{\mu\nu} = \langle \partial_\mu\xi_g, \partial_\nu\xi_g \rangle_{\mathbb{R}^3} + \langle \partial_\mu\xi_p, \partial_\nu\xi_p \rangle_{\mathbb{R}^3}$.

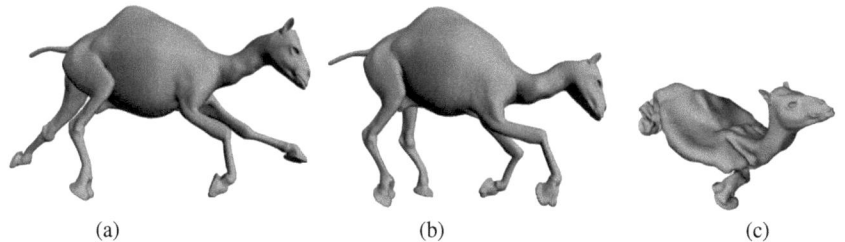

Fig. 5.8 Volumetric (**a, b**) and boundary (**c**) isometric deformations of a camel shape. Figure adapted from [80]. According to [68], volume isometries are a better model of physical objects deformation than boundary isometries

The Laplace-Beltrami operator associated with such a metric gives rise to a heat diffusion equation which takes into consideration both the geometry and the color of the object (simplistically put, the heat flows more slowly across different colors). This, in turn, allows the definition of a color-sensitive HKS (CHKS) that merges geometric and photometric information [47].

5.4.10 Volumetric Heat Kernel Signature (VHKS)

So far, we have considered the shape as a 2D boundary surface of a 3D physical object and represented the deformations of the object as deformation of the 2D surface. While physically realistic transformations of reasonably inelastic objects can be modeled as isometries of the 2D boundary surface ("boundary isometries"), the converse is not true: one can easily think of a transformation that preserves the metric structure of the object boundary, but not the volume (Fig. 5.8). Such transformations are not physically realistic, as they change the object volume or mass. However, all intrinsic descriptors we have discussed (including the HKS) would be invariant to such boundary isometries and thus have "too much invariance".

A different approach is to consider shapes as volumes and require invariance to transformations that preserve the metric structure inside the volume ("volume isometries"). Such descriptors are called *volumetric*. The idea of the heat kernel descriptor can be applied to volumetric shape representations [68]. In this case, given a solid object Ω, the heat diffusion inside the volume is given by the heat equation with Neumann boundary conditions on the boundary $\partial\Omega$,

$$\left(\Delta + \frac{\partial}{\partial t}\right) U(\mathbf{x}, t) = 0, \quad \mathbf{x} \in \text{int}(\Omega), \tag{5.36}$$
$$\langle \nabla U(\mathbf{x}, t), \mathbf{n}(\mathbf{x}) \rangle = 0, \quad \mathbf{x} \in \partial\Omega$$

where $\mathbf{n}$ is the normal to the boundary surface $\partial\Omega$, Δ is the positive-semidefinite Laplacian operator in $\mathbb{R}^3$, and $U : \Omega \times [0, \infty) \to \mathbb{R}$ is the volumetric heat distribution in Ω. The *volumetric heat kernel signature* (VHKS) is defined as the diagonal of the heat kernel of (5.36) at a set of time values t, expressible in the eigenbasis of the Laplacian as

$$K_t(\mathbf{x},\mathbf{x}) = \sum_{l=0}^{\infty} e^{-\Lambda_l t} \Phi_l(\mathbf{x})^2, \qquad (5.37)$$

where Λ_l, Φ_l are the eigenvalues and eigenfunctions of the Laplacian operator with the above boundary conditions,

$$\Delta \Phi_l(\mathbf{x}) = \Lambda_l \Phi_l(\mathbf{x});$$
$$\langle \nabla \Phi_l(\mathbf{x}), \mathbf{n}(\mathbf{x}) \rangle = 0, \quad \mathbf{x} \in \partial \Omega. \qquad (5.38)$$

The descriptor can be computed on any volumetric representation of the shape, allowing for efficient computation of the Laplacian eigenvalues and eigenfunctions. For meshes and other surface representations, it is necessary to perform rasterization to convert them into voxel representation [68].

The VHKS is invariant to volumetric isometries of the shape (i.e. deformations that do not change the metric structure inside the shape). Such transformations are necessarily isometries of the boundary $\partial \Omega$, but not vice versa. Thus, VHKS does not have the extra invariance that HKS has.

5.4.11 Case Study: Shape Retrieval Using Two Heat Kernel Descriptors (HKS and SI-HKS)

We conclude this section with a case study comparing the performance of two descriptors on a shape retrieval application using a "bags of features". For additional details on this application, the reader is referred to Chap. 7. A bag of features is a histogram of vector-quantized descriptors, which allows an efficient computation of similarity between shapes, boiling down to the comparison of two histograms. The bag of features inherits the invariance of the underlying local feature descriptor used for its construction. Thus, the choice of the descriptor is crucial for obtaining desired invariance.

In this test case, we used the cotangent weight scheme to discretize the surface Laplace-Beltrami operator; the heat kernel h was approximated using $k = 100$ largest eigenvalues and eigenvectors. For HKS, we used six scales 1024, 1351, 1783, 2353, 3104 and 4096; for the SI-HKS, we used an exponential scale-space with base $\alpha = 2$ and τ ranging from 1 to 25 with increments of $1/16$. After applying logarithm, derivative, and Fourier transform, the first 6 lowest frequencies were used as the local descriptor. SHREC 2010 dataset was used. The query set consisted of shapes from the dataset undergoing different transformations. Only a single correct match exists in the database, and ideally, it should be the first one.

An example of retrieval using bags of features built from HKS and SI-HKS descriptors is shown in Fig. 5.9. It clearly shows the failure of HKS-based bags of

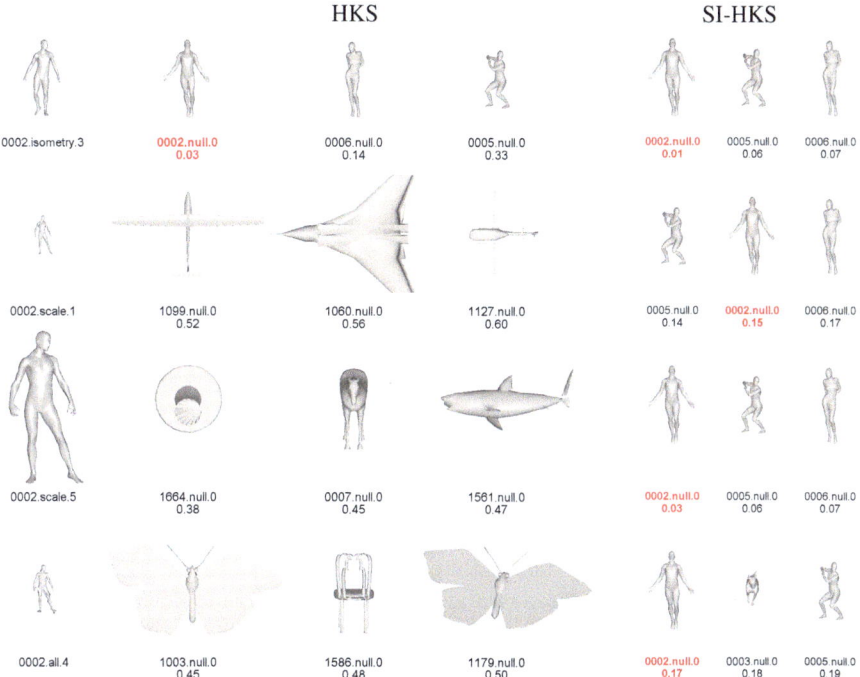

Fig. 5.9 Retrieval results using bags of features computed with HKS and SI-HKS, tested on the SHREC'10 robust large-scale shape retrieval dataset. *Left*: query shapes, *middle*: first three matches obtained with HKS descriptors, *right*: first three matches obtained with SI-HKS descriptors. Only a single correct match exists in the database (marked in *red*), and ideally, it should be the first one

features to correctly find similarity between scaled shapes, which makes the use of SI-HKS preferable over HKS in problems involving arbitrary shape scaling.

5.5 Research Challenges

Current challenges in descriptor research include finding a good proportion between theoretical invariance, discriminativity, sensitivity to noise and computational complexity. A single ideal tradeoff is unlikely to be found, since these parameters heavily depend on the application.

Another important challenge of interest both in 2D image and 3D shape analysis is incorporating spatial relations between features. Most feature descriptors capture only local information of the shape, while it is known that, in many cases, the spatial relations between different features are not less important. For example, on a human hand one would find five similar features corresponding to fingers, while their particular spatial configuration is what makes the object recognizable as a hand. Taking this example *ad absurdum*, one can think of a "soup of features" which have no clear spatial configuration. Recent works on symmetry [40, 59, 62, 66, 67], self-similarity [18, 64] and structure detection is a step in this direction.

5.6 Conclusions

This chapter described feature-based methods in 3D shape analysis that are commonly used in applications such as content-based shape retrieval and invariant shape correspondence. Though not completely new, this field is relatively unexplored in shape analysis and has lagged behind similar methods in 2D image analysis. The success of feature-based methods in computer vision has recently brought significant interest for developing similar approaches in shape analysis, either by finding analogies to 2D image features, or by exploiting 3D shape-specific construction.

This chapter tried to overview the basic ideas and principles in modern feature-based shape analysis models, placing an emphasis on feature detection and description, their invariance and quality. For different applications of these methods (e.g. in shape retrieval), the reader is referred to other chapters in this book.

It should be understood that feature-based shape analysis is a complicated pipeline with inter-dependent stages and, in particular, feature detection and description is a linked pair of operations. In some cases, the link is very natural and homogeneous and falls under the same mathematical model. For example, heat kernels can be used for both detection (heat kernel features) and description (heat kernel signatures).

More generically, it is possible to use different methods for feature detection and description. However, it is important to understand the strengths and limitations of each approach, which are often dependent on the data in hand. For example, one might use Gaussian curvature extrema as a detector, but then using spin images as a descriptor could be a bad idea, since they depend on the normal and Gaussian curvature extrema are exactly where this normal is changing the most.

5.7 Further Reading

For a broad overview of geometric foundations and algorithms in shape analysis, we refer the reader to [16]. For an excellent comprehensive treatment of differential and Riemannian geometry the reader is referred to [28] and [7]. While focusing on *local* features in this chapter, we intentionally completely left aside an interesting and broad field on *global* or *holistic* shape descriptors based on global geometric quantities such as metric distributions. The reader is referred to the chapter on manifold intrinsic similarity in [72] for an overview of these methods. An introduction to diffusion geometry and diffusion maps can be found in [25]. Details of SHREC'10 benchmarks mentioned in this chapter appear in [12–14]. Algorithms for dimensionality reduction and hashing of descriptors in the context of deformable shape retrieval are discussed in [11, 79]. For additional details on shape retrieval, refer to Chap. 7 of this book.

5.8 Questions

1. Give three example applications where feature-based methods in 3D shape analysis are useful.
2. What qualities do we look for in a good feature detector?
3. What qualities do we look for in a good feature descriptor?
4. Explain why descriptor invariance and the information richness of a descriptor often need to be traded-off against each other. Use spin images as an example in your argument.
5. Explain why Gaussian curvature is an intrinsic shape property, whereas mean curvature is not.
6. Outline how heat kernel signatures can be used to determine a set of correspondences across two shapes.
7. Explain the effect of global uniform shape scaling of the shape on the eigenfunctions and eigenvalues of the Laplace-Beltrami operator.

5.9 Exercises

1. Compute the Gaussian curvature map on a 3D shape and display it as a colormap. Which points have positive Gaussian curvature? Negative curvature?
2. Repeat Exercise 1 using several local scales. How does it affect the result?
3. Determine the local extrema of the Gaussian curvature at the most suitable scale. Display the detected points by overlaying them on the 3D shape.
4. Compute a set of descriptors at the points detected in Exercise 3. As the descriptor at each point, use the coordinates x, y, z. Under what circumstances is x, y, z a good/poor choice of descriptor with this particular detector?
5. Match the descriptors across a pair of facial scans of the same person using simple Euclidean metric. Note the problems matching across the symmetrical face. Suggest solutions to this problem of point matching for symmetrical objects.
6. Given a shape represented as a triangular mesh, discretize the Laplace-Beltrami operator using the cotangent weights formula. Compute and show the eigenvalues and eigenfunctions of the Laplace-Beltrami operator.
7. Test the effect of shape transformations on the eigenvalues and eigenfunctions of the Laplace-Beltrami operator. Experimentally confirm their bending-invariance.
8. Using the eigenvalues and eigenfunctions of the Laplace-Beltrami operator, compute the heat kernel. Show the heat kernel diagonal values at points of different curvature.
9. Using the heat kernel diagonal, compute the HKS descriptor. Test its behavior for different values of time scale.
10. Compute dense HKS descriptor on multiple shapes (use for example the SHREC dataset). Create a geometric vocabulary by clustering in the HKS descriptor space. Compute a bag of features by means of vector quantization of

the descriptors in the geometric vocabulary. Compare different settings of hard and soft quantization.
11. Using bags of features computed in Exercise 10, perform shape retrieval on a dataset of shapes undergoing deformations. Experimentally observe invariance and sensitivity of the descriptors.

References

1. Agarwal, P.K., Edelsbrunner, H., Harer, J., Wang, Y.: Extreme elevation on a 2-manifold. In: SCG'04: Proceedings of the twentieth annual symposium on Computational Geometry, pp. 357–365 (2004)
2. Andreetto, M., Brusco, N., Cortelazzo, G.M.: Automatic 3D modeling of textured cultural heritage objects. IEEE Trans. Image Process. **13**(3), 335–369 (2004)
3. Assfalg, J., Bertini, M., Pala, P., Del Bimbo, A.: Content-based retrieval of 3d objects using spin image signatures. IEEE Trans. Multimed. **9**(3), 589–599 (2007)
4. Bay, H., Tuytelaars, T., Van Gool, L.: SURF: speeded up robust features. In: Proc. ECCV, pp. 404–417 (2006)
5. Belongie, S., Malik, J., Puzicha, J.: Shape matching and object recognition using shape contexts. Trans. PAMI, 509–522 (2002)
6. Ben-Chen, M., Weber, O., Gotsman, C.: Characterizing shape using conformal factors. In: Proc. 3DOR (2008)
7. Berger, M.: A Panoramic View of Riemannian Geometry. Springer, Berlin (2003)
8. Besl, P.J.: Surfaces in Range Image Understanding. Springer, Berlin (1988)
9. Besl, P.J., Jain, R.C.: Invariant surface characteristics for 3d object recognition in range images. Comput. Vis. Graph. Image Process. **33**(1), 33–80 (1986)
10. Bronstein, A., Bronstein, M., Bruckstein, A., Kimmel, R.: Partial similarity of objects, or how to compare a centaur to a horse. Int. J. Comput. Vis. **84**(2), 163–183 (2009)
11. Bronstein, A., Bronstein, M., Guibas, L., Ovsjanikov, M.: Shape Google: geometric words and expressions for invariant shape retrieval. ACM Trans. Graph. **30**(1) (2011)
12. Bronstein, A.M., Bronstein, M.M., Bustos, B., Castellani, U., Crisani, M., Falcidieno, B., Guibas, L.J., Isipiran, I., Kokkinos, I., Murino, V., Ovsjanikov, M., Patané, G., Spagnuolo, M., Sun, J.: Shrec 2010: robust feature detection and description benchmark. In: Proc. 3DOR (2010)
13. Bronstein, A.M., Bronstein, M.M., Castellani, U., Falcidieno, B., Fusiello, A., Godil, A., Guibas, L.J., Kokkinos, I., Lian, Z., Ovsjanikov, M., Patané, G., Spagnuolo, M., Toldo, R.: Shrec 2010: robust large-scale shape retrieval benchmark. In: Proc. 3DOR (2010)
14. Bronstein, A.M., Bronstein, M.M., Castellani, U., Guibas, A.D.L.J., Horaud, R.P., Kimmel, R., Knossow, D., von Lavante, E., Mateus, D., Ovsjanikov, M., Sharma, A.: Shrec 2010: robust correspondence benchmark. In: Proc. 3DOR (2010)
15. Bronstein, A.M., Bronstein, M.M., Kimmel, R.: Three-dimensional face recognition. Int. J. Comput. Vis. **64**(1), 5–30 (2005)
16. Bronstein, A.M., Bronstein, M.M., Kimmel, R.: Numerical Geometry of Non-rigid Shapes. Springer, New York (2008)
17. Bronstein, A.M., Bronstein, M.M., Kimmel, R., Mahmoudi, M., Sapiro, G.: A Gromov-Hausdorff framework with diffusion geometry for topologically-robust non-rigid shape matching. In: IJCV (2010)
18. Bronstein, A.M., Bronstein, M.M., Mitra, N.J.: Intrinsic regularity detection in 3D geometry. In: Proc. ECCV (2010)
19. Bronstein, A.M., Bronstein, M.M., Ovsjanikov, M., Guibas, L.J.: Shape Google: a computer vision approach to invariant shape retrieval. In: Proc. NORDIA (2009)

20. Bronstein, M.M., Kokkinos, I.: Scale-invariant heat kernel signatures for non-rigid shape recognition. In: Proc. CVPR (2010)
21. Castellani, U., Cristani, M., Fantoni, S., Murino, V.: Sparse points matching by combining 3D mesh saliency with statistical descriptors. Comput. Graph. Forum **27**, 643–652 (2008)
22. Chazal, F., Guibas, L., Oudot, S., Skraba, P.: Persistence-based clustering in Riemannian manifolds. In: Proceedings of the 27th annual ACM symposium on Computational Geometry (2009)
23. Chum, O., Philbin, J., Sivic, J., Isard, M., Zisserman, A.: Total recall: automatic query expansion with a generative feature model for object retrieval. In: Proc. ICCV (2007)
24. Clarenz, U., Rumpf, M., Telea, A.: Robust feature detection and local classification for surfaces based on moment analysis. IEEE Trans. Vis. Comput. Graph. **10**(5), 516–524 (2004)
25. Coifman, R., Lafon, S.: Diffusion maps. Appl. Comput. Harmon. Anal. **21**(1), 5–30 (2006)
26. Dey, T.K., Li, K., Luo, C., Ranjan, P., Safa, I., Wang, Y.: Persistent heat signature for Pose-oblivious matching of incomplete models. In: Proc. SGP, pp. 1545–1554 (2010)
27. Digne, J., Morel, J., Audfray, N., Mehdi-Souzani, C.: The level set tree on meshes. In: Fifth International Symposium on 3D Data Processing, Visualization and Transmission (3DPVT'10) (2010)
28. Do Carmo, M.: Differential Geometry of Curves and Surfaces, vol. 2. Prentice-Hall, Englewood Cliffs (1976)
29. Edelsbrunner, H., Harer, J.: Computational Topology. An Introduction. Am. Math. Soc., Providence (2010)
30. Edelsbrunner, H., Letscher, D., Zomorodian, A.: Topological persistence and simplification. Discrete Comput. Geom. **28**(4), 511–533 (2002)
31. Elad, A., Kimmel, R.: On bending invariant signatures for surfaces. IEEE Trans. Pattern Anal. Mach. Intell. **25**(10), 1285–1295 (2003)
32. Floater, M.S., Hormann, K.: Surface parameterization: a tutorial and survey. Adv. Multiresol. Geom. Model. **1** (2005)
33. Gebal, K., Bærentzen, J.A., Aanæs, H., Larsen, R.: Shape analysis using the auto diffusion function. Comput. Graph. Forum **28**(5), 1405–1413 (2009)
34. Gelfand, N., Mitra, N.J., Guibas, L.J., Pottmann, H.: Robust global registration. In: Proc. SGP (2005)
35. Glomb, P.: Detection of interest points on 3D data: extending the Harris operator. In: Computer Recognition Systems 3. Advances in Soft Computing, vol. 57, pp. 103–111. Springer, Berlin (2009)
36. Harris, C., Stephens, M.: A combined corner and edge detection. In: Proc. Fourth Alvey Vision Conference, pp. 147–151 (1988)
37. Itti, L., Koch, C., Niebur, E.: A model of saliency-based visual attention for rapid scene analysis. Trans. PAMI **20**(11) (1998)
38. Johnson, A., Spin-images: a representation for 3-d surface matching. Ph.D. thesis, Carnegie Mellon University (1997)
39. Johnson, A.E., Hebert, M.: Using spin images for efficient object recognition in cluttered 3D scenes. IEEE Trans. Pattern Anal. Mach. Intell. **21**(5), 433–449 (1999)
40. Kazhdan, M., Funkhouser, T., Rusinkiewicz, S.: Symmetry descriptors and 3D shape matching. In: Proc. SGP, pp. 115–123 (2004)
41. Kim, V.G., Lipman, Y., Funkhouser, T.: Blended intrinsic maps. In: Proc. SIGGRAPH (2011)
42. Koehl, P.: Protein structure similarities. Curr. Opin. Struct. Biol. **11**(3), 348–353 (2001)
43. Koenderink, J.J., van Doorn, A.J.: Surface shape and curvature scales. Image Vis. Comput. **10**(8), 557–564 (1992)
44. Kokkinos, I., Yuille, A.: Scale invariance without scale selection. In: Proc. CVPR (2008)
45. Kolomenkin, M., Shimshoni, I., Tal, A.: On edge detection on surfaces. In: Proc. CVPR (2009)
46. Körtgen, M., Park, G., Novotni, M., Klein, R.: 3d shape matching with 3d shape contexts. In: Central European Seminar on Computer Graphics (2003)

47. Kovnatsky, A., Bronstein, M.M., Bronstein, A.M., Kimmel, R.: Photometric heat kernel signatures. In: Proc. Conf. on Scale Space and Variational Methods in Computer Vision (SSVM) (2011)
48. Lévy, B.: Laplace-Beltrami eigenfunctions towards an algorithm that "understands" geometry. In: Int. Conf. Shape Modeling and Applications (2006)
49. Litman, R., Bronstein, A.M., Bronstein, M.M.: Diffusion-geometric maximally stable component detection in deformable shapes. In: Computers and Graphics (2011)
50. Lo, T., Siebert, J.: Local feature extraction and matching on range images: 2.5 D SIFT. Comput. Vis. Image Underst. **113**(12), 1235–1250 (2009)
51. Lowe, D.: Distinctive image features from scale-invariant keypoint. In: IJCV (2004)
52. Magid, E., Soldea, O., Rivlin, E.: A comparison of Gaussian and mean curvature estimation methods on triangular meshes of range image data. Comput. Vis. Image Underst. **107**(3), 139–159 (2007)
53. Mahmoudi, M., Sapiro, G.: Three-dimensional point cloud recognition via distributions of geometric distances. Graph. Models **71**(1), 22–31 (2009)
54. Manay, S., Hong, B., Yezzi, A., Soatto, S.: Integral invariant signatures. In: Computer Vision-ECCV 2004, pp. 87–99 (2004)
55. Matas, J., Chum, O., Urban, M., Pajdla, T.: Robust wide-baseline stereo from maximally stable extremal regions. Image Vis. Comput. **22**(10), 761–767 (2004)
56. Mateus, D., Horaud, R.P., Knossow, D., Cuzzolin, F., Boyer, E.: Articulated shape matching using Laplacian eigenfunctions and unsupervised point registration. In: Proc. CVPR (2008)
57. Meyer, M., Desbrun, M., Schroder, P., Barr, A.H.: Discrete differential-geometry operators for triangulated 2-manifolds. In: Visualization and Mathematics III, pp. 35–57 (2003)
58. Mitra, N.J., Guibas, L.J., Giesen, J., Pauly, M.: Probabilistic fingerprints for shapes. In: Proc. SGP (2006)
59. Mitra, N.J., Guibas, L.J., Pauly, M.: Partial and approximate symmetry detection for 3D geometry. ACM Trans. Graph. **25**(3), 560–568 (2006)
60. Najman, L., Couprie, M.: Building the component tree in quasi-linear time. IEEE Trans. Image Process. **15**(11), 3531–3539 (2006)
61. Natarajan, V., Koehl, P., Wang, Y., Hamann, B.: Visual analysis of biomolecular surfaces. In: Visualization in Medicine and Life Sciences, Mathematics and Visualization, pp. 237–255 (2008)
62. Ovsjanikov, M., Sun, J., Guibas, L.J.: Global intrinsic symmetries of shapes. Comput. Graph. Forum **27**(5), 1341–1348 (2008)
63. Pauly, M., Keiser, R., Gross, M.: Multi-scale feature extraction on point-sampled surfaces. Comput. Graph. Forum **22**(3), 281–289 (2003)
64. Pauly, M., Mitra, N.J., Wallner, J., Pottmann, H., Guibas, L.J.: Discovering structural regularity in 3D geometry. In: Proc. SIGGRAPH (2008)
65. Pinkall, U., Polthier, K.: Computing discrete minimal surfaces and their conjugates. Exp. Math. **2**(1), 15–36 (1993)
66. Raviv, D., Bronstein, A.M., Bronstein, M.M., Kimmel, R.: Symmetries of non-rigid shapes. In: Proc. NRTL (2007)
67. Raviv, D., Bronstein, A.M., Bronstein, M.M., Kimmel, R., Sapiro, G.: Diffusion symmetries of non-rigid shapes. In: Proc. 3DPVT (2010)
68. Raviv, D., Bronstein, M.M., Bronstein, A.M., Kimmel, R.: Volumetric heat kernel signatures. In: Proc. ACM Multimedia Workshop on 3D Object Retrieval (2010)
69. Reuter, M.: Hierarchical shape segmentation and registration via topological features of Laplace-Beltrami eigenfunctions. Int. J. Comput. Vis. **89**(2), 287–308 (2010)
70. Reuter, M., Wolter, F.E., Peinecke, N.: Laplace-spectra as fingerprints for shape matching. In: Proc. ACM Symp. Solid and Physical Modeling, pp. 101–106 (2005)
71. Rustamov, R.M.: Laplace-Beltrami eigenfunctions for deformation invariant shape representation. In: Proc. SGP, pp. 225–233 (2007)
72. Scherzer, O.: Handbook of Mathematical Methods in Imaging. Springer, Berlin (2010)

73. Shilane, P., Funkhauser, T.: Selecting distinctive 3D shape descriptors for similarity retrieval. In: Proc. Shape Modelling and Applications (2006)
74. Sipiran, I., Bustos, B.: A robust 3D interest points detector based on Harris operator. In: Proc. 3DOR, pp. 7–14. Eurographics (2010)
75. Sivic, J., Zisserman, A.: Video Google: A text retrieval approach to object matching in videos. In: Proc. CVPR (2003)
76. Skraba, P., Ovsjanikov, M., Chazal, F., Guibas, L.: Persistence-based segmentation of deformable shapes. In: Proc. NORDIA, pp. 45–52 (2010)
77. Sochen, N., Kimmel, R., Malladi, R.: A general framework for low level vision. IEEE Trans. Image Process. **7**(3), 310–318 (1998)
78. Starck, J., Hilton, A.: Correspondence labelling for widetimeframe free-form surface matching. In: Proc. ICCV (2007)
79. Strecha, C., Bronstein, A.M., Bronstein, M.M., Fua, P.: LDAHash: improved matching with smaller descriptors. Technical Report, EPFL (2010)
80. Sumner, R.W., Popović, J.: Deformation transfer for triangle meshes. In: Proc. Conf. Computer Graphics and Interactive Techniques, pp. 399–405 (2004)
81. Sun, J., Ovsjanikov, M., Guibas, L.: A concise and provably informative multi-scale signature based on heat diffusion. Comput. Graph. Forum **28**(5), 1383–1392 (2009)
82. Thorstensen, N., Keriven, R.: Non-rigid shape matching using geometry and photometry. In: Proc. CVPR (2009)
83. Toldo, R., Castellani, U., Fusiello, A.: Visual vocabulary signature for 3D object retrieval and partial matching. In: Proc. 3DOR (2009)
84. Torresani, L., Kolmogorov, V., Rother, C.: Feature correspondence via graph matching: models and global optimization. In: Proc. ECCV, pp. 596–609 (2008)
85. Wang, C., Bronstein, M.M., Bronstein, A.M., Paragios, N.: Discrete minimum distortion correspondence problems for non-rigid shape matching. In: Proc. Conf. on Scale Space and Variational Methods in Computer Vision (SSVM) (2011)
86. Wardetzky, M., Mathur, S., Kälberer, F., Grinspun, E.: Discrete Laplace operators: no free lunch. In: Conf. Computer Graphics and Interactive Techniques (2008)
87. Zaharescu, A., Boyer, E., Varanasi, K., Horaud, R.: Surface feature detection and description with applications to mesh matching. In: Proc. CVPR (2009)

Chapter 6
3D Shape Registration

Umberto Castellani and Adrien Bartoli

Abstract Registration is the problem of bringing together two or more 3D shapes, either of the same object or of two different but similar objects. This chapter first introduces the classical Iterative Closest Point (ICP) algorithm, which represents the gold standard registration method. Current limitations of ICP are addressed and the most popular variants are described to improve the basic implementation in several ways. Challenging registration scenarios are analyzed and a taxonomy of recent and promising alternative registration techniques is introduced. Three case studies are then described with an increasing level of problem difficulty. The first case study describes a simple but effective technique to detect outliers. The second case study uses the Levenberg-Marquardt optimization procedure to solve standard pairwise registration. The third case study focuses on the challenging problem of deformable object registration. Finally, open issues and directions for future work are discussed and conclusions are drawn.

6.1 Introduction

Registration is a critical issue for various problems in computer vision and computer graphics. The overall aim is to find the best alignment between two objects or between several instances of the same object, in order to bring the shape data into the same reference system. The main high level problems that use registration techniques are:

1. **Model reconstruction.** The goal in model reconstruction is to create a complete object model from partial 3D views obtained by a 3D scanner. Indeed, it is rare that a single 3D view captures the whole object structure, mainly due to self occlusions. Registration allows one to obtain the alignment between the partial

U. Castellani (✉)
University of Verona, Verona, Italy
e-mail: Umberto.Castellani@univr.it

A. Bartoli
Université d'Auvergne, Clermont-Ferrand, France
e-mail: Adrien.Bartoli@gmail.com

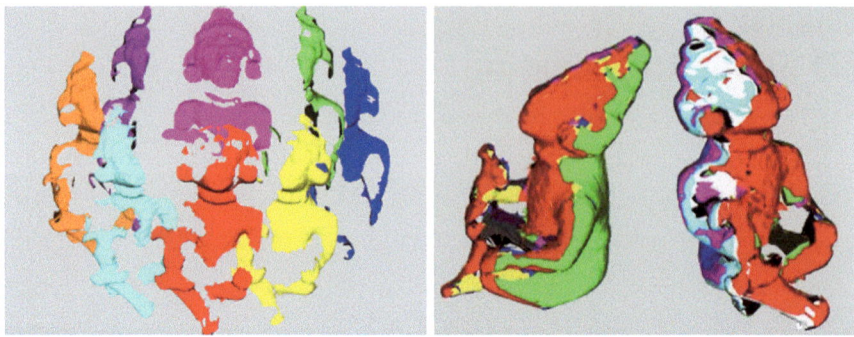

Fig. 6.1 Example of model reconstruction. Partial 3D views of the object of interest are acquired (*left*). After registration all the 3D views are transformed to the common reference system and merged (*right*). Figure generated by Alessandro Negrente, reproduced from [34]

overlapping 3D views in order to build a complete object model, also called a mosaic (see Fig. 6.1). In this context, registration is first applied between pairs of views [7, 78]. The whole model is then reconstructed using multiple view registration refinement [43, 78]. Typically, model reconstruction is employed in *cultural heritage* [6] to obtain 3D models of archaeological findings. It has also been applied in applications such as *reverse engineering* and *rapid prototyping* [95] and for vision in hostile environments [17, 18].

2. **Model fitting.** The goal in model fitting is to compute the transformation between a partial 3D view and a known CAD model of the actual object. Model fitting is used in robotics for object grasping [25, 64] and model-based object tracking [75]. Model fitting is typically used with rigid objects but has recently been extended to deformable objects [19].

3. **Object recognition.** The goal in object recognition is to find, amongst a database of 3D models, which one best matches an input partial 3D view. This problem is more challenging than model fitting since a decision has to be made regarding which model, if any, is the sought one. Solving the recognition problem this way is called *recognition-by-fitting* [92]. Several works have been done for 3D face recognition [9, 10, 83] and for 3D object retrieval [33, 90]. Registration becomes more challenging in a cluttered environment [4, 47, 56].

4. **Multimodal registration.** The goal in multimodal registration is to align several views of the same object taken by different types of acquisition systems. After registration, the information from different modalities can be merged for comparison purposes or for creating a multimodal object model. This problem is typical in medical imaging where it is common to register MRI and CT scans or MRI and PET scans [54, 84]. 3D medical image registration is discussed further in Chap. 11.

This chapter gives a general formulation for the registration problem. This formulation leads to computational solutions that can be used to solve the four above mentioned tasks. It encompasses most of the existing registration algorithms. For a detailed description of registration techniques and experimental comparisons, we refer the reader to recent surveys [48, 57, 76, 78, 79]. It is worth mentioning that most of the existing computational solutions are based on the seminal Iterative Closest Point (ICP) [7] algorithm that we will describe shortly.

Chapter Outline This chapter is organized as follows. We first present the two-view registration problem and the current algorithmic solutions. We then describe some advanced registration techniques. We give a comprehensive derivation of algorithms for registration by proposing three case studies. We give an overview of open challenges with future directions and conclusions. Finally, suggestions for further reading, questions and exercises are proposed.

6.2 Registration of Two Views

Firstly we give a mathematical formulation of the two-view registration problem and then derive the basic ICP algorithm and discuss its main variants.

6.2.1 Problem Statement

Given a pair of views $\mathbb{D}$ and $\mathbb{M}$ representing two scans (partial 3D views) of the same object, registration is the problem of finding the parameters $\mathbf{a}$ of the transformation function $T(\mathbf{a}, \mathbb{D})$ which best aligns $\mathbb{D}$ to $\mathbb{M}$. Typically, $\mathbb{D}$ and $\mathbb{M}$ are either simple point clouds or triangulated meshes [15]. The moving view $\mathbb{D}$ is called the *data-view*, while the fixed view $\mathbb{M}$ is called the *model-view*. The registration problem is solved by estimating the parameters $\mathbf{a}^*$ of the transformation T that satisfy:

$$\mathbf{a}^* = \arg\min_{\mathbf{a}} E\big(T(\mathbf{a}, \mathbb{D}), \mathbb{M}\big), \qquad (6.1)$$

where E is called the *error function* and measures the registration error. Figure 6.2 illustrates the two-view registration process. The data-view and the model-view show different portions of *Bunny*. The transformation function $T(\mathbf{a}, \mathbb{D})$ is applied and the registered views are shown.

Most of the registration methods are based on the paradigm defined directly above and differ in the following aspects:

The transformation function. The transformation function T usually implements a rigid transformation of the 3D space. It uses a translation vector $\mathbf{t}$ and a rotation matrix R whose values are encoded or parametrized in the parameter vector $\mathbf{a}$. The transformation function may also handle deformations; this requires a more complex formulation.

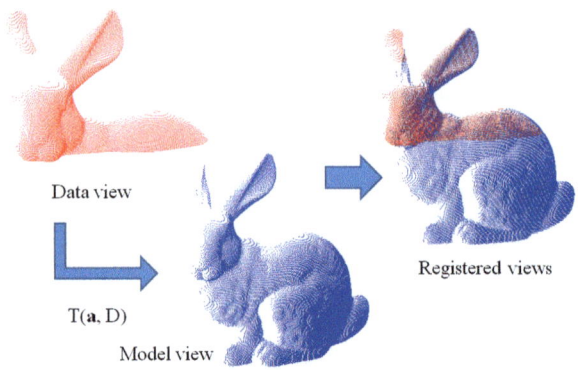

Fig. 6.2 Pairwise registration. The data-view and the model-view (*left*) are to be registered. The transformation function $T(\mathbf{a}, \mathbb{D})$ allows one to move the data-view to the model-view's coordinate frame (*right*) to align the two views

The error function. The error function E measures the registration error or dissimilarity between $\mathbb{D}$ and $\mathbb{M}$ after alignment. When the transformation function T is rigid, E is a measure of *congruence* between the two views. In general E takes the form of an L_2 approximation of the Hausdorff distance, which further involves the so-called *point-to-point* distance [7] or the *point-to-plane* distance [23].

The optimization method. This is the method or algorithm used to find the minimizer $\mathbf{a}$ in Eq. (6.1). The gold standard is the iterative approach used in the ICP algorithm [7], which was specifically designed for the problem at hand. General purpose optimization methods such as Levenberg-Marquardt [32] have also been used for this problem.

6.2.2 The Iterative Closest Points (ICP) Algorithm

In the classical ICP algorithm [7] the overall aim is to estimate a rigid transformation with parameters $\mathbf{a}^* = (\mathsf{R}, \mathbf{t})$. Both views are treated as point clouds $\mathbb{D} = \{\mathbf{d}_1, \ldots, \mathbf{d}_{N_d}\}$ and $\mathbb{M} = \{\mathbf{m}_1, \ldots, \mathbf{m}_{N_m}\}$. The error function is chosen as:

$$E_{ICP}(\mathbf{a}, \mathbb{D}, \mathbb{M}) = \sum_{i=1}^{N_d} \left\| (\mathsf{R}\mathbf{d}_i + \mathbf{t}) - \mathbf{m}_j \right\|^2, \qquad (6.2)$$

where we define $E_{ICP}(\mathbf{a}, \mathbb{D}, \mathbb{M}) = E(T(\mathbf{a}, \mathbb{D}), \mathbb{M})$ and where $(\mathbf{d}_i, \mathbf{m}_j)$ are corresponding points [78].[1] Fixing $\mathbf{d}_i \in \mathbb{D}$ the corresponding point $\mathbf{m}_j \in \mathbb{M}$ is computed such that:

$$j = \underset{k \in \{1, \ldots, N_m\}}{\arg\min} \left\| (\mathsf{R}\mathbf{d}_i + \mathbf{t}) - \mathbf{m}_k \right\|^2. \qquad (6.3)$$

---

[1] Note that the pair $(\mathbf{d}_i, \mathbf{m}_j)$ is initially a tentative correspondence, which becomes a true correspondence when convergence to a global minimum is attained.

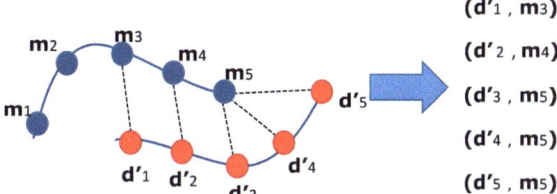

Fig. 6.3 Correspondence estimation in ICP. For each transformed data point $\mathbf{d}'_i = \mathsf{R}\mathbf{d}_i + \mathbf{t}$ the closest model point $\mathbf{m}_j$ is estimated (*left*). The list of corresponding points is then defined (*right*)

More specifically, the value

$$e_i^2 = \|(\mathsf{R}\mathbf{d}_i + \mathbf{t}) - \mathbf{m}_j\|^2 \tag{6.4}$$

is the square of the *residual*. Figure 6.3 illustrates the step of correspondence computation. For each data point (in red) the closest model point (in blue) is computed using the Euclidean distance. The list of correspondences is thus obtained. Note that, given point correspondences, the computation of R and **t** to minimize E_{ICP} in Eq. (6.2) can be solved in closed-form [78]. Several approaches are possible for the closed-form, least-squares estimation of this 3D rigid body transformation. These include approaches based on singular value decomposition (SVD), unit quaternion, dual quaternion, and orthonormal matrices. Although the study of Eggert et al. [30] found little difference in the accuracy and robustness of all these approaches, perhaps the most well-known of these is the SVD approach by Arun et al. [3]. Here, the cross-covariance matrix is formed for the N_d correspondences, $(\mathbf{d}_i, \mathbf{m}_j)$, as

$$\mathsf{C} = \frac{1}{N_d} \sum_{i=1}^{N_d} [\mathbf{d}_i - \bar{\mathbf{d}}][\mathbf{m}_j - \bar{\mathbf{m}}]^T, \tag{6.5}$$

where the means $\bar{\mathbf{d}}, \bar{\mathbf{m}}$ are formed over the N_d correspondences. Performing the SVD of C gives us:

$$\mathsf{USV}^T = \mathsf{C} \tag{6.6}$$

where U and V are two orthogonal matrices and S is a diagonal matrix of singular values. The rotation matrix R can be calculated from the orthogonal matrices as:

$$\mathsf{R} = \mathsf{VU}^T. \tag{6.7}$$

Umeyama states that this solution may fail to give a correct rotation matrix and give a reflection instead when the data is severely corrupted [94]. Thus, it can be modified to always return a correct rotation matrix [94]:

$$\mathsf{R} = \mathsf{VS'U}^T, \tag{6.8}$$

where

$$\mathsf{S'} = \begin{cases} \mathsf{I} & \text{if } \det(\mathsf{U})\det(\mathsf{V}) = 1 \\ \mathrm{Diag}(1, 1, \ldots, 1, -1) & \text{if } \det(\mathsf{U})\det(\mathsf{V}) = -1. \end{cases}$$

Once the rotation matrix has been estimated, the translation vector **t** can be estimated as:

$$\mathbf{t} = \bar{\mathbf{m}} - \mathsf{R}\bar{\mathbf{d}}. \tag{6.9}$$

The ICP algorithm is iterative because it iteratively improves the tentative correspondences. If true correspondences were known, clearly the process could operate in one pass. ICP has two main steps in its inner loop: (i) closest point computation and (ii) rigid transformation estimation. In more detail, the algorithm operates as follows:

1. For each data-point $\mathbf{d}_i \in \mathbb{D}$, compute the closest point $\mathbf{m}_j \in \mathbb{M}$ according to Eq. (6.3).
2. With the correspondences $(\mathbf{d}_i, \mathbf{m}_j)$ from step 1, estimate the new transformation parameters $\mathbf{a} = (\mathsf{R}, \mathbf{t})$.
3. Apply the new transformation parameters **a** from step 2 to the point cloud $\mathbb{D}$.
4. If the change in $E_{ICP}(\mathbf{a}, \mathbb{D}, \mathbb{M})$ between two successive iterations is lower than a threshold then terminate, else go to step 1.

It was proven [7] that this algorithm is guaranteed to converge monotonically to a local minimum of Eq. (6.2). Note that, as for any local iterative method, a strategy for initializing **a** must be used. An overview of the most popular initialization strategies is given in Sect. 6.2.3.1.

6.2.3 ICP Extensions

Although ICP has been successfully applied to many registration problems, there are several critical issues that need to be taken care of. In particular, ICP performs well when the following assumptions are met:

1. *The two views must be close to each other.* If not, ICP will probably get stuck in a local minimum. This issue is typically solved by pre-alignment of the two 3D views, also called *coarse* registration.
2. *The two views must fully overlap or the data-view* $\mathbb{D}$ *must be a subset of the model-view* $\mathbb{M}$. The problem arises from the fact that ICP always assigns a closest model point to every data point. If a data point has no corresponding model point, this will create a spurious correspondence, an *outlier* with respect to the sought transformation, that will bias the solution or prevent the algorithm from finding the correct transformation parameters.

Two other important issues are the *speed* of computation and the *accuracy* of the ICP algorithm. Typically, methods focused on speed improvement try to speed up the closest point computation step, which is the bottleneck of the algorithm. Other interesting approaches address the speed of convergence by proposing new distance formulations for the problem described by Eq. (6.1). Methods focusing on accuracy exploit additional information in order to measure the *similarity* between corresponding points not only in terms of proximity. In the following, we describe

6 3D Shape Registration

Fig. 6.4 A taxonomy of some ICP extensions

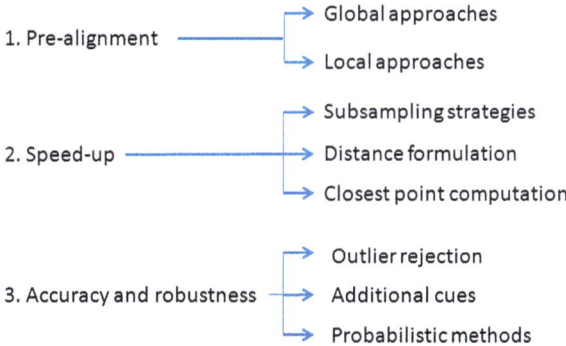

some registration techniques which improve the basic ICP method in several ways. Figure 6.4 illustrates the proposed taxonomy of ICP extensions so as to easily understand the organization of previous work in this field.

6.2.3.1 Techniques for Pre-alignment

The aim of pre-alignment techniques is to estimate a coarse transformation which will allow the two views to get closer. This helps the data-view to be transformed within the basin of attraction of the correct local minimum. In practice, instead of searching *dense* point-to-point correspondences, pre-alignment techniques estimate the best matching between *features* extracted from the views. Roughly speaking the features can be *global* or *local*. The former is a compact representation that effectively and concisely describes the entire view. The latter is a collection of local and discriminative descriptors computed on subparts of the views.

Global Approaches Typically global approaches estimate and match the principal coordinate system of each view. The simplest approach is to compute the main translational alignment by shifting the centroids of the two point clouds to the origin of the coordinate system (i.e. zero-mean). In order to estimate the orientation of the principal axes, Principal Component Analysis (PCA) can be performed on the point clouds. The problems with PCA as a pre-alignment method are (i) a 180 degree ambiguity in the direction of the principal axes, (ii) principal axes may switch for shapes that have eigenvalues similar in value, particularly if the object is able to deform slightly, (iii) a vulnerability to outliers in the raw shape data (as discussed). Even if we enforce a right handed frame using the sign of the cross-product of basis vectors, there still exists an overall 180 degree ambiguity, unless higher order moments are used. Moments of higher orders are also useful to improve accuracy [11]. Of course, these approaches perform well when the two views fully overlap. Otherwise, the non-overlapping parts change the estimation of the principal axes and thus affect the pre-alignment. Some improvements have been made by extracting and matching the *skeletons* of the views [20, 60] but this is feasible for articulated objects only.

Local Approaches Local approaches define a *descriptor* (or signature) for each 3D point which encodes local shape variation in the point neighborhood [16, 47, 49, 62, 89]. Point correspondences are then obtained as the best matches in regard of the point signatures. Various methods to compute signatures were proposed. In their seminal work [47], Johnson and Hebert introduced *Spin Images*. In a spin-image, the neighbors of some selected 3D point (e.g. a 3D interest point) are binned in a 2D cylindrical-polar coordinate system. This consists of a distance from the selected point within that point's tangent plane and a signed height above/below the tangent plane. Thus the spin-image is a 2D histogram of 3D shape, where one dimension of information is sacrificed for pose invariance. In [50] curvilinear features on the object are estimated from a small amount of points of interest. Gaussian and mean curvatures are used to this aim. Similarly, in [99], bitangent curve pairs were used as landmarks on the surface. In [62] a geometric scale-space analysis of 3D models was proposed from which a scale-dependent local shape descriptor was derived. Similarly, in [16], registration involves few feature points by extending the approach for salient point detection to the 3D domain. A *generative model* is then estimated as a point descriptor by using Hidden Markov Models (HMMs). In [49] the proposed descriptor encodes not only local information around the point, but also inter-point relationships. The method is inspired by the so-called *Shape Context* [5] which was improved using the *Bag-of-Words* paradigm [26]. Note that from the analysis of inter-point relationships it is also possible to estimate the overlapping region between two views. It is worth noting that, in general, the estimation of the overlap area is not trivial. An interesting approach was proposed in [82] by combining local geometric features with advanced graph matching techniques. The method consists of representing all tentative point matches as a graph, and then selecting as many *consistent* matches among them as possible. To this aim, a global discrete optimization problem is proposed based on the so called *maximum strict sub-kernel algorithm* [81].

6.2.3.2 Techniques for Improving Speed

The speed of the algorithm is crucial for many applications. Unfortunately, when the number of points is very high, the basic ICP algorithm becomes very slow. In order to address this issue several strategies have been proposed, which we now outline.

Subsampling Subsampling can be applied to either the data-view only or to both the data-view and the model-view. *Random* and *uniform* strategies are common approaches [78]. *Normal space* sampling is a more sophisticated approach based on choosing points such that the distribution of normals among the selected points is as spread as possible. This increases the influence of smaller details which are crucial to better disambiguate the rigid transformation due to translational sliding.

Closest Point Computation As mentioned above, closest point computation is the bottleneck of the registration process due to the quadratic complexity ($O(n^2)$)

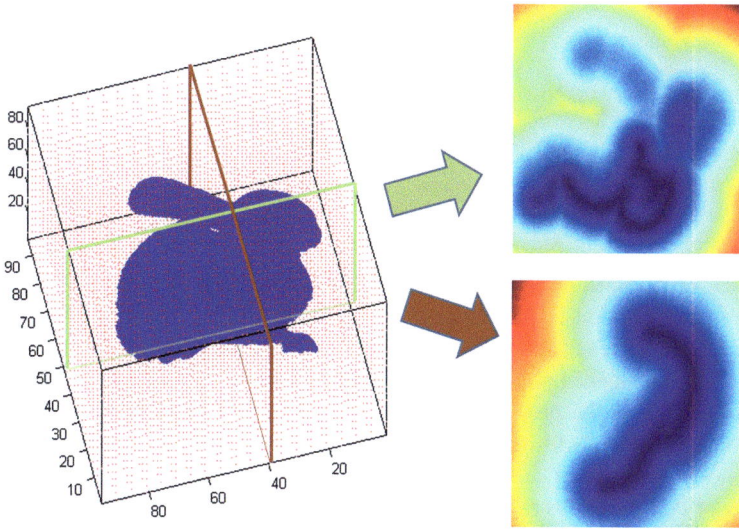

Fig. 6.5 Using the distance transform. The model-view is enclosed in a volumetric grid (*left*). For each point of the grid the closest model-point is computed. *Two planes* are *highlighted* on the XY and YZ axes respectively and the distance transform values of each grid-point are visualized for both planes (*right*). The *cyan color* indicates low distance values, close to the object surface. *Blue colors* are negative and inside the object, *darker blue* meaning further from the surface. *Other colors* are outside the object and, as we move through the *green*, *yellow* and *red colors*, we move further from the surface

in finding the correspondence of each point. Early strategies were based on the organization of the model-points in a k-d tree [87] structure in order to reduce the closest point complexity to $O(n \log n)$. Closest point caching [87] also accelerates the speed of ICP (the data point correspondence search is only among a subset of model points which were the closest at the previous iteration). Indeed, in [63] k-d tree and caching are combined in order to further improve the speed of ICP. Other more effective approaches are based on the so called *reverse calibration* paradigm [8]. The idea is to project the source data point onto the destination model-view which is encoded as a *range* image [76]. In particular, the projection from the 3D domain into the range image is performed by using the calibration parameters of the 3D scanner. In this fashion the correspondence is computed in one-shot. The reverse calibration approach is especially effective for real-time application. For instance in [77] the authors proposed a real-time 3D model reconstruction system, and in [18] on-line registration is performed to build a 3D mosaic of the scene in order to improve the navigation in underwater environments. Also, one-shot computation can be carried out on a generic point cloud (not necessary coming from a range image) by precomputing the so called *distance transform* of the model view [32]. Figure 6.5 illustrates the distance transform. In practice, the distance to closest model-points are precomputed for all grid-points of the discretized volume. The case for using a distance transform computed for the model is particularly compelling when one wishes to align many instances of data scan to the same model scan.

Fig. 6.6 Distance formulation. Point-to-point distance (*left*) and point-to-plane distance (*right*)

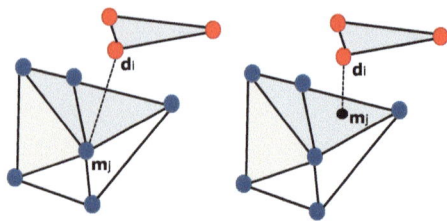

Distance Formulation Another crucial factor affecting the speed of ICP is the point-to-point or point-to-plane distance used in the problem described by Eq. (6.1). Figure 6.6 shows a schema of the two kinds of distances: point-to-point computes the Euclidean distance between the data-point and model-point (left), point-to-plane distance computes the projection of the data-point onto the surface of the model-view, which is encoded in terms of piecewise planar patches (for instance a triangular mesh). In spite of an increased complexity of the distance formulation, the number of ICP iterations required to converge is reduced [65, 69]. Whether this results in a reduced registration time depends on the trade-off between the increased per-iteration time and the reduced number of iterations. Results regarding this aspect on example 3D scans are presented in Sect. 6.4.

Recently a new "distance formulation" has been proposed [66] where the model surface is implicitly represented as the zero-isosurface of a fitted radial basis function (RBF), $s(\mathbf{x}) = 0$, for any 3D point $\mathbf{x}$, where the function s represents *distance-to-surface*. For any point on the data scan (or on a pre-computed 3D grid), the distance and direction (gradient) to the zero isosurface can be computed directly from the RBF. The advantage of this RBF distance formulation is that it interpolates over holes that may exist in the model scan. Particularly for lower resolution scans, the interpolation is more accurate than the piecewise linear point-to-plane method. Both RBF model fitting and RBF model evaluation have a computational complexity of $O(n \log n)$.

6.2.3.3 Techniques for Improving Accuracy

The accuracy of the alignment is the most critical aspect of the registration, since even a small misalignment between two views can affect the whole 3D model reconstruction procedure. The simplest strategy that can be used is outlier rejection. Other methods improve the accuracy by using additional information such as color and texture or local geometric properties. Finally, an effective class of methods devoted to the improvement of accuracy are probabilistic methods.

Outlier Rejection Closest point computation may yield spurious correspondences due to errors or to the presence of non-overlapping parts between the views. Typically, outlier rejection techniques threshold the residuals. The threshold can be fixed manually, or as a percentage of worst pairs (e.g., 10 % [71, 78]). Other techniques perform statistics on the residual vector and set the threshold as 2.5σ or apply the so-called *X84* rule [17, 40]. More recently, statistical analysis has been introduced into the general registration problem (Eq. (6.1)) by proposing a new error function named *Fractional Root Mean Squared Distance* [67].

Additional Information The basic ICP algorithm computes the correspondences by taking into account only the *proximity* of points. However, corresponding points should be similar with respect to other aspects. Several studies have attempted to exploit additional information available from the acquisition process or from the analysis of the surface properties. In practice, the distance formulation is modified to integrate this information, such as local surface properties [36], intensity derived from the sensor [36, 98], or color [72]. In [45] the authors proposed to use color and texture information. In [85] the so-called *ICP using invariant features* (ICPIF) was introduced where several geometric features are employed, namely *curvatures, moments invariants* and *Spherical Harmonics Invariants*. In [14] additional information was integrated in the point descriptors using the spin-image with color.

Probabilistic Methods In order to improve the robustness of the registration, several probabilistic version of the standard ICP have been proposed [38, 73, 74]. In [73, 74] the idea of multiple weighted matches justified by a probabilistic version of the matching problem is introduced. A new matching model is proposed based on Gaussian weights (SoftAssign [74]) and Mutual Information [73], leading to a smaller number of local minima and thus presenting the most convincing improvements. In [38] the authors introduced a probabilistic approach based on the *Expectation Maximization* (EM) paradigm, namely EM-ICP. Hidden variables are used to model the point matching. Specifically, in the case of Gaussian noise, the proposed method corresponds to ICP with multiple matches weighted by normalized Gaussian weights. In practice, the variance of the Gaussian is interpreted as a scale parameter. At high scales EM-ICP gets many matches, while it behaves like standard ICP at lower scales.

6.3 Advanced Techniques

Although registration is one of the most studied problems in computer vision, several cases are still open and new issues have emerged in the recent years. In this section we focus on some scenarios where registration becomes more challenging: registration of *more than two views*, registration in *cluttered scenes* and registration of *deformable objects*. We also describe some emerging techniques based on machine learning to solve the registration problem. Figure 6.7 illustrates the proposed taxonomy for advanced registration techniques.

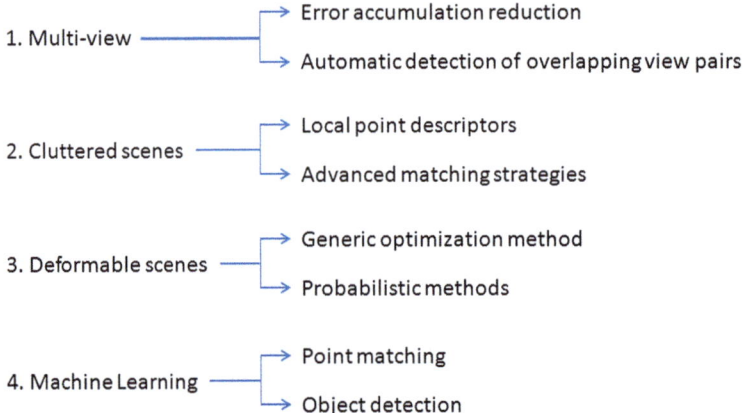

Fig. 6.7 A taxonomy of advanced registration techniques

6.3.1 Registration of More than Two Views

Once registration has been performed pairwise, all the views need to be transformed into a global reference system by applying a *multiple-view* registration technique. There are two main issues: (i) error accumulation and (ii) automation of the process.

Reducing Error Accumulation When the ordering of the sequence of views $N_1, \ldots, N_p$ is available, registration can be performed pairwise between consecutive views (i.e., between views N_i and N_{i+1}). In general, even if all the pairs are apparently well registered, some misalignment typically appears when the full model is reconstructed due to the accumulation and propagation of the registration error. The general idea of multiple-view registration techniques is to solve *simultaneously* for the global registration by exploiting the interdependences between all views at the same time. This introduces additional constraints which reduce the global error. A comparative study of similar multiple-view registration schemes was performed [27]. In [71] a method is presented that first aligns the scans pairwise with each other and then uses the pairwise alignments as constraints in a multi-view step. The aim is to evenly distribute the pairwise registration error, but the method itself is still based on pairwise alignments. In [17] a method that distributes registration errors evenly across all views was proposed. It operates in the space of estimated pairwise registration matrices, however ordering of the views is required. More recently, [91] proposed a new approach based on the well-known Generalized Procrustes Analysis, seamlessly embedding the mathematical theory in an ICP framework. A variant of the method, where the correspondences are non-uniformly weighted using a curvature-based similarity measure was also presented.

Automating Registration Especially when the full model is composed of a large number of scans, the view order might not be available and therefore should be manually specified. Many methods have been proposed to improve the automation of multiple-view registration. In [43] a global optimization process searches a graph constructed from the pairwise view matches for a connected sub-graph containing only correct matches, using a global consistency measure to eliminate incorrect but locally consistent matches. Other approaches use both *global* and *local* pre-alignment techniques to select the overlapping views by computing a coarse alignment between all the pairs. In [55] the pre-alignment is performed by extracting global features from each view, namely extended Gaussian images. Conversely, in [49], the pre-alignment is computed by comparing the signatures of feature points. Then, the best view sequence is estimated by solving a standard Traveling Salesman Problem (TSP).

6.3.2 Registration in Cluttered Scenes

Thanks to the recent availability of large scale scanners it is possible to acquire scenes composed of several objects. In this context registration is necessary to localize each object present in the scene and estimate its pose. However, in cluttered scenes, an object of interest may be made of a small subset of the entire view. This makes the registration problem more challenging. Figure 6.8 shows two examples of highly cluttered scenes: an entire square[2] and a scene composed of several mechanical objects.

Roughly speaking two main strategies have been proposed to address this problem: (i) the use of point signatures to improve point-to-point matching and (ii) the design of more effective matching methods. We now describe each of these in turn.

Point Signatures This approach is similar to local approaches for pre-alignment. Here, due to the cluttered scene, the challenge comes from the fact that the neighborhood of one point of an object can cover part of other objects. Therefore, the descriptor may become useless. In [56] a descriptor that uses two reference points to define a local coordinate system is proposed. In particular, a three-dimensional tensor is built by sampling the space and storing the amount of surface intersecting each sample. In [4] a method that exploits surface scale properties is introduced. The geometric scale variability is encoded in the form of the intrinsic geometric scale of each computed feature, leading to a highly discriminative hierarchical descriptor.

Matching Methods Since the number of corresponding points are very few within cluttered scenes, standard methods for outlier rejection are not useful but more complex matching algorithms can be exploited. In [56], descriptors are stored using a hash table that can be efficiently looked up at the matching phase by a geometric hashing algorithm. In [4], matching is performed in a hierarchical fashion by using the hierarchy induced from the definition of the point-descriptor. In [29], a method

---

[2]Piazza Brà, Verona, Italy. Image courtesy of Gexcel: http://www.gexcel.it.

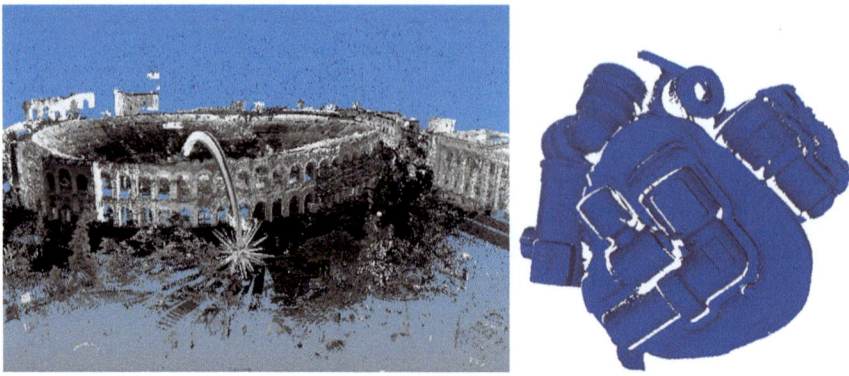

Fig. 6.8 Example of large scan acquisition (*left*) and scene with multiple mechanical objects (*right*)

is proposed that creates a global model description using an oriented point pair feature and matches it using a fast voting scheme. This fast voting scheme, similar to the Generalized Hough Transform, is used to optimize the model pose in a locally reduced search space. This space is parametrized in terms of points on the model and rotation around the surface normals.

6.3.3 Deformable Registration

While rigidity in the aligning transformation is a largely applicable constraint, it is too restrictive in some cases. Imagine indeed that the object that has to be registered is not rigid but deformable. Deformable registration has two main issues: the computation of stable correspondences and the use of an appropriate deformation model. Note that the need for registration of articulated or deformable objects has recently increased due to the availability of real-time range scanners [21, 22, 51, 58]. Roughly speaking, we can emphasize two classes of deformable registration methods: (i) methods based on general optimization techniques, and (ii) probabilistic methods.

Methods Based on General Optimization Techniques The general formulation of deformable registration is more involved than the rigid case and it is more difficult to solve in closed-form. Advanced optimization techniques are used instead. The advantage of using general optimization techniques consists of jointly computing the estimation of correspondences and the deformable parameters [21, 22, 24, 51]. Moreover, other unknowns can be used to model further information like the overlapping area, the reliability of correspondences, the smoothness constraint and so on [51]. Examples of transformation models which have been introduced for surface deformations are (i) affine transforms applied to nodes uniformly sampled from the range images [51], (ii) rigid transforms on patches automatically extracted from the surface [21], (iii) Thin-Plate Splines (TPS) [24, 76], or (iv) linear blend skinning model (LBS) [22]. The error function can be optimized by the Levenberg-Marquardt Algorithm [51], GraphCuts [21], or Expectation-Maximization (EM) [22, 24, 61]. In [42] deformable registration is solved by alternating between correspondence and deformation optimization. Assuming approximately isometric deformations, robust correspondences are generated using a pruning mechanism based on geodesic consistency.

Deformable alignment to account for errors in the point clouds obtained by scanning a rigid object is proposed in [12, 13]. Also, in this case, the authors use TPS to represent the deformable warp between a pair of views, that they estimate through hierarchical ICP [76].

Probabilistic Methods Using probabilistic methods the uncertainty on the correct surface transformation can be addressed by adopting maximum likelihood estimation [2, 28, 41, 46, 61, 96]. Probabilistic approaches are based on modeling each of the point sets by a kernel density function [93]. The dissimilarity among such densities is computed by introducing appropriate distance functions. Registration is carried out without explicitly establishing correspondences. Indeed, the algorithm registers two meshes by optimizing a joint probabilistic model over all point-to-point correspondences between them [2]. In [46], the authors propose a correlation-based approach [93] to point set registration by representing the point sets as Gaussian Mixture Models. A closed-form solution for the L_2 norm distance between two Gaussian mixtures makes fast computation possible. In [96], registration is carried out simultaneously for several 3D range datasets. The method proposes an information-theoretic approach based on the Jensen-Shannon divergence measure. In [61], deformable registration is treated as a Maximum Likelihood estimation problem by introducing the Coherent Point Drift paradigm. Smoothness constraints are introduced based on the assumption that points close to one another tend to move coherently over the velocity field. The proposed energy function is minimized with the EM algorithm. A similar approach has been proposed in [28] to track the full hand motion. A stereo set-up is employed to estimate the 3D surface. To improve the estimation of the hand pose, 2D motion (i.e., optical flow) is combined with 3D information. A well defined hand model is employed to deal with articulated structures and deformations. Also in this case the standard ICP algorithm has been extended to its probabilistic version according to the EM-ICP approach. This approach has been further extended in [41] where the so called Expectation *Conditional* Maximization paradigm is introduced. A formal demonstration is proposed to show that it is convenient to replace the standard M-step by three conditional maximization steps, or CM-steps, while preserving the convergence properties of EM. Experiments are reported for both hand and body tracking.

6.3.4 Machine Learning Techniques

Recently, advanced machine learning techniques have been exploited to improve registration algorithms [1, 37, 44, 59, 88]. The general idea is to use data-driven approaches that learn the relevant registration criteria from examples. The most promising methods have been proposed for (i) improving the matching phase, and (ii) detecting an object which is a general instance of one or more classes.

Improving the Matching In these approaches the emphasis is on the effectiveness of the correspondence computation. In [88] a new formulation for deformable registration (3D faces) is proposed. The distance function from corresponding points is defined as a weighted sum of contributions coming from different surface attributes (i.e. proximity, color/texture, normals). Instead of manually or heuristically choosing the weights, a machine learning technique is proposed to estimate them. A Support Vector Machine (SVM) framework is employed in a supervised manner, based on a dataset of pairs of correct and incorrect correspondences. In [1], the authors propose a novel unsupervised technique that allows one to obtain a fine surface registration in a single step, without the need of an initial motion estimation. The main idea of their approach is to cast the selection of correspondences between points on the surfaces in a *game theoretic* framework. In this fashion, a natural selection process allows one to select points that satisfy a mutual rigidity constraint to thrive, eliminating all the other correspondences.

Object Detection A new class of methods is emerging that employ machine learning techniques for detecting specific classes of objects in large scenes [37, 44, 59]. Several works have focused on the 2D domain, but its extension to 3D scenes is not trivial. In [44], the authors proposed to detect cars in cluttered scenes composed of millions of scanned points. The method is based on integrating *Spin-Images* with *Extended Gaussian Images* in order to combine effectively local and global descriptors. Furthermore, the method is able to detect object classes and not only specific instances. In [59] the Associative Markov Network (AMN) has been extended to integrate the context of local features by exploiting directional information through a new non-isotropic model. In [37], different objects are simultaneously detected by hierarchical segmentation of point clouds. Indeed, clusters of points are classified using standard learning-by-example classifiers.

6.4 Quantitative Performance Evaluation

In this section, we report some experiments using pairwise registration in order to show how basic registration techniques work in practice. Two objects are evaluated: Foot and Frog for which two views are available for pairwise registration.[3] In

---

[3]Experimental material is based on the survey paper [79]. Objects and code are available at http://eia.udg.es/cmatabos/research.htm.

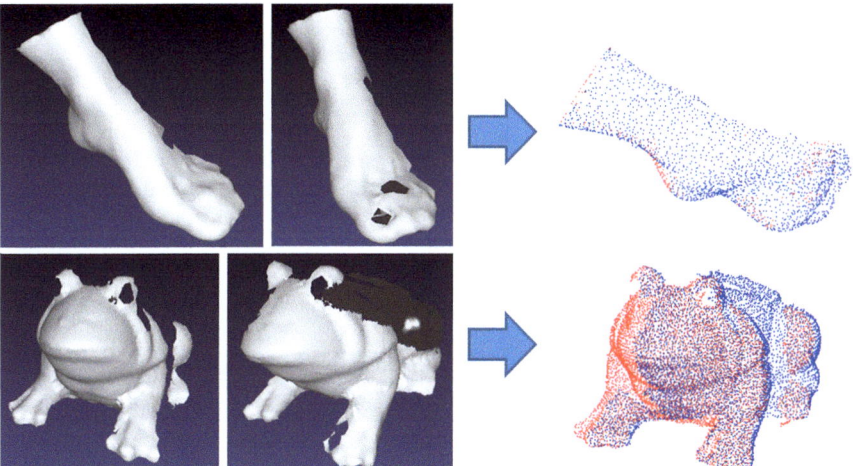

Fig. 6.9 Two views of Foot (*top*) and Frog (*bottom*). Separated views (*left*) and aligned views (*right*). The portion of overlap is large for both of the objects

Fig. 6.9 we show the two objects, the overlapping region of both of the objects in the two views is quite large (i.e. around 80 %). The Foot model has approximately 1500 points, while Frog is composed of around 5000 points for each view. The two views have been acquired separately by two scans and are already aligned by the authors of [79], as shown in Fig. 6.9 (right). In order to evaluate the robustness of pairwise registration methods against the initial pose variation, we define 30 poses by generating random angles sampled from a uniform distribution between 0° and 10° (for the three Euler's angles) and random translations (for the three translation components t_x, t_y, t_z) such that the translation is 5 % of the object's main diagonal. Indeed, such transformations are considered as ground truth. We evaluate the performance of three methods: (i) Besl's ICP [7] (Besl), which is described in Sect. 6.2.2, (ii) Chen and Medioni ICP [23], (Chen) which introduces the point-to-plane distance, and (iii) Picky ICP proposed by Zinsser et al. [101] (Picky) which implements a combination of ICP variations described in Sect. 6.2.3. A hierarchical sampling strategy is introduced to improve the speed, and a thresholding approach on the residual distribution is employed. More specifically, a threshold is defined as $TH = \mu + 2.5\sigma$, where $\mu = \text{mean}(\{e_i\})$, and $\sigma = \text{std}(\{e_i\})$. According to the basic ICP algorithm described in Sect. 6.2.2, the threshold of Step 4 is set as 0.00001 but in most of the evaluated experiments the algorithm stops because it reaches the maximum number of iterations. Therefore, we define two settings with maximum number of iterations 15 and 50 respectively in order to evaluate the speed of convergence for the analyzed cases.

In Fig. 6.10, computational efficiency is evaluated. Experiments were carried out on an entry-level laptop at 1.66 Ghz with 4 Gb. The algorithms are coded using Matlab. The three methods are shown in red (Besl), blue (Chen), and green (Picky). In general, the best results were obtained by the Picky algo-

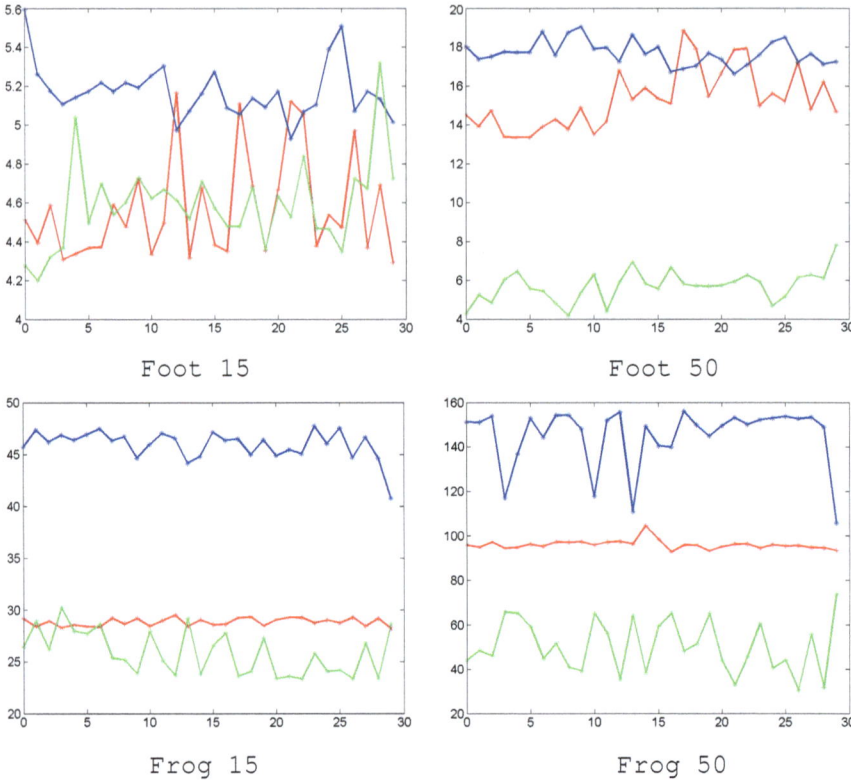

Fig. 6.10 Computational time evaluation. Time (sec) employed for each pairwise registration. The three methods are shown in *red* (Besl), *blue* (Chen), and *green* (Picky)

rithm. Moreover, due to the higher computational cost of the point-to-plane distance, the Chen method is the slowest. Note that a drastic reduction of registration speed is observed when the number of points increases from Foot to Frog.

In Fig. 6.11, the accuracy of registration is evaluated. In general, especially when the ground truth is not available, a good accuracy evaluation criterion is the *Mean Squared Error* (MSE) (i.e. $mean\{e_i\}$). Note that the MSE error is not comparable between the three methods since they compute different distance measures and, in Picky, the error generated by outliers is not considered. Note that, for both the objects, MSE error of Besl does not improve when the number of iterations increases. Conversely, in Picky, the benefit of a higher number of iterations is observed and most of the registrations are able to reach convergence.

In order to get a direct comparison between the methods we use the ground truth transformations, which are available since we have generated them. Indeed, we evaluate the rotation and the translation error, as shown in Figs. 6.12 and 6.13

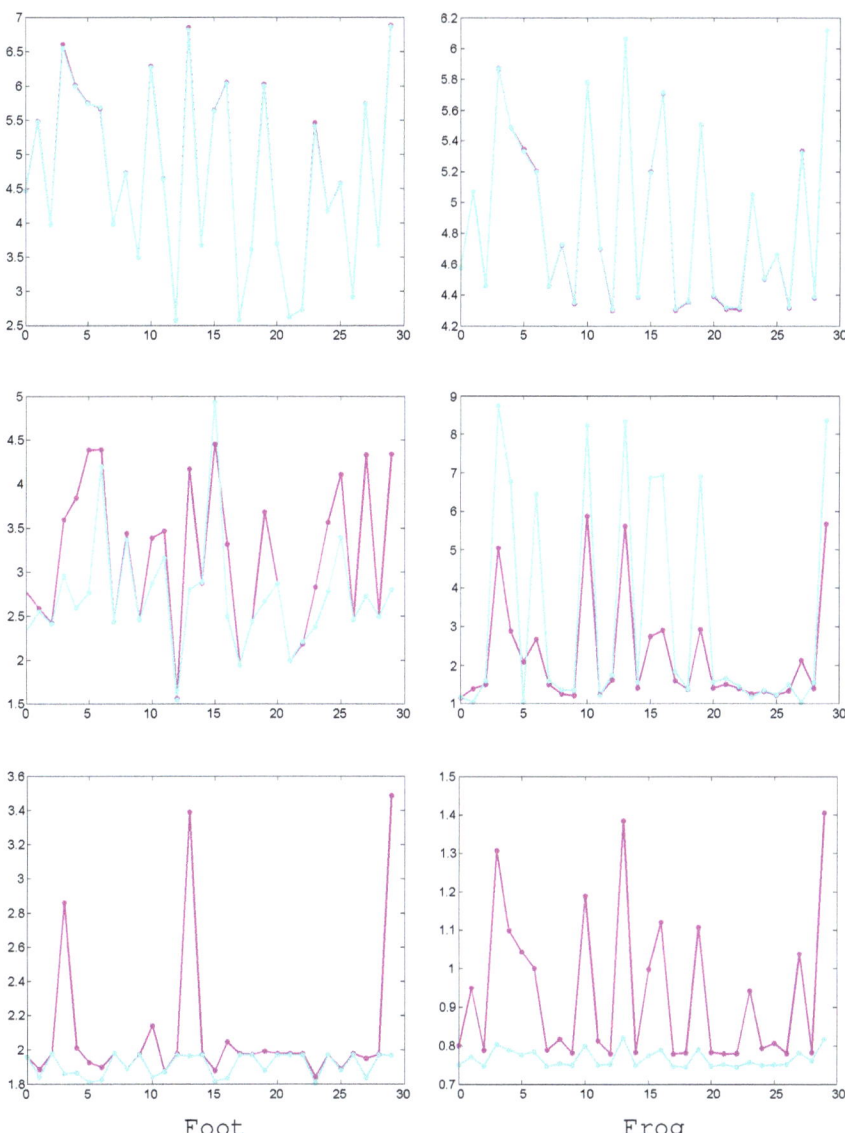

Fig. 6.11 MSE evaluation for Besl (*top*), Chen (*middle*), and Picky (*bottom*). The cases employing 15 iterations are shown in *magenta*, while cases employing 30 iterations are shown in *cyan*

respectively. Rotation error is computed as the mean of the difference between the observed Euler's angles of the estimated transform and the ground truth. Angles are in radians. Translation error is the norm of the difference between the two translation vectors.

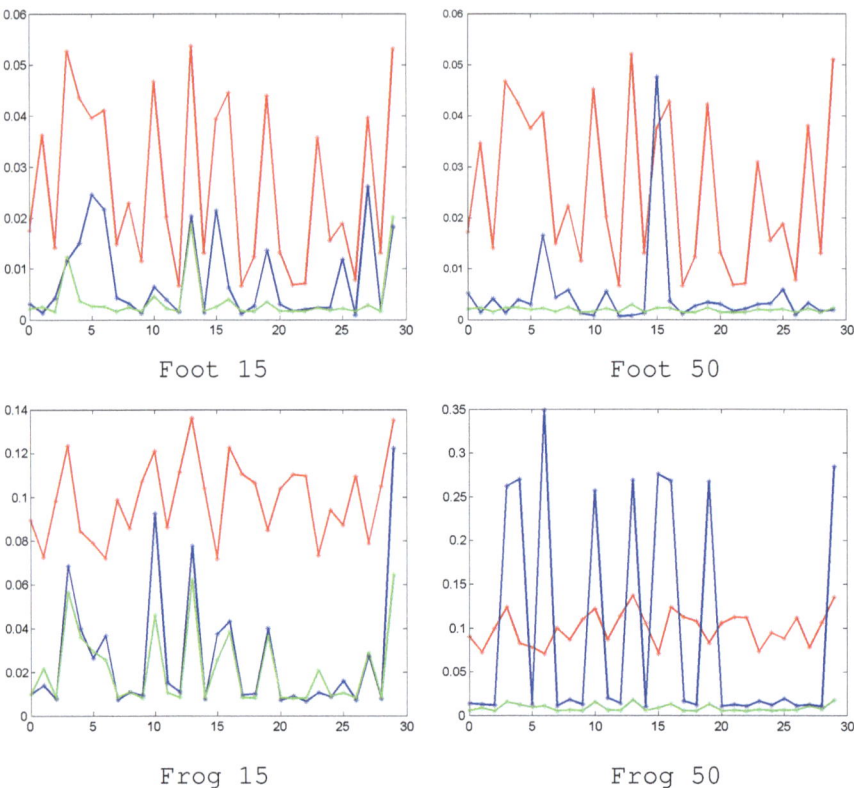

Fig. 6.12 Rotation error. The three methods are shown in *red* (Besl), *blue* (Chen), and *green* (Picky). Note that peaks correspond to failures of the pairwise registration procedure

Table 6.1 summarizes the experiments by showing the mean of the evaluated measures. We observe better accuracy by using Picky. Note also that in general Chen outperforms Besl. Finally, we also show in Table 6.1 the number of failures (or divergences) because a local minimum is reached. We show that in more than half of the cases the convergence is reached within 15 iterations. Again the best results are shown with Picky since no failures are observed after 50 iterations and it always converges after 15 iterations with Foot. We observed also that the cases of failures of Besl and Chen methods are related to the strongest variations of starting pose, thus confirming the importance of a good initialization procedure.

6.5 Case Study 1: Pairwise Alignment with Outlier Rejection

In this section, we describe a simple but effective strategy to make the ICP algorithm resistant to incorrect correspondences. Particularly when views are only par-

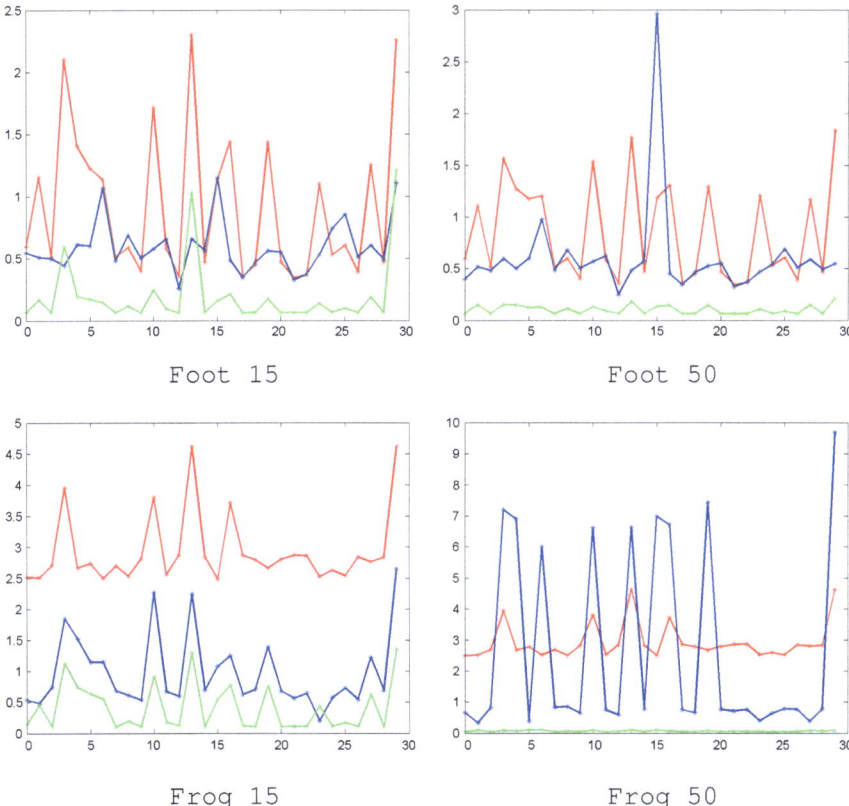

Fig. 6.13 Translation error. The three methods are shown in *red* (Besl), *blue* (Chen), and *green* (Picky). Note that peaks correspond to failures of the pairwise registration procedure

tially overlapped, many points of the data-view do not have a correspondence in the model-view. We call those points *single-points*. However, the basic ICP algorithm enforces single points to be associated to closest points in the model-view, therefore generating outliers. A robust outlier rejection procedure is introduced based on the so-called *X84* rule [17, 40]. The idea is to perform a robust statistical analysis of the residual errors e_i after closest point computation. The underlying hypothesis was pointed out in [100] and consists of considering the residuals of two fully overlapping sets as an approximation of a Gaussian distribution. Non-overlapping points can be detected by estimating a Gaussian distribution from residual errors and by defining a threshold on the tails of the estimated Gaussian.

The *X84* rule is a tool to automatically and robustly estimate this threshold. Given the set of residual errors, $\mathbb{E} = \{e_i\}$, $i = 1 \ldots N_d$, the *Median Absolute Deviation* (MAD) is defined as:

$$MAD = \text{med}(|e_i - location|), \tag{6.10}$$

Table 6.1 Summary of performance evaluation. The mean of the 30 pairwise registrations for each evaluated measure is shown

Exp.	MSE error (mm)	Rot. error (rad.)	Trans. error (mm)	Number of divergences	Time (sec)
Besl Foot 15	4.681	0.026	0.922	13/30	4.568
Chen Foot 15	3.155	0.007	0.593	15/30	5.173
Picky Foot 15	2.084	0.003	0.195	6/30	0.593
Besl Foot 50	4.672	0.025	0.853	13/30	15.309
Chen Foot 50	2.725	0.004	0.601	5/30	17.680
Picky Foot 50	1.910	0.001	0.104	0/30	5.683
Besl Frog 15	4.905	0.099	2.936	14/30	28.811
Chen Frog 15	2.203	0.026	0.976	10/30	45.917
Picky Frog 15	0.932	0.021	0.411	9/30	25.850
Besl Frog 50	4.906	0.099	2.939	5/30	95.882
Chen Frog 50	3.217	0.092	2.608	9/30	145.028
Picky Frog 50	0.765	0.008	0.069	0/30	50.292

where med is the *median* operator and *location* is the median of residual errors (i.e., med($\mathbb{E}$)). The X84 rule prescribes to reject values that violate the following relation:

$$|e_i - location| < k \cdot MAD. \tag{6.11}$$

Under the hypothesis of Gaussian distribution, a value of $k = 5.2$ is adequate in practice, as the resulting threshold contains more than 99.9 % of the distribution.

Now we are ready to define the new procedure for robust outlier rejection:

1. For all data-points $\mathbf{d}_i \in \mathbb{D}$, compute the error e_i according to Eq. (6.4) (i.e. by estimating the closest point and by generating the pair of corresponding points $\mathbf{c}_i = (\mathbf{d}_i, \mathbf{m}_j)$).
2. Estimate *location* by computing the median of residuals, med($\mathbb{E}$).
3. Compute *MAD* according to Eq. (6.10).
4. For each residual error e_i ($i = 1, \ldots, N_d$):
   a. If e_i satisfies Eq. (6.11) then keep $\mathbf{c}_i$ in the list of correspondences,
   b. If not, reject the correspondence.
5. A new list of corresponding points $\hat{\mathbf{c}}_i$ is obtained from which outliers have been filtered out.

In practice, this procedure replaces step 1 in the ICP algorithm described in Sect. 6.2.2. The X84 rejection rule has a breakdown point of 50 %: any majority of the data can overrule any minority. The computational cost of X84 is dominated by the cost of the median, which is $O(n)$, where n is the size of the data point set. The most costly procedure inside ICP is the establishment of point correspondences,

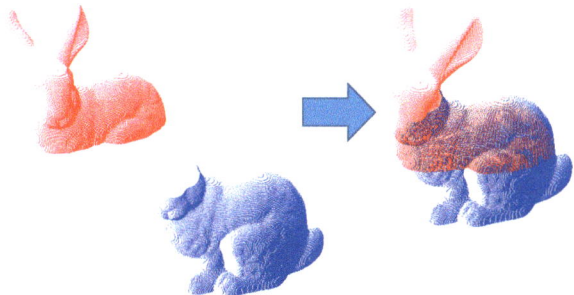

Fig. 6.14 Registration with robust outliers rejection. Two views at starting pose (*left*) and after registration (*right*). Note that the overlap area is quite restricted

which costs $O(n \log n)$. Therefore X84 does not increase the asymptotic complexity of ICP.

In Fig. 6.14, an example of registration between two views with a strong occluded part is shown. The non-overlapping area is wide: the ears and the whole face of *Bunny* are only visible in the data-view while the bottom part of the body is observed in the model-view only. The number of data points is $N_d = 10000$, the number of model points is $N_m = 29150$, and the number of points of the overlap is $\#(\mathbb{D} \cap \mathbb{M}) = 4000$. In this experiment, the two views are synthetically sampled from the whole 3D model. A view mask of 600×500 points is used in order to obtain highly dense views. Moreover, in this fashion, we know the ground truth transformation and no noise affects the views. Figure 6.15 shows the distribution of residual errors after X84-ICP registration. Note that most of the residuals are concentrated around zero. It is confirmed that the behavior of the early part of the distribution is similar to a Gaussian [100]. The X84 rule is employed and the threshold is automatically estimated on the tail of the Gaussian.

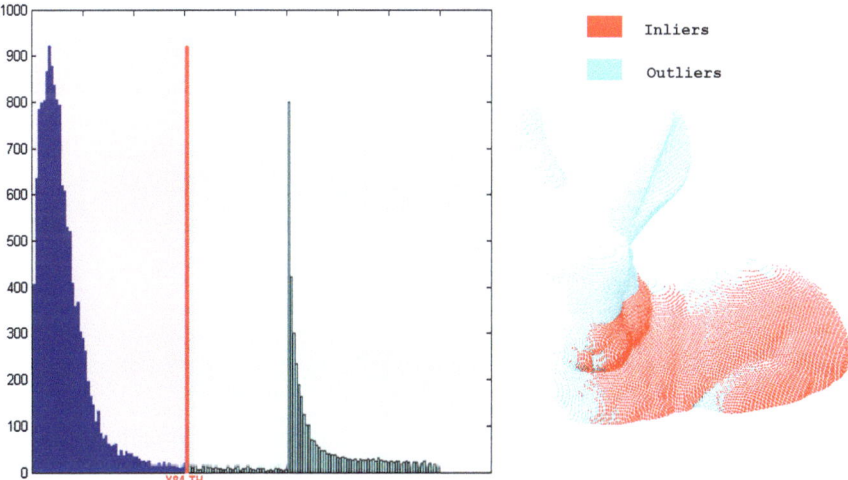

Fig. 6.15 Automatic residuals thresholding. From the distribution of residuals, the threshold is estimated according to the X84 rule. Points under the threshold are inliers (*red*), while outliers are over the threshold (*blue*). Outliers are points in non-overlapping areas

Table 6.2 X-84 performance evaluations. Rotation and translation errors are reported

Method	Rot. error (rad.)	Trans. error (mm)	Number of overlap. points	Number of iterations	Time (sec)
Besl	0.22345	1.2636	10000	20	370
Picky	0.10918	0.9985	9534	28	76
X84-ICP	0.06351	0.4177	4582	21	383
Ground Truth	–	–	4000	–	–

The second peak of the distribution corresponds to residuals generated by the non-overlapping points.[4] In Fig. 6.15 (right), points of the data-view are colored differently between inliers and outliers. Note that non-overlapping parts are correctly registered.

Table 6.2 summarizes the performance of X84-ICP in comparison with Besl and Picky. The ground truth transformation is shown as well. Note that the basic ICP is strongly affected by outliers and is not able to correctly align the two views. The Picky ICP improves the accuracy, but it is not able to correctly estimate the overlapping parts and it does not reach convergence. Conversely, by employing the X84 rule wrong correspondences are well detected and a correct registration is obtained. We highlight that although X84-ICP performs well in this experiment, in more general cases where the number of outliers is greater than 50 % of the residual distribution, the *X84* rule is likely to fail.

6.6 Case Study 2: ICP with Levenberg-Marquardt

In this section, we describe a registration method called Levenberg-Marquardt ICP (LM-ICP), which addresses several of the issues of ICP by modeling the registration as a general optimization problem. LM-ICP [32] was proposed in order to minimize the alignment error by employing a nonlinear optimization procedure. The advantage of the LM-ICP is the versatility in the definition of the optimization function in order to take into account of several aspects of the registration, such as outlier rejection and speed.

6.6.1 The LM-ICP Method

The general problem formulation is defined as for the ICP algorithm. The error function $E(\mathbf{a}) = E_{ICP}(\mathbf{a}, \mathbb{D}, \mathbb{M})$ is Nonlinear Least Squares and can thus be written

---

[4]In order to visualize the peak the second part of the histogram has been quantized with wider intervals.

as the sum of N_d squared residual vectors:

$$E(\mathbf{a}) = \sum_{i=1}^{N_d} (e_i(\mathbf{a}))^2, \qquad e_i(\mathbf{a}) = \|\mathsf{R}\mathbf{d}_i + \mathbf{t} - \mathbf{m}_j\|. \tag{6.12}$$

Defining the residual vector as:

$$\mathbf{e}(\mathbf{a}) = \begin{pmatrix} e_1(\mathbf{a}) & e_2(\mathbf{a}) & \ldots & e_{N_d}(\mathbf{a}) \end{pmatrix}^\mathsf{T}, \tag{6.13}$$

we rewrite the error function as $E(\mathbf{a}) = \|\mathbf{e}(\mathbf{a})\|^2$.

The Levenberg-Marquardt algorithm combines the methods of gradient-descent and Gauss-Newton. The goal at each iteration is to choose an update to the current estimate $\mathbf{a}_k$, say $\mathbf{x}$, so that setting $\mathbf{a}_{k+1} = \mathbf{a}_k + \mathbf{x}$ reduces the registration error.

We first derive the Gauss-Newton update. Expanding $E(\mathbf{a} + \mathbf{x})$ to second order yields:

$$E(\mathbf{a}+\mathbf{x}) = E(\mathbf{a}) + (\nabla E(\mathbf{a}) \cdot \mathbf{x}) + \frac{1}{2!}((\nabla^2 E(\mathbf{a}) \cdot \mathbf{x}) \cdot \mathbf{x}) + h.o.t. \tag{6.14}$$

This is rewritten in terms of $\mathbf{e}$ as:

$$E(\mathbf{a}) = \mathbf{e}^\mathsf{T}\mathbf{e}$$
$$\nabla E(\mathbf{a}) = 2(\nabla \mathbf{e})^\mathsf{T}\mathbf{e}$$
$$\nabla^2 E(\mathbf{a}) = 2(\nabla^2 \mathbf{e})\mathbf{e} + 2(\nabla \mathbf{e})^\mathsf{T}\nabla\mathbf{e}.$$

We now define the $N_d \times p$ *Jacobian* matrix $\mathsf{J} = \nabla \mathbf{e}$, with block (i,j) as $\mathsf{J}_{i,j} = \frac{\partial E_i}{\partial a_j}$ (p is the number of elements in $\mathbf{a}$). Introducing the Gauss-Newton approximation (i.e., neglecting $(\nabla^2 \mathbf{e})\mathbf{e}$) we get:

$$E(\mathbf{a}+\mathbf{x}) \approx \mathbf{e}^\mathsf{T}\mathbf{e} + \mathbf{x}^\mathsf{T}\mathsf{J}^\mathsf{T}\mathbf{e} + \mathbf{x}^\mathsf{T}\mathsf{J}^\mathsf{T}\mathsf{J}\mathbf{x}. \tag{6.15}$$

Differentiating with respect to $\mathbf{x}$ and nullifying yields:

$$\nabla_\mathbf{x} E(\mathbf{a}+\mathbf{x}) = \mathsf{J}^\mathsf{T}\mathbf{e} + \mathsf{J}^\mathsf{T}\mathsf{J}\mathbf{x} = 0, \tag{6.16}$$

and gives the Gauss-Newton update:

$$\mathbf{x}_{GN} = -(\mathsf{J}^\mathsf{T}\mathsf{J})^{-1}\mathsf{J}^\mathsf{T}\mathbf{e}. \tag{6.17}$$

Gauss-Newton is usually fast for mildly nonlinear problems (it has superlinear convergence speed), but there is no guarantee of convergence in the general case (an update may increase the error).

We now derive the gradient descent update. Since we deal with a Least Squares problem, the gradient descent update is simply given by:

$$\mathbf{x}_{GD} = -\lambda^{-1}\mathsf{J}^\mathsf{T}\mathbf{e}, \tag{6.18}$$

where λ is the inverse step length. Gradient descent has the nice property that, unless a local minimum has been reached, one can always decrease the error by making the step length small enough. On the other hand, gradient descent is known to be slow and rather inefficient.

The Levenberg-Marquardt algorithm combines both Gauss-Newton and gradient descent updates in a relatively simple way:

$$\mathbf{x}_{LM} = -(\mathsf{J}^\mathsf{T}\mathsf{J} + \lambda \mathsf{I})^{-1}\mathsf{J}^\mathsf{T}\mathbf{e}. \tag{6.19}$$

A large value of λ yields a small, safe, gradient-descent step while a small value of λ favor large and more accurate steps of Gauss-Newton that make convergence to a local minimum faster. The art of a Levenberg-Marquardt algorithm implementation is in tuning λ after each iteration to ensure rapid progress even where Gauss-Newton fails. The now standard implementation is to multiply λ by 10 if the error increases and to divide it by 10 if the error decreases (with an upper bound at 10^8 and a lower bound at 10^{-4} for instance). In order to make the method robust to outliers, one may attenuate the influence of points with a large error by replacing the square error function by an M-estimator ε and an Iterative Reweighted Least Squared (IRLS)-like reweighting procedure. For instance, the following robust functions can be used:

$$\text{Lorenzian:} \quad \varepsilon(r) = \log\left(1 + \frac{r^2}{\sigma}\right) \quad \text{or}$$

$$\text{Huber:} \quad \varepsilon(r) = \begin{cases} r^2 & r < \sigma \\ 2\sigma|r| - \sigma^2 & \text{otherwise.} \end{cases}$$

6.6.2 Computing the Derivatives

An important issue in how Levenberg-Marquardt is applied to ICP is the one of computing the derivatives of the error function. The simplest approach is based on using finite differencing, assuming that the error function is smooth. However, this leads to a cost of p extra function evaluations per inner loop. In [32] a more effective solution was proposed based on the *distance transform* which also drastically improves the computational efficiency. The distance transform is defined as:

$$D_\varepsilon(\mathbf{x}) = \min_j \varepsilon^2(\|\mathbf{m}_j - \mathbf{x}\|), \tag{6.20}$$

where $\mathbf{x} \in \mathbb{X}$ and $\mathbb{X}$ is a discrete grid representing the volume which encloses the model-view $\mathbb{M}$. Indeed, each data-point d_i can be easily associated to grid-points by obtaining the residual error $e_i = X(d_i)$ in one shot.[5] In other words, LM-ICP merges

---

[5]Note that the volume is discretized into integer values, therefore the data-point d_i should be rounded to recover $X(d_i)$.

the two main steps of ICP, namely closest point computation and transformation estimation, in a single step. Note further that when the mapping $\|\mathbf{x}\| \to \varepsilon^2(\|\mathbf{x}\|)$ is monotonic, we obtain that $D_\varepsilon(\mathbf{x}) = \varepsilon^2(\|D(\mathbf{x})\|)$, so existing algorithms to compute D may be used to compute D_ε, without requiring knowledge of the form of ε.

By combining Eq. (6.12) with Eq. (6.20) the new formulation of the registration problem becomes:

$$E(\mathbf{a}) = \sum_{i=1}^{N_d} D_\varepsilon\big(T(\mathbf{a}, \mathbf{d}_i)\big). \qquad (6.21)$$

This formulation makes it much easier to compute the derivatives of E. In fact, since the distance transform is computed in a discrete form, it is possible to compute finite differences derivatives. More specifically,

$$\nabla_\mathbf{x} D_\varepsilon = \left[\frac{\partial D_\varepsilon}{\partial x}, \frac{\partial D_\varepsilon}{\partial y}, \frac{\partial D_\varepsilon}{\partial z}\right]$$

is computed by defining

$$\frac{\partial D_\varepsilon(x,y,z)}{\partial x} = \frac{D_\varepsilon(x+1,y,z) - D_\varepsilon(x-1,y,z)}{2},$$

$$\frac{\partial D_\varepsilon(x,y,z)}{\partial y} = \frac{D_\varepsilon(x,y+1,z) - D_\varepsilon(x,y-1,z)}{2},$$

and

$$\frac{\partial D_\varepsilon(x,y,z)}{\partial z} = \frac{D_\varepsilon(x,y,z+1) - D_\varepsilon(x,y,z-1)}{2}.$$

In practice, $\nabla_\mathbf{x} D_\varepsilon$ remains constant through the minimization, and we get:

$$\nabla_\mathbf{a} E(\mathbf{a}) = \sum_{i=1}^{N_d} \nabla_\mathbf{x} D_\varepsilon\big(T(\mathbf{a}, \mathbf{d}_i)\big) \nabla_\mathbf{a}^\mathsf{T} T(\mathbf{a}, \mathbf{d}_i). \qquad (6.22)$$

Note that the computation of $\nabla_\mathbf{a}^\mathsf{T} T(\mathbf{a}, \mathbf{d}_i)$ depends on the rigid transformation parametrization being used. In [32], the author proposed to model rotations by unitary quaternions for which the derivatives can be easily computed analytically. Finally, in order to compute the derivatives using matrix operators the *Jacobian* matrix is defined as $J_{i,j} = (\nabla_\mathbf{x} D_\varepsilon(T(\mathbf{a}, \mathbf{d}_i))) \cdot \nabla_{a_j}^\mathsf{T} T(\mathbf{a}, \mathbf{d}_i))$, where $\nabla_{a_j} T(\mathbf{a}, \mathbf{d}_i) = [\frac{\partial T_x(\mathbf{a}, \mathbf{d}_i)}{\partial a_j}, \frac{\partial T_y(\mathbf{a}, \mathbf{d}_i)}{\partial a_j}, \frac{\partial T_z(\mathbf{a}, \mathbf{d}_i)}{\partial a_j}]$.

6.6.3 The Case of Quaternions

Let the quaternion be defined by $\mathbf{q} = [s, \mathbf{v}]$ where s and $\mathbf{v}$ are the scalar and vectorial components respectively [97]. Let $\mathbf{d}$ be the point on which the rotation must be applied. To this aim such a point must be represented in quaternion space, leading to $\mathbf{r} = [0, \mathbf{d}]$. Therefore, the rotated point is obtained by:

$$\mathbf{r}' = \mathbf{q}\mathbf{r}\mathbf{q}^{-1}.$$

By multiplying in quaternion space[6] we obtain:

$$\mathbf{r}' = \left[0, s^2\mathbf{d} + (\mathbf{d} \cdot \mathbf{v}) \cdot \mathbf{v} + 2s(\mathbf{v} \times \mathbf{d}) + \mathbf{v} \times (\mathbf{v} \times \mathbf{d})\right].$$

We represent this rotated point as:

$$\mathbf{r}' = [0, T_x, T_y, T_z],$$

where:

$$\begin{aligned}
T_x &= s^2 d_x + (d_x v_x + d_y v_y + d_z v_z) v_x + 2s(v_y d_z - v_z d_y) + v_y(v_x d_y - v_y d_x) \\
&\quad - v_z(v_z d_x - v_x d_z) \\
&= s^2 d_x + v_x^2 d_x + v_x v_y d_y + v_x v_z d_z + 2s v_y d_z - 2s v_z d_y + v_x v_y d_y - v_y^2 d_x \\
&\quad - v_z^2 d_x + v_x v_z d_z \\
&= (s^2 + v_x^2 - v_y^2 - v_z^2) d_x + 2(v_x v_y - s v_z) d_y + 2(v_x v_z + s v_y) d_z \\
T_y &= s^2 d_y + (d_x v_x + d_y v_y + d_z v_z) v_y + 2s(v_z d_x - v_x d_z) + v_z(v_y d_z - v_z d_y) \\
&\quad - v_x(v_x d_y - v_y d_x) \\
&= s^2 d_y + v_x v_y d_x + v_y^2 d_y + v_y v_z d_z + 2s v_z d_x - 2s v_x d_z + v_y v_z d_z - v_z^2 d_y \\
&\quad - v_x^2 d_y + v_x v_y d_x \\
&= 2(v_x v_y + s v_z) d_x + (s^2 - v_x^2 + v_y^2 - v_z^2) d_y + 2(v_y v_z - s v_x) d_z \\
T_z &= s^2 d_z + (d_x v_x + d_y v_y + d_z v_z) v_z + 2s(v_x d_y - v_y d_x) + v_x(v_z d_x - v_x d_z) \\
&\quad - v_y(v_y d_z - v_z d_y) \\
&= s^2 d_z + v_x v_z d_x + v_y v_z d_y + v_z^2 d_z + 2s v_x d_y - 2s v_y d_x + v_x v_z d_x - v_x^2 d_z \\
&\quad - v_y^2 d_z + v_y v_z d_y \\
&= 2(v_x v_z - s v_y) d_x + 2(v_y v_z + s v_x) d_y + (s^2 - v_x^2 - v_y^2 + v_z^2) d_z.
\end{aligned}$$

Now we introduce the translation component $[t_x, t_y, t_z]$ and normalize the quaternion by obtaining:

---

[6] A multiplication between two quaternions $\mathbf{q}$ and $\mathbf{q}'$ is defined as $[ss' - \mathbf{v} \cdot \mathbf{v}', \mathbf{v} \times \mathbf{v}' + s\mathbf{v}' + s'\mathbf{v}]$.

$$T_x = \frac{(s^2 + v_x^2 - v_y^2 - v_z^2)d_x}{s^2 + v_x^2 + v_y^2 + v_z^2} + \frac{2(v_x v_y - sv_z)d_y}{s^2 + v_x^2 + v_y^2 + v_z^2} + \frac{2(v_x v_z + sv_y)d_z}{s^2 + v_x^2 + v_y^2 + v_z^2} + t_x$$

$$T_y = \frac{2(v_x v_y + sv_z)d_x}{s^2 + v_x^2 + v_y^2 + v_z^2} + \frac{(s^2 - v_x^2 + v_y^2 - v_z^2)d_y}{s^2 + v_x^2 + v_y^2 + v_z^2} + \frac{2(v_y v_z - sv_x)d_z}{s^2 + v_x^2 + v_y^2 + v_z^2} + t_y$$

$$T_z = \frac{2(v_x v_z - sv_y)d_x}{s^2 + v_x^2 + v_y^2 + v_z^2} + \frac{2(v_y v_z + sv_x)d_y}{s^2 + v_x^2 + v_y^2 + v_z^2} + \frac{(s^2 - v_x^2 - v_y^2 + v_z^2)d_z}{s^2 + v_x^2 + v_y^2 + v_z^2} + t_z.$$

According to this model for rotation and translation, the vector of unknowns is $\mathbf{a} = [s, v_x, v_y, v_z, t_x, t_y, t_z]$ (i.e., $\mathbf{a} \in \mathbb{R}^7$). Therefore, the Jacobian part $\nabla_\mathbf{a}^T T(\mathbf{a}, \mathbf{d})$ is a 3×7 matrix:

$$\nabla_\mathbf{a}^T T(\mathbf{a}, \mathbf{d}) = \begin{bmatrix} \frac{\partial T_x}{\partial s} & \frac{\partial T_x}{\partial v_x} & \frac{\partial T_x}{\partial v_y} & \frac{\partial T_x}{\partial v_z} & \frac{\partial T_x}{\partial t_x} & \frac{\partial T_x}{\partial t_y} & \frac{\partial T_x}{\partial t_z} \\ \frac{\partial T_y}{\partial s} & \frac{\partial T_y}{\partial v_x} & \frac{\partial T_y}{\partial v_y} & \frac{\partial T_y}{\partial v_z} & \frac{\partial T_y}{\partial t_x} & \frac{\partial T_y}{\partial t_y} & \frac{\partial T_y}{\partial t_z} \\ \frac{\partial T_z}{\partial s} & \frac{\partial T_z}{\partial v_x} & \frac{\partial T_z}{\partial v_y} & \frac{\partial T_z}{\partial v_z} & \frac{\partial T_z}{\partial t_x} & \frac{\partial T_z}{\partial t_y} & \frac{\partial T_z}{\partial t_z} \end{bmatrix} \quad (6.23)$$

where T_x, T_y, and T_z have been defined above. For instance we can compute the derivative component $\frac{\partial T_x}{\partial v_x}$ as:

$$\frac{\partial T_x}{\partial v_x} = \frac{2v_x d_x}{s^2 + v_x^2 + v_y^2 + v_z^2} - \frac{2v_x(s^2 + v_x^2 - v_y^2 - v_z^2)d_x}{(s^2 + v_x^2 + v_y^2 + v_z^2)^2}$$

$$+ \frac{2v_x d_y}{s^2 + v_x^2 + v_y^2 + v_z^2} - \frac{4v_x(v_x v_y - sv_z)d_y}{(s^2 + v_x^2 + v_y^2 + v_z^2)^2}$$

$$+ \frac{2v_z d_z}{s^2 + v_x^2 + v_y^2 + v_z^2} - \frac{4v_x(v_x v_z + sv_y)d_z}{(s^2 + v_x^2 + v_y^2 + v_z^2)^2}.$$

Similarly, all the other components of the Jacobian can easily be computed.

6.6.4 Summary of the LM-ICP Algorithm

The algorithm for LM-ICP can be summarized as:

1. Set $\lambda \leftarrow \lambda_0 = 10$,
2. compute distance transform $D_\varepsilon(\mathbf{x})$,
3. set $\mathbf{a}_k \leftarrow \mathbf{a}_0$,
4. compute $\mathbf{e}_k = \mathbf{e}(\mathbf{a}_k)$,
5. compute J,
6. repeat

a. compute update $\mathbf{a}_{k+1} = \mathbf{a}_k - (\mathsf{J}^T\mathsf{J} + \lambda\mathsf{I})^{-1}\mathsf{J}^T\mathbf{e}_k$ [7]
b. compute $\Delta E = E(\mathbf{a}_{k+1}) - E(\mathbf{a}_k)$
c. If $\Delta E > 0$ then $\lambda = 10\lambda$, goto a. else $\lambda = \frac{1}{10}\lambda$, goto 4.
7. If $\|\mathbf{e}_k\| > \nu$ goto 3. else terminate.

Note that ν is a constant which defines the convergence of the algorithm. As already highlighted, the algorithm above is the standard LM algorithm. The crucial components are (i) the choice of unknowns $\mathbf{a}$, (ii) the computation of error vector $\mathbf{e}$ and (iii) the computation of the Jacobian matrix J. In particular, the distance transform $D_\varepsilon(\mathbf{x})$, enables an improvement in the computational efficiency of the error computation and makes the computation of the Jacobian feasible. The starting value $\mathbf{a}_0$ can be estimated by employing some of the techniques described in Sect. 6.2.3.1.

6.6.5 Results and Discussion

Figure 6.16 shows an example of LM-ICP alignment between two views. In this experiment the emphasis is on the speed of the algorithm, since the accuracy is guaranteed by the fact that the two views are well overlapped. The LM-ICP takes less than 1 s for an LM iteration. A total of 20 iterations has been run to reach convergence. Both the data-view and the model-view have about 40,000 points. Using the basic *ICP* algorithm the same number of iterations are required but each iteration takes more than 30 s. This confirms that a drastic improvement of speed is observed with LM-ICP, in comparison with basic ICP. Note that a crucial parameter is the grid size. It trades off computational efficiency with memory space. Moreover it requires that the data scan is always inside the volume by requiring large memory space for storage when only a small overlap is observed between the views. Further experiments can be found in [32]. More details on experimental set-up can be found on the LM-ICP website.[8] In practice LM-ICP also enlarges the basin of convergence and estimates a more accurate solution (the minimum is reached with 50 % fewer iterations on average, see [32] for more details).

Finally, it is worth noting that LM-ICP can be easily extended to apply many other variants of the ICP. Multi-view registration could also be solved in the LM-ICP framework.

6.7 Case Study 3: Deformable ICP with Levenberg-Marquardt

In this section, we describe an advanced registration technique: *Deformable-Levenberg-Marquardt Iterative Closest Point* (DLM-ICP) [19]. DLM-ICP extends

---

[7] While we have chosen the identity as the damping matrix, some authors rather choose the diagonal part of the Gauss-Newton Hessian approximation.

[8] http://research.microsoft.com/en-us/um/people/awf/lmicp.

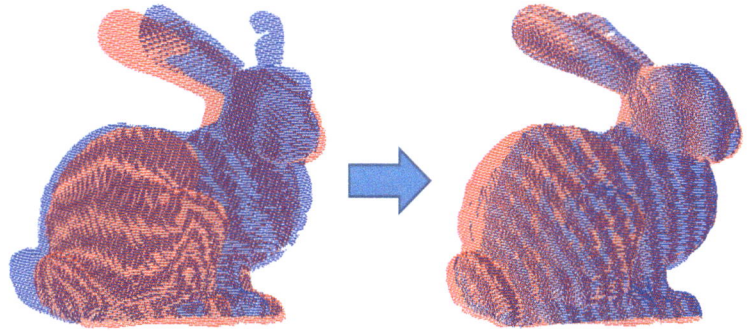

Fig. 6.16 LM-ICP. The starting pose (*left*) and merged views after registration (*right*)

the LM-ICP approach, introduced in Sect. 6.6, to deformable objects. We focus on continuous smooth surfaces such as the page of a book being turned in front of a range sensor. To this aim, a *template* model is warped towards the input scans in order to capture surface deformations. In this case, several instances of almost the entire time-varying object are observed rather than different points of view of an object, and the aim of registration is to align the views over time using a registration-by-fitting approach.

The template model introduces a prior on the acquired shape by providing a joint registration and reconstruction of the object with hole-filling and noise removal. The proposed method exploits only geometric information without the extraction of feature points. According to [32], described in Sect. 6.6, registration is modeled as an optimization problem defined by an error function whose global minimum is the sought after solution, estimated by the Levenberg-Marquardt algorithm. The error function introduces the constraint that data points must be close to model points (i.e. the template). As for [32], it explicitly embeds a min operator, thus avoiding the traditional two steps in ICP-like algorithms, through the use of a distance transform. Furthermore, thanks to the flexibility of LM, many other terms are introduced to model different expected behaviors of the deformation, namely *surface*, and *temporal smoothness* as well as *inextensibility* of the surface. Finally, a boundary constraint is introduced to prevent the computed surface from sliding arbitrarily.

We highlight that, with this method, the unknowns are the template model, represented by a planar-mesh that is deformed to fit each point cloud. More specifically, we directly estimate the position of the model-points without imposing any prior about the kind of transformation function that has been applied. In particular, each unknown (i.e. each vertex of the template) influences a very small portion of the error function. Indeed, another interesting property of DLM-ICP is that the Jacobian matrix, involved in the normal equations to be solved at each iteration, is highly sparse for all the terms. This makes the estimation of dense deformation fields tractable and fast.

6.7.1 Surface Representation

The sequence of 3D point clouds D_i, with $N_d = l_i$ points each, is represented by:

$$D_i = \begin{bmatrix} d_{i,1}^x & d_{i,1}^y & d_{i,1}^z \\ \vdots & \vdots & \vdots \\ d_{i,l_i}^x & d_{i,l_i}^y & d_{i,l_i}^z \end{bmatrix}.$$

The unknown model, $a = M$, has a grid structure and is thus represented by three $R \times C$ matrices, giving the grid's deformation. Each matrix is reshaped in a single vector of size $N_m = RC$, giving M_i as:

$$M_i = \begin{bmatrix} m_{i,1}^x & m_{i,1}^y & m_{i,1}^z \\ \vdots & \vdots & \vdots \\ m_{i,N_m}^x & m_{i,N_m}^y & m_{i,N_m}^z \end{bmatrix}.$$

In practice, the number of data points is much larger than the number of model points (i.e. $l_i \gg N_m$). Upon convergence, the algorithm determines, for each model point, if there is a corresponding point in the current point cloud. Points may be missing because of occlusions or corrupted sensor output. This approach has the advantage that it naturally gives the reconstructed surface by interpolating the mesh points. Point cloud registration is obtained by composing the deformation fields. Note that, in contrast to Sect. 6.6, the registration is from model-points to data-points.

6.7.2 Cost Function

The cost function combines two *data* and three *penalty* terms:

$$E(M) = E_g(M) + \lambda_b E_b(M) + \lambda_s E_s(M) + \lambda_t E_t(M) + \lambda_x E_x(M), \qquad (6.24)$$

where λ_b, λ_s λ_x and λ_t are weights. Note that we drop the frame index i for purposes of clarity, and denote M_i as M and M_{i-1} as $\tilde{M}$.

The data terms are used to attract the estimated surface to the actual point cloud. The first term E_g is for global attraction, while the second one E_b deals with the boundary. In particular, the boundary term aims at preserving the method against possible sliding of the model along the observed surface. Moreover, these terms must account for possible erroneous points by using robust statistics. The penalty terms are E_s, E_t and E_x. The first two account for *spatial smoothness* and *temporal smoothness* E_s respectively. The third one penalizes the *surface stress* and is related to the non-extensibility of the surface, and therefore to material properties of the surface.

This cost function is minimized in an ICP-like manner, as described in the previous section. All five terms are explained below in detail.

Data Term: Global Surface Attraction This term globally attracts the model to the data points in a closest point manner [78]. Denoting $\mathbb{B}_M$ as the set of boundary points in the model, $\mathbb{M}$, where

$$\mathbb{M} = \{[m_i^x \ m_i^y \ m_i^z]^T\}, \quad i = 1\ldots N_m \quad (6.25)$$

and $\mathbb{B}_D$ as the set of boundary points in the data, $\mathbb{D}$, where

$$\mathbb{D} = \{[d_i^x \ d_i^y \ d_i^z]^T\}, \quad i = 1\ldots l_i \quad (6.26)$$

we get the following data term, integrating the model to data points matching step:

$$\sum_{\mathbf{m} \in \mathbb{M} \setminus \mathbb{B}_M} \min_{\mathbf{d} \in \mathbb{D} \setminus \mathbb{B}_D} \|\mathbf{d} - \mathbf{m}\|^2, \quad (6.27)$$

where **d** and **m** are 3-vectors representing a data and a model point respectively. As we mentioned before, the unknowns are not the rigid transformation parameters (i.e. the classical rotation-translation) but correspond to the whole *deformable motion field* in $\mathbb{M}$.

An *outlier rejection* strategy is introduced by defining a robust function ε. Here, the $X84$ rule is employed [17]. Therefore, Eq. (6.27) is modified so as to get the following robustified data term:

$$E_g(\mathbb{M}) = \sum_{\mathbf{m} \in \mathbb{M} \setminus \mathbb{B}_M} \varepsilon \left(\min_{\mathbf{d} \in \mathbb{D} \setminus \mathbb{B}_D} \|\mathbf{d} - \mathbf{m}\|^2 \right). \quad (6.28)$$

Data Term: Boundary Attraction This term attracts boundary model points to boundary data points. It is defined in a similar manner to the global attraction term (Eq. (6.28)) except that the sum and min operators are over the boundary points:

$$E_b(\mathbb{M}) = \sum_{\mathbf{m} \in \mathbb{B}_M} \varepsilon \left(\min_{\mathbf{d} \in \mathbb{B}_D} \|\mathbf{d} - \mathbf{m}\|^2 \right). \quad (6.29)$$

Note that the boundaries can be computed by combining edge detection techniques with morphological operators.[9] More precisely, from the range image, we detect the portion of the image which is covered by the object we want to track (i.e. a piece of paper), and we impose the condition that boundaries of the model and the observed surface must coincide.

Penalty Term: Spatial Smoothness This term discourages surface discontinuities by penalizing its second derivatives, as an approximation to its curvature.

---

[9]The object boundaries can be estimated according to the kind of sensor being used. For instance boundaries on range scans can be estimated on the range image. In stereo sensors, they can be estimated on one of the two optical views.

According to the definition of the geometry image [39], the model $\mathbb{M}$ is a displacement field parameterized[10] by (u, v) with $u = [1\ldots R]$ and $v = [1\ldots C]$, i.e., $\mathbb{M}(u, v) = (M^x(u, v)\ M^y(u, v)\ M^z(u, v))^\mathsf{T}$. The spatial smoothness term can thus be taken as the surface bending energy:

$$E_s(\mathbb{M}) = \iint \left\|\frac{\partial \mathbb{M}^2}{\partial^2 u}\right\|^2 + 2\left\|\frac{\partial \mathbb{M}^2}{\partial u \partial v}\right\|^2 + \left\|\frac{\partial \mathbb{M}^2}{\partial^2 v}\right\|^2 du\, dv.$$

Using a finite difference approximation for the first and second derivatives [70], the bending energy can be expressed in discrete form as a quadratic function of $\mathbb{M}$. More specifically, the derivatives $\frac{\partial M^x}{\partial u}$ at a point (u, v) is discretely approximated as $\frac{\partial M^x(u,v)}{\partial u} = M^x(u+1, v) - M^x(u-1, v)$. This can be conveniently represented by a constant $N_m \times N_m$ matrix C_u such that $\nabla_u \mathbb{M}^x = \mathsf{C}_u \cdot \text{vect}(\mathbb{M}^x)$, where $\text{vect}(\mathbb{M}^x)$ is the vectorization operator which rearranges matrix $\mathbb{M}^x$ to a vector. A similar matrix C_v can be computed with respect to v. Indeed, the second derivatives are computed using Hessian operator matrices, namely $\mathsf{C}_{uu}, \mathsf{C}_{uv}, \mathsf{C}_{vv}$. The surface bending energy can be expressed in discrete form by defining:

$$E_s^x = \text{vect}(\mathbb{M}^x)^\mathsf{T}\left(\mathsf{C}_{uu}^\mathsf{T}\mathsf{C}_{uu} + 2\mathsf{C}_{uv}^\mathsf{T}\mathsf{C}_{uv} + \mathsf{C}_{vv}^\mathsf{T}\mathsf{C}_{vv}\right)\text{vect}(\mathbb{M}^x),$$

and by computing:

$$E_s(\mathbb{M}) = E_s^x(\mathbb{M}^x) + E_s^y(\mathbb{M}^y) + E_s^z(\mathbb{M}^z),$$

which can be further expressed in matrix form as follows:

$$E_s(\mathbb{M}) = \text{vect}(\mathbb{M})^\mathsf{T} \mathscr{H}\, \text{vect}(\mathbb{M}), \qquad (6.30)$$

where $\mathscr{H}$ is a $3N_m \times 3N_m$, highly sparse matrix.

Penalty Term: Temporal Smoothness This term defines a dependency between the current and the previous point clouds, $\mathbb{M}$ and $\tilde{\mathbb{M}}$:

$$E_t(\mathbb{M}) = \|\mathbb{M} - \tilde{\mathbb{M}}\|^2. \qquad (6.31)$$

This makes the surface deformation smooth over time and can be used within a sequential processing approach. Obviously, it is not used on the first frame of the sequence.

Penalty Term: Non-extensibility This term discourages surface stretching. It encourages mesh vertices to preserve their distance with their local neighborhood [80]:

$$E_X(\mathbb{M}) = \sum_{\mathbf{m} \in \mathbb{M}} \sum_{\mathbf{k} \in \mathscr{N}(\mathbf{m})} \left(\|\mathbf{m} - \mathbf{k}\|^2 - L_{m,k}^2\right)^2, \qquad (6.32)$$

where $L_{m,k}$ are constants, which are computed at the first frame after robust initialization, and $\mathscr{N}(\mathbf{m})$ is the 8-neighborhood of the mesh vertex $\mathbf{m}$.

---

[10]Recall that the model points lie on a grid.

6.7.3 Minimization Procedure

The DLM-ICP cost function (6.24) is a sum of squared residuals, nonlinearly depending on the unknowns in M. Therefore, as in Sect. 6.6, the Levenberg-Marquardt algorithm can be used. In order to provide partial derivatives of the residuals through a Jacobian matrix, all five terms in the cost function are separately differentiated and stacked as:

$$J^\mathsf{T} = \begin{bmatrix} J_d^\mathsf{T} & J_b^\mathsf{T} & J_s^\mathsf{T} & J_t^\mathsf{T} & J_x^\mathsf{T} \end{bmatrix}, \tag{6.33}$$

where $J_d^{N_m \times 3N_m}$, $J_b^{N_B \times 3N_m}$, $J_s^{3N_m \times 3N_m}$, $J_t^{N_m \times 3N_m}$, $J_x^{\xi \times 3N_m}$, are related to the global attraction, boundary attraction, spatial smoothness, temporal smoothness and non-extensibility terms respectively, and $\xi = \texttt{size}(\mathcal{N}(M))$. In particular, the Jacobians of global and boundary attraction terms are estimated by finite differences through distance transform, as described in Sect. 6.6.

Note that, in this case, since the Hessian matrix[11] $H = J^\mathsf{T} J + \lambda I$ must be inverted at each LM iteration, the problem is not tractable if the number of model points is too high (if the deformation field is too dense). One advantage of the proposed approach is that the Jacobian matrix J is very sparse. Thus, it uses the sparsity to speed up each iteration using the technique in [68]. In particular, a sparse Cholesky factorization package can be used, as in the Matlab 'mldivide' function.

6.7.4 Summary of the Algorithm

The DLM-ICP algorithm can be summarized as follows:

1. Choose the model-size $R \times C$ (for instance, 10×10)
2. Initialize the template-model M_0
3. For each data-frame $\mathbb{D}_i$
   a. Extract data boundary $\mathbb{B}_D$
   b. Set $M_i = M_{i-1}$ to initialize the LM algorithm
   c. Apply LM-ICP to estimate M_i by minimizing the error function
   d. Goto 3.

Step 3.c is described in Sect. 6.6.4. Here, the unknown is $a = M_i$, the error function $E(M_i)$ is defined by Eq. (6.24), and the Jacobian J is defined by Eq. (6.33).

6.7.5 Experiments

In the following experiment, the sensor is a real-time passive-stereo system.[12] The sensor acquires images at 25 FPS (frames-per-second) and provides both intensity

---
[11] The damped Gauss-Newton approximation to the true Hessian matrix.
[12] Data courtesy of eVS (http://www.evsys.net).

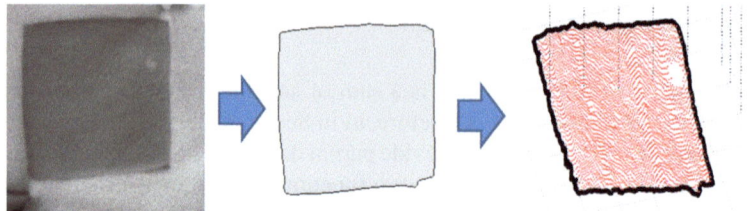

Fig. 6.17 Data acquisition: intensity image of the blanket (*left*), image-boundary (*center*), and the 3D point cloud (*right*)

(i.e. 2D) and 3D information. The deformation of a portion of a blanket is modeled. Figure 6.17 shows a picture of the blanket. Intensity information is used to segment the boundary; more precisely, only the portion delimited by the dark square is considered. Figure 6.17 also shows the image-boundary extracted by combining a binary image segmentation method with 2D morphological operators and depicts the 3D data (i.e. the selected point cloud and 3D boundary).

The sequence is made of 100 point clouds. A model of size $R = 15$ and $C = 20$ is used. Model initialization M_0 is carried out by lying the model-grid on a plane which is fitted to the extracted point cloud. Model initialization is employed in the first frame only. Then, each iteration uses the output of the previous one as an initial condition. Note that a higher value of λ_b is necessary (i.e. $\lambda_b = 1.5$) for a correct convergence of the algorithm to the optimal solution. The other terms are set almost equally to 1. The distance transform parameters are important: the size of the voxels trades off speed and accuracy. In this experiment, the volume is divided into $36 \times 36 \times 18$ voxels. Figure 6.18 shows a selection of the output sequence. For each frame, we visualize: (i) the intensity image with the extracted 2D boundary and the

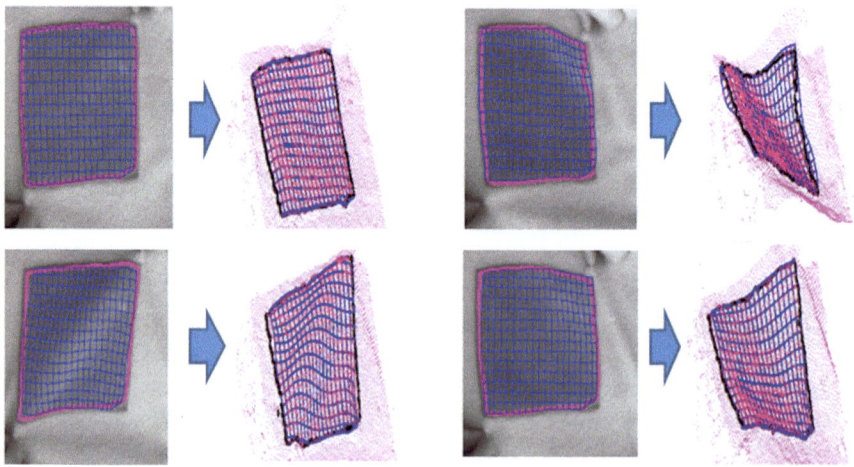

Fig. 6.18 Blanket sequence: 4 selected frames. For each frame the 2D intensity and the 3D data is visualized. The grid models are shown in 3D space, as well as their projection in the 2D image

2D projection of the estimated model and (ii) the point cloud, after the region-of-interest selection, evidencing both the 3D boundary and the grid.

The blanket is handled from the bottom-left and upper-right corners, respectively. On the early frames, the blanket is gradually bent toward the square center, then it is strongly stretched, moving the corners far from each other. Finally, in the late frames, random deformations are generated, especially around the corners. Results are satisfying since the fitting is correct for the whole sequence, in spite of the presence of strong occlusions and deformations. The mesh grids are well superimposed on data points maintaining a smooth shape. Nevertheless, the projection of the grids to the 2D images confirms the accuracy of the registration. More details on performance evaluation are available in [19].

6.8 Research Challenges

In general, new challenges of registration methods arise from advances in acquisition procedures. Structure and motion reconstruction techniques are now available to provide accurate, sparse or dense reconstructed scenes from 2D images. Large-scale scanners are also able to acquire wide scenes. The registration of data coming from these procedures is challenging due to strong clutter and occlusions. Moreover, as observed before, the object to be registered may be very small with respect to the whole scene. An important issue is the local scale estimation of scene sub-parts. On the other hand, texture or color information can be also acquired by the sensor. Therefore, registration can be improved by integrating effectively these additional cues. Another promising direction is the use of machine learning techniques. In particular, new techniques can be exploited, inspired from similar issues already addressed for the 2D domain like face, car or pedestrian detection techniques. Improvements can be achieved by integrating 3D scans and 2D images.

Other problems need to be addressed when real-time scanners are used. In this scenario, objects can move (change their pose) or deform. Therefore, deformable registration techniques should be employed. In particular, all the advances on isometry-invariant point correspondence computation can improve the deformable registration. Other issues are coming from the explosion of data collection. For instance, from real-time scanners a large amount of data can be acquired. In order to avoid exhaustive search some more effective matching strategies can be exploited. Feature based techniques are useful to this aim. In particular, feature point detection and description can reduce drastically the number of analyzed points. Also hierarchical techniques are needed to reduce the search space. Finally, to design a proper surface deformation transform, deformable registration methods can be inspired from 3D animation techniques.

6.9 Concluding Remarks

Registration of 3D data is a well studied problem but new issues still need to be solved. The ICP algorithm is the current standard method, since it works well in general and it is easy to implement. Although the basic version is quite limited, several extensions and strong variants have been introduced that allow it to cope with many scenarios. For instance, the techniques described in Sect. 6.2.3 are sufficient to obtain a full model reconstruction of a single object observed from a few dozen viewpoints. However, in more challenging situations, such as in the presence of cluttered or deformable objects, the problem becomes more difficult. The point matching strategy needs to be improved and the transformation function needs to be properly designed. Therefore, more advanced techniques need to be employed like those described in Sect. 6.3. In order to give some examples of registration algorithms, three case studies were reported. Case study 1 shows how, in practice, a robust outlier rejection strategy can improve the accuracy of registration and estimate the overlapping area. Case study 2 exploits general Levenberg-Marquardt optimization to improve the basic ICP algorithm. In particular, the advantage of using the distance transform is clearly demonstrated. Finally, case study 3 addresses a more challenging problem, namely deformable registration from real-time acquisition. Also in this case, the Levenberg-Marquardt approach enables the modeling of the expected behavior of surface deformations. In particular, effective data and penalty terms can be encoded easily in the general error function.

New challenging scenarios can be addressed as described in Sect. 6.8 by exploiting recent machine learning and computer vision techniques already successfully employed for the 2D domain, as well as new advances inspired from recent computer animation techniques.

6.10 Further Reading

In order to get a more comprehensive overview of 3D registration methods, the reader can refer to recent surveys [48, 57, 78, 79]. In [78], Ruzinkiewicz et al. have analyzed some variants of the ICP technique, focusing on methods and suggestions to improve the computation speed. An extensive review of registration methods based on the definition of surface shape descriptors can be found in [57]. In [79], Salvi et al. proposed an extensive experimental comparison amongst different 3D pairwise registration methods. They evaluated the accuracy of the results for both coarse and fine registration. More recently, Kaick et al. [48] proposed a survey on shape correspondence estimation by extensively reporting and discussing interesting methods for deforming scenarios.

The reader interested in getting in-depth details on the theoretical evaluation of registration convergence should refer to Pottmann et al.'s work [35, 69]. Convergence is discussed also by Ezra et al. [31] who provided lower and upper bounds on the number of ICP iterations. One of these methods [86] defines a new registration metric called the 'surface interpenetration measure'. This is in contrast to the mean square error (MSE) employed by classical ICP and the authors claim that this is more effective when attempting to achieve precise alignments. Finally, we have stated already that most of the registration techniques are based on the ICP algorithm. However, alternative methods in the literature can be considered, such as those based on Genetic Algorithms [52, 53, 86].

6.11 Questions

1. Give four examples of problem where 3D shape registration is an essential component. In each case, explain why registration is required for their automated solution.
2. Briefly outline the steps of the classical iterative closest point (ICP) algorithm.
3. What is usually the most computationally intensive step in a typical ICP application and what steps can be taken to reduce this?
4. What is the common failure mode of ICP and what steps can be taken to avoid this?
5. What steps can be taken to improve the final accuracy of an ICP registration?
6. Explain why registration in clutter is challenging and describe one solution that has been proposed.
7. Explain why registration of deformable objects is challenging and describe one solution that has been proposed.
8. What advantages does LM-ICP have over classical ICP?

6.12 Exercises

1. Given two partial views very close to each other and an implementation of ICP[13] try to register the views by gradually moving the data-view away from the model-view until ICP diverges. Apply the perturbation to both the translational and rotational components. Repeat the exercise, decreasing the overlap area by removing points in the model-view.
2. Implement a pairwise pre-alignment technique based on PCA. Try to check the effectiveness of the pre-alignment by varying the shape of the two views.
3. Implement an outlier rejection technique to robustify ICP registration. Compare the robustness among (i) fixed threshold, (ii) threshold estimated as 2.5σ of the residuals' distribution from their mean and (iii) threshold estimated with the X84 technique.
4. Compute the Jacobian matrix of LM-ICP by encoding rotation with a unit quaternion.[14]
5. Modify LM-ICP in order to work with multiple views, given a sequence of 10 views which surround an object such that N_{10} is highly overlapping N_1. The global reference system is fixed on the first view. Estimate the global registration

---

[13] Matlab implementation at: http://www.csse.uwa.edu.au/ajmal/code.html.

[14] Matlab implementation at: http://research.microsoft.com/en-us/um/people/awf/lmicp.

by including pairwise registration between subsequent views and by view N_{10} to view N_1. *Suggestion:* the number of unknowns is $9p$, where p is the dimension of the transformation vector (i.e., $p = 7$ for quaternions). The number of rows of the Jacobian matrix is given by all residual vectors of each pairwise registration. Here, the key aspect is that view N_{10} should be simultaneously aligned pairwise with both view N_9 and view N_1.

References

1. Albarelli, A., Torsello, A., Rodola, E.: A game-theoretic approach to fine surface registration without initial motion estimation. In: International Conference on Computer Vision and Pattern Recognition (2010)
2. Anguelov, D., Srinivasan, P., Pang, H.C., Koller, D., Thurun, S., Davis, J.: The correlated correspondence algorithm for unsupervised registration of nonrigid surfaces. In: Neural Information Processing Systems Conference (2004)
3. Arun, K.S., Huang, T., Blostein, S.: Least-squares fitting of two 3-d point sets. IEEE Trans. Pattern Anal. Mach. Intell. **9**, 698–700 (1987)
4. Bariya, P., Nishino, K.: Scale-hierarchical 3d object recognition in cluttered scenes. In: International Conference on Computer Vision and Pattern Recognition (2010)
5. Belongie, S., Malik, J., Puzicha, J.: Shape matching and object recognition using shape contexts. IEEE Trans. Pattern Anal. Mach. Intell. **24**(4), 509–522 (2002)
6. Bernardini, F., Rushmeier, H.: The 3D model acquisition pipeline. Comput. Graph. Forum **21**(2), 149–172 (2002)
7. Besl, P., McKay, H.: A method for registration of 3-D shapes. IEEE Trans. Pattern Anal. Mach. Intell. **14**(2), 239–256 (1992)
8. Blais, G., Levine, M.: Registering multiview range data to create 3d computer objects. IEEE Trans. Pattern Anal. Mach. Intell. **17**(8) (1995)
9. Bowyer, K.W., Chang, K., Flynn, P.: A survey of approaches and challenges in 3d and multimodal 3d + 2d face recognition. Comput. Vis. Image Underst. **101**(1) (2006)
10. Bronstein, A.M., Bronstein, M.M., Kimmel, R.: Three-dimensional face recognition. Int. J. Comput. Vis. **64**(1), 5–30 (2005)
11. Bronstein, A.M., Bronstein, M.M., Kimmel, R.: Numerical Geometry of Non-rigid Shapes. Springer, Berlin (2008)
12. Brown, B., Rusinkiewicz, S.: Non-rigid range-scan alignment using thin-plate splines. In: Symposium on 3D Data Processing, Visualization, and Transmission (2004)
13. Brown, B., Rusinkiewicz, S.: Global non-rigid alignment of 3-D scans. ACM Trans. Graph. **26**(3) (2007) (Proc. SIGGRAPH)
14. Brusco, N., Andreetto, M., Giorgi, A., Cortelazzo, G.: 3d registration by textured spin-images. In: 3DIM'05: Proceedings of the Fifth International Conference on 3-D Digital Imaging and Modeling, pp. 262–269 (2005)
15. Campbell, R., Flynn, P.: A survey of free-form object representation and recognition techniques. Comput. Vis. Image Underst. **81**(2), 166–210 (2001)
16. Castellani, U., Cristani, M., Fantoni, S., Murino, V.: Sparse points matching by combining 3D mesh saliency with statistical descriptors. In: Computer Graphics Forum, vol. 27, pp. 643–652. Blackwell, Oxford (2008)
17. Castellani, U., Fusiello, A., Murino, V.: Registration of multiple acoustic range views for underwater scene reconstruction. Comput. Vis. Image Underst. **87**(3), 78–89 (2002)
18. Castellani, U., Fusiello, A., Murino, V., Papaleo, L., Puppo, E., Pittore, M.: A complete system for on-line modelling of acoustic images. Image Commun. J. **20**(9–10), 832–852 (2005)

19. Castellani, U., Gay-Bellile, V., Bartoli, A.: Robust deformation capture from temporal range data for surface rendering. Comput. Animat. Virtual Worlds **19**(5), 591–603 (2008)
20. Chang, M., Leymarie, F., Kimia, B.: 3d shape registration using regularized medial scaffolds. In: International Symposium on 3D Data Processing, Visualization and Transmission (2004)
21. Chang, W., Zwicker, M.: Automatic registration for articulated shapes. Comput. Graph. Forum **27**(5), 1459–1468 (2008) (Proceedings of SGP 2008)
22. Chang, W., Zwicker, M.: Range scan registration using reduced deformable models. Comput. Graph. Forum **28**(2), 447–456 (2009)
23. Chen, Y., Medioni, G.: Object modelling by registration of multiple range images. Image Vis. Comput. **10**(3), 145–155 (1992)
24. Chui, H., Rangarajan, A.: A new point matching algorithm for non-rigid registration. Comput. Vis. Image Underst. **89**(2–3), 114–141 (2003)
25. Corey, G., Matei, C., Jaime, P.: Data-driven grasping with partial sensor data. In: IROS'09: Proceedings of the 2009 IEEE/RSJ International Conference on Intelligent Robots and Systems, pp. 1278–1283 (2009)
26. Cruska, G., Dance, C.R., Fan, L., Willamowski, J., Bray, C.: Visual categorization with bags of keypoints. In: ECCV Workshop on Statistical Learning in Computer Vision, pp. 1–22 (2004)
27. Cunnington, S., Stoddart, A.: N-view point set registration: a comparison. In: British Machine Vision Conference (1999)
28. Dewaele, G., Devernay, F., Horaud, R.: Hand motion from 3d point trajectories and a smooth surface model. In: European Conference on Computer Vision (2004)
29. Drost, B., Ulrich, M., Navab, N., Ilic, S.: Model globally, match locally: efficient and robust 3d object recognition. In: International Conference on Computer Vision and Pattern Recognition (2010)
30. Eggert, D., Lorusso, A., Fisher, R.: Estimating 3-d rigid body transformations: a comparison of four major algorithms. Mach. Vis. Appl. **9**, 272–290 (1997)
31. Ezra, E., Sharir, M., Efrat, A.: On the performance of the ICP algorithm. Comput. Geom. **41**(1–2), 77–93 (2008)
32. Fitzgibbon, A.: Robust registration of 2D and 3D point sets. Image Vis. Comput. **21**(13–14), 1145–1153 (2003)
33. Funkhouser, T., Kazhdan, M., Min, P., Shilane, P.: Shape-based retrieval and analysis of 3d models. Commun. ACM **48**(6), 58–64 (2005)
34. Fusiello, A.: Visione computazionale. Appunti delle lezioni. Pubblicato a cura dell'autore (2008)
35. Gelfand, N., Mitra, N.J., Guibas, L.J., Pottmann, H.: Robust global registration. In: Desbrun, M., Pottmann, H. (eds.) EuroGraphics Association, pp. 197–206 (2005) ISBN 3-905673-24-X
36. Godin, G., Laurendeau, D., Bergevin, R.: A method for the registration of attributed range images. In: 3-D Digital Imaging and Modeling (3DIM), pp. 179–186 (2001)
37. Golovinskiy, A., Kim, V., Funkhouser, T.: Shape-based recognition of 3d point clouds in urban environments. In: International Conference on Computer Vision (2009)
38. Granger, S., Pennec, X.: Multi-scale em-ICP: a fast and robust approach for surface registration. In: European Conference on Computer Vision (2002)
39. Gu, X., Gortler, S.J., Hoppe, H.: Geometry images. ACM Trans. Graph. **21**(3), 355–361 (2002)
40. Hampel, F., Rousseeuw, P., Ronchetti, E., Stahel, W.: Robust Statistics: The Approach Based on Influence Functions. Wiley, New York (1986)
41. Horaud, R., Forbes, F., Yguel, M., Dewaele, G., Zhang, J.: Rigid and articulated point registration with expectation conditional maximization. IEEE Trans. Pattern Anal. Mach. Intell. **33**(3), 587–602 (2011)
42. Huang, Q., Adams, B., Wicke, M., Guibas, L.: Non-rigid registration under isometric deformations. Comput. Graph. Forum **27**(5), 1449–1457 (2008)
43. Huber, D., Hebert, M.: Fully automatic registration of multiple 3D data sets. Image Vis. Comput. **21**(7), 637–650 (2003)

44. IV, A.P., Mordohai, P., Daniilidis, K.: Object detection from large-scale 3d datasets using bottom-up and top-down descriptors. In: Proceedings of the European Conference on Computer Vision (2008)
45. Jhonson, A., Kang, S.: Registration and integration of textured 3d data. Image Vis. Comput. **19**(2), 135–147 (1999)
46. Jian, B., Vemuri, B.C.: A robust algorithm for point set registration using mixture of Gaussians. In: International Conference on Computer Vision and Pattern Recognition (2005)
47. Johnson, A., Hebert, M.: Using spin images for efficient object recognition in cluttered 3D scenes. IEEE Trans. Pattern Anal. Mach. Intell. **21**(5), 433–449 (1999)
48. van Kaick, O., Zhang, H., Hamarneh, G., Cohen-Or, D.: A survey on shape correspondence. In: EuroGraphics: State-of-the-Art Report (2010)
49. Khoualed, S., Castellani, U., Bartoli, A.: Semantic shape context for the registration of multiple partial 3-D views. In: British Machine Vision Conference (2009)
50. Krsek, P., Pajdla, T., Hlaváč, V.: Differential invariants as the base of triangulated surface registration. Comput. Vis. Image Underst. **87**(1–3), 27–38 (2002)
51. Li, H., Sumner, R.W., Pauly, M.: Global correspondence optimization for non-rigid registration of depth scans. Comput. Graph. Forum **27**(5) (2008) (Proc. SGP'08)
52. Liu, Y.: Automatic 3d free form shape matching using the graduated assignment algorithm. Pattern Recognit. **38**, 1615–1631 (2005)
53. Lomonosov, E., Chetverikov, D., Ekárt, A.: Pre-registration of arbitrarily oriented 3d surfaces using a genetic algorithm. Pattern Recognit. Lett. **27**(11), 1201–1208 (2006)
54. Maintz, J., Viergever, M.A.: A survey of medical image registration. Med. Image Anal. **2**(1), 1–36 (1998)
55. Makadia, A., Patterson, A., Daniilidis, K.: Fully automatic registration of 3D point clouds. In: Proceedings of the 2006 IEEE Computer Society Conference on Computer Vision and Pattern Recognition, vol. 1, pp. 1297–1304. IEEE Computer Society, Washington (2006)
56. Mian, A.S., Bennamoun, M., Owens, R.: Three-dimensional model-based object recognition and segmentation in cluttered scenes. IEEE Trans. Pattern Anal. Mach. Intell. **28**(10), 1584–1601 (2006)
57. Mian, A.S., Bennamoun, M., Owens, R.A.: Automatic correspondence for 3d modeling: an extensive review. Int. J. Shape Model. **11**(2), 253–291 (2005)
58. Mitra, N.J., Flory, S., Ovsjanikov, M., Gelfand, N., Guibas, L., Pottmann, H.: Dynamic geometry registration. In: Symposium on Geometry Processing, pp. 173–182 (2007)
59. Munoz, D., Vandapel, N., Hebert, M.: Directional associative Markov network for 3-d point cloud classification. In: International Symposium on 3-D Data Processing, Visualization and Transmission (3DPVT) (2008)
60. Murino, V., Ronchetti, L., Castellani, U., Fusiello, A.: Reconstruction of complex environments by robust pre-aligned ICP. In: 3DIM (2001)
61. Myronenko, A., Song, X., Carreira-Perpinan, M.: Non-rigid point set registration: coherent point drift. In: Neural Information Processing Systems Conference (2006)
62. Novatnack, J., Nishino, K.: Scale-dependent/invariant local 3D shape descriptors for fully automatic registration of multiple sets of range images. In: Proceedings of the 10th European Conference on Computer Vision: Part III, pp. 440–453. Springer, Berlin (2008)
63. Nuchter, A., Lingemann, K., Hertzberg, J.: Cached k-d tree search for ICP algorithms. In: 3DIM'07: Proceedings of the Sixth International Conference on 3-D Digital Imaging and Modeling, pp. 419–426 (2007)
64. Park, K., Germann, M., Breitenstein, M.D., Pfister, H.: Fast and automatic object pose estimation for range images on the GPU. Mach. Vis. Appl. **21**(5), 749–766 (2009)
65. Park, S., Subbarao, M.: An accurate and fast point-to-plane registration technique. Pattern Recognit. Lett. **24**(16), 2967–2976 (2003)
66. Pears, N.E., Heseltine, T., Romero, M.: From 3d point clouds to pose normalised depth maps. Int. J. Comput. Vis. **89**(2), 152–176 (2010)
67. Phillips, J., Liu, R., Tomasi, C.: Outlier robust ICP for minimizing fractional RMSD. In: 3-D Digital Imaging and Modeling (3DIM), pp. 427–434 (2007)

68. Pissanetzky, S.: Sparse Matrix Technology. Academic Press, San Diego (1984)
69. Pottmann, H., Huang, Q., Yang, Y., Hu, S.: Geometry and convergence analysis of algorithms for registration of 3D shapes. Int. J. Comput. Vis. **67**(3), 277–296 (2006)
70. Prasad, M., Zisserman, A., Fitzgibbon, A.W.: Single view reconstruction of curved surfaces. In: International Conference on Computer Vision and Pattern Recognition (2006)
71. Pulli, K.: Multiview registration for large data sets. In: 3DIM'99: Proceedings of the Fifth International Conference on 3-D Digital Imaging and Modeling, pp. 160–168 (1999)
72. Pulli, K., Piiroinen, S., Duchamp, T., Stuetzle, W.: Projective surface matching of colored 3d scans. In: 3-D Digital Imaging and Modeling (3DIM), pp. 531–538 (2005)
73. Rangarajan, A., Chui, H., Duncan, J.: Rigid point feature registration using mutual information. Med. Image Anal. **3**(4), 425–440 (1999)
74. Rangarajan, A., Chui, H., Mjolsness, E., Pappu, S., Davachi, L., Goldman-Rakic, P., Duncan, J.: A robust point-matching algorithm for autoradiograph alignment. Med. Image Anal. **1**(4), 379–398 (1997)
75. Ruiter, H.D., Benhabib, B.: On-line Modeling for Real-Time, Model-Based, 3D Pose Tracking. Springer, Berlin (2007)
76. Rusinkiewicz, S., Brown, B., Kazhdan, M.: 3d Scan Matching and Registration. ICCV Short Course (2005)
77. Rusinkiewicz, S., Hall-Holt, O., Levoy, M.: Real-time 3-D model acquisition. ACM Trans. Graph. **21**(3), 438–446 (2002) (Proc. SIGGRAPH)
78. Rusinkiewicz, S., Levoy, M.: Efficient variants of the ICP algorithm. In: Third International Conference on 3-D Digital Imaging and Modeling, 2001, Proceedings, pp. 145–152 (2001)
79. Salvi, J., Matabosch, C., Fofi, D., Forest, J.: A review of recent range image registration methods with accuracy evaluation. Image Vis. Comput. **25**(5), 578–596 (2007)
80. Salzmann, M., Ilic, S., Fua, P.: Physically valid shape parameterization for monocular 3-D deformable surface tracking. In: British Machine Vision Conference (2005)
81. Sara, R.: Finding the largest unambiguous component of stereo matching. In: Proc. of European Conference on Computer Vision (ECCV), pp. 900–914 (2002)
82. Sara, R., Okatani, I., Sugimoto, A.: Globally convergent range image registration by graph kernel algorithm. In: 3-D Digital Imaging and Modeling (3DIM) (2005)
83. Scheenstra, A., Ruifrok, A., Veltkamp, R.C.: A survey of 3d face recognition methods. In: Audio- and Video-Based Biometric Person Authentication, pp. 891–899 (2005)
84. Shams, R., Sadeghi, P., Kennedy, R.A., Hartley, R.I.: A survey of high performance medical image registration on multi-core, GPU and distributed architectures. IEEE Signal Process. Mag. **27**(2), 50–60 (2010)
85. Sharp, G., Sang, L., Wehe, D.: ICP registration using invariant features. IEEE Trans. Pattern Anal. Mach. Intell. **24**(1), 90–102 (2002)
86. Silva, L., Bellon, O.R.P., Boyer, K.L.: Precision range image registration using a robust surface interpenetration measure and enhanced genetic algorithms. IEEE Trans. Pattern Anal. Mach. Intell. **27**(5), 762–776 (2005)
87. Simon, D.A.: Fast and accurate shape-based registration. Ph.D. thesis, Carnegie Mellon University, Pittsburgh, PA, USA (1996)
88. Steinke, F., Scholkopf, B., Blanz, V.: Learning dense 3d correspondence. In: Annual Conference on Neural Information Processing Systems (NIPS 2006) (2007)
89. Taati, B., Bondy, M., Jasiobedzki, P., Greenspan, M.: Automatic registration for model building using variable dimensional local shape descriptors. In: International Conference on 3-D Digital Imaging and Modeling (2007)
90. Tangelder, J., Veltkamp, R.: A survey of content based 3d shape retrieval methods. Multimed. Tools Appl. **39**(3), 441–471 (2008)
91. Toldo, R., Beinat, A., Crosilla, F.: Global registration of multiple point clouds embedding the generalized procrustes analysis into an ICP framework. In: Symposium on 3D Data Processing, Visualization, and Transmission (2010)
92. Trucco, M., Verri, A.: Introductory Techniques for 3-D Computer Vision. Prentice Hall, New York (1998)

93. Tsin, Y., Kanade, T.: A correlation-based approach to robust point set registration. In: European Conference on Computer Vision, pp. 558–569 (2004)
94. Umeyama, S.: Least-squares estimation of transformation parameters between two points patterns. IEEE Trans. Pattern Anal. Mach. Intell. **13**(4), 376–380 (1991)
95. Vinesh, R., Kiran, F.: Reverse Engineering, an Industrial Perspective. Springer, Berlin (2008)
96. Wang, F., Vemuri, B.C., Rangarajan, A.: Groupwise point pattern registration using a novel CDF-based Jensen-Shannon divergence. In: International Conference on Computer Vision and Pattern Recognition (2006)
97. Watt, A.: 3D Computer Graphics. Addison-Wesley, Reading (2000)
98. Weik, S.: Registration of 3-d partial surface models using luminance and depth information. In: 3-D Digital Imaging and Modeling (3DIM), pp. 93–100 (1997)
99. Wyngaerd, J.V., Gool, L.V.: Automatic crude patch registration: toward automatic 3d model building. Comput. Vis. Image Underst. **87**(1–3), 8–26 (2002)
100. Zhang, Z.: Iterative point matching of free-form curves and surfaces. Int. J. Comput. Vis. **13**(2), 119–152 (1994)
101. Zinsser, T., Schnidt, H., Niermann, J.: A refined ICP algorithm for robust 3D correspondences estimation. In: International Conference on Image Processing, pp. 695–698 (2003)

Chapter 7
3D Shape Matching for Retrieval and Recognition

Benjamin Bustos and Ivan Sipiran

Abstract Nowadays, multimedia information, such as images and videos, are present in many aspects of our lives. Three-dimensional information is also becoming important in different applications, for instance entertainment, medicine, security, art, just to name a few. Therefore, it is necessary to study how to process 3D information in order to take advantage of the properties that it provides. This chapter gives an overview of 3D shape matching and its applications to 3D shape retrieval and 3D shape recognition. In order to present the subject, we describe in detail four approaches with a good balance of maturity and novelty across the different methods. The selected approaches are: the depth buffer descriptor, spin images, salient spectral geometric features and heat kernel signatures.

7.1 Introduction

The ability to store and manipulate large amounts of information has enabled the emergence of a number of applications. Generally, the information is given as text because it is easy to produce and understand by a computer. However, there are situations where information cannot be suitably represented by text, such as a tourist's photo album.

Thus, the use and availability of multimedia information has increased considerably, on the one hand to support new applications and on the other hand due to the proliferation and accessibility of inexpensive capture devices such as digital cameras. A number of applications have benefited from this availability of images, videos and three-dimensional models, such as security, entertainment, and engineering processes. Unlike text, multimedia information is difficult to be compared directly and therefore we require techniques to manipulate it effectively.

This work has been supported by Fondecyt (Chile) Project 1110111.

B. Bustos (✉) · I. Sipiran
Department of Computer Science, University of Chile, Santiago, Chile
e-mail: bebustos@dcc.uchile.cl

I. Sipiran
e-mail: isipiran@dcc.uchile.cl

Our goal in this chapter is to address the problem of comparing two 3D objects based on their shapes. Shape matching refers to the process of finding a correspondence between two shapes based on some similarity criterion. The criterion which has received most attention by the research community is the visual similarity, that is to say, two shapes should be matched if they share visually common features. In this chapter, we are interested in two processes involving 3D shapes matching, namely retrieval and recognition.

Although these processes are related, they are slightly different. On the one hand, shape recognition consists of identifying a given 3D object within a set of possible alternatives. The outcome of this process is generally the class to which the object belongs or the recognized object as stored by the recognition system. The latter is useful when the queried object represents a partial or occluded portion such as a range scan. On the other hand, shape retrieval consists of defining a measure in order to quantify the similarity between shapes. A typical outcome of this process is an ordered list of objects according to their associated measure.

In recent years, we have witnessed increasing interest in the computer graphics and computer vision communities for 3D shape retrieval and recognition. As a result, a number of techniques and approaches have been proposed for shape representation, object and feature description, feature selection, and matching algorithms. It is also important to note the large number of applications that have emerged, such as:

- Geometric 3D comparison for the shoe industry [79].
- 3D hippocampi retrieval [61].
- Classification of pollen in 3D volume datasets [92].
- 3D retrieval for museums [49].
- Human ear recognition in 3D [31].
- 3D object classification for craniofacial research [9].
- 3D protein retrieval and classification [87, 88, 112].
- CAD/CAM [113].
- Archeology [54].
- 3D video sequences [53].

To improve performance in each of these applications, it is important to evaluate and compare new approaches, as they appear, with existing ones. Due to the large amount of research carried out and the large dissemination of 3D information obtained through increasingly better capture devices, several benchmarks have been presented, such as the Princeton Shape Benchmark [96], the Konstanz 3D database [26], the TOSCA dataset [18], and the Shape Retrieval Contest (SHREC) datasets (see Fig. 7.1 with objects from different datasets). Such is the interest in 3D shape retrieval that, for several years now, there have been annual competitions with more tracks and more competitors year after year.

Fig. 7.1 Datasets provide shapes with several characteristics such as size, level of detail and shape classes. This figure shows some examples from (**a**) TOSCA dataset, (**b**) Konstanz database, (**c**) SHREC dataset, and (**d**) Princeton shape benchmark

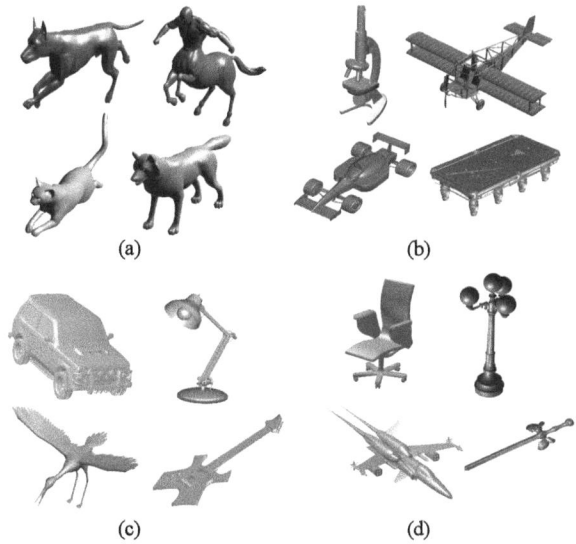

7.1.1 Retrieval and Recognition Evaluation

A very important consideration is the methodology of evaluation for shape retrieval and recognition techniques. In this sense, the evaluation relies on the solid background of mature fields, such as pattern recognition and information retrieval. In the case of shape retrieval, the common evaluation methods are Precision-Recall curves, cumulated gain-based measurements, nearest neighbor, first-tier and second-tier [10]. For shape recognition, *Receiver Operating Characteristic* (ROC) curves and error rates have commonly been used [38]. In order to keep this chapter relatively self-contained, we briefly describe the evaluation measures commonly used in the literature.

In retrieval, the evaluation measures mostly consider the ranked lists retrieved when query objects are presented to the system. The main measures are as follows:

Precision: the extent to which the retrieved objects are relevant to a query. Formally, it is the ratio of correctly retrieved objects with respect to the total number of retrieved objects.

Recall: the extent to which the relevant objects are correctly retrieved. Formally, it is the ratio of correctly retrieved objects with respect to the total number of relevant objects for the query.

R-Precision: precision when the number of retrieved objects equals the number of relevant objects.

Cumulated gain-based measurements: the idea is to use the ranked position of relevant objects. First, we need to convert the retrieved list into a binary list G with 1's in position where relevant objects appear. Second, the discounted cumulated gain vector DCG is defined as follows:

$$DCG[i] = \begin{cases} G[1] & \text{if } i = 1 \\ DCG[i-1] + G[i]/\log_2 i & \text{otherwise} \end{cases} \quad (7.1)$$

where the log function penalizes the ranking of a relevant object.

Nearest neighbor, first tier, and second tier: these evaluation measures check the ratio of relevant objects in the top K objects of the ranked list. Specifically, $K = 1$ for nearest neighbor, $K = |R| - 1$ for first tier and $K = 2 \times (|R| - 1)$ for second tier, where $|R|$ is the number of relevant objects to a query.

In recognition, the common measures are related to error rates after recognition. Some interesting terms are defined as follows:

True positive (TP): ratio of similar shapes identified as similar.
False positive (FP): ratio of dissimilar shapes identified as similar.
False negative (FN): ratio of similar shapes identified as dissimilar.

Using the aforementioned terms, the measures commonly used in recognition are:

Equal error rate (EER): the value of false positive at which it equals the false negative rate. Similarly, a typical measure is the value of false positive at some percentage of false negatives.
ROC curves: is a graphical plot representing the trade-off between the true positives and the false positives.

7.1.2 Chapter Outline

The organization of this chapter is as follows. Section 7.2 provides a brief overview of the proposed approaches and main ideas to date. Section 7.3 presents in detail a selection of techniques for shape retrieval and recognition. The organization of this section is as follows:

- Section 7.3.1 describes a pioneering image-based technique in 3D shape retrieval known as the depth-buffer descriptor.
- Section 7.3.2 presents spin-images, an effective descriptor for 3D shape recognition.
- Section 7.3.3 presents an interesting approach for shape retrieval which uses the Laplace-Beltrami operator to define local descriptors for matching.
- Finally, Sect. 7.3.4 addresses an approach that combines heat kernel signatures with the bag-of-features technique for 3D shape matching.

Section 7.4 is devoted to pose the main challenges in these fields and convenient directions for further research. Section 7.5 presents our concluding remarks. Section 7.6 suggests further readings and finally, in Sects. 7.7 and 7.8 we propose a selection of questions and exercises related to the presented material.

7.2 Literature Review

To support similarity search between two multimedia objects, we must define a model that allows us to compare them. It cannot be done directly because we are interested in retrieving similar objects stored in a database, rather than extracting identical copies. A lot of work has been done to assess the visual similarity between 3D objects when the required model is global. By global, we mean that given a 3D object, an algorithm retrieves those objects in database that look visually similar and the whole shape structure is used for the comparison. The most widely used model consists of obtaining an abstract representation of an object such as feature vectors or graphs, and the similarity is calculated based upon these representations. For example, distance metrics are commonly used to calculate similarity among feature vectors. Another similarity model which has gained much interest involves local features, especially in non-rigid and partial shape retrieval and recognition. The problem of defining a similarity model is very challenging. For example, a visual model allows us to represent a shape by its aspect. However, this model cannot be used to discriminate two shapes semantically similar, but with different aspect.

Bustos et al. [26] described a methodology that consists of representing 3D objects as real vectors of a certain dimension obtained through a transformation function. Then, these vectors can be organized in a multidimensional index, where the similarity corresponds to the proximity in the space where vectors are defined. The Minkowski distance family is usually used to measure the proximity of feature vectors. The authors presented experimental results comparing several transformation functions where the depth-buffer descriptor proposed by Vranic [106] showed the best results. Iyer et al. [55] and Tangelder et al. [100] also discussed techniques for 3D object retrieval, identifying future trends and important issues to be addressed. Also, the Princeton Shape Benchmark [96] provides a reference collection and experimental tests for several descriptors. Other surveys and reports were written by Funkhouser et al. [42], Del Bimbo et al. [15] and Bustos et al. [25, 27]. In 3D shape recognition, Campbell and Flynn [28] presented a comprehensive study of representation and recognition of free-form shapes.

Since then, many other techniques have been proposed to improve effectiveness and efficiency. A brief summary of representative approaches for shape retrieval is given in Table 7.1. Due to space limitations, this table does not show all techniques presented so far. We recommend reading Sect. 7.6 for further references.

Table 7.1 shows a simple taxonomy depending of the extracted shape information which is used in matching. Histogram-based methods summarize certain shape properties such as distribution between points on the surface [82], angle information [86], distribution of face normals [59], and so forth. These properties are used to build histograms which represent shapes and matching is done with common histogram measures. In contrast, transform-based methods apply some transform to the shapes to convert them to a numerical representation of the underlying object. Some examples of such transforms are: Fourier Transform [39], Radon Transform [36], and Wavelet Transform [67]. Image-based methods represent a 3D object as a set of projected images, so the matching becomes an image matching problem. For

Table 7.1 3D shape retrieval methods

Type	Method
Histogram-based	Shape distributions [82]
	Generalized shape distributions [75]
	Angle histogram [86]
	Extended Gaussian images [59]
Transform-based	3D Fourier [39]
	Angular radial transform [91]
	Spherical trace transform [114]
	Rotation invariant spherical harmonics [60]
	Concrete radialized spherical projection [84]
	Spherical wavelet descriptor [67]
Image-based	Depth-buffer descriptor [106]
	Silhouette descriptor [106]
	Light-field descriptor [30]
	Depth-Line descriptor [29]
Graph-based	Reeb graph [104]
	Skeleton graph [99]
Local features	Salient geometric features [44]
	Salient spectral features [52]
	Segmentation-based visual vocabulary [103]
	Heat kernel signatures [83]

instance, Vranic [106] proposed to take the frequency spectrum of depth images, Chen [30] considered silhouettes taken from directions according to the vertices of a dodecahedron, and Chaouch and Verroust-Blondet [29] converted a set of depth images in character strings with the matching being performed with variations of the well-known edit distance. Graph-based methods represent shapes by graph structures such as Reeb graphs [51] which contain information about the connectivity of the shape's parts.

There are several drawbacks with the aforementioned techniques. On the one hand, many of them (especially, image-based and transform-based methods) are pose sensitive. That is, one needs to apply a pose normalization step before the feature extraction process. Clearly, partial and non-rigid matching cannot be addressed with these methods. On the other hand, graph-based methods rely on the topological properties of a 3D object, so topological changes affect the description processes.

Recently, approaches based on local descriptors have received special attention due to its ability to support non-rigid and partial matching. In these approaches, each shape is represented as a set of descriptors and the matching is performed by searching for the best correspondence between them. Gal and Cohen-Or [44] proposed to represent a 3D object as a set of salient geometric features, which determine the complete object. Their scheme entirely relies on curvature information over the shape's surface and the matching is done by indexing the salient features using geometric hashing [108] with a vote scheme to determine similar objects.

An interesting approach was given by Hu and Hua [52] to address the non-rigid and partial matching problem. Their method consists in using the Laplace-Beltrami operator to detect and describe interest points in 3D objects. This operator captures the information of a mesh in different scales, and it is also an isometric invariant, which is an important property to support geometric invariance. The authors proposed an energy function based on the Laplace-Beltrami spectrum to detect interest points with its associated scale. Using these points, along with their respective scales, it is possible to extract descriptors for each interest point from the local Laplace-Beltrami spectrum. The matching is performed by solving an integer quadratic programming problem where two sets of features belonging to shapes to be matched are involved.

One of the most widely used approaches for managing local descriptors is the bag-of-features approach. This begins by clustering all the local descriptors from an entire collection and calculating the centroids for each cluster. Then, each shape is represented as a histogram with a number of bins equal to the number of clusters. Each descriptor adds one into the bin corresponding to the closest centroid. Toldo et al. [103] proposed to segment a given mesh and build a descriptor for each segment. Subsequently, a bag-of-features approach combines all the descriptors in the mesh. Similarly, Ovsjanikov et al. [83] proposed a soft version of the Bag-of-Features approach applied to dense descriptors based on the heat kernel signature, originally introduced by Sun et al. [97], which is related to the Laplace-Beltrami operator. The authors also presented a spatially sensitive bag-of-features technique which gave good results in shape retrieval.

Obviously, the use of local features highlights a new problem: the amount of information used in the matching. With these approaches, a shape is represented with a set of descriptors and the problem of matching becomes non-trivial. In addition, the matching step is more expensive than computing a distance between points, as used in global matching. In this respect, future research directions could be motivated by this kind of matching.

With respect to 3D shape recognition, Table 7.2 shows a selection of techniques proposed to date.

As noted, most presented techniques make extensive use of local features because these can mitigate the effect of occlusion in cluttered scenes. Nevertheless, image-based proposals have also been considered. Lee and Drew [69] extracted contours from 2D projections around a 3D object, and subsequently scale-space curvature image was obtained for each projection. These images were used to identify the class of an object and determine the object in the selected class. In addition, Cyr and Kimia [35] extracted 2D views which were grouped in view sets called aspects. These aspects were represented by a prototype view for accelerating the recognition process given views from new objects.

Table 7.2 3D shape recognition methods

Type	Method
Image-based	Eigen-scale-space contours [69]
	Aspect-graph [35]
Local features	Local features histogram [50]
	Spin images [56]
	Spherical spin images [94]
	3D shape contexts [41]
	Point signatures [33]
	Point fingerprint [98]
	Harmonic shape images [115]
	Cone Curvature [3]
	Local surface patch [32]
	Pyramid Matching [72]

Although it is possible to apply any approach from shape retrieval proposals to object recognition, the general technique that has received most attention is matching by local features. In their seminal work, Chua and Jarvis [33] presented the point signature, a 1D descriptor for points on a surface. To construct the descriptor around some 3D surface point, a 3D space curve is generated as the intersection of a sphere around that point. A plane is fitted to this curve which is translated along its normal until it contains the sphere center (i.e. the surface point). The distance profile of the space curve to this plane, then forms the point's local surface descriptor. In matching, correspondences were found and a voting scheme allowed the determination of objects in a scene.

Following the idea of representing the surrounding geometry of a point, Johnson and Hebert [57] proposed their well-known and well-studied spin images. Given an object, the authors constructed 2D descriptors for points over the surface. As the name suggests, a spin image was obtained by spinning a half plane around the analyzed point's normal and accumulating the points lying in bins of that half plane. The matching was performed by finding correspondences using the spin images between an object and a scene and subsequently a geometric verification with a modified version of the iterative closest point (ICP) algorithm [14] was performed. A variation of this technique was spherical spin images, presented by Ruiz-Correa et al. [94].

Simple information has also been employed. For instance, Hetzel et al. [50] used pixels depth, normals and curvature information in order to combine them in multi-dimensional histograms. Thus, the matching step was performed using χ^2-divergence and a posteriori Bayesian classifier. Sun et al. [98] proposed their point fingerprint, which consisted of geodesic contours projected onto a point's tangent plane. Frome et al. [41] introduced 3D shape contexts and harmonic shape contexts. The idea behind the shape context approach is accumulating the surrounding points using concentric spheres around the analyzed point. The authors proposed to use locality-sensitive hashing for matching. Likewise, Li and Guskov [72] used spin images and normal based signatures to describe selected points over range scans. A combination of pyramid matching and support vector machines (SVMs) were applied for object recognition giving good results on CAD models and faces.

More recently, Chen and Bhanu [32] proposed an approach to recognize highly similar 3D objects in range images. As the authors claimed, several techniques have been proposed to recognize objects in dissimilar classes, however the task of recognizing objects with high similarity is challenging. Given an object, the authors extracted local surface patches on interest points found using curvature information. Due to the high dimensionality of the descriptors, these were embedded in a low dimensional space using FastMap [40]. Then, the low dimensional descriptors were organized in a kd-tree where efficient nearest neighbor algorithms can be applied. Using the kd-tree, it is possible to find correspondences between two objects. A SVM classifier ranks the correspondences according to geometric constraints returning the most promising correspondences which were verified with the iterative closest point algorithm. The object with the least mean square error is selected.

7.3 3D Shape Retrieval Techniques

The aim of this section is to present both mature and promising recent material concerning 3D shape retrieval and recognition. We provide detailed descriptions of four techniques: the depth-buffer descriptor, spin images, salient spectral features for shape matching, and heat kernel signatures.

The aforementioned methods address different aspects of shape matching. Firstly, the depth-buffer descriptor is a technique suitable for global matching. Secondly, the spin image is a pioneering representation and approach in 3D object recognition. Finally, salient spectral features and heat kernel signatures methods are recent proposals to tackle the problems of non-rigid and partial 3D shape matching.

An important issue to be considered before describing the approaches is shape representation. Although there are many ways to represent a 3D object, boundary representations have mostly been used where objects are represented by a limit surface that distinguishes the inside from the outside of the object. Moreover, the surface can be approximated in a piece-wise manner, reducing the amount of information needed to represent it at the expense of losing detail. The most common way is depicting the surface by a set of points (vertices) and polygons (faces) and, in fact, it is preferable to take triangular faces for efficiency and effectiveness in computation. Surprisingly, this representation allows one to conceive almost any object with the desired level of detail.

All the techniques presented in this section use triangular meshes for representing shapes.

7.3.1 Depth-Buffer Descriptor

The *depth-buffer descriptor* [106] is an image-based descriptor. It computes 2D projections of the 3D model, and then computes its feature vector from the obtained projections. This descriptor considers not only the silhouette of each projection of the 3D model, but also considers the depth information (distance from the clipping plane, where the projection starts, to the 3D model).

The process to obtain the feature vector associated to the depth-buffer descriptor is summarized as follows.

1. **Pose normalization:** The depth-buffer descriptor starts with the 3D model oriented and scaled according to a predefined normalized pose.
2. **Depth buffer construction:** The feature extraction method renders six greyscale images using parallel projection (two projections for each principal axis). Each pixel in the 2D projection encodes, to an 8-bit grey value, the orthogonal distance from the viewing plane (i.e. sides of the bounding cube) to the object. These images correspond to the concept of z- or depth-buffers in computer graphics.
3. **Fourier transformation:** After rendering, the method transforms the six images using the standard 2D discrete Fourier transform.
4. **Selection of coefficients:** The magnitudes of certain k low-frequency coefficients of each image contribute to the depth-buffer feature vector of dimensionality $6k$.

7.3.1.1 Computing the 2D Projections

The first step of the depth-buffer descriptor computes 2D projections of the 3D model. To accomplish this, the model must be first normalized in pose (by means of PCA analysis, for example), as this descriptor is not inherently invariant to rotations or scaling. Then, the model must be enclosed in a bounding cube. Each face of this cube is divided into $n \times n$ cells (with initial value 0), which will be used to compute the depth-buffers for each 2D projection. Finally, the 3D model is orthogonally projected to the face of the bounding cube. The value associated to each cell is the normalized orthogonal distance (a value in $[0, 1]$) between the face of the bounding cube and the closest point (orthogonally) in the 3D model.

Formally, let w be the width of the bounding cube. If a point **p** belongs to the surface of the 3D model, its closest orthogonal cell in the face of the bounding cube is **c**, and **p** is the closest point in the mesh to **c**, the associated value of **c** is

$$\text{value}(\mathbf{c}) = \frac{w - \delta(\mathbf{c}, \mathbf{p})}{w},$$

where $\delta(\mathbf{c}, \mathbf{p})$ is the distance from **c** to **p**.

This method works well if the 3D model does not contain a significant number of outliers. Otherwise, the faces of the bounding cube may be too far to the actual surface of the 3D model (it will only be close to the few outliers). This will result in the values of almost all cells in a face of the bounding cube being similar, except for the outliers, thus affecting the computation of the descriptor.

To avoid this problem, Vranic [106] suggests using a canonical cube that does not necessarily enclose the 3D model. The canonical cube is defined by a parameter $t > 0$, such that the vertices of this cube correspond to $(x, y, z) | x, y, z \in \{-t, t\}$. The part of the 3D model that lies outside the canonical cube is not used for computing the descriptor, thus any outlier point will be effectively ignored.

7.3.1.2 Obtaining the Feature Vector

The values associated with the cells on each face of the bounding box could be directly used as the attributes for the feature vector. This feature vector would have a dimensionality of $6n^2$. However, such a descriptor may lead to poor retrieval effectiveness [106]. Instead, the depth-buffer descriptor transforms the values in the spatial domain to the frequency space. Then, it selects some of the obtained coefficients to form the final descriptor.

The depth-buffer descriptor computes the 2D discrete Fourier transform for each of the depth-buffers. Briefly, the 2D discrete Fourier transform of a sequence of two-dimensional complex numbers of equal length (n in our case) is defined as

$$F(u, v) = \frac{1}{n} \sum_{x=0}^{n-1} \sum_{y=0}^{n-1} f(x, y) e^{-2\pi i (xu + yv)/n}$$

where $f(x, y), 0 \le x, y \le n - 1$ is the value of the cell defined by the tuple (x, y). With this definition, it is easy to recover the original values $f(x, y)$:

$$f(x, y) = \frac{1}{n} \sum_{u=0}^{n-1} \sum_{v=0}^{n-1} F(u, v) e^{2\pi i (xu + yv)/n}.$$

The presented formula for $F(u, v)$ takes $O(n^4)$ time ($O(n^2)$ operations must be applied for each cell of the $n \times n$ grid), and it must be computed for each face of the bounding cube, thus it is computationally expensive. However, if n is a power of two, the Fast Fourier Transform (FFT) can be applied to speed the computation of the coefficients, reducing the time complexity to $O(n^2 \log n)$. For this purpose, Vranic [106] recommends setting $n = 256$.

Before computing the Fourier coefficients, the value $f(0, 0)$ is aligned with the cell $(n/2, n/2)$. In this way, the computed low frequency Fourier coefficients correspond to those located in the middle of the resultant image (pixels with values $F(u, v)$). As the inputs of the 2D discrete Fourier transform are real values, the obtained coefficients satisfy a symmetry property:

$$F(u, v) = \overline{F(u, v)}, \qquad (u + u') \bmod n = (v + v') \bmod n = 0,$$

where $\overline{F(u, v)}$ is the complex conjugate of $F(u', v')$.

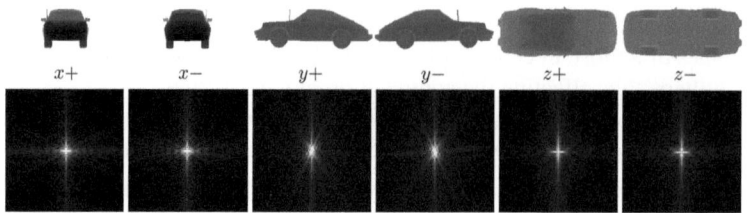

Fig. 7.2 Depth-buffer renderings. The *top row* shows the depth buffers of the 3D model. The *bottom row* shows their coefficient magnitudes of the 2D Fourier transform. Figure courtesy of [27]

After computing the Fourier coefficients, the final depth-buffer descriptor is formed as follows. First, one needs to set a parameter value $k \in \mathbb{N}$. Then, a set of values p and q are computed, such that they hold the inequality

$$|p - n/2| + |q - n/2| \leq k \leq n/2.$$

The absolute values of the coefficients $F(p,q)$ corresponds to the attributes of the final feature vector. It follows that the number of considered coefficients is $k^2 + k + 1$. As we must repeat this process for each face of the bounding cube, the final dimensionality of the descriptor is $6(k^2 + k + 1)$. Vranic [106] recommends setting $k = 8$, thus obtaining a feature vector of 438 dimensions.

Figure 7.2 shows the depth buffer renderings for a 3D model of a car. The first row of images shows the depth buffers of the 3D model. Darker pixels indicate that the distance between the view plane and the object is smaller than at brighter pixels. The second row shows coefficient magnitudes of the 2D Fourier transform of the six images.

7.3.1.3 Evaluation

The effectiveness of the depth-buffer descriptor was compared with several feature-based descriptors for 3D model retrieval [27]. The experimental evaluation showed that descriptors based on 2D projections of the 3D model can be more effective than other global descriptors. In particular, the depth-buffer descriptor got the highest average effectiveness among all descriptors, for queries in a heterogeneous 3D model dataset (Konstanz 3D Model Database). The dataset contained 1838 3D objects collected from the Internet. From the entire collection, 472 objects were used as queries and these contained a manual classification. Table 7.3 shows the results obtained in the experiments. In this case, the R-Precision measure was used in the evaluation.

An advantage of the depth-buffer technique is its low computational cost. In addition, regarding global retrieval, it is the technique with the best effectiveness. However, as can be noted, this method is not suitable to overcome problems such as partial matching and non-rigid retrieval. For more details about the evaluated techniques, we refer the reader to the original paper.

Table 7.3 R-Precision values for evaluated techniques reproduced from Bustos et al. [26]

Method	R-Precision
Depth Buffer	0.3220
Voxel	0.3026
Complex valued shading	0.2974
Rays with spherical harmonics	0.2815
Silhouette	0.2736
3DDFT	0.2622
Shading	0.2386
Ray-based	0.2331
Rotation invariant point cloud	0.2265
Rotation invariant spherical harmonics	0.2219
Shape distribution	0.1930
Ray moments	0.1922
Cords-based	0.1728
3D moments	0.1648
Volume	0.1443
Principal curvature	0.1119

7.3.1.4 Complexity Analysis

Given a 3D object with F triangular faces, and let n be the number of bins for the depth-buffer. In addition, let k be the number of coefficients taken after the FFT. The complexity for each stage of the method is as follows:

- Construction of the depth images: $O(Fn^2)$. In the worst case, each face is projected onto the entire image.
- Fast Fourier Transform: $O(n^2 \log n)$.
- Linear search: $O(P(k^2 + k + 1))$, where P is the number of descriptors stored in the collection. The expression regarding k is because each distance computation is performed between descriptors of dimension $6(k^2 + k + 1)$.

Therefore, the total complexity of this method is dominated by the complexity of the Fourier transform, i.e. $O(n^2 \log n)$

7.3.2 Spin Images for Object Recognition

In this section, we describe a 3D object recognition technique with support for occlusion and cluttered scenes. Originally, this work was proposed by Johnson and Hebert [56, 57] for recognizing objects in complex scenes obtained through a structured light range camera in order to be used in robotic systems. This has been recognized as pioneering work in the use of 3D shape matching for computer vision tasks and its relative success has generated increasing interest in these kinds of techniques to support high level vision tasks. In addition, the central idea behind this technique, the spin image, is one of the pioneering local 3D shape descriptors. Broadly speaking, this technique works as follows:

- Given a set of 3D models (scans), we calculate a spin image for each vertex and store them in a huge collection of spin images.
- Given a scene, possibly cluttered and with occlusions, random vertices are selected for which spin images are computed. Thus, we compare these spin images with those previously stored and select possible correspondences.
- Finally, we need to use geometric consistency and a variation of the iterative closest point algorithm to perform correspondences validation and matching.

In order to calculate the spin images for a 3D shape, a uniform mesh is required. By uniform, we mean that distances between adjacent vertices remain close to the median of all distances. In fact, mesh resolution is defined as the median of all edge lengths from the shape. Johnson [56] proposed an efficient algorithm to control the mesh resolution which is based on mesh simplification schemes [45]. In addition, vertices have to be oriented, so each vertex must have an associated normal pointing towards the outside of the shape. We assume that a shape is uniform and each vertex is properly oriented.

To build a spin image of a vertex, we need to build a local basis defined on this vertex, so accumulating the surrounding vertices around the analyzed vertex using the local basis allows us to create a pose invariant local description. In addition, we can control how local this description is, hence the spin images can be used with large support for alignment and registration tasks and with small support for cluttered recognition.

We denote an oriented point **p** as a pair $\mathbf{O} = (\mathbf{p}, \mathbf{n})$ which maintains coordinate information along with the associated normal vector **n**. The local basis is formed by the following elements:

- The point **p**.
- The normal **n** and the line **L** through **p** parallel to **n**.
- The tangent plane **P** through **p** oriented perpendicularly to **n**.

We can represent any point **q** in this basis, as shown in Fig. 7.3, through two cylindrical coordinates: α, the perpendicular distance from q to the line **L**; and β, the signed perpendicular distance from **q** to the plane **P**. We define the spin-map S_O

Fig. 7.3 Local basis for point **p**

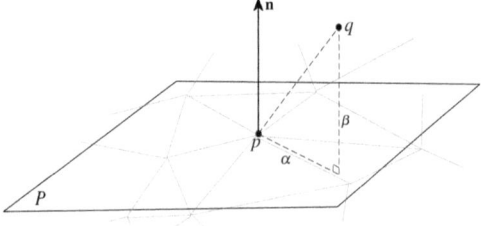

as a function that projects 3D points $\mathbf{q}$ to the local 2D coordinates defined with the previous elements

$$S_O : \mathbb{R}^3 \to \mathbb{R}^2$$
$$S_O(\mathbf{q}) \to (\alpha, \beta) = \left(\sqrt{\|\mathbf{q} - \mathbf{p}\|^2 - (\mathbf{n} \cdot (\mathbf{q} - \mathbf{p}))^2}, \mathbf{n} \cdot (\mathbf{q} - \mathbf{p})\right) \quad (7.2)$$

The process of spin image formation uses the function previously defined accumulating points in the (α, β) image coordinate. This can be seen as spinning a matrix around a point's normal and storing the occurrences of surrounding points in the respective coordinates in the matrix. Finally, the spin image looks like an occurrence histogram in the cylindrical coordinate system defined by the local basis.

In order to create a spin image, three useful parameters have to be defined

- Bin size (*bin*), spatial extent for the bins in the image.
- Image width (W), number of bins in both image directions. Usually, spin images are square.
- Support angle (A_s), the maximum angle between normals for contributing points.

Let $\mathbf{A} = (\mathbf{p}_A, \mathbf{n}_A)$ be an oriented point for which we want to build its spin image. For each oriented point $\mathbf{B} = (\mathbf{p}_B, \mathbf{n}_B)$ on the shape, we use the local basis and the spin-map function to obtain the coordinate (α, β). Then, the bin corresponding to that coordinate is given by

$$i = \left\lfloor \frac{\frac{W * bin}{2} - \beta}{bin} \right\rfloor$$
$$j = \left\lfloor \frac{\alpha}{bin} \right\rfloor \quad (7.3)$$

Instead of directly accumulating the occurrence in the respective bin, the authors suggested the use of bilinear interpolation to accumulate the occurrence in neighboring positions. Therefore, bilinear weights are calculated as follows

$$a = \frac{\alpha}{bin} - j$$
$$b = \frac{\frac{W * bin}{2} - \beta}{bin} - i \quad (7.4)$$

With these weights, the image is updated as follows

$$I(i, j) = I(i, j) + (1 - a)(1 - b)$$
$$I(i, j + 1) = I(i, j + 1) + (1 - a)b$$
$$I(i + 1, j) = I(i + 1, j) + a(1 - b) \quad (7.5)$$
$$I(i + 1, j + 1) = I(i + 1, j + 1) + ab$$

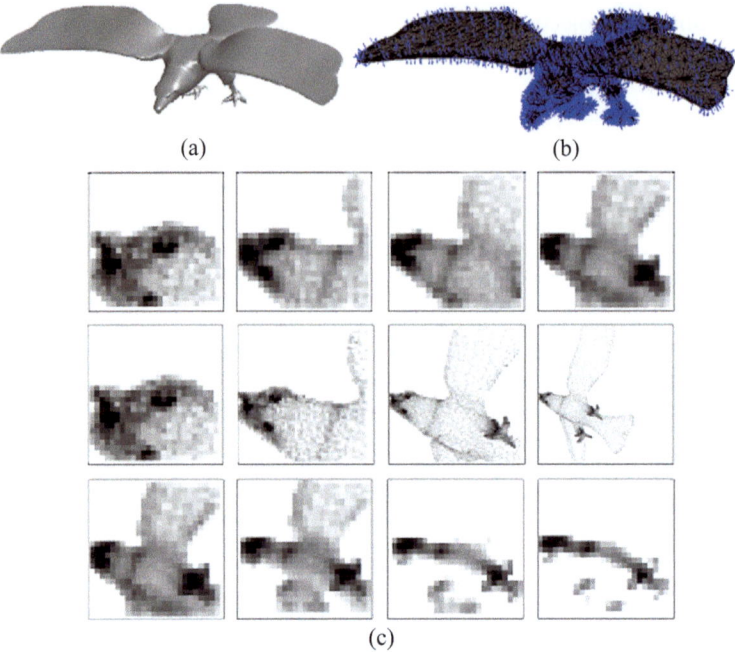

Fig. 7.4 Spin image generation process. (**a**) Input mesh, (**b**) mesh with normals, (**c**) Spin images. At *top*, the parameters were $W = 25$, $A_s = \pi$, and $bin = \{1, 2, 3, 4\}$ times the mesh resolution. At *middle*, the parameters were $W = \{25, 50, 100, 200\}$, $A_s = \pi$, and $bin = 1$ times the mesh resolution. At *bottom*, the parameters were $W = 25$, $bin = 4$ times the mesh resolution, and $A_s = \{\pi, \pi/2, \pi/3, \pi/4\}$ The resolution of the spin images is dependent on W

In addition, there is a constraint that the contributing points must hold with respect to the angle between normals. Only points which hold this condition are used in the spin image generation process.

$$a\cos(\mathbf{n}_A, \mathbf{n}_B) < A_s \qquad (7.6)$$

where A_s is the support angle. When A_s is small, a better support to occlusion is provided, as points on the mesh with considerably different direction can be due to occlusion.

In practice, the bin size must be configured to the mesh resolution in order to preserve a good relation between sampling and descriptiveness. Also, in the original experiments carried out by Johnson [56], the spin image width was 15 and the support angle depends of how much we want to support occlusion, however a common value used in practice is 60 degrees. Figure 7.4 shows spin images generated with different values for each parameter.

Once a spin image is calculated for each vertex within a model, these will be stored for the matching process. Nevertheless, we need to compare spin images in order to determine possible correspondences. Given two spin images P and Q with

N bins each, the cross-correlation can be used to measure their similarity

$$R(P, Q) = \frac{N \sum p_i q_i - \sum p_i \sum q_i}{\sqrt{(N \sum p_i^2 - (\sum p_i)^2)(N \sum q_i^2 - (\sum q_i)^2)}} \quad (7.7)$$

It is easy to note that R is in the range $[-1, 1]$ with high values when the spin images are similar and low values when they are not similar. However, there is a problem when we compare two spin images with this measure. Due to occlusions and cluttered scenes, many times a spin image contains more information than others so, to limit this effect, it is necessary to take only those 'pixels' where data exists. Since the cross-correlation depends of the number of pixels to compute it, the amount of overlap will have an effect on the comparison. Obviously, the confidence in the comparison is better when more pixels are used. In addition, the confidence in the match can be measured by the variance associated with the cross-correlation, so by combining both the cross-correlation R and its variance, we get a new similarity measure C, defined as:

$$C(P, Q) = \left(\operatorname{atanh}(R(P, Q))\right)^2 - \lambda \left(\frac{1}{N-3}\right) \quad (7.8)$$

where N is the number of overlapping pixels (pixels different from zero), λ is a constant and R is calculated using the N overlapping pixels. Note that the hyperbolic arctangent function transforms the correlation coefficient, R, into a distribution that has better statistical properties and the variance of this distribution is $\frac{1}{N-3}$. The measure, C, has a high value when the spin images are highly correlated and a large number of pixels overlap. In experiments, λ was configured to 3.

7.3.2.1 Matching

Given a scene, a random set of points is selected for matching. For each point, a set of correspondences is established using spin images from the scene and those calculated from models. Given a point from the scene, we calculate its spin image as previously described, thus this is compared with all the spin images in the huge collection using Eq. (7.8). From the comparison with the stored spin images, a histogram is built quantizing the similarity measure. This histogram maintains the information about occurrences of similarity measures when a comparison is being performed and it can be seen as a distribution of similarities between the input spin image and the stored ones. As we are interested in high similarity values, these can be found as outliers in the histogram.

In practice, outliers are found by automatically evaluating the histogram. A standard way to localize outliers is to determine the fourth spread of the histogram defined as the difference between the median of the largest $N/2$ measurements and the median of the smallest $N/2$ measurements. Let f_s be the fourth spread, extreme outliers are $3f_s$ units above the median of the largest $N/2$ measurements. Note that with this method, the number of outliers can be greater than or equal to zero, so many correspondences per point can be found.

Once we have the set of correspondences for each point in the scene, we need to organize them in order to recognize the correct model object in the scene. As a large number of correspondences have been detected, it is necessary to filter them. Firstly, correspondences with a similarity measure of less than half of the maximum similarity are discarded. Secondly, by using geometric consistency, it is possible to eliminate bad correspondences. Given two correspondences $\mathbf{C}_1 = (\mathbf{s}_1, \mathbf{m}_1)$ and $\mathbf{C}_2 = (\mathbf{s}_2, \mathbf{m}_2)$, the geometric consistency is defined as follows

$$d_{gc}(\mathbf{C}_1, \mathbf{C}_2) = 2 \frac{\|S_{\mathbf{m}_2}(\mathbf{m}_1) - S_{\mathbf{s}_2}(\mathbf{s}_1)\|}{\|S_{\mathbf{m}_2}(\mathbf{m}_1) + S_{\mathbf{s}_2}(\mathbf{s}_1)\|}$$
$$D_{gc}(\mathbf{C}_1, \mathbf{C}_2) = \max\bigl(d_{gc}(\mathbf{C}_1, \mathbf{C}_2), d_{gc}(\mathbf{C}_2, \mathbf{C}_1)\bigr) \qquad (7.9)$$

where $S_O(\mathbf{p})$ denotes the spin map function of point $\mathbf{p}$ using the local basis of point $\mathbf{O}$, as defined in Eq. (7.2).

This geometric consistency measures the consistency in position and normals. D_{gc} is small when C_1 and C_2 are geometrically consistent. By using geometric consistency, correspondences which are not geometrically consistent with at least a quarter of the complete list of correspondences are eliminated. The final set of correspondences has a high probability of being correct, but it is still necessary to group and verify them.

Now, we group correspondences in order to calculate a good transformation and hence do the matching. A grouping measure is used which prioritizes correspondences that are far apart. The grouping measure is defined as

$$w_{gc}(\mathbf{C}_1, \mathbf{C}_2) = \frac{d_{gc}(\mathbf{C}_1, \mathbf{C}_2)}{1 - \exp(-(\|S_{\mathbf{m}_2}(\mathbf{m}_1)\| + \|S_{\mathbf{s}_2}(\mathbf{s}_1)\|)/2)}$$
$$W_{gc}(\mathbf{C}_1, \mathbf{C}_2) = \max\bigl(w_{gc}(\mathbf{C}_1, \mathbf{C}_2), w_{gc}(\mathbf{C}_2, \mathbf{C}_1)\bigr) \qquad (7.10)$$

The same measure can also be defined between a correspondence C and a group of correspondences $\{\mathbf{C}_1, \mathbf{C}_2, \ldots, \mathbf{C}_n\}$ as follows

$$W_{gc}\bigl(\mathbf{C}, \{\mathbf{C}_1, \mathbf{C}_2, \ldots, \mathbf{C}_n\}\bigr) = \max_i \bigl(W_{gc}(\mathbf{C}, \mathbf{C}_i)\bigr) \qquad (7.11)$$

Therefore, given a set of possible correspondences $\mathbb{L} = \{\mathbf{C}_1, \mathbf{C}_2, \ldots, \mathbf{C}_n\}$, the following algorithm has to be used for generating groups:

- For each correspondence $\mathbf{C}_i \in \mathbb{L}$, initialize a group $\mathbb{G}_i = \{\mathbf{C}_i\}$
  - Find a correspondence $\mathbf{C}_j \in \mathbb{L} - \mathbb{G}_i$, such that $W_{gc}(\mathbf{C}_j, \mathbb{G}_i)$ is minimum. If $W_{gc}(\mathbf{C}_j, \mathbb{G}_i) < T_{gc}$ then update $\mathbb{G}_i = \mathbb{G}_i \cup \{\mathbf{C}_j\}$. T_{gc} is set between zero and one. If T_{gc} is small, only geometrically consistent correspondences remains. A commonly used value is 0.25.
  - Continue until no more correspondences can be added.

As a result, we have n groups, which are used as starting point for final matching. For each group of correspondences $\{(\mathbf{m}_i, \mathbf{s}_i)\}$, a rigid transformation T is calculated by minimizing the following error using the least squares method:

$$E_T = \min_T \sum \|\mathbf{s}_i - T(\mathbf{m}_i)\|^2 \quad (7.12)$$

where $T(\mathbf{m}_i) = \mathsf{R}(\mathbf{m}_i) + \mathbf{t}$, R and $\mathbf{t}$ are the rotation matrix and the translation vector, representing the rotation and position of the viewpoint $\mathbf{s}_i$ in the coordinate system of $\mathbf{m}_i$.

As a last step, each transformation needs to be verified in order to be validated as a matching. The model points in the correspondences are transformed using T. For each point in the scene and the correspondences set, we extend correspondences for neighboring points in both points of a correspondence under a distance constraint. A threshold distance equal to twice the mesh resolution is used. If the final set of correspondences is greater than a quarter or a third of the number of vertices of the model, the transformation is considered valid and the matching is accepted. Finally, with the final correspondences set, the transformation is refined by using an iterative closest point algorithm.

7.3.2.2 Evaluation

Unfortunately, in the original work by Johnson [56], the models used in experiments were obtained using a scanner and they are not available to date. Johnson and Hebert [57] presented results trying to measure the robustness of their method against clutter and occlusion. They built 100 scenes involving four shapes, using a range scanner. The experiments were based on querying an object in a scene and determining if the object was present or not. In addition, the levels of occlusion and clutter were also determined.

The four shapes were used in each scene, so the number of runs was 400. Interestingly, there were no errors at levels of occlusion under 70 % and the rate of recognition was above 90 % at 80 % of occlusion. In addition, the recognition rate was greater than 80 % at levels of clutter under 60 %.

On the other hand, spin images have recently been evaluated in the Robust Feature Detection and Description Benchmark [21] (SHREC 2010 track). In this track, the goal was to evaluate the robustness of the descriptors against mesh transformations such as isometry, topology, holes, micro holes, scale, local scale, sampling, noise, and shot noise. The dataset consisted of three shapes taken from the TOSCA dataset. Subsequently, several transformations, at different levels, were applied to each shape. The resulting dataset contained 138 shapes. In addition, a set of correspondences was available in order to measure the distance between descriptors over corresponding points.

Table 7.4 Robustness results for Spin Images. Table reproduced from Bronstein et al. [21]

Transform.	Strength				
	1	≤2	≤3	≤4	≤5
Isometry	0.12	0.10	0.10	0.10	0.10
Topology	0.11	0.11	0.11	0.11	0.11
Holes	0.12	0.12	0.12	0.12	0.12
Micro holes	0.15	0.15	0.16	0.16	0.16
Scale	0.18	0.15	0.15	0.15	0.15
Local scale	0.12	0.13	0.14	0.15	0.17
Sampling	0.13	0.13	0.13	0.13	0.15
Noise	0.13	0.15	0.17	0.19	0.20
Shot noise	0.11	0.13	0.16	0.17	0.18
Average	0.13	0.13	0.14	0.14	0.15

The evaluation was performed using the normalized Euclidean distance, $Q(X, Y)$, between the descriptors of corresponding points of two shapes X and Y,

$$Q(X, Y) = \frac{1}{|F(X)|} \sum_{k=1}^{|F(X)|} \frac{\|f(y_k) - g(x_j)\|_2}{\|f(y_k)\|_2 + \|g(x_j)\|_2}, \quad (7.13)$$

where (x_j, y_k) are corresponding points, $f(\cdot)$ and $g(\cdot)$ are the descriptors of a point, and $F(X)$ is the set of vertices to be considered. Here, we present the results obtained using $F(X) = X$.

The best results were obtained for isometry and topology transformations with 0.10 and 0.11 average distance respectively. This is because spin images were extracted locally, and these transformations do not modify the local structure of the mesh. On the other hand, the noise and shot noise transformations got higher distances (up to 0.20 and 0.18, respectively). It is clear that stronger levels of noise modify considerably the distribution of points on the surface, so spin images are not constructed robustly. See Tables 7.4 and 7.5 for the complete results. Table 7.5 shows the performance for dense heat kernel signatures calculated on 3D meshes. Clearly, regarding robustness, spin images show some drawbacks. However, an important aspect of this approach is its support to occlusion. In that sense, its application in recognition has been proved.

7.3.2.3 Complexity Analysis

Let S be a 3D object with n vertices. In addition, let W be the number of rows and columns of a resulting spin image (we assume square spin images for the analysis). The complexity of each stage is given as follows:

7 3D Shape Matching for Retrieval and Recognition

Table 7.5 Robustness results for Dense Heat Kernel Signatures. Table reproduced from Bronstein et al. [21]

Transform.	Strength				
	1	≤2	≤3	≤4	≤5
Isometry	0.01	0.01	0.01	0.01	0.01
Topology	0.02	0.02	0.02	0.02	0.02
Holes	0.02	0.02	0.02	0.03	0.03
Micro holes	0.01	0.01	0.01	0.01	0.02
Scale	0.25	0.15	0.13	0.14	0.16
Local scale	0.02	0.03	0.05	0.07	0.10
Sampling	0.02	0.02	0.02	0.02	0.02
Noise	0.03	0.06	0.09	0.12	0.15
Shot noise	0.01	0.01	0.02	0.02	0.02
Average	0.04	0.04	0.04	0.05	0.06

- Computation of spin images for each vertex: $O(n^2)$. Given a vertex, each vertex on the mesh is mapped onto its spin image.
- Find the initial set of correspondences: $O(nPW^2)$, where P is the number of spin images in the collection. For each vertex on the query object, the cross-correlation is calculated with respect to each spin image in the collection.
- Filter the correspondences: $O(n^2)$.
- Group the correspondences: $O(n^2)$. For each correspondence, a group is computed by applying the W_{gc} measure.
- Find the transformation using the least squares method: $O(n)$.
- Validation: $O(n)$.

The total complexity is dominated by the process of finding the initial set of correspondences. This is because $P \gg n$, so the complexity of this method is $O(nPW^2)$.

7.3.3 Salient Spectral Geometric Features

In this section, we present a retrieval method based on local features extracted from the Laplace-Beltrami operator of a shape [52]. Some theoretical background is needed in order to understand the Laplace operator on manifolds and its computation. Detailed information can be found in the works by Reuter et al. [90] and Meyer et al. [77]. In addition, further relevant references can be found in Sect. 7.6.

Let $f \in \mathbb{C}^2$ be a real-valued function defined on a Riemannian manifold $\mathbb{M}$. The Laplace-Beltrami operator is defined as

$$\Delta f = \text{div}(\text{grad } f) \qquad (7.14)$$

with grad f the gradient of f and div the divergence on the manifold.

If $\mathbb{M}$ is a domain in the Euclidean plane, the Laplace-Beltrami operator reduces to the well-known expression

$$\Delta f = \frac{\partial^2 f}{(\partial x)^2} + \frac{\partial^2 f}{(\partial y)^2} \tag{7.15}$$

Thus, we are interested in the Helmholtz equation

$$\Delta f = -\lambda f \tag{7.16}$$

where λ is a real scalar. This equation is important because the family of eigenvalues $0 \leq \lambda_0 \leq \lambda_1 \leq \cdots \leq +\infty$ is the shape spectrum which is isometric invariant[1] as it only depends on the gradient and the divergence, dependent only on the Riemannian structure of the manifold. Another important property is that the Laplace-Beltrami operator is Hermitian, so the eigenvectors $\mathbf{v}_i$ and $\mathbf{v}_j$ corresponding to different eigenvalues λ_i and λ_j are orthogonal:

$$\mathbf{v}_i \cdot \mathbf{v}_j = \int_{\mathbb{M}} \mathbf{v}_i \mathbf{v}_j = 0, \quad i \neq j \tag{7.17}$$

In addition, the i-th eigenvector defines a coefficient over the function f as follows

$$c_i = f \cdot \mathbf{v}_i = \int_{\mathbb{M}} f \mathbf{v}_i \tag{7.18}$$

so the function f can be expanded as

$$f = c_1 \mathbf{v}_1 + c_2 \mathbf{v}_2 + \cdots \tag{7.19}$$

Given a 3D mesh, we can calculate the discrete Laplace-Beltrami operator at each vertex with the cotangent scheme proposed by Meyer et al. [77]:

$$K(\mathbf{p}_i) = \frac{1}{2A_i} \sum_{\mathbf{p}_j \in \mathbb{N}_1(\mathbf{p}_i)} (\cot \alpha_{ij} + \cot \beta_{ij})(\mathbf{p}_i - \mathbf{p}_j) \tag{7.20}$$

where A_i is the Voronoi region area around $\mathbf{p}_i$, α_{ij} and β_{ij} are the angles opposite to the arc $\overline{\mathbf{p}_i \mathbf{p}_j}$ and $\mathbb{N}_1(\mathbf{p}_i)$ is the set of $\mathbf{p}_i$'s adjacent vertices. See Fig. 7.5 for details.

The computation of A_i, the Voronoi region around a vertex $\mathbf{p}_i$, must be performed as follows. We accumulate a region for each adjacent face $\mathbf{T}$ to $\mathbf{p}_i$, if $\mathbf{T}$ is non-obtuse we add the Voronoi region for that face by using Eq. (7.21). If $\mathbf{T}$ is obtuse, we add area($\mathbf{T}$)/2 if the angle of $\mathbf{T}$ at $\mathbf{p}_i$ is obtuse, or area($\mathbf{T}$)/4 otherwise.

$$A_\mathbf{T} = \frac{1}{8} \sum_{j \in \mathbb{N}_1(i)} (\cot \alpha_{ij} + \cot \beta_{ij}) \|\mathbf{p}_i - \mathbf{p}_j\|^2 \tag{7.21}$$

---

[1] The shape spectrum of two shapes with a non-rigid transformation is approximately the same.

Fig. 7.5 Neighborhood configuration around $\mathbf{p}_i$. The *dashed lines* enclose the Voronoi region used in computing the Laplace-Beltrami operator

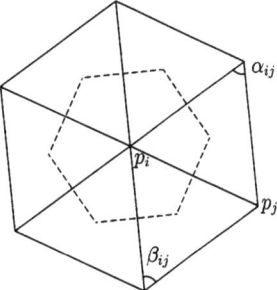

To numerically compute the Laplace-Beltrami operator, a matrix $\mathsf{L} = \{L_{ij}\}$ can be calculated in the following way:

$$L_{ij} = \begin{cases} -\frac{\cot\alpha_{ij}+\cot\beta_{ij}}{2A_i} & \text{if } \mathbf{p}_i \text{ is adjacent to } \mathbf{p}_j \\ \sum_k \frac{\cot\alpha_{ik}+\cot\beta_{kj}}{2A_i} & \text{if } \mathbf{p}_i = \mathbf{p}_j \\ 0 & \text{otherwise,} \end{cases} \quad (7.22)$$

where $\mathbf{p}_k$ are the vertices adjacent to $\mathbf{p}_i$.

We are interested in the eigenvalues and eigenvectors of this matrix. Thus, the problem to be solved is:

$$\mathsf{L}\mathbf{v} = \lambda\mathbf{v} \quad (7.23)$$

However, it is clear to note that L might not be symmetric. This is to say, $L_{ij} \neq L_{ji}$ when $A_i \neq A_j$, which is very likely. Nevertheless, it can be represented as a generalized eigenvalue problem where $\mathsf{L} = \mathsf{S}^{-1}\mathsf{M}$. Then, we have:

$$\mathsf{M}\mathbf{v} = \lambda\mathsf{S}\mathbf{v} \quad (7.24)$$

where $\mathsf{M} = \{M_{ij}\}$ with

$$M_{ij} = \begin{cases} -\frac{\cot\alpha_{ij}+\cot\beta_{ij}}{2} & \text{if } \mathbf{p}_i \text{ is adjacent to } \mathbf{p}_j \\ \sum_k \frac{\cot\alpha_{ik}+\cot\beta_{kj}}{2} & \text{if } \mathbf{p}_i = \mathbf{p}_j \\ 0 & \text{otherwise} \end{cases} \quad (7.25)$$

and $\mathsf{S} = \{S_{ij}\}$ with

$$S_{ij} = \begin{cases} A_i & \text{if } i = j \\ 0 & \text{otherwise} \end{cases} \quad (7.26)$$

The solution to this problem ensures that the eigenvalues and eigenvectors are real. In addition, two eigenvectors $\mathbf{v}_i$ and $\mathbf{v}_j$ corresponding to different eigenvalues λ_i and λ_j are orthogonal with respect to the S dot-product:

$$\mathbf{v}_i \cdot \mathbf{v}_j = \mathbf{v}_i^T \mathsf{S} \mathbf{v}_j = 0, \quad i \neq j \quad (7.27)$$

The shape spectrum is the set of eigenvalues $\{\lambda_0, \lambda_1, \lambda_2, \ldots, \lambda_{n-1}\}$. If the shape is closed, $\lambda_0 = 0$.

7.3.3.1 Feature Points Detection

Recalling the problem of geometric reconstruction, we have the vertices set $\mathsf{P} = [X\ Y\ Z]$ where X, Y and Z are column vectors containing the values of their coordinates. In addition, we define a coefficient matrix $\mathsf{C} = \mathsf{P}^T \mathsf{S} \mathsf{V}$ where S is the diagonal matrix as stated before and V is a $N \times N$ matrix with each column being an eigenvector. The eigenvectors are ordered according to their associated eigenvalues, from low to high. Thus, we can obtain the vertices set with:

$$\mathsf{P} = \mathsf{V}\mathsf{C}^T \tag{7.28}$$

We introduce the matrix notation $\mathsf{A}_{1-p, 1-q}$ as the submatrix with rows from 1 to p and columns from 1 to q. Using this notation, we can express the reconstruction problem using the first k eigenvectors:

$$\mathsf{P}(k) = \mathsf{V}_{1-n, 1-k} \mathsf{C}^T_{1-3, 1-k} \tag{7.29}$$

As can be noted, $\mathsf{P}(k)$ has the same size as P, but the vertex position is dependent on k. We can use $\mathsf{P}(k)$ with the original connections for evaluating the information gained with different k values (see Fig. 7.6). The authors defined a geometric energy at a vertex i corresponding to the kth eigenvector as:

$$E(i,k) = \left\| \mathsf{V}(i,k) \times \mathsf{C}_{1-3,k} \right\|_2 \tag{7.30}$$

The authors evaluated E in order to detect interest points. A vertex $\mathbf{p}_i$ is selected if $E(i,k) > E(j,h)$ for all vertex $\mathbf{p}_j$ adjacent to $\mathbf{p}_i$ in the original mesh and for all $h \in [k-1, k, k+1]$. Furthermore, each selected vertex has an associated scale factor $sf = 1/\sqrt{\lambda_k}$. An important fact to be considered here is that the same vertex can be selected with different associated scale factors. The authors proposed to evaluate only the first 100 eigenvectors because they claimed that more eigenvectors do not contribute significant spatial and spectral energy. The first eigenvectors are associated to the coarse structure of the mesh and later eigenvectors are associated with the detailed geometry. Thus the last eigenvectors could be associated with noise. In this respect, the number of vertices could give us an insight concerning how many eigenvectors might be used, because the maximum number of eigenvectors equals the number of vertices.

Fig. 7.6 Effect of reconstructing P(k) using $k = 5, 20, 50, 100, 300,$ and 1000, respectively over a shape with 8000+ vertices

As the eigenvalues are increasing and the first eigenvectors are related to large scales, taking the scale as previously defined seems to be a good approximation, although the relation between the eigenvalues and the real spatial scale of the interest points is not clear.

7.3.3.2 Local Descriptors

To create local descriptors associated with each interest point, the Laplace-Beltrami operator can be used in a straightforward way. The process starts by selecting a patch based on the scale information of each vertex. Given an interest point, $\mathbf{p}_i$, we select a mesh patch formed by the vertices with geodesic distance from $\mathbf{p}_i$ not exceeding the radius $r \times \text{sf}(\mathbf{p}_i)$ (in the experiments, r was 1.7). The extracted patch is an open boundary surface, so that we need to attach another patch in order to apply the Laplace-Beltrami operator with successful results. The authors proposed to attach the same patch but in the opposite direction. Once we have a closed local surface, we apply the aforementioned method in order to obtain the spectrum.

The local descriptor is defined as the set $\{\lambda_1, \lambda_2, \ldots, \lambda_m\}$ for some value m. For similarity comparison, the spectrum must be normalized in order to allow scale invariance. This can be done by dividing each element in the local descriptor with the first eigenvalue λ_1.

7.3.3.3 Shape Matching

From the preceding stages, each mesh is represented as a set of descriptors, so now we are interested in comparing two objects based on this information. Given two descriptor sets $\mathbb{P} = \{\mathbf{p}_i\}$ and $\mathbb{P}' = \{\mathbf{p}'_i\}$, the problem is to find a transformation function ϕ such that:

$$\phi(\mathbf{p}_i) = \mathbf{p}'_i \tag{7.31}$$

Thus, the similarity function is defined as:

$$\text{Sim}(\phi) = \text{Sim}_s(\phi) + \text{Sim}_p(\phi) \tag{7.32}$$

$\text{Sim}_s(\phi)$ refers to the feature-to-feature comparison and $\text{Sim}_p(\phi)$ to the cluster-to-cluster similarity. The feature-to-feature similarity is defined as follows:

$$\text{Sim}_s(\phi) = \omega_s \sum_{\phi(i)=i'} C(i, i') \tag{7.33}$$

where

$$C(i, i') = \exp\left(\frac{-\|f(i) - f(i')\|^2}{2\sigma_s^2}\right) \tag{7.34}$$

where $f(.)$ is the local descriptor of a point and σ_s is a constant.

In addition, the cluster-to-cluster similarity is defined as:

$$\text{Sim}_p(\phi) = \omega_p \sum_{\phi(i)=i',\phi(j)=j'} H(i,j,i',j') \tag{7.35}$$

where

$$H(i,j,i',j') = \exp\left(\frac{-(d_{pg}(i,j,i',j') + \beta d_{ps}(i,j,i',j'))^2}{2\sigma_p^2}\right) \tag{7.36}$$

where

$$d_{pg}(i,j,i',j') = \left|\frac{g(i,j)}{\text{sf}(i)} - \frac{g(i',j')}{\text{sf}(i')}\right| \tag{7.37}$$

and

$$d_{ps}(i,j,i',j') = \left|\log\left(\frac{\text{sf}(j)}{\text{sf}(i)}\right) - \log\left(\frac{\text{sf}(j')}{\text{sf}(i')}\right)\right| \tag{7.38}$$

where $g(\cdot,\cdot)$ is the geodesic distance between two vertices, $\text{sf}(\cdot)$ is the vertex scale factor calculated in the feature detection stage and σ_p is a constant.

In order to solve the matching problem using the defined similarity measure, we need to define an indicator variable

$$x(i,i') = \begin{cases} 1 & \text{if } \phi(i)=i' \text{ exists} \\ 0 & \text{otherwise} \end{cases} \tag{7.39}$$

We can reformulate the similarity measure using the indicator variable as

$$\text{Sim}(x) = \omega_p \sum_{i,i'} C(i,i')x(i,i') + \omega_s \sum_{i,j,i',j'} H(i,j,i',j')x(i,i')x(j,j') \tag{7.40}$$

subject to $\sum_i x(i,i') \leq 1$ and $\sum_{i'} x(i,i') \leq 1$. These expressions impose the constraint that each point in the first descriptor set has at most one correspondence in the second descriptor set. To numerically solve this problem, we can use Integer Quadratic Programming (IQP) as follows

$$\max_{\mathbf{x}} \; \text{Sim}(\mathbf{x}) = \mathbf{x}^T \mathbf{H} \mathbf{x} + \mathbf{C}^T \mathbf{x} \quad \text{subject to} \quad \mathbf{A}\mathbf{x} \leq \mathbf{b} \tag{7.41}$$

We now describe some details for implementation. Let N be the number of descriptors in $\mathbf{P}$ and M be the number of descriptors in $\mathbf{P}'$. After calculating the matrix C, we have to convert it in a column vector concatenating each column in the matrix so that the dimension of C is $NM \times 1$. Note that the size of H is $NM \times NM$ because we need to calculate $H(i,j,i',j')$ between each pair of descriptor from $\mathbf{P}$ with each pair from $\mathbf{P}'$. With respect to the constraints on the number of correspondences, these have to be located in the matrix A and a vector $\mathbf{b}$. The geodesic distances can be approximated using a shortest path algorithm on the mesh, however another clever algorithm can also be used such as the fast marching method proposed by Kimmel and Sethian [62]. In order to solve the aforementioned optimization problem, there are several alternatives such as the MATLAB's optimization toolbox or the CGAL library [2].

In summary, the method can be described as follows.

1. **Solving the Laplace-Beltrami eigenproblem:** We need to compute the eigenvectors and eigenvalues of the Laplace-Beltrami operator for each shape in the dataset.
2. **Feature points detection:** Computing the geometric energy given in Eq. (7.30), it is possible to select the interest points along with their scales.
3. **Construction of local descriptors:** For each interest point, the method extracts a local patch over which the Laplace-Beltrami operator is calculated. A few normalized eigenvalues of this operator are considered as a local descriptor.
4. **Matching:** The problem of multi-feature matching is considered as an integer quadratic programming problem, as given in Eq. (7.41).

7.3.3.4 Evaluation

In the original work by Hu and Hua [52], several tests were accomplished for shape correspondence and shape retrieval over the SHREC'07 3D shape database available at http://www.aimatshape.net/event/SHREC. The authors proposed to extract 10 shapes from each category of the dataset. Figure 7.7 shows the precision-recall plot for the presented approach compared to the best technique in the SHREC'07 watertight retrieval contest. In addition, Fig. 7.8 present an example of matching between shapes in the same category and between shapes in different categories.

From the results, it is important to note that the method performs well on non-rigid transformations. In fact, it outperforms the best technique in the SHREC'2007

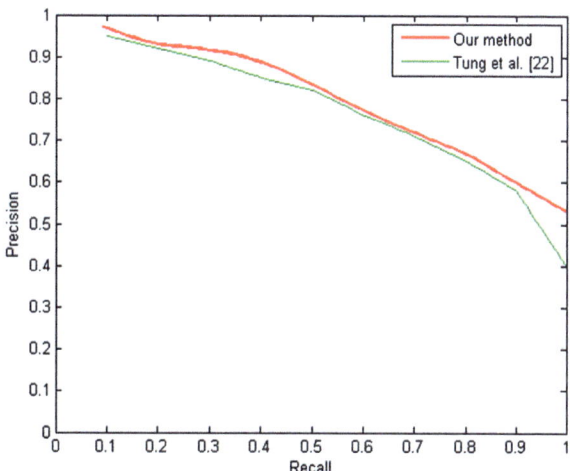

Fig. 7.7 Precision-recall plot for the salient spectral features approach. Figure courtesy of [52]

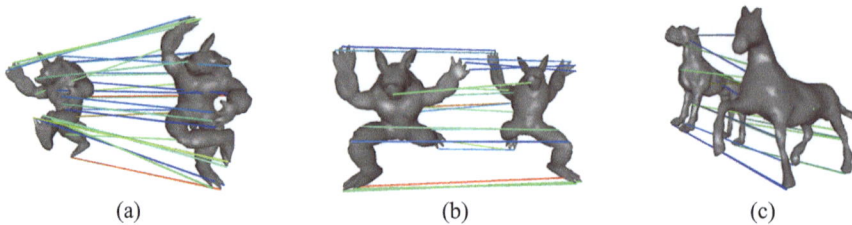

Fig. 7.8 (**a, b**) Matching with shapes from the same category. (**c**) Matching between shapes from different categories. Figure courtesy of [52]

dataset. Also, an important aspect of this technique is that it delivers a set of correspondences between salient points, in addition to the matching score. It is valuable because two problems (matching and correspondences) can be addressed with the same approach.

7.3.3.5 Complexity Analysis

Let $\mathbb{S}$ be a 3D object with n vertices. In the following, we list the computational complexity associated with the various stages of the presented approach.

- Compute the Laplacian matrix: $O(n^2)$.
- Compute eigenvalues and eigenvectors of the Laplacian matrix: $O(n^3)$.
- Interest point detection: $O(nk)$, if k eigenvectors are chosen.
- Interest point description: $O(mq^3)$, where m is the number of detected interest points and q is the number of vertices in the patch associated to each interest point.
- Matching: Let suppose two objects $\mathbb{P}$ and $\mathbb{Q}$ with N and M interest points, respectively. The computational complexities of each step of the matching are:
  - Computation of matrix C: $O(NM)$.
  - Computation of matrix H: $O(N^3 M^2 \log N)$. The matrix H corresponds with all the possible combinations of correspondence pairs. For each pair, the computation of the geodesic distance takes $O(N \log N)$.
  - Solve the IQP problem: $O(N^2 M^2)$.

The total complexity of this method is dominated by the calculation of the matrix H, due to the computation of the geodesic distances between interest points. Therefore, the complexity of this method is $O(N^3 M^2 \log N)$.

7.3.4 Heat Kernel Signatures

We observed in the previous approach the importance and applicability of the Laplace-Beltrami operator and its spectrum in shape description tasks. In this section, we describe the application of heat kernel signatures which are based on the

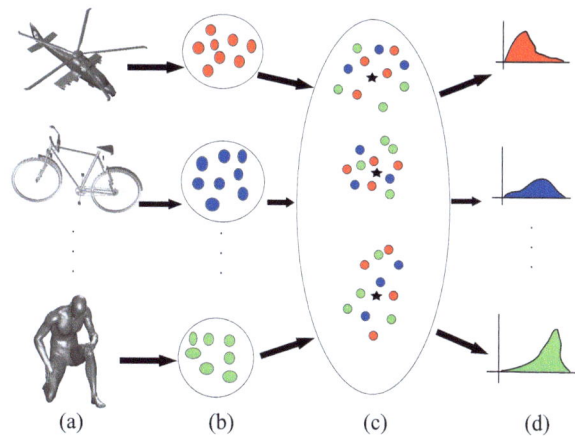

Fig. 7.9 Process to obtain a descriptor for a shape using the heat kernel signatures and bag of features. (**a**) Input shape, (**b**) local descriptors (heat kernel signatures) are extracted, (**c**) clustering of descriptor space (*black stars* are centroids of resulting clusters), and (**d**) Vector quantization, using local descriptors and clusters, results in shape descriptors

intimate relation between the heat diffusion process and the Laplace-Beltrami operator. In addition, the presented technique utilizes a widely-used approach for describing information entities based on their components and frequencies known as Bag-of-Features [83]. Figure 7.9 summarizes the approach.

The heat diffusion process over a compact manifold $\mathbb{S}$, possibly with boundary, is governed by the heat equation

$$\Delta_{\mathbb{S}} u(\mathbf{x}, t) = -\frac{\partial u(\mathbf{x}, t)}{\partial t} \tag{7.42}$$

where $\Delta_{\mathbb{S}}$ is the Laplace-Beltrami operator of $\mathbb{S}$ and $u(., t)$ is the heat distribution over $\mathbb{S}$ over time t.

The fundamental solution of Eq. (7.42) is $K_t(\mathbf{x}, \mathbf{y})$ called the heat kernel. This represents a solution with a point heat source at $\mathbf{x}$ and can be considered as the amount of heat transferred from $\mathbf{x}$ to $\mathbf{y}$ after time t. For compact manifolds, the heat kernel can be expressed using the eigenvalues and eigenvectors of the Laplace-Beltrami operator as follows:

$$K_t(\mathbf{x}, \mathbf{y}) = \sum_{i=0}^{\infty} \exp(-\lambda_i t) \mathbf{v}_i(\mathbf{x}) \mathbf{v}_i(\mathbf{y}) \tag{7.43}$$

where λ_i is the i-th eigenvalue and $\mathbf{v}_i(\cdot)$ is the i-th eigenvector's entry corresponding to a given point.

Sun et al. [97] formally proved that the heat kernel is an isometric invariant, informative (redundant information exists), multi-scale, and stable against perturbations of the surface. In addition, restricting the heat kernel to the temporal domain and fixing the spatial variables, we can obtain a representation for each point on the manifold:

$$K_t(\mathbf{x}, \mathbf{x}) = \sum_{i=0}^{\infty} \exp(-\lambda_i t) \mathbf{v}_i(\mathbf{x})^2 \tag{7.44}$$

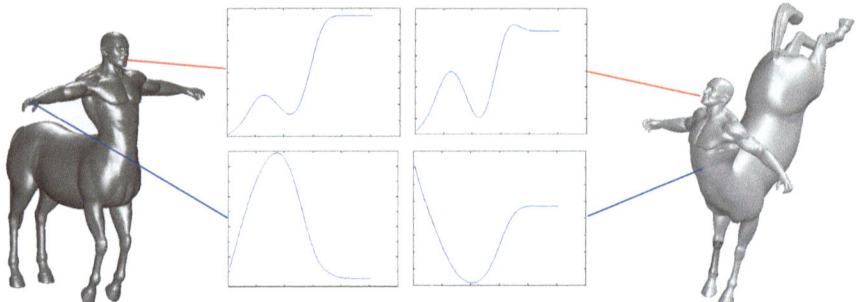

Fig. 7.10 Heat kernel signatures calculated on two isometric shapes. At *top*, signatures in corresponding points look very similar. At *bottom*, signatures in different points on the mesh differ

In Fig. 7.10, we show heat kernel signatures for two isometric shapes. Given a shape $\mathbb{S}$, we need to calculate the heat kernel signature for a point on $\mathbb{S}$. In practice, the heat kernel signature $\mathbf{p}(\mathbf{x})$ of a point $\mathbf{x} \in \mathbb{S}$ is an n-dimensional descriptor vector with each bin corresponding to some value of t:

$$\mathbf{p}(\mathbf{x}) = \big(p_1(\mathbf{x}), \ldots, p_n(\mathbf{x})\big) \tag{7.45}$$

$$p_i(x) = c(x) K_{\alpha^{i-1} t_0}(x, x) \tag{7.46}$$

where $c(x)$ must be selected in order to have $\|\mathbf{p}(\mathbf{x})\|_2 = 1$. Note that we need to restrict the number of eigenvalues and eigenvectors to be considered in Eq. (7.44). As a result, we obtain a descriptor for each vertex on the mesh.

Once we have computed the descriptors for each shape in the database, these must be grouped in a huge collection of local descriptors which will be called the descriptor space. Next, it is necessary to quantize the n-dimensional descriptors space. The idea is to find a point set in the descriptor space in order to better cluster the whole descriptor set. Unsupervised techniques from machine learning field can be used such as k-means and its variants [38]. In order to make this section relatively self-contained, we briefly describe k-means clustering in the descriptor space.

Let $\mathbb{D}$ be the huge set of n-dimensional descriptors and k be the number of clusters we want to find. The algorithm can be summarized as follows:

1. **Initial centroids selection:** Select k points in the n-dimensional space. This step can be performed in different ways, for instance, selecting random points in the n-dimensional space, selecting random descriptors from $\mathbb{D}$, or using information about the distribution of descriptors in $\mathbb{D}$, just to name a few. Let $\mathbb{M} = \{\mathbf{m}_1, \ldots, \mathbf{m}_k\}$ be the set of selected centroids.
2. **Cluster assignment:** Assign each descriptor $\mathbf{d}$ in $\mathbb{D}$ to the closest cluster $\mathbb{C}_i$

$$\mathbb{C}_i = \big\{\mathbf{d} \in \mathbb{D} : \|\mathbf{d} - \mathbf{m}_i\| \leq \|\mathbf{d} - \mathbf{m}_j\|, \forall j = 1 \ldots k\big\} \tag{7.47}$$

3. **Centroids update:** Compute the new centroids for each cluster

$$\mathbf{m}_i = \frac{1}{|\mathbb{C}_i|} \sum_{\mathbf{d} \in \mathbb{C}_i} \mathbf{d} \qquad (7.48)$$

4. **Stop criterion:** If centroids remain unchanged after update step, stop and return $\mathbb{M}$. Otherwise, go to step 2.

Using the set of centroids, $\mathbb{M}$, and the heat kernel signatures previously calculated for a shape, $\mathbb{P}$, we need to compute a single descriptor for $\mathbb{P}$, so it is necessary to combine the local descriptors in a shape descriptor. To tackle this problem, we calculate the feature distribution at a vertex $\mathbf{x} \in \mathbb{P}$ as $\theta(\mathbf{x}) = (\theta_1(\mathbf{x}), \ldots, \theta_k(\mathbf{x}))^T$ where

$$\theta_i(\mathbf{x}) = c(\mathbf{x}) \exp\left(\frac{-\|\mathbf{p}(\mathbf{x}) - \mathbf{m}_i\|_2}{2\sigma^2}\right) \qquad (7.49)$$

where $c(\mathbf{x})$ is a constant selected such that $\|\theta(\mathbf{x})\|_2 = 1$, $\mathbf{p}(\mathbf{x})$ is the heat kernel signature of $\mathbf{x}$, $\mathbf{m}_i$ is the centroid of cluster $\mathbb{C}_i$, and σ is constant. Each bin in $\theta(\mathbf{x})$ can be considered as the probability that $\mathbf{x}$ belongs to the cluster corresponding to such a bin. This is a soft version of quantization because the classic bag of features approach considers placing a one in the bin corresponding to the closest cluster and zeros in the rest. Although the classic way can be performed here, the soft version has proved to be effective in experiments.

To obtain a shape descriptor, the feature distributions are simply added to obtain a shape descriptor of size k, the vocabulary size:

$$f(\mathbb{S}) = \sum_{\mathbf{x} \in \mathbb{S}} \theta(\mathbf{x}) \qquad (7.50)$$

and the matching between two shapes $\mathbb{S}$ and $\mathbb{T}$ is performed by using the L_1 distance

$$d(\mathbb{S}, \mathbb{T}) = \|f(\mathbb{S}) - f(\mathbb{T})\|_1 \qquad (7.51)$$

Nevertheless, during the quantization process, the spatial information is lost. Obviously, this information could be useful in the matching process. To address this problem, Ovsjanikov et al. [83] proposed a feature distribution among pairs of descriptors using a weighting factor related to spatial information. Again, we can use the heat kernel $K_t(\mathbf{x}, \mathbf{y})$ as a spatial factor which will have high values for close points $\mathbf{x}$ and $\mathbf{y}$. Therefore, the following definition for descriptors should be used:

$$F(\mathbb{S}) = \sum_{\mathbf{x} \in \mathbb{S}} \sum_{\mathbf{y} \in \mathbb{S}} \theta(\mathbf{x}) \theta^T(\mathbf{y}) K_t(\mathbf{x}, \mathbf{y}) \qquad (7.52)$$

This descriptor results in a $k \times k$ matrix and the distance between two shapes can be done with the L_1 distance, as usual.

Table 7.6 Performance using bag of features with vocabulary size 48. Table reproduced from Ovsjanikov et al. [83]

Transformation	EER	FPR @ FNR = 1 %	FPR @ FNR = 0.1 %
Null	0.97 %	0.90 %	6.47 %
Isometry	1.34 %	1.56 %	11.13 %
Topology	1.12 %	2.49 %	14.41 %
Isometry+Topology	1.82 %	2.38 %	13.90 %
Triangulation	2.29 %	4.26 %	14.66 %
Partiality	3.81 %	5.68 %	17.28 %
All	1.44 %	1.79 %	11.09 %

7.3.4.1 Evaluation

The main goal of this technique is to be robust in large scale databases, so the authors composed a database with models from the TOSCA dataset, the Princeton shape benchmark and the Sumner dataset. The performance was measured using ROC curves. It is important to note that the shapes in the TOSCA dataset were used as positive examples. These shapes contain transformed versions of the original shapes (null shapes), so the experiments were performed to assess the ability of the algorithm to retrieve shapes under the transformations (isometry, topology, triangulation, partiality).

The parameters used in computing the final descriptor were $t_0 = 1024$ and $\alpha = 1.32$, the size of vocabulary was 48, σ for soft quantization was set to twice the median size of the clusters in the geometric vocabulary. In addition, only 200 eigenvalues were used to compute the heat kernel signatures in Eq. (7.44).

The authors used three criteria to evaluate their method:

- Equal error rate (EER), the value of false positive rate (FPR) at which it equals the false negative rate (FNR).
- FPR at 1 % FNR.
- FPR at 0.1 % FNR.

In terms of EER, when null shapes were used as queries, the method obtained 0.97 %. With respect to the transformations, 'topology' gave the best performance with 1.12 %, followed by 'isometry' with 1.34 %. These results show that this method is robust in the presence of transformations such as topology changes and isometry. We can conjecture that the formulation of the heat kernel signatures, over which the algorithm is based, largely supports these issues. This fact is also noted in the performance of the partiality transformation (3.81 % in terms of EER). As the heat kernel signature is based on the Laplace-Beltrami operator, the partiality transformation reduces the chance of correctly retrieving similar shapes because with partial shapes the intrinsic geometry changes considerably. Tables 7.6 and 7.7 show the complete results.

7 3D Shape Matching for Retrieval and Recognition

Table 7.7 Performance using space-sensitive bag of features with vocabulary size 48. Table reproduced from Ovsjanikov et al. [83]

Transformation	EER	FPR @ FNR = 1 %	FPR @ FNR = 0.1 %
Null	0.58 %	0.33 %	1.98 %
Isometry	1.00 %	1.07 %	6.16 %
Topology	1.12 %	1.67 %	4.77 %
Isometry+Topology	1.41 %	2.14 %	6.80 %
Triangulation	2.11 %	3.43 %	8.57 %
Partiality	3.70 %	6.19 %	8.52 %
All	1.44 %	1.79 %	11.09 %

On the other hand, using the space-sensitive approach, the results were 0.58 % for null shapes, 1.00 % for isometry, 1.12 % for topology, 2.11 % for triangulation, and 3.70 % for partiality; all in terms of EER. A recent track in the Shape Retrieval Contest (SHREC 2010) experimented on large scale retrieval [23], where the presented method and its variations were compared to other state-of-the-art techniques. In this report, heat kernel signatures obtained the best results with the mean average precision close to 100 % in almost all transformations, except partiality.

7.3.4.2 Complexity Analysis

Let $\mathbb{S}$ be a 3D object with n vertices. The computational complexity for each stage of the above method are:

- Computation of the Laplacian matrix: $O(n^2)$.
- Computation of the eigenvalues and eigenvectors: $O(n^3)$.
- Computation of the HKS: $O(nm)$, where m is the dimension of each HKS.
- K-means clustering: $O(IKNm)$, where I is the number of iterations until convergence, K is the number of clusters to be found, N is the number of descriptors of the entire collection, and m is the descriptor dimension.
- Bag of features: $O(Nkm)$.

The total complexity of this method is dominated by the clustering process. Obviously, the number of descriptors N can be extremely large, so the k-means clustering is expensive. Therefore, the total computational complexity of this method is $O(IKNm)$.

7.4 Research Challenges

If we observe the literature on shape retrieval and recognition as briefly reviewed in Sect. 7.2, we can observe that this is a relatively young field and therefore presents a number of areas which require further work and progress. This section is devoted to presenting the trends in future research and the challenges which concern the community.

Query specification. The research is commonly focused on testing the effectiveness and efficiency of the presented proposals, however an important factor is left out, users. As a result, little work has been done in query specification. It is generally assumed that we have a query object in the representation required by the application. Nevertheless, often we are interested in retrieving objects similar to the query, so a natural question arises: *If we have an object (the query) visually similar to our needs, why do we proceed to search?* A more interesting approach is to provide the query as images, video, sketches, or text. However, this proposal will often require human interaction to periodically feed back advisory information to the search. For example, in content-based image retrieval, much research has turned to using sketches as a more natural way of querying an image. This trend has raised new challenges and research interests which are also expected to emerge in the shape retrieval and recognition community.

Efficiency and large scale retrieval. Although a relative level of effectiveness has recently been achieved both in shape retrieval and recognition, important issues related to the efficiency require attention, even if approaches such as local features and the Laplace-Beltrami operator have begun to be extensively used. In addition, most techniques present results over publicly available datasets of no more than 2000 objects and results about efficiency are not even provided. Moreover, Laplace-Beltrami based approaches rely on extensive computations of eigenvalues and eigenvectors of huge matrices, so it is often necessary to simplify the meshes before processing at the expense of losing the level of detail. In this sense, efficient variants and alternatives are expected to be studied.

Object representation. As can be noted from previous sections of this chapter, many approaches rely on a boundary representation for 3D shapes. Perhaps this follows from the fact that this representation is preferred to others because its simplicity and suitability for rendering tasks. In addition, triangle meshes are widely available for processing and the vast majority of 3D objects on the Internet are found in this way. Nevertheless, some potential applications use different representations such as parametric surfaces in CAD and volumetric information in medicine. Each representation has intrinsic advantages which should be considered in order to exploit the information as it is.

Partial matching. A lot of work has been done for 3D objects when the required matching model is global, visual similarity. By global, we mean that given a 3D object, and algorithm retrieves those objects in the database that look visually similar and the whole shape structure is used for comparison. However, many presented methods do not allow partial matching due to the restricted global model that they assume. So given a part of a shape as a query, an interesting problem is to try to retrieve those objects in the database that contain visually similar parts to that query. Difficulties can arise due to the need to represent a model in a compact way, for instance, with local information whose extent is unknown *a-priori*. In addition, the matching becomes an expensive task because of the exponential amount of possible memberships of the query. Moreover, an even harder problem is to quantify the similarity and partiality, since the similarity strongly depends of the level of partiality allowed while searching.

Domain applications. With the increasing interest of the computer vision community in 3D shape retrieval and recognition, a current trend is to research the support that these can give to high level vision tasks. What is more, computer vision aims at recognizing and understanding the real composition of a viewed scene through a camera, where a scene is part of a three-dimensional world. In the future, we could consider the combination of shape retrieval and recognition with 3D reconstructions of scenes from images as an attempt to break the semantic gap between a three-dimensional scene and the image which represents it. In the same way, the field of medicine could take advantage in building 3D image analysis automated systems such as magnetic resonance images (MRI) and computed tomographies. It is easy to obtain three-dimensional representations from this kind of information and further processing can be beneficial. Another interesting application is modeling support, such as is required in videogames, 3D films and special effects; all of these require a large amount of work in modeling. These applications could benefit from shape retrieval and recognition tasks to reduce the time spent modeling.

Automatic 3D objects annotation. In order to increase effectiveness, we may require more semantic information to complement the geometric information extracted from the shape. Information about composition is a good choice, so it is necessary to maintain textual information which represent rich semantic information to be used in retrieval tasks. Nevertheless, attaching tags to shapes by humans is an expensive task, taking into account the amount of objects in a database. Thus, by using shape retrieval and recognition we can assign textual tags based on visual similarity or functionality. In addition, this approach can be used to add semantic information, which can be used to improve the visual search effectiveness.

7.5 Concluding Remarks

This chapter introduces the 3D shape matching process from the point of view of representative approaches in the field, potential applications and the main challenges which need to be addressed. The wide variety of available 3D data allows us to choose between different characteristics such as level of detail, shapes classes, and so forth. In addition to the standard datasets, many shape recognition applications use custom-acquired data in order to test their proposals with respect to domain-oriented information. However it is important to use datasets widely employed and accepted by the community to have consistent research results and valuable performance comparisons.

Just as the amount of available 3D data has considerably grown in recent times, there is also an increasing interest of researchers for proposing new approaches for shape matching and studying the potential applications in several fields. We have witnessed the achieved benefits of fields such as medicine, engineering, art, entertainment, and security, by the development of shape retrieval and recognition techniques. What is more, the interest in computer vision applications based on shape matching is becoming increasingly evident. It is easy to see the great potential that 3D information can provide and how it can be used to complement 2D images and video processing, in order to improve the effectiveness of high-level vision tasks. We believe that 3D information will be used commonly in the future and processes such as retrieval and recognition will be the basis for cutting-edge applications.

Likewise, it is beneficial to have a large catalog of techniques, because we can select an appropriate technique depending of the application context. Often we can combine techniques to improve the performance in general. In this chapter, we selected four techniques, which were explained in detail in Sect. 7.3. The depth buffer descriptor is an effective method based on extracting information of projections. Interestingly, this is one of the most effective methods yet simple, although it just supports a global similarity model. One way of supporting a certain level of partial similarity is by using local features extracted from shapes. Although the amount of information to be extracted increases, it is the cost to be paid for supporting non-global similarity models.

The other three presented techniques assume a non-global similarity model by extracting local descriptors which can be used to do the matching. The first of these is the spin image approach, which has proven to be effective in 3D shape recognition. Its versatility for describing shapes from different aspects has made it a standard technique for recognition tasks and new approaches often compare their results against results using spin images. Nevertheless, its dependency on uniform meshes and normals computation is restrictive. A small difference in calculating normals can produce different spin images, limiting its effectiveness.

Both salient spectral geometric features and heat kernel signature approaches make extensive use of a mathematical tool which has proven to be powerful for shape analysis, namely the Laplace-Beltrami operator. This operator has desirable properties which makes it a valuable tool for shape matching, in addition to the high effectiveness achieved in shape retrieval. Nevertheless, a weak point of this tool is its high computational cost which makes it an interesting challenge to be tackled in the future.

As can be noted, there is a lot of work to be done in proposing new approaches to improve the effectiveness and the efficiency of 3D shape matching, and studying new paradigms, some of which we mention in Sect. 7.4. We are convinced that the future of this research field is promising and the growth in scientific and technological productivity will remain thanks to the enormous efforts that the research communities in various fields are providing.

7.6 Further Reading

As expected, the increasing interest of research communities in shape retrieval and recognition has allowed a rapid advance, both in theory (new approaches) and applications. Obviously, due to space limitations, all the material could not be addressed in this chapter, so this section is devoted to present additional material for interested readers.

A good starting point to introduce the reader further to the subject of shape retrieval and recognition are the surveys [26, 28, 55, 100]. Early evaluations of algorithms were also presented in the reports [15, 25, 27, 42]. For recent experimentation with state-of-the-art techniques, we recommend the reports of the SHREC contest [1]. For instance, recent SHREC tracks are: robust correspondence benchmark [22], robust large-scale shape retrieval benchmark [23], robust feature detection and description benchmark [17, 21], non-rigid 3D shape retrieval [73, 74], and generic 3D warehouse [105]. These reports represent a good reference for reviewing recent approaches and their performance evaluation.

More advanced and recent approaches have been presented, such as retrieval of 3D articulated objects [4], retrieval by similarity score fusion [5], discriminative spherical wavelet features [65], spherical parameterizations [66], compact hybrid shape descriptor [85], matching of point set surfaces [93], probability density-based shape descriptor [6], and spin images for shape retrieval [7, 8, 37], just to name a few. Another interesting approach is to refine the retrieval results using user information about how relevant the results were with a certain query. This approach is commonly called relevance feedback and it was properly applied by Leng and Qin [70], and Giorgi et al. [48] in shape retrieval tasks.

As stated in Sect. 7.4, partial matching is a challenging and still open problem. Nevertheless, some attempts have been proposed in order to tackle this problem. Among the main approaches are objects as metric spaces [20], priority-driven search [43], shape topics [76], reeb pattern unfolding [102], partial matching for real textured 3D objects [58], regularized partial matching of rigid shapes [19], and matching of 3D shape subparts [78]. Additionally, a good reference for non-rigid shape retrieval is due to Bronstein et al. [24].

The use of machine learning techniques has also been involved in shape retrieval and recognition. For instance, the boosting approach [63], supervised learning of similarity measures [64], unsupervised learning approach [80], learning of semantic categories [81], learning of 3D face models [101], face recognition by SVM classification [13], and the neurofuzzy approach [68]. These approaches need some background in pattern recognition and machine learning theory.

For readers interested in the Laplace-Beltrami operator and its applications in shape retrieval and recognition, we recommend the papers by Belkin et al. [11, 12], Bobenko [16], Chuang et al. [34], Ghaderpanah et al. [46], Levy [71], Rustamov [95], Wu et al. [109], and Xu [110, 111]. These papers have highly mathematical content, so it is recommended for a more advanced level of research.

On the other hand, in addition to the applications listed in Sec. 7.1, in the papers by Perakis et al. [89], Zhou et al. [116] and Giorgi et al. [47], we can find applications to face recognition, and in the work by Wessel et al. [107], the authors presented a benchmark for retrieval of architectural data.

7.7 Questions

1. Explain the difference between shape retrieval and shape recognition and give an example application of each.
2. Why is the matching of shapes that can deform (such as bending deformation) more difficult in general than matching of rigid shapes?
3. Why is the matching using partial views of an object (for example, when using single viewpoint 3D scans) more difficult in general than when the complete object surface is available in the query shape?
4. What properties of shape descriptor are desirable when addressing partial matching problems and non-rigid matching problems?
5. Describe the "bag of features" approach to shape retrieval.

7.8 Exercises

1. In the interest point detection of the salient spectral geometric features, the authors recommended to set the number of eigenvectors in the process to 100. Implement the interest point detection method using a higher number of eigenvectors. Investigate the relation between the number of eigenvectors, the number of interest points detected and the magnitude of the scales of them.
2. Consider a neighborhood where four points are coplanar and three of them form an equilateral triangle. The forth point lies in the barycenter of the triangle. Let a be the length of a triangle's side. Compare the triangle area with the following quantities:

    - Voronoi region of **p** by using only Eq. (7.21).
    - Voronoi region of **p** taking into account the obtuse triangles as described in Sec. 7.3.3.

    Argue why it is necessary to be aware of obtuse triangles while calculating the Voronoi region area.
3. Prove that the Laplace-Beltrami operator is not invariant to scale changes. Additionally, suppose a uniform mesh which have edges with the same length denoted by a. Conjecture what happens with the operator when a tends to zero.
4. Explain why the quantity $K_t(\mathbf{x}, \mathbf{y})$ is a good choice for the spatial factor in shape Google technique?
5. The direction of the normal in the spin images defines a horizontal line in the middle of the spin image. A little variation in this normal modifies the image, rotating the pixels around the central point in the first column of the image. Propose a method to tackle with little variation of the normals.
6. The spin image in a point **p** depends of the direction of its normal. Let suppose an object $\mathbb{A}$ with normals computed in each vertex and an object $\mathbb{B}$, equal to $\mathbb{A}$, with opposite normals. Propose a variation to spin image computation in order to generate the same descriptor for corresponding points in $\mathbb{A}$ and $\mathbb{B}$.

7. Implement the spin images construction modifying the accumulation method. Instead of using bilinear interpolation, use a Gaussian weight centered in the corresponding pixel. Is this method more robust against noise and normal variations?

References

1. SHREC—Shape Retrieval Contest: http://www.aimatshape.net/event/SHREC
2. CGAL, Computational Geometry Algorithms Library: http://www.cgal.org
3. Adan, A., Adan, M.: A flexible similarity measure for 3D shapes recognition. IEEE Trans. Pattern Anal. Mach. Intell. **26**(11), 1507–1520 (2004)
4. Agathos, A., Pratikakis, I., Papadakis, P., Perantonis, S.J., Azariadis, P.N., Sapidis, N.S.: Retrieval of 3D articulated objects using a graph-based representation. In: Spagnuolo, M., Pratikakis, I., Veltkamp, R.C., Theoharis, T. (eds.) Proc. Workshop on 3D Object Retr. (3DOR), pp. 29–36. Eurographics Association, Geneve (2009)
5. Akgül, C.B., Sankur, B., Yemez, Y., Schmitt, F.: Similarity score fusion by ranking risk minimization for 3D object retrieval. In: Perantonis, S.J., Sapidis, N., Spagnuolo, M., Thalmann, D. (eds.) Proc. Workshop on 3D Object Retr. (3DOR), pp. 41–48. Eurographics Association, Geneve (2008)
6. Akgul, C.B., Sankur, B., Yemez, Y., Schmitt, F.: 3D model retrieval using probability density-based shape descriptors. IEEE Trans. Pattern Anal. Mach. Intell. **31**(6), 1117–1133 (2009)
7. Assfalg, J., Bimbo, A.D., Pala, P.: Spin images for retrieval of 3D objects by local and global similarity. In: Int. Conf. Pattern Recognit., pp. 906–909 (2004)
8. Assfalg, J., D'Amico, G., Bimbo, A.D., Pala, P.: 3D content-based retrieval with spin images. In: Proc. IEEE Int. Conf. Multimedia and Expo, pp. 771–774. IEEE Press, New York (2004)
9. Atmosukarto, I., Wilamowska, K., Heike, C., Shapiro, L.G.: 3D object classification using salient point patterns with application to craniofacial research. Pattern Recognit. **43**(4), 1502–1517 (2010)
10. Baeza-Yates, R.A., Ribeiro-Neto, B.A.: Modern Information Retrieval. ACM Press/Addison-Wesley, New York (1999)
11. Belkin, M., Sun, J., Wang, Y.: Discrete Laplace operator on meshed surfaces. In: Teillaud, M., Welzl, E. (eds.) Proc. Symposium on Comput. Geom, pp. 278–287. ACM, New York (2008)
12. Belkin, M., Sun, J., Wang, Y.: Constructing Laplace operator from point clouds in rd. In: Mathieu, C. (ed.) Proc. ACM-SIAM Symposium on Discrete Algorithms, pp. 1031–1040. SIAM, Philadelphia (2009)
13. Berretti, S., Bimbo, A.D., Pala, P., Silva-Mata, F.: Face recognition by SVMs classification and manifold learning of 2D and 3D radial geodesic distances. In: Perantonis, S.J., Sapidis, N., Spagnuolo, M., Thalmann, D. (eds.) Proc. Workshop on 3D Object Retr. (3DOR), pp. 57–64. Eurographics Association, Geneve (2008)
14. Besl, P.J., McKay, N.D.: A method for registration of 3D shapes. IEEE Trans. Pattern Anal. Mach. Intell. **14**(2), 239–256 (1992)
15. Bimbo, A.D., Pala, P.: Content-based retrieval of 3D models. ACM Trans. Multimed. Comput. Commun. Appl. **2**(1), 20–43 (2006)
16. Bobenko, A.I.: Delaunay triangulations of polyhedral surfaces, a discrete Laplace-Beltrami operator and applications. In: Teillaud, M., Welzl, E. (eds.) Proc. Symposium on Comput. Geom., p. 38. ACM, New York (2008)
17. Boyer, E., Bronstein, A.M., Bronstein, M.M., Bustos, B., Darom, T., Horaud, R., Hotz, I., Keller, Y., Keustermans, J., Kovnatsky, A., Litman, R., Reininghaus, J., Sipiran, I., Smeets, D., Suetens, P., Vandermeulen, D., Zaharescu, A., Zobel, V.: SHREC 2011: robust feature de-

tection and description benchmark. In: Proc. Workshop on 3D Object Retrieval (3DOR'11). Eurographics Association, Geneve (2011). doi:10.2312/3DOR/3DOR11/071-078
18. Bronstein, A., Bronstein, M., Kimmel, R.: Numerical Geometry of Non-rigid Shapes. Springer, Berlin (2008)
19. Bronstein, A.M., Bronstein, M.M.: Regularized partial matching of rigid shapes. In: Forsyth, D.A., Torr, P.H.S., Zisserman, A. (eds.) Proc. Eur. Conf. Comput. Vis. (ECCV). Lecture Notes in Computer Science, vol. 5303, pp. 143–154. Springer, Berlin (2008)
20. Bronstein, A.M., Bronstein, M.M., Bruckstein, A.M., Kimmel, R.: Partial similarity of objects, or how to compare a centaur to a horse. Int. J. Comput. Vis. **84**(2), 163–183 (2009)
21. Bronstein, A.M., Bronstein, M.M., Bustos, B., Castellani, U., Crisani, M., Falcidieno, B., Guibas, L.J., Kokkinos, I., Murino, V., Sipiran, I., Ovsjanikov, M., Patanè, G., Spagnuolo, M., Sun, J.: SHREC 2010: robust feature detection and description benchmark. In: Proc. Workshop on 3D Object Retrieval (3DOR'10). Eurographics Association, Geneve (2010)
22. Bronstein, A.M., Bronstein, M.M., Castellani, U., Dubrovina, A., Guibas, L.J., Horaud, R., Kimmel, R., Knossow, D., von Lavante, E., Mateus, D., Ovsjanikov, M., Sharma, A.: SHREC 2010: robust correspondence benchmark. In: Proc. Workshop on 3D Object Retrieval (3DOR'10). Eurographics Association, Geneve (2010)
23. Bronstein, A.M., Bronstein, M.M., Castellani, U., Falcidieno, B., Fusiello, A., Godil, A., Guibas, L., Kokkinos, I., Lian, Z., Ovsjanikov, M., Patanè, G., Spagnuolo, M., Toldo, R.: SHREC 2010: robust large-scale shape retrieval benchmark. In: Proc. Workshop on 3D Object Retrieval (3DOR'10). Eurographics Association, Geneve (2010)
24. Bronstein, A.M., Bronstein, M.M., Kimmel, R.: Topology-invariant similarity of nonrigid shapes. Int. J. Comput. Vis. **81**(3), 281–301 (2009)
25. Bustos, B., Keim, D., Saupe, D., Schreck, T.: Content-based 3D object retrieval. IEEE Comput. Graph. Appl. **27**(4), 22–27 (2007)
26. Bustos, B., Keim, D.A., Saupe, D., Schreck, T., Vranic, D.V.: Feature-based similarity search in 3D object databases. ACM Comput. Surv. **37**(4), 345–387 (2005)
27. Bustos, B., Keim, D.A., Saupe, D., Schreck, T., Vranic, D.V.: An experimental effectiveness comparison of methods for 3D similarity search. Int. J. Digit. Libr. **6**(1), 39–54 (2006)
28. Campbell, R.J., Flynn, P.J.: A survey of free-form object representation and recognition techniques. Comput. Vis. Image Underst. **81**(2), 166–210 (2001)
29. Chaouch, M., Verroust-Blondet, A.: 3D model retrieval based on depth line descriptor. In: Proc. IEEE Int. Conf. Multimedia and Expo, pp. 599–602. IEEE Press, New York (2007)
30. Chen, D.Y., Tian, X.P., Shen, Y.T., Ouhyoung, M.: On visual similarity based 3D model retrieval. Comput. Graph. Forum **22**(3), 223–232 (2003)
31. Chen, H., Bhanu, B.: Human ear recognition in 3D. IEEE Trans. Pattern Anal. Mach. Intell. **29**(4), 718–737 (2007)
32. Chen, H., Bhanu, B.: Efficient recognition of highly similar 3D objects in range images. IEEE Trans. Pattern Anal. Mach. Intell. **31**(1), 172–179 (2009)
33. Chua, C.S., Jarvis, R.: Point signatures: a new representation for 3D object recognition. Int. J. Comput. Vis. **25**(1), 63–85 (1997)
34. Chuang, M., Luo, L., Brown, B.J., Rusinkiewicz, S., Kazhdan, M.M.: Estimating the Laplace-Beltrami operator by restricting 3D functions. Comput. Graph. Forum **28**(5), 1475–1484 (2009)
35. Cyr, C.M., Kimia, B.B.: A similarity-based aspect-graph approach to 3D object recognition. Int. J. Comput. Vis. **57**(1), 5–22 (2004)
36. Daras, P., Zarpalas, D., Tzovaras, D., Strintzis, M.G.: Shape matching using the 3D radon transform. In: Proc. Int. Symposium on 3D Data Proces., Vis. and Transm., pp. 953–960. IEEE Computer Society, Los Alamitos (2004)
37. de Alarcón, P.A., Pascual-Montano, A.D., Carazo, J.M.: Spin images and neural networks for efficient content-based retrieval in 3D object databases. In: Lew, M.S., Sebe, N., Eakins, J.P. (eds.) Proc. ACM Int. Conf. on Image and Video Retrieval (CIVR). Lecture Notes in Computer Science, vol. 2383, pp. 225–234. Springer, Berlin (2002)

38. Duda, R.O., Hart, P.E., Stork, D.G.: Pattern Classification, 2nd edn. Wiley-Interscience, New York (2000)
39. Dutagaci, H., Sankur, B., Yemez, Y.: Transform-based methods for indexing and retrieval of 3D objects. In: Proc. Int. Conf. 3D Digital Imaging and Modeling, pp. 188–195. IEEE Computer Society, Los Alamitos (2005)
40. Faloutsos, C., Lin, K.: Fastmap: a fast algorithm for indexing, data-mining and visualization of traditional and multimedia datasets. In: Proc. ACM Int. Conf. on Management of Data (SIGMOD), pp. 163–174 (1995)
41. Frome, A., Huber, D., Kolluri, R., Bülow, T., Malik, J.: Recognizing objects in range data using regional point descriptors. In: Pajdla, T., Matas, J. (eds.) Proc. Eur. Conf. Comput. Vis. (ECCV). Lecture Notes in Computer Science, vol. 3023, pp. 224–237. Springer, Berlin (2004)
42. Funkhouser, T.A., Kazhdan, M.M., Min, P., Shilane, P.: Shape-based retrieval and analysis of 3D models. Commun. ACM **48**(6), 58–64 (2005)
43. Funkhouser, T.A., Shilane, P.: Partial matching of 3D shapes with priority-driven search. In: Sheffer, A., Polthier, K. (eds.) Proc. Symposium on Geom. Process. ACM International Conference Proceeding Series, vol. 256, pp. 131–142. Eurographics Association, Geneve (2006)
44. Gal, R., Cohen-Or, D.: Salient geometric features for partial shape matching and similarity. ACM Trans. Graph. **25**(1), 130–150 (2006)
45. Garland, M., Heckbert, P.S.: Surface simplification using quadric error metrics. In: Proc. Int. Conf. and Exhib. on Comput. Graph. and Interact. Tech. (SIGGRAPH), pp. 209–216 (1997)
46. Ghaderpanah, M., Abbas, A., Hamza, A.B.: Entropic hashing of 3D objects using Laplace-Beltrami operator. In: Proc. Int. Conf. Image Process. (ICIP), pp. 3104–3107. IEEE, New York (2008)
47. Giorgi, D., Attene, M., Patanè, G., Marini, S., Pizzi, C., Biasotti, S., Spagnuolo, M., Falcidieno, B., Corvi, M., Usai, L., Roncarolo, L., Garibotto, G.: A critical assessment of 2D and 3D face recognition algorithms. In: Tubaro, S., Dugelay, J.L. (eds.) Proc. Int. Conf. on Advanc. Video and Signal Based Surveill. (AVSS), pp. 79–84. IEEE Computer Society, Los Alamitos (2009)
48. Giorgi, D., Frosini, P., Spagnuolo, M., Falcidieno, B.: Multilevel relevance feedback for 3D shape retrieval. In: Spagnuolo, M., Pratikakis, I., Veltkamp, R.C., Theoharis, T. (eds.) Proc. Workshop on 3D Object Retr. (3DOR), pp. 45–52. Eurographics Association, Geneve (2009)
49. Goodall, S., Lewis, P.H., Martinez, K., Sinclair, P.A.S., Giorgini, F., Addis, M., Boniface, M.J., Lahanier, C., Stevenson, J.: Sculpteur: Multimedia retrieval for museums. In: Proc. ACM Int. Conf. on Image and Video Retrieval (CIVR). Lecture Notes in Computer Science, vol. 3115, pp. 638–646. Springer, Berlin (2004)
50. Hetzel, G., Leibe, B., Levi, P., Schiele, B.: 3D object recognition from range images using local feature histograms. In: Proc. IEEE Conf. Comput. Vision and Pattern Recognit. (CVPR), pp. 394–399. IEEE Computer Society, Los Alamitos (2001)
51. Hilaga, M., Shinagawa, Y., Komura, T., Kunii, T.L.: Topology matching for fully automatic similarity estimation of 3d shapes. In: Proc. Int. Conf. and Exhib. on Comput. Graph. and Interact. Tech. (SIGGRAPH), pp. 203–212 (2001)
52. Hu, J., Hua, J.: Salient spectral geometric features for shape matching and retrieval. Vis. Comput. **25**(5–7), 667–675 (2009)
53. Huang, P., Hilton, A., Starck, J.: Shape similarity for 3D video sequences of people. Int. J. Comput. Vis. **89**(2–3), 362–381 (2010)
54. Huang, Q.X., Flöry, S., Gelfand, N., Hofer, M., Pottmann, H.: Reassembling fractured objects by geometric matching. ACM Trans. Graph. **25**(3), 569 (2006)
55. Iyer, N., Jayanti, S., Lou, K., Kalyanaraman, Y., Ramani, K.: Three-dimensional shape searching: state-of-the-art review and future trends. Comput. Aided Des. **37**(5), 509–530 (2005)
56. Johnson, A., Spin-images: a representation for 3D surface matching. Ph.D. thesis, Robotics Institute, Carnegie Mellon University, Pittsburgh, PA (1997)

57. Johnson, A.E., Hebert, M.: Using spin images for efficient object recognition in cluttered 3D scenes. IEEE Trans. Pattern Anal. Mach. Intell. **21**(5), 433–449 (1999)
58. Kanezaki, A., Harada, T., Kuniyoshi, Y.: Partial matching for real textured 3D objects using color cubic higher-order local auto-correlation features. In: Spagnuolo, M., Pratikakis, I., Veltkamp, R.C., Theoharis, T. (eds.) Proc. Workshop on 3D Object Retr. (3DOR), pp. 9–12. Eurographics Association, Geneve (2009)
59. Kang, S.B., Ikeuchi, K.: The complex egi: a new representation for 3D pose determination. IEEE Trans. Pattern Anal. Mach. Intell. **15**(1), 707–721 (1993)
60. Kazhdan, M., Funkhouser, T., Rusinkiewicz, S.: Rotation Invariant Spherical Harmonic Representation of 3D Shape Descriptors (2003)
61. Keim, D.A.: Efficient geometry-based similarity search of 3D spatial databases. In: Delis, A., Faloutsos, C., Ghandeharizadeh, S. (eds.) Proc. ACM Int. Conf. on Management of Data (SIGMOD), pp. 419–430. ACM Press, New York (1999)
62. Kimmel, R., Sethian, J.A.: Computing geodesic paths on manifolds. In: Proc. Natl. Acad. Sci. USA, pp. 8431–8435 (1998)
63. Laga, H., Nakajima, M.: A boosting approach to content-based 3D model retrieval. In: Rohl, A. (ed.) Proc. Int. Conf. and Exhib. on Comput. Graph. and Interact. Tech. in Australasia (SIGGRAPH), pp. 227–234. ACM, New York (2007)
64. Laga, H., Nakajima, M.: Supervised learning of similarity measures for content-based 3D model retrieval. In: Tokunaga, T., Ortega, A. (eds.) Proc. Int. Conf. Large-Scale Knowledge Resources. Lecture Notes in Computer Science, vol. 4938, pp. 210–225. Springer, Berlin (2008)
65. Laga, H., Nakajima, M., Chihara, K.: Discriminative spherical wavelet features for content-based 3D model retrieval. Int. J. Shape Model. **13**(1), 51–72 (2007)
66. Laga, H., Takahashi, H., Nakajima, M.: Spherical parameterization and geometry image-based 3D shape similarity estimation. Vis. Comput. **22**(5), 324–331 (2006)
67. Laga, H., Takahashi, H., Nakajima, M.: Spherical wavelet descriptors for content-based 3D model retrieval. In: Proc. Shape Modeling Int, p. 15. IEEE Computer Society, Los Alamitos (2006)
68. Lazaridis, M., Daras, P.: A neurofuzzy approach to active learning based annotation propagation for 3D object databases. In: Perantonis, S.J., Sapidis, N., Spagnuolo, M., Thalmann, D. (eds.) Proc. Workshop on 3D Object Retr. (3DOR), pp. 49–56. Eurographics Association, Geneve (2008)
69. Lee, T.K., Drew, M.S.: 3D object recognition by eigen-scale-space of contours. In: Sgallari, F., Murli, A., Paragios, N. (eds.) Proc. Int. Conf. on Scale Space and Var. Methods in Comput. Vision. Lecture Notes in Computer Science, vol. 4485, pp. 883–894. Springer, Berlin (2007)
70. Leng, B., Qin, Z.: A powerful relevance feedback mechanism for content-based 3D model retrieval. Multimed. Tools Appl. **40**(1), 135–150 (2008)
71. Lévy, B.: Laplace-Beltrami eigenfunctions towards an algorithm that understands geometry. In: Proc. Shape Modeling Int, p. 13. IEEE Computer Society, Los Alamitos (2006)
72. Li, X., Guskov, I.: 3d object recognition from range images using pyramid matching. In: Proc. Int. Conf. Comput. Vision (ICCV), pp. 1–6. IEEE Press, New York (2007)
73. Lian, Z., Godil, A., Bustos, B., Daoudi, M., Hermans, J., Kawamura, S., Kurita, Y., Lavoue, G., Nguyen, H., Ohbuchi, R., Ohishi, Y., Porikli, F., Reuter, M., Sipiran, I., Smeets, D., Suetens, P., Tabia, H., Vandermeulen, D.: SHREC'11 track: shape retrieval on non-rigid 3d watertight meshes. In: Proc. Workshop on 3D Object Retrieval (3DOR'11). Eurographics Association, Geneve (2011). doi:10.2312/3DOR/3DOR11/079-088
74. Lian, Z., Godil, A., Fabry, T., Furuya, T., Hermans, J., Ohbuchi, R., Shu, C., Smeets, D., Suetens, P., Vandermeulen, D., Wuhrer, S.: SHREC'10 track: non-rigid 3D shape retrieval. In: Proc. Workshop on 3D Object Retrieval (3DOR'10), pp. 1–8. Eurographics Association, Geneve (2010)
75. Liu, Y., Zha, H., Qin, H.: The generalized shape distributions for shape matching and analysis. In: Proc. Shape Modeling Int., p. 16. IEEE Computer Society, Los Alamitos (2006)

76. Liu, Y., Zha, H., Qin, H.: Shape topics: A compact representation and new algorithms for 3D partial shape retrieval. In: Proc. IEEE Conf. Comput. Vision and Pattern Recognit. (CVPR), pp. 2025–2032. IEEE Computer Society, Los Alamitos (2006)
77. Meyer, M., Desbrun, M., Schroder, P., Barr, A.H.: Discrete differential-geometry operators for triangulated 2-manifolds. Vis. Math. **III**, 35–57 (2003)
78. Novotni, M., Degener, P., Klein, R.: Correspondence generation and matching of 3D shape subparts. Tech. Rep., University of Bonn (2005)
79. Novotni, M., Klein, R.: A geometric approach to 3D object comparison. In: Proc. Shape Modeling Int., pp. 167–175. IEEE Computer Society, Los Alamitos (2001)
80. Ohbuchi, R., Kobayashi, J.: Unsupervised learning from a corpus for shape-based 3D model retrieval. In: Wang, J.Z., Boujemaa, N., Chen, Y. (eds.) Proc. ACM Int. Conf. Multimedia Infor. Retr., pp. 163–172. ACM, New York (2006)
81. Ohbuchi, R., Yamamoto, A., Kobayashi, J.: Learning semantic categories for 3D model retrieval. In: Wang, J.Z., Boujemaa, N., Bimbo, A.D., Li, J. (eds.) Proc. ACM Int. Conf. Multimedia Infor. Retr., pp. 31–40. ACM, New York (2007)
82. Osada, R., Funkhouser, T.A., Chazelle, B., Dobkin, D.P.: Shape distributions. ACM Trans. Graph. **21**(4), 807–832 (2002)
83. Ovsjanikov, M., Bronstein, A.M., Guibas, L.J., Bronstein, M.M.: Shape Google: a computer vision approach to invariant shape retrieval. In: Proc. Workshop on Non-Rigid Shape Anal. and Deform. Image Alignment (NORDIA) (2009)
84. Papadakis, P., Pratikakis, I., Perantonis, S.J., Theoharis, T.: Efficient 3D shape matching and retrieval using a concrete radialized spherical projection representation. Pattern Recognit. **40**(9), 2437–2452 (2007)
85. Papadakis, P., Pratikakis, I., Theoharis, T., Passalis, G., Perantonis, S.J.: 3D object retrieval using an efficient and compact hybrid shape descriptor. In: Perantonis, S.J., Sapidis, N., Spagnuolo, M., Thalmann, D. (eds.) Proc. Workshop on 3D Object Retr. (3DOR), pp. 9–16. Eurographics Association, Geneve (2008)
86. Paquet, E., Rioux, M.: Nefertiti: A query by content software for three-dimensional models databases management. In: Proc. Int. Conf. 3D Digital Imaging and Modeling, pp. 345–352. IEEE Computer Society, Los Alamitos (1997)
87. Paquet, E., Viktor, H.: Exploring protein architecture using 3D shape-based signatures. In: Proc. Int. Conf. Eng. in Med. and Biol., pp. 1204–1208 (2007)
88. Paquet, E., Viktor, H.L.: Capri/mr: exploring protein databases from a structural and physicochemical point of view. Proc. VLDB **1**(2), 1504–1507 (2008)
89. Perakis, P., Theoharis, T., Passalis, G., Kakadiaris, I.A.: Automatic 3D facial region retrieval from multi-pose facial datasets. In: Spagnuolo, M., Pratikakis, I., Veltkamp, R.C., Theoharis, T. (eds.) Proc. Workshop on 3D Object Retr. (3DOR), pp. 37–44. Eurographics Association, Geneve (2009)
90. Reuter, M., Biasotti, S., Giorgi, D., Patanè, G., Spagnuolo, M.: Discrete Laplace-Beltrami operators for shape analysis and segmentation. Comput. Graph. **33**(3), 381–390 (2009)
91. Ricard, J., Coeurjolly, D., Baskurt, A.: Generalizations of angular radial transform for 2D and 3D shape retrieval. Pattern Recognit. Lett. **26**(14), 2174–2186 (2005)
92. Ronneberger, O., Burkhardt, H., Schultz, E.: General-purpose object recognition in 3D volume data sets using gray-scale invariants—classification of airborne pollen-grains recorded with a confocal laser scanning microscope. In: Int. Conf. Pattern Recognit., vol. 2 (2002)
93. Ruggeri, M.R., Saupe, D.: Isometry-invariant matching of point set surfaces. In: Perantonis, S.J., Sapidis, N., Spagnuolo, M., Thalmann, D. (eds.) Proc. Workshop on 3D Object Retr. (3DOR), pp. 17–24. Eurographics Association, Geneve (2008)
94. Ruiz-Correa, S., Shapiro, L.G., Melia, M.: A new signature-based method for efficient 3D object recognition. In: Proc. IEEE Conf. Comput. Vision and Pattern Recognit. (CVPR), vol. 1 (2001)
95. Rustamov, R.M.: Laplace-Beltrami eigenfunctions for deformation invariant shape representation. In: Belyaev, A.G., Garland, M. (eds.) Proc. Symposium on Geom. Process. ACM In-

ternational Conference Proceeding Series, vol. 257, pp. 225–233. Eurographics Association, Geneve (2007)
96. Shilane, P., Min, P., Kazhdan, M.M., Funkhouser, T.A.: The Princeton shape benchmark. In: Proc. Shape Modeling Int., pp. 167–178. IEEE Computer Society, Los Alamitos (2004)
97. Sun, J., Ovsjanikov, M., Guibas, L.J.: A concise and provably informative multi-scale signature based on heat diffusion. Comput. Graph. Forum **28**(5) (2009)
98. Sun, Y., Paik, J.K., Koschan, A., Page, D.L., Abidi, M.A.: Point fingerprint: a new 3D object representation scheme. IEEE Trans. Syst. Man Cybern. **33**(4), 712–717 (2003)
99. Sundar, H., Silver, D., Gagvani, N., Dickinson, S.: Skeleton based shape matching and retrieval. In: Proc. Shape Modeling Int., p. 130. IEEE Computer Society, Washington (2003)
100. Tangelder, J.W.H., Veltkamp, R.C.: A survey of content based 3D shape retrieval methods. Multimed. Tools Appl. **39**(3), 441–471 (2008)
101. Taniguchi, M., Tezuka, M., Ohbuchi, R.: Learning 3D face models for shape based retrieval. In: Proc. Shape Modeling Int., pp. 269–270. IEEE Press, New York (2008)
102. Tierny, J., Vandeborre, J.P., Daoudi, M.: Partial 3D shape retrieval by reeb pattern unfolding. Comput. Graph. Forum **28**(1), 41–55 (2009)
103. Toldo, R., Castellani, U., Fusiello, A.: Visual vocabulary signature for 3D object retrieval and partial matching. In: Spagnuolo, M., Pratikakis, I., Veltkamp, R.C., Theoharis, T. (eds.) Proc. Workshop on 3D Object Retr. (3DOR), pp. 21–28. Eurographics Association, Geneve (2009)
104. Tung, T., Schmitt, F.: The augmented multiresolution reeb graph approach for content-based retrieval of 3D shapes. Int. J. Shape Model. **11**(1), 91–120 (2005)
105. Vanamali, T., Godil, A., Dutagaci, H., Furuya, T., Lian, Z., Ohbuchi, R.: SHREC'10 track: generic 3D warehouse. In: Proc. Workshop on 3D Object Retrieval (3DOR'10). Eurographics Association, Geneve (2010)
106. Vranic, D.: 3D model retrieval. Ph.D. thesis, University of Leipzig (2004)
107. Wessel, R., Blümel, I., Klein, R.: A 3D shape benchmark for retrieval and automatic classification of architectural data. In: Spagnuolo, M., Pratikakis, I., Veltkamp, R.C., Theoharis, T. (eds.) Proc. Workshop on 3D Object Retr. (3DOR), pp. 53–56. Eurographics Association, Geneve (2009)
108. Wolfson, H.J., Rigoutsos, I.: Geometric hashing: an overview. Comput. Sci. Eng. **4**, 10–21 (1997)
109. Wu, H.Y., Wang, L., Luo, T., Zha, H.: 3D shape consistent correspondence by using Laplace-Beltrami spectral embeddings. In: Spencer, S.N., Nakajima, M., Wu, E., Miyata, K., Thalmann, D., Huang, Z. (eds.) Proc. ACM Int. Conf. on Virtual Real. Contin. and Its Appls. in Ind., pp. 307–309. ACM, New York (2009)
110. Xu, G.: Convergent discrete Laplace-Beltrami operators over triangular surfaces. In: Proc. Geom. Modeling and Process., pp. 195–204. IEEE Computer Society, Los Alamitos (2004)
111. Xu, G.: Discrete Laplace-Beltrami operators and their convergence. Comput. Aided Geom. Des. **21**, 767–784 (2004)
112. Yeh, J.S., Chen, D.Y., Chen, B.Y., Ouhyoung, M.: A web-based three-dimensional protein retrieval system by matching visual similarity. Bioinformatics **21**(13), 3056–3057 (2005)
113. You, C.F., Tsai, Y.L.: 3D solid model retrieval for engineering reuse based on local feature correspondence. Int. J. Adv. Manuf. Technol. **46**(5–8), 649–661 (2009)
114. Zarpalas, D., Daras, P., Axenopoulos, A., Tzovaras, D., Strintzis, M.G.: 3D model search and retrieval using the spherical trace transform. EURASIP J. Appl. Signal Process. **2007**(1), 207 (2007)
115. Zhang, D.: Harmonic shape images: A 3D free-form surface representation and its applications in surface matching. Ph.D. thesis, Robotics Institute, Carnegie Mellon University, Pittsburgh, PA (1999)
116. Zhou, X., Seibert, H., Busch, C., Funk, W.: A 3D face recognition algorithm using histogram-based features. In: Perantonis, S.J., Sapidis, N., Spagnuolo, M., Thalmann, D. (eds.) Proc. Workshop on 3D Object Retr. (3DOR), pp. 65–71. Eurographics Association, Geneve (2008)

Part III
3D Imaging Applications

In this final part of this book, we discuss four applications areas of 3D imaging and analysis, in each of four chapters. The first of these is 3D face recognition and the second is 3D Digital Elevation Model generation. The third concerns how such 3D remote sensing technology can be applied to the measurement of forests. A final chapter discusses 3D medical imaging. This is a little different from the other applications in the sense that internal structures are imaged and many data representations employed are volume-based (voxelized) rather than surface mesh based.

Chapter 8
3D Face Recognition

Ajmal Mian and Nick Pears

Abstract Face recognition using standard 2D images struggles to cope with changes in illumination and pose. 3D face recognition algorithms have been more successful in dealing with these challenges. 3D face shape data is used as an independent cue for face recognition and has also been combined with texture to facilitate multimodal face recognition. Additionally, 3D face models have been used for pose correction and calculation of the facial albedo map, which is invariant to illumination. Finally, 3D face recognition has also achieved significant success towards expression invariance by modeling non-rigid surface deformations, removing facial expressions or by using parts-based face recognition. This chapter gives an overview of 3D face recognition and details both well-established and more recent state-of-the-art 3D face recognition techniques in terms of their implementation and expected performance on benchmark datasets.

8.1 Introduction

Measurement of the intrinsic characteristics of the human face is a socially acceptable biometric method that can be implemented in a non-intrusive way [48]. Face recognition from 2D images has been studied extensively for over four decades [96]. However, there has been a lot of research activity and media publicity in 3D face recognition over the last decade. With the increased availability of affordable 3D scanners, many algorithms have been proposed by researchers and a number of competitions have been arranged for benchmarking their performance. Some commercial products have also appeared in the market and one can now purchase a range of *Commercial Off-The-Shelf* (COTS) 3D face recognition systems.

A. Mian (✉)
School of Computer Science and Software Engineering, University of Western Australia,
35 Stirling Highway, Crawley, WA 6009, Australia
e-mail: ajmal.mian@uwa.edu.au

N. Pears
Department of Computer Science, University of York, Deramore Lane, York, YO10 5GH, UK
e-mail: nick.pears@york.ac.uk

This chapter will introduce the main concepts behind 3D face recognition algorithms, give an overview of the literature, and elaborate upon some carefully selected representative and seminal techniques. Note that we do not intend to give a highly comprehensive literature review, due to the size of the field and the tutorial nature of this text.

A 2D image is a function of the scene geometry, the imaging geometry, the scene reflectance and the illumination conditions. The same scene appears completely different from different viewpoints or under different illuminations. For images of human faces, it is known that the variations due to pose and illumination changes are greater than the variations between images of different subjects under the same pose and illumination conditions [3]. Therefore, 2D image-based face recognition algorithms usually struggle to cope with such imaging variations.

On the other hand, a captured face surface[1] much more directly represents the geometry of the viewed scene, and is much less dependent on ambient illumination and the viewpoint (or, equivalently, the facial pose). Therefore, 3D face recognition algorithms have been more successful in dealing with the challenges of varying illumination and pose.

Strictly, however, we observe that 3D imaging is not fully independent of pose, because when imaging with a single 3D camera with its limited field of view, the part of the face imaged is clearly dependent on pose. In other words, self-occlusion is a problem, and research issues concerning the fact that the surface view is *partial* come into play. Additionally, 3D cameras do have some sensitivity to strong ambient lighting as, in the active imaging case, it is more difficult to detect the projected light pattern, sometimes leading to missing parts in the 3D data. Camera designers often attempt to counter this by the use of optical filters and modulated light schemes. Finally, as pose varies, the orientation of the imaged surface affects the footprint of the projected light and how much light is reflected back to the camera. This varies the amount of noise on the measured surface geometry.

Despite these issues, 3D imaging for face recognition still provides clear benefits over 2D imaging. 3D facial shape is used both as an independent cue for face recognition, in multimodal 2D/3D recognition schemes [18, 64], or to assist (pose correct) 2D image-based face recognition. These last two are possible because most 3D cameras also capture color-texture in the form of a standard 2D image, along with the 3D shape, and the data from these two modalities (2D and 3D) is registered.

3D face recognition developments have also achieved significant success towards robust operation in the presence of facial expression variations. This is achieved either by building expression-invariant face surface representations [15], or modeling non-rigid surface deformations [58], or by avoiding expression deformations by only considering the more rigid upper parts of the face [64] or regions around the nose [19].

---

[1]This may be referred to as a *3D model*, a *3D scan* or a *3D image*, depending on the mode of capture and how it is stored, as discussed in Chap. 1, Sect 1.1. Be careful to distinguish between a *specific* face model relating to a single specific 3D capture instance and a *general* face model, such as Blanz and Vetter's morphable face model [11], which is generated from many registered 3D face captures.

Data from 3D scanners can be used to construct generative 3D face models offline, where such models can synthesize the face under novel pose and illumination conditions. Using such models, an online recognition system can employ standard 2D image probes, obviating the need for a 3D scanner in the live system. For example, 3D face models have been used to estimate the illumination invariant facial albedo map. Once a 3D model and face albedo are available, any new image can be synthetically rendered under novel poses and illumination conditions. A large number of such images under different illuminations are used to build the illumination cones of a face [38] which are subsequently used for illumination invariant face recognition. Similarly, synthesized images under different poses are used to sample the pose space of human faces and to train classifiers for pose invariant face recognition [38]. In another approach of this general modeling type, Blanz and Vetter [11] built a statistical, morphable model, which is learnt offline from a set of textured 3D head scans acquired with a laser scanner. This model can be fitted to single probe images and the model parameters of shape and texture are used to represent and recognize faces.

Thus there are a lot of different possibilities when using 3D face captures in face recognition systems. Although we examine several of these, the emphasis of this chapter is on recognition from 3D shape data only, where geometric features are extracted from the 3D face and matched against a dataset to determine the identity of an unknown subject or to verify his/her claimed identity. Even within these 3D facial shape recognition systems, there are many different approaches in the literature that can be categorized in several different ways. One of the main categorizations is the use of *holistic* face representations or *feature-based* face representations. Holistic methods encode the full visible facial surface after its pose has been normalized (to a canonical frontal pose) and the surface and its properties are resampled to produce a standard size feature vector. The feature vector could contain raw depth values and/or any combination of surface property, such as gradients and curvature. This approach has been employed, for example, using depth maps and the associated surface feature maps in nearest neighbor schemes within both *Principal Component Analysis* (PCA) and *Linear Discriminant Analysis* (LDA) derived subspaces [45]. (Note that the counterpart of these methods for 2D images are often called *appearance-based* methods, since their low-dimensional representation is faithful to the original image.)

Although holistic methods often do extract features, for example to localize a triplet of fiducial points (landmarks) for pose normalization, and a feature vector (e.g. of depths, normals, curvatures, etc.) is extracted for 3D face matching, the term *feature-based method* usually refers to those techniques that only encode the facial surface around extracted *points of interest*, also known as *keypoints*. For example, these could be the local extrema of curvature on the facial surface or keypoints for which we have learnt their local properties. Structural matching (e.g. graph matching) approaches can then be employed where the relative spatial relations of features is key to the face matching process [65]. Alternatively, a 'bag of features' approach could be employed, where spatial relations are completely discarded and the content of more complex 'information rich' features is the key to the face matching process.

An advantage of holistic methods is that they try to use all of the visible facial surface for discrimination. However, when 3D scans are noisy or low resolution, accurate and reliable pose normalization is difficult and feature-based approaches may perform better.

An outline of the *broad* steps involved in a typical 3D face recognition system are as follows:

1. *3D face scan acquisition.* A 3D face model is acquired using one of the techniques described in Chap. 2 (passive techniques) or Chap. 3 (active techniques). Currently, most cameras used for 3D face recognition are active, due to the lack of sufficiently large scale texture on most subject's facial surface.
2. *3D face scan preprocessing.* Unlike 2D images from a digital camera, the 3D data is visibly imperfect and usually contains spikes, missing data and significant surface noise. These anomalies are removed during preprocessing and any small holes, both those in the original scan and those created by removal of data spikes and pits (negative spikes), are filled by some form of surface interpolation process. Surface smoothing, for example with Gaussians, is often performed as a final stage of 3D data preprocessing.
3. *Fiducual point localization and pose normalization.* Holistic face recognition approaches require pose normalization so that when a feature vector is generated, specific parts of the feature vector represent properties of specific parts of the facial surface. Generally this can be done by localizing a set of three fiducial points (e.g. inner eye corners and tip of the nose), mapping them into a canonical frame and then refining the pose by registering the rigid upper face region to a 3D facial template in canonical pose, using some form of *Iterative Closest Points* (ICP) [9] variant. Note that many feature-based methods avoid this pose normalization stage as, in challenging scenarios, it is often difficult to get a sufficiently accurate normalization.
4. *Feature vector extraction.* A set of features are extracted from the refined 3D scan. These features represent the geometry of the face rather than the 2D color-texture appearance. The choice of features extracted is crucial to the system performance and is often a trade-off between invariance properties and the richness of information required for discrimination. Example 'features' include the raw depth values themselves, normals, curvatures, spin images [49], 3D adaptations of the *Scale-Invariant Feature Transform* (SIFT) descriptor [57] and many others.
5. *Facial feature vector matching/classification.* The final step of feature matching/classification is similar to any other pattern classification problem, and most, if not all, of the well-known classification techniques have been applied to 3D face recognition. Examples include k-nearest neighbors (k-NN) in various subspaces, such as those derived from PCA and LDA, neural nets, *Support Vector Machines* (SVM), *Adaboost* and many others.

8 3D Face Recognition

Chapter Outline The remainder of this chapter is structured as follows: Sect. 8.2 gives an overview of how facial surfaces are represented and visualized. More detail on these aspects can be found in Chap. 4, but the overview here keeps this chapter more self-contained. Section 8.3 gives an overview of the datasets that researchers have used to conduct comparative performance evaluations. The following section presents the types of performance evaluation that are made for both verification and recognition. Section 8.5 looks at a typical processing pipeline for a 3D face recognition system and includes face detection, spike removal, hole filling, smoothing, pose correction, resampling, feature extraction and classification. Sections 8.6 to 8.9 give a tutorial presentation of a set of well-established techniques for 3D face recognition, including ICP, holistic subspace-based methods (PCA, LDA) and curvature-based methods. Section 8.10 presents more recent state-of-the-art approaches, including annotated face models, local feature-based methods and expression-invariant 3D face recognition. Towards the end of the chapter, we present future challenges for 3D face recognition systems, conclusions, suggested further reading, and questions and exercises for the reader.

8.2 3D Face Scan Representation and Visualization

The fundamental measurement provided by most 3D cameras is a set of 3D point coordinates, $\mathbf{p}_i = [x_i, y_i, z_i]^T$, described in some defined 3D camera frame. Since we are concerned with shape, encoded by relative depths of points and not absolute depths, knowledge of the exact definition of this frame is usually unimportant. If the set of points are unordered, it is termed a *point cloud* and there is no neighborhood or surface connectivity information explicit or implicit in the representation.

In contrast, a *range image* may be generated, which is a 2D arrangement of depth (Z coordinate) values of the scene corresponding to the pixels of the image plane of the 3D sensor. A range image only retains the Z coordinates of the sensed points and the corresponding (X, Y) coordinates can be obtained from the (calibrated) camera model parameters. It is possible to convert a point cloud representation to a centrally projected range image or orthogonally projected *depth map* (see Fig. 8.1), which is similar to a range image but resampled with orthogonal projection.

Since range only is retained in a range image, the inverse is also possible only if the camera model (i.e. projection model) is given, so that the correct (X, Y) coordinates can be computed for each range image pixel.

The software of many stereo-based 3D cameras augment 3D point data with surface connectivity information and thus provide the user with a *polygonal mesh* (e.g. in the OBJ format). This makes the object scan more suitable for the purposes of rendering and processing. Mesh representations are common in computer graphics and are generated by constructing polygons from neighboring points such that each polygon is planar and simple (i.e. has non-intersecting edges). Both of these

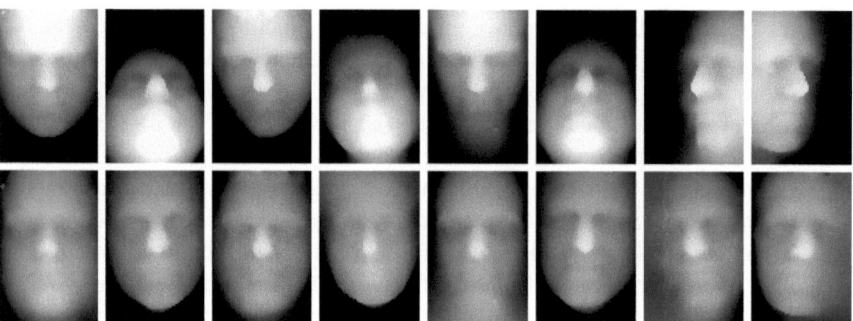

Fig. 8.1 Facial depth maps: the *top row* shows the captured pose when the subject has been asked to move their head 45 degrees relative to frontal. The rendering is the same as a range image i.e. brighter pixels are closer to the 3D camera. The *bottom row* shows resampled depth maps after a pose normalization process has been applied to the captured point cloud. Figure adapted from [72]

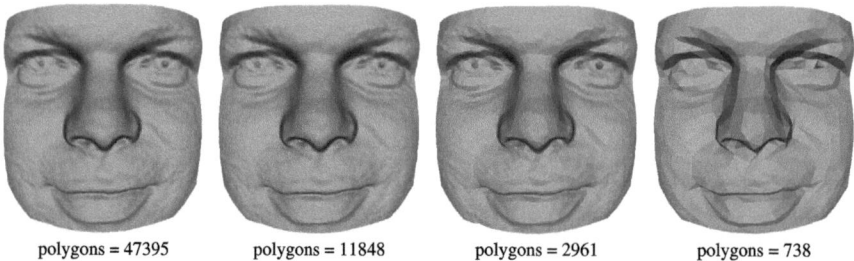

polygons = 47395   polygons = 11848   polygons = 2961   polygons = 738

Fig. 8.2 A 3D face mesh (rendered as flat shaded view in MeshLab [68]) is decimated three times using the *quadric error algorithm* [37]

constraints are always satisfied with triangles, therefore, most meshes are made of triangles only. Delaunay triangulation is a common method used to generate triangular meshes from point clouds.

Range sensors sample a surface according to their relative orientation and the perspective view of the sensor. Therefore, surfaces that are closer and orthogonal to the sensor are sampled more densely compared to surfaces that are far or oblique to the sensor. For efficient memory utilization and rendering, points/vertices from the oversampled parts of the scene are removed using mesh decimation [42]. Mesh decimation works on the principle of collapsing edges that would minimally alter the surface geometry hence the decimated mesh contains only a fraction of points/polygons and yet retains the original 3D shape. Figure 8.2 shows a sample 3D face decimated three times using the *quadric error algorithm* [37].

Polygonal models are linear approximations of surfaces with flat polygons. A more accurate mathematical representation is given by *non-uniform rational B-splines* (NURBS). In addition to having greater accuracy, a NURBS representation is also more compact compared to the polygonal representation. NURBS represent surfaces continuously in two parametric directions with the help of control points and knots. Details of NURBS and B-splines can be found in [74].

A large number of visualization tools are available for rendering and manipulating 3D data. Most are built using the *Open Graphics Library* (OpenGL) and can render point clouds, meshes, filled polygons with constant shading or texture mappings. Likewise, file formats are numerous, however, they all follow the same convention i.e. a header followed by the X, Y, Z coordinates of the point cloud and the list of polygons. The header usually contains information about the sensor, rendering parameters, the number of points and polygons and so on. The polygon list contains index numbers of points that form a polygon. A few examples of free visualization and manipulation tools are *PCL*, *MeshLab* [68], *Plyview*, *Blender* and *Scanalyze*. Proprietary softwares include *Maya*, *Rhino* and *Poser*. Online datasets of 3D faces are also on the increase and the most well-known of these are discussed in the following section.

8.3 3D Face Datasets

A range of 3D face datasets have been employed by the research community for 3D face recognition and verification evaluations. Examples with a large number (>1000) of images include

- The Face Recognition Grand Challenge v2 3D dataset (FRGC v2) [73].
- The Bosphorus 3D face dataset (Bosphorus) [13].
- The Texas 3D face recognition dataset (Texas3DFRD) [86].
- The Notre Dame 3D face dataset (ND-2006) [30].
- The Binghamton University 3D facial expression dataset(BU-3DFE) [93].
- The Chinese Academy of Sciences Institute of Automation 3D dataset (CASIA) [16].
- The University of York 3D face dataset (York3DFD) [45].

Datasets are characterized by the number of 3D face images captured, the number of subjects imaged, the quality and resolution of the images and the variations in facial pose, expression, and occlusion. Table 8.1 outlines this characterization for the datasets mentioned above.

Datasets comprising several thousand images, gathered from several hundred subjects, allow researchers to observe relatively small differences in performance in a statistically significant way. Different datasets are more or less suitable for evaluating different types of face recognition scenario. For example, a frontal view, neutral expression dataset is suitable for 'verification-of-cooperative-subject' evaluations but a dataset with pose variations, expression variations and occlusion by head accessories (such as hat and spectacles) is necessary for evaluating a typical 'identification-at-a-distance' scenario for non-cooperating subjects who may even be unaware that they are being imaged. This type of dataset is more challenging to collect as all common combinations of variations need to be covered, leading to a much larger number of captures per subject.

Table 8.1 A selection of 3D face datasets used for face recognition evaluation

Dataset	Subj.	Samp.	Size	Exp.	Pose	Occ.
FRGC v2	466	1–22	4950	Yes	No	No
Bosphorus	105	29–54	4666	Yes	Yes	Yes
Texas3DFRD	118	1–89	1149	Yes	No	No
ND-2006	888	1–63	13450	Yes	Yes	No
BU-3DFE	100	25	2500	Yes	No	No
CASIA	123	15	1845	Yes	No	No
York3DFD	350	15	5250	Yes	Yes	No

Due to space limitations, we only describe the most influential of these, the FRGC v2 3D face dataset and the Bosphorus dataset. The reader is referred to the literature references for the details of other datasets.

8.3.1 FRGC v2 3D Face Dataset

Over recent years, the *Face Recognition Grand Challenge* version 2 (FRGC v2) 3D face dataset [73] has been the most widely used dataset in benchmark face identification and verification evaluations. Many researchers use this dataset because it allows them to compare the performance of their algorithm with many others. Indeed, it has become almost expected within the research community that face recognition evaluations will include the use of this dataset, at least for the cooperating subject verification scenario.

The FRGC v2 dataset contains a 3D dataset of 4950 3D face images, where each capture contains two channels of information: a structured 3D point cloud[2] and registered color-texture image (i.e. a standard 2D image). An example of both of these channels of information, each of which has a 640 × 480 resolution, is shown in Fig. 8.3. Thus, in addition to 3D face recognition, 2D/3D multimodal recognition is supported. Results comparing 2D, 3D and multi-modal PCA-based recognition on this dataset are given in [18]. There is a direct correspondence between the 3D points in the 640 × 480 range data (abs format) and pixels in the 640 × 480 color-texture image (ppm format). The range data file is an ASCII text file, containing some header information, a 640 × 480 array of binary flags indicating where a valid range reading has been made, and the (X, Y, Z) tuples over a 640 × 480 array. Where a range flag reads invalid, each value in the tuple is set to -999999.0.

The range sensor employed collects the texture data just after the range data. This opens up the possibility of the subject moving their face slightly between these two captures and can lead to poor registration between the range and texture channels.

---

[2]3D points are structured in a rectangular array and since (x, y) values are included, strictly it is not a range image, which contains z-values only.

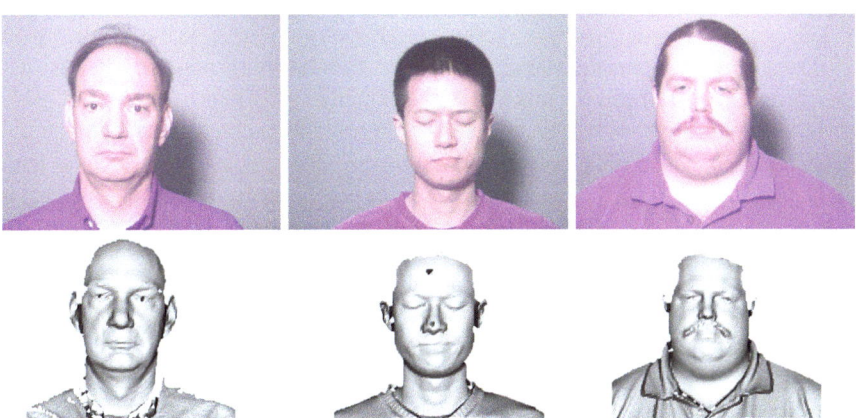

Fig. 8.3 *Top row*: 2D images reprinted from the FRGC v2 dataset [73]. *Second row*: a rendering of the corresponding 3D data, after conversion from ABS to OBJ format

Often the texture channel is used to mark up fiducial points on the face, such as eye corners, nose-tip and mouth corners, and these are then mapped onto the range data using the known, implicit registration to give 3D landmarks. In this case, and in other cases where channel registration is important, these 3D scans must not be used.

A key point in the proper evaluation of any supervised training system is that the differences between the training and testing 3D face scans must be comparable to what is expected when test data is gathered in a live operational recognition scenario. In dataset development, capturing consecutive scans of the same person leads to train/test data that is too similar for proper evaluation, hence the different collection periods of the FRGC v2 dataset, which is divided into three sections, *Spring-2003*, *Fall-2003* and *Spring-2004*, named after their periods of collection. The Spring-2003 set is regarded by Phillips et al. [73] as a training set. It consists of 943 3D face images, with subjects in a cooperating, near frontal pose and a neutral facial expression. The majority of the images in this subset are at a depth such that the neck and shoulder areas are also imaged. In contrast, a small number of the images contain close-up shots, where only the facial area is imaged. Thus the resolution of imaged facial features is higher in these scans. Also, within this training subset, ambient lighting is controlled.

In the Fall-2003 and Spring-2004 datasets, ambient lighting is uncontrolled, and facial expressions are varied. Expressions include any of anger, happiness, sadness, surprise, disgust and 'puffy cheeks', although many subjects are not scanned with the full set of these expressions. Additionally, there is less depth variation than in the Spring-2003 subset and all of the images are close ups with little shoulder area captured. Again pose can be regarded as frontal and cooperative, but there are some mild pose variations. In these data subsets there are 4007 two-channel scans of 466 subjects (1–22 scans per subject) and Phillips et al. [73] regard these as validation datasets.

The development of this dataset has made a huge contribution to the advancement of 3D face recognition algorithms. However, an interesting point to note is that pose invariance has been an often quoted advantage of 3D face recognition over 2D face recognition, and yet many recognition evaluations have been made on the FRGC dataset, which only contains the very mild pose variations associated with cooperative subjects. In non-cooperative subject face recognition applications, other datasets are needed that contain scans from a wide range of different head poses including, for example, full profile views, thus challenging the recognition system in terms of its ability to represent and match partial surfaces. One example of such a dataset is the Bosphorus dataset, which we now briefly outline.

8.3.2 The Bosphorus Dataset

The Bosphorus dataset contains 4666 3D face images of 105 subjects, with 29–54 3D captures per subject [13, 79]. Thus, compared to FRGC v2, there are fewer subjects, but there are more images per subject so that a wider variety of natural, unconstrained viewing conditions, associated with non-cooperative image capture, can be explored. There are three types of variation: expression, pose and occlusion. The standard set of 6 expressions is included, which includes happiness, surprise, fear, anger, sadness and disgust, but these are augmented with a set of more primitive expressions based on facial action units (FACS) to give 34 expressions in total. There are 14 different poses (with neutral expression) comprising 8 yaw angles, 4 pitch angles, and two combined rotations of approximately 45 degrees yaw and ± 20 degrees pitch. Finally there are up to 4 scans with occlusions, including *hand over eye*, *hand over mouth*, *spectacles* and *hair over face*.

The data is captured with an *Inspeck Mega Capturor II 3D* camera. Subjects sit at around 1.5 m from the camera and (X, Y, Z) resolution is 0.3 mm, 0.3 mm, 0.4 mm for each of these dimensions respectively. The associated color-texture images are 1600×1200 pixels. Example captures from the Bosphorus dataset, which are stored as structured depth maps, are shown in Fig. 8.4. Registration with an associated 2D image is stored as two arrays of texture coordinates. More details of capture conditions can be found in [79].

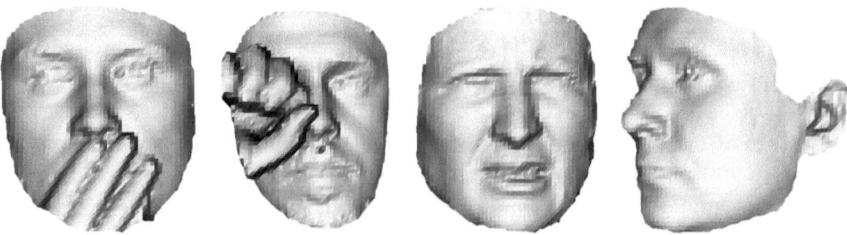

Fig. 8.4 Example 3D scans from the Bosphorus dataset with occlusions, expression variations and pose variations [13, 79]. Figure adapted from [25]

8.4 3D Face Recognition Evaluation

The evaluation of a 3D face recognition system depends on the application that it is intended for. In general, a face recognition system operates in either a *verification* application, which requires one-to-one matching, or an *identification* application, which requires one-to-many matching. We discuss each of these in turn in the following subsections.

8.4.1 Face Verification

In a verification application, the face recognition system must supply a binary *accept* or *reject* decision, as a response to the subject's claimed identity, associated with one of a stored set of *gallery* scans. It does this by generating a match score between the captured 3D data (the *probe* or *query*) and the gallery data of the subject's claimed identity. Often this is implemented as a distance metric between feature vectors, such as the Euclidean distance, cosine distance or Mahalanobis distance (in the case of multiple images of the same person in the gallery). A low score on the distance metric indicates a close match and application of a suitable threshold generates the accept/reject decision. Verification systems are mainly used by authorized individuals, who want to gain their rightful access to a building or computer system. Consequently, they will be cooperative when adopting a neutral expression and frontal pose at favorable distance from the camera. For cooperative scenarios, datasets such as FRGC v2 provide suitable training and validation datasets to perform verification tests.

In order to evaluate a verification system, a large number of verification tests need to be performed, where the subject's identity associated with the test 3D capture is known, so that it can be established whether the accept/reject decision was correct. This identity can be extracted from the filename of a 3D face capture within a dataset by means of a unique subject identifier.

A key point is that the accept/reject decision is threshold dependent and it is desirable to explore the system performance over a wide range of such thresholds. Given that a set of 3D face scans is available, all with known identities, and there are at least two scans of each subject, we now describe a way of implementing this. Every image in the set is compared with every other, excluding itself, and a match score is formed. Two lists are then formed, one containing matches of the same subject identity and the other containing matches of different subjects. We then vary the threshold from zero so that all decisions are reject, to the maximum score value, so that all decisions are accept. For each threshold value, we examine the two lists and count the number of *reject* decisions from the *same identity* (SI) list to form a *false rejection rate* (FRR) as a percentage of the SI list size and we count the number of *accept* decisions in the *different identity* (DI) list to form a *false acceptance rate* (FAR) as a percentage of the DI list size. Ideally both FAR and FRR would be both zero and this describes a perfect system performance. However, in reality, verification systems are not perfect and both *false accepts* and *false rejects* exist. False accepts can be reduced by decreasing the threshold but this increases false rejects and vice-versa. A *receiver operating characteristic* or ROC curve, as defined in biometric verification tests, is a plot of FRR against FAR for all thresholds, thus giving a visualization of the tradeoff between these two performance metrics. Depending on the dataset size and the number of scans per person, the SI and DI list sizes can be very different, with DI usually much larger than SI. This has the implication that values on the FRR axis are noisier than on the FAR axis.

In order to measure system performance using a ROC curve we can use the concept of an *equal error rate* (EER), where $FAR = FRR$, and a lower value indicates a better performance for a given face verification system. Given that a false accept is often a worse decision with a higher penalty than a false reject, it is common practise to set a suitably low FAR and then performance is indicated by either the FRR, the lower the better, or the *true accept rate*, $TAR = 1 - FRR$, the higher the better. TAR is commonly known as the *verification rate* and is often expressed as a percentage. In FRGC benchmark verification tests this FAR is set at 0.001 (0.1 %).

At the time of writing, high performance 3D face recognition systems are reporting verification rates that typically range from around 96.5 % to 98.5 % (to the nearest half percent) at 0.1 % FAR on the full FRGC v2 dataset [51, 64, 76]. This is a significant performance improvement of around 20 % on PCA-based baseline results [71]. It is reasonable to assume that, in many verification scenarios, the subject will be cooperating with a neutral expression. Verification rates for probes with neutral expressions only range from around 98.5 % to 99.5 % [51, 64] at 0.1 % FAR.

8.4.2 Face Identification

In face identification, the probe (query) 3D capture is matched to a stored gallery of 3D captures ('models'), with known identifier labels, and a set of matching scores is generated. Thus identification requires a *one-to-many* match process in contrast to verification's *one-to-one* match. The match with the highest match score (or, equivalently, lowest distance metric) provides the identity of the probe. If the closest match is not close enough by application of some threshold, the system may return a null response, indicating that the probe does not match to any subject in the gallery. This is a more difficult problem than verification, since, if there are 1000 subjects in the gallery, the system has to provide the correct response in 1001 possible responses (including the null response).

In order to test how good a 3D face recognition system is at identification, a large number of identification tests are performed, with no 3D model being compared to itself, and we determine the percentage of correct identifications. This gives the *rank-1 identification rate*, which means that the match is taken as the best (rank-1) score achieved when matching to the gallery. However, we can imagine real-world identification scenarios where the rank-1 identification test is too severe and where we may be interested in a wider performance metric. One such scenario is the *watch list*, where 3D models of a small number of known criminals may be stored in the

8 3D Face Recognition

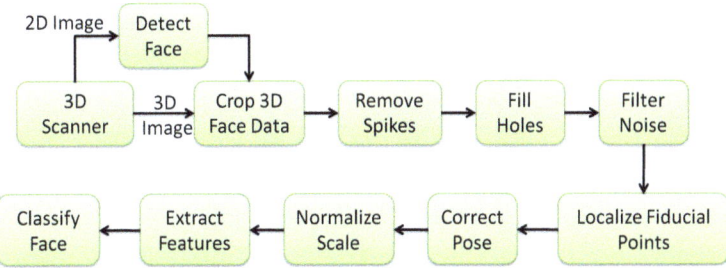

Fig. 8.5 Block diagram showing typical processing steps in a 3D face recognition system. There are several possible reorderings of this pipeline, depending on the input data quality and the performance priorities of the application

gallery, along with a larger set of the general public. If a probe matches reasonably well to any one of these criminal identities, such that the match score is ranked in the top ten, then this can trigger an alarm for a manual inspection of the probe image and top 10 gallery matches. In this case the *rank-10 identification rate* is important.

In practice, curves are generated by recording the rank of the correct match and then counting the percentage of identifications that are less than or equal to r, where r is the allowable rank. The allowable rank starts at 1 and is incremented until 100 % recognition is attained for some r, or the graph may be terminated before then, for example $r = 100$. Plotting such a *Cumulative Match Curve* (CMC) of percentage identification against rank allows us to compare systems at a range of possible operating points, although rank-1 identification is the most important of these.

At the time of writing, high performance 3D face recognition systems are reporting rank-1 identification rates that typically range from around 96 % to 98.5 % [51, 64, 76] on the FRGC v2 3D face dataset. We note that the FRGC v2 3D face dataset does not contain significant pose variations and performance of identification systems may fall as more challenging large scale datasets are developed that do contain such variations.

8.5 Processing Stages in 3D Face Recognition

When developing a 3D face recognition system, one has to understand what information is provided from the camera or from the dataset, what format it is presented in and what imperfections are likely to exist. The raw data obtained from even the most accurate scanners is imperfect as it contains spikes, holes and noise. Preprocessing stages are usually tailored to the form and quality of this raw data. Often, the face scans must be normalized with respect to pose (e.g. holistic approaches) and spatial sampling before extracting features for 3D face recognition. Although the 3D face processing pipeline shown in Fig. 8.5 is typical, many variations on this exist;

in particular, there are some possible reorderings and not all of the preprocessing and pose normalization stages are always necessary. With this understanding, we discuss all of the stages of the pipeline in the following subsections.

8.5.1 Face Detection and Segmentation

Images acquired with a 3D sensor usually contain a larger area than just the face area and it is often desirable to segment and crop this extraneous data as early as possible in the processing pipeline in order to speed up processing in the downstream sections of the pipeline. This face detection and cropping process, which yields 3D face segmentation, can be done on the basis of the camera's 3D range data, 2D texture image or a combination of both.

In the case of 2D images, face detection is a mature field (particularly for frontal poses) and popular approaches include skin detection, face templates, eigenfaces, neural networks, support vector machines and hidden Markov models. A survey of face detection in images is given by Yang et al. [92]. A seminal approach for real-time face detection by Viola and Jones [88] is based on Haar wavelets and adaptive boosting (Adaboost) and is part of the *Open Computer Vision* (OpenCV) library.

However, some face recognition systems prefer not to rely on the existence of a 2D texture channel in the 3D camera data and crop the face on the basis of 3D information only. Also use of 3D information is sometimes preferred for a more accurate localization of the face. If some pose assumptions are made, it is possible to apply some very basic techniques. For example, one could take the upper most vertex (largest y value), assume that this is near to the top of the head and crop a sufficient distance downwards from this point to include the largest faces likely to be encountered. Note that this can fail if the upper most vertex is on a hat, other head accessory, or some types of hair style. Alternatively, for co-operative subjects in frontal poses, one can make the assumption that the nose tip is the closest point to the camera and crop a spherical region around this point to segment the facial area. However, the chin, forehead or hair is occasionally closer. Thus, particularly in the presence of depth spikes, this kind of approach can fail and it may be better to move the cropping process further down the processing pipeline so that it is after a spike filtering stage.

If the system's computational power is such that it is acceptable to move cropping even further down the pipeline, more sophisticated cropping approaches can be applied, which could be based on facial feature localization and some of the techniques described earlier for 2D face detection. The nose is perhaps the most prominent feature that has been used alone [64], or in combination with the inner eye corners, for face region segmentation [22]. The latter approach uses the principal curvatures to detect the nose and eyes. The candidate triplet is then used by a PCA-based classifier for face detection.

8.5.2 Removal of Spikes

Spikes are caused mainly by specular regions. In the case of faces, the eyes, nose tip and teeth are three main regions where spikes are likely to occur. The eye lens sometimes forms a real image in front of the face causing a positive spike. Similarly, the specular reflection from the eye forms an image of the laser behind the eye causing a negative spike. Shiny teeth seem to be bulging out in 3D scans and a small spike can sometimes form on top of the nose tip. Glossy facial makeup or oily skin can also cause spikes at other regions of the face. In medical applications such as craniofacial anthropometry, the face is powdered to make its surface Lambertian and the teeth are painted before scanning. Some scanners like the Swiss Ranger [84] also gives a confidence map along with the range and grayscale image. Removing points with low confidence will generally remove spikes but will result in larger regions of missing data as points that are not spikes may also be removed. Spike detection works on the principle that surfaces, and faces in particular, are generally smooth.

One simple approach to filtering spikes is to examine a small neighborhood for each point in the mesh or range image and replace its depth (Z-coordinate value) by the median of this small neighborhood. This is a standard *median filter* which, although effective, can attenuate fine surface detail. Another approach is to threshold the absolute difference between the point's depth and the median of the depths of its neighbors. Only if the threshold is exceeded is the point's depth replaced with the median, or deleted to be filled later by a more sophisticated scheme. These approaches work well in high resolution data, but in sufficiently low resolution data, problems may occur when the facial surface is steep relative to the viewing angle, such as the sides of the nose in frontal views. In this case, we can detect spikes relative to the local surface orientation, but this requires that surface normals are computed, which are corrupted by the spikes. It is possible to adopt an iterative procedure where surface normals are computed and spikes removed in cycles, yielding a clean, uncorrupted set of surface normals even for relatively low resolution data [72]. Although this works well for training data, where processing time is non-critical, it may be too computationally expensive for live test data.

8.5.3 Filling of Holes and Missing Data

In addition to the holes resulting from spike removal, the 3D data contains many other missing points due to occlusions, such as the nose occluding the cheek when, for example, the head pose is sufficiently rotated (in yaw angle) relative to the 3D camera. Obviously, such areas of the scene that are not visible to either the camera or the projected light can not be acquired. Similarly, dark regions which do not reflect sufficient projected light are not sensed by the 3D camera. Both can cause large regions of missing data, which are often referred to as *missing parts*.

In the case of cooperative subject applications (e.g. a typical verification application) frontal face images are acquired and occlusion is not a major issue. However, dark regions such as the eyebrows and facial hair are usually not acquired. Moreover, for laser-based projection, power cannot be increased to acquire dark regions of the face due to eye-safety reasons.

Thus the only option is to fill the missing regions using an interpolation technique such as nearest neighbor, linear or polynomial. For small holes, linear interpolation gives reasonable results however, bicubic interpolation has shown to give better results [64]. Alternatively one can use implicit surface representations for interpolation, such as those provided by radial basis functions [72].

For larger size holes, symmetry or PCA based approaches can be used, although these require a localized symmetry plane and a full 6-DOF rigid alignment respectively, and hence would have to be moved further downstream in the processing pipeline. Alternatively, a model-based approach can be used to morph a model until it gives the best fit to the data points [95]. This approach learns the 3D face space offline and requires a significantly large training data in order to generalize to unseen faces. However, it may be very useful if the face being scanned was previously seen and obviously this is a common scenario in 3D face recognition.

For better generalization to unseen faces, an anthropometrically correct [32] *annotated face model* (AFM) [51] is used. The AFM is based on an average 3D face constructed using statistical data and the anthropometric landmarks are associated with its vertices. The AFM is then fitted to the raw data from the scanner using a deformable model framework. Blanz et al. [12] also used a morphable model to fit the 3D scan, filling up missing regions in addition to other preprocessing steps, in a unified framework.

8.5.4 Removal of Noise

For face scans acquired by laser scanners, noise can be attributed to optical components such as the lens and the mirror, or mechanical components which drive the mirror, or the CCD itself. Scanning and imaging conditions such as ambient light, laser intensity, surface orientation, texture, and distance from the scanner can also affect the noise levels in the scanner. Sun et al. [89] give a detailed analysis of noise in the Minolta Vivid scanner and noise in active sensors is discussed in detail in Chap. 3 of this book.

We have already mentioned the median filter as a mechanism for spike (impulsive noise) removal. More difficult is the removal of surface noise, which is less differentiated from the underlying object geometry, without removing fine surface detail or generally distorting the underlying shape, for example, from volumetric shrinkage. Clearly, there is a tradeoff to be made and an optimal level of filtering is sought in order to give the best recognition performance. Removal of surface noise is particularly important as a preprocessing step in some methods of extraction of the differential properties of the surface, such as normals and curvatures.

If the 3D data is in range image or depth map form, there are many methods available from the standard 2D image filtering domain, such as convolution with

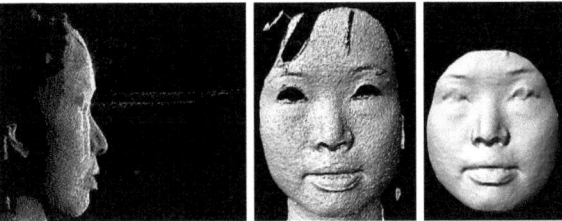

Fig. 8.6 From left to right. A 3D capture of a face with spikes in the point cloud. *Shaded* view with holes and noise. Final preprocessed 3D data after cropping, removal of spikes, hole filling and noise removal. Figure courtesy of [64]

Gaussian filters. Many of these methods have been adapted so that they can be applied to 3D meshes. One example of this is *Bilateral Mesh Denoising* [35], which is based on shifting mesh vertices along their normal directions.

Figure 8.6 shows a face scan with spikes, holes and noise before and after preprocessing.

8.5.5 Fiducial Point Localization and Pose Correction

The pose of different subjects or the same subject can vary between scans even when they are cooperative. Therefore, pose correction is a necessary preprocessing step for holistic approaches that require normalized resampling of the facial surface in order to generate a feature vector. (Such feature vectors are often subsequently mapped into a subspace; for example, in PCA and LDA-based methods described later.) This may also be necessary for other algorithms which rely on features that are not inherently pose-invariant.

A common approach to pose correction uses fiducial points on the 3D face. Three points are necessary to normalize the pose to a canonical form. Often these points are manually identified, however, automatic detection of such points is desirable particularly for online verification and identification processes.

The shape index, derived from principle curvatures, has been used to automatically detect the inside eye corners and the nose tip for facial pose correction [59]. Although, a minimum of three fiducial points are sufficient to correct the pose, it has proved a challenging research problem to detect these points, where all three are identified correctly and localized with high repeatability. This problem is more difficult in the presence of varying facial expression, which can change the local shape around a point. Worse still, as pose changes, one of the three fiducial points selected may become occluded. For example, the nose bridge occludes an inner eye corner as the head is turned from frontal view towards a profile view. To counter this, some approaches have attempted to extract a large number of fiducial points so that three or more are always visible [24].

In addition to a shape scan, most 3D cameras capture a registered color-texture map of the face (i.e. a standard 2D image, where the color associated with each 3D point is known). Fiducial point detection can be performed on the basis of 2D images or both 2D and 3D images. Gupta et al. [41] detected 10 anthropometric fiducial points to calculate cranio-facial proportions [32]. Three points were detected using the 3D face alone and the rest were detected based on 2D and 3D data. Mian et al. [64] performed pose correction based on a single point, the nose tip, which is automatically detected. The 3D face was cropped using a sphere of fixed radius centered at the nose tip and its pose was then corrected by iteratively applying PCA and resampling the face on a uniform grid. This process also filled the holes (due to self occlusions) that were exposed during pose correction. Pears et al. [72] performed pose correction by detecting the nose tip using pose invariant features based on the spherical sampling of a radial basis function (RBF) representation of the facial surface. Another sphere centered on the nose tip intersected the facial surface and the tangential curvature of this space curve was used in a correlation scheme to normalize facial pose. The interpolating properties of RBF representations gave all steps in this approach a good immunity to missing parts, although some steps in the method are computationally expensive.

Another common pose correction approach is to register all 3D faces to a common reference face using the *Iterative Closest Points* (ICP) algorithm [9]. The reference is usually an average face model, in canonical pose, calculated from training data. Sometimes only the rigid parts of the face are used in this face model, such as upper face area containing nose, eyes and forehead. ICP can find the optimal registration only if the two surfaces are already approximately registered. Therefore, the query face is first coarsely aligned with the reference face, either by zero-meaning both scans or using fiducial points, before applying ICP to refine the registration [59]. In refining pose, ICP establishes correspondences between the closest points of the two surfaces and calculates the rigid transformation (rotation and translation) that minimizes the mean-squared distance between the corresponding points. These two steps are repeated until the change in mean-squared error falls below a threshold or the maximum number of iterations is reached. In case of registering a probe face to an average face, the surfaces are dissimilar. Hence, there may be more than one comparable local minima and ICP may converge to a different minimum each time a query face is registered to the reference face. The success of ICP depends upon the initial coarse registration and the similarity between the two surfaces.

As a final note on pose correction, Blanz et al. [12] used a morphable model in a unified framework to simultaneously optimize pose, shape, texture, and illumination. The algorithm relies on manual identification of seven fiducial points and uses the Phong lighting model [6] to optimize shape, texture and illumination (in addition to pose) which can be used for face recognition. This algorithm would be an expensive choice if only pose correction is the aim and it is not fully automatic.

8.5.6 Spatial Resampling

Unlike 2D images, 3D scans have an absolute scale, which means that the distance between any two fiducial points (landmarks), such as the inner corners of the eye, can be measured in absolute units (e.g. millimeters). Thus scanning the same face from near or far will only alter the spatial sampling rate and the measured distance between landmarks should vary very little, at least in scans of reasonable quality and resolution.

However, many face recognition algorithms require the face surface, or parts of the face surface, to be sampled in a uniform fashion, which requires some form of *spatial sampling normalization* or *spatial resampling* via an interpolation process. Basic interpolation processes usually involve some weighted average of neighbors, while more sophisticated schemes employ various forms of implicit or explicit surface fitting.

Assuming that we have normalized the pose of the face (or facial part), we can place a standard 2D resampling grid in the x, y plane (for example, it could be centered on the nose-tip) and resample the facial surface depth orthogonally to generate a resampled depth map. In many face recognition schemes, a standard size feature vector needs to be created and the standard resampling grid of size $p \times q = m$ creates this. For example, in [64], all 3D faces were sampled on a uniform x, y grid of 161×161 where the planar distance between adjacent pixels was 1 mm. Although the sampling rate was uniform in this case, subjects had a different number of points sampled on their faces, because of their different facial sizes. The resampling scheme employed cubic interpolation. In another approach, Pears et al. [72] used RBFs as implicit surface representations in order to resample 3D face scans.

An alternative way of resampling is to identify three non-collinear fiducial points on each scan and resample it such that the number of sample points between the fiducial points is constant. However, in doing this, we are discarding information contained within the absolute scale of the face, which often is useful for subject discrimination.

8.5.7 Feature Extraction on Facial Surfaces

Depth maps may not be the ideal representations for 3D face recognition because they are quite sensitive to pose. Although the pose of 3D faces can be normalized with better accuracy compared to 2D images, the normalization is never perfect. For this reason it is usually preferable to extract features that are less sensitive to pose before applying holistic approaches. The choice of features extracted is crucial to the system performance and is often a trade-off between invariance properties and the richness of information required for discrimination. Example 'features' include the raw depth values themselves, normals, curvatures, spin images [49], 3D adaptations of the *Scale-Invariant Feature Transform* (SIFT) descriptor [57] and many others. More detail on features can be found in Chaps. 5 and 7.

8.5.8 Classifiers for 3D Face Matching

In the large array of published 3D face recognition work, all of the well-known classification schemes have been applied by various researchers. These include k-nearest neighbors (k-NN) in various subspaces, such as those derived from PCA and LDA, neural nets, Support Vector Machines (SVM), Adaboost and many others. The choice (type, complexity) of classifier employed is related to the separation of subjects (classes) within their feature space. Good face recognition performance depends on choosing a classifier that fits the separation of the training data well without overfitting and hence generalizes well to unseen 3D face scans, either within testing or in a live operational system.

Pattern classification is a huge subject in its own right and we can only detail a selection of the possible techniques in this chapter. We refer the reader to the many excellent texts on the subject, for example [10, 28].

8.6 ICP-Based 3D Face Recognition

In this section and the following three sections, we will present a set of well-established approaches to 3D face recognition, with a more tutorial style of presentation. The aim is to give the reader a solid grounding before going on to more modern and more advanced techniques that have better performance. We will highlight the strengths and limitations of each technique and present clear implementation details.

One of the earliest algorithms employed for matching surfaces is the *iterative closest points* (ICP) algorithm [9], which aims to iteratively minimize the mean square error between two point sets. In brief, ICP has three basic operations is its iteration loop, as follows.

1. Find pairs of closest points between two point clouds (i.e. probe and gallery face scans).
2. Use these *putative* correspondences to determine a rigid 6-DOF Euclidean transformation that moves one point cloud closer to the other.
3. Apply the rigid transformation to the appropriate point cloud.

The procedure is repeated until the change in mean square error associated with the correspondences falls below some threshold, or the maximum number of iterations is reached. In the context of 3D face recognition, the remaining mean square error then can be used as a matching metric.

Due to its simplicity, ICP has been popular for rigid surface registration and 3D object recognition and many variants and extensions of ICP have been proposed in the literature [77]. Readers interested in a detailed description of ICP variants are referred to Chap. 6 of this book, which discusses ICP extensively in the context of surface registration.

Here, we will give a presentation in the context of 3D face recognition. Surface registration and matching are similar procedures except that, in the latter case, we are only interested in the final registration error between the two surfaces. A fuller and more formal outline of ICP is presented in the following subsection.

8.6.1 ICP Outline

Let $\mathbf{p}_j = [x_j\ y_j\ z_j]^T$ where $j = 1\ldots M$ be a zero-mean set of 3D points of a probe face scan and let $\mathbf{g}_i = [x_i\ y_i\ z_i]^T$ where $i = 1\ldots N$ be a zero-mean set of 3D points of a gallery face scan. Since both point clouds are zero mean, they have an implicit coarse translational alignment. An initial coarse orientation alignment *may* also be required to avoid convergence to a local minimum but, for now, we will assume that it is not required and we will discuss this issue later.

We can stack the points in $M \times 3$ and $N \times 3$ data matrices to give:

$$\mathsf{P} = \begin{bmatrix} \mathbf{p}_1^T \\ \vdots \\ \mathbf{p}_M^T \end{bmatrix}, \quad \mathsf{G} = \begin{bmatrix} \mathbf{g}_1^T \\ \vdots \\ \mathbf{g}_N^T \end{bmatrix}. \tag{8.1}$$

Let F be a function that, for each point in P, finds the nearest point in G:

$$(\mathbf{c}, \mathbf{d}) = F(\mathsf{P}, \mathsf{G}), \tag{8.2}$$

where $\mathbf{c}$ and $\mathbf{d}$ are vectors of size M each, such that $\mathbf{c}$ and $\mathbf{d}$ contain, respectively, the index number and distance of the jth point of P to its nearest point in G. This is called the *closest points* step where the pairs of closest points within the two point clouds are assigned as *tentative correspondences*. (We use the word *tentative* because they are not accurate correspondences until ICP has converged to the correct global minimum.) This is the most critical and computationally the most expensive step of the algorithm. It is critical because highly inaccurate tentative correspondences could, in the worst case, cause ICP convergence to a local minimum. Even if this is not the case, they will affect the accuracy of the final registration and hence the matching metric between the two point clouds. Typically, the following filters are applied to minimize these effects:

1. Tentative correspondences whose distance is greater than a threshold are removed. The threshold is usually chosen as a multiple of the point cloud resolution which is initially set relatively high, depending on the quality of the initial registration. It is then gradually reduced through the iterations until it is equal to the resolution.
2. Tentative correspondences whose surface normals have a mutual angle above a threshold are removed. The threshold is chosen based on the accuracy of the normals and the quality of the initial registration. Also, it is possible to reduce this threshold through the iterations.
3. Tentative correspondences at the boundary points are avoided. This step is useful when the two point clouds only partially overlap, as occurs with partial views of the probe face.

4. Sometimes additional information such as texture is also used to remove poor quality tentative correspondences.

To speed up the search for nearest points within the gallery scan, the points in each gallery scan are arranged in a k-d tree (see Chap. 4) and these structures are precomputed offline. A further speed up can be achieved by storing the index of the nearest neighbor from the centers of a set of voxels in a voxelized space around the gallery scan [91]. Again this can be precomputed offline. (Note that the ICP technique based on Levenberg-Marquardt minimization [34], described in Chap. 6, also uses a pre-computed distance transform.)

Let $\mathbf{p}_k = [x_k\ y_k\ z_k]^T$ and $\mathbf{g}_k = [x_k\ y_k\ z_k]^T$ (where $k = 1 \ldots m$) be the remaining m corresponding pairs of points of the probe and gallery face respectively. The next step is to find the rotation matrix R and translation vector $\mathbf{t}$ that minimizes the mean square error (MSE) between these tentative correspondences. The error to be minimized is given by:

$$e = \frac{1}{m} \sum_{k=1}^{m} \|\mathsf{R}\mathbf{p}_k + \mathbf{t} - \mathbf{g}_k\|^2. \tag{8.3}$$

The unknowns (R and $\mathbf{t}$) in Eq. (8.3) can be calculated using a number of approaches including *quaternion* methods and *Singular Value Decomposition* (SVD). We will give details of the widely-used SVD approach [7]. The means of $\mathbf{p}_k$ and $\mathbf{g}_k$ are given by

$$\bar{\mathbf{p}} = \frac{1}{m} \sum_{k=1}^{m} \mathbf{p}_k \tag{8.4}$$

$$\bar{\mathbf{g}} = \frac{1}{m} \sum_{k=1}^{m} \mathbf{g}_k \tag{8.5}$$

and the cross-covariance matrix C is given by the mean of outer products:

$$\mathsf{C} = \frac{1}{m} \sum_{k=1}^{m} (\mathbf{p}_k - \bar{\mathbf{p}})(\mathbf{g}_k - \bar{\mathbf{g}})^T. \tag{8.6}$$

Equivalently, this can be expressed as:

$$\mathsf{C} = \frac{1}{m} \mathsf{P}_m^T \mathsf{G}_m, \tag{8.7}$$

where $\mathsf{P}_m, \mathsf{G}_m$ are the zero-centered data matrices in Eq. (8.1) trimmed to $m \times 3$ matrices of m tentative correspondences. Performing the SVD of C gives us:

$$\mathsf{USV}^T = \mathsf{C}, \tag{8.8}$$

where U and V are two orthogonal matrices and S is a diagonal matrix of singular values. The rotation matrix R can be calculated from the orthogonal matrices as [7]:

$$\mathsf{R} = \mathsf{VU}^T. \tag{8.9}$$

Note that if this is indeed a rotation matrix, then det(R) = +1. However, in principle, it is possible to obtain det(R) = −1, which corresponds to a reflection. This degeneracy is not what we want but, according to Arun et al. [7] and in our own experience, it usually does not occur. Once the rotation matrix has been computed, the translation vector **t** can be calculated as:

$$\mathbf{t} = \bar{\mathbf{g}} - R\bar{\mathbf{p}}. \tag{8.10}$$

Then the original point cloud of the probe face is transformed as:

$$P'^T = RP^T + \mathbf{t}J_{1,n}, \tag{8.11}$$

where $J_{1,n}$ is a $1 \times n$ matrix of ones.

Subsequently, tentative correspondences are established again between the transformed probe face and the gallery face (Eq. (8.2)). This process is iterated until e approaches a minimum value, detected by its change over one iteration falling below some threshold. If the initial coarse alignment is within the convergence zone of the global minimum MSE, the final value of e is a good measure of the similarity between two face scans, where smaller values of e mean that the faces are more similar. In identification scenarios, the probe face is matched with every gallery face and the identity of the one with the minimum value of e is declared as the probe's identity. If two gallery identities have very similar low e values, sometimes the number of correspondences, m, in the final iteration can also be used to make a better judgement. Alternatively, a probe can be verified against a claimed gallery identity if the computed value of e falls below some appropriate threshold.

8.6.2 A Critical Discussion of ICP

The main advantage of the ICP algorithm is that it iteratively corrects registration errors as it matches two faces, provided that the initial alignment of the surfaces is within the zone of convergence of the global minimum. If the initial coarse registration is not good enough ICP can converge to a local minimum and hence the algorithm fails. Iterative realignment comes at a heavy computational cost, particularly in the establishment of closest points. For this step, a basic search has complexity $O(MN)$, where M and N are the number of points in the probe and gallery scans respectively. This is reduced to $O(M \log N)$ when using k-d tree structures for the closest points search in the gallery scans. It is important to remember that the average time per gallery scan match is also scaled by the average number of iterations per match which is often different for different ICP variants.

Another disadvantage of ICP is that it does not extract features from the face, thus ruling out the possibilities of training classifiers on multiple instances of a face, and ruling out indexing of features from gallery faces for faster matching or feature-level fusion. Thus, the probe must be matched to the complete gallery, thereby making the recognition time linear to the gallery size. This means that, in relation to scan resolution and gallery size, N_G, a single ICP-based probe to gallery match has overall complexity $O(N_G M \log N)$.

As a consequence of this, many variants of ICP try to reduce the face scan match time. Coarse to fine resolution schemes can be used and we can precompute as many aspects of the algorithm as possible on the whole gallery in an offline batch process. Examples include extracting fiducial points for coarse registration, cropping to spherical volumes relative to the nose tip, building k-d trees and placing the galley scans in voxel structures for fast look up of closest points.

The ICP algorithm can accurately match rigid surfaces. However, faces are not rigid and the facial surface can significantly deform due to expressions. Consequently, the performance of standard ICP degrades under facial expressions. For example, one study cropped the 3D face region manually and then applied standard ICP for neutral and non-neutral subsets of the FRGC dataset for a rank-1 recognition test. The neutral dataset gave an average result of 91 % while the non-neutral subset was only 61.5 % [19].

However, a second advantage of ICP is that it can operate in partial surface matching schemes. Thus the problem of facial expressions can be significantly mitigated by applying ICP to the relatively rigid regions of the face [19, 64], which can be identified in the gallery scans in an offline batch process. The ability to do partial matching also allows ICP to handle pose variations by matching 2.5D scans to complete face models [59]. In the case of large pose variations, coarse prealignment using fiducial points (landmarks) may be necessary.

8.6.3 A Typical ICP-Based 3D Face Recognition Implementation

We now outline typical steps involved in a standard ICP-based 3D face recognition application. This is intended as a guide on how to implement and start using this approach, but please note that there are many variants of this algorithm available in the literature. A MATLAB implementation of ICP can be downloaded and adapted as necessary from [63].

We assume that the probe and gallery faces are near-frontal in pose. Some minor pose variations are allowable, such as is found in the FRGC v2 dataset and as might be seen in a typical cooperative verification application. Padia and Pears [69] show that, when registering a 3D face scan to an average face model, ICP converges to the correct global minimum for an initial misalignment between the scans of at least 30 degrees in any of three orthogonal rotational axes. We preprocess each gallery scan, according to the steps below.

1. Determine the closest vertex to the camera. In most reasonable quality scans, this will be close to the nose-tip. (Occasionally, the chin, lips or forehead can be closest to the camera and, in a first implementation, a quick visual check may be required so that the nose tip can be selected manually for these failure cases.)
2. Crop to a spherical region of radius 100 mm around this point. For smaller faces this may include some neck and hair area.
3. Filter spikes and interpolate over any holes.

8 3D Face Recognition

4. Compute the mean of the point cloud and perform a zero-mean operation (i.e. subtract the mean from each vertex).
5. Use an off-the-shelf algorithm to organize each gallery scan into a k-d tree. Many are publicly available on the web.

For each probe scan to be matched to the gallery, we follow the steps below.

1. Perform the processing steps 1–4 described for the gallery scans above. Given that both probe and gallery face scans are now zero-mean, this constitutes an initial coarse translational alignment.
2. Use a standard off-the-shelf algorithm to perform a closest-point search in the k-d tree of the gallery scan, for each point in the probe scan.
3. Delete tentative correspondences according to the filters given in the earlier 4-point list. (Use the distance and surface normal filters, at least.)
4. From the tentative correspondences, form the cross-covariance matrix using Eq. (8.7). (Note that the means used for this matrix are associated with the list of filtered tentative correspondences, not the full scans.)
5. Perform SVD on the cross-covariance matrix and hence extract the rotation matrix, **R**, according to Eq. (8.9).
6. Compute the translation, **t** using Eq. (8.10).
7. Update the alignment of the probe scan with the gallery scan using Eq. (8.11).
8. Compute e and, unless on first iteration, determine the change in e from the previous iteration. If this is below a threshold, or if the maximum number of iterations has been reached, finish. Otherwise go to step 2.

The smallest final value of e is used to determine the best match in the gallery for a rank-1 identification, although if e is not sufficiently low, it could be determined that the probe subject is not present in the gallery. Alternatively, the e value could be determined from a single gallery face scan match and thresholded in a verification test against a claimed gallery identity.

Once this basic implementation described above is operational, there are several immediate improvements that can be made. For those readers that want to improve the implementation, we suggest the following.

- The final number of correspondences may vary and this number may be included, along with e, in a cost function in order to make the verification or identification decision. (i.e. A slightly higher e value could be preferable if it is accompanied by a significantly higher number of correspondences.)
- Particularly for large datasets where a fast per-scan match is required, it is preferable to construct a voxel space around the gallery scans where, for the center of each voxel, the index of the nearest gallery surface point is stored. This means that for some probe point, we determine the voxel that it lies in and we just look up the corresponding gallery surface point [91].

When dealing with large pose variations of the probe, such as may be encountered in a non-cooperating subject identification scenario, more sophisticated techniques than the above are required. The cropping of the probe based on the nose-tip being the nearest point to the camera will often fail and, in profile views, the nose tip will often not be detected by many current methods. Worse still, the probe will often be outside of the global minimum convergence zone of the near frontal gallery scan poses. To deal with these scenarios, techniques are needed to extract three fiducial points (landmarks) on the probe scans when they are in an arbitrary pose. Then, if a sufficiently wide range of these fiducial points is precomputed on the gallery scans, an initial coarse pose registration is possible. However, reliable landmarking of 3D face scans in arbitrary poses is not trivial and is a focus of current research. For example Creusot et al. [24] extract keypoints on 3D face scans and then label them from a set of fourteen possible labels [23].

8.6.4 ICP Variants and Other Surface Registration Approaches

Medioni and Waupotitsch [67] used a variant of ICP for 3D face recognition. Unlike other techniques, they acquired the face data using passive stereo. Maurer et al. [61] report the recognition performance of Geometrix AcitiveID^{TM} which uses ICP for 3D face recognition. Lu et al. [59] used *shape index* features along with some anchor points to perform an initial coarse registration of the faces which was later refined with ICP. They matched partial 2.5D scans to 3D face models in order to deal with large pose variations.

Chang et al. [19] proposed an *adaptive rigid multiregion selection* (ARMS) approach for ICP-based 3D face recognition. They automatically locate the inner eye corners, nose tip, and bridge of the nose based on mean and Gaussian curvatures. These landmarks are used to define an elliptical region around the nose of the gallery face. For a probe face, these landmarks are used to define multiple overlapping surface regions, which are individually matched to the gallery face using ICP and the results are combined. The results of Chang et al. show that using smaller regions around the nose can result in better recognition performance. A cross comparison of their ARMS approach with standard approaches on the FRGC v2 dataset gave a rank-1 performance of 97.1 % on neutral faces and 86.1 % on non-neutral faces, as compared to a PCA performance of 77.7 % (neutral) and 61.3 % (non-neutral), and a standard ICP performance of 91 %(neutral) and 61.5 % (non-neutral).

Mian et al. [64] used a variant of ICP for separately matching the *eyes-forehead* region and the nose. Their results show that the eyes-forehead region is more robust to facial expressions compared to the nose. Accurate automatic segmentation of the two regions was performed by first detecting the nose tip, aligning the face using PCA and then detecting the points of inflection around the nose. In the ICP variant, correspondences were established along the z-dimension. Point clouds were projected to the xy-plane before establishing correspondences and reprojected to the xyz-space for alignment. Mian et al. [64] argued that correspondences should be forced between points that are far along the viewing direction as it gives useful information about the dissimilarity between faces.

Faltemier et al. [31] aligned the face using the nose tip and selected 28 subregions on the face that remain relatively consistent in the presence of expressions and matched each region independently using ICP. They used *Borda Count* and consensus voting to combine the scores. Matching expression insensitive regions of the face is a potentially useful approach to overcome the sensitivity of ICP to expressions. However, determining such regions is a problem worth exploring because these regions are likely to vary between individuals as well as expressions. Another challenge in matching sub-regions is that it requires accurate segmentation of the sub-regions.

Finally we note that, rather than minimizing a mean squared error metric between the probe and gallery surfaces, other metrics are possible, although a significantly different approach to minimization must be adopted and the approach is no longer termed 'ICP'. One such metric is termed the *Surface Interpenetration Measure* (SIM) [81] which measures the degree to which two aligned surfaces cross over each other. The SIM metric has recently been used with a *Simulated Annealing* approach to 3D face recognition [76]. A verification rate of 96.5 % was achieved on the FRGC v2 dataset at 0.1 % FAR and a rank-one accuracy of 98.4 % was achieved in identification tests.

In the following two sections we discuss PCA and LDA-based 3D face recognition systems that operate on depth maps and surface feature maps (e.g. arrays of curvature values) rather than on point clouds.

8.7 PCA-Based 3D Face Recognition

Once 3D face scans have been filtered, pose normalized and re-sampled so that, for example, standard size depth maps are generated, the simplest way to implement a face recognition system is to compare the depth maps directly. In this sense we see a $p \times q$ depth map as an $m \times 1$ feature vector in an $m = pq$ dimensional space and we can implement a 1-nearest neighbor scheme, for example, based on either a Euclidean (L2 norm) metric or cosine distance metric. However, this is not generally recommended. Typical depth map sizes mean that m can be a large dimensional space with a large amount of redundancy, since we are only imaging faces and not other objects. Dimension reduction using *Principal Component Analysis* (PCA) can express the variation in the data in a smaller space, thus improving speed of feature vector comparisons, and removing dimensions that express noise, thus improving recognition performance. Note that PCA is also known in various texts as the *Hotelling transform* or the *Karhunen-Lóeve transform*. The transform involves a zero-mean operation and a rotation of the data such that the variables associated with each dimension become uncorrelated. It is then possible to form a reduced dimension subspace by discarding those dimensions that express little variance in the (rotated) data. This is equivalent to a projection into a subspace of the zero-mean dataset that decorrelates the data. It is based on the second order statistical properties of the data and maps the general covariance matrix in the original basis to a diagonal matrix in the new, rotated basis.

PCA based 3D face recognition has become a benchmark at least in near-frontal poses, such as is provided in the FRGC v2 dataset [73]. This implies that, when a researcher presents a new 3D face recognition method for this kind of 3D scan, it is expected to at least improve upon a standard PCA performance (for the given set of features employed). The method is similar to the seminal approaches where 2D facial images are decomposed into a linear combination of eigenvectors [82] and employed within a face recognition scenario [87], except that, instead of 2D images, depth maps are used as the input feature vectors. Another important difference is that in 2D 'eigenfaces', the three most significant eigenvalues are usually affected by illumination variations and discarding them improves recognition performance [8]. Since depth maps do not contain any illumination component, all significant eigenvalues are used for 3D face recognition.

One of the earliest works on PCA based 3D face recognition is of Achermann et al. [2]. Hesher et al. [46] explored the use of different numbers of eigenvectors and image sizes for PCA based 3D face recognition. Heseltine et al. [44] generated a set of twelve feature maps based on the gradients and curvatures over the facial surface, and applied PCA-based face recognition to these maps. Pan et al. [70] constructed a circular depth map using the nose tip as center and axis of symmetry as starting point. They applied a PCA based approach to the depth map for face recognition. Chang et al. [17] performed PCA based 3D face recognition on a larger dataset and later expanded their work to perform a comparative evaluation of PCA based 3D face recognition with 2D eigenfaces and found similar recognition performance [18].

In order to implement and test PCA-based 3D face recognition, we need to partition our pose-normalized 3D scans into a training set and a test set. The following sub-sections provide procedures for training and testing a PCA-based 3D face recognition system.

8.7.1 PCA System Training

1. For the set of n training images, $\mathbf{x}_i$, $i = 1\ldots n$, where each training face is represented as an m-dimensional point (column vector) in depth map or surface feature space,

$$\mathbf{x} = [x_1, \ldots, x_m]^T, \tag{8.12}$$

stack the n training face vectors together (as rows) to construct the $n \times m$ training data matrix:

$$\mathsf{X} = \begin{bmatrix} \mathbf{x}_1^T \\ \vdots \\ \mathbf{x}_n^T \end{bmatrix}. \tag{8.13}$$

2. Perform a mean-centering operation by subtracting the mean of the training face vectors, $\bar{\mathbf{x}} = \frac{1}{n}\sum_{i=1}^{n} \mathbf{x}_i$, from each row of matrix X to form the zero-mean training data matrix:

$$\mathsf{X}_0 = \mathsf{X} - \mathsf{J}_{n,1}\bar{\mathbf{x}}^T, \tag{8.14}$$

where $\mathsf{J}_{n,1}$ is an $n \times 1$ matrix of ones.

3. Generate the $m \times m$ covariance matrix of the training data as:

$$C = \frac{1}{n-1} X_0^T X_0. \quad (8.15)$$

Note that dividing by $n-1$ (rather than n) generates an unbiased covariance estimate from the training data (rather than a maximum likelihood estimate). As we tend to use large training sets (of the order of several hundred images), in practice there is no significant difference between these two covariance estimates.

4. Perform a standard eigendecomposition on the covariance matrix. Since the covariance matrix is symmetric, its eigenvectors are orthogonal to each other and can be chosen to have unit length such that:

$$VDV^T = C, \quad (8.16)$$

where both V and D are $m \times m$ matrices. The columns of matrix V are the eigenvectors, v_i, associated with the covariance matrix and D is a diagonal matrix whose elements contain the corresponding eigenvalues, λ_i. Since the covariance is a symmetric positive semidefinite matrix, these eigenvalues are real and non-negative. A key point is that these eigenvalues describe the variance along each of the eigenvectors. (Note that eigendecomposition can be achieved with a standard function call such as the MATLAB `eig` function.) Eigenvalues in D and their corresponding eigenvectors in V are in corresponding columns and we require them to be in descending order of eigenvalue. If this order is not automatically performed within the eigendecomposition function, column reordering should be implemented.

5. Select the number of subspace dimensions for projecting the 3D faces. This is the *dimensionality reduction* step and is usually done by analyzing the ratio of cumulative variance associated with the first k dimensions of the rotated image space to the total variance associated with the full set of m dimensions in that space. This *proportion of variance* ratio is given by:

$$a_k = \frac{\sum_{i=1}^{k} \lambda_i}{\sum_{i=1}^{m} \lambda_i} \quad (8.17)$$

and takes a value between 0 and 1, which is often expressed as a percentage 0–100 %. A common approach is to choose a minimum value of k such that a_k is greater than a certain percentage (90 % or 95 % are commonly used). Figure 8.7 shows a plot of a_k versus k for 455 3D faces taken from the FRGC v2 dataset [73]. From Fig. 8.7 one can conclude that the shape of human faces lies in a significantly lower dimensional subspace than the dimensionality of the original depth maps. Note that the somewhat arbitrary thresholding approach described here is likely to be sub-optimal and recognition performance can be tuned later by searching for an optimal value of k in a set of face recognition experiments.

6. Project the training data set (the *gallery*) into the k-dimensional subspace:

$$\tilde{X} = X_0 V_k. \quad (8.18)$$

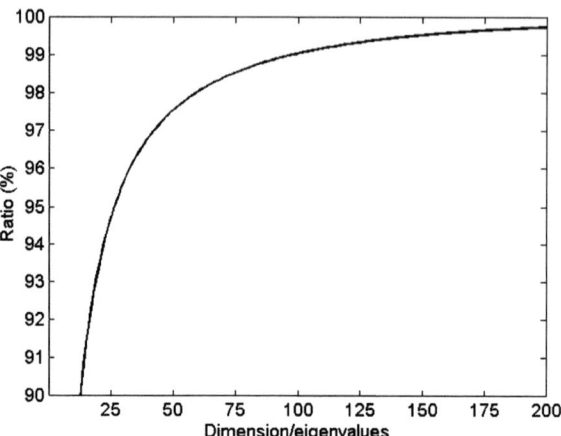

Fig. 8.7 Proportion of variance (%) of the first k eigenvalues to the total variance for 455 3D faces. The first 26 most significant eigenvalues retain 95 % of the total variance and the first 100 eigenvalues retain 99 % of the total variance [73]

Here V_k is a $m \times k$ matrix containing the first k eigenvectors (columns, $\mathbf{v}_i$) of V and $\tilde{X}$ is a $n \times k$ matrix of n training faces (stored as rows) in the k-dimensional subspace (k dimensions stored as columns).

8.7.2 PCA Training Using Singular Value Decomposition

Several variants of PCA-based 3D face recognition exist in the literature and one of the most important variants is to use *Singular Value Decomposition* (SVD) directly on the $n \times m$ zero-mean training data matrix, X_0, thus replacing steps 3 and 4 in the previous subsection. The advantage of using SVD is that it can often provide superior numerical stability compared to eigendecomposition algorithms, additionally the storage required for a data matrix is often much less than a covariance matrix (the number of training scans is much less than the dimension of the feature vector). The SVD is given as:

$$\mathsf{USV}^T = \mathsf{X}_0, \qquad (8.19)$$

where U and V are orthogonal matrices of dimension $n \times n$ and $m \times m$ respectively and S is a $n \times m$ matrix of *singular values* along its diagonal. Note that, in contrast to the eigendecomposition approach, no covariance matrix is formed, yet the required matrix of eigenvectors, V, spanning the most expressive subspace of the training data is obtained. Furthermore, we can determine the eigenvalues from the corresponding singular values. By substituting for X_0 in Eq. (8.15), using its SVD in Eq. (8.19), and then comparing to the eigendecomposition of covariance in Eq. (8.16) we see that:

$$\mathsf{D} = \frac{1}{n-1}\mathsf{S}^2. \qquad (8.20)$$

The proof of this is given as one of the questions at the end of this chapter. Typically SVD library functions order the singular values from highest to lowest along the leading diagonal allowing a suitable number of eigenvectors to be selected for the subspace, as in step 5 of the previous subsection.

8.7.3 PCA Testing

Once the above PCA training phase is completed, it is straightforward to implement a simple nearest neighbor face identification scheme, within the reduced k-dimensional space. We can also threshold a suitable distance metric to implement a face verification scheme.

Each test or *probe* face, $\mathbf{x}_p$, must undergo the same transformations as the training faces, namely subtraction of the training data mean and projection into the subspace:

$$\tilde{\mathbf{x}}_p^T = (\mathbf{x}_p - \bar{\mathbf{x}})^T \mathsf{V}_k. \tag{8.21}$$

Euclidean distance and cosine distance are common metrics used to find the nearest neighbor in the gallery. Given some probe face, $\tilde{\mathbf{x}}_p$, and some gallery face, $\tilde{\mathbf{x}}_g$, both of which have been projected into the PCA-derived subspace, the Euclidean distance between them is given as:

$$d_e(\tilde{\mathbf{x}}_p, \tilde{\mathbf{x}}_g) = \|\tilde{\mathbf{x}}_p - \tilde{\mathbf{x}}_g\| = \sqrt{(\tilde{\mathbf{x}}_p - \tilde{\mathbf{x}}_g)^T (\tilde{\mathbf{x}}_p - \tilde{\mathbf{x}}_g)} \tag{8.22}$$

and the cosine distance is given as:

$$d_c(\tilde{\mathbf{x}}_p, \tilde{\mathbf{x}}_g) = 1 - \frac{\tilde{\mathbf{x}}_p^T \tilde{\mathbf{x}}_g}{\|\tilde{\mathbf{x}}_p\| \cdot \|\tilde{\mathbf{x}}_g\|}. \tag{8.23}$$

In both cases, a small value of the metric (preferably close to zero) indicates a good match. In testing of a PCA-based 3D face recognition system Heseltine et al. [44] found that, usually the Euclidean distance outperformed the cosine distance, but the difference between the two metrics depended on the surface feature type (depth, curvature or gradient) and in a minority of cases, the cosine distance gave a marginally better performance.

The distance metrics described above don't take any account of how the training data is spread along the different axes of the PCA-derived subspace. The *Mahalanobis distance* normalizes the spread along each axis, by dividing by its associated variance to give:

$$d_m(\tilde{\mathbf{x}}_p, \tilde{\mathbf{x}}_g) = \sqrt{(\tilde{\mathbf{x}}_p - \tilde{\mathbf{x}}_g)^T \mathsf{D}^{-1} (\tilde{\mathbf{x}}_p - \tilde{\mathbf{x}}_g)}. \tag{8.24}$$

This expresses the distance in units of standard deviation. Note that the inverse of D is fast to compute due to its diagonal structure. Equivalently, we can *whiten* the training and test data, by premultiplying all feature vectors by $\mathsf{D}^{-\frac{1}{2}}$, which maps the covariance of the training data to the identity matrix, and then Eq. (8.22) for the Euclidean distance metric can be used in this new space. Similarly, we can use the cosine distance metric in the whitened feature space. Heseltine et al. [44] found that using information in D generally improved performance in their PCA-based 3D face recognition system. For many surface features, the cosine distance in the whitened space improved on the standard cosine distance so much that it became the best performing distance metric. This metric is also reported to be the preferred metric in the PCA-based work of Chang et al. [18].

Finally, 3D face recognition systems often display the match between the probe and the gallery. This can be done in terms of the original images, or alternatively the two $m \times 1$ 3D face vectors can be *reconstructed* from their k-dimensional subspace vectors as:

$$\mathbf{x} = \mathsf{V}_k \tilde{\mathbf{x}} + \bar{\mathbf{x}}. \tag{8.25}$$

We summarize a PCA face recognition testing phase as follows:

1. Project the test (probe) face into the PCA derived subspace using Eq. (8.21).
2. For every face in the training data set (gallery), compute a distance metric between the probe and gallery. Select the distance metric with the smallest value as the rank-1 identification match.
3. Optionally display the probe and gallery as reconstructions from the PCA space using Eq. (8.25).

For a verification system, we replace step 2 with a check against the *claimed identity* gallery capture only, and if the distance metric is below some threshold, then the identity is verified. Performance metrics are then evaluated with reference to the true identities of probe and gallery, which are generally contained with the 3D face scan filenames. Obviously, for large scale performance evaluations, step 3 is omitted.

8.7.4 PCA Performance

PCA has been tested on 3D face datasets by many researchers. It is often used as a baseline to measure the performance of other systems (i.e. reported new systems are expected to be better than this.) As mentioned earlier, Chang et al. [19] report the PCA performance of rank-1 recognition on the FRGC dataset as 77.7 % and 61.3 % for neutral and non-neutral expressions respectively. Problems with the PCA include (i) a vulnerability to expressions due to the holistic nature of the approach and (ii) the difficulty to get good pose normalization, which is a requirement of the preprocessing stages of the method. The most time-consuming part of on-line face processing is usually the pose normalization stage, particularly if automatic feature localization and cropping is used as a precursor to this. Once we have sampled the face scan into a standard size feature vector, its projection into 3D face space is a fast operation (linear in the dimension of the feature vector) and, in a nearest neighbor matching scheme, matching time is linear in the size of the gallery.

Fig. 8.8 A two-class classification problem in which we wish to reduce the data dimension to one. The standard PCA result is given as the *black axis* passing through the pooled data mean, and the LDA result is given by the *green axis*

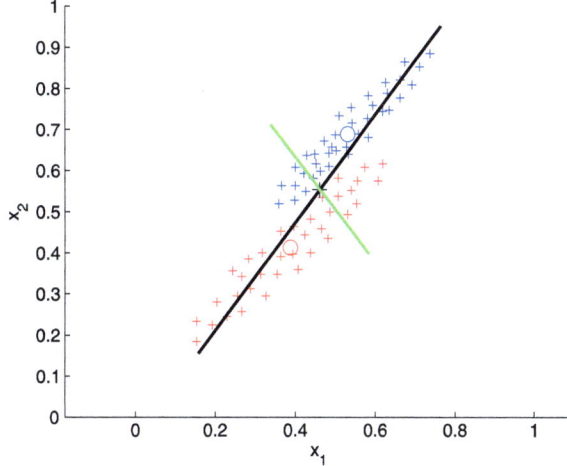

8.8 LDA-Based 3D Face Recognition

One reason that PCA-based approaches have been popular is that they can operate with only one training example per subject. This is because it does not take account of the per-subject (within-class) distribution of the training data. However, because of this reason, the projection axes computed by PCA may make class discrimination difficult. Indeed, in the worst case for some surface feature type, it could be that the very dimensions that are discarded by PCA are those that provide good discrimination between classes. With the advent of more sophisticated datasets with several (preferably many) 3D scans per subject, more sophisticated subspaces can be used, which attempt to find the linear combination of features that best separates each subject (class). This is the aim of *Linear Discriminant Analysis (LDA)*, while simultaneously performing dimension reduction. Thus, while PCA finds the most *expressive* linear combinations of surface feature map dimensions (in the simplest case, depth map pixels), LDA finds the most *discriminative* linear combinations.

Although 3D face recognition is an inherently multi-class classification problem in a high dimensional space, it is easier to initially look at LDA for a two-class problem in a two-dimensional space and compare it to PCA. Subsequently we will look at the issues involved with high dimensional feature vectors and we will also generalize to multi-class problems.

8.8.1 Two-Class LDA

Suppose that we have the two-class, 2D problem shown in Fig. 8.8. Intuitively we want to project the data onto a direction for which there is the largest separation of the class means, relative to the within-class scatter in that same projection direction.

A scatter matrix is simply a scaled version of a covariance matrix, and for each set of training scans, $\mathbb{C}_c$, belonging to class $c \in \{1, 2\}$, they are formed as:

$$S_c = X_{0c}^T X_{0c}, \qquad (8.26)$$

where X_{0c} is a zero-mean data matrix, as described in Sect. 8.7.1 (although it is now class-specific), and n_c is the number of training scans in the set $\mathbb{C}_c$. We note that these scatter matrices are often expressed as a sum of outer products:

$$S_c = \sum_{i=1}^{n_c} (\mathbf{x}_i - \bar{\mathbf{x}}_c)(\mathbf{x}_i - \bar{\mathbf{x}}_c)^T, \quad \mathbf{x}_i \in \mathbb{C}_c, \qquad (8.27)$$

where $\bar{\mathbf{x}}_c$ is the mean of the feature vectors in class $\mathbb{C}_c$. Given that we have two classes, the *within-class scatter matrix* can be formed as:

$$S_W = S_1 + S_2. \qquad (8.28)$$

The *between-class scatter* is formed as the outer product of the difference between the two class means:

$$S_B = (\bar{\mathbf{x}}_1 - \bar{\mathbf{x}}_2)(\bar{\mathbf{x}}_1 - \bar{\mathbf{x}}_2)^T. \qquad (8.29)$$

Fisher proposed to maximize the ratio of between class scatter to within class scatter relative to the projection direction [28], i.e. solve

$$J(\mathbf{w}) = \max_{\mathbf{w}} \frac{\mathbf{w}^T S_B \mathbf{w}}{\mathbf{w}^T S_W \mathbf{w}} \qquad (8.30)$$

with respect to the 2×1 column vector $\mathbf{w}$. This is known as Fisher's criterion. A solution to this optimization can be found by differentiating Eq. (8.30) with respect to $\mathbf{w}$ and equating to zero. This gives:

$$S_W^{-1} S_B \mathbf{w} - J \mathbf{w} = \mathbf{0}. \qquad (8.31)$$

We recognize this as a generalized eigenvalue-eigenvector problem, where the eigenvector of $S_W^{-1} S_B$ associated with its largest eigenvalue (J) is our desired optimal direction, $\mathbf{w}^*$. (In fact, the other eigenvalue will be zero because the between class scatter matrix, being a simple outer product, can only have rank 1.) Figure 8.8 shows the very different results of applying PCA to give the most expressive axis for the pooled data (both classes), and applying LDA which gives a near orthogonal axis, relative to that of PCA, for the best class separation in terms of Fisher's criterion. Once data is projected into the new space, one can use various classifiers and distance metrics, as described earlier.

8.8.2 LDA with More than Two Classes

In order to extend the approach to a multiclass problem ($K > 2$ classes), we could train $\frac{K(K-1)}{2}$ pairwise binary classifiers and classify a test 3D face according to the class that gets most votes. This has the advantage of finding the projection that best separates each pair of distributions, but often results in a very large number of classifiers in 3D face recognition problems, due to the large number of classes (one per subject) often experienced. Alternatively one can train K *one-versus-all* classifiers where the binary classifiers are of the form *subject X* and *not subject X*. Although this results in fewer classifiers, the computed projections are usually less discriminative.

Rather than applying multiple binary classifiers to a multi-class problem, we can generalize the binary LDA case to multiple classes. This requires the assumption that the number of classes is less than or equal to the dimension of the feature space (i.e. $K \leq m$ where m is the dimension of our depth map space or surface feature map space). For high dimensional feature vectors, such as encountered in 3D face recognition, we also require a very large body of training data to prevent the scatter matrices from being singular. In general, the required number of 3D face scans is not available, but we address this point in the following subsection.

The multi-class LDA procedure is as follows: Firstly, we form the means of each class (i.e. each subject in the 3D face dataset). Using these means, we can compute the scatter matrix for each class using Eqs. (8.26) or (8.27). For the within-class scatter matrix, we simply sum the scatter matrices for each individual class:

$$S_W = \sum_{i=1}^{K} S_i. \qquad (8.32)$$

This is an $m \times m$ matrix, where m is the dimension of the feature vector. We form the mean of all training faces, which is the weighted mean of the class means:

$$\bar{x} = \frac{1}{n} \sum_{i=1}^{K} n_i \bar{x}_i, \qquad (8.33)$$

where n_i is the number of training face scans in each class and n is the total number of training scans. The between-class scatter matrix is then formed as:

$$S_B = \sum_{i=1}^{K} n_i (\bar{x}_i - \bar{x})(\bar{x}_i - \bar{x})^T. \qquad (8.34)$$

This scatter matrix is also $m \times m$. Rather than finding a single m-dimensional vector to project onto, we now seek a reduced dimension subspace in which to project our data, so that a feature vector in the new subspace is given as:

$$\tilde{x} = W^T x. \qquad (8.35)$$

We formulate Fisher's criterion as:

$$J(W) = \max_W \frac{|W^T S_B W|}{|W^T S_W W|}, \qquad (8.36)$$

where the vertical lines indicate that the determinant is to be computed. Given that the determinant is equivalent to the product of the eigenvalues, it is a measure of the square of the scattering volume. The projection matrix, W, maps the original

m-dimensional space to, at most, $K-1$ dimensions and so its maximum size is $m \times (K-1)$. This limit exists because S_B is the sum of K outer products and matrices formed from outer products are rank 1 or less. Additionally, only $K-1$ of these are independent due to their dependence on the overall mean $\bar{x}$ of the pooled training data. As with the two class case, the optimal projection is found from the generalized eigenvalue-eigenvector problem:

$$S_W^{-1} S_B W - JW = 0, \qquad (8.37)$$

and the optimal projection W^* is the one whose columns are the eigenvectors corresponding to the largest eigenvalues. At most, there will be $K-1$ non-zero eigenvalues. In practise we select the subset of eigenvectors with eigenvalues above some small threshold, as those close to zero provide little useful discrimination. Note that we can only form the solution in this way if S_W is non-singular and we discuss this issue in the following subsection.

8.8.3 LDA in High Dimensional 3D Face Spaces

When applying LDA to 3D face recognition, we have to address the problems associated with working in high dimensional spaces. In [45], for example, range maps of 60 pixels wide and 90 high are employed to give feature vectors of length $m = 5400$. Thus the scatter matrices, both S_W and S_B are extremely large (dimension $m \times m$) and worse still, due to the typically small number (10–100) of training images per class, they are singular (non invertible). This is referred to as LDA's *small sample size* problem. The more traditional approach to dealing with this is to initially apply PCA as a dimensional reduction stage, before LDA can proceed, as was done in Belhumeur et al.'s [8] seminal work in 2D face recognition and later in 3D face recognition work [39, 43, 45].

If the total number of pooled training vectors is n, then the rank of S_W is at most $k = n - K$. Thus PCA can be applied to the data and the k eigenvectors with the largest eigenvalues are selected to give the $m \times k$ projection matrix V_k. This is then reduced to $K-1$ dimensions using the LDA derived $k \times (K-1)$ projection matrix, as described in the previous subsection.

Assuming that 3D faces can be represented as an m-dimensional vector, we can summarize this approach with the following training steps:

1. Determine the projection matrix of a PCA-derived subspace, of dimension $n-K$, as described in Sect. 8.7.
2. Project all of the 3D faces that constitute the training data into this subspace.
3. Form the within-class and between-class scatter matrices of the training data in this reduced dimension PCA-derived subspace, as described in Sect. 8.8.2.
4. Determine the smaller (maximum dimension $K-1$) LDA-derived subspace of this PCA subspace by solving the generalized eigenvalue-eigenvector problem of the form of Eq. (8.37).
5. Project the training data from the PCA subspace into the LDA subspace.

Then, when we wish to classify a 3D face scan (a probe), it must be projected into the new space. Therefore, we combine the two projections by multiplying them together, and each probe feature vector is mapped directly into the smaller subspace (of maximum dimension $K - 1$) as:

$$\tilde{\mathbf{x}}_p = \mathsf{W}^T \mathsf{V}_k^T (\mathbf{x}_p - \bar{\mathbf{x}}). \tag{8.38}$$

Although this approach can often give better results than PCA alone when there is enough training data within each class, a criticism of this two-stage approach is that the initial PCA stage could still discard dimensions that have useful discriminative information, as discussed earlier. Therefore, more recent approaches to applying LDA to high dimensional approaches have tried to avoid this and these techniques go under various names such as *direct LDA*. It is worth noting, however, that for some of these approaches there have been different viewpoints in the literature (e.g. in [94] and [36]) and we encourage the reader to investigate direct approaches after becoming comfortable with this more established two-stage approach.

8.8.4 LDA Performance

The work of Heseltine et al. [43] shows that LDA can give significantly better performance than PCA when multiple scans of the same subject are available in the training data, although this work pre-dates the wide use of benchmark FRGC 3D face data. As with PCA, the most computationally expensive process is usually pose normalization. Again, projection into a sub-space is a fast operation (linear in the dimension of the feature vector) and, in a nearest neighbor matching scheme, matching time is linear in the size of the gallery.

8.9 Normals and Curvature in 3D Face Recognition

When PCA, LDA and other techniques are applied to 3D face recognition problems, surface features are often extracted. The simplest of these are related to the differential properties of the surface, namely the surface normals and the surface curvature. In *normal maps*, each pixel value is represented by the surface normal. Gokbert et al. [39] used the normal vectors in Cartesian form (n_x, n_y, n_z) and concatenated them to perform PCA-based 3D face recognition. Note that this form has redundancy and a more compact way is to use the spherical coordinates, (θ, ϕ), which are the elevation and azimuth angles respectively. Normals can be computed using the cross product on the mesh data, as described in Chap. 4, or we can fit a planar surface using orthogonal least squares to the spherical neighborhood of a 3D point or range pixel. This is implemented via SVD and the eigenvector with the smallest eigenvalue is the surface normal. Figure 8.9 shows sample images of normal maps of a 3D face.

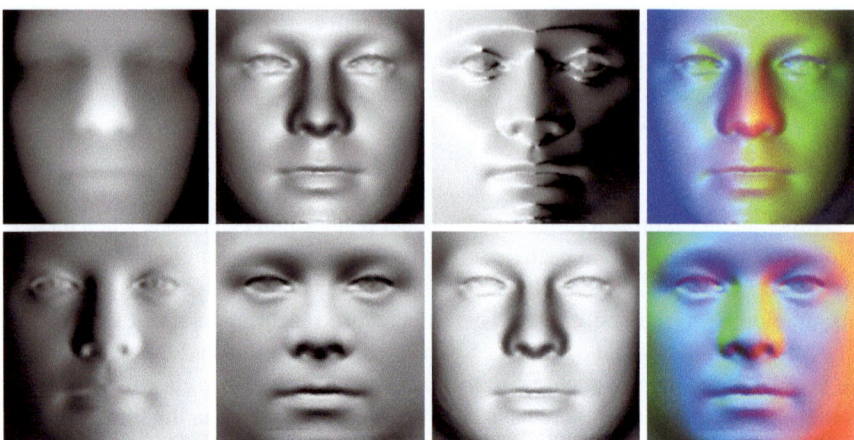

Fig. 8.9 *Top row*: a range image (Z values) and its normal maps of elevation ϕ and azimuth θ angles. The three (Z, ϕ, θ) values rendered as an RGB image. *Bottom row*: normal maps of x, y and z normal components. The three (X, Y, Z) values rendered as an RGB image

Surface normals can capture minor variations in the facial surface however, being first order derivatives, they are more sensitive to noise compared to depth maps. Often, to overcome this problem, the 3D face is smoothed before computing the normals, or the normals are computed over a larger neighborhood. In either case, the ability of surface normals to capture subtle features is somewhat attenuated.

The surface normals of a shape can be represented by points on a unit sphere. This sphere is often called the Gaussian sphere. By associating weights to the normals based on the surface area with the same normal, an *extended Gaussian image* (EGI) is formed [47]. The EGI cannot differentiate between similar objects at different scales which is not a major problem in 3D face recognition. Another limitation, which can impact face recognition, is that the EGI of only convex objects is unique and many non-convex objects can have the same EGI. To work around this limitation, Lee and Milios [55] represent only the convex regions of the face by EGI and use a graph matching algorithm for face recognition.

Curvature based measures, which are related to second-order derivatives of the raw depth measurements, have also been used to extract features from 3D face images and these measures are pose invariant. Several representations are prominent in this context, most of which are based on the principal curvatures of a point on a three dimensional surface. To understand principal curvatures, imagine the normal on a surface and an infinite set of planes (a *pencil of planes*) each of which contains this normal. Each of these planes intersects the surface in a plane curve and the principal curvatures are defined as the maximum curvature, κ_1, and minimum curvature, κ_2, of this infinite set of plane curves. The directions that correspond to maximum and minimum curvatures are always perpendicular and are called the principal directions of the surface. Principal curvatures are in fact the eigenvalues of the *Weingarten matrix*, which is a 2×2 matrix containing the parameters of a

Fig. 8.10 Maximum (*left*) and minimum (*right*) principal curvature images of a 3D face

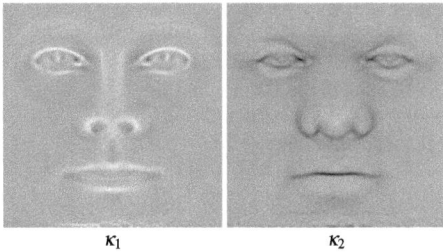

quadratic local surface patch, fitted in a local plane that is aligned to the surface tangent plane. Figure 8.10 shows images of the maximum and minimum curvatures of a 3D face. Tanaka et al. [85] constructed a variant of the EGI by mapping the principal curvatures and their directions onto two unit spheres representing ridges and valleys respectively. Similarity between faces was calculated by Fisher's spherical correlation [33] of their EGIs.

Gaussian curvature, K, is defined as the product of these principal curvatures, while *mean curvature*, H, is defined as the average, i.e.

$$K = \kappa_1 \kappa_2, \qquad H = \frac{\kappa_1 + \kappa_2}{2}. \qquad (8.39)$$

Both of these are invariant to rigid transformations (and hence pose), but only Gaussian curvature is invariant to the surface bending that may occur during changes of facial expression. Lee and Shim [56] approximated 3×3 windows of the range image by quadratic patches and calculated the minimum, maximum and Gaussian curvatures. Using thresholds, edge maps were extracted from these curvatures and a depth weighted Hausdorff distance was used to calculate the similarity between faces. Using depth values as weights in fact combines the range image with the curvatures giving it more discriminating power. The advantages of combining depth with curvature for face recognition have been known since the early 90's [40].

The *shape index* was proposed by Koenderink and van Doorn [54] as a surface shape descriptor. It is based on both principal curvatures and derived as:

$$s = \frac{2}{\pi} \arctan\left(\frac{\kappa_2 + \kappa_1}{\kappa_2 - \kappa_1}\right) \quad (-1 \leq s \leq +1). \qquad (8.40)$$

It can be thought of a polar description of shape in the $\kappa_1 - \kappa_2$ plane, where different values distinguish between caps, cups, ridges, valleys and saddle points. Since a ratio of curvatures is used in Eq. (8.40), the size of the curvature is factored out and hence the descriptor is scale invariant. Koenderink and van Doorn combine the principal curvatures in a different measure to measure the magnitude of the curvature, which they called *curvedness*, c, where $c = \sqrt{\frac{\kappa_1^2 + \kappa_2^2}{2}}$. Since, principal curvatures are pose invariant, the shape index is also pose invariant. Lu et al. [59] used the shape index to find a rough estimate of registration which was then refined with a variant of the ICP algorithm [9]. In their earlier work, they also used the shape index map of the registered faces for recognition along with the texture and the Cartesian coordinates of the 3D face. This is an example where curvatures are combined with

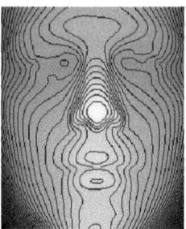

Fig. 8.11 Facial curves mapped on the range image of a face [78]. These are the intersection of the 3D face with planes orthogonal to the camera, at different depths

the point cloud, instead of the range image, for face recognition. Thus we can conclude that curvatures offer viewpoint invariant and localized features that are useful for face alignment and matching. Moreover, face recognition performance generally improves when curvature based features are combined with the range image or point cloud.

Samir et al. [78] represented a 3D face with continuous facial curves which were extracted using a depth function. We can think of these curves as the intersection of the 3D face with planes orthogonal to the camera and at different depths. Face recognition was performed by matching their corresponding facial curves using geodesic distance criteria [53]. Although, the facial curves of a face change with changes in curvature of different identities, they are not completely invariant to pose [78]. Figure 8.11 shows a sample 3D face with facial curves.

8.9.1 Computing Curvature on a 3D Face Scan

Here we present a standard technique for computing curvatures on a 3D face scan. We assume that we start with a preprocessed mesh, which has spikes filtered and holes filled. Then, for each surface point, we implement the following procedure:

1. Find the neighbors within a local neighborhood, the neighbor set includes the point itself. The size of this neighborhood is a tradeoff that depends on the scan resolution and the noise level. We can use connectivity information in the mesh or the structure in a range image to compute neighborhoods quickly. Otherwise some form of data structuring of a point cloud is required to do a fast cuboidal region search, usually refined to a spherical region. Typically k-d trees and octrees are employed and standard implementations of these can be found online.
2. Zero-mean the neighbors and either use an eigendecomposition or SVD to fit a plane to those neighbors. The eigenvector with the smallest eigenvalue is the estimated surface normal. The other two eigenvectors lie in the estimated tangent plane and can be used as a local basis.
3. Project all neighbors into this local basis. (This is the same procedure as was outlined for a full face scan in Sect. 8.7.1.)
4. Recenter the data on the surface point.
5. Using least-squares fitting, fit a local quadratic surface patch, $z = \frac{A}{2}x^2 + Bxy + \frac{C}{2}y^2$, where $[x, y, z]^T$ are the neighboring points expressed in the recentered local basis and $[A, B, C]^T$ are the surface parameters to be found by least-squares.

6. Form the Weingarten matrix as:

$$W = \begin{pmatrix} A & B \\ B & C \end{pmatrix}. \quad (8.41)$$

7. Determine the principal curvatures, κ_1, κ_2 as the eigenvalues of the Weingarten matrix.
8. Form the Gaussian curvature, mean curvature and shape index, as required, using Eqs. (8.39) and (8.40).

Of course there are many variants of this approach. For example, in step 2, it is faster to compute normals using cross products rather than SVD, in which case we would use an arbitrary local basis to do the quadratic surface fit.

8.10 Recent Techniques in 3D Face Recognition

In this section we present a selection of promising recent techniques in the field of 3D face recognition including 3D face recognition using *Annotated Face Models* (AFMs) [51], local feature-based 3D face recognition [65], and expression-invariant 3D face recognition [15].

8.10.1 3D Face Recognition Using Annotated Face Models (AFM)

Kakadiaris et al. [50, 51] proposed a deformable *Annotated Face Model* (AFM), which is based on statistical data from 3D face meshes and anthropometric landmarks identified in the work of Farkas [32]. Farkas studied 132 measurements on the human face and head which are widely used in the literature. For example, DeCarlo and Metaxas [26] used 47 landmarks and their associated distance/angular measurements to describe a 3D deformable face model for tracking. Kakadiaris et al. [51] associated a subset of the facial anthropometric landmarks [32] with the vertices of the AFM and using knowledge of the facial physiology, segmented the AFM into different annotated areas. Figure 8.12 illustrates the AFM.

The input data is registered to the AFM using a multistage alignment procedure. Firstly, spin images [49] are used to coarsely align the data with the AFM. In the second step, the ICP algorithm [9] is used to refine the registration. In the final step, the alignment is further refined using *Simulated Annealing* to minimize the z-buffer difference. The z-buffers uniformly resample the data resulting in better registration. Uniform sampling was also used by Mian et al. [64] for better pose correction in an iterative approach. The AFM is fitted to the registered data using an elastically deformable model framework [62]. Additional constraints were imposed on the AFM similar to DeCarlo and Metaxas [26] to ensure that the fitting result is anthropometrically correct. Kakadiaris et al. [51] used a *Finite Element Approximation* to solve this equation and used a subdivision surface [60] as the model for greater flexibility

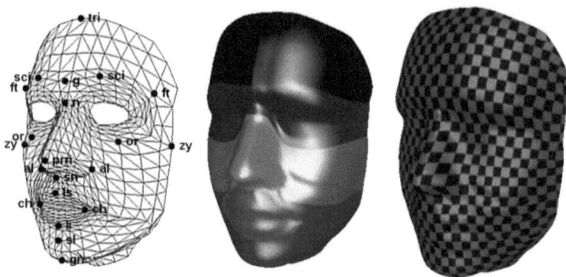

Fig. 8.12 Anthropometric landmarks on a 3D face mesh. Annotated Face Model (AFM) with different annotated areas shown different shaded. Demonstration of parameterization using a checkerboard texture mapped on the AFM. Figure courtesy of [50]

(compared to parametric surfaces). To speed up the fitting process, space partitioning techniques are used to reduce the cost of the nearest neighbor search per model vertex required at each iteration.

After the fitting, a continuous UV parameterization was applied to the AFM (polygonal mesh) transforming it to an equivalent geometry image. The geometry image has three channels each recording one of the three x, y or z position coordinates of the fitted AFM points. However, most of the information is contained in the z channel. Mapping between the AFM and the deformation image is performed using a spherical mapping function such that the ratio of area in 3D space to the area in UV space is approximately the same for every part of the surface.

A three channel (X, Y, Z) normal map is also extracted from the geometry image. The geometry and normal map images are treated as separate images and their individual wavelet coefficients are computed. Haar wavelets were used to extract features from the normal and geometry images. Additionally, the pyramid transform was also used to extract features from only the geometry images.

The Haar wavelet transform consisted of the tensor product of the 1D Walsh wavelet system, namely low-pass $\mathbf{g} = \frac{1}{\sqrt{2}}[1\ 1]$ and high-pass $\mathbf{h} = \frac{1}{\sqrt{2}}[1\ -1]$. The tensor product resulted in the four channel filter bank $\mathbf{g}^T * \mathbf{g}$, $\mathbf{g}^T * \mathbf{h}$, $\mathbf{h}^T * \mathbf{g}$ and $\mathbf{h}^T * \mathbf{h}$, which were applied to the images and the same subset of coefficients were used directly for comparison of two faces.

The pyramid transform [75] performs a linear multiscale, multiresolution image decomposition. The image is first divided into high and low-pass subbands and the latter is passed through a set of steerable bandpass filters resulting in a set of oriented subbands and a lower-pass subband. The latter is subsampled by a factor of two and recursively passed through the set of steerable bandpass filters resulting in a pyramid representation which is translation and rotation-invariant. These properties provide robustness to facial expressions. Kakadiaris et al. [51] applied 3 scale, 10 orientations decomposition and used the oriented subbands at the farthest scale only for comparison of two faces.

The AFM 3D face recognition system was evaluated on the FRGC v2 dataset and the Haar wavelet performed slightly better than the pyramid transform with approximately 97 % verification rate at 0.1 % FAR, as compared to 95 %. A fusion of the two transforms provided a marginal improvement of around 0.3 % over Haar wavelets alone. If the evaluation was limited to neutral expressions, a reasonable verification scenario, verification rates improved to as high as 99 %. A rank-1 identification rate of 97 % was reported.

8.10.2 Local Feature-Based 3D Face Recognition

Three-dimensional face recognition algorithms that construct a global representation of the face using the full facial area are often termed *holistic*. Often, such methods are quite sensitive to pose, facial expressions and occlusions. For example, a small change in the pose can alter the depth maps and normal maps of a 3D face. This error will propagate to the feature vector extraction stage (where a feature vector represents a 3D face scan) and subsequently affect matching. For global representation and features to be consistent between multiple 3D face scans of the same identity, the scans must be accurately normalized with respect to pose. We have already discussed some limitations and problems associated with pose normalization in Sect. 8.5.5. Due to the difficulty of accurate localization of fiducial points, pose normalization is never perfect. Even the ICP based pose normalization to a reference 3D face cannot perfectly normalize the pose with high repeatability because dissimilar surfaces have multiple comparable local minima rather than a single, distinctively low global minimum. Another source of error in pose normalization is a consequence of the non-rigid nature of the face. Facial expressions can change the curvatures of a face and displace fiducial points leading to errors in pose correction.

In contrast to holistic approaches, a second category of face recognition algorithms extracts local features [96] from faces and matches them independently. Although local features have been discussed before for the purpose of fiducial point localization and pose correction, in this section we will focus on algorithms that use local features for 3D face matching. In case of pose correction, the local features are chosen such that they are generic to the 3D faces of all identities. However, for face matching, local features may be chosen such that they are unique to every identity.

In feature-based face recognition, the first step is to determine the locations from where to extract the local features. Extracting local features at every point would be computationally expensive. However, detecting a subset of points (i.e. keypoints) over the 3D face can significantly reduce the computation time of the subsequent feature extraction and matching phases. Uniform or arbitrary sparse sampling of the face will result in features that are not unique (or sufficiently descriptive) resulting in sub-optimal recognition performance. Ideally keypoints must be repeatedly detectable at locations on a 3D face where invariant and descriptive features can be extracted. Moreover, the keypoint identification (if required) and features should be robust to noise and pose variations.

8.10.2.1 Keypoint Detection and Local Feature Matching

Mian et al. [65] proposed a keypoint detection and local feature extraction algorithm for 3D face recognition. Details of the technique are as follows. The point cloud is first resampled at uniform intervals of 4 mm on the x, y plane. Taking each sample point p as a center, a sphere of radius r is used to crop a local surface from the face. The value of r is chosen as a trade-off between the feature's descriptiveness and sensitivity to global variations, such as those due to varying facial expression. Larger r will result in more descriptive features at the cost of being more sensitive to global variations and vice-versa.

This local point cloud is then translated to zero mean and a decorrelating rotation is applied using the eigenvectors of its covariance matrix, as described earlier for full face scans in Sect. 8.7.1. Equivalently, we could use SVD on the zero-mean data matrix associated with this local point cloud to determine the eigenvectors, as described in Sect. 8.7.2. The result of these operations is that the local points are aligned along their principal axes and we determine the maximum and minimum coordinate values for the first two of these axes (i.e. the two with the largest eigenvalues). This gives a measure of the spread of the local data over these two principal directions.

We compute the difference in these two principal axes spreads and denote it by δ. If the variation in surface is symmetric as in the case of a plane or a sphere, the value of δ will be close to zero. However, in the case of asymmetric variation of the surface, δ will have a value dependent on the asymmetry. The depth variation is important for the descriptiveness of the feature and the asymmetry is essential for defining a local coordinate basis for the subsequent extraction of local features.

If the value of δ is greater than a threshold t_1, p qualifies as a keypoint. If t_1 is set to zero, every point will qualify as a keypoint and as t_1 is increased, the total number of keypoints will decrease. Only two thresholds are required for keypoint detection namely r and t_1 which were empirically chosen as $r_1 = 20$ mm and $t_1 = 2$ mm by Mian et al. [65]. Since the data space is known (i.e. human faces), r and t_1 can be chosen easily. Mian et al. [65] demonstrated that this algorithm can detect keypoints with high repeatability on the 3D faces of the same identity. Interestingly, the keypoint locations are different for different individuals providing a coarse classification between different identities right at the keypoint detection stage. This keypoint detection technique is generic and was later extended to other 3D objects as well where the scale of the feature (i.e. r) was automatically chosen [66].

In PCA-based alignment, there is an inherent two-fold ambiguity. This is resolved by assuming that the faces are roughly upright and the patch is rotated by the smaller of the possible angles to align it with its principal axis. A smooth surface is fitted to the points that have been mapped into a local frame, using the approximation given in [27] for robustness to noise and outliers. The surface is sampled on a uniform 20×20 xy lattice. To avoid boundary effects, a larger region is initially cropped using $r_2 > r$ for surface fitting using a larger lattice and then only the central 20×20 samples covering the r region are used as a feature vector of dimension 400. Note that this feature is essentially a depth map of the local surface defined

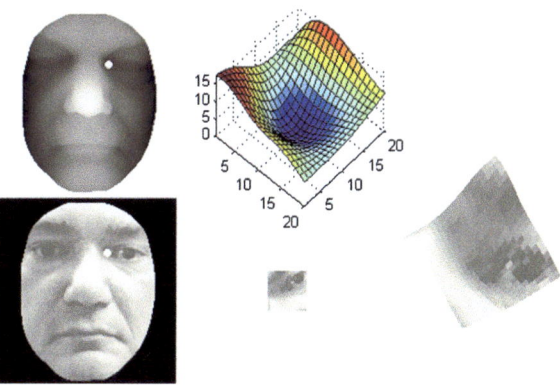

Fig. 8.13 Illustration of a keypoint on a 3D face and its corresponding texture. Figure courtesy of [65]

in the local coordinate basis with the location of the keypoint p as origin and the principal axes as the direction vectors. Figure 8.13 shows a keypoint and its local corresponding feature.

A constant threshold t_1 usually results in a different number of keypoints on each 3D face scan. Therefore, an upper limit of 200 is imposed on the total number of local features to prevent bias in the recognition results. To reduce the dimensionality of the features, they are projected to a PCA subspace defined by their most significant eigenvectors. Mian et al. [65] showed that 11 dimensions are sufficient to conserve 99 % of the variance of the features. Thus each face scan is represented by 200 features of dimension 11 each. Local features from the gallery and probe faces are projected to the same 11 dimensional subspace and whitened so that the variation along each dimension is equal. The features are then normalized to unit vectors and the angle between them is used as a matching metric.

For a probe feature, the gallery face feature that forms the minimum angle with it is considered to be its match. Only one-to-one matches are allowed i.e. if a gallery feature matches more than one probe feature, only the one with the minimum angle is considered. Thus gallery faces generally have a different number of matches with a probe face.

The matched keypoints of the probe face are meshed using Delaunay triangulation and its edges are used to construct a similar 3D mesh from the corresponding keypoints of the gallery face. If the matches are spatially consistent, the two meshes will be similar (see Fig. 8.14). The similarity between the two meshes is given by:

$$\gamma = \frac{1}{n_\varepsilon} \sum_i^{n_\varepsilon} |\varepsilon_{pi} - \varepsilon_{gi}|, \qquad (8.42)$$

where ε_{pi} and ε_{gi} are the lengths of the corresponding edges of the probe and gallery meshes, respectively. The value n_ε is the number of edges. Note that γ is invariant to pose.

A fourth similarity measure between the faces is calculated as the mean Euclidean distance d between the corresponding vertices (keypoints) of the meshes after least squared minimization. The four similarity measures namely the average

Fig. 8.14 Graph of feature points matched between two faces. Figure courtesy of [65]

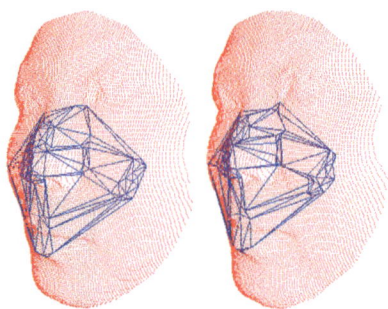

angle between the matching features, the number of matches, γ and d are normalized on a scale of 0 to 1 and combined using a confidence weighted sum rule:

$$s = \kappa_\theta \bar{\theta} + \kappa_m(1-m) + \kappa_\gamma \gamma + \kappa_d d, \tag{8.43}$$

where κ_x is the confidence in individual similarity metric defined as a ratio between the best and second best matches of the probe face with the gallery. The gallery face with the minimum value of s is declared as the identity of the probe. The algorithm achieved 96.1 % rank-1 identification rate and 98.6 % verification rate at 0.1 % FAR on the complete FRGC v2 data set. Restricting the evaluation to neutral expression face scans resulted in a verification rate of 99.4 %.

8.10.2.2 Other Local Feature-Based Methods

Another example of local feature based 3D face recognition is that of Chua et al. [21] who extracted point signatures [20] of the rigid parts of the face for expression robust 3D face recognition. A point signature is a one dimensional invariant signature describing the local surface around a point. The signature is extracted by centering a sphere of fixed radius at that point. The intersection of the sphere with the objects surface gives a 3D curve whose orientation can be normalized using its normal and a reference direction. The 3D curve is projected perpendicularly to a plane, fitted to the curve, forming a 2D curve. This projection gives a signed distance profile called the point signature. The starting point of the signature is defined by a vector from the point to where the 3D curve gives the largest positive profile distance. Chua et al. [21] do not provide a detailed experimental analysis of the point signatures for 3D face recognition.

Local features have also been combined with global features to achieve better performance. Xu et al. [90] combined local shape variations with global geometric features to perform 3D face recognition. Finally, Al-Osaimi et al. [4] also combined local and global geometric cues for 3D face recognition. The local features represented local similarities between faces while the global features provided geometric consistency of the spatial organization of the local features.

8.10.3 *Expression Modeling for Invariant 3D Face Recognition*

Bronstein et al. [15] developed expression-invariant face recognition by modeling facial expressions as surface isometries (i.e. bending but no stretching) and constructing expression-invariant representations of faces using canonical forms. The facial surface is treated as a deformable object in the context of Riemannian geometry. Assuming that the intrinsic geometry of the facial surface is expression-invariant, an isometry-invariant representation of the facial surface will exhibit the same property.

The Gaussian curvature of a surface is its intrinsic property and remains constant for isometric surfaces. (Clearly, the same is not true for mean curvature.) By isometrically embedding the surface into a low-dimensional space, a computationally efficient invariant representation of the face is constructed. Isometric embedding consists of measuring the geodesic distances between various points on the facial surface followed by *Multi-Dimensional Scaling* (MDS) to perform the embedding.

Once an invariant representation is obtained, comparing deformable objects, such as faces, becomes a problem of simple rigid surface matching. This, however, comes at the cost of loosing some accuracy because the facial surface is not perfectly isometric. Moreover, isometric modeling is only an approximation and can only model facial expressions that do not change the topology of the face, such as an open mouth.

Given a surface in discrete form, consisting of a finite number of sample points on surface S, the geodesic distances between the points $d_{ij} = d(x_i, x_j)$ are measured and described by the matrix D. The geodesic distances are measured with $O(N)$ complexity using a variant of the *Fast Marching Method* (FMM) [80] which was extended to triangular manifolds in [52]. The FMM variant used was proposed by Spira and Kimmel [83] and has the advantage that it performs computation on a uniform Cartesian grid in the parameterization plane rather than the manifold itself.

Bronstein et al. [15] numerically measured the invariance of the isometric model by placing 133 markers on a face and tracking the change in their geodesic and Euclidean distances due to facial expressions. They concluded that the change in Euclidean distances was two times greater than the change in geodesic distances. Note that the change in geodesic distances was not zero.

The matrix of geodesic distances D itself can not be used as an invariant representation because of the variable sampling rates and the order of points. Thus the Riemannian surface is represented as a subset of some manifold $\mathcal{M}^m$ which preserves the intrinsic geometry and removes the extrinsic geometry. This is referred to as isometric embedding. The embedding space is chosen to simplify the process. Bronstein et al. [15] treat isometric embedding as a simple mapping:

$$\varphi : (\{x_1, x_2, \ldots, x_N\} \subset S, \mathsf{D}) \to (\{x'_1, x'_2, \ldots, x'_N\} \subset \mathcal{M}^m, \mathsf{D}'), \qquad (8.11)$$

between two surfaces such that the geodesic distances between any two points in the original space and the embedded space are equal. In the embedding space, geodesic distances are replaced by Euclidean distances. However, in practice, such an embed-

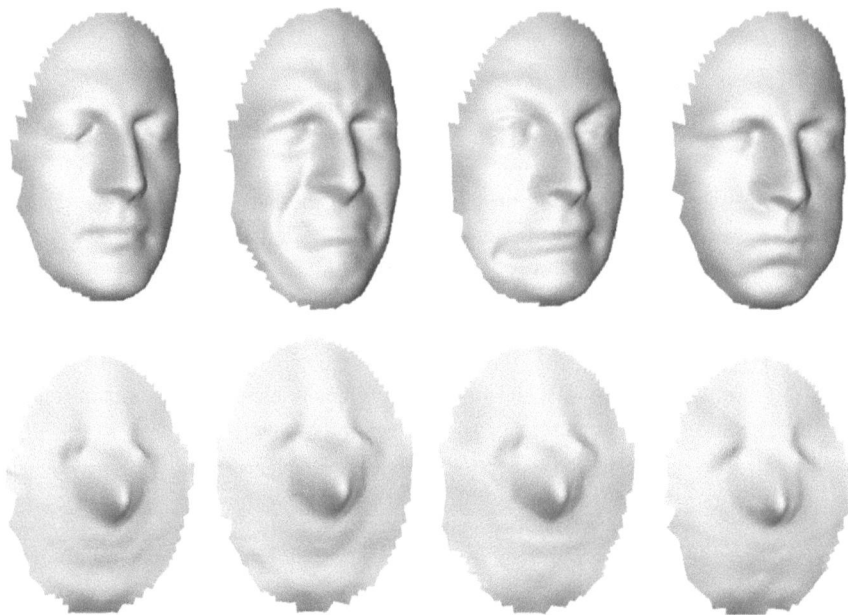

Fig. 8.15 The canonical representations (*second row*) are identical even though the original face surface is quite different due to facial expressions (*top row*). (Image courtesy of [15])

ding does not exist. Therefore, Bronstein et al. [15] try to find an embedding that is near-isometric by minimizing the embedding error given by:

$$\varepsilon(\mathsf{X}'; \mathsf{D}, \mathsf{W}) \equiv \sum_{i<j} w_{ij} \big(d'_{ij}(\mathsf{X}') - d_{ij}\big)^2, \qquad (8.45)$$

where d'_{ij} and d_{ij} are the distances between points i, j in the embedding and original spaces respectively. $\mathsf{X}' = (x_1, x_2, \ldots, x_N)$ is an N by m matrix of parametric coordinates in $\mathcal{M}^m$ and $\mathsf{W} = (w_{ij})$ is a symmetric matrix of weights determining the relative contribution of the distances between all pairs of points to the total error. The minimization of the above error with respect to X' can be performed using gradient descent.

In addition to the limitations arising from the assumptions discussed above, another downside of this approach is that the isometric embedding also attenuates some important discriminating features which are not caused by expressions. For example, the 3D shape of the nose and the eye sockets is somewhat flattened. Figure 8.15 shows sample 3D faces of the same person. Although the facial surface changes significantly in the original space due to different facial expressions, the corresponding canonical representations in the embedded space look similar.

The approach was evaluated on a dataset consisting of 30 subjects with 220 face scans containing varying degrees of facial expression. The gallery consisted of neutral expressions only and the results were compared with rigid face matching [15].

8.10.3.1 Other Expression Modeling Approaches

Another example of facial expression modeling is the work of Al-Osaimi et al. [5]. In this approach, the facial expression deformation patterns are first learned using a linear PCA subspace called an *Expression Deformation Model*. The model is learnt using part of the FRGC v2 data augmented by over 3000 facial scans under different facial expressions. More specifically, the PCA subspace is built from shape residues between pairs of scans of the same face, one under neutral expression and the other under non-neutral facial expression. Before calculating the residue, the two scans are first registered using the ICP [9] algorithm applied to the semi-rigid regions of the faces (i.e. forehead and nose). Since the PCA space is computed from the residues, it only models the facial expressions as opposed to the human face.

The linear model is used during recognition to morph out the expression deformations from unseen faces leaving only interpersonal disparities. The shape residues between the probe and every gallery scan are calculated. Only the residue of the correct identity will account for the expression deformations and other residues will also contain shape differences. A shape residue $\mathbf{r}$ is projected to the PCA subspace E as follows:

$$\mathbf{r}' = \mathsf{E}(\mathsf{E}^T \mathsf{E})^{-1} \mathsf{E}^T \mathbf{r}. \quad (8.46)$$

If the gallery face from which the residue was calculated is the same as the probe, then the error between the original and reconstructed shape residues

$$\varepsilon = (\mathbf{r} - \mathbf{r}')^T (\mathbf{r} - \mathbf{r}') \quad (8.47)$$

will be small, otherwise it will be large. The probe is assigned the identity of the gallery face corresponding to the minimum value of ε. In practice, the projection is modified to avoid border effects and outliers in the data. Moreover, the projection is restricted to the dimensions of the subspace E where realistic expression residues can exist. Large differences between $\mathbf{r}$ and $\mathbf{r}'$ are truncated to a fixed value to avoid the effects of hair and other outliers. Note that it is not necessary that one of the facial expressions (while computing the residue) is neutral. One non-neutral facial expression can be morphed to another using the same PCA model. Figure 8.16 shows two example faces morphed from one non-neutral expression to another. Using the FRGC v2 dataset, verification rates at 0.001 FAR were 98.35 % and 97.73 % for face scans under neutral and non-neutral expressions respectively.

8.11 Research Challenges

After a decade of extensive research in the area of 3D face recognition, new representations and techniques that can be applied to this problem are continually being released in the literature. A number of challenges still remain to be surmounted. These challenges have been discussed in the survey of Bowyer et al. [14] and include

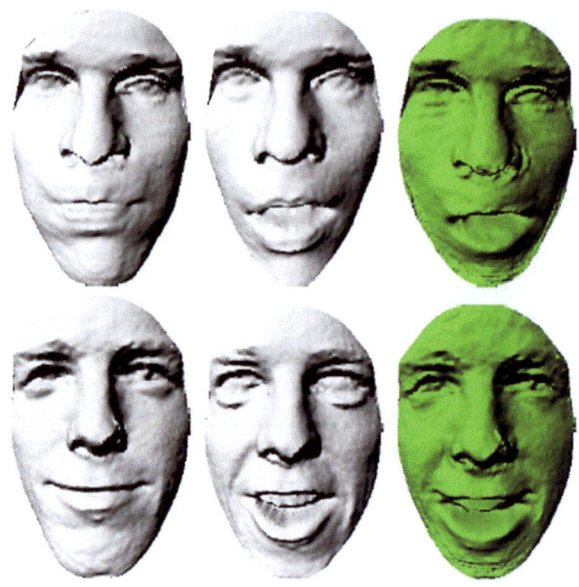

Fig. 8.16 *Left*: query facial expression. *Centre*: target facial expression. *Right*: the result of morphing the left 3D image in order to match the facial expression of the central 3D image. Figure courtesy of [5]

improved 3D sensing technology as a foremost requirement. Speed, accuracy, flexibility in the ambient scan acquisition conditions and imperceptibility of the acquisition process are all important for practical applications. Facial expressions remain a challenge as existing techniques lose important features in the process of removing facial expressions or extracting expression-invariant features. Although relatively small pose variations can be handled by current 3D face recognition systems, large pose variations often can not, due to significant self-occlusion. In systems that employ pose normalization, this will affect the accuracy of pose correction and, for any recognition system, it will result in large areas of missing data. (For profile views, this may be mitigated by the fact that the symmetrical face contains redundant information for discrimination.) Additional problems with capturing 3D data from a single viewpoint include noise at the edges of the scan and the inability to reliably define local regions (e.g. for local surface feature extraction), because these become eroded if they are positioned near the edges of the scan. Dark and specular regions of the face offer further challenges to the acquisition and subsequent preprocessing steps.

In addition to sensor technology improving, we expect to see improved 3D face datasets, with larger numbers of subjects and larger number of captures per subject, covering a very wide range of pose variation, expression variation and occlusions caused by hair, hands and common accessories (e.g. spectacles, hats, scarves and phone). We expect to see publicly available datasets that start to combine pose variation, expression variation, and occlusion thus providing an even greater challenge to 3D face recognition algorithms.

Passive techniques are advancing rapidly, for example, some approaches may no longer explicitly reconstruct the facial surface but directly extract features from multiview stereo images. One problem with current resolution passive stereo is that there is insufficient texture at a large enough scale to perform correspondence matching. As imaging technology improves, we will be able to see the fine detail of skin pores and other small-scale skin surface textures, which may provide enough distinctive texture for matching. Of course, with a much increased input data size associated with high resolution images, a commensurate increase in computational power is required and that depends on the complexity of the state-of-the-art feature extraction and dense matching algorithms.

3D video cameras are also appearing in the market opening up yet another dimension for video based 3D face recognition. Current 3D cameras usually have one or more drawbacks which may include: low resolution, offline 3D scene reconstruction, noisy reconstructions or high cost. However, it is likely that the technology will improve and the cost will decrease with time, particularly if the cameras are used in mass markets, such as computer games. A prime example of this is Microsoft's Kinect camera, released in 2010.

8.12 Concluding Remarks

In this chapter we presented the basic concepts behind 3D face recognition algorithms. In particular we looked at the individual stages in a typical 3D face scan processing pipeline that takes raw face scans and is able to make verification or identification decisions. We presented a wide range of literature relating to all of these stages. We explained several well-established 3D face recognition techniques (ICP, PCA, LDA) with a more tutorial approach and clear implementation steps in order to familiarize the reader with the area of 3D face recognition. We also presented a selection of more advanced methods that have shown promising recognition performance on benchmark datasets.

8.13 Further Reading

The interested reader is encouraged to refer to the original publications of the methods described in this chapter, and their references, for more details concerning the algorithms discussed here. There are several existing 3D face recognition surveys which give a good overview of the field, including those by Bowyer et al. [14], and Abate et al. [1]. Given that a range image can in many ways be treated like a standard 2D image, a good background in 2D face recognition is desirable. To this end we recommend starting with the wide ranging survey of Zhao et al. [96], although this relates to work prior to 2003. No doubt further surveys on 3D, 2D and 3D/2D face recognition will be published periodically in the future. In addition, the website www.face-rec.org [29] provides a range of information an all common face recognition modalities. Several of the chapters in this book are highly useful to the 3D face recognition researcher, particularly Chaps. 2–7 which include detailed discussions on 3D image acquisition, surface representations, 3D features, shape registration and shape matching. For good general texts on pattern recognition and machine learning we recommend the texts of Duda et al. [28] and Bishop [10].

8.14 Questions

1. What advantages can 3D face recognition systems have over standard 2D face recognition systems?
2. How can a 3D sensor be used such that the 3D shape information that it generates aids 2D-based face recognition? Discuss this with respect to the probe images being 3D and the gallery 2D and vice-versa.
3. What are the main advantages and disadvantages of feature-based 3D face recognition approaches when compared to holistic approaches?
4. Outline the main processing stages of a 3D face recognition system and give a brief description of the primary function of each stage. Indicate the circumstances under which some of the stages may be omitted.
5. Briefly outline the main steps of the ICP algorithm and describe its advantages and limitations in the context of 3D face recognition.
6. Provide a short proof of the relationship between eigenvalues and singular values given in (8.20).
7. Compare and contrast PCA and LDA in the context of 3D face recognition.

8.15 Exercises

In order to do these exercises you will need access to the FRGC v2 3D face dataset.

1. Build (or download) some utilities to load and display the 3D face scans stored in the ABS format files of the FRGC dataset.
2. Implement the cropping, spike removal and hole filling preprocessing steps as described in Sect. 8.5. Apply them to a small selection of scans in the FRGC v2 data and check that they operate as expected.
3. Implement an ICP-based face verification system, as described in Sect. 8.6 and use the pre-processed scans as input.
4. Implement a PCA-based 3D face recognition system, as described in Sect. 8.7, using raw depth data only and compare your results with the ICP-based system.
5. Use a facial mask to only include the upper half of the 3D face scan in training and testing data. Rerun your experimentations for ICP and PCA and compare with your previous results, particularly with a view to those scans that have non-neutral facial expressions.

References

1. Abate, A.F., Nappi, M., Riccio, D., Sabatino, G.: 2D and 3D face recognition: a survey. Pattern Recognit. Lett. **28**, 1885–1906 (2007)

2. Achermann, B., Jiang, X., Bunke, H.: Face recognition using range images. In: Int. Conference on Virtual Systems and MultiMedia, pp. 129–136 (1997)
3. Adini, Y., Moses, Y., Shimon, U.: Face recognition: the problem of compensating for changes in illumination direction. IEEE Trans. Pattern Anal. Mach. Intell. **19**(7), 721–732 (1997)
4. Al-Osaimi, F., Bennamoun, M., Mian, A.: Integration of local and global geometrical cues for 3D face recognition. Pattern Recognit. **41**(3), 1030–1040 (2008)
5. Al-Osaimi, F., Bennamoun, M., Mian, A.: An expression deformation approach to non-rigid 3D face recognition. Int. J. Comput. Vis. **81**(3), 302–316 (2009)
6. Angel, E.: Interactive Computer Graphics. Addison Wesley, Reading (2009)
7. Arun, K.S., Huang, T.S., Blostein, S.D.: Least-squares fitting of two 3-D point sets. IEEE Trans. Pattern Anal. Mach. Intell. **9**(5), 698–700 (1987)
8. Belhumeur, P., Hespanha, J., Kriegman, D.: Eigenfaces vs. fisherfaces: recognition using class specific linear projection. IEEE Trans. Pattern Anal. Mach. Intell. **19**, 711–720 (1997)
9. Besl, P., McKay, H.: A method for registration of 3-d shapes. IEEE Trans. Pattern Anal. Mach. Intell. **14**(2), 239–256 (1992)
10. Bishop, C.M.: Pattern Recognition and Machine Learning. Springer, Berlin (2006)
11. Blanz, V., Vetter, T.: Face recognition based on fitting a 3D morphable model. IEEE Trans. Pattern Anal. Mach. Intell. **25**, 1063–1074 (2003)
12. Blanz, V., Scherbaum, K., Seidel, H.: Fitting a morphable model to 3D scans of faces. In: IEEE Int. Conference on Computer Vision, pp. 1–8 (2007)
13. The Bosphorus 3D face database: http://bosphorus.ee.boun.edu.tr/. Accessed 5th July 2011
14. Bowyer, K., Chang, K., Flynn, P.: A survey of approaches and challenges in 3D and multi-modal 3D + 2D face recognition. Comput. Vis. Image Underst. **101**, 1–15 (2006)
15. Bronstein, A., Bronstein, M., Kimmel, R.: Three-dimensional face recognition. Int. J. Comput. Vis. **64**(1), 5–30 (2005)
16. CASIA-3D FaceV1: http://biometrics.idealtest.org. Accessed 5th July 2011
17. Chang, K., Bowyer, K., Flynn, P.: Face recognition using 2D and 3D facial data. In: Multi-modal User Authentication Workshop, pp. 25–32 (2003)
18. Chang, K., Bowyer, K., Flynn, P.: An evaluation of multimodal 2D+3D face biometrics. IEEE Trans. Pattern Anal. Mach. Intell. **27**(4), 619–624 (2005)
19. Chang, K., Bowyer, K., Flynn, P.: Multiple nose region matching for 3D face recognition under varying facial expression. IEEE Trans. Pattern Anal. Mach. Intell. **28**(10), 1695–1700 (2006)
20. Chua, C., Jarvis, R.: Point signatures: a new representation for 3D object recognition. Int. J. Comput. Vis. **25**(1), 63–85 (1997)
21. Chua, C., Han, F., Ho, Y.: 3D human face recognition using point signatures. In: Proc. IEEE Int. Workshop Analysis and Modeling of Faces and Gestures, pp. 233–238 (2000)
22. Colombo, A., Cusano, C., Schettini, R.: 3D face detection using curvature analysis. Pattern Recognit. **39**(3), 444–455 (2006)
23. Creusot, C., Pears, N.E., Austin, J.: 3D face landmark labelling. In: Proc. 1st ACM Workshop on 3D Object Retrieval (3DOR'10), pp. 27–32 (2010)
24. Creusot, C., Pears, N.E., Austin, J.: Automatic keypoint detection on 3D faces using a dictionary of local shapes. In: The First Joint 3DIM/3DPVT Conference on 3D Imaging, Modeling, Processing, Visualization and Transmission, pp. 16–19 (2011)
25. Creusot, C.: Automatic landmarking for non-cooperative 3d face recognition. Ph.D. thesis, Department of Computer Science, University of York, UK (2011)
26. DeCarlo, D., Metaxas, D.: Optical flow constraints on deformable models with applications to face tracking. Int. J. Comput. Vis. **38**(2), 99–127 (2000)
27. D'Erico, J.: Surface Fitting Using Gridfit. MATLAB Central File Exchange (2006)
28. Duda, R.O., Hart, P.E., Stork, D.G.: Pattern Classification, 2nd edn. Wiley-Interscience, New York (2001)
29. Face recognition homepage: http://www.face-rec.org. Accessed 24th August 2011
30. Faltemier, T.C., Bowyer, K.W., Flynn, P.J.: Using a multi-instance enrollment representation to improve 3D face recognition. In: 1st IEEE Int. Conf. on Biometrics: Theory, Applications, and Systems (BTAS'07) (2007)

31. Faltemier, T., Bowyer, K., Flynn, P.: A region ensemble for 3-D face recognition. IEEE Trans. Inf. Forensics Secur. **3**(1), 62–73 (2008)
32. Farkas, L.: Anthropometry of the Head and Face. Raven Press, New York (1994)
33. Fisher, N., Lee, A.: Correlation coefficients for random variables on a unit sphere or hypersphere. Biometrika **73**(1), 159–164 (1986)
34. Fitzgibbon, A.W.: Robust registration of 2D and 3D point sets. Image Vis. Comput. **21**, 1145–1153 (2003)
35. Fleishman, S., Drori, I., Cohen-Or, D.: Bilateral mesh denoising. ACM Trans. Graph. **22**(3), 950–953 (2003)
36. Gao, H., Davis, J.W.: Why direct LDA is not equivalent to LDA. Pattern Recognit. **39**, 1002–1006 (2006)
37. Garland, M., Heckbert, P.: Surface simplification using quadric error metrics. In: Proceedings of SIGGRAPH (1997)
38. Georghiades, A., Belhumeur, P., Kriegman, D.: From few to many: illumination cone models for face recognition under variable lighting and pose. IEEE Trans. Pattern Anal. Mach. Intell. **6**(23), 643–660 (2001)
39. Gokberk, B., Irfanoglua, M., Arakun, L.: 3D shape-based face representation and feature extraction for face recognition. Image Vis. Comput. **24**(8), 857–869 (2006)
40. Gordon, G.: Face recognition based on depth and curvature feature. In: IEEE Computer Society Conference on CVPR, pp. 808–810 (1992)
41. Gupta, S., Markey, M., Bovik, A.: Anthropometric 3D face recognition. Int. J. Comput. Vis. doi:10.1007/s11263-010-0360-8 (2010)
42. Heckbert, P., Garland, M.: Survey of polygonal surface simplification algorithms. In: SIGGRAPH, Course Notes: Multiresolution Surface Modeling (1997)
43. Heseltine, T., Pears, N.E., Austin, J.: Three-dimensional face recognition: an fishersurface approach. In: Proc. Int. Conf. Image Analysis and Recognition, vol. II, pp. 684–691 (2004)
44. Heseltine, T., Pears, N.E., Austin, J.: Three-dimensional face recognition: an eigensurface approach. In: Proc. IEEE Int. Conf. Image Processing, pp. 1421–1424 (2004)
45. Heseltine, T., Pears, N.E., Austin, J.: Three dimensional face recognition using combinations of surface feature map subspace components. Image Vis. Comput. **26**(3), 382–396 (2008)
46. Hesher, C., Srivastava, A., Erlebacher, G.: A novel technique for face recognition using range imaging. In: Int. Symposium on Signal Processing and Its Applications, pp. 201–204 (2003)
47. Horn, B.: Robot Vision. MIT Press, Cambridge (1986). Chap. 16
48. Jain, A., Ross, A., Prabhakar, S.: An introduction to biometric recognition. IEEE Trans. Circuits Syst. Video Technol. **14**(1), 4–20 (2004)
49. Johnson, A., Hebert, M.: Using spin images for efficient object recognition in cluttered 3D scenes. IEEE Trans. Pattern Anal. Mach. Intell. **21**(5), 674–686 (1999)
50. Kakadiaris, I., Passalis, G., Theoharis, T., Toderici, G., Konstantinidis, I., Murtuza, N.: Multimodal face recognition: combination of geometry with physiological information. In: Proc. IEEE Int. Conf on Computer Vision and Pattern Recognition, pp. 1022–1029 (2005)
51. Kakadiaris, I., Passalis, G., Toderici, G., Murtuza, M., Lu, Y., Karampatziakis, N., Theoharis, T.: Three-dimensional face recognition in the presence of facial expressions: an annotated deformable model approach. IEEE Trans. Pattern Anal. Mach. Intell. **29**(4), 640–649 (2007)
52. Kimmel, R., Sethian, J.: Computing geodesic on manifolds. Proc. Natl. Acad. Sci. USA **95**, 8431–8435 (1998)
53. Klassen, E., Srivastava, A., Mio, W., Joshi, S.: Analysis of planar shapes using geodesic paths on shape spaces. IEEE Trans. Pattern Anal. Mach. Intell. **26**(3), 372–383 (2004)
54. Koenderink, J.J., van Doorn, A.J.: Surface shape and curvature scales. Image Vis. Comput. **10**(8), 557–564 (1992)
55. Lee, J., Milios, E.: Matching range images of human faces. In: Int. Conference on Computer Vision, pp. 722–726 (1990)

56. Lee, Y., Shim, J.: Curvature-based human face recognition using depth-weighted Hausdorff distance. In: Int. Conference on Image Processing, pp. 1429–1432 (2004)
57. Lo, T., Siebert, J.P.: Local feature extraction and matching on range images: 2.5D SIFT. Comput. Vis. Image Underst. **113**(12), 1235–1250 (2009)
58. Lu, X., Jain, A.K.: Deformation modeling for robust 3D face matching. In: Proc IEEE Int. Conf. on Computer Vision and Pattern Recognition, vol. 2, pp. 1377–1383 (2006)
59. Lu, X., Jain, A., Colbry, D.: Matching 2.5D scans to 3D models. IEEE Trans. Pattern Anal. Mach. Intell. **28**(1), 31–43 (2006)
60. Mandal, C., Qin, H., Vemuri, B.: A novel FEM-based dynamic framework for subdivision surfaces. Comput. Aided Des. **32**(8–9), 479–497 (2000)
61. Maurer, T., Guigonis, D., Maslov, I., Pesenti, B., Tsaregorodtsev, A., West, D., Medioni, G.: Performance of Geometrix ActiveID 3D face recognition engine on the FRGC data. In: IEEE Workshop on Face Recognition Grand Challenge Experiments (2005)
62. Metaxas, D., Kakadiaris, I.: Elastically adaptive deformable models. IEEE Trans. Pattern Anal. Mach. Intell. **24**(10), 1310–1321 (2002)
63. Mian, A.: http://www.csse.uwa.edu.au/~ajmal/code.html. Accessed on 6th July 2011
64. Mian, A., Bennamoun, M., Owens, R.: An efficient multimodal 2D–3D hybrid approach to automatic face recognition. IEEE Trans. Pattern Anal. Mach. Intell. **29**(11), 1927–1943 (2007)
65. Mian, A., Bennamoun, M., Owens, R.: Keypoint detection and local feature matching for textured 3D face recognition. Int. J. Comput. Vis. **79**(1), 1–12 (2008)
66. Mian, A., Bennamoun, M., Owens, R.: On the repeatability and quality of keypoints for local feature-based 3D object retrieval from cluttered scenes. Int. J. Comput. Vis. (2010)
67. Medioni, G., Waupotitsch, R.: Face recognition and modeling in 3D. In: IEEE Int. Workshop Analysis and Modeling of Faces and Gestures, pp. 232–233 (2003)
68. MeshLab.: Visual computing Lab. ISTI-CNR. http://meshlab.sourceforge.net/. Cited 14 June, 2010
69. Padia, C., Pears, N.E.: A review and characterization of ICP-based symmetry plane localisation in 3D face data. Technical Report YCS 463, Department of Computer Science, University of York (2011)
70. Pan, G., Han, S., Wu, Z., Wang, Y.: 3D face recognition using mapped depth images. In: IEEE Workshop on Face Recognition Grand Challenge Experiments (2005)
71. Passalis, G., Kakadiaris, I.A., Theoharis, T., Toderici, G., Murtuza, N.: Evaluation of the UR3D algorithm using the FRGC v2 data set. In: Proc. IEEE Workshop on Face Recognition Grand Challenge Experiments (2005)
72. Pears, N.E., Heseltine, T., Romero, M.: From 3D point clouds to pose normalised depth maps. Int. J. Comput. Vis. **89**(2), 152–176 (2010). Special Issue on 3D Object Retrieval
73. Phillips, P., Flynn, P., Scruggs, T., Bowyer, K., Chang, J., Hoffman, K., Marques, J., Min, J., Worek, W.: Overview of the face recognition grand challenge. In: IEEE CVPR, pp. 947–954 (2005)
74. Piegl, L., Tiller, W.: The NURBS Book. Monographs in Visual Communication, 2nd edn. (1997)
75. Portilla, J., Simoncelli, E.: A parametric texture model based on joint statistic of complex wavelet coefficients. Int. J. Comput. Vis. **40**, 49–71 (2000)
76. Queirolo, C.Q., Silva, L., Bellon, O.R.P., Segundo, M.P.: 3D face recognition using simulated annealing and the surface interpenetration measure. IEEE Trans. Pattern Anal. Mach. Intell. **32**(2), 206–219 (2010)
77. Rusinkiewicz, S., Levoy, M.: Efficient variants of the ICP algorithm. In: Int. Conf. on 3D Digital Imaging and Modeling, pp. 145–152 (2001)
78. Samir, C., Srivastava, A., Daoudi, M.: Three-dimensional face recognition using shapes of facial curves. IEEE Trans. Pattern Anal. Mach. Intell. **28**(11), 1858–1863 (2006)
79. Savran, A., et al.: In: Bosphorus Database for 3D Face Analysis. Biometrics and Identity Management. Lecture Notes in Computer Science, vol. 5372, pp. 47–56 (2008)
80. Sethian, J.: A review of the theory, algorithms, and applications of level set method for propagating surfaces. In: Acta Numer., pp. 309–395 (1996)

81. Silva, L., Bellon, O.R.P., Boyer, K.L.: Precision range image registration using a robust surface interpenetration measure and enhanced genetic algorithms. IEEE Trans. Pattern Anal. Mach. Intell. **27**(5), 762–776 (2005)
82. Sirovich, L., Kirby, M.: Low-dimensional procedure for the characterization of human faces. J. Opt. Soc. Am. A **4**, 519–524 (1987)
83. Spira, A., Kimmel, R.: An ecient solution to the eikonal equation on parametric manifolds. Interfaces Free Bound. **6**(3), 315–327 (2004)
84. Swiss Ranger. Mesa Imaging. http://www.mesa-imaging.ch/. Cited 10 June, 2010
85. Tanaka, H., Ikeda, M., Chiaki, H.: Curvature-based face surface recognition using spherical correlation principal directions for curved object recognition. In: Int. Conference on Automated Face and Gesture Recognition, pp. 372–377 (1998)
86. Texas 3D face recognition database. http://live.ece.utexas.edu/research/texas3dfr/. Accessed 5th July 2011
87. Turk, M., Pentland, A.: Eigenfaces for recognition. J. Cogn. Neurosci. **3**, 71–86 (1991)
88. Viola, P., Jones, M.: Robust real-time face detection. Int. J. Comput. Vis. **57**(2), 137–154 (2004)
89. Xianfang, S., Rosin, P., Martin, R., Langbein, F.: Noise analysis and synthesis for 3D laser depth scanners. Graph. Models **71**(2), 34–48 (2009)
90. Xu, C., Wang, Y., Tan, T., Quan, L.: Automatic 3D face recognition combining global geometric features with local shape variation information. In: Proc. IEEE Int. Conf. Pattern Recognition, pp. 308–313 (2004)
91. Yan, P., Bowyer, K.W.: A fast algorithm for ICP-based 3D shape biometrics. Comput. Vis. Image Underst. **107**(3), 195–202 (2007)
92. Yang, M., Kriegman, D., Ahuja, N.: Detecting faces in images: a survey. IEEE Trans. Pattern Anal. Mach. Intell. **24**(1), 34–58 (2002)
93. Yin, L., Wei, X., Sun, Y., Wang, J., Rosato, M.J.: A 3D facial expression database for facial behavior research. In: 7th Int. Conf. on Automatic Face and Gesture Recognition (FGR06), pp. 211–216 (2006)
94. Yu, H., Yang, J.: A direct LDA algorithm for high-dimensional data—with application to face recognition. Pattern Recognit. **34**(10), 2067–2069 (2001)
95. Zhang, L., Snavely, N., Curless, B., Seitz, S.: Spacetime faces: high resolution capture for modeling and animation. ACM Trans. Graph. **23**(3), 548–558 (2004)
96. Zhao, W., Chellappa, R., Phillips, P., Rosenfeld, A.: Face recognition: a literature survey. In: ACM Computing Survey, vol. 35, pp. 399–458 (2003)

Chapter 9
3D Digital Elevation Model Generation

Hong Wei and Marc Bartels

Abstract This chapter presents techniques used for the generation of 3D digital elevation models (DEMs) from remotely sensed data. Three methods are explored and discussed—optical stereoscopic imagery, Interferometric Synthetic Aperture Radar (InSAR), and LIght Detection and Ranging (LIDAR). For each approach, the state-of-the-art presented in the literature is reviewed. Techniques involved in DEM generation are presented with accuracy evaluation. Results of DEMs reconstructed from remotely sensed data are illustrated. While the processes of DEM generation from satellite stereoscopic imagery represents a good example of passive, multi-view imaging technology, discussed in Chap. 2 of this book, InSAR and LIDAR use different principles to acquire 3D information. With regard to InSAR and LIDAR, detailed discussions are conducted in order to convey the fundamentals of both technologies.

9.1 Introduction

A digital elevation model (DEM) is a digital representation of a terrain's surface, created from terrain elevation data, with horizontal coordinates X and Y, and altitude Z. The methods used for DEM generation are roughly categorized as follows.

- DEM generation by passive remote sensors relying on natural energy sources like the sun. These could be airborne or spaceborne multispectral/panchromatic images evaluated as stereo-pairs to extract 3D information. This is also referred to as classical photogrammetry.
- DEM generation by active remote sensors, which sense artificial energy sources deliberately transmitted to a target. These include radar (Radio Detection And

---

H. Wei (✉) · M. Bartels
Computational Vision Group, School of Systems Engineering, University of Reading,
Reading RG6 6AY, UK
e-mail: h.wei@reading.ac.uk

M. Bartels
e-mail: marc.bartels.berlin@gmail.com

Ranging) stereo-pairs, InSAR (Interferometric Synthetic Aperture Radar), and LIDAR (LIght Detection And Ranging), which involves laser scanning.
- DEM generation by geodetic measurements. Geodetic instruments, which are integrated devices measuring lengths, angles, and levels of land surface, collect the measured coordinates (X, Y) and altitude (Z) point by point in a designated coordinate system (e.g. WGS84[1]). With these data, a topographic map of the area is made with contour lines. Digitizing these contour lines and gridding them if needed, turns the hardcopy map to digital data format (i.e. DEM). This is a traditional method.

Techniques discussed in this chapter are mainly concerned with DEM generation from remote sensing, and cover both passive and active approaches. Three key remote sensing methods for DEM generation are discussed as optical stereo imaging, InSAR, and LIDAR. Although optical stereo images and InSAR data can be acquired from both airborne and spaceborne remote sensing, only spaceborne is considered in the discussion, whereas for an airborne representative, LIDAR is presented. A brief literature review of these three techniques in DEM generation is given in each of Sects. 9.2, 9.3, and 9.4, respectively.

There are three relevant technical terms that we need to distinguish: DEM, DTM (Digital Terrain Model), and DSM (Digital Surface Model). A DEM is a general term referring to an elevation model; a DSM is a surface model representing sensor detected height including all visible objects on the top of a surface; and a DTM is a terrain model showing bare ground surface topography. In using spaceborne stereoscopic imagery and InSAR to generate DEMs, there is hardly any difference between DSM and DTM due to the typical elevation accuracy of ± 10 meters [38, 73], especially in rural areas where buildings and other man-made objects are absent from remotely sensed data. Under this circumstance, the term DEM is generally used to represent the 3D reconstruction in the photogrammetry and remote sensing community. However, with airborne LIDAR, the vertical accuracy and the capability to capture multiple returns (or echoes) necessitate the extension of the term DEM to the terms of DSM and DTM [143]. It is possible to remove objects and generate a more accurate DTM from the original DSM.

For many reasons, it has been a longstanding goal of mankind to be able to look at the Earth and find out what its surface or terrain looks like. With the development of remote sensing technologies and image interpretation techniques, it has become possible to see the Earth surface from a bird's eye view, as shown in Fig. 9.1. Such data has been used to monitor changes in the Earth's surface as a function of time, especially after natural disasters, such as volcanoes, earthquakes and tsunamis. It has also been used to predict land erosion and slides. In these applications, DEMs play an important role to recover the surface topography. Associated with co-registered satellite images, a vivid land surface can be displayed for visualization. Apart from visualization, DEMs are also required by many disciplines of scientific research involving studies of the Earth's land surface, such as cartography, climate modeling,

---

[1] WGS84: World Geodetic Systems dating from 1984 and last revised in 2004.

9 3D Digital Elevation Model Generation

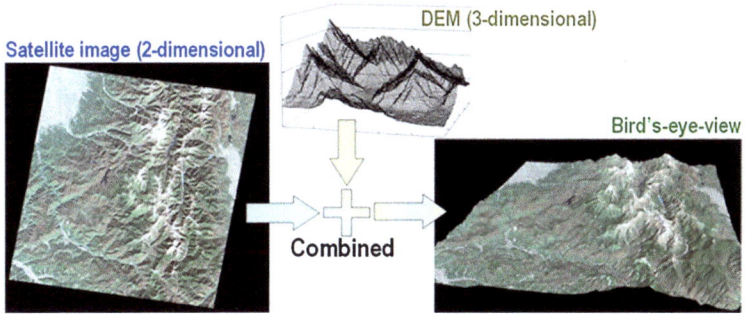

Fig. 9.1 Bird's eye view of a mountainous area from a 3D DEM mapped with texture from a satellite image. Copyright METI/NASA, reprinted with permission from ERSDAC (Earth Remote Sensing Data Analysis Center), http://www.ersdac.or.jp/GDEM/E/2.html

biogeography, geology, and soil science [80]. With the development of new remote sensing technologies with which data accuracy has dramatically improved, DEMs are also being used within an increasingly wide range of applications. These include site suitability studies for urban developments, telecommunications base stations and intelligent transportation systems, floodplain mapping and land erosion analysis, and applications in agriculture and forestry [105].

Chapter Outline   After this introduction, the chapter is organized in the following main sections.

- Section 9.2 introduces DEM generation from stereoscopic imagery. In this section, a detailed literature review is presented on the technique, followed by accuracy evaluation. A step-by-step guide is given in an example of DEM generation from stereoscopic imagery.
- Section 9.3 discusses the principle and techniques for DEM generation from InSAR and accuracy analysis is conducted with regards to error sources. Examples of DEM generation from InSAR show the detailed process.
- Section 9.4 details DEM generation from LIDAR. It covers LIDAR data acquisition, data types and accuracy, and LIDAR interpolation. Comprehensive literature review is given for LIDAR filtering, an important step towards an accurate DEM (or DTM). The algorithm of Skewness Balancing in DEM generation from LIDAR is presented in detail.
- Section 9.5 discusses the research challenges remaining in the area of 3D DEM generation from remote sensing.
- Section 9.6 summarizes the chapter and lists clear learning targets for readers to achieve.
- Section 9.7 gives additional reading material for readers to further expand their knowledge in the areas of remote sensing, geographical information systems, and InSAR and LIDAR techniques.

- Finally a set of questions and exercises is provided in Sects. 9.8 and 9.9 respectively.

9.2 DEM Generation from Stereoscopic Imagery

Compared to the traditional manual methods that use human operators, automated methods of DEM generation from remote sensing provide efficient, economic and reasonably accurate products covering extended areas of the Earth's surface. Remote sensing of the Earth's surface started with photographic film cameras and has been evolving to digital cameras with selective sensing bands, for example, multispectral, thermal, hyperspectral, and radar. In this section, we discuss the issues associated with DEM generation from stereo images that are sensed from natural light in spaceborne missions. As with all stereo 3D reconstruction, two or more images that sense a scene with overlapping areas are required. A stereo image pair can be formed by along-track or across-track arrangement of sensors as shown in Fig. 9.2.

Along-track is defined by the forward motion of the satellite along its orbital path, whereas across-track refers to a satellite traveling on different orbits, hence images covering the same area are taken from different orbits. In general, a stereo pair captured in an along-track mission has a shorter time interval between two images than that captured in an across-track mission [101]. Thus variable weather conditions have less effect on along-track stereo pairs than on across-track stereo pairs in these passive imaging scenarios. The distance between two sensors is called the baseline (B), and the nadir distance (vertical distance) from satellite to ground is referred to as the height (H), as illustrated in Fig. 9.2. The base to height (B/H) ratio is a key parameter in DEM generation from stereoscopic imagery. It is a criterion for choosing an adequate number of stereo pairs from the same or different orbits. This section presents a literature review of the techniques used for DEM generation

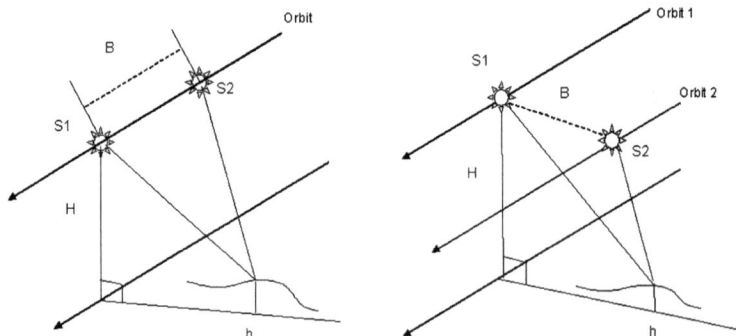

Fig. 9.2 DEM generation from satellite stereoscopic imagery. The *arrows* refer to the satellite's direction of flight. The *low arrowed lines* are the orthographic projection of the orbit onto the ground. Orbits 1 and 2 are two designated orbits that meet the requirements of stereo pairs. *Left*: Along-track. *Right*: Across-track

from remotely sensed stereoscopic imagery, followed by a discussion on quality evaluation of reconstructed DEMs. A step-by-step process to generate a DEM from a stereo pair is also presented.

9.2.1 Stereoscopic DEM Generation: Literature Review

The first space mission to provide stereoscopic imagery of the Earth's surface was the American CORONA[2] spy satellite program [52]. Over the past decades, a number of Earth observation satellites have been launched with high resolution imaging systems, such as Landsat (1972), IKONOS (1999), QUICKBIRD (2001), SPOT-5 (2002), ENVISAT (2002), ALOS (2006) and GeoEye-1 (2008). Stereo images acquired by these satellites can be along-track image pairs or across-track image pairs. DEM generation from a stereoscopic image pair involves the following processes [51, 68].

- Pre-processing of image pairs for noise removal: this is a process to mitigate the effects of noise introduced by the image sensors.
- Image matching: this is the process of finding corresponding points in two or more images and is implemented by either area-based or feature-based matching, or a combination of both.
- Triangulation process: image coordinates of matched points from the image pairs are transformed into ground coordinates using the cameras' interior and exterior parameters.[3] This process involves geometric modeling of the satellite camera system and the ground coordinate system.
- Evaluation of the reconstructed DEM: this process can be achieved by means of ground control points (GCPs), if available.

As indicated in Marr and Poggio's pioneering research on the computational theory of human stereo vision [109], there are two issues to address with respect to 3D reconstruction from stereo image pairs: correspondence and reconstruction (please refer to Chap. 2 of this book for the details). A key issue in automatic DEM generation is the process of image matching (solving the correspondence problem). Great efforts have been made by researchers from both remote sensing and computer vision communities in the 1980s [2, 11, 45, 57, 117, 130] to explore approaches in this field. In contrast to area-based cross-correlation, which dominated the field of image matching since the early 1950s, techniques developed in the period of the 1980s involved feature-based approaches. The combination of area-based and edge-based matching was attempted and applied by Förstner [45], Ackermann [2], and

---

[2]The CORONA program started in 1956 as a series of American strategic reconnaissance satellites. CORONA mission 9031 launched on 27th Feb. 1962 and was the first satellite providing stereoscopic images of the Earth.

[3]The terms 'interior' and 'exterior' are used in the DEM generation research community. In other research communities, such as computer vision, they are called 'intrinsic' and 'extrinsic' parameters, as discussed in Chap. 2.

Pertl [119] in DEM generation. Gruen developed a powerful model in which information from both image grey-level and first-order derivatives were incorporated for image matching [57]. With this model, adaptive least square correlation was performed to select the best match based on the fusion of point positioning with grey level information. It was claimed that the adaptive least square correlation provided a high matching accuracy. In terms of feature-based matching, Förstner and Gulch identified a series of feature points such as road intersections or centers of circular features which could be incorporated in matching algorithms [46]. Otto and Chau developed a region-growing algorithm for matching of terrain images [117]. They declared that their algorithm was an extension of Gruen's adaptive least squares correlation algorithm so that whole images can be automatically processed, instead of only selected patches. It was demonstrated that the developed algorithm was capable of producing high quality and dense range maps when the scene being viewed had significant texture and few discontinuities. Feature-based algorithms in satellite stereo image matching complement the situations in which the scene has a sparse texture and presents large discontinuities.

In the 1990s, the development of passive stereo imaging techniques in the field of Computer Vision made it possible to have more automated solutions for DEM generation from stereoscopic imagery. Techniques, such as the stereo matching algorithm with an adaptive window [87], the coarse-to-fine pyramidal area correlation stereo matching method [116], and the robust approach for matching using the epipolar constraint [183] were adapted by the remote sensing community. By using the main principles of passive stereo vision from the Faugeras' book [41], Gabet et al. worked out a solution for automatic generation of high resolution urban zone digital elevation models [51]. The work made use of an image sequence acquired with different base to height (B/H) ratios, hence, several stereo pairs are jointly used for DEM generation in a fixed area. With combinations of multiple algorithms covering both area-based and feature-based approaches, a fixed window size was used for cross-correlation in image matching. The authors claimed that the developed approach was universal to both airborne and spaceborne stereoscopic imagery, although only airborne data was tested due to the scope of the research. Wang [165] proposed an interesting structural image matching algorithm, in which an image descriptor was used for matching, which included points, lines, and regions structured by pre-defined relationships. The author demonstrated that the algorithm could achieve higher automation in DEM generation. The demand of automation for DEM generation within commercial software can also be seen in Heipke's review paper [69] and significant improvements had been made to aerial stereo images in the 1990s.

In the 21st century, researchers have continued their efforts on automated DEM generation from satellite images and developed methodologies aimed at improving DEM accuracy and the level of automation. More robust computer vision algorithms were developed for stereo image matching [106]. Commercial software, such as PCI Geomatics, Desktop Mapping System, ERDAS Imagine, ENVI software, amongst others appeared on the market including algorithms for automated DEM generation from stereoscopic imagery. Hirano et al. [73] examined ASTER[4] stereo image data for DEM generation. ASTER provides along-track stereo image data in near-infrared with a 15 m horizontal resolution at a B/H ratio of 0.6. Computed elevations from commercial software were compared with results from topographic map and USGS[5] DEMs at a few testing sites and conclusions were made that DEMs generated from ASTER could expect ± 7 m to ± 15 m elevation accuracy and up to 99 % correlation success rate with images of good quality and adequate ground control. Lee, et al. [98] argued that DEM generation from satellite images was time-consuming and error-prone. This was due to the fact that most DEM generation software used for processing satellite images was originally developed for aerial photos taken by perspective cameras, while satellite images may be formed by linear push-broom cameras. Hence, image matching and geometric modeling implemented in the software for aerial photos had to be modified for satellite imaging applications. In their paper, linear pushbroom cameras were modeled with the geometric properties in designing the matching strategy optimized in three aspects: conjugate search method, correlation patch design, and match sequence determination. It was claimed that the developed approach was universal for linear pushbroom images with various correlation algorithms and sensor models. DEM generation from SPOT-5 stereoscopic imagery was investigated in [21, 92, 125, 150]. SPOT-5 is equipped with two High Resolution Stereoscopic (HRS) cameras that are tilted $\pm 20°$ to acquire stereo pairs of 120 km swath, along the track of the satellite with a B/H ratio of 0.8, and the nadir looking-HRG (high resolution geometric) panchromatic camera providing additional images. HRS has a horizontal resolution of 10 m and HRG has a resolution of 5 m. A summary of the SPOT-5 payload and mission characteristics is given in [21]. In the above work, bundle adjustments were conducted to correct cameras' interior and exterior parameters in the geometric model. The best result was claimed in [150] with the vertical accuracy of 2.2 m for a smooth bare surface. In general, the DEM generated from SPOT-5 stereo images could achieve 5–10 m elevation accuracy with accurate and sufficient GCPs. DEMs generated from the IKONOS triplet (forward, nadir and backward) of stereoscopic imagery were investigated by Zhang and Gruen [182]. In their work, a multi-image matching approach was developed by using a coarse-to-fine hierarchical solution with an effective fusion of several matching algorithms and automatic quality control. It was reported that the DSM achieved 2–3 m elevation accuracy in the test area. With this accuracy, it is possible to consider DTMs to be extracted from the DSMs.

In June 2009, Japan's Ministry of Economy, Trade and Industry (METI) and NASA[6] jointly announced the release of Global Digital Elevation Model (GDEM) by stereo-correlating about 1.3 million scenes from ASTER data [85], as shown in Fig. 9.3. It has been indicated in its validation summary report [9] that ASTER

---

[4]ASTER: Advanced Spaceborne Thermal Emission and Reflection Radiometer, an imaging instrument flying on Terra satellite launched in December 1999 as part of NASA's Earth Observing System.

[5]USGS: United States Geological Survey.

[6]NASA: National Aeronautics and Space Administration.

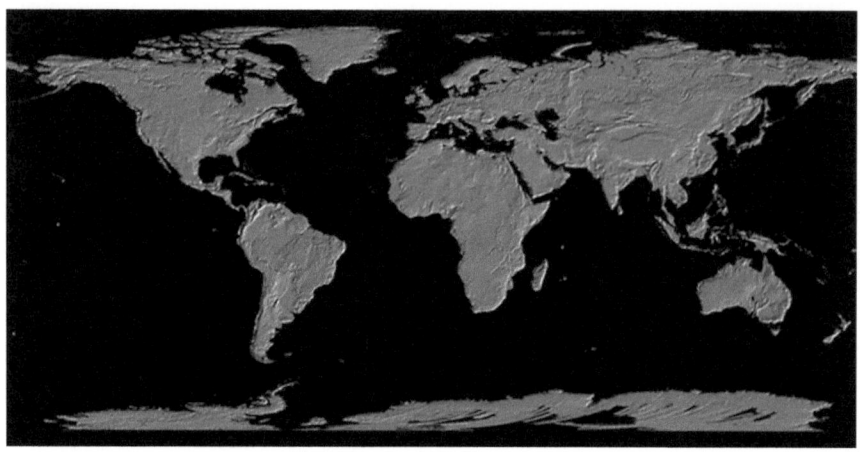

Fig. 9.3 Global DEM from ASTER. Copyright METI/NASA, reprinted with permission from ERSDAC, http://www.ersdac.or.jp/GDEM/E/4.htm

GDEM covers land surfaces between 83°N and 83°S with estimated accuracy of 20 m at 95 % confidence for vertical data and 30 m at 95 % confidence for horizontal data. Although ASTER GDEM was found to contain significant anomalies and artifacts, METI and NASA decided to release it for public use with belief of its potential benefits outweighing its flaws and with expectation of improving it via the user community.

Research into DEM generation has also expanded to Mars by a combination of stereoscopic imagery and the Mars orbiter's laser altimeter [58]. It can be foreseen that there will be the following improvements.

1. Further evaluation of geometric models to adaptively correct DEM errors caused by sensor platform attitude instability.
2. Development of more robust image matching algorithms for increasing automation and matching coverage.

For advanced stereo vision techniques that can be used for DEM generation from stereoscopic imagery, please refer to Chap. 2 of this book.

9.2.2 Accuracy Evaluation of DEMs

Quantitative evaluation of DEMs generated by satellite stereoscopic imagery can be conducted by comparing the reconstructed elevation values with GCPs collected by ground surveys or compared with corresponding DEMs generated by higher accuracy devices, such as LIDAR. In both cases, the measure of Root Mean Square Error

9 3D Digital Elevation Model Generation

(RMSE) is used in assessing the DEM accuracy. It is defined as

$$RMSE = \sqrt{\frac{\sum_{i=1}^{n} \Delta h_i^2}{n}} \qquad (9.1)$$

where n is the number of assessed points in evaluation, and Δh is the height difference between the assessed DEM and GCPs or reference DEM at point i. The standard deviation of the height difference can be calculated in Eq. (9.2).

$$\sigma = \sqrt{\frac{\sum_{i=1}^{n} (\Delta h_i - \Delta \bar{h})^2}{n}} \qquad (9.2)$$

where the mean height difference is given as $\Delta \bar{h} = \frac{1}{n} \sum_{i=1}^{n} \Delta h_i$. Assuming that the measured data has a normal distribution, $\pm 1\sigma$ gives 68 % level of confidence and $\pm 2\sigma$ gives 95 % level of confidence in measurements. In the remote sensing community, the elevation accuracy is usually represented by RMSE with a level of confidence, for example, 20 m with LE95 (Linear Error with confidence of 95 %).

Possible error sources are considered in order to improve DEM accuracy. Error propagation can be tracked along the processes of DEM generation, for example, errors due to image matching and 3D reconstruction from the geometric modeling. Geometric modeling to recover elevations from stereo images is the well-known perspective projection from image coordinates to cartographic coordinates. The projection involves elementary transformations (rotations and translations), which are functions of the cameras' interior and exterior parameters. This requires prior knowledge of the cameras, platforms, and cartographic coordinate systems. Based on such prior knowledge, a rigorous model based on collinearity conditions can be used for DEM generation. This geometric model integrates the following transformations [149, 150], where the xoy refers to the image coordinate system, rotations and translations are also referred to images, and the z-axis represents the direction perpendicular to the image common plane (usually same as the z-axis to the cartographic system).

- Rotation from the camera reference to the platform reference.
- Translation to the Earth's center (refers to the cartographic coordinate system).
- Rotation that takes into account the platform variation over time.
- Rotation to align the z-axis with the image center on the Earth's surface.
- Translation to the image center.
- Rotation to align the y-axis in the meridian plane.
- Rotation to have xoy (the image plane) tangential to the Earth.
- Rotation to align the x-axis in the image scan direction.
- Rotation-translation into the cartographic coordinate system.

With the geometric model and possible errors introduced by each step of the process, the integration of different distortions and their impact to the final elevation can be derived [147]. In the derivation, each of the model parameters is the combination of several correlated variables of the total viewing geometry. These include the following.

- The orientation of the image is a combination of the platform heading due to orbital inclination, the yaw of the platform, and the convergence of the meridian.
- The scale factor in the along-track direction is a combination of the velocity, the altitude and the pitch of the platform, the detection signal time of the sensor and the component of the Earth's rotation in the along-track direction.
- The leveling angle in the across-track direction is a combination of platform roll, the viewing angle, the orientation of the sensor and the Earth's curvature.

Mathematical models establishing geometrical relationships between the image and cartographic coordinates can be rigorous or approximate [64]. Rigorous modeling can be applied when a comprehensive understanding of the imaging geometry exists. However in many cases, it is difficult to obtain accurate interior and exterior parameters of the imaging system due to the lack of sufficient control. Therefore, approximate modeling has been developed for real-world use. Approximate models include direct linear transformation (DLT), self-calibration DLT, rational function models, and parallel projection [64]. In analyzing the accuracy potential of DEMs generated by high-resolution satellite stereoscopic imagery, Fraser [48] pointed out that a mathematical model, such as collinearity equations, needs to be modified for different settings in a rigorous model with stereo-bundle adjustments, while in the absence of the sensors' attitude data and sensors' orbital parameters, approximate models are recommended.

To improve the imaging geometry, researchers have paid special attention to the B/H ratio in acquiring satellite stereo pairs. A systematic investigation was conducted by Hasegawa et al. [67]. In their research, the impact of the B/H ratio to DEM accuracy was analyzed and the conclusion was made that B/H ratios ranging from 0.5 to 0.9 give better results for automatic DEM generation from stereo pairs. Li et al. designed an accurate model of the intersection angle and B/H ratio for a spaceborne three linear array camera system [100]. It was indicated that the B/H ratio was directly related to the DEM accuracy. A favourable imaging geometry can be achieved by a B/H ratio of 0.8 or more [48]. With SPOT-5, the viewing angle can be adjusted to tune the across-track B/H ratio between 0.6 and 1.1 and the along-track B/H ratio to around 0.8 [150].

From an application point of view, errors of terrain representation (ETR) are also taken into account since these may propagate through GIS operations and affect the quality of final products which use DEMs [31]. When interpolation is needed, the way to represent the terrain surface contributes to DEM accuracy. Chen and Yue [31] developed a promising method of surface modeling based on the theorem of surface. In their work, a terrain surface was defined by the first and second fundamental coefficients with information of the surface geometric properties and its deviation from the tangent plane at the point under consideration. It was demonstrated in their work that a good criterion for DEM accuracy evaluation should have included not only errors generated in 3D reconstruction from stereoscopic geometry but also ETR at a global level. When using a DEM in an application product, ETR should be counted as an input error.

9 3D Digital Elevation Model Generation

Table 9.1 Characteristics of the SPOT-5 stereo-pair acquired over the study site

Acquisition date	Sun angle	Stereo	View angle	B/H	Image (km)	Pixel (m)	No. GCPs
05 May 2003	52°	Multidate	+23°	0.77	60 × 60	5 × 5	33
25 May 2003	55°	across-track	−19°				

9.2.3 An Example of DEM Generation from SPOT-5 Imagery

In this section, the main steps in DEM generation from a satellite stereoscopic image pair are outlined. The example presented in this section is from [149]. The study site is the area around Quebec City, QC, Canada (47°N, 71°30′W). The information of the SPOT-5 stereo images in panchromatic mode is listed in Table 9.1.

A perspective projection model is established based on the geometric positions of the satellite, the camera, and the cartographic coordinate. This model links the 3D cartographic coordinate to the image coordinates, and the mathematical expression is given by Eqs. (9.3) and (9.4) [147, 148]:

$$\kappa_u u + y(1 + \delta\gamma X) - \beta H - H_0 \Delta T^* = 0 \quad (9.3)$$

$$X + \theta \frac{H}{\cos \chi} + \alpha v \left(k_v + \theta X - \frac{H}{\cos \chi} \right) - k_v \Delta R = 0 \quad (9.4)$$

where

$$X = (x - ay)\left(1 + \frac{z}{N_0}\right) + by^2 + cxy \quad (9.5)$$

and

$$H = z - \frac{x^2}{2N_0} \quad (9.6)$$

Parameters involved in Eqs. (9.3)–(9.6) are explained as follows.

H	is the altitude of the point corrected for Earth curvature;
H_0	is the satellite elevation at the image center line;
N_0	is the normal to the Earth;
a	is mainly a function of the rotation of the Earth;
α	is the instantaneous field-of-view;
u, v	are the image coordinates;
k_u, k_v	are the scale factors in along-track and cross-track, respectively;
β and θ	are a function of the leveling angles in along-track and across-track, respectively;
ΔT^* and ΔR	are the non-linear attitude variations (ΔT^*: combination of pitch and yaw; ΔR: roll);
$x, y,$ and z	are the ground coordinates;
b, c, χ and $\delta\gamma$	are second-order parameters, which are a function of the total geometry (e.g. satellite, image, and Earth).

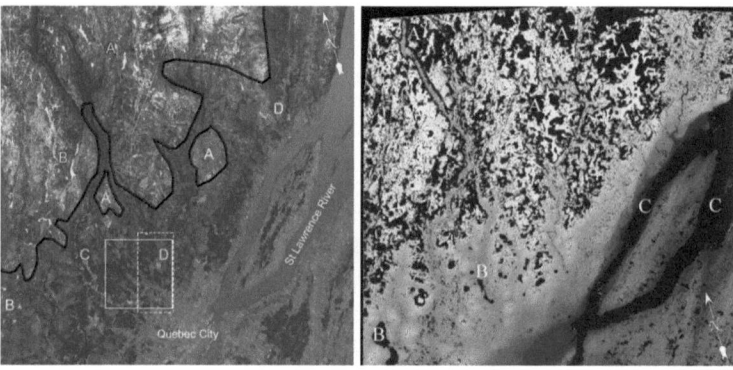

Fig. 9.4 *Left*: SPOT-5 image captured on 5 May 2003. *Right*: DEM generated from the stereo pair. *A*: melting snow; *B*: frozen lakes; *C*: the St. Lawrence River with significant melting ice; *D*: down-hill ski stations with snow. Figure courtesy of [149]

The ground control points (GCPs) with known (x, y, z) coordinates and corresponding (u, v) image coordinates are employed for the bundle adjustment to obtain parameters in the mathematical model. The processing steps of DEM generation from SPOT-5 stereo images (see Fig. 9.4(left)) are as follows.

1. Acquisition and pre-processing of the remote sensed data (images and metadata showing configuration of image acquisition) to determine an approximate value for each parameter of the 3D projection model.
2. Collection of GCPs with their 3D cartographic coordinates and 2D image coordinates. GCPs covered the total surface with points at the lowest and highest elevation to avoid extrapolations, both in x, y and elevation.
3. Computation of the 3D projection model, initialized with the approximate parameter values and refined by an iterative least-squares bundle adjustment with the GCPs.
4. Extraction of matching points from the two stereo images by using a multi-scale normalized cross-correlation method with computation of the maximum of the correlation coefficient.
5. Computation of (x, y, z) cartographic coordinates from the matching points in a regular grid spacing using the adjusted projection model (from step 3).

The full DEM (60 km × 60 km with a 5 m grid spacing) is extracted as shown in Fig. 9.4(right). It reproduces the terrain features, such as the St. Lawrence River and a large island in the middle. The black areas correspond to mismatched areas due to radiometric differences between the multi-date images. In this case, they are a result of snow in the mountains and on frozen lakes. The quantitative evaluation is conducted by comparison of the DEM generated from the SPOT-5 stereo images to a LIDAR acquired DEM with the accuracy of 0.15 m in elevation. Accuracies of 6.5 m (LE68) and 10 m (LE90) were achieved, corresponding to an image matching error of ±1 pixel.

9.3 DEM Generation from InSAR

Interferometric Synthetic Aperture Radar (InSAR) is the combination of SAR and interferometry techniques. SAR systems, operating at microwave frequencies, provide unique images representing the geometrical and electrical properties of the surface in nearly all weather conditions. DEM generation from InSAR is an active sensing process which is largely independent of weather conditions and can operate at any time throughout the day or night. A conventional SAR only produces 2D images reflecting the location of a target in the along-track axis, which is the axis along the flight track (azimuth range, X), and the across-track axis, which is the axis defined as the range from the SAR to the target (slant range, Y). The altitude-dependent distortion of SAR images can only be viewed in X and Y with ambiguous interpretation. Therefore, it is impossible to use a single SAR image to recover surface elevation. The development of InSAR techniques has enabled measurement of the third dimension (the elevation), which relies on the phase difference from two SAR images covering the same area and acquired from slightly different angles.

DEM generation from satellite-based SAR was reviewed by Toutin and Gray [151] with four different categories: stereoscopy, clinometry, polarimetry and interferometry (InSAR). Stereoscopy employs the same geometric triangulation principle used in optical stereoscopy for recovering elevation information, clinometry utilises the concept of shape from shading and polarimetry works on a complex scattering matrix based on a theoretical scattering model for tilted and slightly rough dielectric surfaces to calculate the azimuthal slopes, hence generating the elevation. InSAR also employs triangulation, but in a different implementation to stereoscopy, and can measure to an accuracy of millimeters to centimeters, which is a fraction of the SAR wavelength, whereas the other three methods are only accurate to the order of the SAR image resolution (several meters or more) [129]. DEM generation from InSAR is introduced in this section. For the other categories, please refer to [151] for details.

9.3.1 Techniques for DEM Generation from InSAR

The concept of incorporating interferometry to radar for topographic measurement can be traced back to Roger and Ingalls' Venus research in 1969 [127]. Zisk used the same method for moon topography measurements [184], while Graham employed InSAR for Earth observation by an airborne SAR system [56]. However the real development of InSAR in DEM generation from spaceborne SAR instruments has been supported by the availability of suitable globally acquired SAR data from ERS-1 (1991), JERS-1 (1992), ERS-2 (1995), RADARSAT-1 (1995), SRTM (2000), Envisat (2002), RADARSAT-2 (2007), and TanDEM-X (2010). The technique has been considered mature since the late 1990s. The following section introduces InSAR concepts and their application to DEM generation.

Fig. 9.5 InSAR imaging geometry: The radar signal is transmitted from antenna S_1 and received simultaneously at S_1 and S_2. The phase difference of the two echoes is proportional to Δr, which depends on the baseline angle α, look angle θ, satellite altitude H, range vectors r_1 and r_2, and target elevation h

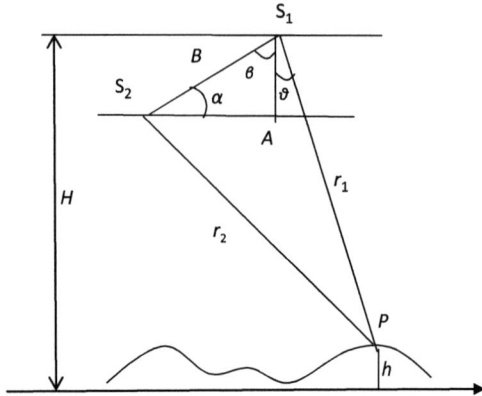

9.3.1.1 Basic Principle of InSAR in Elevation Measurement

InSAR in DEM generation requires that two SAR images of a target are acquired from different positions by a sensor (or sensors) with nearly the same observation angles. The phase difference between these two observations is then used to derive the elevation. The two SAR images can be taken at the same time (single-pass interferometry) or at different times (repeat-pass interferometry) over the target. Figure 9.5 depicts a simplified InSAR imaging geometry [1]. S_1 and S_2 are two sensor positions, r_1 and r_2 are range vectors from the two sensors to the target point **P** with elevation h, satellite altitude is H, the baseline is B, α is the baseline orientation angle, and θ is the look angle.

A complex signal returning to the SAR from the target **P** is expressed by

$$S = Ae^{j\phi} \tag{9.7}$$

where A is the amplitude and ϕ is the phase. Two complex SAR images (a 'master' and a 'slave') are formed from positions S_1 and S_2. Therefore the phase difference ψ between S_1 and S_2 is directly related to the path difference between r_1 and r_2, as follows:

$$\psi = -\frac{4\pi}{\lambda}\Delta r \tag{9.8}$$

where λ is the SAR signal wavelength, and $\Delta r = r_2 - r_1$.

The imaging geometry in Fig. 9.5 demonstrates the relationship of B, r_1, r_2, α, and θ. In order to derive the formula which expresses the relationship quantitatively, two additional elements are introduced: one is point A, a perpendicular intersection point of line $S_1 A$ and line $S_2 A$, and the other is angle β, the complementary angle of $90°$ to α in the right angled triangle $S_1 S_2 A$. According to a trigonometric theorem, applied to the triangle $S_1 S_2 P$, the following equation is satisfied:

$$\cos(\beta + \theta) = \frac{r_2^2 - r_1^2 - B^2}{-2r_1 B} \quad \text{or} \quad r_2^2 = r_1^2 + B^2 - 2r_1 B \cos(\beta + \theta) \tag{9.9}$$

In Eq. (9.9), $\cos(\beta + \theta)$ can be expanded to

$$\cos(\beta + \theta) = \cos\beta \cos\theta - \sin\beta \sin\theta \tag{9.10}$$

9 3D Digital Elevation Model Generation

In the right angled triangle $S_1 S_2 A$ of Fig. 9.5, $\sin\beta = \cos\alpha$ and $\cos\beta = \sin\alpha$. Substituting these into the right-hand side of Eq. (9.10), we have

$$\cos(\beta + \theta) = \sin\alpha \cos\theta - \cos\alpha \sin\theta = -\sin(\theta - \alpha) \tag{9.11}$$

Substituting Eq. (9.11) to Eq. (9.9), the relationship of B, r_1, r_2, α, and θ is expressed in Eq. (9.12), and the target elevation h can be calculated from Eq. (9.13) based on the geometric relation shown in Fig. 9.5.

$$\sin(\theta - \alpha) = \frac{r_2^2 - r_1^2 - B^2}{2 r_1 B} \tag{9.12}$$

$$h = H - r_1 \cos\theta \tag{9.13}$$

In Eq. (9.12), r_1 is replaced by r, and r_2 by $r + \Delta r$, then it can be re-written as

$$\sin(\theta - \alpha) = \frac{(r + \Delta r)^2 - r^2 - B^2}{2 r B} \tag{9.14}$$

Replacing $\cos\theta$ in Eq. (9.13) by $\sin(\theta - \alpha)$ in such a way that it can be rewritten as

$$h = H - r\{\cos\alpha \sqrt{1 - [\sin^2(\theta - \alpha)]} - \sin\alpha \sin(\theta - \alpha)\} \tag{9.15}$$

In practice, the SAR altitude H, the baseline B, and the baseline orientation angle α are estimated from knowledge of the orbit, and the range r, half the round-trip distance of radar signal, is measured by the SAR internal clock. Knowing the phase difference ψ from the interferometric fringes of two SAR images, the path difference Δr can be calculated from Eq. (9.8), hence $\sin(\theta - \alpha)$ can be derived from Eq. (9.14), and finally the elevation value is calculated from Eq. (9.15).

The phase difference between the two SAR images is normally represented as an interferogram, an image which is the product of the complex master image convolved with the complex slave image. It is important to appreciate that only the principal values of the phase, (i.e. modulo 2π), can be measured from the interferogram. The 2π phase difference corresponds to one cycle of interferometric fringe. The total path difference of the two receivers is multiples of the radar wavelength, (i.e. multiples of 2π in terms of phase). The process of *phase unwrapping* estimates this integer number in the interferometry. It is a key process in DEM generation from InSAR.

In many cases, the InSAR imaging geometry may differ from that demonstrated in Fig. 9.5. However, the principle of deriving the target elevation from the interferogram is similar and involves the following two steps:

1. Find out the path difference from the phase difference.
2. Calculate the topography based on the path difference with other known geometric parameters.

Figure 9.5 is a simplified model and the phase of SAR signals contains other information beyond topography. For a detailed description of InSAR and a better understanding of the signal modeling, please refer to [72].

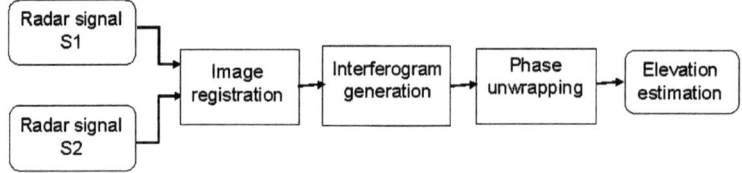

Fig. 9.6 Processing stages of DEM generation from InSAR

9.3.1.2 Processing Stages of DEM Generation from InSAR

DEM generation from InSAR may involve different approaches, as presented in various published work [1, 38, 71, 95, 123, 135, 180]. In general, the processing stages to generate DEMs from spaceborne InSAR can be summarized in Fig. 9.6.

When two radar signals are acquired, image registration is accomplished either based on cross-correlation of the image radiometry (speckle correlation) or by optimizing phase patterns for the area extracted from the two images. All image registration techniques developed in the image processing community can be used for this purpose [185]. Visual identification of a corresponding point in both images sometimes is needed. Sub-pixel registration accuracy has been reported in the remote sensing community for InSAR image registration [102]. For those co-registered pixels, an interferogram is formed by averaging the corresponding amplitudes and differencing the corresponding phase at each pixel. The phase of the interferogram contains information on the differential range from the target to the SAR antenna in the two paths, which is related to the elevation of the target. Normally the interferogram needs to be filtered for noise removal. Many algorithms have been developed for interferogram filtering, such as filtering based on pivoting median [97], adaptive phase noise [86], locally adaptive [173], and adaptive contoured window approaches [178]. In case of the presence of large co-registration errors, various techniques can be used for error correction to ensure a high quality interferogram [99]. Figure 9.7 shows an example of interferogram images in the form of magnitude (left) and phase (right).

As mentioned previously, the interferogram phase shown in Fig. 9.7(right) only reflects the principal value of modulo 2π. The phase difference that corresponds to the path difference of the two SAR positions to a target, is a multiple of the 2π in terms of phase. The phase unwrapping process aims to recover the integer number, which gives the multiple of modulo 2π. InSAR phase unwrapping has remained an active research area for several decades. Many approaches have been proposed and applied. In their pioneering research, Goldstein et al. [54] proposed the integration of a branch-cut approach in 2D phase-unwrapping. Least squares methods for phase unwrapping were developed in 1970s [49, 79] and have been widely adapted in InSAR elevation estimation [71, 121]. In the last two decades, further methods have been developed including network programming [36], region growing [174], hierarchical network flow [29], data fusion by means of Kalman filtering [103], multichannel phase unwrapping with graph cuts [42], complex-valued Markov random field

9 3D Digital Elevation Model Generation

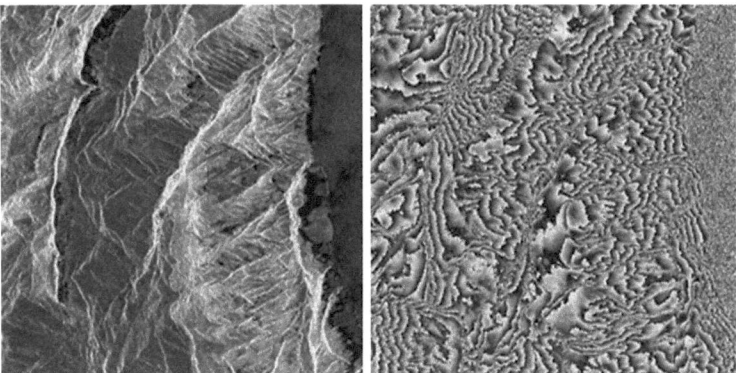

Fig. 9.7 Interferogram images from InSAR. *Left*: magnitude. *Right*: phase. The original two SAR images are ERS-1 data, imaging Sardinia, Italy, from frame 801, orbit 241, August 2, 1991 and orbit 327, August 8, 1991, centered at $40°8'$N, $9°32'$E. 512×512 pixels represent a 16 km $\times$ 16 km portion of the scene. Figure courtesy of http://sar.ece.ubc.ca/papers/UNWRAPPING/PU.html

model [176], particle filtering [110], phase unwrapping by Markov chain Monte Carlo energy minimization [5], and cluster-analysis-based multi-baseline phase unwrapping [177].

Fundamentally all existing phase unwrapping algorithms start from the fact that it is possible to determine the discrete derivatives of the unwrapped phase, that are the neighbouring pixel differences in the wrapped phase when these differences are mapped into the interval of $(-\pi, \pi)$. By summing these discrete derivatives (or phase differences), the unwrapped phase can be calculated. This is based on the assumption that the original scene is sampled densely enough and the true (unwrapped) phase does not change by more than $\pm\pi$ between adjacent pixels. If the hypothesis fails, so-called phase inconsistencies occur, that can lead to phase unwrapping errors. Phase unwrapping algorithms differ in the way that they deal with the difficulty of phase inconsistencies. Two classical approaches to phase unwrapping, branch cuts and least squares, are now detailed [129].

The Branch-Cut Method of Phase Unwrapping The basic idea is to unwrap the phase by choosing only paths of integration that lead to self-consistent solutions [54]. Theoretically the unwrapped solution should be independent of the integration path. This implies that the integral of the differenced phase of a closed path is zero in the error-free case. In other words, phase inconsistencies occur when the phase difference summed around a closed path formed by each mutually neighbouring set of four pixels is non-zero. Referred as *residues*, these points are classified as either positively or negatively 'charged' depending on the sign of the sum in a clockwise path. Branch-cuts connect nearby positive and negative residues such that no net residues can be encircled and no global errors can be accumulated. Figure 9.8 illustrates an example of a branch cut and allowable and forbidden paths of integration.

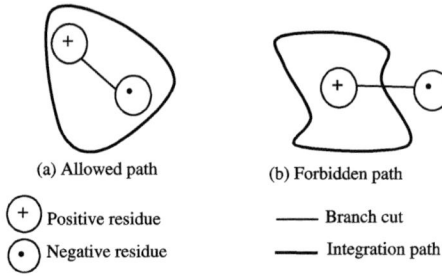

Fig. 9.8 Integration paths in phase unwrapping under the branch-cut rule

One key issue in the design of branch cuts based unwrapping algorithms is the selection of optimum cuts, especially when the density of the residue population is high. The algorithm developed by Goldstein et al. [54] gives the following steps to connect residues with branch cuts.

1. The interferogram is scanned until a residue is found.
2. A box of size 3×3 pixels is placed around the residue and is searched for another residue.
3. If found, a cut is placed between them.
   - If the sign of the two residue is opposite, the cut is designated 'uncharged' and the scan continues for another residue.
   - If the sign of the residue is the same as the original, the box is moved to the new residue and the search continues until either an opposite sign residue is located or no new residues can be found within the boxes.
4. For the latter case in step 3, the size of the box is increased by 2 pixels and the algorithm repeats from the current starting residue.

Finally, all of the residues lie on cuts that are uncharged, allowing no global error. The phase differences are integrated in such a way that there is no integration path crossing any of the cuts. Although branch-cuts based algorithms provide an effective way in phase unwrapping, the main disadvantage is that it may need operator intervention to succeed [44].

The Least Squares (LS) Method of Phase Unwrapping LS algorithms minimize the mean square difference between the gradients of the unwrapped phase (estimated solution) and the wrapped phase. Ghiglia and Romero gave the following expression for the sum t to be minimized [53]:

$$t = \sum_{i=0}^{M-2} \sum_{j=0}^{N-1} \left(\phi_{i+1,j} - \phi_{i,j} - \Delta_{i,j}^x\right)^2 + \sum_{i=0}^{M-1} \sum_{j=0}^{N-2} \left(\phi_{i,j+1} - \phi_{i,j} - \Delta_{i,j}^y\right)^2 \quad (9.16)$$

where $\phi_{i,j}$ is the unwrapped estimate corresponding to the wrapped value $\varphi_{i,j}$ and:

$$\begin{aligned}\Delta_{i,j}^x &= W(\varphi_{i,j} - \varphi_{i-1,j}) \\ \Delta_{i,j}^y &= W(\varphi_{i,j} - \varphi_{i,j-1})\end{aligned} \quad (9.17)$$

with the operator $W()$ wrapping values into the range of $-\pi \leq \varphi \leq \pi$. M and N refer to the image size in two dimensions. To find the minimum in Eq. (9.16) is equivalent to solving the following system of linear equations:

$$(\phi_{i+1,j} - 2\phi_{i,j} + \phi_{i-1,j}) + (\phi_{i,j+1} - 2\phi_{i,j} + \phi_{i,j-1}) = \rho_{i,j} \quad (9.18)$$

where

$$\rho_{i,j} = \left(\Delta^x_{i,j} - \Delta^x_{i-1,j}\right) + \left(\Delta^y_{i,j} - \Delta^y_{i,j-1}\right). \quad (9.19)$$

Equation (9.18) represents a discretized version of Poisson's equation [121]. The LS problem can be formulated as the solution of the set of linear equations:

$$A\phi = \rho \quad (9.20)$$

where A is an $MN \times MN$ sparse matrix, vector ρ contains values of wrapped phase, and vectors ϕ is the unwrapped values to be estimated. Although LS based methods are computationally very efficient when they make use of Fast Fourier transform (FFT) techniques, they are not very accurate because local errors tend to spread without means of limitation [53].

In practice, it is hard to operate the phase unwrapping process in a totally automated fashion in spite of vast investigation and research in this aspect of InSAR [151]. Human interventions are always needed. Therefore, in order to improve automation, phase unwrapping remains an active research area.

9.3.2 Accuracy Analysis of DEMs Generated from InSAR

The accuracy of the final DEMs generated from InSAR may be affected by many factors from SAR instrument design to image analysis. The major problems can be summarized as follows [1].

1. Inaccurate knowledge of acquisition geometry.
2. Atmospheric or ionospheric delays.
3. Phase unwrapping errors.
4. Decorrelation on land use types (scattering composition or geometry) which increases phase noise in the interferogram.
5. Layover or shadowing, which may directly affect interferometry.

For InSAR operational conditions, a critical baseline was defined for choosing SAR image pairs to generate an interferogram [112]. The concept of the critical baseline was introduced to describe the maximum separation of the satellite orbits in the direction orthogonal to both the along-track (azimuth) and the across-track (slant). If the critical value is exceeded, it would not be expected to have clear phase fringes in the interferogram. Toutin and Gray [151] indicated that the optimum baseline is terrain dependent; moderate to large slopes can generate a phase that can be difficult to process in the phase unwrapping stage and a baseline between a third and a half of the critical baseline is good for DEM generation, if terrain slope is moderate.

The final elevation error can be propagated from each variable presented in Eqs. (9.8), (9.14) and (9.15), as a function of H, B, α, r, and Δr (i.e. phase difference ψ). Based on geometric errors caused by H, B, α, r, and ψ, the related elevation error can be calculated by partially differentiating these functions [126], as shown in Eq. (9.21).

$$\begin{aligned} \delta h_H &= \delta H \\ \delta h_B &= -r \tan(\theta - \alpha)(\sin\theta + \cos\theta \tan\tau)\frac{\delta B}{B} \\ \delta h_\alpha &= r(\sin\theta + \cos\theta \tan\tau)\delta\alpha \\ \delta h_r &= -\cos\theta \delta r \\ \delta h_\psi &= \frac{4\pi r(\sin\theta + \cos\theta \tan\tau)}{\lambda B \cos(\theta - \alpha)}\delta\psi \end{aligned} \quad (9.21)$$

where τ is the terrain surface slope in the slant range direction. The overall elevation error can be a sum of the errors presented in Eq. (9.21). To rectify errors in Eqs. (9.21), a useful way to identify errors is from the following three aspects.

1. *Random errors.* These are errors randomly introduced in the DEM generation procedures, such as, electronic noise of SAR instruments and interferometric phase estimation error. They cannot be compensated by tie points, which are the corresponding points where their corrected ground positions are known. The random errors affect the precision of the InSAR system, while the following errors determine the elevation accuracy.
2. *Geometric distortion.* These include altitude errors, baseline errors, and SAR internal clock timing errors (or atmospheric delay). They are systematic errors that may be corrected by tie points.
3. *Position errors.* These errors include orbit errors and SAR processing azimuth-location errors and may be removed by a simple vertical or horizontal shift in the topographical surface.

From the above discussion, it can be seen that the elevation accuracy of DEMs generated from InSAR is influenced by various factors. Atmospheric irregularities affect the quality of SAR images and induce errors in the interferogram phase. Terrain types also contribute to the accuracy as scattering composition and geometry. This can be seen from Eq. (9.21) where the terrain surface slope along the slant range direction makes contributions to a few original errors, such as the original baseline error and phase error. Theoretically the interferometric nature used in DEM generation from InSAR gives the height accuracy to the level of the SAR wavelength (i.e. millimeters to centimeters), which match the phase difference. However this is hard to achieve in practice due to the errors mentioned above and the uncertainty introduced by imaging geometry and atmospheric irregularities (especially for repeat-pass interferometry). It was reported that atmospheric effects on a repeat-pass InSAR could induce significant variations in an interferogram of 0.3 to 2.3 phase cycles. For an ERS interferogram with a baseline of 100 m, elevation errors of up to about 100–200 m can be caused by the atmospheric effects on DEMs [70].

9 3D Digital Elevation Model Generation   387

Quantitative validation of DEMs generated from InSAR needs ground truth for comparison, such as GCPs or DEMs generated by higher accuracy instruments. As with DEM generation from optical stereoscopic imagery, RMSE and standard deviation can be used as metrics in accuracy evaluation. Reported elevation accuracy for the SRTM[7] data [82], created using C-band InSAR, was 2–25 m, with a significant variation depending on the terrain and ground cover types (i.e. vegetation). When vegetation is dense, InSAR does not provide good DEM results, while there is only sparse/low vegetation, the elevation accuracy can achieve 2 m. Horizontal resolution of SRTM SAR data is typically about 90 m for most areas, which is much worse than 2–20 m resolution of optical satellite images. ERS-1 and ERS-2 were exploited in DEM generation by Mora et al. [113], and the reconstructed DEMs were compared with those from SRTM InSAR in the same areas with maximum difference of 35–60 m and standard deviation of 3–11 m. Normally ±10 m elevation accuracy is expected from SRTM InSAR generated DEMs [123].

Due to difficulties in meeting the geometric requirement to the coherent conditions for two complex SAR images in interferometry, InSAR is not yet as popular as its counterpart of stereoscopic imagery in DEM generation [88]. In comparison with satellite stereoscopic imagery, the major advantage of InSAR is that it is independent from weather conditions—SAR illuminates its target with the emitted electromagnetic wave and the antenna receives the coherent radiation reflected from the target. In areas where optical sensors fail to provide data, such as heavy cloud areas, InSAR can be used as a complementary sensing mode for global DEM generation.

9.3.3 Examples of DEM Generation from InSAR

The first example presented in this section is a DEM from SRTM data [123]. The parameters of the interferometer are listed in Table 9.2.

Figure 9.9 (top left) shows the magnitude (or amplitude) of SRTM raw data from the master antenna. The imaging area consists of 600×450 pixels. Each pixel of the image is a complex value of amplitude and phase as shown in Eq. (9.7). Figure 9.9 (top right) is the phase of the interferogram, and the reconstructed DEM is presented in Fig. 9.9 (bottom).

The processing of the SRTM InSAR data to the DEM is split into two parts: the InSAR data processing part and the geocoding part. The first part covers the steps necessary to get from the sensor raw data to the unwrapped phase, while the second part deals with precise geometric transformation from the sensor domain to map the cartographic coordinate space.

---

[7]SRTM: Shuttle Radar Topography Mission aimed to obtain DEMs on a near global scale from 56°S to 60°N.

Table 9.2 Important parameters of the SRTM SAR interferometer

Wavelength (cm)	3.1
Range pixel spacing (m)	13.3
Azimuth pixel spacing (m)	4.33
Range bandwidth (MHz)	9.5
Range sampling frequency (MHz)	11.25
Effective baseline length (m)	59.9
Baseline angle (degree)	45
Look angle at scene center (degree)	54.5
Orbit height (km)	233
Slant range distance at scene center (km)	392
Height ambiguity per 2π fringe (m)	175

1. InSAR data processing steps.
    a. *SAR focusing*. When the site was selected, the corresponding SAR images need to go through focusing process. The physical reason for SAR image defocusing is the occurrence of unknown fluctuations in the microwave path length between the antenna and the scene [115]. For SAR focusing, several algorithms exist, and in this example, the chirp scaling algorithm was selected [124].
    b. *Motion compensation*. Oscillations from the mounting device of SAR equipment introduces distortion to images. The oscillations can be filtered in the received signals before performing azimuth focusing. The SAR image after focusing and motion compensation is shown in Fig. 9.9(top left).
    c. *Co-registration and interpolation*. Due to the Earth's curvature, different antenna positions and delays in the electronic components, the two images may both be shifted and stretched with respect to each other to the order of a couple of pixels. In this example, instead of correlation methods, the image registration was conducted solely from the baseline geometry that was measured by the instruments of Attitude and Orbit Determination Avionics.
    d. *Interferogram formation and filtering*. The interferogram is formed by multiplication and subsequent weighted averaging of complex samples of the master and slave images. The average corresponds to 8 pixels in azimuth and 2 pixels in slant range. It has proved that this combination provides the best tradeoff between spatial resolution and height error.
    e. *Phase unwrapping*. The phase unwrapping was produced by a version of the minimum cost flow algorithm [36] and the computational time for the phase unwrapping process took about 5 minutes (on a parallel computer) for moderate terrain to several hours for complicated fringe patterns in mountainous regions.
2. Geocoding steps.
    a. The unwrapped phase image is converted into an irregular grid of geolocated points of height, latitude and longitude on the Earth's surface using WGS84 as horizontal and vertical reference.

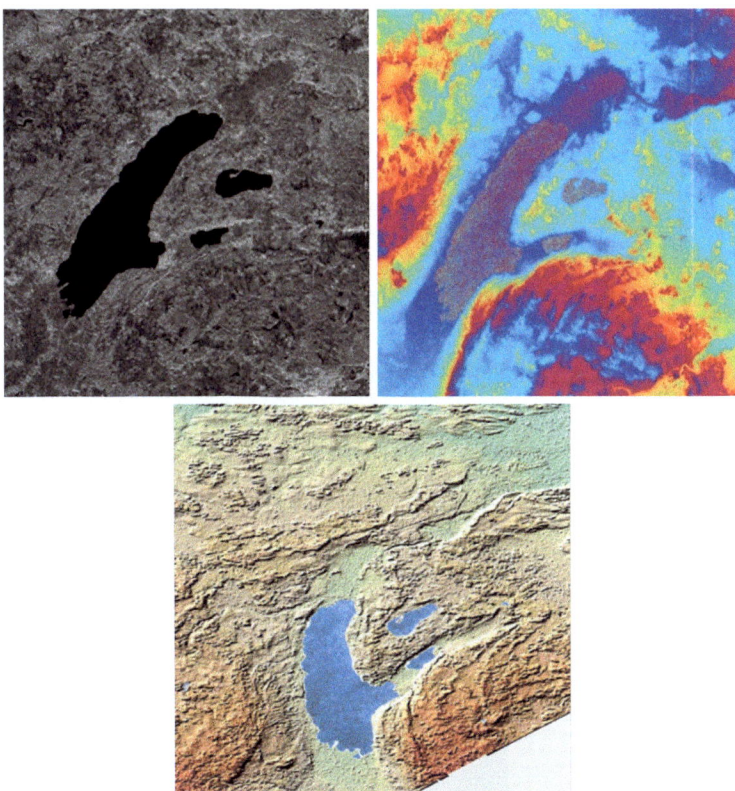

Fig. 9.9 InSAR generated DEM of Lake Ammer, Germany. *Top left*: Magnitude of raw data. *Top right*: Interferogram phase. *Bottom*: DEMs from phase. Figure courtesy of [123]

b. The irregular grid is interpolated to a corresponding regular grid.
c. Slant range images are converted into their regular grid equivalents. The mapped DEM is demonstrated in Fig. 9.9(bottom).

The reconstructed DEM has horizontal accuracy, relative vertical accuracy, and absolute vertical accuracy of 20 m, 6 m and 16 m with LE90, respectively.

The second example is taken from a pair of ERS-1 SAR images of a mountainous region of Sardinia, Italy [37]. The image has 329×641 pixels. Figure 9.10(a) is the interferogram phase image, and Fig. 9.10(b) is the unwrapped phase image with the white points representing existing values. The phase unwrapping was done by a fast algorithm based on LS methods. It was claimed that the reconstructed DEM was in qualitative agreement with the elevation reported in geographic maps. Although the overall accuracy was not given because the published research was concentrated on the phase unwrapping algorithm, the computational time required for phase unwrapping process was achieved as 25 minutes on a Silicon Graphics Power Onyx RE2 machine for the mountainous region of Sardinia.

Fig. 9.10 InSAR generated DEMs from a pair of ERS-1 SAR images of a mountainous region of Sardinia, Italy. Figure courtesy of [37]

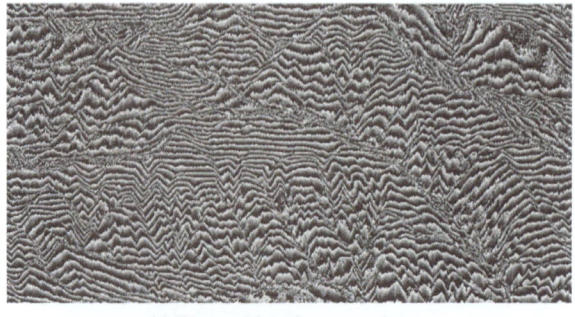

(a) Wrapped interferogram phase

(b) Unwrapped phase

(c) DEM

9.4 DEM Generation from LIDAR

9.4.1 LIDAR Data Acquisition

Airborne Laser Scanning (ALS) or LIght Detection And Ranging (LIDAR) has revolutionized topographic surveying for fast acquisition of high-resolution elevation data, which has enabled the development of highly accurate 3D products. LIDAR was developed by NASA in the 1970s [3]. Since the early 1990s, LIDAR has made significant contributions to many environmental, engineering and civil applications. It is being used increasingly by the public and commercial sectors [108] for forestry, archeology, 3D city map generation, flood simulations, coastal erosion monitoring,

9 3D Digital Elevation Model Generation

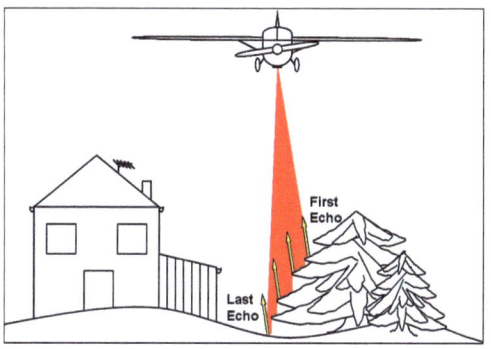

Fig. 9.11 LIDAR acquisition principle

landslide prediction, corridor mapping and wave propagation models for mobile telecommunication networks.

From an airborne platform, a LIDAR system estimates the distance between the instrument and a point on the surface by measuring the time for a round-trip of a laser pulse, as illustrated in Fig. 9.11. Differential Global Positioning System (DGPS) and Inertial Navigation System (INS) complement the data with position and orientation, respectively [78]. The result is the collection of surface height information in the form of a dense 3D point cloud. LIDAR is an active sensor which relies on the amount of backscattered light. The portion of light returning back to the receiver depends on the scene surface type illuminated by the laser pulse. Consequently, there will be gaps and overlaps in the data which is therefore not homogeneously and regularly distributed [14]. Additionally, since LIDAR is an active sensor and is independent of external lighting conditions, it can be used at night, a great advantage compared to traditional stereo matching [93]. Typical flight heights range from 600 m to 950 m [14, 81], scan angles 7–23°, wavelengths 1047–1560 nm, scan rates 13–653 Hz, and pulse rates 5–83 kHz [25, 78]. Average footprint sizes range typically from 0.4–1.0 m, depending on the flight height [20, 91]. Scan and pulse rates, in particular, have grown in recent years, leading to higher point densities as a function of flight height, velocity of the aircraft, scan angle, pulse rate and scan rate [10, 13].

The capability of the laser to penetrate gaps in vegetation allows the measurement of occluded ground. This is due to the laser's large footprint relative to the vegetation gaps. At least the First Echo (FE) and the Last Echo (LE) can be recorded, as schematically depicted in Fig. 9.11. Ideally, the FE and LE are arranged in two different point clouds as subsets within LIDAR data [122] and clearly the differentiation of multiple echoes is a challenge. Modern LIDAR systems can record up to four echoes (or more if derived from full waveform datasets), while the latest survey techniques, such as low-level LIDAR, allow point densities up to 100 points per square meter [28]. The latest developments of the full waveform LIDAR have introduced a new range of applications. The recording of multiple echoes allows modeling of the vertical tree profile [14]. Acquired FE points mostly comprise canopies, sheds, roofs, dormers and even small details such as aerials or chimneys, whereas LEs are reflections of the ground or other lower surfaces after the laser has

Table 9.3 LIDAR versus aerial photogrammetry

Property	LIDAR	Aerial photogrammetry
Sensor	Active	Passive
Georeferencing	Direct	Post-acquisition
Point distribution	Irregular	Regular
Vertical accuracy	High	Low
Horizontal accuracy	Low	High
Height information	Directly from data	Stereo matching required
Degree of automation	High	Low
Maintenance	Intensive and expensive	Inexpensive
Life time	Limited	Long
Contrast	High	Low
Texture	None	Yes
Color	Monochrome	Multispectral
Shadows	Minimal effect	Clearly visual
Ground captivity	Vegetation gap penetration	Wide open spaces required
Breakline detection	Difficult due to irregular sampling	Suitable
DTM generation source	Height data	Textured overlapping imagery
Planimetry	Random irregular point cloud	Rich spatial context
Land cover classification	Unsuitable, fusion required	Suitable

penetrated gaps within the foliage. The occurrence of multiple echoes at the same geo-referenced point indicates vegetation but also edges of hard objects [10]. The difference between FE and LE therefore reveals, in the best case, building outlines and vegetation heights [138]. Table 9.3 summarizes the pros and cons of LIDAR versus traditional aerial photogrammetric techniques.

9.4.2 Accuracy, Error Types and Countermeasures

LIDAR is the most accurate remote sensing source for capturing height. It has revolutionized photogrammetry with regard to vertical accuracy, with values ranging between 0.10–0.26 m [3, 4, 34, 74, 104, 107, 167, 179]. Like any other physical measurements, LIDAR errors are composed of both systematic and random errors. Systematic errors are due to the setting of the equipment; generally they have a certain pattern and are therefore reproducible. Examples are systematic height shifts as a function of flight height, which are due to uncertainty of GPS, georeferencing and orientation. Time errors of assigning range and position are reported to be $<10\ \mu s$ [167]. Calibration can be carried out by using known mounting angles, the redundancy from overlapping (crossing) strips and ground truth (i.e. manually measured

GCPs which have been acquired in an accompanying field survey). Problems occur if the positions of GCPs and measured LIDAR points do not correspond with each other [137]. This can be solved using a high point density, acquired with a low altitude, low velocity and a steep scan angle.

In contrast, random errors are not reproducible and are thus more difficult to eliminate. Gross errors, blunders and 'no data' situations are due to a temporal malfunction of the LRF or occasional perturbations such as birds or low flying aircrafts [143]. Data voids are due to the irregular sampling nature of the LIDAR and have to be corrected using interpolation if required. The total number of gross errors and blunders may be small, but their overall impact on the data is strong. Kidner et al. [89] reported that local blunders can be large as 20 m and can be detected if the height of all neighbouring points is below a certain threshold, for example ≤ 5 m. Extreme blunders can be greater than 767 m [89] and can be removed by comparing the mean and standard deviation of the height differences of each LIDAR point in a defined neighborhood.

Point density and scan range per scanned line are a function of scan angle, however it is also known that the greater the scan angle the greater its elevation error [179]. The error caused by the scan angle becomes smaller when the flight height and pulse rate are lower [7]. A small scan angle ensures that terrain or object edges are resolved more clearly and vertical tree profiles can be sampled due to the fact that laser pulses reach lower tree branches [104]. In general, the smaller the scan angle, the higher the point density, the better the edges on man-made structure are sampled, and the better the laser can be pushed forward to lower branch levels of trees [138].

Multipath propagation causes backscattered laser light to travel a longer time. Consequently, some points will appear below the actual surface [91, 143]. Multipath effects of LE LIDAR data can be compensated for by exploiting the redundant information of FE and LE [166].

Finally, wind, atmospheric distortions and bright sunlight can all influence the accuracy of LIDAR data as the laser beam is narrow [12]. The best laser ranging conditions are achieved if the weather is dry, cool and clear [12]. Furthermore, water vapour and humidity such as rain and fog attenuate the power of the laser. This disturbing effect can be deliberately exploited for investigating clouds and aerosols in the atmosphere using ground-based LIDAR [77]. To generalize, studies have revealed that the greater slope, terrain roughness, amount of vegetation and the larger the flight velocity and height, the smaller the scan angle, the larger the random error will be [14, 74, 93, 179].

To reduce inaccuracies within the acquired data, error models are applied. A popular method to estimate the total error can be done by calculating the Root Mean Square Error (RMSE) of equal georeferenced GCPs and LIDAR points as defined in [74]:

$$RMSE = \sqrt{\frac{1}{N_{GCP}} \sum_{j=1}^{N_{GCP}} (X_j - GCP_j)^2} \qquad (9.22)$$

Table 9.4 Typical systematic and random errors in LIDAR point clouds

Error (Type)	Order	Counter measure
Height shift (Systematic)	≤20 cm	Ground control points
GPS shift (Systematic)	10 cm	Differential GPS
Georeferencing (Systematic)	<10 µs	Strip adjustment, redundancy, revisit
Orientation (Systematic)	<10 µs	Strip adjustment, redundancy, revisit
Mounting angles (Systematic)	N/A	Calibrate and recalculate
Slope of terrain (Random)	(15–20) cm	Slope adaptive algorithm
Gross errors/blunders (Random)	>100 cm	FE/LE redundancy, manual intervention
Object roughness (Random)	<10 cm	Surveys in leaf-off season
Multipath (Random)	<10 cm	Small scan angle, FE/LE redundancy
Bright sun light (Random)	N/A	Surveys at night
Atmosphere, weather (Random)	N/A	Avoid forest fires, clouds, fog
Strong winds (Random)	N/A	Avoid rough weather

where N_{GCP} is the total number of GCP_j and X_j the corresponding LIDAR points with $j \in \{1, 2, \ldots, N_{GCP}\}$. To break the absolute error down, mean height differences (systematic error) and standard deviation of difference (random error) can be calculated. Yu [179] observed that the random error decreases at greater vegetation penetration rates (i.e. the more open the space is), greater point densities and lower flight heights, while the systematic error remains stable at different flight heights. Even if there is no initial vertical error evident, a horizontal error still has an impact on the vertical error. Hodgson et al. [75] established a link between the terrain slope angle α and the horizontal displacement e_h of the LIDAR point yielding the vertical error e_v:

$$e_v = e_h \tan(\alpha) \quad (9.23)$$

where the horizontal error e_h is dominated by the flight height h, which is a general rule of thumb [74]

$$e_h \approx 0.1 \ \% \ h \quad (9.24)$$

Systematic and random errors can be corrected by GCPs, surveyed at the same time with LIDAR data. From another point of view, LIDAR itself can be used to provide GCPs for accuracy assessment of photogrammetric products as recently demonstrated by James et al. [84]. Systematic errors can either be eliminated by careful calibration or, if known, calculated and removed from the error budget. Random errors can only be estimated after the survey in a post-processing analysis. Table 9.4 summarizes all typical systematic and random errors and states countermeasures.

9.4.3 LIDAR Interpolation

In general, there are two principal ways to prepare LIDAR data for filtering techniques: gridding or working on the original point cloud. On the one hand, some researchers suggest the use of the original data for accuracy reasons, since gridding and interpolation may omit original data and induce additional non-existent data. On the other hand, gridding and interpolation allows the use and further advancement of well-known image processing techniques [47], such as filtering in the spatial and frequency domain. For applications requiring data fusion, different bands have to be co-registered to obtain a consistent format. Typical spatial resolutions for gridding are in the order of 0.25–2 m [104]. Commonly used interpolation techniques include nearest neighborhood and bilinear interpolation [34, 111, 146, 167, 181].

Bater et al. [20] compared seven interpolation methods applied to LIDAR data at different resolutions and measured the interpolation error as RMSE. Conclusions were that, although the interpolation error is independent of the interpolation method, it is a function of the resolution, where 0.5 m increase in spatial resolution yields an RMSE increase of 1 cm on average. Therefore, the authors suggested employing a natural neighbor algorithm with minimal interpolation error and computational costs. Natural or nearest neighbor interpolation suggests that missing data can be synthesized by the mean (or median) of adjacent data points based on the assumption that they are similar.

9.4.4 LIDAR Filtering

The main interest in airborne LIDAR data is to generate accurate elevation maps and to identify objects within the point cloud. The main products include Digital Surface Models (DSM), Digital Terrain Models (DTM) and normalized DSMs (nDSM) [143]. A DSM includes all sampled top surfaces of objects and ground [14, 136, 138], including tree canopies, roof tops, chimneys or above ground power transmission lines, as illustrated in Fig. 9.12. A DSM can also be directly produced from the LIDAR point cloud. Since many applications require accurate ground data, one major goal in LIDAR filtering is to separate object and ground points. If object points are of interest, an nDSM can then be generated very conveniently by subtracting the DTM from the DSM [172]. Again, an interpolation step is required to create a DEM from the filtered data (to fill those patches where objects were with appropriate data).

LIDAR filtering is the bottle-neck in the processing chain from acquisition to real applications. Friess [50] reported that the ratio of post-processing to acquisition time for correcting the points' geometry is up to 14:1 and DEM generation demands an even higher ratio of 20:1. Filtering algorithms constitute the major contribution to a final product derived from LIDAR [167], taking three times longer than the acquisition. Flood [43] reported that at least 60 % of the production time to obtain DEMs is allocated for filtering and other post-processing steps. Although LIDAR

Fig. 9.12 From top to bottom: Original scene, DSM, DTM, nDSM

systems are considered to be mature, there is much work to de done to develop filtering algorithms that are robust, accurate and efficient [10, 13, 162]. In the following, a brief overview of the different categories of LIDAR filtering techniques is given.

Morphological filtering does two things: filters object points and interpolates the missing terrain at the same time. Based on set theory, morphological filtering consists of two basic operators, erosion and dilation [65, 66], usually applied in a sliding window. Further derived operators are cleaning, filling, bridging and the watershed algorithm. When applied to LIDAR data, the major assumption is that there is a distinct difference between slopes of objects and of ground [172]. The first step is to find the minimum LIDAR point in a window [90] where the difficulty here is to select the right window size according to shape, size and orientation of objects [8]. Small windows relative to large objects result in treating them as ground. Large windows, however, may erode terrain irreversibly. Therefore, the latest developments in morphological filtering make use of progressive [181] increasing window sizes [90]. In general, morphological filtering is considered to be robust and works well for isolated objects. However, some drawbacks include the indifference of this filtering technique towards object and terrain details, which can be eroded irreversibly [32].

Slope-based filtering exploits slope and discontinuities between adjacent single or grouped points (e.g. buildings) since LIDAR data is vertically accurate in the range of decimeters. Vosselman [155] employed a predetermined cut-off plane to measure and classify slopes of lines between two points with parameters to adapt the plane to highly sloped terrain [142]. Slope-based filtering is non-trivial since extreme slopes and flat terrain can cause failure of the algorithm. Therefore, the Laplacian of Gaussian (LoG) is often used to differentiate objects from the ground [55]. A grid based DTM generation approach was developed by Wack et al. [163, 164] who downsampled the data coarsely first to a 9 m spacing. By doing so, most of the object points were discarded. Roggero [128] derived a DTM by using weighted linear regression on original, irregular LIDAR data. The authors then employed a local inverted cone adapted to the terrain slope in order to estimate ground points, regarding the maximum height difference between two points. Objects were then detected using a LoG. In general, slope-based algorithms pick up precisely edges, lines, corners and other discontinuities. If spatial masks are used, gridding is required. Slope-based filtering algorithms fail if their major assumption *steep slopes are only caused by objects* is violated; for example, in mountainous terrain with discontinuities such as trenches, manhole covers for canalisation, holes, caves or outliers.

Geometry-based filtering is a popular method to describe man-made and natural objects in LIDAR data, assuming that object properties such as shape, length, width, height, position and orientation are known. From an nDSM obtained by means of morphological filtering, Weidner and Förstner [172] extracted buildings from a parametric and prismatic building model [169] based on the Minimum Description Length (MDL) principle [170]. First, a bounding box for each building is estimated using a defined threshold with respect to known building heights. Second, the segmentation is refined based on a height threshold calculated from the median of 10 % lowest and 10 % highest points of the preselected data. Sparse Triangular Irregular Network (TIN) densification for DTM generation is also very popular [145] since neither gridding and interpolation nor dense point clouds are required [96]. Axelsson [10] classified vegetation, buildings and power transmission lines in original LIDAR data, based on their surface in a TIN using MDL criteria. The underlying assumption was that objects consist of planar faces and therefore, neighbouring TIN facets had a similar orientation with a second derivative of zero whereas the second derivatives of breaklines and vegetation points were non-zero. One of the biggest advantages of geometry-based filtering is that structures in LIDAR data can be described directly from point clouds. Buildings can be recovered very efficiently and initial gridding and interpolating the data is not necessary. However, geometry-based filtering requires many predefined parameters and becomes more difficult when the level of object complexity is high.

Curvature-based filters have been developed to detect classes of curved areas (i.e. convex, concave and plane) within the point cloud [6, 153]. Vosselman [154] assumed that buildings consist of planar faces which can be recognized by applying the Hough transform in LIDAR point clouds. The data had been segmented with existing 2D ground plans [156, 157]. The spatial structure chosen for the geometric description of the planar faces were 2D Delaunay triangles [154]. If a connected component was greater than a specified threshold, a planar face was found. The buildings' outlines were estimated using the planar faces projected into the 2D space [154]. Working on non-gridded data, Rottensteiner and Briese [131] detected non-ground building regions in the first stage. Then, roofs were detected using surface normals of a DSM [134]. The biggest advantage of curvature-based LIDAR filters is that they are directly applicable to the original data to detect structures in a LIDAR point cloud. Drawbacks, however, are that only man-made objects that have planar, convex or concave faces can be detected with pre-defined thresholds and that vegetation is difficult to recognize due to its random character.

Linear prediction can be used for DTM generation and gross error removal [26], as was developed by Kraus and Pfeifer [93]. The supervized algorithm contained a combination of filtering (object point classification) and interpolation of the ground. First, a rough approximation of a DTM was calculated using linear prediction employing overlapping patches. The difference of this DTM and the original LIDAR point cloud was estimated to obtain residuals as the basis for assigning weights to LIDAR points from a parametric weighting function. Points above a certain threshold were classified as object points. The whole algorithm was iteratively executed until either a stable situation or a predefined number of iterations was reached [93]. Based on linear prediction, Kobler et al. [91] addressed the challenge of filtering LIDAR data in steep wooded terrain with a repetitive interpolation algorithm by setting empirically estimated parameters, thresholds and a buffer zone [94]. A major advantage of linear prediction models is their applicability to different terrain types and that DTMs can be derived from sloped terrain. The compromise to this solution however is that prior knowledge of the terrain for the weighting factors and thresholds are required. Those parameters can be adjusted depending on the application and terrain. Also, some approaches lack a clear termination criterion, as either a stable situation has to be reached or the number of iterations has to be specified in advance.

Coarse-to-fine filters and *multi-resolution filters* benefit from both detailed and coarse views of the LIDAR data [93]. Pfeifer et al. [120] presented a series of LIDAR post-processing steps aimed at flood modeling: data calibration, strip adjustment, 'robust linear prediction' and terrain structure recovery (i.e. breakline modeling). The new element contributing to the robustness of the filtering approach was the use of hierarchical pyramids. DTMs of different resolutions were compared to each other, however, still requiring some thresholds [120]. References [139–141] presented a semi-automatic, multi-resolution approach for filtering LIDAR data based on the Hermite transform. Gaussian pyramids were employed to transform the data in the first step. An assumption was made that any change from ground and off-terrain is a linear combination of shifted, rotated and scaled error functions, similar to a kernel function in Wavelet analysis. A multi-resolution algorithm for DTM generation from LIDAR data was proposed by Vu et al. [159–162] who compared successive median-filtered resolutions of gridded LIDAR data to detect boundaries. The final segmentation of the LIDAR data was achieved using both the boundaries and the actual height as features. A Wavelet approach to separate ground and object points on gridded LIDAR data was proposed by Vu and Tokunaga [158]. The authors applied K-means on height to segment buildings, motorways, boundaries and trees. The advantage of multi-resolution filtering algorithms is the separation of low and high frequencies (i.e. approximations and details) of a LIDAR scene. However, it is not always clear what resolution to choose since energy (i.e. information contents) becomes smaller the further the signal is decomposed [18]. When using approximations (i.e. discarding the high frequency components) a loss of information occurs. Also, higher computational costs and memory requirements have to be considered, when using multi-resolution filters.

Knowledge-based filters make use of predefined models of different height and shape [22]. Haala and Brenner [60] presented a complete solution of a realistic 3D city model from LIDAR derived DSMs. To get the buildings' ground planes, the authors segmented the DSM using a 2D GIS map whose incompleteness and inaccuracy was complemented with a cadastral map. Their algorithm was based on region growing using straight lines of pixels [59] and histogram analysis of surface vector normals which yielded planar surfaces [62]. Having obtained the ground planes, the actual buildings were modeled by fitting a limited number of predefined 3D building primitives into the DSM. Location and rough type of vegetation were estimated with three bands of aerial Color Infra-Red (CIR) images (i.e. NIR, red and green) and the geometric information from the nDSM [63]. A hierarchical rule-based filtering solution was presented by Nardinocchi et al. [114]. LIDAR data was gridded and three classes—terrain, building and vegetation—were estimated by exploiting their geometric (height differences) and topological (spatial distribution) properties and their relationships among each other using region growing and local slope analysis. Employing hierarchical rules and fitting in 3D geometric primitives is very efficient for identifying objects in LIDAR data [114], provided that urban area is presented. However, this approach involves prior knowledge of the buildings and other man-made structures and becomes extremely difficult for complex objects. Furthermore, it is almost impossible to model vegetation geometrically. Hence, additional information such as CIR or Normalized Difference Vegetation Index (NDVI) has to be integrated.

Data fusion for land cover classification exploits complementary properties of both LIDAR and photogrammetry. It requires registration and orientation of gridded and interpolated LIDAR data with all spectral bands [136, 137]. Popular spectral data are NIR, red and green from CIR imagery [61] to be combined with height information from LIDAR data. Processing co-registered remotely sensed data involves solving a multivariate statistical problem. Typical classifiers are used such as ML, distance classifiers, Support Vector Machine (SVM), Principal Component Analysis (PCA), Independent Component Analysis (ICA) and Artificial Neural Networks (ANN). CIR imagery combined with LIDAR data can be used for detecting sealed and non-sealed surfaces for water waste management and council taxing [138] or for tree crown volume estimation. Further applications with fused LIDAR data and aerial images are building reconstruction [131], building outline extraction with fused NDVIs from IKONOS multispectral panchromatic imagery [144], roof segmentation [23, 24], building detection based on Dempster-Shafer [132, 133], roofs, trees and grass classification using Gaussian Mixture Model (GMM) and Expectation Maximization (EM) [30], per-pixel minimum distance classification of streets, grass, trees, buildings and shadows [61], including empirical ground truth collection [118]. For data fusion applications, it is popular to use open source software such as the Geographic Resources Analysis Support System (GRASS) [27] or commercial software packages such as eCognition, Arc/Info, TerraSolid and TerraModeler [76, 152, 171]. In general, fusing LIDAR and additional space and airborne remotely sensed data has great potential for improving accuracy for land cover classification as it combines advantages of complementary bands. The gain, however, has a limit due to the curse of dimensionality in that an extensive adding of further bands may result in attenuation of accuracy [83]. Furthermore, it is non-trivial to find contemporary 2D GIS maps, imagery and ground truth. Moreover, the data has to be co-registered, and if necessary downsampled, gridded and interpolated due to different resolution and orientation. This process, however, omits data and adds additional non-existent information. The use of commercial software packages involves experimental tuning of the settings and most algorithms are hidden to the user. Furthermore, expensive licenses cannot always be purchased due to funding limitations.

Statistical classification filters are a means to segment and classify objects and terrain in LIDAR data in an unsupervized manner [168]. Cobby et al. [34] generated a DTM for flood simulation from LIDAR data recorded by the Environment Agency, UK. The authors segmented the rural area close to the River Severn and classified the objects into three vegetation height classes: short (crops and grasses), intermediate (hedges and shrubs) and tall (trees). Using a 5×5 window, the semi-automatic segmenter employed the standard deviation of local height as a feature because tall vegetation was assumed to constitute the highest objects [35]. For simplicity, the authors declared the limited number of houses in this area as high vegetation. Since the authors were interested in vegetation height, they separated the slightly hilly terrain from the actual object using detrending [39]. By subtracting the bilinear interpolated surface from the LIDAR data, an nDSM for a hydraulic model was obtained, as developed by [33]. Skewness balancing [19] and its adaptation to hilly terrain [17] are an alternative to object-based filtering. Yao et al. [175] have adapted skewness balancing to address the challenging task in detecting cars in LIDAR data. Bao et al. [15] further improved the algorithm by incorporating the measure of kurtosis, where the authors exploited the different changes of both statistical measures with respect to vegetation and ground. Advantages of statistical filtering algorithms are that they can work unsupervized directly on the original, non-gridded data. They fail, however, if the statistical model boundaries are insufficiently described.

A comparison of LIDAR filtering methods is illustrated in Table 9.5.

Table 9.5 Comparison of LIDAR filtering techniques

Filtering technique	Details	Pros	Cons	Application
Morphology	Erosion, dilation, cleaning, filling, watershed algorithm	Robust, works well for isolated objects, DTM directly derived from point cloud	Imprecise towards little details, knowledge of minimum structure required	Forestry (canopy modeling), flood modeling
Slope-based	Derivatives of slope (directional), gradients, edge, corner, line detectors, Laplacian, LoG	Precise for discontinuities	Threshold required, fails at mountainous, highly sloped or completely flat terrain	Object detection
Curvature-based	Convex, concave, plane hulls, Hough transform, TIN densification	Direct recognition of structure in point cloud	Thresholds, surfaces of man-made objects only	Building detection
Geometry-based	MDL, shape, length, width, height, position, orientation	Direct recognition of structure in point cloud	Many prior parameters required, fails at complex objects	Building detection
Linear prediction	Detrending, robust linear prediction	Robust against sloped terrain	Threshold, weighting factors	DTM generation
Multi-resolution	Gaussian, median pyramids, wavelets, hierarchical robust linear prediction	Robust, separation of high and low frequencies	Computational costs and memory requirements	DTM generation
Knowledge-based	3D primitives	High quality models	Huge database required due complexity, vegetation difficult to model	Building detection
Data fusion	ML, distance classifiers, neural networks, PCA, ICA, SVM	Combination of complementary advantages	Co-registration, need for contemporary maps, curse of dimensionality	Land cover estimation, forestry
Statistical classification algorithms	Detrending, Gaussian models, skewness balancing	Unsupervised, works on original point clouds	Fails if model boundaries are invalid	Object and ground point separation

9.4.5 DTM from Statistical Properties of the Point Cloud

Unsupervised statistical filtering algorithms are an alternative to object-based filtering. Separation of ground and object points within the LIDAR point cloud is a prerequisite for DTM generation. Bartels and Wei [17] developed a LIDAR filtering technique, purely based on the statistical distribution of the point cloud. For the definition of the algorithm, three assumptions can be made to exploit the statistics of a 2.5 dimensional point cloud.

- From a global perspective, there is a normal distribution of ground point elevation, similar to samples collected from a population [40].
- Object points may disturb or 'skew' this normal distribution [16].
- The number of visible ground points must dominate the LIDAR point cloud to ensure validity of the first assumption.

The last assumption is essential to avoid misclassification of object points as ground points, for example, large flat roofs in dense urban areas. Furthermore, there has to be a minimum number of LIDAR ground points available to be able to make a solid statistical statement over the point cloud's distribution. Based on these assumptions, the unsupervised object and ground point separator is formulated [17]. First, the skewness of the point cloud is calculated. If it is greater than zero, peaks (i.e. objects) dominate the point cloud distribution. The greatest value of the point cloud is then removed by classifying it as an object point. These steps are iteratively executed while the skewness of the point cloud is greater than zero. Finally, the remaining points are normally distributed and belong to the ground. By doing so, the skewed distribution of the data is balanced, and the algorithm is therefore called *Skewness Balancing* [16].

A limitation of the basic algorithm is the assumption that object points are located above the ground. This is valid for large classes of terrain types, but in mountainous areas, the algorithm would misclassify ground points as object points. Skewness balancing is therefore extended to sloped terrain with the following reasoning. After termination of basic skewness balancing on the original positively skewed LIDAR point cloud, the extracted subset of LIDAR points (which still contains misclassified ground points) can still be positively skewed. The remaining object point cloud is now re-considered as a new model, DSM*, which is statistically independent from the original DSM. It is now re-filtered by skewness balancing and misclassified ground points are thus iteratively corrected. The extended algorithm terminates as the remaining object points converge to zero, as depicted in Fig. 9.13.

The advantages of this unsupervised approach are obvious: skewness balancing does not require pre-defined thresholds, a pre-determined number of iterations or tunable (i.e. application-dependent) weighting factors. It does not incorporate prior knowledge about the terrain or objects and is independent from format (gridded or non-gridded) and resolution of the data. Ground points between gaps and in narrow streets are picked up without thinning out the data. In doing so, object and terrain details are preserved. Skewness balancing is therefore ideal for integration

9 3D Digital Elevation Model Generation

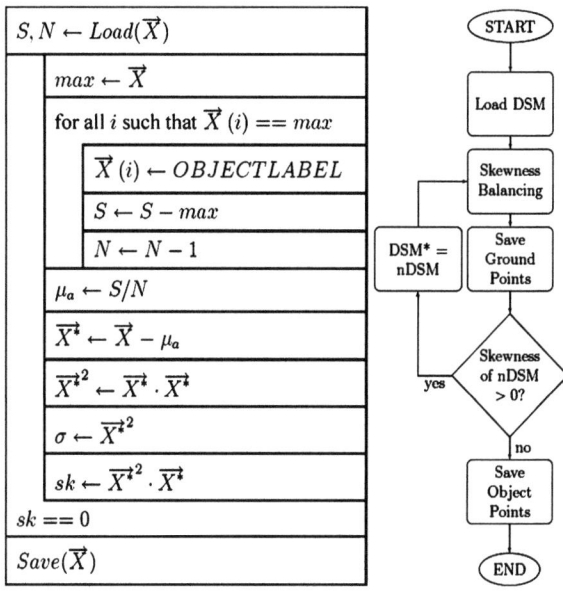

Fig. 9.13 Skewness balancing algorithm and adaptation to sloped terrain [17]. *Left*: Original algorithm. *Right*: Adapted to sloped terrain

into GIS software packages, while having the option to improve it by deriving an optimization-localization operator.

Figure 9.14 depicts a large number of key terrain elements in rural and urban area filtered out by the algorithm. Bare earth (streets, pavements and court yards), detached objects (buildings and vegetation) and ambiguously attached objects (bridges, motorway junctions, ramps and slopes) are separated from the two tiles of LIDAR point clouds. Figure 9.14(bottom left) shows that skewness balancing even picks up power transmission lines, while vegetation in rural and forestry areas is correctly filtered at an accuracy of 96 % [19].

To create a DEM or DTM after the object points are removed from LIDAR point cloud, the following possibilities should be taken into account, and a proper approach should be taken accordingly.

- For areas where high vegetation are removed, the corresponding LIDAR LE can be used for filling the patches because the LIDAR can penetrate vegetation.
- For areas where the removed points represent buildings or other hard objects, there are two situations.
  - For those areas with reasonable size, TIN linear interpolation, bilinear interpolation, and Kriging interpolation [181] could be used to fill the empty space.
  - For a large area where object points are removed, the true information of terrain is unknown. The common practice is to leave the space as empty (data missing).

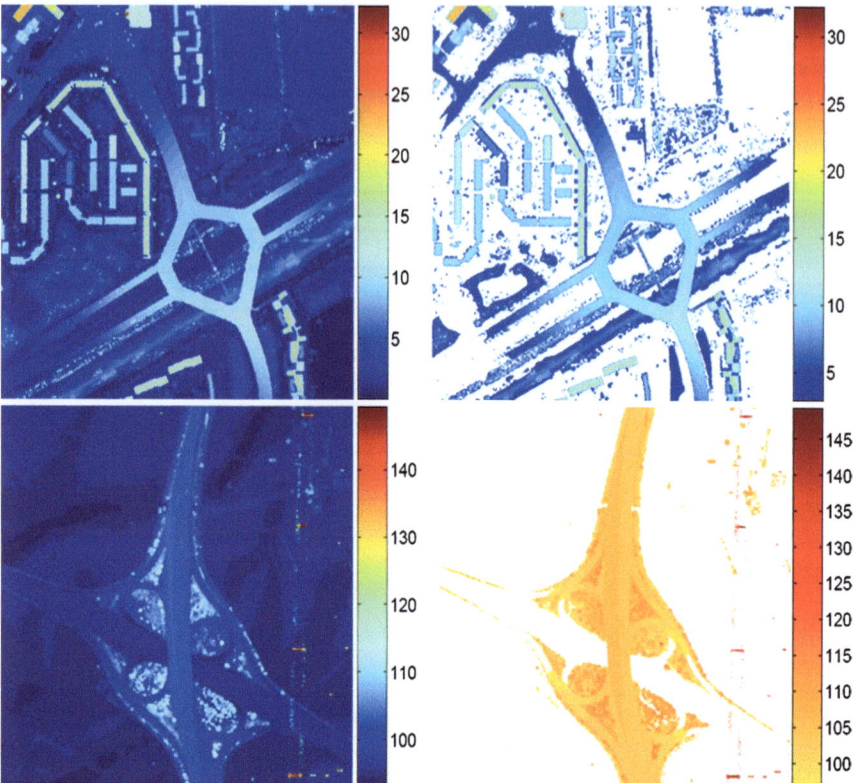

Fig. 9.14 DSM (*left column*) and filtered object points (*right column*) obtained from skewness balancing of two different LIDAR tiles. *Top*: Thamesmead, London, UK (courtesy of Environment Agency, UK). *Bottom*: Mannheim, Germany (courtesy of TopoSys GmbH and the Stadt Mannheim, Germany)

9.5 Research Challenges

With the development of remote sensing technology and advanced signal processing algorithms, 3D DEM generation from remote sensing has demonstrated enormous potential with advantages of automation, economy, and large coverage of terrain. Related techniques have been maturing due to significant investment in sensing devices, instruments, processing algorithms, and software development. The launch of Earth observation satellites, such as, Envisat, Landsat, GeoEye, and Worldview has brought opportunities as well as challenges to the research communities.

- When the high accuracy, high resolution, and high density data are continuously acquired from various Earth observation satellites, huge datasets are generated. How to store and retrieve these datasets is the first challenge. These may require reliable servers and tangible databases for data storage, and robust algorithms for information retrieval from the databases if needed.

- For DEM generation from stereoscopic imagery, further improving DEM accuracy requires better mathematical models which can adaptively correct errors caused by sensors' platform attitude instability and geometric distortion of images. Automation demands more robust algorithms for image matching processes.
- As described previously, most current techniques used in 3D DEM generation from remote sensing need intensive interaction from operators. They are time-consuming and the accuracy of the final product is difficult to control. This demands researchers' further understanding of physical properties of sensing elements (e.g. SAR) with accurate theoretical models for signal interpretation, and better knowledge of satellite orbits and imaging geometry (for both stereo images and SAR images).
- For LIDAR, power consumption is the key issue for spaceborne missions although lasers can provide more accurate elevation data compared with other devices. Quantitative analysis of the effects caused by weather and atmospheric conditions to LIDAR is required to ensure that the raw signal/data is interpreted correctly.

The above aspects need to be addressed in order to bring more automation and higher accuracy to the DEMs generated from remote sensing.

9.6 Concluding Remarks

In this chapter, three methods used for 3D DEM generation from remote sensing have been introduced. These are DEM generation from optical stereoscopic imagery, InSAR, and airborne LIDAR. All of these have shown enormous potential in many application areas. After working through this chapter, it is expected that readers appreciate the achievements and are aware of the problems remaining in this research area. Readers should have sufficient knowledge to answer the questions presented in Sect. 9.8 and carry out the exercises in Sect. 9.9, with the comprehensive references listed at the end of this chapter. Also, readers should be able to do the following.

- Outline processing procedures of DEM generation from satellite stereoscopic imagery, InSAR, and airborne LIDAR.
- Explain how the 3D passive vision technology developed in the computer vision community (Chap. 2) can be applied to DEM generation from satellite stereoscopic imagery.
- Explain how the 3D active vision technology can be used for DEM generation from InSAR and LIDAR.
- Appreciate various algorithms developed in the area of DEM generation for stereo-matching, image registration, phase unwrapping, and data filtering.
- Estimate DEM accuracy based on knowledge of imaging geometry and relative physical properties of sensing devices.

- Identify advantages and disadvantages for DEM generation from different remote sensing approaches.
- Perform DEM generation with available data (possibly through the use of commercial software packages).

9.7 Further Reading

The following books are recommended for the purposes of broadening knowledge in the field, from instruments for raw data acquisition to DEM applications.

1. James B. Campbell (1996), *Introduction to Remote Sensing*, 2nd edition, Taylor & Francis Ltd—This book provides an introduction level of remote sensing including image acquisition, analysis, and applications. Both passive imaging and active radar are discussed. Spaceborne as well as airborne remote sensing techniques are covered.
2. Peter Burrough, and Rachael A. McDonnell (1998), *Principles of Geographical Information Systems*, Oxford University Press. Readers may access this book to gain knowledge of spatial science and geographical information systems (GIS).
3. Chris Oliver and Shaun Quegan (1998), *Understanding Synthetic Aperture Radar Images*, Artech House Inc. This book describes insight of SAR and SAR image analysis and processing. It helps readers gain knowledge of SAR principles and image formation.
4. Ramon F. Hanssen (2001), *Radar Interferometry: Data Interpretation and Error Analysis*, Kluwer Academic Publishers. This book is specifically dedicated to InSAR. It details fundamentals of radar system theory, interferometric processing, functional models for InSAR, data analysis and error estimation.
5. Norbert Pfeifer and Gottfried Mandlburger (2009), Chap. 11—LIDAR data filtering and DTM generation, *Topographic Laser Ranging and Scanning—Principles and Processing*, Edited by Jie Shan and Charles K. Toth, CRC Press. This book explores LIDAR's potentials and capabilities in topographic mapping. Chapter 11 describes DEM/DTM generation from LIDAR.

9.8 Questions

1. Outline the procedure of DEM generation from satellite stereoscopic image pairs, and indicate possible advantages of using satellite imagery (relative to the use of airborne imagery) in DEM generation.
2. Briefly discuss the physical principle of InSAR in DEM generation, and outline the processing stages of DEM generation from satellite InSAR.
3. Explain possible issues involved in the processes stated in Q. (2), and explain the related solutions.

4. Compare and contrast DEM generation methods of satellite stereoscopic imagery and InSAR, consider aspects of sensor type, resolution, scale, orbit, timing, wavelengths used, and satellite altitude. You may need additional information from the further reading materials to answer this question.
5. Explain LIDAR operation in DEM/DTM generation and outline the key steps to generate the final DEM/DTM from the raw LIDAR point cloud.

9.9 Exercises

1. Simulate an along-track satellite stereoscopic imaging geometry and establish the geometric model of the prospective projection based on the setting illustrated in Fig. 9.2(left).
2. For the across-track satellite stereoscopic imaging shown in Fig. 9.2(right), derive the mathematical model of the perspective projection geometry associated with the cameras and the terrain surface and speculate possible errors which affect the accuracy of final DEMs generated from this setting.
3. Write an essay which discusses state-of-the-art stereo image matching algorithms specifically used for DEM generation from satellite stereoscopic imagery. In preparation of this essay, you may look for image matching algorithms used in commercial DEM generation software products.
4. Based on the discussion in Sect. 9.3.1.2, derive the phase unwrapping algorithms of branch-cuts and least squares.
5. Earth observation based on satellite missions normally is very expensive so that it requires resources of a national government to fund the related projects. Many people question whether it is necessary to spend government funds for such programs. Write an essay, with your argument, to justify the costs. You may choose positive or negative views.
6. Compare LIDAR filtering techniques introduced in this chapter and implement them in your choice of programming language.
7. Implement the Skewness Balancing algorithm in a programming language of your choice, and apply it to a LIDAR point cloud data set to generate a DEM. You may access the LIDAR data at http://www.commission3.isprs.org/wg4/.

References

1. Abdelfattah, R., Nicolas, J.M.: Topographic SAR interferometry formulation for high-precision DEM generation. IEEE Trans. Geosci. Remote Sens. **40**(11), 2415–2426 (2002)
2. Ackermann, F.: Digital image correlation: performance and potential application in photogrammetry. Photogramm. Rec. **11**(64), 429–439 (1984)
3. Ackermann, F.: Airborne laser scanning present status and future expectations. ISPRS J. Photogramm. Remote Sens. **54**, 64–67 (1999)
4. Adams, J.C., Chandler, J.H.: Evaluation of LIDAR and medium scale photogrammetry for detecting soft-cliff coastal change. Photogramm. Rec. **17**(99), 405–418 (2002)

5. Adi, K., Suksmono, A.B., Mengko, T.L.R., Gunawan, H.: Phase unwrapping by Markov chain Monte Carlo energy minimization. IEEE Geosci. Remote Sens. Lett. **7**(4), 704–707 (2010)
6. Ahlberg, S., Soderman, U., Elmqvist, M., Persson, A.: On modeling and visualization of high resolution virtual environments using LIDAR data. In: Proc. 12th International Conference on Geoinformatics, pp. 299–306 (2004)
7. Ahokas, E., Yu, X., Oksanen, J., Hyyppa, J., Kaartinen, H., Hyyppa, H.: Optimization of the scanning angle for countrywide laser scanning. Int. Arch. Photogramm. Remote Sens. Spatial Inf. Sci. **XXXVI**(3/W19), 115–119 (2005)
8. Arefi, H., Hahn, M.: A morphological reconstruction algorithm for separating off-terrain points from terrain points in laser scanner data. Int. Arch. Photogramm. Remote Sens. Spatial Inf. Sci. **XXXVI**(3/W19), 120–125 (2005)
9. ASTER GDEM Validation Team: ASTER Global DEM Validation Summary Report (2009)
10. Axelsson, P.: Processing of laser scanner data—algorithms and applications. ISPRS J. Photogramm. Remote Sens. **54**(2–3), 138–147 (1999)
11. Baker, H.H., Binford, T.D.: A system for automated stereo mapping. In: Proceedings of the Symposium of the ISPRS Commission II, Ottawa, Canada (1982)
12. Baltsavias, E.P.: Airborne laser scanning: basic relations and formulas. ISPRS J. Photogramm. Remote Sens. **54**, 199–214 (1999)
13. Baltsavias, E.P.: Airborne laser scanning: existing firms and other resources. ISPRS J. Photogramm. Remote Sens. **54**, 199–214 (1999)
14. Baltsavias, E.P.: A comparison between photogrammetry and laser scanning. ISPRS J. Photogramm. Remote Sens. **54**, 83–94 (1999)
15. Bao, Y., Li, G., Cao, C., Li, X., Zhang, H., He, Q., Bai, L., Chang, C.: Classification of LIDAR point cloud and generation of DTM from LIDAR height and intensity data in forested area. Int. Arch. Photogramm. Remote Sens. Spatial Inf. Sci. **XXXVII**(3/W19), 313–318 (2008)
16. Bartels, M., Wei, H.: Segmentation of LIDAR data using measures of distribution. Int. Arch. Photogramm. Remote Sens. Spatial Inf. Sci. **XXXVI**(7), 426–431 (2006)
17. Bartels, M., Wei, H.: Threshold-free object and ground point separation in LIDAR data. Pattern Recognit. Lett. **31**(10), 1089–1099 (2010)
18. Bartels, M., Wei, H., Mason, D.C.: Wavelet packets and co-occurrence matrices for texture-based image segmentation. In: IEEE International Conference on Advanced Video and Signal-Based Surveillance, vol. 1, pp. 428–433 (2005)
19. Bartels, M., Wei, H., Mason, D.C.: DTM generation from LIDAR data using skewness balancing. In: Proceedings of 18th International Conference on Pattern Recognition, I, pp. 566–569 (2006)
20. Bater, C.W., Coops, N.C.: Evaluating error associated with LIDAR-derived DEM interpolation. Comput. Geosci. **35**(2), 289–300 (2009)
21. Bouillon, A., Bernard, M., Gigord, P., Orsoni, A., Rudowski, V., Baudoin, A.: SPOT 5 HRS geometric performances: using block adjustment as a key issue to improve quality of DEM generation. ISPRS J. Photogramm. Remote Sens. **60**(3), 134–146 (2006)
22. Brenner, C.: Towards fully automatic generation of city models. Int. Arch. Photogramm. Remote Sens. Spatial Inf. Sci. **33**(3), 85–92 (2000)
23. Bretar, F., Roux, M.: Hybrid image segmentation using LIDAR 3D planar primitives. Int. Arch. Photogramm. Remote Sens. Spatial Inf. Sci. **XXXVI**(3/W19), 72–78 (2005)
24. Bretar, F., Pierrot-Deseilligny, M., Roux, M.: Recognition of building roof facets by merging aerial images and 3D LIDAR data in a hierarchical segmentation framework. In: Proceedings of 18th International Conference on Pattern Recognition, IV, pp. 5–8 (2006)
25. Briese, C., Pfeifer, N.: Airborne laser scanning and derivation of digital terrain models. Opt. 3-D Meas. Tech. **V**, 81–87 (2001)
26. Briese, C., Pfeifer, N., Dorninger, P.: Applications of the robust interpolation for DTM determination. Int. Arch. Photogramm. Remote Sens. Spatial Inf. Sci. **XXXIV**(3A), 55–61 (2002)

27. Brovelli, M.A., Cannata, M., Longoni, U.M.: Managing and processing LIDAR data within GRASS. In: Proceedings of the Open Source GIS—GRASS Users Conference, I (2002). 29 pages
28. Burton, T., Neill, L.: Use of low-level LIDAR systems for commercial large-scale survey applications. In: Annual Conference of the Remote Sensing and Photogrammetry Society, I(1), (2007). 6 pages
29. Carballo, G.F., Fieguth, P.W.: Hierarchical network flow phase unwrapping. IEEE Trans. Geosci. Remote Sens. **40**(8), 1695–1708 (2002)
30. Charaniya, A.P., Manduchi, R., Lodha, S.K.: Supervised parametric classification of aerial LIDAR data. In: Proceedings of IEEE Conference on Computer Vision and Pattern Recognition Workshop, pp. 30–38 (2004)
31. Chen, C., Yue, T.: A method of DEM construction and related error analysis. Comput. Geosci. **36**(6), 717–725 (2010)
32. Chen, Q., et al.: Filtering airborne laser scanning data with morphological methods. Photogramm. Eng. Remote Sens. **73**(2), 175–185 (2007)
33. Cobby, D.M.: The use of airborne scanning laser altimetry for improved river flood prediction. University of Reading (2002)
34. Cobby, D.M., Mason, D.C., Davenport, I.J.: Image processing of airborne scanning laser altimetry data for improved river flood modeling. ISPRS J. Photogramm. Remote Sens. **56**, 121–138 (2001)
35. Cobby, D.M., et al.: Two-dimensional hydraulic flood modeling using a finite-element mesh decomposed according to vegetation and topographic features derived from airborne scanning laser altimetry. Hydrol. Process. **17**(10), 1979–2000 (2002)
36. Costantini, M.: A novel phase unwrapping method based on network programming. IEEE Trans. Geosci. Remote Sens. **36**(3), 813–821 (1998)
37. Costantini, M., Farina, A., Zirilli, F.: A fast phase unwrapping algorithm for SAR interferometry. IEEE Trans. Geosci. Remote Sens. **37**(1), 452–460 (1999)
38. Crosetto, M.: Calibration and validation of SAR interferometry for DEM generation. ISPRS J. Photogramm. Remote Sens. **57**, 213–227 (2002)
39. Davenport, I.J., et al.: Improving bird population models using airborne remote sensing. Int. J. Remote Sens. **21**(13 & 14), 2705–2717 (2000)
40. Duda, R.O., Stork, D.G.: Pattern Classification. Wiley, New York (2001)
41. Faugeras, O.: Three-Dimensional Computer Vision—A Geometric Viewpoint. MIT Press, Cambridge (1993)
42. Ferraioli, G., et al.: Multichannel phase unwrapping with graph cuts. IEEE Geosci. Remote Sens. Lett. **6**(3), 562–566 (2009)
43. Flood, M.: LIDAR activities and research priorities in the commercial sector. Int. Arch. Photogramm. Remote Sens. Spatial Inf. Sci. **XXXIV**(3/W4), 3–7 (2001)
44. Fornaro, G., Franceschetti, G., Lanari, R.: Interferometric SAR phase unwrapping using green's formulation. IEEE Trans. Geosci. Remote Sens. **34**(3), 720–727 (1996)
45. Förstner, W.: On the geometric precision of digital correlation. Int. Arch. Photogramm. **24**(III), 176–189 (1982). Helsinki
46. Förstner, W., Gulch, E.: A fast operator for detection and precise location of distinct points, corners and centres of circular features. In: Inter-commission Conference on Fast Processing of Photogrammetric Data, Interlaken, Switzerland, pp. 281–305 (1987)
47. Fraile, R., Maybank, S.: Comparing probabilistic and geometric models on LIDAR data. Int. Arch. Photogramm. Remote Sens. Spatial Inf. Sci. **34**(3/W4), 67–70 (2001)
48. Fraser, C.S.: High-resolution satellite imagery: a review of metric aspects. In: International Archives of Photogrammetry and Remote Sensing, XXXIII, Part B7, Amsterdam (2000)
49. Fried, D.L.: Least-squares fitting a wave-front distortion estimate to an array of phase-difference measurements. J. Opt. Soc. Am. **67**, 370–375 (1977)
50. Friess, P.: Toward a rigorous methodology airborne laser mapping. In: ISPRS International Calibration and Orientation Workshop (EuroCOW 2006), I (2006). 7 pages

51. Gabet, L., Giraudon, G., Renouard, L.: Automatic generation of high resolution urban zone digital elevation models. ISPRS J. Photogramm. Remote Sens. **52**(1), 33–47 (1997)
52. Galiatsatos, N., Donoghue, D.N.M., Philip, G.: High resolution elevation data derived from stereoscopic CORONA imagery with minimal ground control: an approach using ikonos and SRTM data. Photogramm. Eng. Remote Sens. **74**(9), 1093–1106 (2008)
53. Ghiglia, D.C., Romero, L.A.: Robust two-dimensional weighted and unweighted phase unwrapping that uses fast transforms and iterative methods. J. Opt. Soc. Am. **11**(1), 107–117 (1994)
54. Goldstein, R.M., Zebker, H.A., Werner, C.L.: Satellite radar interferometry: two-dimensional phase unwrapping. Radio Sci. **23**(4), 713–720 (1988)
55. Gomes Pereira, L.M., Janssen, L.L.F.: Suitability of laser data for DTM generation: a case study in the context of road planning and design. ISPRS J. Photogramm. Remote Sens. **54**, 244–253 (1999)
56. Graham, L.C.: Synthetic interferometric radar for topographic mapping. Proc. IEEE **62**(6), 763–768 (1974)
57. Gruen, A.W.: Adaptive least squares correlation: a powerful image matching technique. J. Photogramm. Remote Sens. Cartography **14**(3), 175–185 (1985)
58. Gwinner, K., et al.: Topography of mars from global mapping by HRSC high-resolution digital terrain models and orthoimages: characteristics and performance. Earth Planet. Sci. Lett. **294**(3–4), 506–519 (2010)
59. Haala, N., Brenner, C.: Generation of 3D city models from airborne laser scanning data. In: Proceedings of EARSEL Workshop on LIDAR Remote Sensing of Land and Sea, pp. 105–112 (1997)
60. Haala, N., Brenner, C.: Fast production of virtual reality city models. Int. Arch. Photogramm. Remote Sens. Spatial Inf. Sci. **32**(4), 77–84 (1998)
61. Haala, N., Brenner, C.: Extraction of buildings and trees in urban environments. ISPRS J. Photogramm. Remote Sens. **54**, 130–137 (1999)
62. Haala, N., Brenner, C., Anders, K.-H.: 3D urban GIS from laser altimeter and 2D map data. ISPRS Congress Commission III, Working Group **4**(32(3/1)), 339–346 (1998)
63. Haala, N., Brenner, C., Staetter, C.: An integrated system for urban model generation. Proceedings ISPRS Congress Commission II, Working Group **6**, 96–103 (1998)
64. Habib, A., et al.: DEM generation from high resolution satellite imagery using parallel projection model. In: ISPRS Congress, Istanbul (2004)
65. Haralick, R.M., Shapiro, L.G.: Computer and Robot Vision, vol. I. Addison-Wesley, Reading (1992)
66. Haralick, R.M., Sternberg, S.R., Zhuang, X.: Image analysis using mathematical morphology. IEEE Trans. Pattern Anal. Mach. Intell. **9**(4), 532–550 (1987)
67. Hasegawa, H., et al.: DEM accuracy and the base to height (B/H) ratio of stereo images. In: International Archives of Photogrammetry and Remote Sensing, XXXIII, Part B4, Amsterdam (2000)
68. Hashimoto, T.: DEM generation from stereo AVNIR images. Adv. Space Res. **25**(5), 931–936 (2000)
69. Heipke, C.: Automation of interior, relative, and absolute orientation. ISPRS J. Photogramm. Remote Sens. **52**(1), 1–19 (1997)
70. Hellwich, O.: Basic principles and current issues of SAR interferometry. In: ISPRS Workshop, Commission I, Working Group I/3, Hannover, Germany (1999)
71. Hellwich, O., Ebner, H.: Geocoding SAR interferograms by least squares adjustment. ISPRS J. Photogramm. Remote Sens. **55**(4), 277–288 (2000)
72. Henssen, R.F.: Radar interferometry: data interpretation and error analysis. In: Meer, F.V.D. (ed.) Remote Sensing and Digital Image Processing, vol. 2. Kluwer Academic, London (2001)
73. Hirano, A., Welch, R., Lang, H.: Mapping from ASTER stereo image data: DEM validation and accuracy assessment. ISPRS J. Photogramm. Remote Sens. **57**(5–6), 356–370 (2003)

74. Hodgson, M.E., Bresnahan, P.: Accuracy of airborne LIDAR-derived elevation: empirical assessment and error budget. Photogramm. Eng. Remote Sens. **70**(3), 331–339 (2004)
75. Hodgson, M.E., et al.: An evaluation of LIDAR-derived elevation and terrain slope in leaf-off conditions. Photogramm. Eng. Remote Sens. **71**(7), 817–823 (2005)
76. Hofmann, A.D., Maas, H.-G., Streilein, A.: Knowledge-based building detection based on laser scanner data and topographic map information. Int. Arch. Photogramm. Remote Sens. Spatial Inf. Sci. **34**(3A), 169–174 (2002)
77. Hogan, R.J., et al.: Characteristics of mixed-phase clouds. I: LIDAR, radar and aircraft observations from CLARE98. Q. J. R. Meteorol. Soc. **129**(592), 2089–2116 (2003)
78. Huising, E.J., Gomes Pereira, L.M.: Errors and accuracy estimates of laser data acquired by various laser scanning systems for topographic applications. ISPRS J. Photogramm. Remote Sens. **53**, 245–261 (1998)
79. Hunt, B.R.: Matrix formulation of the reconstruction of phase values from phase differences. J. Opt. Soc. Am. **69**, 393–399 (1979)
80. Hutchinson, M.F.: Development of a continent-wide DEM with applications to terrain and climate analysis. In: Goodchild, M.F., et al. (eds.) Environmental Modeling with GIS. Oxford University Press, Oxford (1993)
81. Hyyppä, H., et al.: Factors affecting the quality of DTM generation in forested areas. Int. Arch. Photogramm. Remote Sens. Spatial Inf. Sci. **XXXVI**(3/W19), 85–90 (2005)
82. Jacobsen, K.: DEM generation from satellite data. In: Remote Sensing in Transition—23rd EARSeL Symposium, Ghent, Belgium (2003)
83. Jain, A.K., Duin, R.P.W., Mao, J.: Statistical pattern recognition: a review. IEEE Trans. Pattern Anal. Mach. Intell. **22**(1) (2000)
84. James, T.D., et al.: Extracting photogrammetric ground control from LIDAR DEMs for change detection. Photogramm. Rec. **21**(116), 312–328 (2006)
85. Jet Propulsion Laboratory: ASTER Global Digital Elevation Map Announcement. http://asterweb.jpl.nasa.gov/gdem.asp (2009)
86. Jong-Sen, L., et al.: A new technique for noise filtering of SAR interferometric phase images. IEEE Trans. Geosci. Remote Sens. **36**(5), 1456–1465 (1998)
87. Kanade, T., Okutomi, M.: A stereo matching algorithm with an adaptive window: theory and experiment. IEEE Trans. Pattern Anal. Mach. Intell. **16**(9), 920–932 (1994)
88. Kervyn, F.: Modeling topography with SAR interferometry: illustrations of a favourable and less favourable environment. Comput. Geosci. **27**(9), 1039–1050 (2001)
89. Kidner, D.B., et al.: Coastal monitoring with LIDAR: challenges, problems, and pitfalls. Proc. SPIE **5574**, 80–89 (2004)
90. Kilian, J., Haala, N., Englich, M.: Capture and evaluation of airborne laser data. Int. Arch. Photogramm. Remote Sens. **31**(3), 383–388 (1996)
91. Kobler, A., et al.: Repetitive interpolation: a robust algorithm for DTM generation from aerial laser scanner data in forested terrain. Remote Sens. Environ. **108**(1), 9–23 (2007)
92. Kornus, W., et al.: DEM generation from SPOT-5 3-fold along track stereoscopic imagery using autocalibration. ISPRS J. Photogramm. Remote Sens. **60**(3), 147–159 (2006)
93. Kraus, K., Pfeifer, N.: Determination of terrain models in wooded areas with airborne laser scanner data. ISPRS J. Photogramm. Remote Sens. **53**, 193–203 (1998)
94. Kraus, K., Pfeifer, N.: Advanced DTM generation from LIDAR data. ISPRS J. Photogramm. Remote Sens. **53**, 193–203 (2001)
95. Krieger, G., et al.: TanDEM-X: a satellite formation for high-resolution SAR interferometry. IEEE Trans. Geosci. Remote Sens. **45**(11), 3317–3341 (2007)
96. Krzystek, P.: Filtering of laser scanning data in forest areas using finite elements. Int. Arch. Photogramm. Remote Sens. Spatial Inf. Sci. **XXXIV**(3/W13) (2003). 6 pages
97. Lanari, R., et al.: Generation of digital elevation models by using SIR-C/X-SAR multifrequency two-pass interferometry: the Etna case study. IEEE Trans. Geosci. Remote Sens. **34**(5), 1097–1114 (1996)
98. Lee, H.-Y., et al.: Extraction of digital elevation models from satellite stereo images through stereo matching based on epipolarity and scene geometry. Image Vis. Comput. **21**(9), 789–796 (2003)

99. Li, H., Liao, G.: An estimation method for InSAR interferometric phase based on MMSE criterion. IEEE Trans. Geosci. Remote Sens. **48**(3), 1457–1469 (2010)
100. Li, J., et al.: The research and design of the base-height ratio for the three linear array camera of satellite photogrammetry. In: International Archives of the Photogrammetry, Remote Sensing and Spatial Information Sciences, XXXVII, Part B1, Beijing (2008)
101. Lillesand, T.M., Kiefer, R.W., Chipman, J.W.: Remote Sensing and Image Interpretation. Wiley, New York (2004)
102. Lin, Q., Vesecky, J.F., Zebker, H.A.: New approaches in interferometric SAR data processing. IEEE Trans. Geosci. Remote Sens. **30**(3), 560–567 (1992)
103. Loffeld, O., et al.: Phase unwrapping for SAR interferometry—a data fusion approach by Kalman filtering. IEEE Trans. Geosci. Remote Sens. **46**(1), 47–58 (2008)
104. Löffler, G.: Aspects of raster DEM data derived from laser measurements. Int. Arch. Photogramm. Remote Sen. Spatial Inf. Sci. **XXXIV**(3/W13) (2003). 5 pages
105. Lohr, U.: Laserscan DEM for various applications. In: Fritsch, M.E.D., Sester, M. (eds.) ISPRS Commission IV Symposium on GIS—Between Visions and Applications, vol. 32/4 (1998)
106. Lowe, D.G.: Distinctive image features from scale-invariant keypoints. Int. J. Comput. Vis. **60**(2), 91–110 (2004)
107. Luethya, J., Stengele, R.: 3D mapping of Switzerland—challenges and experiences. Int. Arch. Photogramm. Remote Sens. Spatial Inf. Sci. **XXXVI**(3/W19), 42–47 (2005)
108. Maas, H.-G.: Akquisition von 3D-GIS Daten durch Flugzeuglaserscanning. Kartogr. Nachr. **55**(1), 3–11 (2005)
109. Marr, D., Poggio, T.: A computational theory of human stereo vision. Proc. R. Soc. Lond., Ser. B **204**(1156), 301–328 (1979)
110. Martinez-Espla, J.J., Martinez-Marin, T., Lopez-Sanchez, J.M.: A particle filter approach for InSAR phase filtering and unwrapping. IEEE Trans. Geosci. Remote Sens. **47**(4), 1197–1211 (2009)
111. Mason, D.C., Scott, T.R., Wang, H.-J.: Extraction of tidal channel networks from airborne scanning laser altimetry. ISPRS J. Photogramm. Remote Sens. **61**(2), 67–83 (2006)
112. Massonnet, D., Rabaute, T.: Radar interferometry: limits and potential. IEEE Trans. Geosci. Remote Sens. **31**(2), 455–464 (1993)
113. Mora, O., et al.: Generation of accurate DEMs using DInSAR methodology (TopoDInSAR). IEEE Geosci. Remote Sens. Lett. **3**(4), 551–554 (2006)
114. Nardinocchi, C., Forlani, G., Zingaretti, P.: Classification and filtering of laser data. Int. Arch. Photogramm. Remote Sen. Spatial Inf. Sci. **XXXIV**(3/W13) (2003). 8 pages
115. Oliver, C., Quegan, S.: Understanding Synthetic Aperture Radar Images. Artech House, London (1998)
116. O'Neill, M., Denos, M.: Automated system for coarse-to-fine pyramidal area correlation stereo matching. Image Vis. Comput. **14**(3), 225–236 (1996)
117. Otto, G.P., Chau, T.K.W.: Region-growing algorithm for matching of terrain images. Image Vis. Comput. **7**(2), 83–94 (1989)
118. Oude Elberink, S., Maas, H.-G.: The use of anisotropic height texture measures for the segmentation of laser scanner data. Int. Arch. Photogramm. Remote Sens. Spatial Inf. Sci. **XXXIII**(B3), 678–684 (2000)
119. Pertl, A.: Digital image correlation with the analytical plotter PLANICOMP C-100. In: Int. Archives of Photogrammetry and Remote Sensing, XXV, A3b, Commission III, Rio de Janeiro (1984)
120. Pfeifer, N., Stadler, P., Briese, C.: Derivation of digital terrain models in the SCOP++ environment. In: Proceedings of OEEPE Workshop on Airborne Laserscanning and Interferometric SAR for Detailed Digital Terrain Models (2001)
121. Pritt, M.D., Shipman, J.S.: Least-squares two-dimensional phase unwrapping using FFT's. IEEE Trans. Geosci. Remote Sens. **32**(3), 706–708 (1994)

122. Raber, G.T., et al.: Creation of digital terrain models using an adaptive LIDAR vegetation point removal process. Photogramm. Eng. Remote Sens. **68**(12), 1307–1315 (2002)
123. Rabus, B., et al.: The shuttle radar topography mission—a new class of digital elevation models acquired by spaceborne radar. ISPRS J. Photogramm. Remote Sens. **57**(4), 241–262 (2003)
124. Raney, R.K., et al.: Precision SAR processing using chirp scaling. IEEE Trans. Geosci. Remote Sens. **32**(4), 786–799 (1994)
125. Reinartz, P., et al.: Accuracy analysis for DSM and orthoimages derived from SPOT HRS stereo data using direct georeferencing. ISPRS J. Photogramm. Remote Sens. **60**(3), 160–169 (2006)
126. Rodriguez, E., Martin, J.M.: Theory and design of interferometric synthetic aperture radars. IEE Proc., F, Radar Signal Process. **139**(2), 147–159 (1992)
127. Rogers, A.E.E., Ingalls, R.P.: Venus: mapping the surface reflectivity by radar interferometry. Science **165**, 797–799 (1969)
128. Roggero, M.: Airborne laser scanning: clustering in raw data. Int. Arch. Photogramm. Remote Sens. Spatial Inf. Sci. **34**(3/W4), 227–232 (2001)
129. Rosen, P.A., et al.: Synthetic aperture radar interferometry. Proc. IEEE **88**(3), 333–382 (2000)
130. Rosenfeld, A.: Image analysis: problems, progress and prospects. Pattern Recognit. **17**(1), 3–12 (1984)
131. Rottensteiner, F., Briese, C.: Automatic generation of building models from LIDAR data and the integration of aerial images. Int. Arch. Photogramm. Remote Sens. Spatial Inf. Sci. ISPRS **34**(3/W13), 174–180 (2003)
132. Rottensteiner, F., et al.: Building detection by fusion of airborne laser scanner data and multi-spectral images: performance evaluation and sensitivity analysis. ISPRS J. Photogramm. Remote Sens. **62**, 135–149 (2007)
133. Rottensteiner, F., et al.: Using the Dempster-Shafer method for the fusion of LIDAR data and multi-spectral images for building detection. Inf. Fusion **6**, 283–300 (2005)
134. Rottensteiner, F., et al.: Automated delineation of roof planes from LIDAR data. Int. Arch. Photogramm. Remote Sens. Spatial Inf. Sci. **XXXVI**(3/W19), 42–47 (2005)
135. Rufino, G., Moccia, A., Esposito, S.: DEM generation by means of ERS tandem data. IEEE Trans. Geosci. Remote Sens. **36**(6), 1905–1912 (1998)
136. Schenk, T., Csathó, B.: Fusion of LIDAR data and aerial imagery for a more complete surface description. Int. Arch. Photogramm. Remote Sens. Spatial Inf. Sci. **XXXIV**(3A/B), 310–317 (2002)
137. Schenk, T., Seo, S., Csathó, B.: Accuracy study of airborne laser scanning data with photogrammetry. Int. Arch. Photogramm. Remote Sens. Spatial Inf. Sci. **XXXIV**(3/W4), 113–118 (2001)
138. Schnadt, K., Katzenbeißer, R.: Unique airborne fiber scanner technique for application-oriented LIDAR products. Int. Arch. Photogramm. Remote Sens. Spatial Inf. Sci. **XXXVI**(8/W2), 19–23 (2004)
139. Silván-Cárdenas, J.L., Wang, L.: A multi-resolution approach for filtering LIDAR altimetry data. ISPRS J. Photogramm. Remote Sens. **61**, 11–22 (2006)
140. Silván-Cárdenas, J.L., Wang, L.: The multiscale Hermite transform for local orientation analysis. IEEE Trans. Image Process. **15**(5), 1236–1253 (2006)
141. Silván-Cárdenas, J.L., Wang, L.: Multiscale-based filtering of LIDAR altimetry data. MAPPS/ASPRS, I (2006). 6 pages
142. Sithole, G.: Filtering of laser altimetry data using a slope adaptive filter. Int. Arch. Photogramm. Remote Sens. Spatial Inf. Sci. **XXXIV**(3/W4), 203–210 (2001)
143. Sithole, G., Vosselman, G.: Experimental comparison of filter algorithms for bare-earth extraction from airborne laser scanning point clouds. ISPRS J. Photogramm. Remote Sens. **59**(1–2), 85–101 (2004)
144. Sohn, G.: Extraction of buildings from high-resolution satellite data and LIDAR. Int. Arch. Photogramm. Remote Sens. Spatial Inf. Sci. **XXXV**(7), 1036–1042 (2004)

145. Sohn, G., Dowman, I.: Terrain surface reconstruction by the use of tetrahedron model with the MDL criterion. Int. Arch. Photogramm. Remote Sens. Spatial Inf. Sci. **XXXIV**(3A), 336–344 (2002)
146. Tarsha-Kurdi, F., et al.: New approach for automatic detection of buildings in airborne laser scanner. Int. Arch. Photogramm. Remote Sens. Spatial Inf. Sci. **XXXVI**(3), 25–30 (2006)
147. Toutin, T.: Error tracking in ikonos geometric processing using a 3D parametric model. Photogramm. Eng. Remote Sens. **69**(1), 43–51 (2003)
148. Toutin, T.: Spatiotriangulation with multisensor VIR/SAR images. IEEE Trans. Geosci. Remote Sens. **42**(10), 2096–2103 (2004)
149. Toutin, T.: Comparison of stereo-extracted DTM from different high-resolution sensors: SPOT-5, EROS-A, IKONOS-II, and QuickBird. IEEE Trans. Geosci. Remote Sens. **42**(10), 2121–2129 (2004)
150. Toutin, T.: Generation of DSMs from SPOT-5 in-track HRS and across-track HRG stereo data using spatiotriangulation and autocalibration. ISPRS J. Photogramm. Remote Sens. **60**(3), 170–181 (2006)
151. Toutin, T., Gray, L.: State-of-the-art of elevation extraction from satellite SAR data. ISPRS J. Photogramm. Remote Sens. **55**(1), 13–33 (2000)
152. Viñas, O., et al.: Combined use of LIDAR and QuickBird data for the generation of land use maps. Int. Arch. Photogramm. Remote Sens. Spatial Inf. Sci. **XXXVI**(7), 155–159 (2006)
153. von Hansen, W., Vögtle, T.: Extraktion der geländeoberfläche aus flugzeuggetragenen Laserscanner-Aufnahmen. Photogramm. Fernerkund. Geoinf. (PFG) **4**, 229–236 (1999)
154. Vosselman, G.: Building reconstruction using planar faces in very high density height data. Int. Arch. Photogramm. Remote Sens. Spatial Inf. Sci. **32**(3/2W5), 87–92 (1999)
155. Vosselman, G.: Slope based filtering of laser altimetry data. Int. Arch. Photogramm. Remote Sens. Spatial Inf. Sci. **33**(B3/2), 935–942 (2000)
156. Vosselman, G., Dijkman, S.: 3D building model reconstruction from point clouds and ground plans. Int. Arch. Photogramm. Remote Sens. Spatial Inf. Sci. **XXXIV**(3/W4), 37–43 (2001)
157. Vosselman, G., Suveg, I.: Map based building reconstruction from laser data and images. Proc. Autom. Extract. Man-Made Obj. Aerial Space Images **32**(3/2W5), 231–239 (2001)
158. Vu, T.T., Tokunaga, M.: Wavelet and scale-space theory in segmentation of airborne laser scanner data. In: Proc. 22nd Asian Conference on Remote Sensing, I (2001). 5 pages
159. Vu, T.T., Tokunaga, M.: Wavelet-based clustering method to detect building in urban area from airborne laser scanner data. In: MapAsia 2002, I (2002). 2 pages
160. Vu, T.T., Tokunaga, M.: Wavelet-based filtering the cloud points derived from airborne laser scanner. In: Proceeding of the 23rd Asian Conference on Remote Sensing, I (2002). 2 pages
161. Vu, T.T., et al.: Wavelet-based system for classification of airborne laser scanner data. In: IEEE International Geoscience and Remote Sensing Symposium, IGARSS 2003, vol. 7, pp. 4404–4406 (2003)
162. Vu, T.T., Tokunaga, M., Yamazaki, F.: In: LIDAR signatures to update Japanese building inventory database. 25th Asian Conference on Remote Sensing, I (2004). 6 pages
163. Wack, R., Stelzl, H.: Laser DTM generation for South-Tyrol and 3D-visualization. Int. Arch. Photogramm. Remote Sens. Spatial Inf. Sci. **XXXVI**(3/W19), 48–53 (2005)
164. Wack, R., Wimmer, A.: Digital terrain models from airborne laser scanner data—a grid based approach. Int. Arch. Photogramm. Remote Sens. Spatial Inf. Sci. **34**(3B), 293–296 (2002)
165. Wang, Y.: Principles and applications of structural image matching. ISPRS J. Photogramm. Remote Sens. **53**(3), 154–165 (1998)
166. Weed, C.A., et al.: Classification of LIDAR data using a lower envelope follower and gradient-based operator. IEEE International Geoscience and Remote Sensing Symposium **3**, 1384–1386 (2002)
167. Wehr, A., Lohr, U.: Airborne laser scanning—an introduction and overview. ISPRS J. Photogramm. Remote Sens. **54**, 68–82 (1999)
168. Wei, H., Bartels, M.: Unsupervized segmentation using Gabor wavelets and statistical features in LIDAR data analysis. In: Proceedings of 18th International Conference on Pattern Recognition, I, pp. 667–670 (2006)

169. Weidner, U.: An approach to building extraction from digital surface models. Int. Arch. Photogramm. Remote Sens. Spatial Inf. Sci. **31**(B3), 924–929 (1996)
170. Weidner, U.: Digital Surface Models for Building Extraction. Automatic Extraction of Man-Made Objects from Aerial and Space Images (II). Birkhäuser, Basel (1997). A. Grün (ed.)
171. Weidner, U.: Analysis and comparison of different high-resolution data sets for urban applications. Int. Arch. Photogramm. Remote Sens. Spatial Inf. Sci. **XXXVI**(7), 750–755 (2006)
172. Weidner, U., Förstner, W.: Towards automatic building extraction from high resolution digital elevation models. ISPRS J. Photogramm. Remote Sens. **50**(4), 38–49 (1995)
173. Wu, N., Feng, D.-Z., Li, J.: A locally adaptive filter of interferometric phase images. IEEE Geosci. Remote Sens. Lett. **3**(1), 73–77 (2006)
174. Xu, W., Cumming, I.: A region-growing algorithm for InSAR phase unwrapping. IEEE Trans. Geosci. Remote Sens. **37**(1), 124–134 (1999)
175. Yao, W., Hinz, S., Stilla, U.: Automatic vehicle extraction from airborne LIDAR data of urban areas using morphological reconstruction. In: Proceedings of 5th IAPR Workshop on Pattern Recognition in Remote Sensing (PRRS 2008) (2008). 4 pages
176. Yamaki, R., Hirose, A.: Singular unit restoration in interferograms based on complex-valued Markov random field model for phase unwrapping. IEEE Geosci. Remote Sens. Lett. **6**(1), 18–22 (2009)
177. Yu, H., Li, Z., Bao, Z.: A cluster-analysis-based efficient multibaseline phase-unwrapping algorithm. IEEE Trans. Geosci. Remote Sens. **49**(1), 478–487 (2011)
178. Yu, Q., et al.: An adaptive contoured window filter for interferometric synthetic aperture radar. IEEE Geosci. Remote Sens. Lett. **4**(1), 23–26 (2007)
179. Yu, X., et al.: Applicability of first pulse derived digital terrain models for Boreal forest studies. Int. Arch. Photogramm. Remote Sens. Spatial Inf. Sci. **XXXVI**(3/W19), 97–102 (2005)
180. Zebker, H.A., et al.: The TOPSAR interferometric radar topographic mapping instrument. IEEE Trans. Geosci. Remote Sens. **30**(5), 933–940 (1992)
181. Zhang, K., et al.: A progressive morphological filter for removing nonground measurements from airborne LIDAR data. IEEE Trans. Geosci. Remote Sens. **41**(4), 872–882 (2003)
182. Zhang, L., Gruen, A.: Multi-image matching for DSM generation from IKONOS imagery. ISPRS J. Photogramm. Remote Sens. **60**(3), 195–211 (2006)
183. Zhang, Z., et al.: A robust technique for matching two uncalibrated images through the recovery of the unknown epipolar geometry. Artif. Intell. **78**(1–2), 87–119 (1995)
184. Zisk, S.H.: A new Earth-based radar technique for the measurement of lunar topography. Moon **4**, 296–300 (1972)
185. Zitová, B., Flusser, J.: Image registration methods: a survey. Image Vis. Comput. **21**(11), 977–1000 (2003)

Chapter 10
High-Resolution Three-Dimensional Remote Sensing for Forest Measurement

Hans-Erik Andersen

Abstract High-resolution, optical, airborne remote sensing systems can capture detailed information on three-dimensional (3D) forest canopy structure. Individual tree biomass, volume, and carbon are highly correlated to tree height, so if individual tree heights can be efficiently measured using high-resolution remote sensing, it significantly reduces the cost of forest inventory and increase the quality of the information available to resource managers. We describe several techniques for the 3D remote sensing of forests. In the first category, we describe how aerial photogrammetric measurements, acquired from overlapping stereo digital imagery, can provide accurate 3D measurements of individual tree crowns. In the second category, we describe airborne laser scanning (LIDAR), which provides a 3D point cloud of laser returns from the forest canopy and underlying terrain.

10.1 Introduction

Accurate estimates of aboveground forest biomass, three-dimensional (3D) forest structure, and forest type and condition class are critical for monitoring of carbon dynamics, timber production, wildlife habitat, and canopy fuels. Typically, natural resource managers use measurements acquired at field plots to characterize the forest type, structure, and biomass resources within a particular area. The basic tree measurements and qualitative information collected at field plots usually include tree species, tree height, stem diameter at breast height (DBH, where breast height is defined as 1.3 m), crown ratio (the length of the crown as a percentage of total tree height), as well as the percentage of the merchantable stem that is rotten or otherwise not suitable for timber. Often, the position of the tree stem relative to the plot center (distance and azimuth) is noted so as to facilitate re-measurement in subsequent years. Although plot sizes vary depending on the available resources and forest types, measurements on small trees (seedlings and saplings) are usually acquired on a smaller *regeneration plot*. For example, in the national forest inventory system

H.-E. Andersen (✉)
United States Department of Agriculture Forest Service, Pacific Northwest Research Station, Seattle, WA, USA
e-mail: handersen@fs.fed.us

in the United States (Forest inventory and Analysis (FIA)), each plot consists of a cluster of four 1/60th hectare subplots spaced 36 meters apart, while trees smaller than 12.5 cm DBH are only measured on smaller 1/300th hectare microplots [7].

10.1.1 Allometric Modeling of Biomass

While these individual tree dimensions are sometimes of interest in their own right (e.g. for characterizing site productivity), often resource managers are interested in using these basic dimensional measurements to acquire indirect estimates of other tree attributes with more direct commercial and ecological significance, such as biomass, merchantable volume, and aboveground carbon. Allometric scaling principles in biology dictate that individual tree dimensions (height, DBH) will be functionally related to the total weight of the tree [55]. While DBH is the most common basic tree dimension used to estimate volume and biomass, tree height is also highly correlated with these variables (see Fig. 10.1). As Fig. 10.1 indicates, the relationship between tree height and biomass has the functional form: $m = ah^2$, where m is biomass and h is tree height [31].

While the relationship between tree height and biomass is influenced by stand density, an advantage of using tree height, as opposed to DBH, to estimate biomass is that direct measurements of tree height can be acquired using high-resolution remote sensing data. Therefore, if allometric relationships are available relating tree height to biomass (possibly supplemented with stand density or crown width information), then it is theoretically possible to estimate individual tree biomass or volume using remote sensing data alone, obviating the need for field plots and thereby significantly reducing the cost of inventory.

In some forest types, however, it is very difficult, or even impossible, to accurately detect and measure individual tree crowns making up the dominant forest canopy layer. In this case, aggregate measures of forest structure obtained from three-dimensional remote sensing, such as airborne laser scanning, can be obtained over a specific area (usually a square grid cell or plot extent) and these structural metrics can be used to estimate the aggregate biomass level within this same area of forest using a predictive modeling (i.e. inferential) approach.

10.1.2 Chapter Outline

In this chapter, we will describe several techniques that can be used to detect and measure individual tree crowns using high-resolution remote sensing data, including aerial photogrammetry and airborne laser scanning (LIDAR), as well as approaches that can be used to infer aggregate biomass levels within areas of forest (plots and grid cells), using information on three-dimensional forest structure obtained from airborne laser scanning.

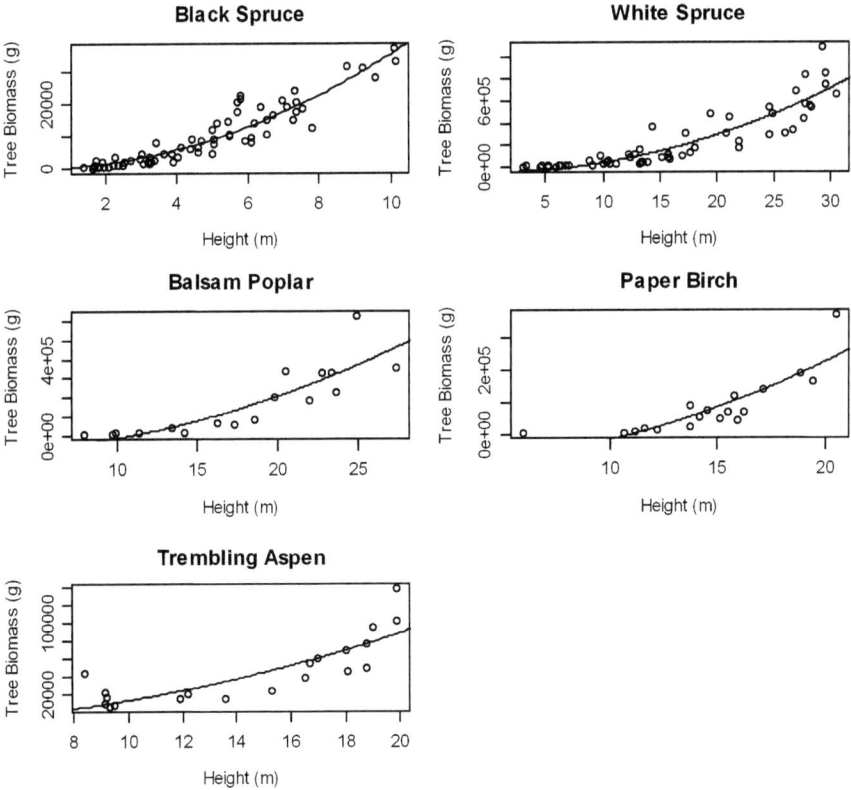

Fig. 10.1 Relationships between tree height and aboveground biomass for several boreal forest species in interior Alaska, USA [57]. *Line* shows the predicted values from the regression model, $m = ah^2$

10.2 Aerial Photo Mensuration

In this section, we firstly describe the principles of aerial photogrammetry and then we go on to describe how this is used to form tree height measurements.

10.2.1 Principles of Aerial Photogrammetry

Aerial photogrammetry,[1] or the science of making measurements from aerial photographs, has been used to support forestry applications for well over half a century

---

[1] It should be noted that the terminology describing identical geometric principles and analytical procedures often differs between the fields of photogrammetry and computer vision. For the purposes of clarity, the following table denotes the photogrammetry terminology and the corresponding computer vision terms:

[43, 51]. Furthermore, aerial photo mensuration, or forest photogrammetry, is the science of acquiring forest measurements from aerial photographs [40]. As mentioned above, tree height is one of the most fundamental measurements in forest inventory and the use of aerial photogrammetry to collect accurate and precise tree height measurements from a remote platform is a primary goal of aerial photo mensuration. Although there are several methods used to acquire tree height information from aerial photos, the most reliable method of tree height measurement, if also the most complex and difficult to carry out in practice, is based on the measurement of stereo disparity on overlapping pairs of aerial photographs (see Fig. 10.2). From a mathematical standpoint, the measurement of tree heights within the overlap area of a stereo pair is carried out by taking the distance between the elevation measured at the base of the tree (X_p, Y_p, Z_{base}) and the elevation measured at the top of the tree (X_p, Y_p, Z_p) (see Fig. 10.2). Once the exact position and orientation of each photo in the stereo pair is determined (using ground control points and a procedure known as exterior orientation), then these elevations can be determined using the collinearity condition, which states that the ray from the optical center to the image feature and the ray from the optical center to the corresponding world feature are collinear. Given that two collinearities are formed on the same scene point, we can intersect them to determine the 3D location of the scene point (see Fig. 10.2) [56].

10.2.1.1 Geometric Basis of Photogrammetric Measurement

In mathematical terms, the collinearity condition for a feature on the ground (**P**) that is seen at point ($\mathbf{p}_1$) in image 1 (Fig. 10.2) is expressed by the so-called collinearity equations, based on the geometric principle that the ray from the optical center to the image feature and the ray from the optical center to the corresponding real world feature are collinear [56]:

$$x_{p_1} - x_{o_1} = -f \left[\frac{m_{11_1}(X_p - X_{o_1}) + m_{12_1}(Y_p - Y_{o_1}) + m_{13_1}(Z_p - Z_{o_1})}{m_{31_1}(X_p - X_{o_1}) + m_{32_1}(Y_p - Y_{o_1}) + m_{33_1}(Z_p - Z_{o_1})} \right] \quad (10.1)$$

$$y_{p_1} - y_{o_1} = -f \left[\frac{m_{21_1}(X_p - X_{o_1}) + m_{22_1}(Y_p - Y_{o_1}) + m_{23_1}(Z_p - Z_{o_1})}{m_{31_1}(X_p - X_{o_1}) + m_{32_1}(Y_p - Y_{o_1}) + m_{33_1}(Z_p - Z_{o_1})} \right] \quad (10.2)$$

Here the elements of the rotation matrix $\mathbf{M} = \{m_{ij}\}_{i,j=1,1}^{3,3}$ are functions of the rotation angles $(\kappa, \varphi, \omega)$ that define the orientation of camera for each exposure:

Photogrammetry	Computer vision
Exterior orientation	Extrinsic calibration
Interior orientation	Intrinsic calibration
Conjugate points	Corresponding points
Exposure stations	3D capture positions
Space forward intersection	Triangulation

Fig. 10.2 Geometric basis for measurement of tree heights using the collinearity principle and space forward intersection from a stereo pair of aerial photographs. For the purposes of clarity, the untilted image coordinate system (x, y, z) is only shown the top figure

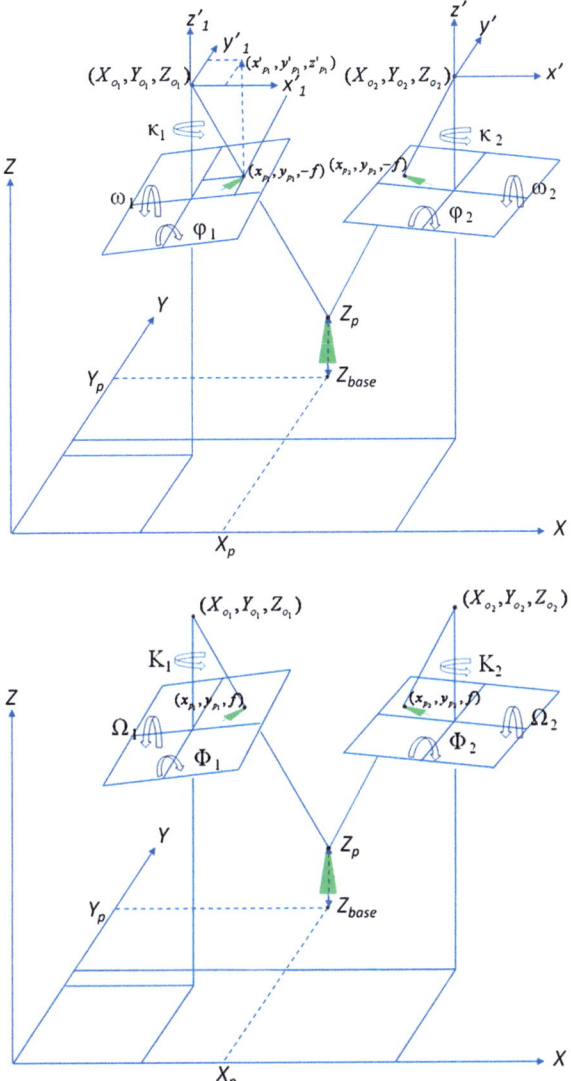

$$m_{11} = \cos(\varphi)\cos(\kappa)$$
$$m_{12} = \sin(\omega)\sin(\varphi)\cos(\kappa) + \cos(\omega)\sin(\kappa)$$
$$m_{13} = -\cos(\omega)\sin(\varphi)\cos(\kappa) + \sin(\omega)\sin(\kappa)$$
$$m_{21} = -\cos(\varphi)\sin(\kappa)$$
$$m_{22} = -\sin(\omega)\sin(\varphi)\sin(\kappa) + \cos(\omega)\cos(\kappa) \quad (10.3)$$
$$m_{23} = \cos(\omega)\sin(\varphi)\sin(\kappa) + \sin(\omega)\cos(\kappa)$$
$$m_{31} = \sin(\varphi)$$

$$m_{32} = -\sin(\omega)\cos(\varphi)$$
$$m_{33} = \cos(\omega)\cos(\varphi)$$

and $(X_{o_1}, Y_{o_1}, Z_{o_1})$ is the exposure station coordinate corresponding to image 1 (see Fig. 10.2).

In stereo imagery (i.e. when the same feature is imaged in two photographs taken from different perspectives), then two collinearities are formed for each scene point and these rays can be intersected to determine the 3D position of the scene point. Thus, when a feature is imaged within the overlap area on two stereo images, the pair of Eqs. (10.1) and (10.2) can be formed for each image, giving a system of four equations and three unknowns (X_p, Y_p, Z_p). This coordinate can therefore be determined via a least-squares solution. As an alternative to the least-squares solution and for the purposes of demonstration, the coordinates of an object on the ground can be obtained using space intersection via the following approach described in [56]. If the image point in each photo (x_p, y_p) is described in terms of the coordinate system of the tilted photography $(x, y, -f)$ and another untilted image coordinate system whose respective axes (x, y, z) are parallel to the axis of the ground coordinate system (X, Y, Z), then the coordinates of object point (X_p, Y_p, Z_p) can be expressed as a scaled version of the untilted image 1 coordinate system $(x'_{p_1}, y'_{p_1}, z'_{p_1})$:

$$\begin{aligned} X_p &= \lambda_{p_1} x'_{p_1} + X_{o_1} \\ Y_p &= \lambda_{p_1} y'_{p_1} + Y_{o_1} \\ Z_p &= \lambda_{p_1} z'_{p_1} + Z_{o_1} \end{aligned} \tag{10.4}$$

and the untilted coordinates of the image point **p** can be obtained from the tilted image coordinates via:

$$\begin{aligned} x'_{p_1} &= m_{11_1} x_{p_1} + m_{21_1} y_{p_1} + m_{31_1} z_{p_1} \\ y'_{p_1} &= m_{12_1} x_{p_1} + m_{22_1} y_{p_1} + m_{32_1} z_{p_1} \\ z'_{p_1} &= m_{13_1} x_{p_1} + m_{23_1} y_{p_1} + m_{33_1} z_{p_1} \end{aligned} \tag{10.5}$$

Since the object point with coordinates (X_p, Y_p, Z_p) is imaged in both photos, the coordinate can also be expressed as a scaled version of the untilted image 2 coordinate system $(x'_{p_2}, y'_{p_2}, z'_{p_2})$ using Eqs. (10.4).

Solving for the scaling factor λ_{p_1} in these six equations yields:

$$\lambda_{p_1} = \frac{y'_{p_1}(X_{O_1} - X_{O_2}) - x'_{p_1}(Y_{O_1} - Y_{O_2})}{x'_{p_1} y'_{p_1} - x'_{p_2} y'_{p_2}} \tag{10.6}$$

which can then be used in Eqs. (10.4) to calculate the coordinate of the point (X_p, Y_p, Z_p).

Example Given two images taken with a digital camera with a pixel size of 5.3 microns and a calibrated focal length of 35.1138 mm, and with exterior orientation parameters $(X, Y, Z, \omega, \varphi, \kappa)$ of (404829.1, 7029981.0, 1202.1, 5.71, 2.42, 93.14) for image 1 and (404962.9, 7029992.0, 1197.9, 4.65, 4.87, 91.63) for image 2, calculate the object space coordinate for a feature with pixel coordinates (3445.88, 2435.13) in image 1 and (3561.62, 1482.28) in image 2.

Solution Using Eqs. (10.3), the elements of the rotation matrix for each image can be calculated from the $(\omega, \varphi, \kappa)$ angles provided in the exterior orientation. This yields:

$$
\begin{aligned}
m_{11} &= -0.055 (image1) & -0.029 (image2) \\
m_{12} &= 0.99 (image1) & 1.0 (image2) \\
m_{13} &= 0.10 (image1) & 0.083 (image2) \\
m_{21} &= -0.98 (image1) & -1.0 (image2) \\
m_{22} &= -0.059 (image1) & -0.035 (image2) \\
m_{23} &= -0.047 (image1) & -0.087 (image2) \\
m_{31} &= 0.042 (image1) & 0.085 (image2) \\
m_{32} &= -0.099 (image1) & -0.08 (image2) \\
m_{33} &= 0.99 (image1) & 0.99 (image2)
\end{aligned}
$$

$$
\begin{aligned}
x'_{p_1} &= (-0.055)(6.90) + (-1.0)(-5.36) + (0.042)(-35.11) = 3.49 \\
y'_{p_1} &= (0.99)(6.90) + (-0.059)(-5.36) + (-0.099)(-35.11) = 10.66 \quad (10.7) \\
z'_{p_1} &= (0.10)(6.90) + (-0.047)(-5.36) + (0.99)(-35.11) = -33.96
\end{aligned}
$$

The untilted image coordinates for image 2 can be calculated in a similar manner, yielding $x'_{p_2} = -2.88$, $y'_{p_2} = 10.33$, $z'_{p_2} = -34.22$. The scaling factor λ_{p_1} can then be calculated as:

$$
\begin{aligned}
\lambda_{p_1} &= \frac{y'_{p_1}(X_{O_1} - X_{O_2}) - x'_{p_1}(Y_{O_1} - Y_{O_2})}{x'_{p_1} y'_{p_1} - x'_{p_2} y'_{p_2}} \\
&= \frac{10.66(404829.1 - 404962.9) - 3.49(7029981.1 - 7029991.7)}{(3.49)(10.66) - (-2.88)(10.33)} \\
&= 21.15
\end{aligned}
$$

The object coordinates for the feature of interest can then be calculated as:

$$
\begin{aligned}
X_p &= \lambda_{p_1} x'_{p_1} + X_{o_1} = (21.15)(3.49) + 404829.1 = 404975.1 \\
Y_p &= \lambda_{p_1} y'_{p_1} + Y_{o_1} = (21.15)(10.66) + 7029981.1 = 7029868.8 \\
Z_p &= \lambda_{p_1} z'_{p_1} + Z_{o_1} = (21.15)(-35.11) + 1202.1 = 484.1
\end{aligned}
$$

With the advent of the digital computer, it is possible to measure tree heights on digital imagery within a digital (or softcopy) photogrammetric workstation environment. In a digital photogrammetric workstation, a pair of overlapping photographs can be viewed in stereo on a computer monitor using either special hardware (shutter glasses and an emitter to synchronize the display and the glasses) or color anaglyph display and glasses with red-cyan filters (see Fig. 10.3).

Furthermore, a digital photogrammetric workstation provides the capability to digitize features within a stereo model, such as the 3D coordinate of a tree top and

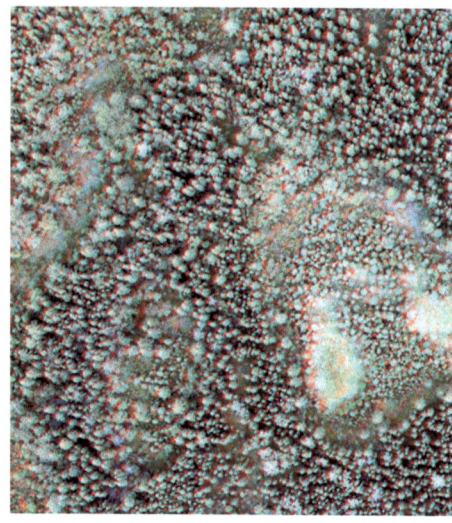

Fig. 10.3 Stereo aerial photography of a forest scene viewed in a digital photogrammetric environment using color anaglyph, upper Tanana valley of interior Alaska, USA. (*Red-blue* glasses are necessary to view this scene in stereo). Significant radial displacement: apparent shift of an object having height in relation to its base in an image with a central projection of trees (layover) is evident in the top left corner of the scene

crown base (tree height) or a (planimetrically-correct) polygon delineating a distinct forest condition class, such as its size class[2] or species class[3] or density class.[4]

10.2.1.2 Ground Control and Direct Georeferencing

As the collinearity conditions indicate above, it is essential to know the coordinates of each camera station and the elements of the rotation matrix (M) of each camera before aerial photographs can be used to acquire three-dimensional measurements of forest features (X_p, Y_p, Z_p). Typically, this information is obtained through the use of ground control points, which are features on the ground, with known (X_p, Y_p, Z_p) coordinates, that are also visible in the overlap area of the stereo pair of aerial photographs (technically, three vertical control points for leveling the model and two horizontal control points for scaling the model is the minimum requirement for controlling a single stereo pair [56]). If additional ground control points are available, a least-squares solution can be obtained with an estimate of uncertainty. When there are a large number of overlapping stereo models covering an area, the requirement of three control points per stereo model is relaxed, and the exterior orientation parameters for all photos within the block can be obtained through a procedure known as a *bundle block adjustment* [56]. As stated

---

[2]Size class refers to the predominant size (diameter, or DBH) of the trees within a stand; e.g. regeneration (*DBH* < 12.7 cm), poletimber (12.7 cm < *DBH* < 30.48 cm), sawtimber (*DBH* > 30.48 cm).

[3]Species class refers to the predominant species (or species mixture) of the stand (e.g. black spruce, mixed spruce-hemlock, etc.).

[4]Density class refers to the number of tree stems in a given area (i.e. trees per hectare).

in [56], a bundle adjustment is a procedure for simultaneously "adjusting all photogrammetric measurements to ground control values in a single solution." However, when using aerial photographs in a sampling mode, where plots are widely spaced, the need for sufficient ground control can introduce a significant and potentially prohibitive additional cost to the aerial photo-based inventory.

If smaller scale (i.e. lower resolution), controlled aerial photography is available that covers the same area as the uncontrolled large scale photography, ground control points can be measured photogrammetrically in the small scale photography and subsequently used to control the large scale photography (a method known as bridging control) [46]. However, in very remote areas, such as interior Alaska, it is unlikely that even recent small-scale, controlled imagery will be available. Fortunately, in recent years, technology has become available that allows for precise, and accurate, measurement of the position and orientation of the camera in the aircraft at the moment of exposure, which significantly reduces, or even eliminates entirely, the need for surveyed ground control. The use of two tightly-coupled technologies: (1) the global positioning systems (GPS) and (2) inertial measurement unit (IMU), now allow the exterior orientation parameters for each camera station to be obtained without the need for ground control, an approach known as *direct georeferencing* [34]. The GPS instrument uses a system of satellites to triangulate the position of the camera, while the inertial measurement unit uses a system of accelerometers and gyroscopes to determine the orientation of the camera. Furthermore, because the GPS acquires accurate, but relatively noisy, positional information, while the IMU provides trajectory and orientation information with relatively little noise but with systematic drift, the positional error can be dramatically reduced by merging these two complementary sources of positional information via a Kalman filter signal processing procedure. In the Kalman filter, the estimate of the position at time $k+1$ is given by the so-called *state estimate equation*:

$$\mathbf{x}_{k+1} = \mathbf{A}\mathbf{x}_k + \mathbf{B}\mathbf{u}_k + \mathbf{w}_k$$
$$\mathbf{y}_k = \mathbf{C}\mathbf{x}_k + \mathbf{z}_k$$
$$\mathbf{K}_k = \mathbf{A}\mathbf{P}_k\mathbf{C}^T\left(\mathbf{C}\mathbf{P}_k\mathbf{C}^T + \mathbf{S}_z\right)^{-1}$$
$$\hat{\mathbf{x}}_{k+1} = (\mathbf{A}\hat{\mathbf{x}}_k + \mathbf{B}\mathbf{u}_k) + \mathbf{K}_k(\mathbf{y}_{k+1} - \mathbf{C}\hat{\mathbf{x}}_k)$$
$$\mathbf{P}_{k+1} = \mathbf{A}\mathbf{P}_k\mathbf{A}^T + \mathbf{S}_w - \mathbf{A}\mathbf{P}_k\mathbf{C}^T\mathbf{S}_z^{-1}\mathbf{C}\mathbf{P}_k\mathbf{A}^T$$

In the above equation, A, B, and C are matrices that describe how the state changes and can be measured, k is the time index, **x** is the state of the system, **u** is the known input to the system, **y** is the measured output, **w** is the process noise, **z** is the measurement noise, $\mathbf{K}_k$ is the Kalman gain, $\mathbf{S}_w$ is the process noise covariance: $\mathbf{S}_w = E(\mathbf{w}_k\mathbf{w}_k^T)$, and $\mathbf{S}_z$ is the measurement noise covariance: $\mathbf{S}_z = E(\mathbf{z}_k\mathbf{z}_k^T)$, and P is the estimation error covariance. The first term in the fourth equation is basically A times the estimated position $\hat{\mathbf{x}}$ at time k, plus B times the known input **u** (IMU-based acceleration information) at time k. The second term is K (the so-called Kalman gain that minimizes the error covariance of the position at time $k+1$) times the difference (residual) between the measured position $\mathbf{y}_{k+1}$ and the prediction of the measured position ($C\hat{x}_k$). The Kalman gain (K) incorporates the measurement error such that when the measurement error (i.e. GPS error in our case) is large, the gain K is small, and the measured GPS position (y_{k+1}) will not have as much influence on the estimated position $\hat{x}_{k+1}$ [50].

Although differential post-processing of the GPS data previously required base station data, even these requirements are now disappearing with the advent of processing techniques such as precise point positioning (PPP), which can provide accurate GPS coordinates without base station data [37]. These developments could dramatically reduce the cost of aerial photo acquisitions, especially in remote, unpopulated areas.

10.2.2 Tree Height Measurement Using Forest Photogrammetry

In this section, we first consider manual and then automatic methods of forest photogrammetry.

10.2.2.1 Manual Forest Measurements Using Large-Scale Aerial Photogrammetry

The ability to accurately identify and measure individual tree crowns using aerial photographs is heavily dependent on scale and image quality [23]. Scale is a function of focal length of the camera lens and the flying height, while image quality is determined by many factors, including film characteristics and processing, camera lens design, atmospheric and lighting conditions, image motion compensation (blur), resolution (pixel size), color balance, etc.

The other important consideration in determining the efficacy of tree height measurement using forest photogrammetry is image geometry and radial displacement. Many newer digital imaging systems have significantly shorter effective focal lengths than older film mapping cameras, leading to severe layover of trees throughout most of the image area (see Fig. 10.3). Layover (radial displacement) can make it very difficult to view forested scenes in stereo, leading to difficulties in tree height measurement. For this reason, relatively long lenses (e.g. 305 mm) were usually used on mapping cameras in forest photogrammetry applications [23].

Image motion, or blurring due to movement of the aircraft during the time that the camera shutter is open, is another significant concern when acquiring large-scale photography for forestry applications. Before the advent of Forward Motion Compensation (FMC) technology in the late 1980s, image motion with film cameras could only be minimized through the use of a short exposure time, which in turn required a fast film with larger grain size [39]. FMC technology actually involved moving the film plate a minute amount during the time that the shutter is open, thereby reducing image blurring. In the case of modern digital imaging systems, a technology called Time Delayed Integration (TDI) is used. In TDI, the image is read continuously by the detector and the accumulated images are digitally shifted in such a way as to correct for the movement of the aircraft during the time that the shutter is open [39].

The accuracy of manual tree height measurements using photogrammetry usually depends upon the ability of the interpreter to see both the base and top of the tree. Due to the characteristics of the tree crown and in particular, the size of the crown apex, the species of tree will influence the accuracy of photogrammetric tree height measurements. For example, Kovats [23] found that with large-scale photographs measured under an analytical stereo plotter instrument, lodge pole pine tree tops were larger and could be measured more accurately than relatively small Douglas-fir tree tops [13]. This study found that when tree tops were visible, tree heights could be measured very accurately (0.05 ± 0.59 m (mean error $\pm$ standard deviation (SD))) with large scale (1 : 1200) photography. In dense, closed canopy forests on mountainous terrain it is often impossible to see through the forest canopy and therefore the base of trees cannot be accurately measured. This leads to increasing tree height error as forest canopy closure and terrain roughness increase. Other studies have shown that large scale non-metric (i.e. non-mapping) 35-mm camera could be used to accurately measure stem counts and determine species in a loblolly pine plantation in Virginia [38].

In general, the process to obtain individual tree measurements and attributes from digital aerial images within a digital photogrammetric workstation consists of the following steps:

1. Obtain overlapping aerial stereo imagery (using digital camera or scanned film imagery)
2. Carry out interior orientation using camera calibration information
3. Carry out exterior orientation using either direct georeferencing (obtained using airborne GPS and IMU) or ground control points
4. Manually measure tree dimensions and digitize features using collinearity condition and space forward intersection (Fig. 10.2).
5. Export coordinates and attributes of trees for further analysis within a geographical information system (GIS).

10.2.2.2 Automated Methods in Forest Photogrammetry

To a large extent, acquisition of accurate individual tree measurements from digital aerial photographs requires the use of manual techniques. Given the complexity and irregularity of imaged forest scenes, which are composed of various vegetation and ground surface components with differing textures, spectral signatures, shadow patterns, as well as the fact that every image represents a different perspective on these complex and irregular features, it is very difficult to efficiently automate the acquisition of forest photogrammetric measurements. However, this has been an active area of research over the last 10–15 years, and progress has been made.

Several studies in the 1990s and early 2000s investigated the possibility of automatically extracting individual tree-level measurements from high resolution imagery in a two-dimensional space. Gougeon developed a shadow-following technique that effectively delineated individual tree crowns in both aerial photographs and high resolution satellite images [17]. Brandtberg and Walter used multiple scale analysis to extract individual tree crowns from aerial images [9]. Both Larsen and Rudemo [24] and Pollock [42] used template-matching techniques to detect individual trees in aerial images. Lund and Rudemo [27] developed a probabilistic approach to identifying individual tree crown tops in digital imagery based on a stochastic point process model. Larsen and Rudemo [24] have since extended this model to a three-dimensional point pattern using multiple image views, although the technique is still largely theoretical in nature. Gong et al. [15] developed a semi-automated method to extract tree measurements using a three-dimensional generalized ellipsoid model for tree crown shape. Culvenor [10] developed a technique called the tree identification and delineation algorithm (TIDA) based on (1) identification of local maxima, (2) identification of local minima, and (3) clustering of crown pixels, where local maxima are used as seed points for the clustering and local minima are used to constrain the clustering. Due to the difficulty of finding individual tree crown positions, however, this method relied on manual determination of tree top and base.

Other approaches have concentrated on the automated measurement of canopy surface models from digital stereo imagery, instead of direct extraction of individual tree crowns. This approach involves the automated identification of conjugate points (image points corresponding to the same object on the ground) in the overlapping areas of stereo imagery, and then uses the collinearity equations (described above) to calculate the elevation of each surface point throughout the overlap area. The process of locating conjugate points throughout the overlap area is called *image matching*. Although this approach does not attempt to isolate individual tree crowns, image matching in a forested area is also complicated by many of the same factors as the individual tree methods, including (1) occlusions, (2) repetitive patterns, (3) shadows, perspective differences, (4) semi-transparent surfaces, and (5) rough, discontinuous surfaces [25]. Although most digital photogrammetric software packages provide image matching and surface generation capabilities, these systems are usually designed to generate digital terrain models in relatively unvegetated areas and usually yield disappointing results over forests. That being said, attempts have been made to develop image matching algorithms that are more effective in forested areas. For example, Li and Gruen [25] developed an approach that matches both grid points, textural and edge features, uses geometric constraints to limit the search space, and employs two different matching techniques (sum of modified cross-correlation and least-squares matching) to improve the accuracy of matching results in complex forested scenes. The technique combines both area-based matching (ABM) and feature-based matching (FBM) approaches, and employs a hierarchical approach moving from coarse to finer resolutions in the matching process. A triangular irregular network (TIN) surface is generated at each level of the resolution hierarchy, and a modified multi-photo geometrically constrained (MPGC) matching algorithm is used to further refine the surface, remove any remaining errors, and achieve sub-pixel accuracy [25]. The results obtained from this algorithm were compared to surfaces generated using commercial digital photogrammetric image matching algorithm (SocetSet) and airborne laser scanning (LIDAR, 1 m point spacing) in a mire environment in Switzerland, and found that results from their algorithm were better than those obtained with the commercial system and at least as dense and of similar accuracy as those obtained from LIDAR [5]. It should be noted that the LIDAR data used in this study was relatively low resolution (1 m). However, the results from this study indicate that there is potential for using automated image matching techniques to generate accurate forest canopy surface models.

10.3 Airborne Laser Scanning

In this section, we firstly describe the principles of airborne laser scanning and then go on to detail how individual tree-level measurement are made using LIDAR. Finally, we outline the area-based approach to estimating biomass with LIDAR.

10.3.1 Principles of Airborne Laser Scanning

The other optical remote sensing technology capable of providing high resolution measurements of forest canopy structure is airborne laser scanning (also known as light detection and ranging, or LIDAR). Airborne LIDAR systems consist of a laser system that emits pulses at a very high rate (typically 100,000–167,000 Hz) in a scanning pattern beneath the aircraft. Precise measurement of the time-of-flight of an individual laser pulse, multiplied by the speed of light (a known constant), provides the range between the laser instrument and reflecting surfaces below. If the exact position and orientation of the laser system is also known at the moment each pulse is emitted, provided by airborne GPS and an inertial measurement unit respectively (the same enabling technologies used in direct georeferencing of aerial photography), then the 3D coordinate associated with each laser reflection can be calculated [4]. These so-called *discrete-return* airborne scanning systems generate a dense cloud of 3D points in a swath along the flight path of the aircraft. Most commercial LIDAR systems can record multiple returns from a single pulse, therefore, in a forested area, the point cloud provides information on the 3D forest canopy structure in a given area (see Fig. 10.4).

In recent years, airborne LIDAR systems have provide the entire waveform associated with each LIDAR pulse, instead of the discretized point data. These *full-waveform* LIDAR systems depict the full measurement process of the LIDAR system and therefore have the potential to provide even more detailed picture of the three-dimensional distribution of forest canopy components beyond what is available from discrete-return systems [54]. Although processing and analysis of full

Fig. 10.4 Lidar data swath, upper Tanana valley of interior Alaska, USA. *Points* are *color-coded* by height (*blue*: low, *green*: medium, *yellow/red*: high)

waveform LIDAR data is still an evolving research field, recent progress has been made in establishing the theoretical basis for modeling the signal obtained from a full-waveform LIDAR system, where the signal is modeled as a series of Gaussian pulses [54]. Other studies have indicated great potential for using the additional information from full-waveform to characterize tree species composition and other forest attributes [45, 52].

The intensity (reflected energy level) associated with each LIDAR return (reflection) is also provided along with the 3D coordinate. Since most LIDAR systems operate in the near infrared portion of the electromagnetic spectrum (e.g. 1064 nm), which is sensitive to the chorophyll content and condition of vegetation, LIDAR intensity can provide additional information for forest characterization.

As with aerial photography, the properties of airborne LIDAR data are a function of the specific LIDAR system employed and system settings, such as pulse frequency, scan rate, beam divergence, scan angle, as well as a number of variable flight parameters, such as nominal flying height above ground level (AGL) and aircraft ground speed. In addition, LIDAR intensity information can be affected by the specific settings of the automatic gain control system and the AGL [13]. Previous studies carried out in Australia have indicated that, although acquiring LIDAR from platform altitudes as high as 3000 meters can still allow for quantification of forest structure, data acquired from higher altitudes will have fewer ground points available for generation of accurate digital terrain models, and the lower data density will have a detrimental effect on the accuracy of individual tree crown detection and measurement [16].

10.3.1.1 Lidar-Based Measurement of Terrain and Canopy Surfaces

Because LIDAR provides direct measurements of three-dimensional canopy structure, as well as the underlying terrain surface, the most fundamental products provided by airborne LIDAR are the canopy surface model and digital terrain model. Previous research has indicated that LIDAR-derived terrain models can be highly accurate (i.e. root mean square error (RMSE) <0.50 m), even under relatively dense coniferous forest canopy conditions found in the Pacific Northwest region of the

United States [47]. Several algorithms have been developed for filtering out the ground returns from LIDAR data, although much of this research and development work has been carried out in the commercial sector and is considered proprietary. Even after the ground reflections have been filtered out from the all-return data set, there is variability in the derived terrain model due to the choice of the gridding algorithm. Bater and Coops [6] evaluated the error in the LIDAR-derived terrain models associated with various interpolation algorithms including linear, quintic, natural neighbor, regularized spline, spline with tension, a finite difference approach, and an inverse distance weighted interpolation algorithm at spatial resolutions of 0.5, 1.0, and 1.5 meters, and found that 0.5 meter terrain models were the most accurate, and the natural neighbor algorithm provided the best results for interpolation, although the differences in accuracy between the algorithms were minor.

Given the highly irregular and ill-defined nature of a forest canopy surface, the characteristics of LIDAR-derived canopy surface models are highly dependent upon type of filtering and interpolation algorithms employed as well as the input parameters of these algorithms. The most common approach to generating LIDAR canopy surface models is to extract the highest LIDAR return within a given grid cell area and then employ an interpolation algorithm, such as kriging, linear, or inverse distance weighting (IDW), to generate a regular grid [44]. Often, additional processing is required to remove anomalous elevations within the surface and produce an accurate representation of the true canopy surface [8].

10.3.2 Individual Tree-Level Measurement Using Lidar

Airborne LIDAR can be used to acquire highly accurate measurements of individual tree height (Fig. 10.5). In a test carried out in western Washington, Andersen et al. [1] investigated the influence of beam divergence setting (i.e. laser footprint size), species type (pine vs. fir), and digital terrain model error on the accuracy of height measurements. This study found that tree height measurements obtained from narrow-beam (0.33 m), high-density (6 points/m^2) LIDAR were more accurate (mean error $\pm$ SD $= -0.73 \pm 0.43$ m) than those obtained from wide-beam (0.8 m) LIDAR (-1.12 ± 0.56 m). This was likely due to the fact that with wide-beam LIDAR the energy is spread out over a large area, which decreases the strength of the returns from a tree top and lessens the likelihood that they exceed the noise threshold [35]. In addition, this study found that tree height measurements on Ponderosa pine were more accurate (-0.43 ± 0.13 m) than those obtained for Douglas-fir (-1.05 ± 0.41 m), largely because the size of the Douglas-fir leader is a smaller target than the top of a Ponderosa pine tree. These results were consistent with the accuracies for LIDAR-based tree height measurements reported in other studies in various forest types [14, 28, 48].

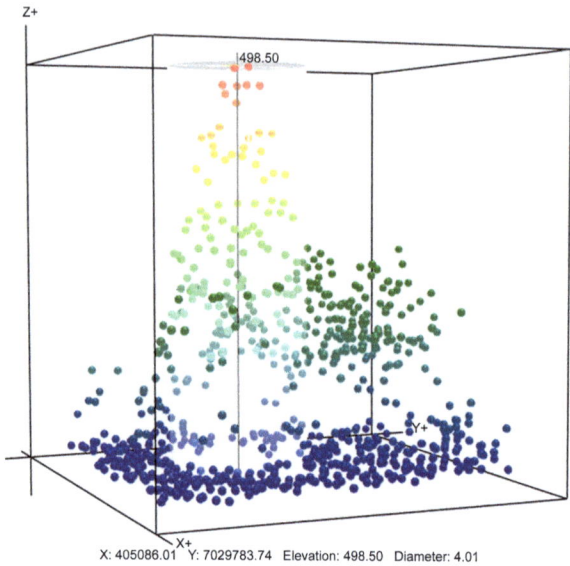

Fig. 10.5 Lidar-based individual tree height measurement, upper Tanana valley of interior Alaska, USA. Units are meters

10.3.2.1 Automated Individual Tree Measurement Using Lidar

Because LIDAR represents direct, and automatically georeferenced, digital measurements of 3D forest canopy structure, it is considerably easier to automate the individual tree detection and measurement process with LIDAR than is the case with digital photogrammetry. In fact, over the last ten years, a considerable amount of attention has been devoted to analysis of airborne LIDAR at the individual tree level. In general, these approaches tend to operate upon the high-density LIDAR canopy height model that is formed from gridding the LIDAR returns from the top of the canopy surface and subtracting the elevation of the underlying LIDAR terrain model. A variety of computer vision algorithms have been proposed for isolating the features within this canopy height model that correspond to individual tree crowns, including spectral analysis using wavelets [12], morphological watershed segmentation [20, 49], valley-following [41], and level-set analysis [21]. Of these techniques, morphological watershed segmentation is probably the most robust and widely used. This algorithm is based on the *immersion process*, as described in [53]. In this process, the canopy height model is inverted, and then starting at the local minima, water is poured in that fills up various catchment basins (watersheds). At each point where water from two different catchment basins merge, a dam is built. The result of the process is a complete tessellation of the image defined by the locations of the dams surrounding every watershed [53]. In a forestry context, these individual watersheds often correspond to individual tree crowns.

The morphological watershed segmentation technique can be very effective in situations where the tree crowns are distinct morphological features, even if the trees are closely spaced in a closed canopy. However, the technique is not as effective in stands where crowns are intermixed (e.g. deciduous stands). Figure 10.6

Fig. 10.6 Lidar-based individual tree crown segmentation, upper Tanana valley of interior Alaska, USA. *Black circles* indicate position and size of crown segments. Surface is color-coded by canopy height (*blue*: low canopy height, *red*: high canopy height). *Inset* shows area surround around a field plot, and green circles indicated field-measured trees

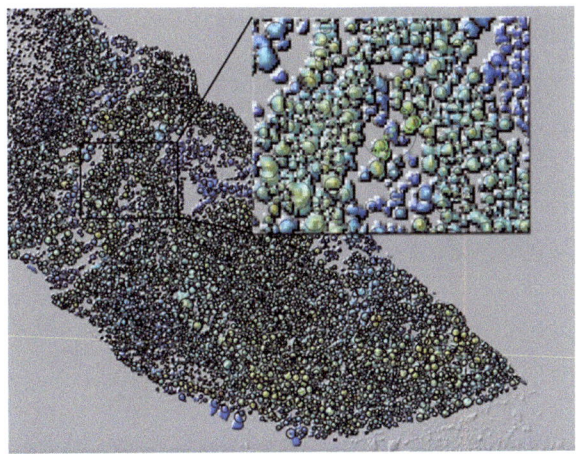

shows the result of a watershed-based individual tree crown segmentation algorithm applied to high-density airborne LIDAR collected over a boreal forest area in interior Alaska. As is evident from the inset in this graphic, which shows a comparison of the field-measured tree crowns to the watershed-based tree crowns (estimated locations and crown widths indicated by the black circles) within a 1/30th ha plot area, the segmentation algorithm successfully identified several of the larger crowns within the plot, but does not successfully delineate the smaller tree crowns that are not resolved in the 1-meter resolution LIDAR canopy height model. This algorithm also tends to over-segment in complex stands, since there is often morphological complexity even within a single tree crown

Once the forest area is segmented into individual tree crowns, the raw LIDAR can be extracted for each segment and used to obtain more detailed information on the tree. For example, the highest LIDAR return within the segment provides an estimate of the tree top [1]. In leaf-off conditions, the intensity values of the raw LIDAR returns within a crown segment can be used to classify the segment into conifer or deciduous species class. For example, Kim et al. [22] used a linear discriminant function to classify various species of trees in the Pacific Northwest of the United States using mean intensity of LIDAR returns in the upper portion of the crown as the primary metric and reported a classification rate of 83.4 % for separating coniferous and deciduous trees using leaf-off LIDAR data, and 73.1 % using leaf-on LIDAR data.

10.3.2.2 Comparison of Lidar-Based and Photo-Based Individual Tree Measurements

Individual tree measurements, acquired using high-density LIDAR and large-scale aerial photography, were compared to field-based measurements acquired on an inventory plot established in the upper Tanana valley of interior Alaska (Fig. 10.7). The aerial photography was acquired using a low-cost, non-metric digital single

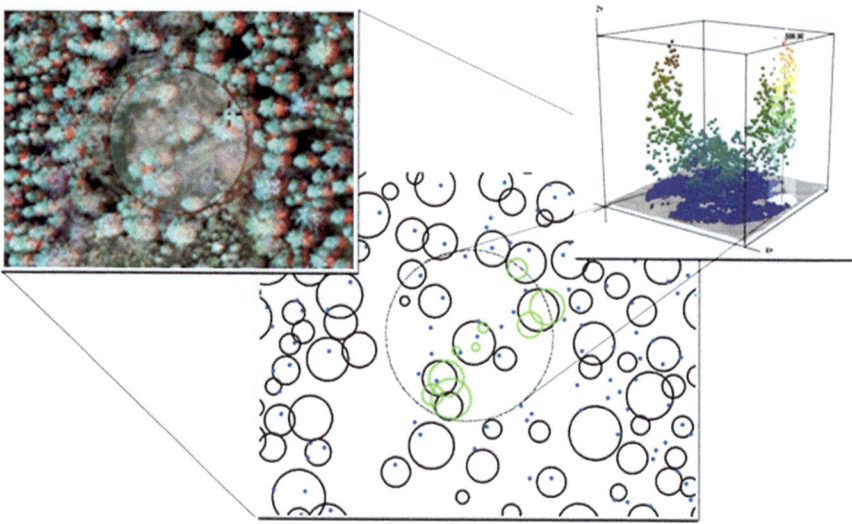

Fig. 10.7 Comparison of photogrammetric and LIDAR individual tree height measurement techniques, upper Tanana valley of interior Alaska, USA. Center graphic shows 1/30th ha circular plot (*dashed line*), *black circles* indicate locations and estimated crown sizes from automated segmentation of LIDAR canopy height model, *green circles* indicate location of field-measured trees within plot, and *blue dots* indicate locations of individual tree crowns observed in aerial photo stereo model. *Upper left inset graphic* shows the plot area in stereo (*red-blue* glasses are needed for stereo viewing) and the *black cross* is positioned to measure the top of a selected tree in the plot. The *upper right inset graphic* shows this same tree top measured in the LIDAR point cloud (color coded by height). The field-measured height of this white spruce tree is 22.25 meters, the LIDAR-measured height is 22.03 m, and the photogrammetrically-measured height is 23.8 m. The error in the LIDAR measurement is likely due to the LIDAR pulses missing the top of the tree crown [1], while the error in the photogrammetric measurement is likely a combination of the errors in the coarse terrain model and difficulty in identifying the true elevation of the tree top when viewed in stereo

lens reflex (SLR) camera mounted on a Cessna 185 aircraft flying at approximately 1000 meters above ground level (AGL). It should also be noted that this low-cost system did not have image motion compensation. In order to remove one source of error in the comparisons, the ground control points for the exterior orientation of the non-metric imagery were acquired from the airborne LIDAR, using the FUSION interactive LIDAR measurement environment [11, 30]. The photo-based tree height measurements were acquired by the following process: (1) photogrammetrically measuring the elevations of several points on bare ground distributed throughout the area, (2) using these points to generate a terrain model, (3) photogrammetrically measuring tree top elevation for all visible trees in the area, and (4) estimating tree heights as the difference between the tree top elevation and the elevation of the underlying terrain model. Lidar-based tree height measurements were generated similarly by subtracting the elevation of the LIDAR-based terrain elevation from the elevation of the highest LIDAR return within an individual tree crown segment.

The measurements for a selected white spruce tree within this 1/30th ha plot provide an indication of the correspondence between these various measurement techniques (see caption on Fig. 10.7). In this case, the LIDAR-based height measurement (22.03 m) slightly underestimated the field-measured tree height (22.25 m), while the photo-based height was slightly higher (23.8 m). It is also evident from Fig. 10.7 that in general, the stem count obtained from the automated crown segmentation (black circles) is much lower than the number of stems observed in the large scale aerial photography (blue dots). It is also notable that the photo-based stem count corresponds fairly closely to the field-measured trees within the inventory plot, although there appears to be a systematic discrepancy between the horizontal locations (possibility due to registration error, image parallax, field measurement errors, or a combination of the above). It appears that the automated segmentation captures the large structural features (large crowns, clumps of small trees) but likely does not represent an accurate measurement of true stem counts.

The process to obtain individual tree measurements and attributes from airborne LIDAR consists of the following steps:

1. Filter out terrain and canopy-level points from raw LIDAR point cloud
2. Grid both terrain and canopy-level LIDAR points at desired resolution to generate a digital terrain model (DTM[5]) and canopy surface model (CSM)
3. Subtract DTM from CSM to obtain a canopy height model (CHM)
4. Apply morphological watershed operation to CHM to delineate segments associated with individual tree crowns (Fig. 10.6).
5. Extract LIDAR points within each individual tree crown segment
   a. Use intensity data to classify into species type (e.g. conifer vs. deciduous, etc.)
   b. Use maximum LIDAR return height within the segment as an estimate of total tree height (Fig. 10.5).
   c. Use segment area as an estimate of crown area
   d. Use either estimated tree height alone (see Fig. 10.1) or estimated tree height and crown area to estimate individual tree biomass
   e. Estimate total biomass over coverage area as the sum of estimated individual tree biomass estimates over entire LIDAR coverage area.

The development of high-resolution aerial imaging and laser scanning systems, both making use of recent technological advances in geopositioning and inertial navigation, are providing resource managers with an impressive array of tools for measuring forest structural characteristics, such as volume, biomass and aboveground carbon. High density airborne LIDAR can provide highly detailed information on the 3D structural attributes of the forest canopy (including individual tree heights, etc.), but cannot yet provide reliable information on species or condition. In contrast,

---

[5] The term digital terrain model (DTM) specifically refers to the model of the terrain surface. Digital elevation model (DEM) is a more generic term that can refer to either the terrain surface or canopy surface.

high-resolution (large-scale) digital aerial imagery can provide highly detailed information on forest type and density and at a significantly lower cost than LIDAR, but provides less accurate measurements of individual tree dimensions. It is expected that these highly complementary remote sensing systems will both play an important role in reducing the cost and increasing the efficiency of forest inventory systems in the future.

10.3.3 Area-Based Approach to Estimating Biomass with Lidar

Given the structural and compositional complexity of many forests, there is a need for alternative techniques for quantifying biomass and aboveground carbon using LIDAR that are not dependent upon accurate detection and measurement of individual tree crowns. Aggregate measures of forest structure, including basal area (m^2/ha), biomass (MG/ha), and volume (m^3/ha), calculated from all trees within a given area (above a certain minimum diameter) are typically highly correlated to structural metrics calculated using the LIDAR point cloud data extracted over the same area. Most of the variability in biomass within a given area can be explained by three LIDAR-derived structural metrics: (1) mean height of canopy-level LIDAR returns, (2) LIDAR-derived percent canopy cover, and (3) standard deviation of canopy-level LIDAR returns [26]. Collectively, these three metrics provide a quantitative description of the three-dimensional spatial distribution of canopy material within a given area, which in turn, is strongly related to the amount of aboveground biomass present in this area. However, many other LIDAR-derived structural metrics can be generated from the LIDAR point cloud (maximum height of canopy level returns, 10th, 25th, 50th, 75th, 90th, percentile height of canopy-level returns, canopy density by layer, etc.). For example, Fig. 10.8 shows the vertical distribution of LIDAR data, extracted LIDAR structural metrics, and the biomass level for four selected field plots in interior Alaska. Magnussen and Boudewyn established the theoretical basis for the relationship between LIDAR height quantiles and the vertical distribution of canopy materials [29]. Given the tremendous variability in forest composition and structure in forests throughout the world, the specific models describing the relationship between biomass and LIDAR metrics can also vary by forest type, and often will incorporate different predictor variables and regression coefficients. A practical approach to estimate biomass and other inventory parameters (density, volume, etc.) using LIDAR was developed in Norway [35, 36], in which field inventory data was collected at a limited number of accurately-georeferenced plots, then empirical relationships were established between field-based inventory estimates and a selection of LIDAR structural metrics extracted for the area associated with each plot. An automated variable selection procedure (stepwise regression) was used to select the predictor variables for each regression model. Figure 10.9 shows the relationship between field- and LIDAR-based estimates of (square root-transformed) aboveground tree biomass on seventy-nine (79) field plots established in the upper Tanana valley of interior Alaska, where the model is obtained via a stepwise regression procedure.

10 High-Resolution Three-Dimensional Remote Sensing for Forest Measurement 437

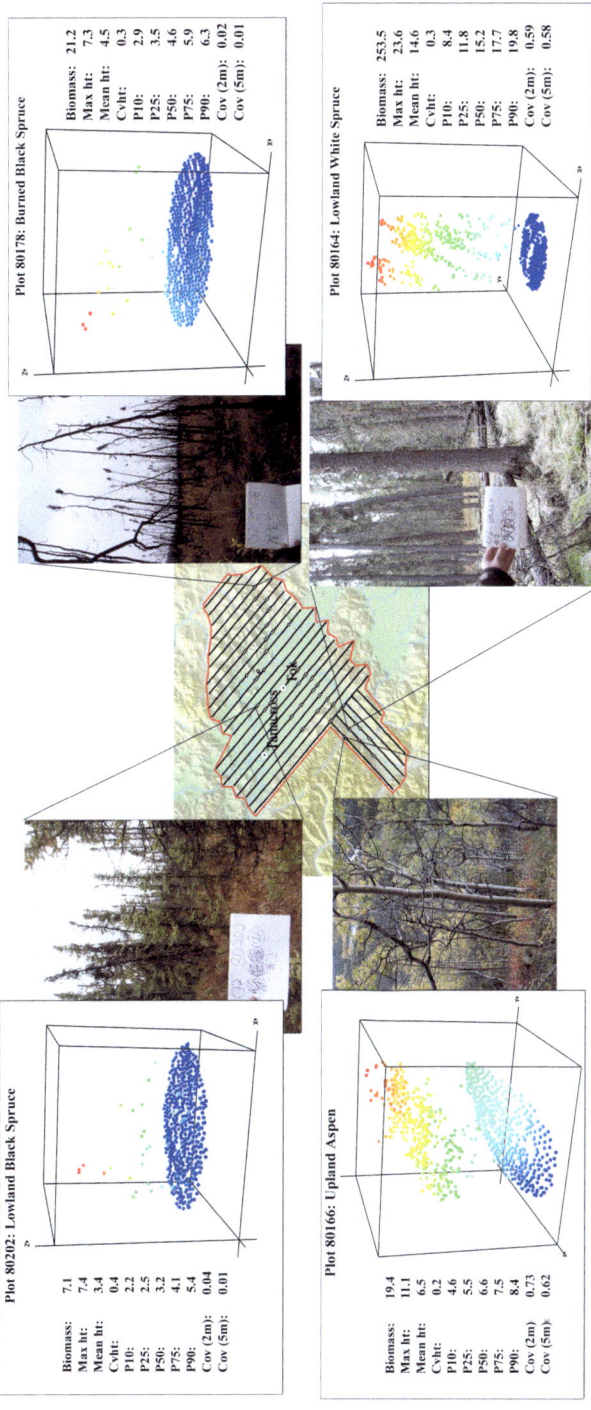

Fig. 10.8 Photographs show several representative forest types in the study area, located in the upper Tanana valley of interior Alaska, USA. *Insets* show the LIDAR point cloud within each 1/30th ha plot, as well as the estimated biomass and the list of LIDAR-based structural metrics for each plot. *Background* graphic shows outline of study area, with diagonal lines indicating location of LIDAR flight lines (reprinted from [12])

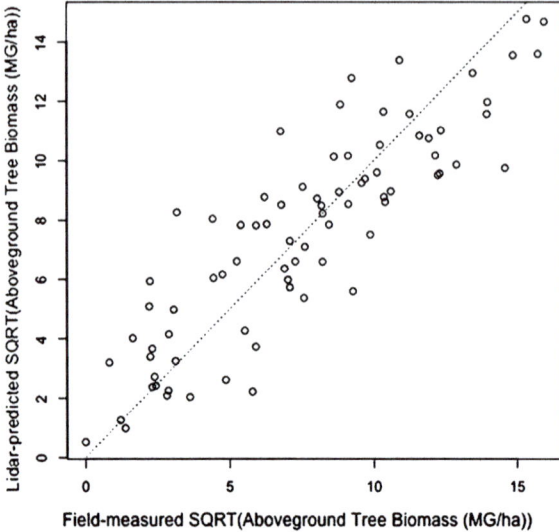

Fig. 10.9 Relationship between (transformed) field- and LIDAR-based estimates of aboveground tree biomass (MG/ha) for seventy-nine (79) plots in the upper Tanana valley of interior Alaska

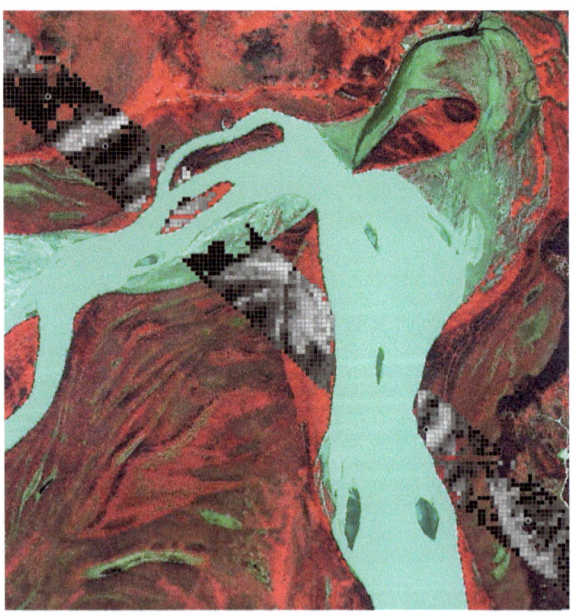

Fig. 10.10 Example of LIDAR-derived biomass measurements (*black*: low biomass, *white*: high biomass) within single LIDAR swath, upper Tanana valley of interior Alaska. Background is a false-color SPOT 5 image (2.5 meter resolution), and circles represent field plots (with same color ramp as the LIDAR grid cells)

This model is then applied to each grid cell within the LIDAR coverage area (where the grid cell size is a comparable grain size as the field plots (i.e. 1/30th hectare ∼18 m × 18 m grid cells) (see Fig. 10.10).

The LIDAR-based estimates of precision acquired over the coverage area can then be used to develop estimates of total (or mean) biomass. Due to the interest (to date) in using LIDAR to acquire better topographical information, most LIDAR acquisitions are wall-to-wall acquisitions, and in this case the LIDAR data is, from a statistical standpoint, a complete census of the population. In very remote and extensive areas, the cost of obtaining wall-to-wall LIDAR coverage may be prohibitive, and in this case LIDAR may be acquired in a strip sampling mode [2, 3, 18]. The area-based approach to estimating biomass consists of the following steps:

1. Filter out ground-level LIDAR points.
2. Grid filtered ground-level points into digital terrain model (DTM).
3. Extract LIDAR point cloud within each field inventory plot area.
4. Generate structural metrics from extracted LIDAR point cloud (maximum height, mean height, canopy cover, height percentiles, etc.) (Fig. 10.8).
5. Develop regression model to predict plot-level biomass using LIDAR structural metrics as predictor variables (Fig. 10.9).
6. At each grid cell over the entire LIDAR coverage area (where the grid cell area corresponds to the field plot area), extract the same LIDAR structural metrics as in Step 4 above.
7. Apply the regression model developed in Step 5 above to predict biomass within each grid cell (Fig. 10.10).
8. Use resulting map of biomass to estimate (mean or total) biomass over entire LIDAR coverage area.

10.4 Future Developments

It should also be noted that both airborne digital imaging systems and laser scanners will continue to develop and provide increasingly accurate, precise, and information-rich measurements. For example, the increasing availability of *full waveform*, discrete-return airborne LIDAR has the potential to significantly increase the spatial resolution at which we measure and characterize canopy structure [45, 52, 54]. The coupling of high-resolution hyperspectral and multispectral imagers with high-density airborne scanners, or eventually the development of a true multispectral LIDAR system, has tremendous potential for simultaneously determining vegetation condition, species, and spatial dimension [3, 33].

10.5 Concluding Remarks

The convergence of a new generation of high-resolution remote sensing systems, including digital imagery and airborne laser scanning, advanced geopositioning technologies, and ever-increasing computational capability has led to dramatic improvements in our ability to measure and characterize forests from remote platforms over the last 10–15 years. Forest inventory specialists can now extract detailed tree height measurements and individual tree attributes from high-resolution, low-altitude stereo digital imagery. High-density airborne LIDAR data can also be used to extract detailed information on individual tree dimensions and attributes through the application of automated image analysis algorithms. In areas where individual tree-based analysis is not appropriate or feasible, due to the data resolution or forest characteristics, area-based LIDAR analysis techniques can be used to develop spatially-explicit information for various inventory parameters across the landscape, which in turn can provide highly useful information to support forest management applications.

10.6 Further Reading

More details on analytical and digital photogrammetry can be found in the texts by Wolf [56] and Mikhail et al. [32]. Basic formulas and technical details related to airborne LIDAR scanning are provided in the article by Baltsavias [4]. Further background on field-measurement of individual trees and a comparison to LIDAR-based tree heights are found in [1], and further background on the principles of full-waveform airborne laser scanning are found in [54]. Further details on the principles of LIDAR-based individual-tree detection and measurement are provided in [20] and [41]. Details on using LIDAR intensity and crown structure to determine individual tree species type are provided in [22] and [19]. Further reading on the area-based approach to estimating biomass using airborne LIDAR is provided in [35].

10.7 Questions

1. This question is about the effect of the quality of digital imagery on the measurement of tree heights:
    a. Describe the data requirements for measuring tree heights from stereo digital imagery.
    b. Describe how image motion affects the quality of digital imagery and how this can be mitigated.
2. Describe the expected accuracy of manual tree height measurements acquired from airborne LIDAR and how these may be affected by species and sensor settings.
3. Explain the difference between an individual-tree and area-based approach to estimating biomass using airborne LIDAR. When would an area-based approach be preferable to an individual tree approach?
4. Describe one technique for automatically extracting individual tree measurements from LIDAR.
5. List five LIDAR-based structural metrics that can be used in the area-based LIDAR biomass estimation technique.

References

1. Andersen, H.-E., Reutebuch, S., McGaughey, R.: A rigorous assessment of tree height measurements obtained using airborne LIDAR and conventional field methods. Can. J. Remote Sens. **32**(5), 355–366 (2006)
2. Andersen, H.-E., Strunk, J., Temesgen, H.: Using airborne light detection and ranging as a sampling tool for estimating forest biomass resources in the upper Tanana Valley of interior alaska. Western J. Appl. For. **26**(4), 157–164 (2011)
3. Asner, G., Knapp, D., Jones, M., Kennedy-Bowdoin, T., Martin, R., Boardman, J., Field, C.: Carnegie airborne observatory: in-flight fusion of hyperspectral imaging and waveform light detection and ranging for three-dimensional studies of ecosystems. J. Appl. Remote Sens. **1**(1) (2007)
4. Baltasavias, E.: Airborne laser scanning: basic relations and formulas. ISPRS J. Photogramm. Remote Sens. **54**, 199–214 (1999)
5. Baltsavias, E., Gruen, A., Kuchler, M., Thee, P., Waser, L., Zhang, L.: Tree height measurements and tree growth estimation in a mire environment using digital surface models. In: Proceedings of the Workshop on 3D Remote Sensing in Forestry, Feb. 14–15, 2006, Vienna, Austria (2006)
6. Bater, C., Coops, N.: Evaluating error associated with LIDAR-derived DEM interpolation. Comput. Geosci. **35**(2), 289–300 (2009)
7. Bechtold, W., Patterson, P. (eds.): The enhanced forest inventory and analysis program, national sampling design and estimate procedures. Gen. Tech. Rep. SRS-80, Asheville, NC, U.S. Department of Agriculture, Forest Service, Southern Research Station, 85 p. (2005)
8. Ben-Arie, J., Hay, G., Powers, R., Castilla, G., Onge, B.St.: Development of a pit filling algorithm for LiDAR canopy models. Comput. Geosci. **35**(9), 1940–1949 (2009)
9. Brandtberg, T., Walter, F.: Automated delineation of individual tree crowns in high spatial resolution aerial images by multiple scale analysis. Mach. Vis. Appl. **11**, 64–73 (1998)
10. Culvenor, D.: TIDA: an algorithm for the delineation of tree crowns in high spatial resolution remotely sensed imagery. Comput. Geosci. **28**(1), 33–44 (2002)
11. Delara, R., Mitishita, E., Habib, A.: Bundle adjustment of images from non-metric CCD camera using LIDAR data as control points. Int. Arch. Photogramm. Remote Sens. **35**(B3), 470–475 (2004)
12. Falkowski, M.J., Smith, A.M.S., Hudak, A.T., Gessler, P.E., Vierling, L.A., Crookston, N.L.: Automated estimation of individual conifer tree height and crown diameter via Two-dimensional spatial wavelet analysis of LIDAR data. Can. J. Remote Sens. **32**(2), 153–161 (2006)
13. Gatziolis, D.: Dynamic range-based intensity normalization for airborne, discrete return LIDAR data for forest canopies. Photogramm. Eng. Remote Sens. **77**(3), 251–259 (2011)
14. Gaveau, D., Hill, R.: Quantifying canopy height underestimation by laser pulse penetration in small-footprint airborne laser scanning data. Can. J. Remote Sens. **29**(5), 650657 (2003)
15. Gong, R., Sheng, Y., Biging, G.: 3D model-based tree measurement from high-resolution aerial imagery. Photogramm. Eng. Remote Sens. **68**(11), 1203–1212 (2002)
16. Goodwin, N., Coops, N., Culvenor, D.: Assessment of forest structure with airborne LIDAR and the effects of platform altitude. Remote Sens. Environ. **103**(2), 140–152 (2006)
17. Gougeon, F.A.: Crown-following approach to the automatic delineation of individual tree crowns in high spatial resolution aerial images. Can. J. Remote Sens. **21**(3), 274–284 (1995)
18. Gregoire, T., Stahl, G., Naesset, E., Gobakken, T., Nelson, R., Holm, S.: Model-assisted estimation of biomass in a LiDAR sample survey in Hedmark county, Norway. Can. J. For. Res. **41**, 83–95 (2010)
19. Holmgren, J., Persson, A.: Identifying species of individual trees using airborne laser scanner. Remote Sens. Environ. **90**(4), 415–423 (2009)
20. Hyyppa, J., Kelle, O., Lehihoinen, M., Inkinen, M.: A segmentation-based method to retrieve stem volume estimates from 3D tree height models produced by laser scanners. IEEE Trans. Geosci. Remote Sens. **39**, 969–975 (2001)

21. Kato, A., Moskal, M., Schiess, P., Swanson, M., Calhoun, D., Stuetzle, W.: Capturing tree crown formation through implicit surface reconstruction using airborne LIDAR data. Remote Sens. Environ. **113**(6), 1148–1162 (2009)
22. Kim, S., McGaughey, R.J., Andersen, H.-E., Schreuder, G.: Tree species differentiation using intensity data derived from leaf-on and leaf-off airborne laser scanner data. Remote Sens. Environ. **113**, 1575–1586 (2009)
23. Kovats, M.: A large-scale aerial photographic technique for measuring tree heights on long-term forest installations. Photogramm. Eng. Remote Sens. **63**(3), 741–747 (1997)
24. Larsen, M., Rudemo, M.: Approximate Bayesian estimation of a 3D point pattern from multiple views. Pattern Recognit. Lett. **25**, 1359–1368 (2004)
25. Li, Z., Gruen, A.: Automatic DSM generation from LIDAR array imagery data. Int. Arch. Photogramm. Remote Sens. **35**(B3), 128–133 (2003)
26. Li, Y., Andersen, H.-E., McGaughey, R.: A comparison of statistical methods for estimating forest biomass from light detection and ranging data. Western J. Appl. For. **23**(4), 223–231 (2008)
27. Lund, J., Rudemo, M.: Models for point processes observed with noise. Biometrika **87**(2), 235–249 (2000)
28. Maltamo, M., Mustonen, K., Hyyppa, J., Pitkanen, J., Yu, X.: The accuracy of estimating individual tree variables with airborne laser scanning in a boreal nature reserve. Can. J. For. Res. **34**(9), 1791–1801 (2004)
29. Magnussen, S., Boudewyn, P.: Derivations of stand heights from airborne laser scanner data with canopy-based quantile estimators. Can. J. For. Res. **28**, 1016–1031 (1998)
30. McGaughey, R., Carson, W., Reutebuch, S., Andersen, H.-E.: Direct measurement of individual tree characteristics from LIDAR data. In: Proceedings of the Annual ASPRS Conference, 23–24 May 2004, Denver, Colorado, USA. American Society of Photogrammetry and Remote Sensing (ASPRS), Bethesda (2004)
31. Mette, T., Hajnsek, I., Papathanassiou: Height-biomass allometry in temperate forests: performance accuracy of height-biomass allometry. In: Proceedings of the 2003 IEEE Geoscience and Remote Sensing Symposium, IGARRS'03 (2003)
32. Mikhail, E., Bethel, J., McGlone, J.: Introduction to Modern Photogrammetry. Wiley, New York (2001)
33. Morsdorf, F., Nichol, C., Malthus, T., Woodhouse, I.: Assessing forest structural and physiological information content of multi-spectral LiDAR waveforms by radiative transfer modelling. Remote Sens. Environ. **113**(10), 2152–2163 (2009)
34. Mostafa, M.: PE&RS direct georeferencing column: an introduction. Photogramm. Eng. Remote Sens. **67**(10), 1105–1109 (2001)
35. Naesset, E.: Predicting forest stand characteristics with airborne scanning laser using a practical two-stage procedure and field data. Remote Sens. Environ. **80**, 88–99 (2002)
36. Naesset, E., Bjerknes, K.-O.: Estimating tree heights and number of stems in young forest stands using airborne laser scanner data. Remote Sens. Environ. **78**, 328–340 (2001)
37. Natural Resources Canada: On-line precise point positioning 'How to use' document. Natural Resources Canada, Canada Centre for Remote Sensing, Ontario, Canada (2004)
38. Needham, T., Smith, J.: Stem count accuracy and species determination in loblolly pine plantations using 35-mm aerial photography. Photogramm. Eng. Remote Sens. **53**(12), 1675–1678 (1987)
39. Pacey, R., Fricker, P.: Forward motion compensation (FMC) is it the same in the digital imaging world? Photogramm. Eng. Remote Sens. **71**(11), 1241–1242 (2005)
40. Paine, D., Kiser, J.: Aerial Photography and Image Interpretation. Wiley, New York (2003)
41. Persson, A., Holmgren, J., Soderman, U.: Detecting and measuring individual trees using a airborne laser scanner. Photogramm. Eng. Remote Sens. **68**(9), 925–932 (2002)
42. Pollock, R.: The automatic recognition of individual trees in aerial images of forests based on a synthetic tree crown image model. Ph.D. thesis, University of British, Columbia, Vancouver, Canada (1996). 172 pp.

43. Pope, R., Maclean, C., Bernstein, D.: Forest uses of aerial photos. U.S. Department of Agriculture, Forest Service, Pacific Northwest Forest and Range Experiment Station (1961)
44. Popescu, S., Wynne, R.: Seeing the trees in the forest: using LIDAR and multispectral data fusion with local filtering and variable window size for estimating tree height. Photogramm. Eng. Remote Sens. **70**, 589–604 (2004)
45. Reitberger, J., Krzystek, P., Stilla, U.: Analysis of full waveform LiDAR for tree species classification. Int. J. Remote Sens. **36**, 228–233 (2006)
46. Reutebuch, S., Shea, R.: A method to control large-scale aerial photos when surveyed ground control is unavailable. In: Proceedings of the 2nd Forest Service Remote Sensing Applications Conference, 11–15 April, Slidell, Louisiana, USA. American Society of Photogrammetry and Remote Sensing, Falls Church, pp. 231–236 (1997)
47. Reutebuch, S., McGaughey, R., Andersen, H.-E., Carson, W.: Accuracy of a high-resolution LIDAR terrain model under a conifer forest canopy. Can. J. Remote Sens. **29**(5), 527–535 (2003)
48. Rönnholm, P., Hyyppa, H., Haggren, H., Yu, X., Kaartinen, H.: Calibration of laser-derived tree height estimates by means of photogrammetry techniques. Scand. J. For. Res. **19**, 524–528 (2004)
49. Schardt, M., Ziegler, M., Wimmer, A., Wack, R., Hyyppa, J.: Assessment of forest parameters by means of laser scanning. Int. Arc. Photogramm. Remote Sens. **24**(3A) (2002)
50. Simon, D.: Kalman filtering. Embedded Systems Programming, June, 2001, 72–79 (2001)
51. Spurr, S.: History of forest photogrammetry and aerial mapping. Photogramm. Eng. **20**, 551–560 (1954)
52. Vaughn, N., Moskal, L.M., Turnblom, E.: Fourier transformation of waveform LIDAR for species recognition. Remote Sens. Lett. **2**(4), 347–356 (2010)
53. Vincent, L., Soille, P.: Watersheds in digital spaces: an efficient algorithm based on immersion simulations. IEEE Trans. Pattern Anal. Mach. Intell. **13**(6), 583–598 (1991)
54. Wagner, W., Ullrich, A., Ducic, V., Melzer, T., Studnicka, N.: Gaussian decomposition and calibration of a novel small-footprint full-waveform digitising airborne laser scanner. ISPRS J. Photogramm. Remote Sens. **60**(2), 100–112 (2006)
55. West, G., Brown, J., Enquist, B.: A general model for the origin of allometric scaling laws in biology. Science **276**(5309), 122–126 (1997)
56. Wolf, P., DeWitt, B.: Elements of Photogrammetry with Applications in GIS. McGraw-Hill, New York (2000)
57. Yarie, J., Kane, E., Mack, M.: Aboveground biomass equations for the trees of interior Alaska. University of Alaska Fairbanks; Agricultural and Forestry Experiment Station Bulletin, vol. 115 (2007)

Chapter 11
3D Medical Imaging

Philip G. Batchelor, P.J. "Eddie" Edwards, and Andrew P. King

Abstract This chapter overviews three-dimensional (3D) medical imaging and the associated analysis techniques. The methods described here aim to reconstruct the inside of the human body in three dimensions. This is in contrast to optical methods that try to reconstruct the surface of viewed objects, although there are similarities in some of the geometries and techniques used. Due to the wide scope of medical imaging it is unrealistic to attempt an exhaustive or detailed description of techniques. Rather, the aim is to provide some illustrations and directions for further study for the interested reader. The first section gives an overview of the physics of data acquisition, where images come from and why they look the way they do. The next section illustrates how this raw data is processed into surface and volume data for viewing and analysis. This is followed by a description of how to put images in a common coordinate frame and a more specific case study illustrating higher dimensional data manipulation. Finally, we describe some clinical applications to show how these methods can be used to provide effective treatment of patients.

11.1 Introduction

Medical imaging dates back to the discovery of X-rays by Wilhelm Röntgen in November 1895. His discovery was published in early 1896 and rapidly led to the proliferation of 2D X-Ray imaging equipment. The clinical implications of the fact that X-rays pass through the soft tissue and can image bone was quickly realized

---

P.G. Batchelor · A.P. King
King's College, London, UK

P.G. Batchelor
e-mail: philip.batchelor@kcl.ac.uk

A.P. King
e-mail: andrew.king@kcl.ac.uk

P.J. "Eddie" Edwards (✉)
Imperial College, London, UK
e-mail: eddie.edwards@imperial.ac.uk

and X-rays were used to image fractures and diagnose the presence and location of foreign bodies such as gunshot wounds.

Much of the 3D imaging described in the earlier chapters of this book is based on one or more optical cameras imaging a visible surface. In contrast, the aim of 3D medical imaging is to model structures beneath the surface of the skin. The techniques of stereo and multi-view reconstruction, such as those described in Chap. 2, can also be applied to X-rays, which have the same projective geometry as camera images. For example, the 3D shape of vessels can be reconstructed from biplanar 2D X-rays [32]. However, such applications have been largely part of research and, for over 70 years since its inception, the field of medical imaging remained largely 2D.

In the 1970s, however, research began on imaging modalities that produce a fully 3D representation of the patient. The first of these was computed tomography (CT), a 3D reconstruction using X-rays. The second was magnetic resonance imaging (MRI) which utilizes the nuclear magnetic resonance effect. These developments were in part only possible due to the increasing power of computing occurring at the same time. Both of these modalities produce volumetric images. These can be considered as a series of aligned slices but really form a continuous 3D block of data. The individual elements are generally referred to as voxels rather than pixels. In a sense, the surface data described in much of this book is not truly 3D, since it represents a 2D surface, albeit a surface embedded in 3D space. In this chapter, we will concentrate on fully volumetric 3D medical imaging modalities, but also look at how surfaces can be extracted from or registered to such images.

Despite being three dimensional imaging modalities, the most common way for a radiologist to view these images is as a series of 2D slices. Until remarkably recently, these would actually be viewed as printed films on a light box. However, with the widespread adoption of standardized networking and reviewing of images via picture archiving and communication systems (PACS), viewing on a computer screen is now the norm. Viewing as 2D slices does enable the full image data to be explored, but viewing in 3D can provide improved perception and the majority of radiologists are now used to navigating and viewing datasets in 3D.

Chapter Outline In Sect. 11.2, we will summarize the principles behind the leading 3D anatomical medical imaging modalities, namely CT and MRI, as well as briefly touching on positron emission tomography (PET). CT and MRI are sometimes described as anatomical modalities, whereas PET is considered functional, in the sense that it shows where metabolism is occurring. There are also functional forms of MRI, however, but discussion of this is beyond the scope of this chapter. In Sect. 11.3, we present methods for surface extraction and volumetric visualization. The following section deals with volumetric image registration, while Sect. 11.5 presents segmentation methods. Section 11.6 considers higher dimensional imaging with the example of diffusion tensor MRI and the final main section describes some clinical applications of 3D imaging; in particular, surgical guidance.

There are, of course, many other medical imaging modalities. Ultrasound is a real-time and largely 2D modality, but can be made 3D by the addition of tracking or 2D phased array probes. There is nuclear medicine, SPECT, thermography, electrical impedance tomography, elastography, optical coherence tomography, confocal microscopy, magnetoencephalography, fluorescence lifetime imaging, near infrared optical tomography and spectroscopy and the list goes on. It is not possible to cover the huge field of medical imaging in one chapter. Rather, we provide an introduction to the subject that summarizes the basics of 3D medical imaging. For more details, we refer the reader to some excellent textbooks [4, 16, 39], as well as online references; for example, the online Encyclopedia of Medical Physics (EMITEL) [77].

11.2 Volumetric Data Acquisition

Before discussing how we can process and analyze 3D medical imaging data, it is important to examine the issues relating to data acquisition. The human body is largely opaque to optical imaging, so medical images must use other physical processes to image tissue properties. The techniques used will have significant influence on the types of tissue that can be imaged and the quality of the 3D data obtained in terms of contrast, noise characteristics and artifacts.

In this section, we will summarize the methods behind volumetric data acquisition. For 3D imaging of human anatomy, two modalities dominate, CT and MRI. We describe briefly the physics and the computational methods used to reconstruct these modalities, as well as considering the functional modality, PET. We consider the characteristics of the reconstructed data from the point-of-view of 3D and describe some of the artifacts that can occur.

11.2.1 Computed Tomography

Computed tomography (CT) is essentially a 3D version of classical X-Rays. The overall idea is fairly simple. An X-Ray is a projection through the object, in the sense that the pixel intensities can be interpreted as related to an integral along projected rays through the object. If we take multiple X-Rays at different angles, we might be able to solve for the 3D voxel intensities. In fact, the process really reconstructs a single 2D slice and the patient is moved through the scanning plane to collect multiple slices and create a 3D volume.

So, how is such a 2D slice reconstructed? The object (slice through the patient) can be considered as a 2D array of X-ray attenuation coefficients $\mu(x, y)$. The aim of CT imaging is then to reconstruct the function $\mu(x, y)$. If the incident intensity from the X-ray source is I_0, the transmitted intensity I having passed along a single ray through the patient will be:

$$I(\theta) = I_0 e^{-\int_{-\infty}^{\infty} \mu(x(s,\theta), y(s,\theta))\, ds}$$

where $(x(s, \theta), y(s, \theta))$ denotes a point along the ray making an angle θ with an arbitrary but fixed axis, and s is distance along the ray. We can convert this to a direct integral along the line by taking log intensities, in which case the process corresponds mathematically to a *Radon transform*. We are integrating the function $\mu(x, y)$ along a given line. If we have a parallel beam geometry, many such lines are integrated through the object at the same angle, θ, but different offsets, d, providing a linear projection profile, P, of the object. The 1D projection at this angle becomes:

$$P(d, \theta) = \ln(I/I_0) = -\int \mu(x, y) \, ds \qquad (11.1)$$

This corresponds to the Radon transform, but to reconstruct $\mu(x, y)$ we must solve for the inverse Radon transform. There is a nice theorem that helps in this process, known as the *central slice theorem* or the *projection slice theorem*. It turns out that the 1D Fourier transform of the projection P is actually the same as a line through the 2D Fourier transform of $\mu(x, y)$. Hence, we can take the 1D Fourier transform of all our projections at different angles and use these to interpolate the full 2D Fourier transform. The final image is then obtained by a 2D inverse Fourier transform of the result.

A simpler approach is merely to back-project (spread the value associated to a line uniformly among all pixels on the line) the profiles at all angles and average them. This produces images which are rather blurred and this blurring has an analytical expression. Correct results are achieved if the individual slice spectra are filtered before undergoing a 1D inverse Fourier transform and then being projected back into the 2D spatial image. Each filtered projection is simply projected back into the 2D image at the same angle as it was taken and the sum of all projections is then averaged. This process is known as *filtered back-projection*. An excellent online demo is available [45].

We have described how a 2D slice is produced. By incrementing the slice position, we end up with a stack of slices corresponding to the full 3D volume. In modern scanners, the reconstruction is not from parallel beams, but fan beams (single source to multiple detectors in a ring). The acquisition is often taken using a spiral motion with the patient continually moving through the scanner and reconstruction being fully 3D. An example CT scan is shown in Fig. 11.1. Multiple slices are often detected in one acquisition and the latest scanners may be 256 or even 512 slice devices. This enables, for example, coronary scans to be taken in a single heartbeat.

11.2.1.1 Characteristics of 3D CT Data

Since CT images the X-ray attenuation coefficient, it is good at imaging dense objects such as bones. The contrast for soft tissues may not be so high, but certainly fat and muscle can be differentiated and often pathological tissue such as cancerous lesions can be identified. The intensity corresponding to a given tissue density should always be the same and CT voxels are generally provided in Hounsfield units

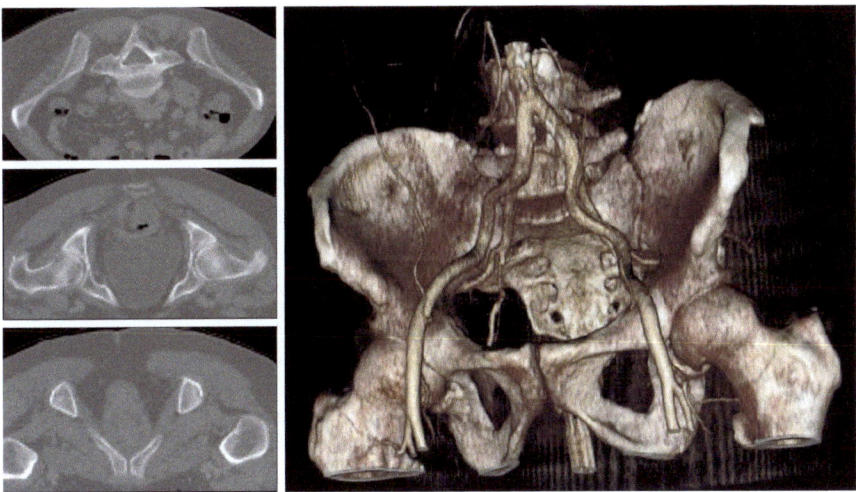

Fig. 11.1 Slices from an abdominal CT and volume rendering showing pelvic bone and major vessels

(HU) (-1000 for air, 0 for water) or CT number (HU $+ 1000$). Hounsfield units are named after Sir Godfrey Hounsfield, who received the Nobel Prize for Medicine in 1979 for his pioneering work in constructing the first CT scanner.

The resolution of a CT slice is generally less than 1 mm. Image dimensions are typically a power of 2 and in-slice matrix will typically be 512×512. The thickness and separation of slices varies depending on the application, but will typically be a few millimeters unless there is a specific desire for an accurate 3D model. Since CT consists of multiple X-rays, radiation dose is a major issue. As with X-rays, there is a compromise between image quality and dose. The relationship between dose, D, and signal-to-noise ratio (SNR) can be expressed as:

$$D \propto \frac{\text{SNR}^2}{d^3 h}$$

where d is in-plane pixel size, and h is slice thickness [16]. At the same time there is a pay-off between resolution and SNR. Greater resolution, whether in-plane or in terms of slice thickness, will mean a reduction in SNR.

There are many artifacts that can arise in CT scanning. If very dense objects, such as metal fillings, are visible in the scan, the back-projection process will mean that these appear as streaks in the reconstructed image [37]. If there is a region of high density material, for example a thick area of skull bone, this effectively filters out lower energy X-rays and leaves a higher energy beam that is less easily absorbed. The result can be shadows beyond such regions and these are known as beam hardening artifacts. Motion can also cause significant artifacts in CT (see Fig. 11.2).

Despite the potential for artifacts and radiation dose, CT is able to produce some spectacular anatomical reconstructions (see Fig. 11.1). It is also worth noting that

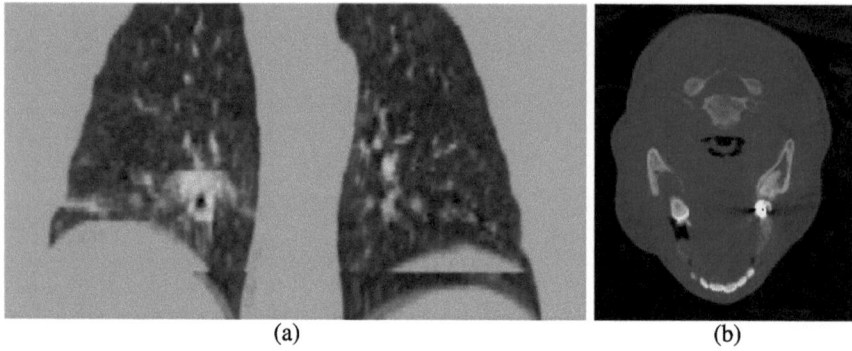

Fig. 11.2 (a) Lung CT with multiple motion artifacts. There are step changes visible at various points, especially towards the bottom of the image, as the patient moves due to breathing. (b) Head CT with visible streak artifact from a filling. There are radial *dark* and *light lines* centered on the filling

CT imaging should be entirely geometrically correct—there should be no warping or distortion and the reconstruction should be an accurate reflection of the anatomy of the subject.

11.2.2 Positron Emission Tomography (PET)

The mathematics of PET is superficially very similar to that of CT, since the signals are related to absorptions along linear trajectories. The physics is very different, however, and quite fascinating, as it involves anti-matter. There are a number of isotopes that emit positrons, including ^{11}C, ^{13}N, ^{15}O and ^{18}F. These have short half lives of only a few minutes and are not easy to produce. They require a cyclotron in close vicinity to or in the hospital and care must be taken in transporting these radioactive chemicals. These are crucial elements in organic chemistry, however, which makes it possible to image the uptake of a wide range of organic molecules. The process of producing these molecules is known as radiochemistry. The most common is Fluorodeoxyglucose (FDG), in which a OH group in glucose is replaced with ^{18}F. This is readily used in imaging due to the relatively long half life of ^{18}F (110 minutes) compared to ^{15}O (2 minutes). The action of FDG within the body is very similar to glucose, in the sense that it is taken up by cells that are highly metabolizing (i.e. using energy). This includes active brain cells and also rapidly developing cancer cells. An example of a PET scan is shown in Fig. 11.3.

Having labeled a particular molecule, the radioactive marker is injected or ingested by the patient. The take-up of the radio-labeled molecule can then be imaged. As the nucleus decays, it emits a positron—the anti-matter equivalent of an electron. Within a short range, perhaps a few millimeters in tissue, this will annihilate with an electron. Two high energy (511 kEv) photons are given off at nearly 180°. A ring of

Fig. 11.3 A sagittal section through a PET scan showing activity in the brain but also in a cancerous lesion within the mouth

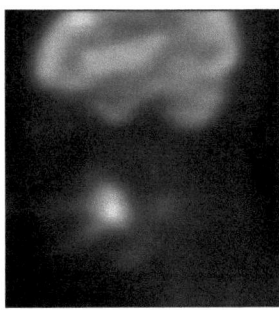

highly sensitive photon detectors is used and the coincidence of two nearly simultaneous photons is considered to be a positive count, which means that there was a positron emitted somewhere along the line between the detectors. The lines forming the combinations of all sets of detectors can be organized into parallel sets at a given angle and considered as similar to tomographic projections, and methods similar to CT reconstruction can be used. Correction for attenuation is required and, for this purpose, a transmission scan similar to a CT scan is taken.

Being based on a photon counting device, the accuracy and quality of PET strongly depend on the number of events being measured. There are several effects that can impact the resolution and the SNR. These may involve physical effects (e.g. photon scattering and attenuation), counting effects (e.g. amount of injected tracer, limited photon statistics, random photon counting) and physiological effects (e.g. subject motion, tracer metabolites, tracer selectivity). For this reason, it is not possible to state a single typical number for SNR.

Due to the large number of factors that can impact PET quality, the subject of PET image reconstruction is an ongoing research field. One of the more successful range of algorithms is the use of statistical methods to provide expectation maximization. The maximum likelihood expectation maximization (ML-EM) algorithm, originally suggested by Dempster in 1977 [23] can be applied to emission tomography in a manner suggested by Shepp and Vardi [73]. An estimate of the concentration distribution of the metabolite $I_j(0)$ is forward projected to provide a predicted set of measurements at the detectors.

This method is very time consuming and the efficiency can be significantly improved using the ordered subsets EM algorithm which uses subsets of the input voxels at each iteration [36].

11.2.2.1 Characteristics of 3D PET Data

PET is particularly suitable for imaging molecular, functional processes, but has a much lower resolution and SNR than the anatomic techniques such as MRI or CT (see Fig. 11.3). There is, in fact, a physical limit on the possible resolution of PET. This is in part due to the distance travelled by the positron before annihilation with an electron (typically a few millimeters) and also due the fact that the emitted photons from the annihilation are not exactly at 180°. Despite the resolution limits, PET is very useful for displaying metabolism.

11.2.3 MRI

It is often said that CT provides structural, or anatomical information, at high resolution, while PET provides 'functional' information. MRI is a third piece of the puzzle: it is most sensitive to hydrogen present in water and is therefore good at imaging soft tissues, as they contain a lot of water.

The principles of MRI are completely different from those of the tomographies. It is inherently 3D and where, for other modalities, 'depth' and 'absorption' play a role, this is not the case for MRI: deep lying tissues are as well visualized, often better, than superficial ones. The reason is that the scanning doesn't happen in the actual image space but in the Fourier domain, also called 'k-space'. It is there that different positions play a role.

The basis of MRI is the nuclear magnetic resonance (NMR) effect. This is observed for any nucleus but, in the case of medical imaging, we are almost exclusively interested in hydrogen. Since a large quantity of the body is water, which contains two hydrogen and one oxygen atoms, hydrogen is the most common atomic nucleus in the body, in fact accounting for about 63 % of the atoms in the body. In the presence of a high magnetic field, spin state of the hydrogen nucleus (in fact a single proton) is split into two energy levels: being aligned with the field, or against it.

Main Field: B_0 Hence, the first ingredient of MRI is a very strong, permanent, spatially uniform, magnetic field, B_0. Protons have their own magnetization, proportional to their 'spin'. Thus they act as little magnet. When introduced in the scanner, they will tend to be parallel to this main field. In fact, they precess around it at a resonant frequency proportional to the external field: the Larmor frequency ω_0. Although NMR is a quantum effect, the sum of all spins induced is a small but macroscopic magnetization for each voxel position.

RF Field: B_1 A second, much smaller, field is switched on. This field is a function of time and oscillates at the frequency ω_0. This means it is in *resonance* with the hydrogen nuclei. The plane in which B_1 oscillates is chosen at an angle α from B_0 (in an ideal experiment perpendicular, but in practice different 'flip' angles, α, are used). This excites nuclei to be aligned against the field and causes them to precess in synchrony.

Gradient Field $G^t x$ As a result of B_0 and B_1, we have a small but measurable magnetization oscillating in the measurement coils in a plane transversal to the main field. By linearity, all pixels contributions add up and we end up with an oscillating magnetic field whose strength depends on the amount and environment of water molecules. In *NMR* or MR spectroscopy, what we would change is the resonance frequency, to investigate different types of molecules. In MRI, we want images. Thus the resonant frequency stays similar, but the main field is modified by the addition of a linearly varying field. This makes the resonance frequency linear in position, in direction 'x'. Each pixel or voxel now contributes with a slightly different frequency. Before applying this gradient, another perpendicular gradient is applied in the third direction, for a short while. This makes spins precess faster in that direction for a short while, thus when this 'phase-encode' gradient is switched, they get back to their previous frequency of rotation, but with an additional dephasing proportional to their 'y'-coordinate. Thus, when we 'read' the magnetization, what we read is the contribution from each pixel, but weighted by a term dependent on position, and the gradients applied. It is not too hard to see that this term can be written $e^{-ik_x x + k_y y}$, where k_* is a function of gradients and when they were switched on and off. This is the k-space often described for MRI and the measured signal corresponds to a *Fourier transform*. It is actually possible to excite an entire 3D volume and, for example, frequency encode the x direction and phase encode the y, z directions, although this is relatively slow.

Relaxation If left alone, the spins interact with their environment and with each other, leading to exponential decays, which are the source of the main image contrasts (T1 and T2) mentioned below.

11.2.3.1 Characteristics of the 3D MRI Data

As for CT, classical MRI is thus a 3D modality, which can be imagined as a stack of 2D slices. The most common acquisition is indeed to excite one slice at a time, and frequency encode and phase encode in two directions in that plane. MRI can be acquired directly as a full 3D volume. This means phase-encoding two directions. It is possible to have non-standard, non-lattice acquisition patterns, such as radial, spiral and rose-like. Modern advances in reconstruction theory have led to the use of different types of random sampling patterns.

Image Quality and Artifacts The most typical artifacts for MR acquisition are 'Nyquist' artifacts, also known as 'aliasing' artifacts, which are artifacts related to a spatial sampling rate that is too low. 3D MR acquisitions can be particularly affected by them. In particular, *Gibbs ringing* artifacts are frequent near edges. These are due to unavoidable truncations in the acquisition. Further to this, the contrast of the image is determined by the center of the k-space. It can happen that outer parts are then undersampled, leading to *blurred* images. The phase encode direction is the slowest to acquire. So, to make scans faster, this direction may be undersampled. This can lead to *foldover* or *wrap-around* artifacts, where parts of the image which are out of the field-of-view seem to fold inside it. Related motion artifacts are also more visible in this direction. Examples of MRI artifacts are shown in Fig. 11.4.

Apart from the main magnetic field, all fields change with time. This creates eddy currents, which induce fields and thus distort the picture. The typical artifact

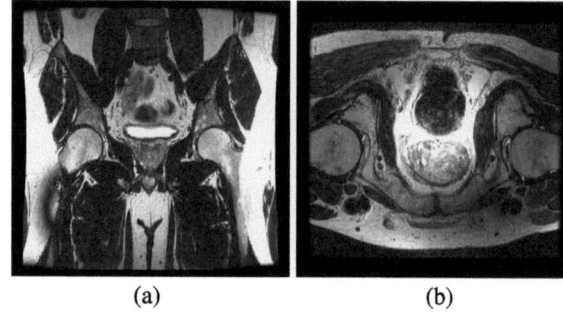

Fig. 11.4 Examples of MRI artifacts—(**a**) aliasing causing wrap-around near the sides of the image and (**b**) intensity inhomogeneity (*brightness at the center*) and ringing (wave-like patterns *inside dark prostate region*) in an image taken with a transrectal coil

(a) (b)

due to such eddy currents is a distortion, possibly affine (shear, etc.). See Erasmus et al. [27] for further reading on MRI artifacts.

A different type of artifact can arise due to the main field being non-uniform or the gradients not being perfectly linear functions. Such inhomogeneities lead to spatial distortions of the image. There are also local imperfections of the magnetic field due to local changes in magnetic susceptibility. These artifacts lead to non-affine, localized distortions at interfaces; for example, tissue-air. So, unlike CT, it cannot be guaranteed that MRI is a geometrically correct representation of the patient.

Resolution δx is inversely proportional to the width in k-space, $\delta x \propto 1/\Delta k$. Small voxels are also noisier, thus there is always a trade-off between resolution and other desirable qualities of the image, such as SNR. This again is something that can be decided by operators, thus might be influenced by the application. Typical resolutions for human, *in vivo* MRI, are between 1 mm and 2 mm, with typical image sizes between 128×128 to 256×256.

MR images are, from the Fourier transform reconstruction, complex by nature, with the magnitudes of the complex numbers being used to display the image. Although *noise in MRI* is Gaussian, provided we consider their complex form, the noise on the displayed magnitudes is Rician. It is important for the computer scientists performing post-processing operations to keep this in mind.

Standard MR modalities have sufficient SNR that the noise can be approximated as Gaussian (with some correction factors) but for some other techniques, such as diffusion MRI (see Sect. 11.6), this is usually not true. We refer the reader to Rajan et al. [66] for more details on SNR in MRI.

Note that there are always trade-offs. With longer scan times, we can improve SNR at the risk of augmenting sensitivity to motion.

Contrasts: There is a wealth of different contrast weighting in MRI, thus, for a specific 3D application, it is nearly always useful to discuss the requirements with MR physicists, as it is often possible to tune the scan. However, one should keep in mind that, in most cases, these contrasts are not mutually exclusive. Images are weighted more towards one type of property, but always contain some element of the other.

The simplest contrast conceptually is the proton density scan, but this has few clinical applications. Typical clinical images are 'T1' or 'T2'-weighted, which means that the contrast is a relaxation rate relating to the spin-lattice or spin-spin

11 3D Medical Imaging

Fig. 11.5 Example MRI images: a T1 image of the knee (*left*) and a T2 image of the head (*right*)

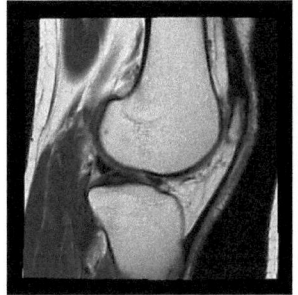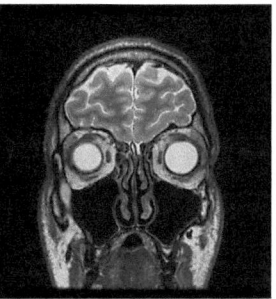

interactions. Examples of such images are given in Fig. 11.5. It is also possible to use phase contrast (remember the complex number nature of the data), to visualize flows and even tensor contrast in diffusion tensor MRI (see Sect. 11.6).

11.2.4 Summary

For the three modalities that we have considered, this section has tried to underline where artifacts come from and what kind of 3D data to expect. In summary, CT is good for very high quality 3D images of specific regions focussing on bone and other dense tissues. MRI is the method of choice for visualization of soft tissue and is very flexible, but is slightly lower resolution than CT and more sensitive to motion. PET is lower resolution again, but provides functional data, since it shows where metabolism is occurring. Another message is that some knowledge of signal processing is a vital skill for understanding why medical images look as they do, in particular issues relating to the Nyquist-Shannon sampling theorem. Note that recent developments in reconstruction for all modalities are tending towards iterative reconstruction methods. This is the default in PET and there are algebraic methods in CT and conjugate gradient methods in MRI. So basic knowledge of inverse problems and numerical linear algebra can also be helpful. We haven't covered ultrasound due to lack of space and also because it is less commonly used in a 3D modality.

11.3 Surface Extraction and Volumetric Visualization

As previously mentioned, much of this book concentrates on 2D surfaces embedded in 3D space. Although medical images are volumetric 3D representations of the patient, there are times when such a surface representation is useful. For example, triangulated surfaces are readily rendered by graphics hardware. A surface representation would be useful to provide an interactive 3D model of the patient. In this section, we will consider how such a representation can be created from a volume image, but also consider ways that a volume image can be rendered without extracting a surface.

Fig. 11.6 *Left*: A grid of voxel intensities and *Right*: the contour corresponding to a threshold of 9.5

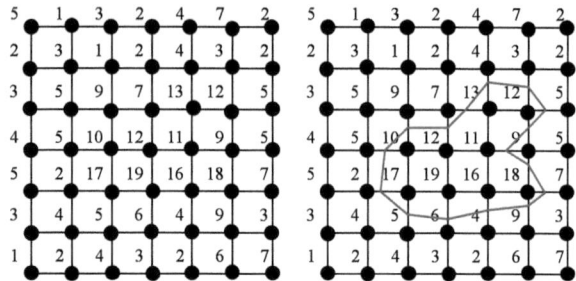

11.3.1 Surface Extraction

In order to extract a surface from a volume image, let's first assume that we know the threshold corresponding to the object to be described. This may seem a strong assumption but, in the case of CT, if we want the bone surface, we already know that bone corresponds to a specific density for most people. If we want to extract a surface corresponding to a given threshold, the algorithm to use is *marching cubes* [47].

Consider the 2D case. If we draw a grid of points centered on our pixels, let's assume we have the values shown in Fig. 11.6 and we want to extract a contour at a threshold of 9.5. It is clear that we will have a point on our contour along any of the lines between voxel centers where one voxel is above the threshold and the other is below. This point should be linearly interpolated to find its position along this line. However, there still remains the task of deciding how these points connect. In the example, shown in Fig. 11.6, this is clear and trivial to decide. However, in other cases, it is not so clear. Figure 11.7 shows such a case, where two opposite corners are above the threshold and the other two are not. There are two ways to connect the lines. As is always the case, making a different choice with such ambiguities leads to changes in topology—there will either be one or two objects in the case shown in Fig. 11.7.

When moving into 3D, the situation becomes more complicated. The different possible connections between points can be placed in a 'case' table depending on which points are above and below the threshold in a group of 8 neighboring voxels

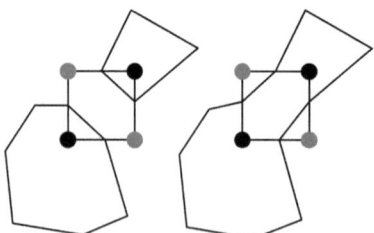

Fig. 11.7 Example of ambiguity in the 2D marching squares algorithm. A vertex must be placed along each of the four edges, since the one of the corner values is above and one below the threshold. These can be joined in one of two ways, making either one or two regions

11 3D Medical Imaging

Fig. 11.8 A skull surface extracted from a CT image showing typical staircase artifacts. These can be reduced by smoothing the surface or by blurring the 3D image before applying marching cubes. This latter approach is often better

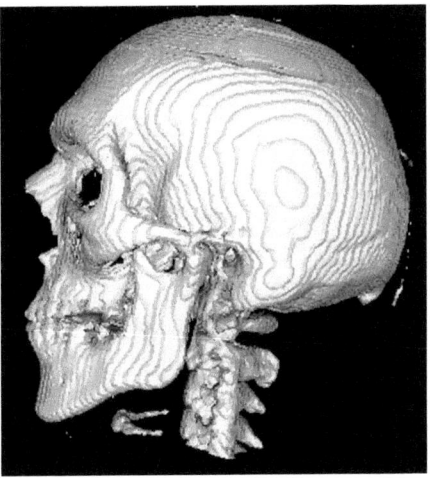

(the corners of a cube). This could provide 256 potential cases, but by adjusting for rotational and other symmetries these can be reduced to 15 cases. Ambiguities in 3D, if not dealt with correctly, can lead to holes in the resulting surface. There are a number of possible solutions to this, for example using tetrahedra rather than cubes.

Volumetric medical images usually do not have resolutions of comparable quality to what is achieved with range data. Partly as a consequence of this, surface extraction algorithms such as marching cubes [47] may produce surfaces with typical 'staircase' effects. Further processing may smooth the surface or decimate it. It is often better to smooth the 3D volume before running marching cubes as this reduces the noise in the dataset. As mentioned above, the triangulation can contain singularities (zero angled triangles), holes, duplicate triangles, folds and so on, if the implementation is not robust.

Example: Curvatures and Geometric Tools Once the surface has been extracted, different operations are possible for medical imaging applications. We will illustrate briefly with the example of curvatures. Curvatures are an intuitive quantity but, since they involve *second* derivatives, they tend to be very sensitive to surface irregularities [6, 7] They can be used as a quantification of the surface or as a tool to evolve the surface [5]. Figure 11.9 shows some illustrative examples.

11.3.2 Volume Rendering

It is also possible to produce a rendering of the anatomy from a model without extracting a surface first. This method is known as volume rendering. The idea originated in computer graphics before its application to medical imaging, but this method is ideally suited to rendering of volumetric data such as CT or MRI scans. A volume rendering of a CT image is shown in Fig. 11.10. The idea is very similar to

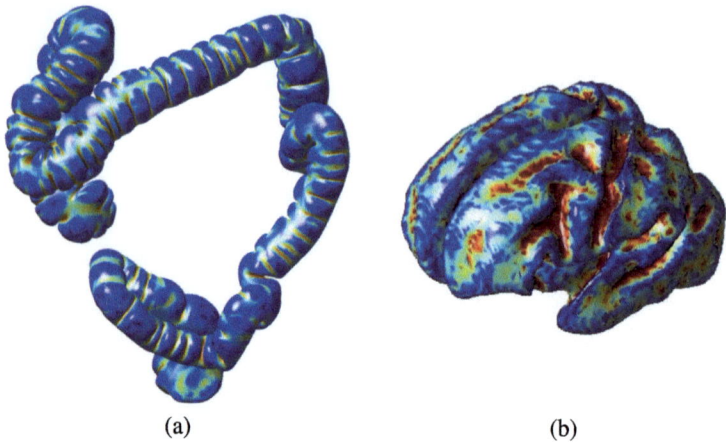

Fig. 11.9 (**a**) Colon image *colored* by curvature. The colon is deformed by a curvature ('Ricci') flow into a cylinder, from which comparisons can be made [69]. (**b**) Mean curvature of the cortical surface. These are used to quantify the folding of the cortex, as a biomarker of brain shape [6]

raytracing, in that a ray is cast from a given 2D image pixel through the volume. The process aims to simulate the passage of light through a semi-transparent medium. If the ray has a current color C_r^n, as it passes through a voxel v with color C_v and opacity α_v, the color of the ray is changed using the *over operator*:

$$C_r^{n+1} = (1 - \alpha_v)C_r^n + \alpha_v C_v. \qquad (11.2)$$

The scalar values in the image need to be mapped to color and opacity by the *transfer function*, which determines the color and opacity of a voxel depending on the greyscale values in the image (i.e. $C_v(I)$ and $\alpha_v(I)$ are functions of the image intensity, I). There are some simple transfer functions, such as the maximum intensity projection, which just calculates the maximum value along the ray. This has proven useful in viewing vessels in angiography images.

It is also possible to composite the rays back to front rather than front to back, in which case the slightly different *under operator* is used:

$$\begin{aligned}\alpha_r^{n+1} &= \alpha_r^n + \alpha_v(1 - \alpha_r^n) \\ \hat{C}_r^{n+1} &= \hat{C}_r^n + \hat{C}_v(1 - \alpha_r^n),\end{aligned} \qquad (11.3)$$

where $\hat{C}_r = \alpha_r C_r$ and $\hat{C}_v = \alpha_v C_v$. There are numerous implementation issues with volume rendering and many tricks to speed up the process. Even on modern graphics cards and CPUs, however, the interactivity of volume rendering is not the same as surface rendering. A common option is to display the volume rendered scene at a lower resolution during interaction and display the full image only when interaction stops. This will become less of a problem as graphics performance increases.

In general, to achieve a good result, it is necessary to roughly segment the organ of interest first before performing surface or volume rendering. In the next section

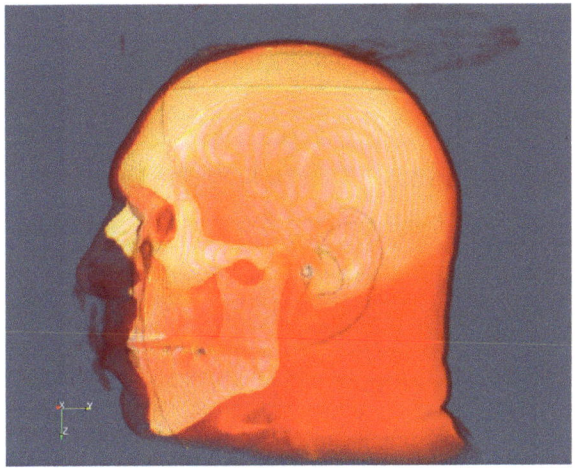

Fig. 11.10 A volume rendering of the CT image from Fig. 11.8. There is smoothing of the skull surface, and we are able to view this through the transparent skin

we will look at the problem of segmentation. A further issue is how to incorporate a lighting model into volume rendering. In the volumetric lighting approach, a normal is calculated at each voxel from finite difference approximation of the scalar gradient:

$$\nabla I = \begin{bmatrix} \frac{\partial I}{\partial x} \\ \frac{\partial I}{\partial y} \\ \frac{\partial I}{\partial z} \end{bmatrix} = \begin{bmatrix} \frac{I(x+\Delta x,y,z)-I(x-\Delta x,y,z)}{2\Delta x} \\ \frac{I(x,y+\Delta y,z)-I(x,y-\Delta y,z)}{2\Delta y} \\ \frac{I(x,y,z+\Delta z)-I(x,y,z-\Delta z)}{2\Delta z} \end{bmatrix}. \quad (11.4)$$

The normal is calculated as $n = \frac{\nabla I}{|\nabla I|}$ and the interaction of the light with each voxel is calculated during composition.

11.3.3 Summary

This section illustrated how some of the techniques described in this book can be applied to medical imaging data. Bear in mind the message from the previous section about limitations of the original images. If there is one message to take from surfaces from medical images, it is that they can be rather low quality, with discretization ('staircase' artifacts), holes, missing parts, foldovers and so on. On the other hand, the number of triangles in a triangulated surface can be huge and feel unnecessary with regards to graphics requirements, but one has to be very careful when smoothing or performing other manipulations. In medical imaging, the clinician may not be interested in final image quality, but might want to focus on small imperfections or other nearly indistinguishable features that could be indicative of disease. Medical diagnosis is inherently different from computer graphics in this respect. Volume rendering has the nice property that the voxel data is rendered without significant modification, so the chances of smoothing out important information in the name of rendering quality is reduced.

11.4 Volumetric Image Registration

An important field in medical imaging is *registration*, which is the process of aligning multiple images. The images may be of the same modality (e.g. MRI to MRI), known as intra-modality registration, or of different modalities (e.g. MRI to CT), known as inter-modality registration. They may be images of the same patient at different times, for example longitudinal studies looking at normal or pathological growth. Alternatively they may be images of different patients, for example group studies which attempt to quantify similarities and differences within a particular patient cohort. Registering images of different patients can also be useful in segmentation, as we will see in Sect. 11.5.2.1.

11.4.1 A Hierarchy of Transformations

The first consideration when describing the problem of registration is the form of the aligning transformation. How many degrees of freedom are appropriate? This will very much depend on the given situation. Are the images of the same patient? Is there likely to be change of shape, for example due to growth, either natural or due to disease or by deformation of the tissue.

Here we consider the most common transformations and they can be thought to exist in a hierarchy, ranging from simple transformations with few degrees of freedom to more general transformations with more degrees of freedom. An interesting point to note is that, as the generality of the transformation increases, fewer properties remain unchanged (e.g. lengths, angles). Such properties are known as *invariance* properties of the transformations. See [31] for further details on transformations.

11.4.1.1 Rigid Body Transformation

In aligning 3D images, the simplest form is the *rigid body* transformation. This is the same as a change of coordinate systems and consists of a simple translation, $\mathbf{t} = [t_x, t_y, t_z]^T$, and rotation:

$$R = \begin{bmatrix} r_{11} & r_{12} & r_{13} \\ r_{21} & r_{22} & r_{23} \\ r_{31} & r_{32} & r_{33} \end{bmatrix}, \tag{11.5}$$

where $\det(R) = 1$ and $R^T R = I$ and I is the identity matrix. In 3D there are three degrees of freedom for each making six in total. This can be represented by a matrix in homogeneous form:

$$\begin{bmatrix} x' \\ y' \\ z' \\ 1 \end{bmatrix} = \begin{bmatrix} r_{11} & r_{12} & r_{13} & t_x \\ r_{21} & r_{22} & r_{23} & t_y \\ r_{31} & r_{32} & r_{33} & t_z \\ 0 & 0 & 0 & 1 \end{bmatrix} \begin{bmatrix} x \\ y \\ z \\ 1 \end{bmatrix}. \tag{11.6}$$

Alternatively, the rotations can also be represented by quaternions. Note that all lengths and angles are invariants under a rigid body transformation and, therefore, properties derived from length and angle, such as volume, are also invariant.

11.4.1.2 Similarity Transformations and Anisotropic Scaling

Adding a further degree of freedom we have the *similarity* transformation. This allows for a uniform scale factor, s, in all dimensions (i.e. isotropic scaling), making 7 degrees of freedom in all. In a similarity transformation, angles and length ratios are invariant, but lengths are not. In effect, shape remains the same, but size changes.

In anisotropic scaling, the scaling factors, s_x, s_y and s_z, along each of the axes x, y and z of the coordinate system can be different, providing 9 degrees of freedom. This can be easily expressed in homogeneous matrix form:

$$\begin{bmatrix} x' \\ y' \\ z' \\ 1 \end{bmatrix} = \begin{bmatrix} s_x & 0 & 0 & 0 \\ 0 & s_y & 0 & 0 \\ 0 & 0 & s_z & 0 \\ 0 & 0 & 0 & 1 \end{bmatrix} \begin{bmatrix} r_{11} & r_{12} & r_{13} & t_x \\ r_{21} & r_{22} & r_{23} & t_y \\ r_{31} & r_{32} & r_{33} & t_z \\ 0 & 0 & 0 & 1 \end{bmatrix} \begin{bmatrix} x \\ y \\ z \\ 1 \end{bmatrix}. \tag{11.7}$$

11.4.1.3 Affine Transformations

The *affine* transformation enables skew to be taken into account. These can be expressed as a linear skew of one axis in the direction of another; for example, $S_x y$. The skews $S_x y$ and $S_y x$ do not represent the same transformation so, at first sight, there are 6 skews. However, these are not independent and, again, 3 degrees of freedom are added. The overall 12 degrees of freedom for the affine transformation can be represented by a single homogeneous matrix:

$$\begin{bmatrix} x' \\ y' \\ z' \\ 1 \end{bmatrix} = \begin{bmatrix} a_{11} & a_{12} & a_{13} & a_{14} \\ a_{21} & a_{22} & a_{23} & a_{24} \\ a_{31} & a_{32} & a_{33} & a_{34} \\ 0 & 0 & 0 & 1 \end{bmatrix} \begin{bmatrix} x \\ y \\ z \\ 1 \end{bmatrix}, \tag{11.8}$$

which has 12 variables. In the general affine transformation, neither lengths nor angles are invariant, but parallelism is preserved.

11.4.1.4 Perspective Transformations

Finally there is the set of perspective projections, in which lines remain lines and any features that are collinear remain collinear but parallelism is not invariant:

$$\lambda \begin{bmatrix} x' \\ y' \\ z' \\ 1 \end{bmatrix} = \begin{bmatrix} p_{11} & a_{12} & p_{13} & p_{14} \\ p_{21} & a_{22} & p_{23} & p_{24} \\ p_{31} & a_{32} & p_{33} & p_{34} \\ p_{41} & p_{42} & p_{43} & 1 \end{bmatrix} \begin{bmatrix} x \\ y \\ z \\ 1 \end{bmatrix}. \qquad (11.9)$$

The division by λ to find $(x', y', z')^T$ makes the transformation non-linear (in inhomogeneous coordinates) and 3 further degrees of freedom are added. These transformations are very rarely used for mapping 3D datasets to each other, but perspective projections are key to mapping 3D data onto 2D images, for example when aligning a 3D preoperative model to video or X-ray images. As a final observation note that, as we move to more general transformations, the more specific transformations are specialized subsets within these, i.e. perspective transformations include all affine transformations, which include all similarity transformations, which include all rigid body transformations.

11.4.1.5 Non-rigid Transformations

When moving into the realm of non-linear or non-rigid transformations there are a huge number of possibilities to choose from. It is also possible to use global polynomials, piecewise linear transformations over triangulations, or piecewise polynomials. Desirable functions for a non-linear mapping are that it is one-to-one, continuous (at least C1 and preferably in higher dimensions). When matching anatomical shapes, one of the earliest examples was the thin-plate spline [13], which is a radial basis function technique that can interpolate between given landmark points. It is highly dependent on the location and accuracy of the landmarks and is therefore very much a point-based technique.

As a more general scheme for describing non-linear transformations, the freeform deformation has proved very successful in medical imaging [71]. Here, the transformation is described by a cubic B-spline surface controlled by the position of a regular grid of node points. The cubic B-spline interpolation function is designed to approximate a Gaussian and has the following four basis functions:

$$B_0(u) = (1 - u)^3 / 6$$
$$B_1(u) = \left(3u^3 - 6u^2 + 4\right)/6$$
$$B_2(u) = \left(-3u^3 + 3u^2 + 3u + 1\right)/6$$
$$B_3(u) = u^3/6.$$

Given a uniform grid of control points $\phi_{i,j,k}$, we can produce a free form deformation of space using a local transformation:

$$T_{local}(x, y, z) = \sum_{l=0}^{3}\sum_{m=0}^{3}\sum_{n=0}^{3} B_l(u) B_m(v) B_n(w) \phi_{i+l, j+m, k+n} \qquad (11.10)$$

where i, j, k is the index of the node preceding x, y, z and u, v, w represents the fraction of the grid beyond the point that the position x, y, z is located. The free form deformation can interpolate the whole of the domain smoothly and has some nice properties. It is locally controlled, which means that the movement of a control point only affects the local region. This makes it more computationally efficient than methods such as the thin-plate spline, where motion of a single landmark affects the whole of the domain. The complexity of the free form deformation can be controlled by setting the control point spacing.

11.4.2 Points and Features Used for the Registration

Having chosen an appropriate transformation for our problem, the next step is to decide what type of features should be used to calculate the registration. There will, in general, be some sort of corresponding anatomical points or regions. These can be categorized by their dimension.

11.4.2.1 Landmark Features

The simplest feature to consider is the landmark, where landmarks are well-defined points in 3D space within the 3D images to be registered. If *corresponding* landmarks can be found in the two images, these can form the basis of the registration. Landmarks may be anatomical features, such as the centers of the eyes, bony protrusions, or crossing points of vessels. Alternatively, there may be markers attached to the patient for the purposes of registration. It is common for these landmarks to be called *fiducial points* or, more succinctly, *fiducials*.

The points to be aligned are represented by two corresponding landmark sets, $\{\mathbf{x}_i\}, \{\mathbf{y}_i\}$. Given one of the above spatial transforms, T, the standard similarity function is the target registration error, *TRE*, and we wish to find an instance of the selected class of transformations, such that this error is minimized:

$$TRE^* = \min_{\mathsf{T}} \sum_i \|\mathsf{T}\mathbf{x}_i - \mathbf{y}_i\|^2. \qquad (11.11)$$

The squared norm can be replaced by more general functions. Note that we assume that landmarks are already matched, in general this might require either manual intervention, or algorithmic search.

11.4.2.2 Surface-Based Registration

Rather than using 3D points, one could imagine a registration based on linear features, such as blood vessels or ridges on the surface of an object. In practice, such registrations are rare and it is more common to use surfaces. This approach was first proposed for medical imaging by Pelizzari et al. [61] as the *head and hat* algorithm. This led to a number of techniques to register 3D images using distance maps, or chamfer maps, which are images showing the distance to a given surface. These techniques have been very much taken over by intensity-based registration for fully 3D volumes, but there is still a place for surface matching in image-guided surgery, which we will discuss later, and in situations where an accurate segmentation of two images has been created. The surface may be a polygonal surface or a set of surface points, but typically the preoperative surface will be triangulated and intraoperative measurements will be points. A surface-based similarity measure can be generated as the sum-of-squared distance from the surface points to the nearest points on the triangulated surface.

11.4.2.3 Intensity-Based Registration

One of the most successful methods in medical image registration in the last few decades has been the use of intensity-based similarity measures. Given that we have a transformation T from image $I_A(\mathbf{x})$ to image $I_B(\mathbf{y})$, we are able to calculate corresponding voxel intensities. For a given voxel at position $\mathbf{x}$ in image $I_A(\mathbf{x})$ the corresponding point in image I_B will be $I_B(\mathsf{T}(\mathbf{x}))$. We can now start to calculate some image statistics in the region of the overlap, Ω, between the two images.

For example, if we are trying to register images from the same modality and patient, we could assume that corresponding voxels will have the same intensity. This means that, at registration, all voxels should be equal and we can minimize a cost function, C_{SSD}, to give:

$$C^\star_{SSD}(\mathsf{T}) = \min_{\mathsf{T}} \frac{1}{N} \sum_{\mathbf{x} \in \Omega} |I_A(\mathbf{x}) - I_B(\mathsf{T}(\mathbf{x}))|^2 \qquad (11.12)$$

where N is the number of voxels in the overlap. This is simply the mean sum of squared differences of intensities between the images. Thus, by minimizing $C_{SSD}(\mathsf{T})$ over the parameters of our transformation, T, we can achieve registration without needing to extract landmarks.

If we know the voxel intensities of the two images are an increasing function of each other, but we can't be sure that they have the same intensities, then perhaps cross-correlation would be a more appropriate measure. When the relationship between intensities in the two images is not known we can use information theoretic measures to provide a similarity measure. We start by producing a 2D histogram. For each corresponding pixel we have an intensity I_A and an intensity I_B. These form a point on a graph of intensity in image type A (CT, say) vs image type B (MRI,

11 3D Medical Imaging

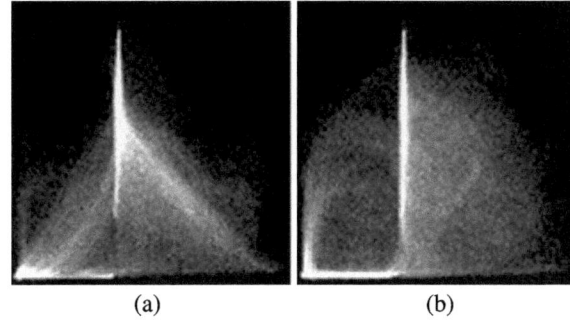

Fig. 11.11 MR vs CT joint histogram—at registration (**a**) and misregistered (**b**). The bright vertical line corresponds to soft tissue (large variation in MR, little in CT)

say). By choosing appropriately sized bins, we can form a probability distribution $p(A, B)$, which is described by the joint histogram (see Fig. 11.11).

Mutual information (MI) can now be calculated as:

$$MI(A, B) = \sum_A \sum_B p(A, B) \log\left(\frac{p(A, B)}{p(A)p(B)}\right) \quad (11.13)$$

where $p(A, B)$ is the probability of a pixel having intensity A in the first image and intensity B in the second image and $p(A)$, $p(B)$ are the marginal probabilities that a pixel has a given value in each separate image. In practical applications MI, and a normalized version (NMI) [75], have proven to be highly robust as a means of registering 3D medical images for rigid and non-rigid applications.

11.4.3 Registration Optimization

There are many optimization strategies that can be employed to calculate the registration. In general, we will have a cost function that can be calculated over the degrees of freedom of the transformation. In the case of point-based rigid registration, there is an analytic solution that can be solved either by singular value decomposition (SVD) or by quaternion methods [28]. The general problem of calculating a rotation given a set of corresponding points is known as the Procrustes problem. This rather disingenuous term refers to a character from Greek mythology, who would stretch or cut the limbs of his guest to make them fit the bed. This originally referred data being fitted to a model when there was no real relationship but the term is still used to refer to the respectable problem of shape alignment.

For surface matching, there is the simple algorithm known as iterative closest points (ICP) [10]. Here, we have a set of points $\mathbf{x}_i$ on one surface and we find the closest points $\mathbf{y}_i^0$ on the other surface. The next step in the algorithm is a standard rigid registration on the two point sets. After this, a new set of nearest points $\mathbf{y}_i^1$ is calculated and a new transformation calculated. After each iteration of this two-stage cycle, the error between the data sets is reduced and will rapidly converge to a local minimum, which may or may not be a global minimum. The method requires computation of nearest points on a surface, which can be made much more efficient using data structures such as k-d trees [8]. It should be mentioned that surface registrations such as this are very prone to multiple local minima (i.e. that are not globally minimal). Thus, depending on the starting alignment, the algorithm may get stuck an undesired local minimum. A combination of landmark and surface registration may be better behaved in terms of this problem. ICP and other methods of surface registration are discussed in more detail in Chap. 6.

For any type of non-linear transformation and for rigid or non-rigid intensity-based registration, the solution must be calculated iteratively. A hierarchical coarse-to-fine approach aids smoothness and convergence. A technique known as Parzen windowing can be used to estimate gradients in the cost function [79]. There are potentially a large number of parameters to optimize with intensity-based non-rigid registration (three times the number of control points) and registrations can take several hours. Various implementations incorporating GPU calculations have been proposed to speed up this process and efficient intensity-based non-rigid registration is the subject of ongoing research.

11.4.3.1 Estimation of Registration Errors

In all cases of registration, it is important to consider the problem of error estimation. Again, for the simple case of isotropic errors in point-based registration, an analytic solution is given by Fitzpatrick [28]. This relates the expected squared value of target registration error, $\langle TRE^2(\mathbf{r})\rangle$, (at some target point, $\mathbf{r}$, other than the fiducials used to register) to the expected squared value of the fiducial localization error, $\langle FLE^2\rangle$, (the error at which individual fiducials are localized) as follows:

$$\langle TRE^2(\mathbf{r})\rangle \approx \frac{\langle FLE^2\rangle}{N}\left(1+\frac{1}{3}\sum_{k=1}^{3}\frac{d_k^2}{f_k^2}\right), \quad (11.14)$$

where N is the number of fiducials, d_k is the distance from the target point to the kth principal axis of the fiducials, and f_k is the RMS distance of the fiducials to the same axis. The second term in brackets is similar to a moment-of-inertia. The centroid is the most accurately located point and rotational errors mean that TRE increases further away from the principal axes. This equation tells us that not only an increase in the number of fiducials improves the registration error, but also their spread with respect to the principal axes. Any configuration of points that approaches being on a line can lead to significant rotational errors away from the fiducials even if the residual error is low.

For higher dimensional data, such as surfaces, there is no analytic solution for the errors. Experience tells us that surface registration can be unreliable and should not be used alone without some validation or involvement of landmark data. In particular, surface registration is likely to fail if the surface shape has any rotational or translational symmetry or where there is non-rigid tissue motion. Intensity-based registrations have been used for many years and are found to be highly robust.

11 3D Medical Imaging

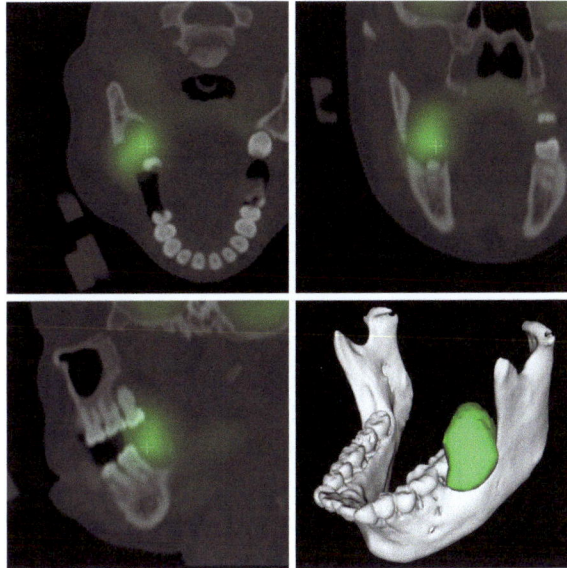

Fig. 11.12 A CT image registered to a PET scan showing cancer of the mouth. Three orthogonal cuts through the dataset are shown along with a 3D rendering (*bottom right*). The PET scan (*green*) shows the presence of cancer whereas the CT scan shows the surrounding bone. The anatomical location of the lesion in the mandible is much clearer from the registered image than from either CT scan or PET scan alone

11.4.4 Summary

We have described the methods of registration with respect to 3D medical images. There are three considerations of any registration algorithm: the form of the aligning transformation, the similarity measure and the optimization strategy. One of the big challenges in medical imaging is that the object of interest, the human body, is composed of rigid parts, tissues which have complex mechanical properties (visco-elastic), and fluids. The section on data acquisition showed that there is no single modality which can account for all phenomena, thus registration is an essential tool, but one of its main challenges is the non-rigidity of soft tissue, which induces non-unicity. As such, non-rigid registration remains an important research topic. Figure 11.12 shows an example registration of CT and PET. CT is able to show the bony anatomy well, whereas PET shows the metabolising function of the cancerous tumour. PET is inherently lower resolution but, by registration, we are better able to see the relationship between anatomy and disease.

11.5 Segmentation

The term *segmentation* refers to the process of identifying or delineating a structure of interest, typically for the purpose of some further processing. For example, in medical imaging, a segmentation of the heart might be required for quantitative measurements of blood flow or electrical activation [72]; in image-guided interventions, segmentations are often required for visualization in surgical planning or guidance [63]. Segmentation techniques have been applied to delineate a wide variety of organs from medical imaging data acquired using a wide range of modalities.

Approaches to segmentation vary a lot in terms of their sophistication and the amount of user input required. Purely manual techniques allow users to outline structures using software such as the ANALYZE[1] package. Manual segmentation can be very accurate, but time-consuming, and is subject to inter-observer variation or bias. Semi-automatic techniques allow the user to have some control or input into the segmentation process, combined with automatic processing using computer algorithms. Finally, fully automatic techniques require no user input and often make use of some prior knowledge to produce the segmentation. The following sections review a number of semi-automatic and fully automatic approaches to medical image segmentation. Our coverage of this huge research area is not exhaustive, but we provide a few examples that give an introduction to the field.

11.5.1 Semi-automatic Methods

In this section, we consider three semi-automatic approaches to segmentation based on thresholding, region growing and deformable models.

11.5.1.1 Thresholding

Perhaps the simplest example of user interaction in segmentation is the specification of a *threshold*. Typically, a thresholding operation involves comparing every intensity in the image to the threshold value and setting it to 1 if it is greater than or equal to the threshold, or 0 otherwise, thereby creating a binary image. Figure 11.13 illustrates this operation on cardiac MRI data. Software such as ITK-SNAP can be used to interactively adjust the threshold to produce the desired result. Thresholding is commonly applied as one step in a segmentation pipeline, but the presence of noise, image artifacts and other structures in the image mean that it is rarely enough on its own to produce an accurate and reliable segmentation. This fact can be observed in Fig. 11.13b, in which several pixels outside of the left and right ventricles are set to 1, despite not being the target structures of the segmentation.

---

[1]Biomedical Imaging Resource, Mayo Foundation, Rochester, MN, USA or ITK-SNAP [84], http://www.itksnap.org.

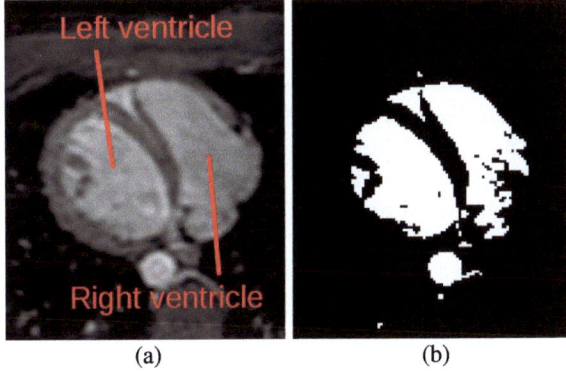

Fig. 11.13 Thresholding an axial cardiac MRI slice. (**a**) Original slice. (**b**) Result of thresholding operation

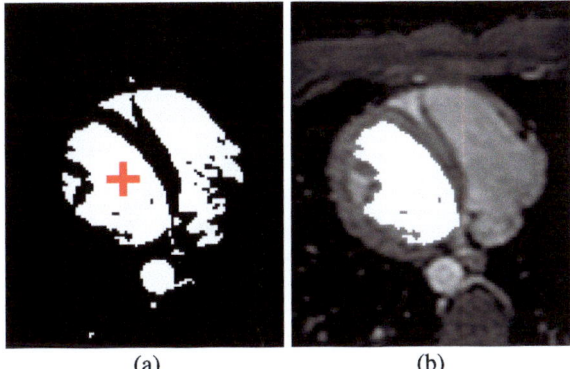

Fig. 11.14 Segmenting the left ventricle using region growing on the thresholded axial cardiac MR slice. (**a**) Thresholded image with seed point in the left ventricle indicated by the *red cross*. (**b**) Result of region growing, overlaid onto original cardiac MRI slice

11.5.1.2 Region Growing

One technique that can be used to refine thresholded images, such as that shown in Fig. 11.13b, is known as *region growing*. Region growing involves user interaction in the form of specifying a *seed point*. This is a pixel in the image that is known to lie inside the structure being segmented. The region is then iteratively grown by adding neighboring pixels that have similar appearance. The concept of similarity needs to be defined: for example, by specifying a range of intensity values around that of the seed pixel. If region growing is applied to a thresholded image then, to be considered similar, pixels should have the same binary value as the seed pixels. In addition, the concept of neighborhood needs to be defined, with 4-neighborhoods (i.e. only directly adjacent pixels) and 8-neighborhoods (i.e. including diagonally adjacent) commonly used in 2D images. Figure 11.14 illustrates the operation of the region growing algorithm for segmenting the left ventricle from the cardiac MRI data introduced in Fig. 11.13. A seed point has been placed in the left ventricle (indicated by the red cross) and the region growing algorithm has included all pixels that were connected to this seed, excluding all others. The resulting segmentation is of the left ventricle only.

Algorithm 11.1 REGION GROW on seed pixel

Require: Initialize all pixels to unknown region
  Set current pixel to be inside region
  for all neighboring pixels **do**
    if it is inside image bounds and currently has an unknown region **then**
      Compute similarity to current pixel
      if similar **then**
        REGION GROW on neighboring pixel
      else
        Set neighboring pixel to background
      end if
    end if
  end for

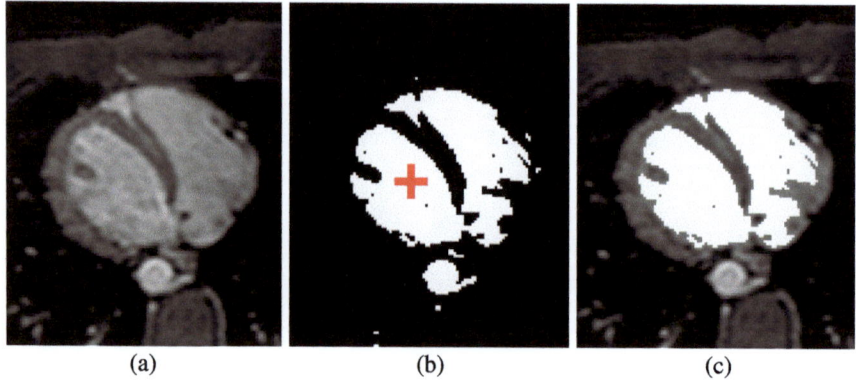

Fig. 11.15 The problem of leaks in region growing. (**a**) An axial cardiac MRI slice. (**b**) Result of thresholding operation, seed point for region growing in the left ventricle indicated by the *red cross*. (**c**) Result of region growing. The segmentation has 'leaked' into the right ventricle

The region growing algorithm can be implemented in a number of ways. The simplest, although not the most computationally efficient, is a recursive implementation. There are many implementations and this is the same problem as flood-fill or area-fill in graphics or vision. Pseudocode for recursive region growing is given in Algorithm 11.1.

One problem that the region growing algorithm can encounter is that of *leaks*. This problem is illustrated in Fig. 11.15. This shows a different axial cardiac MRI slice from that used in Fig. 11.13 and Fig. 11.14. This time the region growing has 'leaked' the segmentation into the right ventricle. Therefore, in region growing, care must be taken when selecting threshold values and specifying the similarity term to avoid such cases. The region growing algorithm can be extended to 3D, in which case the neighborhood in Algorithm 11.1 will extend to 3D accordingly. However, in 3D the problem of leaks can be exacerbated.

11.5.1.3 Deformable Models

Both thresholding and region growing are relatively straightforward techniques that can be important steps in a segmentation pipeline. However, they work only using the intensities in the image and impose no constraints on the shape of the resulting segmented object. A more sophisticated class of techniques that do incorporate such constraints is known as *deformable models* [53]. Deformable models are contours (in 2D) or surfaces (in 3D) that move and deform according to an energy term. The energy term comprises two components:

- an *internal* energy, which typically constrains the contour/surface to remain approximately smooth with no sharp discontinuities, and
- an *external* energy, which pulls the contour/surface towards certain features in the image data, such as strong gradients.

The segmentation problem then becomes one of optimizing the parameters of the contour/surface to minimize the energy.

Deformable models come in many different forms, but they can be broadly split into two types: *parametric deformable models* and *geometric deformable models*. In parametric deformable models the contour/surface is *explicitly* parameterized, for example by specifying a set of control points between which a contour is interpolated. We describe in more detail two of the more popular parametric techniques below. In geometric deformable models, the contour/surface is defined *implicitly*. An example of such an approach is the 'level set' technique [33, 50], in which a 2D contour is defined as the zero-crossing of a signed 2D function. In this case, it is the function that is parameterized and the contour is encoded implicitly in this parameterization. Examples of the use of level sets in medical imaging include segmentation of brain images from MRI [2], segmentation of the left ventricle of the heart from MRI and ultrasound [60] and segmentation of the cerebral vasculature from CT angiography [51].

Snakes One of the most famous examples of a parametric deformable model is known as *Active Contour Models* or *Snakes* [40]. In the Snakes algorithm, the user initially defines an approximate contour for the object being segmented. The algorithm refines this contour by minimizing the energy term. Formally, if a 2D contour is defined by $\mathbf{v}(s) = [x(s), y(s)]$ with s varying between 0 and 1, the energy is defined as:

$$E_{snake} = \int_0^1 E_{int}(v(s)) + E_{ext}(v(s)) \, ds. \qquad (11.15)$$

The internal and external energy terms E_{int} and E_{ext} must be defined to suit the particular application. For example, how does the object appear in the image data? If the object's boundary is defined by a strong gradient in the image then E_{ext} should be high in cases where the Snake does not overlay such gradients. Similarly, E_{int} will be high for contours which have sharp changes in direction and low for smooth contours. Once these terms have been defined, an optimization strategy such as gradient descent is employed to iteratively adjust the contour definition to minimize the

Algorithm 11.2 SNAKES

Require: Initialize contour parameters
$i = 0$
Compute energy at iteration 0: $E_{snake,0}$
repeat
    Compute gradient of energy term $E_{snake,i}$
    Modify contour parameters to minimize energy
    $i = i + 1$
until $E_{snake,i} - E_{snake,i-1} < \varepsilon$ or maximum iterations reached

energy, E_{snake}. Fast implementations of the Snakes algorithm have been proposed that have a computational complexity of $O(nm)$, where n is the number of control points and m is the size of the neighborhood in which the points can move [82].

There are several variants of the Snakes algorithm and the precise implementation details will depend on the choice of optimization strategy and the nature of the contour parameterization. However, pseudocode for a generic version of Snakes is given in Algorithm 11.2. In general, snakes work well where there are clearly defined edges in the image and the shape of the object is reasonably smooth, since sharp edges will be smoothed out by the snake's internal energy, which resists high curvature. Finally, they can be interactively manipulated towards the edge of choice in semi-automatic applications. Examples of the use of Snakes for 2D medical image segmentation include segmentation of intra-vascular US [85] and annotation of specular masses from mammography images [56].

Balloons The original work on Snakes was designed for 2D image segmentation. A similar concept can be extended to 3D images. The *3D balloons* technique [19] is one such example. This algorithm is illustrated in Fig. 11.16, which shows a 3D segmentation of the left ventricle from an MRI image, implemented in ITK-SNAP (the 3D MRI image is the same image that the 2D slices in Figs. 11.13, 11.14 and 11.15 were extracted from). This shows how the internal energy term of the 3D balloons algorithm can constrain the shape of the segmented object to avoid the problem of leaks that we saw in Fig. 11.15. Each screenshot shows the current segmentation in red overlaid onto sagittal (top left), coronal (top right) and axial (bottom right) views through the MRI image, together with a rendering of the current segmentation (bottom left). The axial slice shown is the same slice used in Fig. 11.15, although the 3D segmentation operated on all slices in the MRI volume. The user initializes the segmentation by placing a 'balloon' (a spherical surface) inside the structure to be segmented, as shown in Fig. 11.16a. The algorithm then iteratively 'inflates' the balloon (see Fig. 11.16b, c) until it is stopped by forces based on the image data (see Fig. 11.16d). In the example in Fig. 11.16 the inflation of the balloon is stopped by the intensity gradient where the bright intensities of the left ventricle are next to the darker intensities of the surrounding myocardium. This iterative optimization works in a similar way to the original 2D Snakes technique. 3D balloons have been used for cardiac segmentation from US data [42] and cerebral cortex segmentation from MRI images [83].

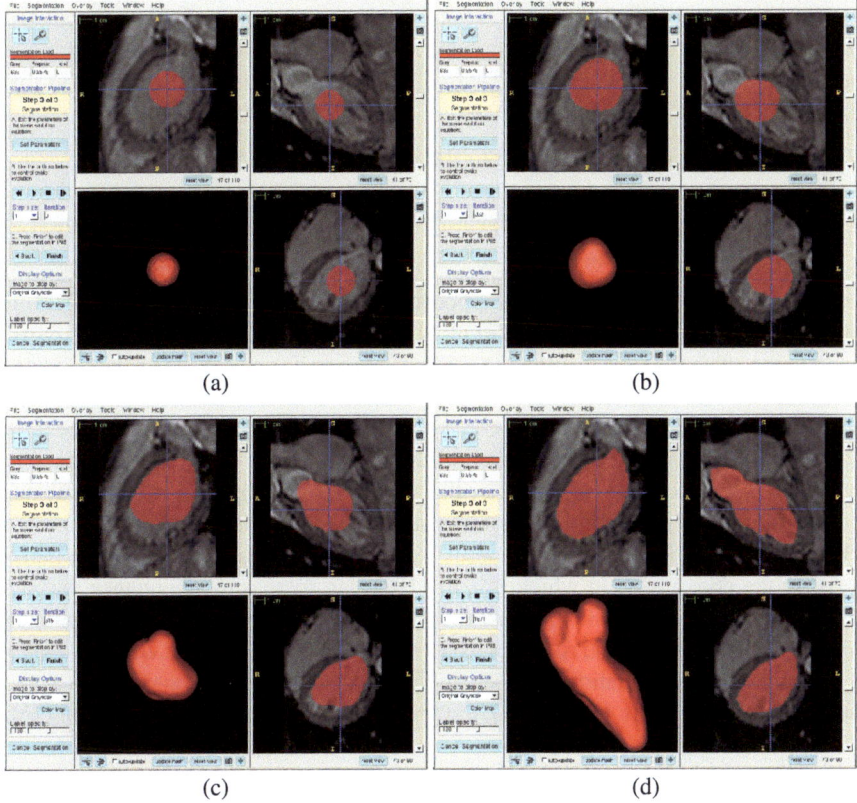

Fig. 11.16 Segmenting the left ventricle from MRI using the 3D balloons technique implemented in ITK-SNAP. (**a**) Initial balloon placement. (**b**), (**c**) Intermediate stages. (**c**) Final segmentation. Each image contains 4 panels: sagittal slice (*top left*), coronal slice (*top right*), axial slice (*bottom right*) and rendering of segmented surface (*bottom left*). The segmentation took approximately 5 seconds to complete

11.5.2 Fully Automatic Methods

Development of robust, fully automatic segmentation techniques has proved a challenging task and has been an active research topic for many years now. A common approach is to introduce some prior knowledge of the likely shape of the object being segmented. There are many different ways of introducing such knowledge. Here we discuss two of the most common ways, which introduce prior knowledge in slightly different ways.

11.5.2.1 Atlas-Based Segmentation

Atlas-based segmentation techniques introduce prior knowledge in the form of an *atlas*. Here, an atlas refers to a sample intensity image of the region of interest together with a corresponding segmentation. The segmentation need only be produced once, so a time-consuming (but accurate) manual or semi-automatic approach can be used. The basic approach of atlas-based segmentation can be summarized as follows:

- register the atlas intensity image to the subject image that we want to segment, then
- use the motion fields from the registration to propagate the atlas segmentation to the subject image.

An example for the purpose of hippocampus segmentation from brain MRI images was described by Carmichael et al. [17]. The atlas intensity image was registered to the subject image resulting in a geometric transformation. The atlas segmentation then underwent the same geometric transformation to produce the subject's segmentation estimate.

Due to the sometimes large variation in anatomy, there may be some cases in which the registration phase fails. For this reason a more sophisticated scheme has been proposed using multiple atlas intensity images and segmentations. These are known as *multi-atlases* [68]. With multi-atlases, a new subject image can be registered to the atlas image to which it is most similar, increasing the chance that the registration will be successful. Alternatively, a database of images can be combined to form a single average atlas image [67] or a probabilistic atlas [22, 49].

Atlas-based segmentation has been applied to many different organs, such as the heart [49, 86], the brain [17, 18, 22], the prostate [41] and the liver and spleen [46].

11.5.2.2 Statistical Shape Modeling and Analysis

Another way to introduce prior knowledge into an automatic segmentation technique is to use a *statistical shape model* (SSM). SSMs explicitly capture the likely shape and variation in shape across a population. They have also been known as active shape models or point distribution models [21].

Based on a set of instances of a shape (the training set), SSMs use principal component analysis to compute a mean shape and its principal *modes of variation*. In medicine, the training set is typically derived from medical imaging data such as CT or MRI images.

The construction of a SSM involves a number of distinct steps. First, the n instances in the training set must be aligned to a common coordinate system. This can be done using image registration techniques. Next, for each shape instance we define a 1D *shape vector*, which we denote by **x**, where:

$$\mathbf{x} = [x_1 \ldots x_k]^T. \tag{11.16}$$

This vector represents a parameterization of the shape. Common parameterizations used for SSMs include surface landmark coordinates [21] or interior control points [70]. Whatever the parameterization used, the values must be extracted from the training images, either manually or automatically.

11 3D Medical Imaging

Next, we form a mean shape by taking the mean of all n shape vectors,

$$\bar{\mathbf{x}} = \frac{1}{n} \sum_{i=1}^{n} \mathbf{x}_i. \tag{11.17}$$

From the mean shape and the training set of shape vectors, we compute the covariance matrix, S,

$$S = \frac{1}{n} \sum_{i=1}^{n} [\mathbf{x}_i - \bar{\mathbf{x}}][\mathbf{x}_i - \bar{\mathbf{x}}]^T. \tag{11.18}$$

The covariance matrix contains information about how the different parameters of the shape vectors vary with each other (or *co-vary*) away from their mean values. The eigenvectors of this covariance matrix summarize the major *modes of variation* of the shape vectors. Therefore, next we compute the non-zero eigenvalues of S and their corresponding eigenvectors. These, along with the mean shape, define the SSM. We denote the eigenvectors by ϕ_i and the eigenvalues by λ_i. The eigenvectors will be 1D vectors of the same length as the shape vectors. Intuitively, they represent the ways in which the shape parameters (e.g. surface landmarks) change together. Each eigenvector defines a particular change in the value of all shape parameters, e.g. a direction of variation for all surface landmarks. The larger the eigenvalue, λ_i, the more of the total variation of the shape population that the corresponding eigenvector represents. If there are n samples in the training set and the eigenmodes are sorted from largest to smallest eigenvalue, then the cumulative variance for the first m modes is given by $\sum_{i=1}^{m} \lambda_i / \sum_{i=1}^{n} \lambda_i$. If there are n samples, then the covariance matrix has rank $n - 1$ and only the first $n - 1$ eigenvalues will be non-zero.

Finally, we can compute a new shape instance from the SSM by defining a set of weights, b_i, for the eigenvectors. For example, using the largest m eigenvalues, a new shape instance $\hat{\mathbf{x}}$ is produced as follows,

$$\hat{\mathbf{x}} = \bar{\mathbf{x}} + \sum_{i=1}^{m} b_i \phi_i. \tag{11.19}$$

It is common to choose the value of m so that the eigenvectors used account for a certain percentage of the total variation (e.g. 95 %) in the shape population. Since the eigenvalues represent the variance of the data in the direction of the corresponding eigenvector, they can be used to compute the proportion of the total variance that the eigenvectors represent. Also, when specifying values for the weights, it is common to restrict their range of values so that $-3\sqrt{\lambda_i} \leq b_i \leq +3\sqrt{\lambda_i}$, i.e. they cover about 99.7 % of the variation in each mode.

Figure 11.17 shows an illustration of a SSM of the femur. The left column shows two femur surfaces generated by varying only the weight for the most significant mode of variation, i.e. b_1 in Eq. (11.19), between $-3\sqrt{\lambda_1}$ and $+3\sqrt{\lambda_1}$. The middle and right columns show femur surfaces generated from the second and third most significant modes respectively.

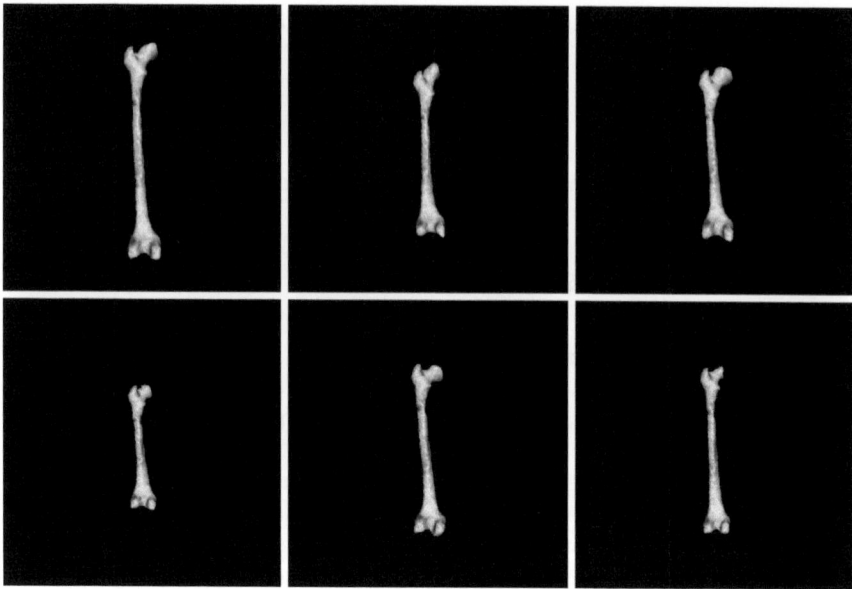

Fig. 11.17 An illustration of the largest three modes of variation of a SSM of the femur ($+3\sigma$ on *top row* and -3σ on the *bottom* for modes 1–3 (left to right). The first mode largely corresponds to size, whereas the second mode is dominated by the angle of the femoral head

SSMs can be applied to the problem of segmentation by using them to constrain a registration between the shape vector and a subject image of the organ. A similarity measure between the shape vector and the subject image is defined, typically based upon image intensities [15, 29] or gradients [24], or features extracted from the images [48, 78]. The SSM weights are typically optimized to produce a shape vector that maximizes this similarity measure.

SSMs have been applied to segmentation in a wide range of anatomy. For example, Fripp et al. [29] used SSMs to segment knee bones from MRI images, Tao et al. [78] used them for segmentation of sulcal curves from MRI images of the brain and de Bruijne et al. [14, 15] for segmenting abdominal aortic aneurysms from CT data. In addition, whole heart segmentation has been demonstrated from CT [24, 48], MRI [62] and rotational X-ray images [52].

Figure 11.18 illustrates a sample whole heart segmentation from CT produced using the SSM-based algorithm described in [24]. The segmentation is visualized using ITK-SNAP and shows three orthogonal views through the CT volume (top-left, top-right and bottom-right panels), overlaid with color-coded segmentations of the four chambers and major vessels of the heart. The bottom-left panel shows a 3D rendering of the segmented surfaces from an anterior-posterior view. A good review on the use of SSMs for 3D medical image segmentation can be found in [34].

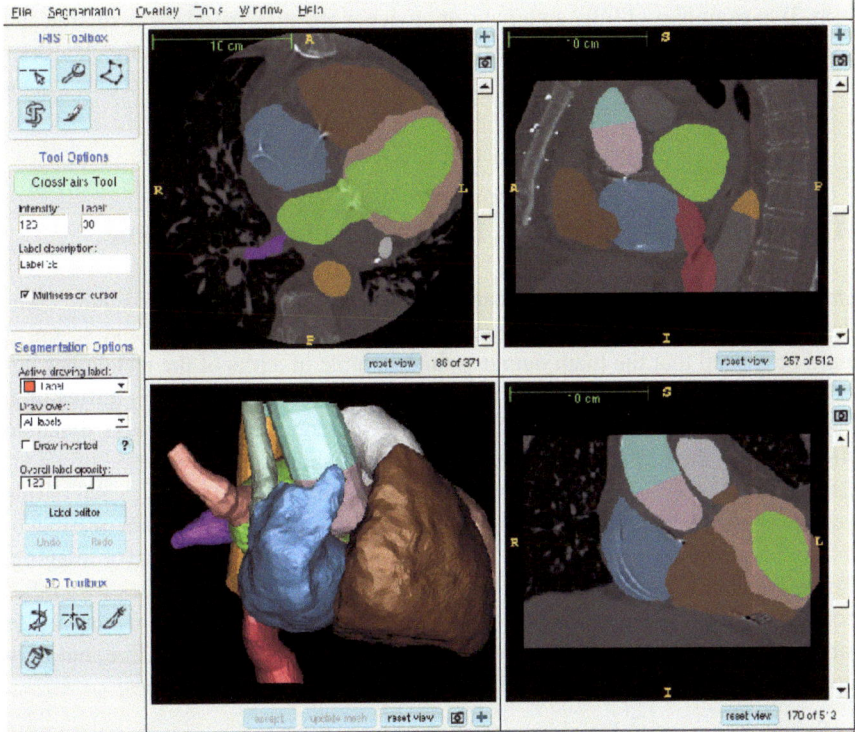

Fig. 11.18 Statistical shape model based whole heart segmentation from CT [24], visualized using ITK-SNAP. *Top left*, *top right*, *bottom right panels*: three orthogonal slices through the CT volume. *Bottom left panel*: surface rendering of segmentation. The four chambers and major vessels of the heart are rendered in different colors: *green* indicates left ventricle; *light brown* indicates left ventricular myocardium; *dark brown* indicates right ventricle; *blue* indicates right atrium; *pink* indicates left atrium

11.5.3 Summary

Segmentation is the process of delineating structures of interest from images. This is an important task in medical imaging as it forms a preprocessing step for many operations, such as making quantitative measurements to monitor disease progression. Segmentation can be performed manually, semi-automatically or fully automatically. Manual segmentation can be accurate but time-consuming and prone to observer error or bias. Deformable models can be used for semi-automatic segmentation and one of the most well-known examples is the 2D Snakes algorithm, with Balloons being the analogous process in 3D. In fact, if algorithms for automatic placement of the initial contour/surface are available, deformable model based approaches can sometimes be close to fully automatic. Such algorithms would probably involve some sort of prior knowledge of the anatomy being segmented and, in general, fully automatic approaches make use of such prior knowledge in some form. Two examples of fully automatic approaches are atlas-based segmentation and statistical shape models. No automatic methods are perfect, but given the laborious nature of manual segmentation and the pressures on clinicians' time, segmentation is a very active research field.

11.6 Diffusion Imaging: An Illustration of a Full Pipeline

Although the physics of the 3D imaging modalities can be considered quite complex, involving different wavelengths, different fields, radioactivity and so on, it could be argued that the main output is fairly simple in terms of the techniques described in this chapter. Essentially, we get grayscale images. But this is misleading, medical imaging can also provide dynamic frame images from ultrasound, dynamic MRI or CT of the heart, contrast enhanced images showing the evolution of a contrast agent (MRI, CT, PET), flow images, and even tensor matrix images. All of this requires sophisticated post-processing and data analysis. Clearly, it is not possible to describe every technique, rather, in this section, we concentrate on tensor imaging. This relates to the most complex objects (tensors) and illustrates issues with other techniques, thus we use it as a case study of data processing in medical imaging. In particular, we use this to illustrate that nice images do not come for free, but only after processing steps that all require care. Specifically, we see the steps:

1. From raw images to the object which is a tensor field; this requires spatial alignment of different images, the input is a set of scalar images; the output consists of tensor images;
2. Data processing from the tensor field to a field of glyphs: input is a tensor image; the output is a visualization (glyphs), or vector images (showing principal direction of diffusion);
3. Information extraction from the glyph shapes, first pointwise: the input is a tensor image; the output consists of different quantitative scalar images;
4. We can also extract global information by connectivity: the input is a vector image, the output consists of a collection of 3D streamlines.

Processing requires different steps mentioned in previous sections, such as segmentation to delineate white matter, smoothing and thresholding to stop lines with unrealistic shapes and so on.

11.6.1 From Scalar Images to Tensors

This entire chapter tries to convey the message that the underlying physics of imaging cannot be ignored. Understanding where the images come from, and why they look like how they do is important. In some cases one might waste months of work trying to perform an imaging operation that would have just required a radiographer

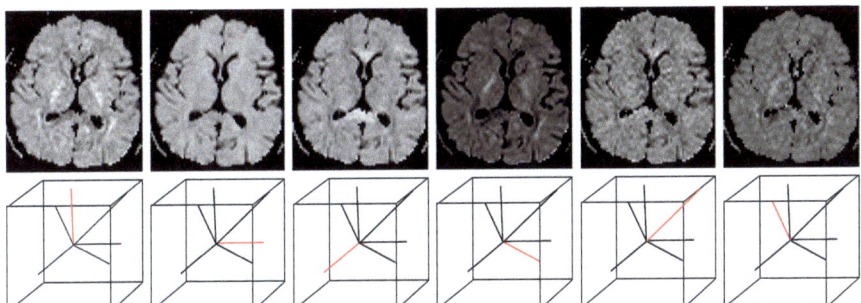

Fig. 11.19 Diffusion weighted images with corresponding gradient directions below. Note that differences are subtle—for each gradient direction (*red line* in lower row), the image has darker voxels when it contains structures forcing diffusion in that direction. For this reason, such images are rarely used directly, but replaced by the FA, MD, etc. below, which are orientation independent

to change scan settings or inject a different contrast agent. In diffusion MRI, we can and do manipulate magnetic field gradients in different directions, **g**. As a second order diffusion tensor can be represented by a symmetric 3 × 3 matrix, it contains six independent components. Thus, provided we have a model of the physics of how these gradients affect images, we should be able to reconstruct the matrix. The images in Fig. 11.19 show the diffusion weighted images corresponding to the gradient directions below.

One model, the default for diffusion imaging, is that each of these 6 images obeys the equation $S(g) = S_0 \exp(-bg^t Dg)$ where $\mathbf{g} = [x, y, z]^T$ is a unit vector in the gradient direction, the scalar b comprises several acquisition parameters, such as gradient strength and duration, and D is the unknown tensor matrix with unknowns $[D_{xx}, D_{yy}, D_{zz}, D_{xy}, D_{xz}, D_{yz}]$. A more compact way to describe them is via a matrix, or *tensor* **D**, which is a table of numbers called diffusion coefficients:

$$\mathbf{D} = \begin{bmatrix} D_{xx} & D_{xy} & D_{xz} \\ D_{yx} & D_{yy} & D_{yz} \\ D_{zx} & D_{zy} & D_{zz} \end{bmatrix}$$

Thus, we have the equations

$$s(\mathbf{G}_1) = s_0 e^{-b\mathbf{G}_1^t \mathbf{D}\mathbf{G}_1} \rightarrow -\frac{1}{b} \log \frac{s(\mathbf{G}_1)}{s_0} = \mathbf{G}_1^t \mathbf{D}\mathbf{G}_1$$

$$= \begin{bmatrix} x_1^2 & y_1^2 & z_1^2 & 2x_1y_1 & 2x_1z_1 & 2y_1z_1 \end{bmatrix}$$

$$\times \begin{bmatrix} D_{xx} & D_{yy} & D_{zz} & D_{xy} & D_{xz} & D_{yz} \end{bmatrix}^t$$

$$s(\mathbf{G}_2) = s_0 e^{-b\mathbf{G}_2^t \mathbf{D}\mathbf{G}_2} \rightarrow -\frac{1}{b} \log \frac{s(\mathbf{G}_2)}{s_0} = \mathbf{G}_2^t \mathbf{D}\mathbf{G}_2$$

$$= \begin{bmatrix} x_2^2 & y_2^2 & z_2^2 & 2x_2y_2 & 2x_2z_2 & 2y_2z_2 \end{bmatrix}$$

$$\times \begin{bmatrix} D_{xx} & D_{yy} & D_{zz} & D_{xy} & D_{xz} & D_{yz} \end{bmatrix}^t$$

$$\vdots = \vdots$$

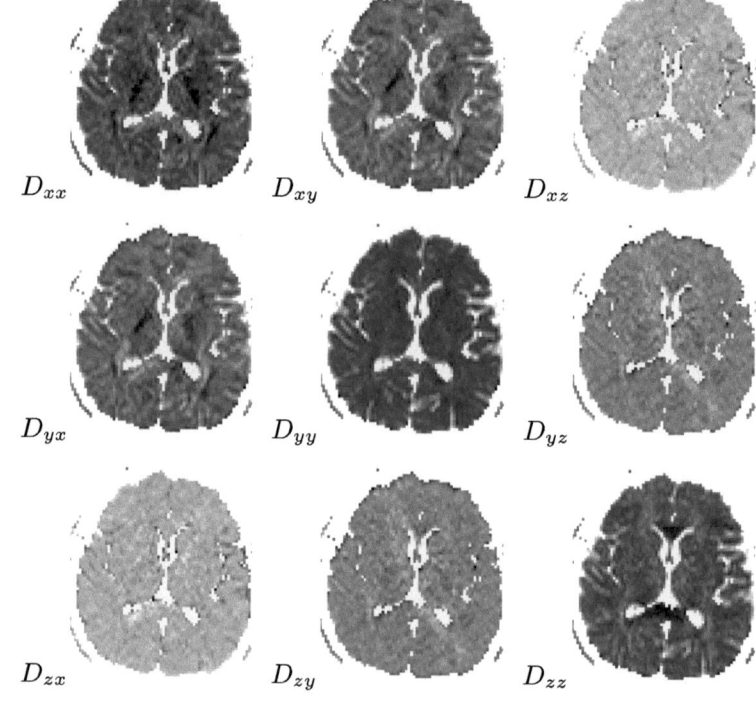

Fig. 11.20 Components of the diffusion tensor image. In other words, this is a matrix of images, or the image of a matrix (tensor). This provides very rich information, but MD shown in Fig. 11.21 and FA shown in Fig. 11.22 are easier to interpret directly, although they have lost information

By solving the equations using least squares, we can get *tensor images* as output, as shown in Fig. 11.20.

11.6.2 From Tensor Image to Information

Although, in theory, the diffusion tensor image in Fig. 11.20 contains all available information on diffusion, it is hard to interpret. For this reason, we construct images which display the information in a more intuitive way. The main tool for this is that the 3×3 diffusion tensor can be decomposed in *orientation* and *anisotropy* information. Shape information is encoded by three numbers describing the specific diffusivities in three orthogonal directions.

The *Mean Diffusivity* (MD) describes how 'strong' the diffusion is, or how unhindered, or how far in average water molecules diffuse. It is a mean, over all directions, and thus contains *no* directional information. To interpret it, higher MD, i.e. with a light to white contrast, correspond to regions where there are few barriers. For example, a region with higher MD than normal could describe a degradation of the

Fig. 11.21 An image of Mean Diffusivity (MD). *Bright areas* correspond to voxels containing water able to diffuse relatively freely. *Dark regions* contain more restricted water molecules

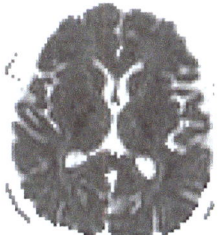

cellular structure. On the other hand, dark regions indicate that the water molecules find it harder to move around. Macroscopically it would be as if the medium has become more viscous, or microscopically cells could have swollen. In units, MD has the same units as the diffusion tensor, mm^2/s, see Fig. 11.21.

The *Fractional Anisotropy* (FA) measures, as its name suggests, how anisotropic the diffusion is. It is an index, thus has no units, and ranges between 0–1, where 0 indicates fully isotropic diffusion and 1 indicates that diffusion happens in a single direction. The definition of FA is the standard deviation of the specific diffusivities, suitably normalized. Typically, cerebro-spinal fluid (CSF) has a low FA as it is essentially a liquid, so should not have a preferred direction. FA is high in white matter, in particular in the *Corpus Callosum*, or in any fibre like structure such as muscle fibres. (See Fig. 11.22a.)

Both MD and FA indicate nothing about direction. A useful way to do this is to use colors. The three components in RGB are matched to spatial directions. Note the blue large balls in the 'smarties' picture above a FA region. They indicate strong diffusion, but not very directional. The smaller ellipsoids show that in regions where diffusion is directional it is also much smaller (see Fig. 11.22b).

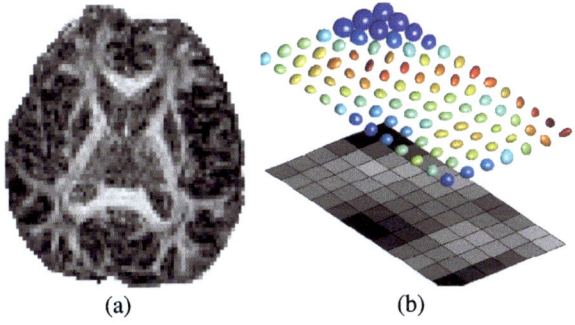

(a) (b)

Fig. 11.22 An image of Fractional Anisotropy (FA). *Bright regions* indicate high anisotropy; note that this information complements the MD, also note that ventricles, for example, contain fully isotropic voxels (*dark* in FA) as they contain Cerebro Spinal Fluid (CSF), but the corresponding voxels are bright in MD, as the water molecules are essentially free. Regions of the *Corpus Callosum*, on the other hand, contain lots of white matter fibres pointing in a single direction thus they appear dark in MD, as molecules cannot move much, but bright in FA as, when they move, they do so preferably in a single direction. (**b**) Colored FA, with *colors* indicating direction

Fig. 11.23 Fibre tracts in the heart. Since water diffuses more along the fibres we can use DTI to show the direction of these fibres

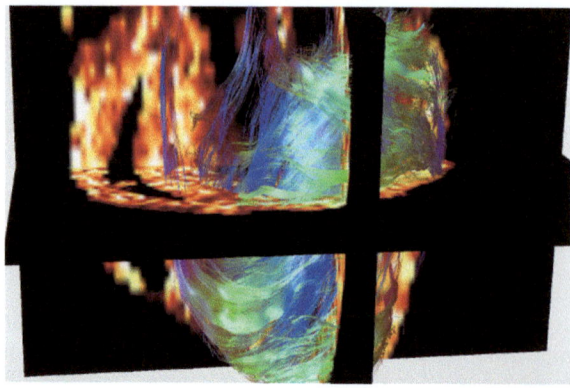

The directions can also be displayed as lines, and we can join these lines in by tracking the most natural connection. These are *fibre tracking* images. Figure 11.23 shows a less common cardiac fibre tracking. It should be stressed that all stages of diffusion imaging introduce errors. At the fibre tracking stage, these may end up causing totally spurious lines. Thus fibre tracking results should be interpreted very cautiously.

11.6.3 Summary

This section illustrated manipulation of higher order data. It showed that we need to take account of the model of the physics producing the images in order to extract maximal information. It also illustrated something typical of medical images and perhaps less often considered in standard optical imaging. Medical images can be *quantitative* in the sense that they sometimes have units. Thus, instead of being just a visualization, they are also measurements. This has the advantage that they can be validated against other data: for example, data from non-imaging sensors.

11.7 Applications

We have shown how 3D images of human anatomy can be produced and analyzed to create 3D models of the patient. However, we still need to answer the question of clinical usability of such models. Now, we will briefly describe some applications, which show how 3D imaging can be used to influence treatment.

11.7.1 Diagnosis and Morphometry

The shape modeling example from Sect. 11.5.2.2 showed how such models can be used for segmentation. The reduced dimensional space of the shape model also makes it possible to describe shape in a succinct way. This shape space provides a useful coordinate system for analysis of shape or morphometry. If diseased groups can be seen to occupy certain regions within shape space, then statistical shape analysis can be used for diagnosis. There have been numerous studies, for example, looking at the shape of brain structures such as the hippocampus in schizophrenia patients using statistical shape models.

11.7.2 Simulation and Training

It has long been agreed that the existing method of training surgeons is inadequate. The standard phrase that sums up the traditional method of surgical training was "see one, do one, teach one". The learning curve of new surgeons is often significant and the results for patients may be catastrophic. This was particularly noticed with the introduction of keyhole or laparoscopic surgery. Other options for laparoscopic surgery include box trainers, for example suturing rubber gloves, but these are limited in scope. If a sufficiently high-fidelity virtual simulator can be developed, this has several advantages. The movements of the surgeon are known and measured, so scores of dexterity and ability can be derived. A significant database of cases can be created, including rare but important difficulties. This gives the surgeons experience that would otherwise take years in the normal apprenticeship model.

Simulation is a wide research field in itself. A simulator must model not only the 3D graphical data to produce a convincing view, but also the physics and motion of soft tissue as it deforms under the influence of surgical tools. The surgeon should ideally receive haptic information—touch feedback that is similar to the real situation. From a software point of view, there is a good research resource in this field, available from the SOFA[2] network.

11.7.3 Surgical Planning and Guidance

Until recently, the standard way of viewing 3D medical images was as a series of slices printed on X-ray film and displayed on a light box. This has traditionally been the way such images are displayed to surgeons and, despite the availability of high resolution screens, it is still the norm for radiological images to be displayed in 2D. In surgery, the relationship between the preoperative imaging model and the patient is established entirely in the mind of the surgeon. The question is: given the 3D nature of the data, can we provide a more useful presentation of the patient to the surgeon?

The idea of image-guided surgery is that the preoperative model should be aligned to the physical space of the patient on the operating table. This has long

---

[2] www.sofa-framework.org.

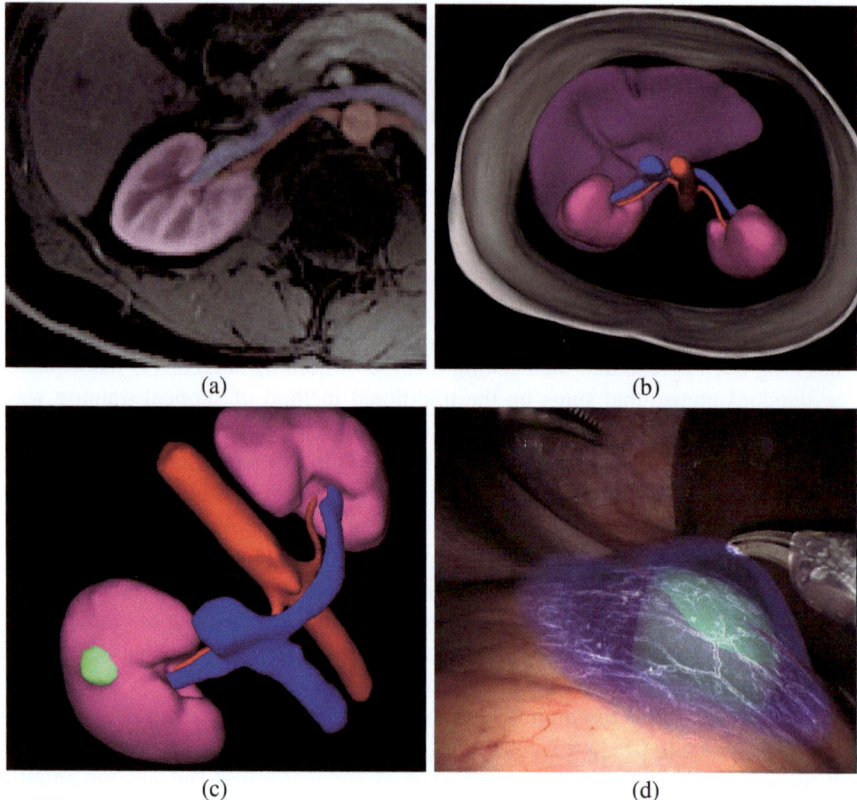

Fig. 11.24 Augmented reality image overlay for partial nephrectomy, showing CT derived model (**a**), (**b**), (**c**) and $p - q$ space rendering (**d**) of the model superimposed on the surgical view [43, 65]

been used in neurosurgery and orthopaedics where the operation is close to bone, which means that the rigid body registration approximation should hold. To align a preoperative model to the patient, it is necessary for a coordinate system to be established in the operating room. This part of the process can use techniques from computer vision. The most common commercial navigation devices use an optical camera to track markers which are either active, retro-reflective or passive.

An aligned preoperative model can then be displayed using augmented reality [65] to blend the real operative view with the 3D model (see Fig. 11.24).

The majority of surface data in medical imaging is extracted from volumetric acquisitions, mostly CT and MRI. However, there is the potential to use surfaces from video sources during therapy or surgery. These surfaces will come from one or more of the techniques described in the other chapters in this book. In radiotherapy, for example, 3D surface reconstruction from projected patterned light is used to track the chest and abdomen position in real-time. This information can be linked with previous volumetric data, such as the CT derived model in Fig. 11.24, to estimate the position of a tumour in real-time, as shown in Fig. 11.25.

Fig. 11.25 VisionRT 3D surface—intended for surface registration to pre-treatment CT scans for guidance of radiotherapy

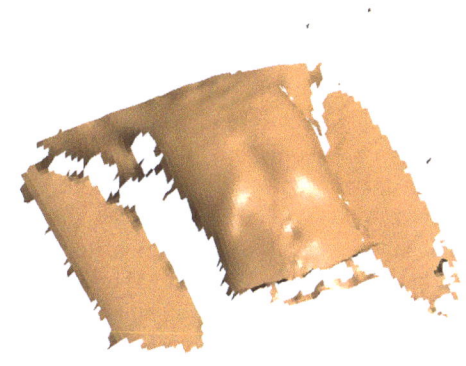

11.7.4 Summary

In this section, we have looked at some of the clinical applications of 3D modeling from medical images. These are not exhaustive and not covered in detail. The aim is that the reader gets some understanding of how 3D imaging models can impact clinical practice.

11.8 Concluding Remarks

This chapter has introduced the field of 3D medical imaging. Although the methods and the physics of medical imaging are significantly different from that of computer vision-based reconstruction, there are definitely areas of overlap in terms of research. An example is the use of vision-based trackers, which are now very common in surgical guidance systems. The idea of live surface reconstruction during surgery is potentially very powerful, if a robust surface alignment method can be found. We hope that this chapter has provided some new insights into methods of 3D reconstruction, segmentation, analysis and clinical applications in 3D medical imaging.

11.9 Research Challenges

There are many research challenges facing all the areas of 3D medical imaging covered in this chapter. MICCAI,[3] the premier medical image analysis conference, has grown significantly in the last decade, which indicates the rapid expansion of research in this field. In this section, we will briefly summarize a few of the research challenges in each area.

---

[3] The International Conference on Medical Image Computing and Computer Assisted Intervention.

In registration, the issue of how to cope with non-rigid soft tissue motion is key to providing accurate alignment. In particular, for image guidance one needs to deform a 3D preoperative model to match the (often 2D) intraoperative scene. The incorporation of physical finite element models into this process helps to keep deformations realistic, but significantly increases the required processing power.

In image segmentation, there is no generic automatic algorithm that has been shown to work reliably. Given the amount of time a clinician must spend doing manual segmentation, more automated approaches are vital if segmentation is to be adopted into routine practice. The segmentation workshop of the MICCAI conference incorporates grand challenges[4] for specific clinical applications and algorithms compete in automatic and semi-automatic categories. Although some impressive developments have been made, there is as yet no perfect automated method.

There are some significant unanswered questions in the field of shape modeling. Little attention has been paid to the number of modes that should be retained and what constitutes a sufficient sample. Instead, in most cases, models are built on a limited sample and the number of modes retained uses a simple heuristic such as fitting 95 % of the data. Mei et al. [54, 55] suggest using bootstrapping as a means of assessing the stability of mode directions across replicates. For real and simulated data, the number of modes retained stabilizes at a given sample size and this is taken as an indication of sample sufficiency.

There is also the question of how to establish correspondence. Much work has focused on producing diffeomorphic transformations and the use of the minimum description length to establish optimal correspondences [20]. Other interesting research areas include non-linear models, such as kernel PCA and manifold learning. On a well chosen manifold, the shape model may well be more compact and can be represented by a smaller sample.

Within diffusion tensor imaging, the dominant issues are those surrounding how to generate fibre tracts in the brain or heart. The field of tractography looks at methods to cope with error accumulation and difficult cases, such as fibre tracts that cross each other. There is increasing interest in tractography in neuroscience, since imaging of the connectivity of the brain can potentially help to understand its function.

11.10 Further Reading

As mentioned, the premier conference on medical imaging is MICCAI. The papers in this conference are the best source to find the latest research developments in this field. On a more algorithmic level, IPMI[5] provides a smaller but more focussed conference. A superb introduction to medical image processing, with examples in Matlab, is given in [11].

---

[4]See www.grand-challenge.org.

[5]International Conference on Information Processing in Medical Imaging. See www.ipmi-conference.org.

Data Acquisition There are many medical physics textbooks and books that specialize in certain modalities. There are too many to give a comprehensive list here, but [76] is a good overview and we can mention a few noteworthy references. The Encyclopedia of Medical Imaging [77] is a good source of information and further references. As a reference on the mathematics of imaging, we would recommend [9]. Readers with an interest in the most mathematical texts should read [57] or [3, 26]. A classic reprint is [39]. For theoretical problems, inspired from tomography but without applications in mind, see [30]. An overview of PET can be found in [1]. For MRI, a signal processing perspective is given in [44] (one of the authors is Paul Lauterbur who was awarded the Nobel prize for inventing MRI).

Surface Extraction The manipulation of surface objects, for example triangulated surfaces, is presented in [25] and gives the basic concepts. For further investigation, again distanced from the medical imaging motivation, see also [12].

Volume Registration For a full review of medical image registration see [35] or the book [31], while the book [74] collects classical papers in information theory.

Segmentation For the latest developments in segmentation visit the 'grand challenge' web pages.[6] In specific areas, there are some excellent review papers. For deformable models, there is the original paper by McInerney [53]. In statistical shape modeling, an excellent review is given by [34]. Further reviews are available of semi-automatic and fully-automatic segmentation [64], the role of user interaction [59] and ultrasound segmentation [58].

Diffusion Imaging The book [38] is an excellent overview of this application topic. The books [80, 81] contain a range of articles on tensor processing in the spirit of this book.

Image-Guided Surgery An excellent textbook on image guidance is provided by Peters and Cleary [63]. The latest research is also well covered by the conferences IPCAI[7] and MICCAI.

Software Medical images come in a number of formats. The standard is DICOM,[8] considered clumsy sometimes, but it is the standard that main manufacturers of medical imaging equipment use. Besides manufacturers' tools, MRIcro, ImageJ, Matlab, and OsiriX are software packages that can read and display them. The most popular open source library is `dicom4chee` and the C++ libraries vtk and itk also provide lots of tools that can be used as plugins in ImageJ, for example, via Java wrappers. Matlab is commonly used in research environments, in particular in reconstruction

---

[6] www.grand-challenge.org.
[7] International Conference on Information Processing in Computer-Assisted Interventions.
[8] Digital Imaging and Communications in Medicine.

contexts, as it provides an all-in-one solution (but it is not free software, although student licenses are fairly affordable at time of writing). Free software packages such as Octave, vtk, the GNU Scientific Library GSL, BLAS-LAPACK and FFTW can, in theory, be used for the same purposes, but with more effort. For some surface manipulation, the CGAL library is emerging as a standard and there is the excellent package: Meshlab. Currently, GPU computing is playing an important role in some medical imaging applications, see, for example, OpenCL and CUDA.

11.11 Questions

1. For the grid in Fig. 11.6, sketch the result of marching squares for a threshold of 11.5. Comment on any issues that arise and suggest possible solutions.
2. In volume rendering, a ray sent out from a pixel on the viewing plane encounters the following scalar values with increasing distance from the viewpoint: 22, 80, 45, 40, 120, 100. The color and opacity transfer function is:

α	C_{red}	C_{green}	C_{blue}	Scalar value
0.0	0.7	0.3	1.0	$10 < x < 30$
1.0	0.5	0.6	1.0	$30 < x < 70$
0.5	0.5	0.2	0.5	$70 < x < 90$
0.5	1.0	1.0	0.0	$90 < x < 150$

   Calculate the pixel color using back-to-front rendering as well as front-to-back rendering (the results should be the same).
3. How would the MRI intensity inhomogeneity effect (see Fig. 11.4) be likely to affect the result of a region growing algorithm? What measures could be taken to reduce such effects?
4. For diffusion tensor imaging, build the equations in $[D_{xx}, D_{xy}, \ldots]$ that need to be solved from the model equation.
5. Four markers are placed on a patient's head as fiducials for registration. In the preoperative CT scan these are found to be at the following locations:

x	y	z
23.5	40.4	13.3
50.2	−35.5	8.5
−43.7	28.4	35.0
−18.4	38.7	18.2

   (i) Calculate the position of the point in the CT scan that is most accurately located with these fiducials.
   (ii) Define the terms fiducial registration error (FRE), fiducial localization error (FLE) and target registration error (TRE).

(iii) The fiducial points are translated to the centroid and rotated to lie along their principal axes. Their new positions are:

x	y	z
−3.5	30.6	−2.6
−70.8	−13.5	0.4
45.4	−21.7	−2.8
28.9	4.6	5.0

A target is located at $(13.1, -1.0, -61.4)$ in this coordinate system. If the fiducials can be located to an accuracy of 3 mm, what is the TRE at this point?

(iv) The resulting transformation is used as an input to a surface matching algorithm. In what situations can surface registration give a poor result? How might this affect the choice of regions on the head where the fiducials are placed? What methods can be used to overcome these issues?

11.12 Exercises

1. The aim of this exercise is to explore the effects of some of the image reconstruction algorithms on images. By using the libraries described in the Software section, you can try to do it in C++, but we will describe it as Matlab tasks for simplicity. Firstly, write code to generate simple test images of cubes, spheres and so on. Compute their 'MRI data' (Fourier transform) and 'CT or PET data' (Radon transform). Explore the undersampling effects by (a) removing odd lines of data; (b) removing outer parts of data; (c) removing inner parts of data; and (d) removing random parts of data. To make it more sophisticated, instead of simply removing, you can apply spatial transforms to corresponding undersampled data, and then merge back. The following code gives a template:

```
N = 256; M = N; P = M;
R = 1; r = R/2;
[X,Y,Z] = meshgrid(linspace(-R,R),N,M,P);
cube = ( X < r \& Y < r \& Z < r );
mri = fftn(cube);
ct = radon(cube);
% 1) subsample:
% a) remove odd lines of data and reconstruct
% b) remove outer parts of data and reconstruct
% c) remove inner parts of data and reconstruct
% d) remove random parts of data and reconstruct
```

```
% 2) motion:
% a) move odd lines of data and reconstruct
% b) move outer parts of data and reconstruct
% c) move inner parts of data and reconstruct
% d) move random parts of data and reconstruct

% 3) noise:
% Add noise to the date before reconstruction in
% all examples above

% 4) surface extraction:
% Hint: isosurface

% 5) curvature computation: compute curvatures
% of the object. As it is a cube, you should get
% very high curvatures at corners and edges, and
% zero otherwise. Is that the case?
%
% Hint: you have to ensure that the surface is
% oriented, i.e. that all the normals point
% outwards or inwards. For curvatures (mean
% curvature) you need the dihedral angle at an,
% edge and for Gauss curvature, you need the
% angle defect 2pi − sum(angles) at vertices.
% See chapter 2 in this book for more details
```

2. Write code in Matlab to implement the recursive region growing algorithm introduced in Algorithm 11.1. The recursive function should take six arguments: the image being segmented, the current region map (-1 = unknown, 0 = background, 1 = foreground), the x and y coordinates of the current pixel, the intensity of the original seed pixel and the intensity distance used to determine if a pixel is similar to the original seed pixel. The following sample code sets up a simple test image, calls the recursive function and displays the result.

```
% input image
im = [0 3 0 0 0; ...
1 5 4 2 1; ...
2 4 5 5 0; ...
1 5 6 0 1; ...
0 0 4 1 0];

% initialize output to unknown
r = −1 * ones(size(im));
```

```
% call region growing function
% args: image, region, seed x, seed y,
% seed intensity, intensity distance
r = regionGrow(im, r, 3, 3, im(3,3), 1.0);

% any unvisited pixels are set to background
r(find(r == -1)) = 0;

% display original image and region
figure; imagesc(im); colormap(gray);
figure; imagesc(r); colormap(gray);
```

If you have implemented the region growing algorithm correctly, the result of the segmentation should be as follows:

```
r =
0  0  0  0  0
0  1  1  0  0
0  1  1  1  0
0  1  1  0  0
0  0  1  0  0
```

3. Implement the marching squares algorithm to create a connected series of vertices for a given threshold. You will need to interpolate the position of the vertices and consider the case table of 16 possibilities to decide how to connect these. Run this on the same image as for Exercise 2 with a threshold of 2.5.
4. Implement a simple volume renderer that accumulates voxels from back-to-front along the z-axis of a 3D image and produces a rendering in the x–y plane. Render the images of the sphere (perfect and with noise or missing data) from Exercise 1 with a transfer function that gives a color of white and an opacity somewhere between 0 and 1. To introduce volumetric lighting, calculate the voxel gradient by finite difference and scale the voxel color by the dot product of the normalized gradient with $(0, 0, 1)$. Comment on the differences between these renderings and the previous isosurfaces.
5. Download the segmentation package ITK-SNAP[9] and work through the tutorial using their example MRI image. How do the region competition and edge-based snakes differ from simple region growing? In what situations would region growing be better or worse than the ITK-SNAP methods?

---

[9] www.itksnap.org/download.

References

1. Bailey, D., Townsend, D., Valk, P., Maisey, M.N. (eds.): Positron Emission Tomography. Springer, Berlin (2005)
2. Baillard, C., Hellier, P., Barillot, C.: Segmentation of brain 3D MR images using level sets and dense registration. Med. Image Anal. **5**, 185–194 (2001)
3. Barret, H.H., Myers, K.J.: Foundations of Image Science. Pure and Applied Optics. Wiley, New York (2004)
4. Barrett, J.F., Keat, N.: Artifacts in CT: recognition and avoidance. Radiograph., Rev. Publ. Radiol. Soc. N. Am. **24**(6), 1679–1691 (2004). doi:10.1148/rg.246045065. http://radiographics.rsna.org/content/24/6/1679.full
5. Batchelor, P., Castellano Smith, A., Hill, D., Hawkes, D., Cox, T., Dean, A.: Measures of folding applied to the development of the human fetal brain. IEEE Trans. Med. Imaging **21**(8), 953–965 (2002)
6. Batchelor, P.G., Calamante, F., Tournier, D., Atkinson, D., Hill, D.L.G., Connelly, A.: Quantification of the shape of fiber tracts. Methods **903**(2005), 894–903 (2006). doi:10.1002/mrm.20858
7. Batchelor, P.G., Calamante, F., Tournier, J., Atkinson, D., Hill, D.L.G., Connelly, A.: Quantification of the shape of fiber tracts. Magn. Reson. Med. **55**, 894–903 (2006)
8. de Berg, M., Cheong, O., van Kreveld, M., Overmars, M. (eds.): Computational Geometry: Algorithms and Applications. Springer, Berlin (2008)
9. Bertero, M., Boccacci, P.: Introduction to Inverse Problems in Imaging. Institute of Physics Publishing, Bristol (1998)
10. Besl, P.J., McKay, N.D.: A method for registration of 3-d shapes. IEEE Trans. Pattern Anal. Mach. Intell. **14**(2), 239–256 (1992)
11. Birkfellner, W.: Applied Medical Image Processing: A Basic Course. CRC Press, Boca Raton (2010)
12. Boissonnat, J.D., Yvinec, M.: Algorithmic Geometry. Cambridge University Press, Cambridge (1998)
13. Bookstein, F.L.: Principal warps: thin-plate splines and the decomposition of deformations. IEEE Trans. Med. Imaging **11**, 567–585 (1989)
14. de Bruijne, M., van Ginneken, B., Viergever, M.A., Niessen, W.J.: Adapting active shape models for 3D segmentation of tubular structures in medical images. In: Proceedings IPMI (2003)
15. de Bruijne, M., van Ginneken, B., Viergever, M.A., Niessen, W.J.: Interactive segmentation of abdominal aortic aneurysms in CTA images. Med. Image Anal. **8**, 127–138 (2004)
16. Bushberg, J.T.: The Essential Physics of Medical Imaging. Lippincott Williams & Wilkins, Baltimore (2002)
17. Carmichael, O.T., Aizenstein, H.A., Davis, S.W., Becker, J.T., Thompson, P.M., Meltzer, C.C., Liu, Y.: Atlas-based hippocampus segmentation in Alzheimer's disease and mild cognitive impairment. Neuroimage **27**, 979–990 (2005)
18. Ciofolo, C., Barillot, C.: Atlas-based segmentation of 3d cerebral structures with competitive level sets and fuzzy control. Med. Image Anal. **13**, 456–470 (2010)
19. Cohen, L.D.: On active contour models and balloon. CVGIP, Image Underst. **53**, 211–218 (1991)
20. Cootes, T., Twining, C., Babalola, K., Taylor, C.: Diffeomorphic statistical shape models. Image Vis. Comput. **26**(3), 326–332 (2008)
21. Cootes, T.F., Taylor, C.J., Cooper, D.H., Graham, J.: Active shape models—their training and application. Comput. Vis. Image Underst. **61**, 38–59 (1995)
22. Cuadra, M.B., Pollo, C., Bardera, A., Cuisenaire, O., Villemure, J.G., Thiran, J.P.: Atlas-based segmentation of pathological MR brain images using a model of lesion growth. IEEE Trans. Med. Imaging **23**, 1301–1314 (2004)
23. Dempster, A., Laird, N., Rubin, D.: Maximum likelihood from incomplete data via the em algorithm. J. R. Stat. Soc. **39**, 1–38 (1977)

24. Ecabert, O., Peters, J., Schramm, H., Lorenz, C., von Berg, J., Walker, M.J., Vembar, M., Olszewski, M.E., Subramanyan, K., Lavi, G., Weese, J.: Automatic model-based segmentation of the heart in CT images. IEEE Trans. Med. Imaging **27**, 1189–1201 (2008)
25. Edelsbrunner, H.: Geometry and Topology for Mesh Generation. Monographs on Applied and Computational Mathematics. Cambridge University Press, Cambridge (2001)
26. Epstein, C.L.: Introduction to the Mathematics of Medical Imaging, 2nd edn. SIAM, Philadelphia (2003)
27. Erasmus, L.J., Hurter, D., Naudé, M., Kritzinger, H.G., Acho, S.: A short overview of MRI artefacts. SA J. Radiol. **8**(2), 13–17 (2004)
28. Fitzpatrick, M.J., West, J.B., Maurer, C.R. Jr.: Predicting error in rigid-body point-based registration. IEEE Trans. Med. Imaging **17**(5), 694–702 (1998)
29. Fripp, J., Crozier, S., Warfield, S., Ourselin, S.: Automatic segmentation of the knee bones using 3D active shape models. In: Proceedings ICPR (2006)
30. Gardner, R.J.: In: Geometric Tomography. Cambridge University Press, Cambridge (2006)
31. Hajnal, J.V. (ed.): Medical Image Registration. CRC Press, Boca Raton (2001)
32. Hall, P., Ngan, M., Andreae, P.: Reconstruction of vascular networks using three-dimensional models. IEEE Trans. Med. Imaging **16**(6), 919–929 (1997)
33. Han, X., Xu, C., Prince, J.L.: A topology preserving level set method for geometric deformable models. IEEE Trans. Pattern Anal. Mach. Intell. **25**(6), 755–768 (2003)
34. Heimann, T., Meinzer, H.P.: Statistical shape models for 3D medical image segmentation: a review. Med. Image Anal. **13**, 543–563 (2009)
35. Hill, D.L.G., Batchelor, P.G., Holden, M., Hawkes, D.J.: Medical image registration. Phys. Med. Biol. **46**, R1–R45 (2001)
36. Hudson, H.M., Larkin, R.S.: Accelerated image reconstruction using ordered subsets of projection data. IEEE Trans. Med. Imaging **13**, 601–609 (1994)
37. Imai, K., Ikeda, M., Wada, S., Enchi, Y., Niimi, T.: Analysis of streak artefacts on CT images using statistics of extremes. Br. J. Radiol. **80**(959), 911–918 (2007). http://bjr.birjournals.org/cgi/content/abstract/80/959/911. doi:10.1259/bjr/93741044
38. Johansen-Berg, H., Behrens, T.E. (eds.): Diffusion MRI from Quantitative Measurement to In-Vivo Neuroanatomy. Elsevier, Amsterdam (2009)
39. Kak, A.C., Slaney, M.: Principles of Computerized Tomographic Imaging. SIAM, Philadelphia (2001). Unabridged edn.
40. Kass, M., Witkin, A., Terzopoulos, D.: Snakes—active contour models. Int. J. Comput. Vis. **1**(4), 321–331 (1987)
41. Klein, S., van der Heide, U.A., Lips, I.M., van Vulpen, M., Staring, M., Pluim, J.P.: Automatic segmentation of the prostate in 3D MR images by atlas matching using localized mutual information. Med. Phys. **35**, 1407–1417 (2008)
42. Kucera, D., Martin, R.W.: Segmentation of sequences of echocardiographic images using a simplified 3D active contour model with region-based external forces. Comput. Med. Imaging Graph. **21**, 1–21 (1997)
43. Lerotic, M., Chung, A., Mylonas, G., Yang, G.Z.: Pq-space based non-photorealistic rendering for augmented reality. In: Ayache, N., Ourselin, S., Maeder, A. (eds.) MICCAI 2007. Lecture Notes in Computer Science, vol. 4792, pp. 102–109. Springer, Berlin (2007)
44. Liang, Z.P., Lauterbur, P.C.: Principles of Magnetic Resonance Imaging: a Signal Processing Perspective. Series on Biomedical Engineering. IEEE Press, New York (2000)
45. Liebling, M.: CT Reconstruction Demo Applet. Online (2001). http://bigwww.epfl.ch/demo/jtomography/demo.html
46. Linguraru, M.G., Sandberg, J.K., Li, Z., Pura, J.A., Summers, R.M.: Atlas-based automated segmentation of spleen and liver using adaptive enhancement estimation. In: Proceedings MICCAI, pp. 1001–1008 (2009)
47. Lorensen, W.E., Cline, H.E.: Marching cubes: a high resolution 3D surface reconstruction algorithm. Comput. Graph. **21**(3), 163–169 (1987)
48. Lorenz, C., von Berg, J.: A comprehensive shape model of the heart. Med. Image Anal. **10**, 657–670 (2006)

49. Lorenzo-Valdés, M., Sanchez-Ortiza, G.I., Elkington, A.G., Mohiaddin, R.H., Rueckert, D.: Segmentation of 4D cardiac MR images using a probabilistic atlas and the EM algorithm. Med. Image Anal. **8**, 255–265 (2004)
50. Malladi, R., Sethian, J., Vemuri, B.C.: Shape modeling with front propagation: a level set approach. IEEE Trans. Pattern Anal. Mach. Intell. **17**(2), 158–175 (1995)
51. Manniesing, R., Velthuis, B.K., can Leeuwen, M.S., van der Schaaf, I.C., van Laar, P.J., Niessen, W.J.: Level set based cerebral vasculature segmentation and diameter quantification in ct angiography. Med. Image Anal. **10**(2), 200–214 (2006)
52. Manzke, R., Meyer, C., Ecabert, O., Peters, J., Noordhoek, N.J., Thiagalingam, A., Reddy, V., Chan, R.C., Weese, J.: Automatic segmentation of rotational X-ray images for anatomic intra-procedural surface generation in atrial fibrillation ablation procedures. IEEE Trans. Med. Imaging **29**, 260–272 (2010)
53. McInerney, T., Terzopoulos, D.: Deformable models in medical image analysis: a survey. Med. Image Anal. **1**(2), 91–108 (1996)
54. Mei, L., Figl, M., Darzi, A., Rueckert, D., Edwards, P.: Sample sufficiency and PCA dimension for statistical shape models. In: Proceedings of the 10th European Conference on Computer Vision: Part IV, pp. 492–503. Springer, Berlin (2008). http://portal.acm.org/citation.cfm?id=1478237.1478274
55. Mei, L., Figl, M., Rueckert, D., Darzi, A., Edwards, P.: Sample sufficiency and number of modes to retain in statistical shape modelling. In: Metaxas, D., Axel, L., Fichtinger, G., Szkely, G. (eds.) Medical Image Computing and Computer-Assisted Intervention MICCAI 2008. Lecture Notes in Computer Science, vol. 5241, pp. 425–433. Springer, Berlin (2008)
56. Muralidhar, G.S., Bovik, A.C., Giese, J.D., Sampat, M.P., Whitman, G.J., Haygood, T.M., Stephens, T.W., Markey, M.K.: Snakules: a model-based active contour algorithm for the annotation of spicules on mammography. IEEE Trans. Med. Imaging **29**, 1768–1780 (2010)
57. Natterer, F., Wübbeling, F.: Mathematical Methods in Image Reconstruction. Monographs on Mathematical Modeling and Computation. SIAM, Philadelphia (2001)
58. Noble, J.A., Boukerroui, D.: Ultrasound image segmentation: a survey. IEEE Trans. Med. Imaging **25**(8), 987–1010 (2006)
59. Olabarriaga, S.D., Smeulders, A.W.M.: Interaction in the segmentation of medical images: a survey. Med. Image Anal. **5**(2), 127–142 (2001)
60. Paragios, N.: A level set approach for shape-driven segmentation and tracking of the left ventricle. IEEE Trans. Med. Imaging **22**(6), 773–776 (2003)
61. Pelizzari, C.A., Tan, K.K., Levin, D.N., Chen, G.T.Y., Balter, J.: Interactive 3D patient-image registration. In: Colchester, A.C.F., Hawkes, D.J. (eds.) Information Processing in Medical Imaging, pp. 133–141. Springer, Berlin (1991)
62. Peters, J., Ecabert, O., Meyer, C., Schramm, H., Kneser, R., Groth, A., Weese, J.: Automatic whole heart segmentation in static magnetic resonance image volumes. In: Proceedings MICCAI, pp. 402–410 (2007)
63. Peters, T.M., Cleary, K.R.: Image-Guided Interventions: Technology and Applications. Springer, Berlin (2008)
64. Pham, D.L., Xu, C., Prince, J.L.: A survey of current methods in medical image segmentation. Annu. Rev. Biomed. Eng. **2**, 315–338 (2000)
65. Pratt, P., Mayer, E., Vale, J., Cohen, D., Edwards, E., Darzi, A., Yang, G.Z.: An effective visualisation and registration system for image-guided robotic partial nephrectomy. J. Robotic Surgery (2012)
66. Rajan, J., Poot, D., Juntu, J., Sijbers, J.: Noise measurement from magnitude MRI using local estimates of variance and skewness. Phys. Med. Biol. **55**(16), N441-9 (2010). http://www.ncbi.nlm.nih.gov/pubmed/20679694. doi:10.1088/0031-9155/55/16/N02
67. Rohlfing, T., Brandt, R., Maurer, C. Jr., Menzel, R.: Bee brains, b-splines and computational democracy: generating an average shape atlas. In: Proceedings MMBIA, pp. 187–194 (2001)
68. Rohlfing, T., Brandt, R., Menzel, R., Maurer, C.R. Jr.: Evaluation of atlas selection strategies for atlas-based image segmentation with application to confocal microscopy images of bee brains. Neuroimage **21**, 1428–1442 (2004)

69. Roth, H., McClelland, J., Modat, M., Boone, D., Hu, M., Ourselin, S., Slabaugh, G.G., Halligan, S., Hawkes, D.J.: Establishing spatial correspondence between the inner colon surfaces from prone and supine ct colonography. In: Proceedings MICCAI (Beijing), pp. 497–504 (2010)
70. Rueckert, D., Frangi, A.F., Schnabel, J.A.: Automatic construction of 3D statistical deformation models of the brain using nonrigid registration. IEEE Trans. Med. Imaging **22**, 1014–1025 (2003)
71. Rueckert, D., Sonoda, L.I., Hayes, C., Hill, D.L.G., Leach, M.O., Hawkes, D.J.: Nonrigid registration using free-form deformations: application to breast MR images. IEEE Trans. Med. Imaging **18**(8), 712–721 (1999)
72. Rhode, K., Sermesant, M.: Modeling and registration for electrophysiology procedures based on three-dimensional imaging. Curr. Cardiovasc. Imaging Rep. **4**, 116–126 (2011)
73. Shepp, L., Vardi, Y.: Maximum likelihood reconstruction for emission tomography. IEEE Trans. Med. Imaging **1**, 113–122 (1982)
74. Slepian, D. (ed.): Key Papers in the Development of Information Theory. Reprint Series. IEEE Press, New York (1974)
75. Studholme, C., Hill, D.L.G., Hawkes, D.J.: An overlap invariant entropy measure of 3D medical image alignment. Pattern Recognit. **32**(1), 71–86 (1999)
76. Suetens, P.: Fundamentals of Medical Imaging. Cambridge University Press, Cambridge (2002)
77. Tabakov, S., Smith, P.H.S., Milano, F., Strand, S.E., Lewis, C. (eds.): Encyclopedia of Medical Physics. Taylor & Francis, London (2012). ISBN 9781439846520 http://www.emitel2.eu/. available [Online]
78. Tao, X., Prince, J.L., Davatzikos, C.: Using a statistical shape model to extract sulcal curves on the outer cortex of the human brain. IEEE Trans. Med. Imaging **21**, 513–524 (2002)
79. Viola, P.A., Wells, W.M.: Alignment by maximisation of mutual information. In: Proceedings of the 5th International Conference on Computer Vision, pp. 15–23 (1995)
80. Weickert, J., Laidlaw, D. (eds.): Visualization and Processing of Tensor Fields. II. Mathematics+Visualization. Springer, Berlin (2009)
81. Weickert, J., Hagen, H. (eds.): Visualization and Processing of Tensor Fields. Mathematics+Visualization. Springer, Berlin (2006)
82. Williams, D.J., Shah, M.: A fast algorithm for active contours and curvature estimation. CVGIP, Image Underst. **55**, 14–26 (1992)
83. Xu, C., Pham, D.L., Rettmann, M.E., Yu, D.N., Prince, J.L.: Reconstruction of the human cerebral cortex from magnetic resonance images. IEEE Trans. Med. Imaging **18**, 467–480 (1999)
84. Yushkevich, P.A., Piven, J., Hazlett, H.C., Smith, R.G., Ho, S., Gee, J.C., Gerig, G.: User-guided 3D active contour segmentation of anatomical structures: significantly improved efficiency and reliability. Neuroimage **31**(3), 1116–1128 (2006)
85. Zhu, X.J., Zhang, P.F., Shao, J.H., Cheng, Y.Z., Zhang, Y., Bai, J.: A snake-based method for segmentation of intravascular ultrasound images and its in vivo validation. Ultrasonics **51**, 181–189 (2011)
86. Zhuang, X., Rhode, K.S., Razavi, R.S., Hawkes, D.J., Ourselin, S.: A registration-based propagation framework for automatic whole heart segmentation of cardiac MRI. IEEE Trans. Med. Imaging **29**, 1612–1625 (2010)

Index

A
Active triangulation, 98
    calibration, 114
    experimental characterization, 121
    Gray code methods, 107
    measurement uncertainty, 116
    Scheimpflug condition, 129
    sheet-of-light projector model, 105
    spot scanner, 99
    stripe scanner, 102, 105
    structured light systems, 106

B
B-reps, 154
Binary space partitioning, 153
Bundle adjustment, 80

C
Camera calibration, 48
    extrinsic parameters, 48
    intrinsic parameters, 48
    stereo rig, 54
Camera model, 41, 103
    pinhole camera model, 41, 103
Camera obscura, 96
Computed tomography, 447
Constructive solid geometry, 154
Correlation, 68
Correspondences, 68
Curvature, 205
    Gaussian, 205, 349
    mean, 205, 349
Curvedness, 205

D
Datasets, 317
    3D face, 317
    Bosphorus 3D face dataset, 320
    FRGC 3D face dataset, 318
Deformable models, 471
    balloons, 472
    snakes, 471
DEM, 367
    generation from InSAR, 379
    generation from LIDAR, 390
    generation from stereo, 370
    InSAR phase unwrapping, 381
Depth buffer descriptor, 276
Depth map, 141
Digital elevation model, *see* DEM

E
Epipolar geometry, 56
Essential matrix, 57

F
Face identification, 322
Face recognition
    ICP, 334
    LDA, 343
    PCA, 337
    using curvature, 350
Face verification, 321
Features, 195
    descriptors, 203
    detectors, 195
    heat kernel signature, 208
    HOG, 208
    SIFT, 208
    spectral features, 285
    spin images, 277
Fundamental matrix, 59
    computation, 60
    eight point algorithm, 61
    pure translation, 59

G
Gaussian curvature, 349

H
Heat kernel, 199
  heat kernel signature, 208, 292
Homogeneous coordinates, 42
Homography, 49
  for planar scene, 64
  for pure rotation, 63

I
ICP, 224
  3D face recognition, 330
  critical discussion, 333
  deformable ICP, 250
  outline, 331
  using LM minimization, 244
Implicit surface, 145
InSAR, 380
Interest points, 195
Interferometry, 97
Isosurface, 145
Iterative Closest Points, *see* ICP

K
K-d tree, 152
Keypoints, 195

L
Level set, 145
LIDAR, 390, 429
  filtering, 395
Linear Discriminant Analysis, 343

M
Magnetic resonance imaging, *see* MRI
Mean curvature, 349
Mesh, 143
  DOG operator, 197
  halfedge structure, 159
  Laplacian, 169
  quadrilateral, 144
  simplification, 172
  triangular, 143
Morphable model, 144
MRI, 452
  diffusion MRI, 479

N
Needle map, 142
NURBS, 149

O
Object recognition, 267, 271
Object retrieval, 267, 269

P
PCA, 337
  in medical applications, 474
PET scan, 450
Phase unwrapping, 381
  branch-cut method, 383
  least squares method, 384
Photogrammetry, 419
  forest measurement, 426
Point cloud, 140
  structured point cloud, 141
Positron emission tomography, *see* PET scan
Principal component analysis, *see* PCA
Projectivity, 49

R
Radial distortion, 47
Range image, 141
RANSAC, 61
Registration, 223
  intensity-based, 464
  rigid body alignment, 225
  volumetric, 460
Resampling, 329

S
Segmentation, 467
  atlas-based, 473
Shape context, 206
Shape from X, 11
  shape from focus, 40
  shape from shading, 39
  shape from texture, 40
Shape index, 205, 349
Shape recognition, *see* Object recognition
Shape retrieval, *see* Object retrieval
SLAM, 86
Spin images, 20, 205, 277, 351
Statistical shape models, 474
Stereo, 37
  commercial rigs, 81
  dense matching, 73
  epipolar constraint, 73
  reconstruction, 72
  rectification, 65
  stereo rig, 37
  stereo rig calibration, 54

Stereo (*cont.*)
    triangulation, 75
    uniqueness constraint, 73
Structure from Motion, 39, 78
Subdivision surfaces, 144, 162
    Catmull-Clark scheme, 164
    Doo-Sabin scheme, 162
    Loop scheme, 165
Surface, 147
    from volumetric image, 456
    interest points, 195
    keypoints, 195
    local descriptors, 203
    normals, 167
    NURBS surface patch, 149
    parametric, 147

T
3D image, 2
3D model, 2
    compression, 170
    visualization, 174
3D scan, 2

U
UV coordinates, 143

V
Volume rendering, 457
Voxels, 151

X
X84 outlier rejection rule, 242

MIX
Papier aus verantwortungsvollen Quellen
Paper from responsible sources
FSC® C105338

If you have any concerns about our products,
you can contact us on
ProductSafety@springernature.com

In case Publisher is established outside the EU,
the EU authorized representative is:
**Springer Nature Customer Service Center GmbH
Europaplatz 3, 69115 Heidelberg, Germany**

Printed by Libri Plureos GmbH
in Hamburg, Germany